Previous page: *Royal Oak* during the stormy Fleet Manoeuvres in the Atlantic during March 1934.
Below: *Repulse* entering Valetta Harbour, Malta, in March 1937. Note the Spanish Civil War stripes on 'B' turret.

BRITISH
BATTLESHIPS
1919–1939

R. A. BURT

ARMS AND
ARMOUR

To my Mother

Arms and Armour Press
A Cassell Imprint
Villiers House, 41-47 Strand, London WC2N 5JE.

Distributed in Australia by Capricorn Link
(Australia) Pty. Ltd, P.O. Box 665, Lane Cove,
New South Wales 2066.

British Library Cataloguing-in-Publication Data:
a catalogue record for this book is available from
the British Library

ISBN 1-85409-068-2

Designed and edited by DAG Publications Ltd.
Designed by David Gibbons; edited by Michael
Boxall; layout by Anthony A. Evans; typeset by
Ronset Typesetters, Darwen, Lancashire;
printed and bound in Great Britain by
The Bath Press, Avon.

Acknowledgments
During the five years this book has been in
preparation, the author has been indebted to the
following establishments and persons:
    The staff of the National Maritime Museum,
Greenwich.
    The staff of the Public Records Office, Kew.
    In particular I should like to extend sincere
thanks to John Roberts for all his help; to J.
Hitchon, A. S. Norris and R. Wilson for help
with material; and appreciation is also due to T.
W. Ferrers-Walker for material and for great
encouragement throughout the preparation of
this book.
    Once again my gratitude is expressed for my
publishers; and in particular to David Gibbons
and Anthony Evans, who always point out items
I might otherwise have missed; and to Michael
Boxall, my editor, for checking everything and
putting up with me in general.
    Finally to my wife, Janice, who has put a lot
of effort into this book in the way of research,
typing and checking, etc.
    Life has not been easy for any of my family
whilst this book was in preparation, and for all of
their for suffering in silence I am truly grateful.

                                    R. A. Burt

CONTENTS

PREFACE

The period from 1919 to 1939, although a time of peace between the major powers, probably produced more wartime ideas than hostilities themselves. The naval treaties that brought a halt to capital ship construction (from 1921) meant that the time and money available was spent either on the reconstruction of existing warships, or on basically new designs to be built as soon as new programmes could begin. It was a time when 'Jack' could join up and see the world without fear of having to fight for his country (although always ready to do so).

Commissions came and went, bringing a much needed showing of the flag, and no memories are fonder than when an old 'salt' recalls his happy days aboard one of His Majesty's battleships. During those years it seemed that the Royal Navy was still the major force on the oceans, even though her ships had reduced in number to parity with the US Navy. The Union 'Jack' still counted for something and the Royal Navy was still the Senior Service in more ways than one. Indeed, it had the most battle experienced ships and crews, and had carried out some of the most meticulous tests against old battleships ever witnessed.

Although there was much change so far as reconstruction was concerned, on the whole the administration and policies of the Royal Navy were little altered and Fleet practice and exercises were carried out in a fashion similar to those current during the First World War. The Admiralty saw no reason to change its thinking in this regard; it considered the battleship to be supreme despite the many critics who believed that the day of the big ship had passed. The aircraft carrier, still not fully developed, came into its own during the inter-war years, but at that time the main strength was still envisaged as lying in straight battle divisions that would engage an enemy line when required to do so.

True, future action would differ from the Great War, given the greatly reduced numbers in the type, but even though Japan and the USA were looking towards the aircraft-carrier and submarine, all major powers still struck up a massive construction programme of battleships during the years leading up to the Second World War. British battleship designs often take a knock, and lately it has become trendy to highlight their faults, but this is probably because it is comparatively easy to analyse a service that has such a long history of battle experience. Most British battleships were a compromise – no battleship ever constructed was perfect, but they contended with attacking aircraft, torpedoes, mines, submersibles, contemporary battleships and finally all weathers in all sea conditions throughout the world.

It is a simple matter to compare ship against ship statistics on paper, but it means very little in practical terms; actions speak louder than words and when one examines the record of the British battleship from 1919 to 1945, the Royal Navy's designers, the crews serving them and the vessels themselves, it becomes clear that they had little reason to pay heed to derogatory opinions. They did all that was asked of them – and sometimes paid a heavy price. As war approached in 1939 the Admiralty was all too aware that the Royal Navy was ill equipped and unready, but naval treaties, politics and financial restrictions had all taken their toll of the service since 1919. War was hard for the Navy the second time around, and by 1941 capital ships had been seriously depleted. There were few new ships and many of the older ones were in great need of modernization and long-awaited refits. The battle was pursued, however, and by 1942 the tide had turned, but the battleship had taken second place to the aircraft carrier as the most important unit in the fleet. Policy and battle tactics in the Atlantic and Pacific had altered drastically and it no longer seemed imperative to have a massive battlefleet as had been the case in 1939. The all-important weapons were carriers and fast light AA cruisers to look after them. The new enemy would now come from the air, not from over the horizon.

And what of the ships themselves, the mighty battleships – those floating leviathans of the world's oceans, that had inspired the serviceman, the journalist and the general public for generations. The sight of a 'friendly' battleship imparted a sense of visual pleasure and powerful reassurance. Crowds would flock to the sea front at Portsmouth and Devonport to see one return from a commission. On many a visit to a foreign port hundreds would gather to see the British Fleet entering their harbour. They would glide in, gondola like, over a sun-blessed sea through schools of dolphins, while overhead convoys of seagulls kept close vigil for titbits. On board, a cacophony of noise as the off-duty watch prepared to come up on deck. Many were sun-worshippers, particularly those that had just left the inclement weather of Pompey or Guz. Hatches and scuttles were opened and the awnings would go up as soon as the anchor had been dropped. The King's ships had entered harbour in all their glory – usually with main armament at salute elevation – freshly painted in the light grey (almost bleached white in the bright sunshine) Mediterranean colours. 'Anchors aweigh!' sounded and the Fleet came to rest – 'Jack' was in for some well-earned leave ashore and he would hope, a good stretch before having to return to a home port. Romantic it may sound, an idyllic picture it may seem, but this was the scene that had not changed for hundreds of years; this was the life to which 'Jack' was accustomed (even though times in general were extremely hard during the 1920s and 1930s), and these were the battleships with which he was so familiar.

In January 1948, when Lord Hall announced the scrapping of certain ships, he said: 'The First Sea Lord and I feel like padres taking a funeral service for a number of old friends. The ships the Admiralty is scrapping are old friends in every sense of the word to every officer and man in the Navy.' Without doubt, this was also the feeling of the general public. The period itself is probably the most popular with naval historians, enthusiasts and collectors alike, and when casting bait to ascertain what kind of book they would next like to see, the answer came back loud and clear – another battleship book, but with fresh information if possible, new drawings and different photographs. The first two requirements have not proved easy to furnish and the latter were even more difficult. There have been a few books on the subject over the past twenty years and a real 'dig' was needed to secure the required items. Masses of official documents have been consulted, but unfortunately many have been either destroyed or have gone missing over the years so a certain degree of continuity in the material is lacking. Private papers have been included and the drawings are from official Admiralty sources as well as unofficial ones from the author's archives. The photographs have been carefully selected so as to avoid the oft-repeated shots; those seen here will, in most cases, not have been published for 40 years.

Although the sailors and the man in the street were fiercely proud of the fleet, they probably

The labours of the battle being ended, a rest is called before entering harbour.

Life was never dull for long when serving on board a capital ship – one day nothing much, but the next might well bring a double shift. During the lull in capital ship construction (1919 to 1939) the crews carried on regardless with what ships they had. The following views show a lifestyle that was familiar to the British matelot.

Far left, top: Coaling. Certainly one of the most arduous and backbreaking tasks the crews underwent. The chore was obsolete after *Marlborough* and her sisters when the *Queen Elizabeth* and *Royal Sovereign* classes were designed to burn oil-fuel only. The photograph shows *Marlborough* c.1923.

Far left centre: 'In for a dip' – nothing would be more welcome after coaling or heavy work on the anchor party than a refreshing swim, especially when at a tropical port. Some of the lads are shown here working their way along a boom on *Royal Sovereign*, 9 August 1920.

Far left, bottom: Hoisting a torpedo on *Ramillies*. Careful procedure was needed when handling torpedoes because a slip could mean broken bodies as well as damage to the weapon itself – worth more than £2,000 each.

Left: 'Stand easy'. After work there was a period when crews could either relax, play cards or write letters, etc. Here some of the crew are seen lazing on the forecastle on a *Queen Elizabeth* class battleship

Top right: 'The concert party'. A spot of light relief to cheer up the crews and restore morale. Often the acting members would 'send up' the officers, which always received good applause. *Royal Oak*.

Centre right: 'Football team'. Each capital ship had its own team, and there was fierce competition between the squadrons. Often there were periodicals for service use only to show who was winning what in football, rowing or boxing. *Repulse*, BCS, 1931.

Right: 'Crossing the line'. Every time a ship crossed the Equator there were ceremonies and games on board. Any new rating or officer certainly went through it. The photograph shows some of the crew on *Repulse* receiving a ducking c.1926. Note the ever-present Neptune on the extreme left.

Above left: One of Jacks' favourite pastimes was to get his head down for 'forty winks'. Newcomers to hammocks said that they took a lot of getting used to but once mastered they were more comfortable than conventional beds.

Above right: Christmas day at sea. The festive season was not the best time to be away from home. Nevertheless Jack made the most of it and there was much 'splicing of the Mainbrace' and plenty to eat.

Left: 'All lit up at night'. A familiar and spectacular sight in foreign ports and one that is remembered with great fondness. The superstructure and forward 15in turrets of *Ramillies* are illuminated while anchored at Alexandria, 1930.

Below: A visit to a foreign port and welcome shore leave. HM ships *Queen Elizabeth*, *Resolution*, *Revenge* (in dry dock), *Resource* and a *London* class cruiser are seen in the favourite port of Malta *c.*1935.

never took much account of the technical changes that were taking place, perhaps because the general way of life itself was undergoing profound change. This book contains, I hope, a blend of ingredients to interest not only the technical man, but also the enthusiast, naval photograph collector, model maker and the general public, and is a tribute to all the crews that served in the Royal Navy's capital ships from 1919 until the end of the war in 1945.

R. A. Burt, Rayleigh, 1993

EVOLUTION OF THE DREADNOUGHT

The beginning of the 20th century saw the metamorphosis in British battleship design that signalled a departure from the practice of the previous ten years during which the basic design had adhered to a uniform layout (*Majestic*, 1893) with little or no improvement (see R. A. Burt *British Battleships 1889–1904*). By 1902 there was a growing appreciation of the advantages of long range and it was being realized as a result of practical experience that action could be commenced at ranges up to 10,000 yards rather than the 3–4,000 yards that had been the norm up to this time. It also became obvious that fire control would have to improve greatly if the all-important accurate spotting of the fall of shot were to be achieved. Moreover there was a need to give British battleships a heavier armament (only 4x12in for the last ten years) so that an enemy ship could be overwhelmed by a huge weight of broadside before he could bring his own guns to bear.

In 1904–5 intelligence reports from the Russo–Japanese War confirmed many of these theories and suggested that it would only be a matter of time before one of the leading maritime powers seriously considered building an all big gunned ship to suit long-range fighting requirements. After hearing a general intimation from abroad that Russia and Japan were thinking along these lines for any future construction, and that the United States had indeed gone farther by actually laying down such a vessel, the Admiralty needed no further stimulus.

When Admiral Sir John Fisher was appointed First Sea Lord in October 1904, the first thing he did was to gather a staff who were of the same mind as himself – that Britain should be the first to build the first new type of ship. His position and drive ensured that a prototype was laid down in October 1905. Named HMS *Dreadnought* at Fisher's instigation, the vessel was built in an unprecedentedly short time (1 year and 1 day) and became the first all big gunned turbine-driven battleship to go to sea.

Fred Jane, the eminent naval historian, once asked 'What is a Dreadnought?' and for some strange reason the question agitated many people. In the columns of *The Scientific American* during 1909, a Major Boerum Wetmore of Allenhurst, New Jersey put forward the vessel *Roanoke* as the first true Dreadnought type and stated that with her two 15in and one 11in guns she should rightfully take this position in history. What he forgot to mention, however, was the fact that *Roanoke* was a converted frigate which had been razed, plated with iron, armed with large guns and was, on the whole, very experimental. She also proved to be quite unsatisfactory. She was precluded from service in Confederate waters and although serving with the North Atlantic Squadron for a year proved to be a terrible seaboat, the weight of her giant turrets making her roll dangerously and the thrust of her spindles always threatening to force her out of keel when the turrets were keyed up for action.

A Mr Percival Hislam replied to the Major's letter, defending the claims of early British vessels and putting forward the *Royal Sovereign* of 1864 as a contender. 'This ship was the first true Dreadnought type,' he said. As was *Roanoke*, *Royal Sovereign* was a converted wooden hulled ship which had been iron plated and armed with five 10.5in guns mounted along the centre line, and could rightfully claim to be the first British turret ship.

The undaunted Major returned the charge with *Onandanga*, another monitor authorized by Congress in 1861. He stated that, '... she was of high freeboard and, armed with two 5in guns, must take preference to the *Royal Sovereign*'. This small war of words swelled the columns in the Press for some time, and it seems as if the conclusion was that the definition of a Dreadnought was a seagoing all big gunned ship' in which case the United States can rightfully lay claim to having had the first vessels of this type. In 1859 in his book *The Navies of the World*, Hans Busk, MA wrote 'At all events the authorities in the United States have not yet abandoned the principle of building gigantic vessels, in order to carry a few heavy guns.' The context referred to criticisms that had been voiced about the American idea, and predicted that it would be short lived. These ships were officially rated as 40-gun frigates, but actually carried only twelve, all mounted so as to ensure that seven could fire on either broadside. They were 345ft long and displaced 5,013 tons. The largest British warship of the day was *Marlborough*, a three-decker, 131-gunned screw ship displacing 4,000 tons. Clearly, those American ships embodied the principles of the true Dreadnought concept.

Although these facts should not be forgotten, the naval historian of today when asked the question 'What is a Dreadnought?' would almost certainly refer to the British *Dreadnought* herself, built in 1906, and others that followed her being loosely dubbed dreadnoughts or super dreadnoughts. This in no way reflects on any of the vessels previously mentioned, but there is a difference between modifying and experimenting with an existing vessel, and the design and construction of a true sea-going all big gunned ship. It would, however, be incorrect to claim that HMS *Dreadnought* of 1906 was the first to be designed as such, or indeed even the first to be laid down. Nevertheless, when one compares her innovatory features with existing or even proposed designs of 1906, a clear margin of superiority is apparent and at the time of her completion there was no comparable ship afloat; regardless of debate then and now, she can rightfully claim her position in naval history as the first true all big gunned dreadnought type.

When F. T. Jane gave his first opinion of HMS *Dreadnought* in 1906 after he had seen her in Portsmouth Harbour, it was obvious that he was more than a little impressed. His reactions published in *The Naval and Military Record* say it all:

'As regards those details which most strike the eye, perhaps the chief one is the bigness of everything. The mast, which is the most conspicuous object, has a peculiar massiveness about it. It is a tripod affair but each tripod-leg is like the trunk of some enormous forest tree. Similarly the funnels. They are not particularly high, and end-on they are narrow to reduce wind resistance, but seen from the broadside they have the characteristic immenseness of the Dreadnought. Aft, the eye is caught by a couple of square box-like erections. They are apparently some kind of ventilator. Each is about the size of the tower of a village church. Everything is big; everything is on the grand scale.

'She is not in any way one's conception of a ship. Regarded as a ship I suppose she is ugly, because she is unconventional. But her ugliness is that of one of Brangwyn's best pictures alongside the oleographic effort of the conventional R.A. There is no Alma-Tadema about her. But she looks what she is – the embodiment of power, of solidity of all that we delight to call English and which some neurotics call Philistine.

One's first and last conception of her is that.'

It is well documented that *Dreadnought* started one of the greatest arms races ever known, but for all that it was Great Britain that had managed to lead the field in construction technology by the time the Great War had started in 1914. Suffice to say that never before had a single type of ship caused such controversial mayhem and practical upset – and certainly never since.

From *Dreadnought* onwards the vessels remained a source of debate, but remain they would for the next forty years as the supreme capital ship in the navies of the world. Toppled somewhat by the ever-increasing submarine warfare and finally the arrival of the accurate airborne torpedo-bomber launched from aircraft carriers, the battleship was slowly relegated to subsidiary duties. Its demise was forecast as long ago as 1920, but she still served on with distinction throughout the Second World War and in fact is still at sea today (1990) in the US Navy, proving that there has been little to compare with her power even by today's standards; the battleship has no equal, and there is still a demand for heavy gunfire – not a bad record for a type of vessel primarily designed more than 80 years ago.

Some of the British battleships that followed *Dreadnought* were as different from her as she had been from the *Majestic* of 1893, but they all had one thing in common in that they were all designed to carry the heaviest possible armament on a load displacement. In fact, gun sizes increased dramatically from 12in diameter to a massive 15in in just a short period of time when it was realized that modern layouts could only muster ten big guns in different arrangements without cramping the basic design. After *Dreadnought* in 1906 came the following classes: *Bellerophon, St Vincent, Neptune, Colossus, Orion, King George V, Iron Duke, Queen Elizabeth* and *Royal Sovereign*.

Three war purchases supplemented the Royal Navy's inventory during the war, *Agincourt, Erin* and *Canada*, and the world's first battlecruiser was laid down in 1906 (*Invincible* class) followed by the *Indefatigable, Lion, Queen Mary, Tiger, Renown, Courageous* and *Furious* classes.

During the Great War many improvements were made internally and externally of necessity because of action damage, and by 1918 the British capital ship was the most capable of its type in the world. The early Dreadnoughts saw limited appearance changes which usually amounted to little more than bridge and searchlight development, but the vessels that escaped the great scrapping programme of 1921 underwent drastic measures to keep pace with modern-day requirements. With no new ships (except *Nelson* and *Rodney*) entering service from 1920, it became difficult to keep some of the vessels fit for front-line duties and some of the designs suffered as a result. Nevertheless, it was a task that all navies had to undertake.

It is difficult go give a comprehensive account of internal alterations made from 1920 to 1945 because many of the refit documents have been lost or destroyed, but at least photographic evidence, where existing, shows us the external alterations that were made, and it is hoped that the small-scale drawings that follow will give an insight to the procedure of development from *Dreadnought* in 1906 through to *Royal Sovereign* of 1913 (the last battleships to be built during the Great War. Some of the basic changes to look for are:

Extended bridgework.
Anti-torpedo net removal.
Drastic searchlight redistribution.
AA guns added.
Searchlight towers around funnels.
Removal of all flying decks.
Secondary armament closed in and given some protection.
Fire control installed.
New heavy foretops.
Reduction of topmasts.
Clinker screens to funnels.
Aircraft flying-off platforms on top of main turrets.

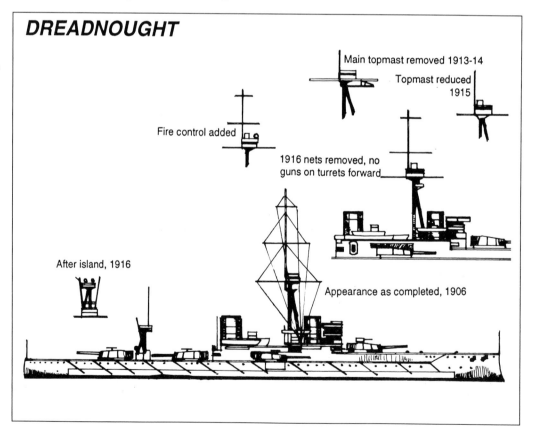

DREADNOUGHT

Main topmast removed 1913-14

Topmast reduced 1915

Fire control added

1916 nets removed, no guns on turrets forward

After island, 1916

Appearance as completed, 1906

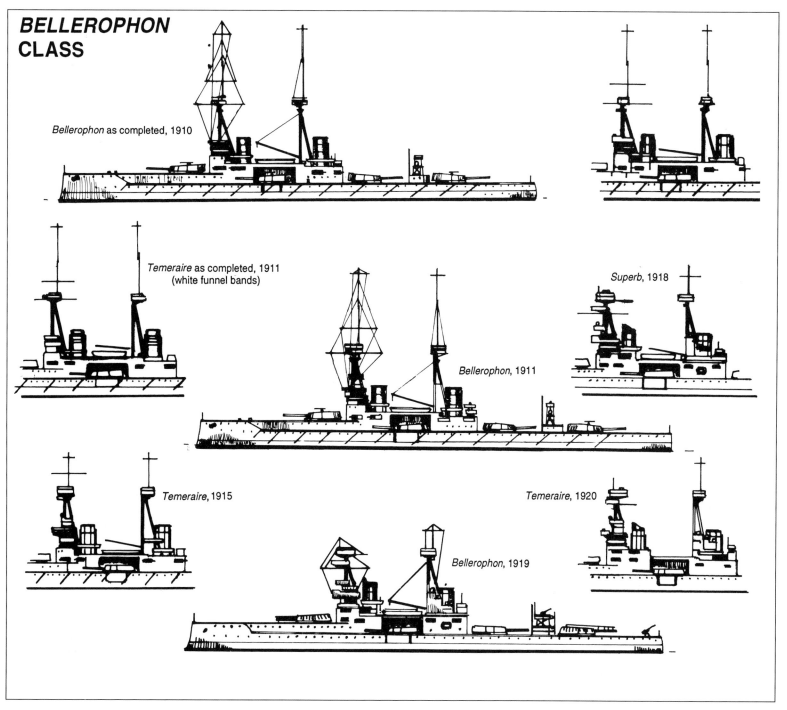

BELLEROPHON CLASS

Bellerophon as completed, 1910

Temeraire as completed, 1911
(white funnel bands)

Bellerophon, 1911

Superb, 1918

Temeraire, 1915

Temeraire, 1920

Bellerophon, 1919

ST VINCENT CLASS

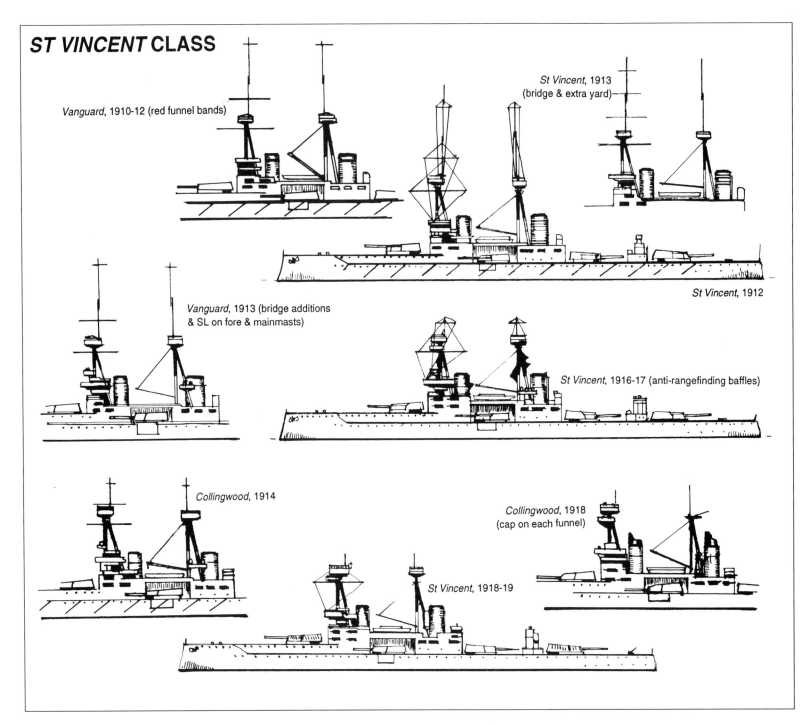

Vanguard, 1910-12 (red funnel bands)

St Vincent, 1913
(bridge & extra yard)

St Vincent, 1912

Vanguard, 1913 (bridge additions
& SL on fore & mainmasts)

St Vincent, 1916-17 (anti-rangefinding baffles)

Collingwood, 1914

Collingwood, 1918
(cap on each funnel)

St Vincent, 1918-19

NEPTUNE AS COMPLETED

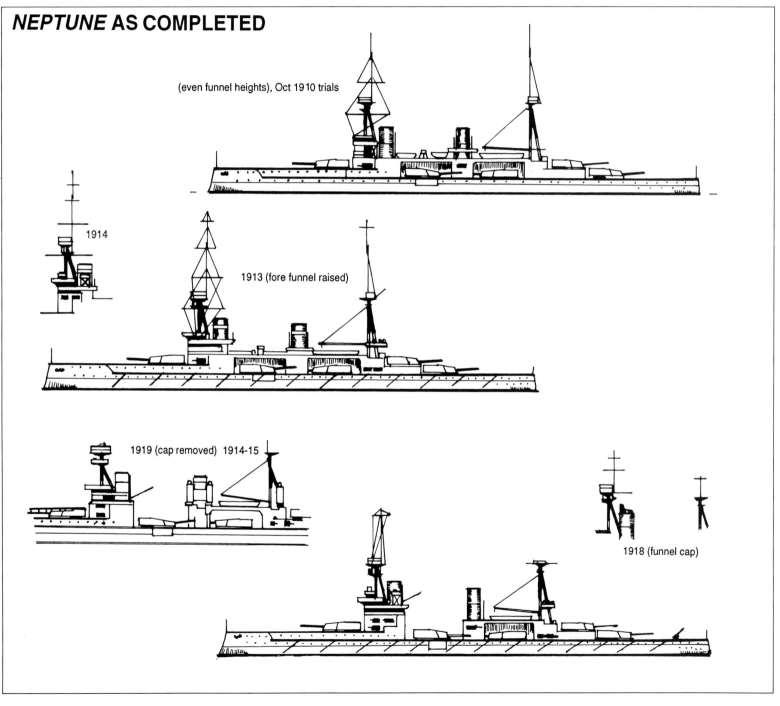

(even funnel heights), Oct 1910 trials

1914

1913 (fore funnel raised)

1919 (cap removed) 1914-15

1918 (funnel cap)

HERCULES AND COLOSSUS

1913, white band on after funnel

(Very similar to each other) *Hercules* as completed, 1911

Hercules, 1920

Colossus, 1913-14 (Enlarged bridge & extra SL around tripod)

Colossus, 1918 (Bridge differences in both during this period)

ORION CLASS

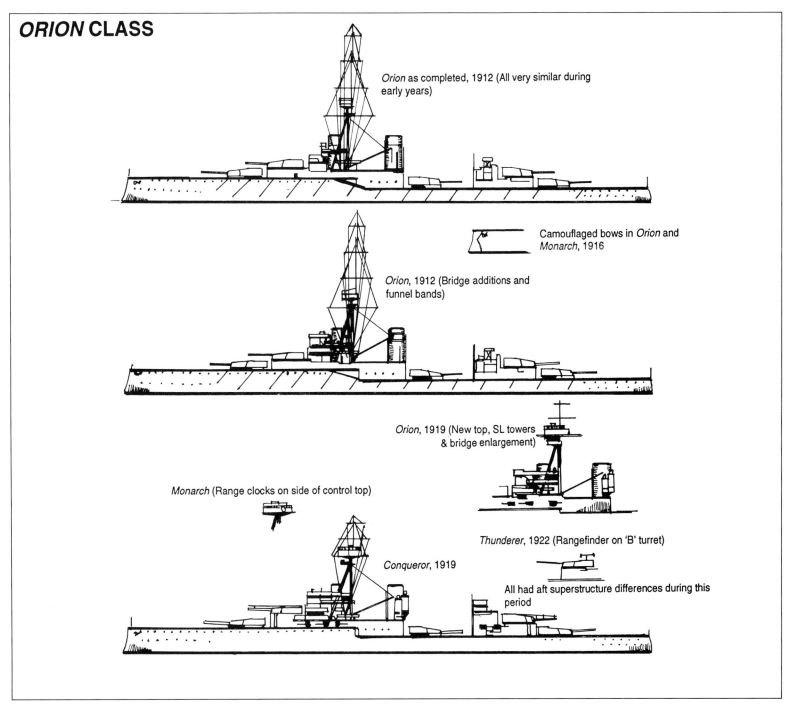

Orion as completed, 1912 (All very similar during early years)

Camouflaged bows in *Orion* and *Monarch*, 1916

Orion, 1912 (Bridge additions and funnel bands)

Orion, 1919 (New top, SL towers & bridge enlargement)

Monarch (Range clocks on side of control top)

Thunderer, 1922 (Rangefinder on 'B' turret)

Conqueror, 1919

All had aft superstructure differences during this period

KING GEORGE V
CLASS

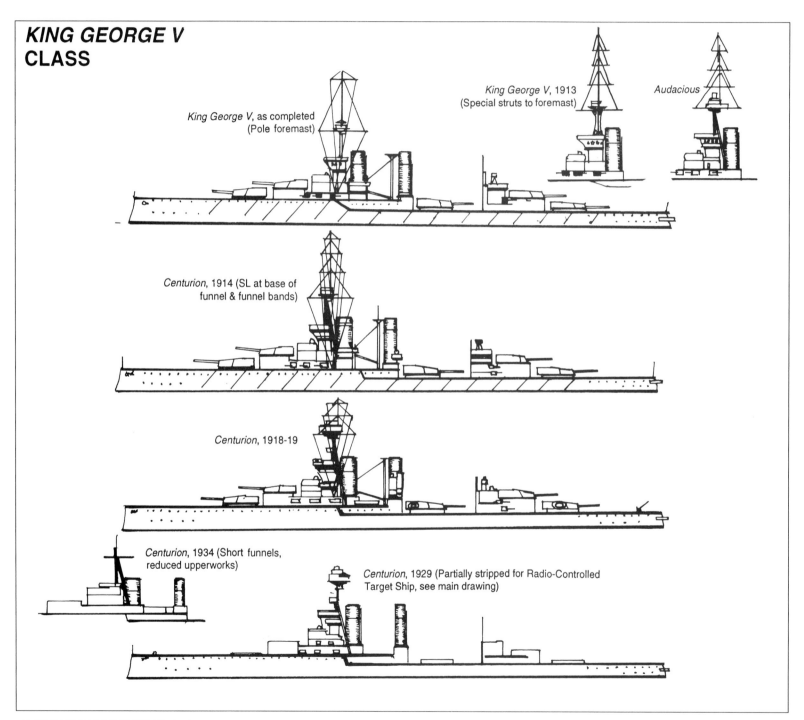

King George V, as completed
(Pole foremast)

King George V, 1913
(Special struts to foremast)

Audacious

Centurion, 1914 (SL at base of
funnel & funnel bands)

Centurion, 1918-19

Centurion, 1934 (Short funnels,
reduced upperworks)

Centurion, 1929 (Partially stripped for Radio-Controlled
Target Ship, see main drawing)

IRON DUKE CLASS

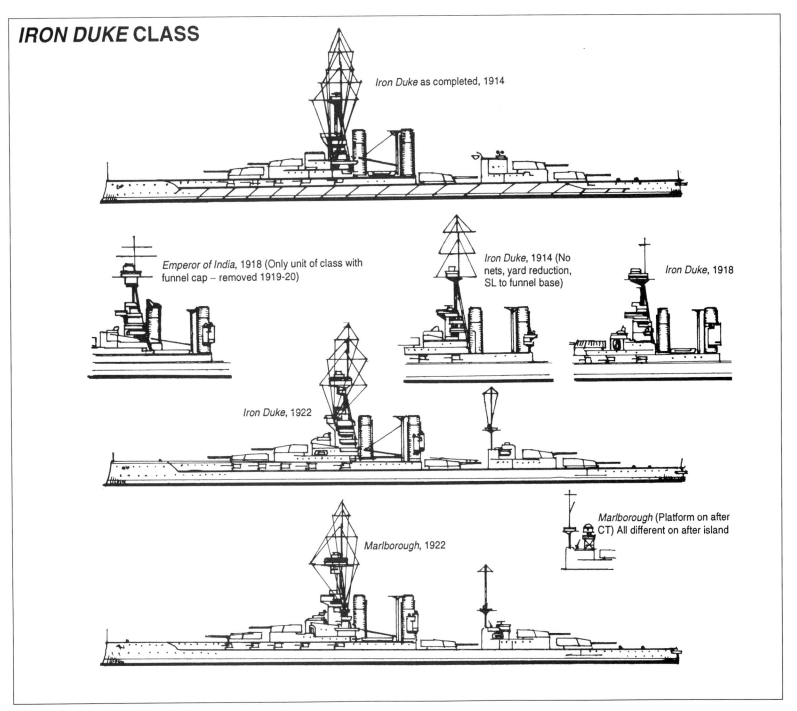

Iron Duke as completed, 1914

Emperor of India, 1918 (Only unit of class with funnel cap – removed 1919-20)

Iron Duke, 1914 (No nets, yard reduction, SL to funnel base)

Iron Duke, 1918

Iron Duke, 1922

Marlborough, 1922

Marlborough (Platform on after CT) All different on after island

QUEEN ELIZABETH CLASS

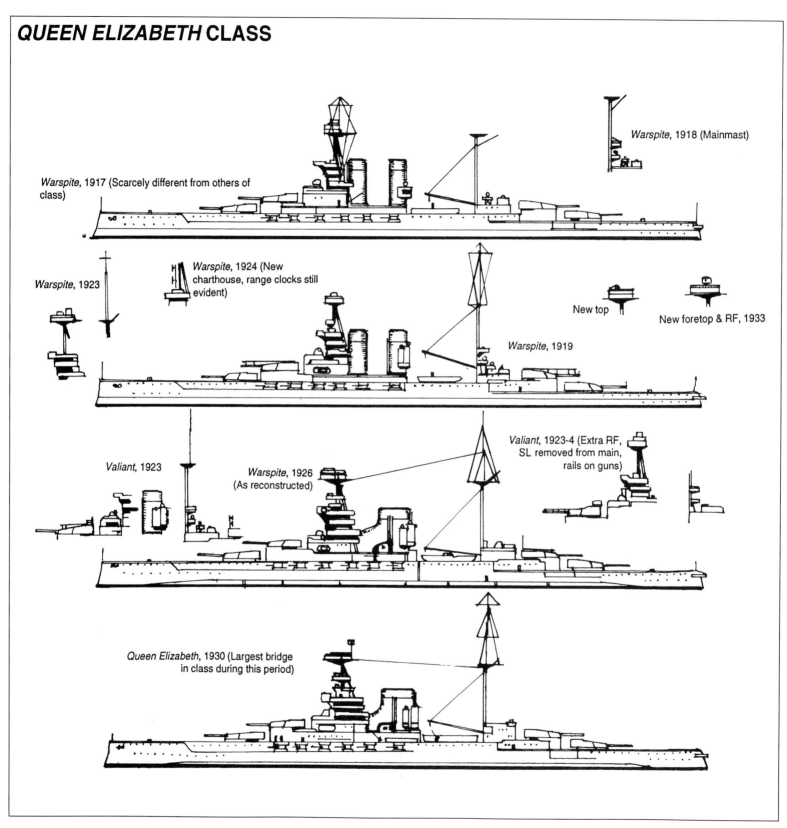

Warspite, 1918 (Mainmast)

Warspite, 1917 (Scarcely different from others of class)

Warspite, 1923

Warspite, 1924 (New charthouse, range clocks still evident)

New top

New foretop & RF, 1933

Warspite, 1919

Valiant, 1923

Warspite, 1926 (As reconstructed)

Valiant, 1923-4 (Extra RF, SL removed from main, rails on guns)

Queen Elizabeth, 1930 (Largest bridge in class during this period)

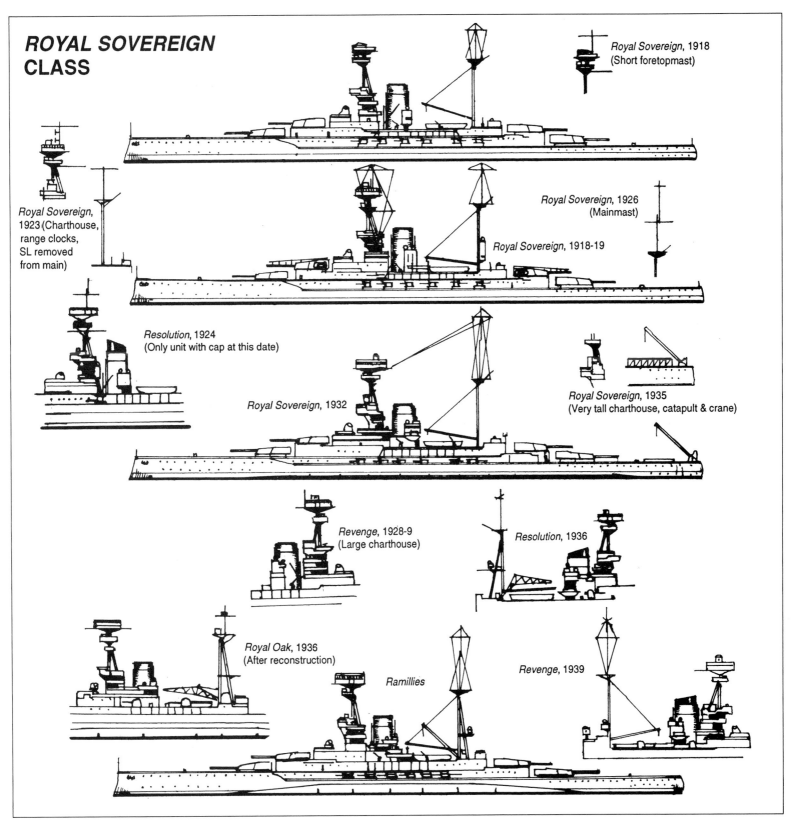

ROYAL SOVEREIGN CLASS

Royal Sovereign, 1918
(Short foretopmast)

Royal Sovereign,
1923 (Charthouse,
range clocks,
SL removed
from main)

Royal Sovereign, 1926
(Mainmast)

Royal Sovereign, 1918-19

Resolution, 1924
(Only unit with cap at this date)

Royal Sovereign, 1935
(Very tall charthouse, catapult & crane)

Royal Sovereign, 1932

Revenge, 1928-9
(Large charthouse)

Resolution, 1936

Royal Oak, 1936
(After reconstruction)

Ramillies

Revenge, 1939

POST-WAR REORGANIZATION
AND NAVAL TREATIES

Although the Great War had hit Britain's economy hard, it was realized that no reduction in her navy could be planned immediately hostilities ceased because of a great deal of uncertainty about the future. Burdened with a massive fleet it certainly did not need in peacetime, the Royal Navy was anxious to reduce it, but both America and Japan were busy planning massive construction programmes. Faced with these problems and the fact that the Treasury was not exactly forthcoming with the appropriate funds, the Admiralty had to decide whether it would be beneficial to build new ships or reconstruct some of the many warships in service that were fast becoming obsolete. Either measure represented severe financial outlay, but, given its international commitments, the Admiralty was practically forced into an uneasy situation of a battle fleet reconstruction. The war ended in November 1918, but it was an uneasy peace so far as the Royal Navy was concerned. What was to be done with the massive German fleet that had just arrived in Scapa Flow – not to mention the crews aboard the ships? Writing for the Admiralty Reconstruction Committee Sir William May stated:

'The work of the A.R.C. cannot be satisfactorily proceeded with unless a definition of policy on which to work is decided upon. The majority of questions to be considered hinge exactly on the peace terms and consequently the strength at which the Navy is to be maintained. What peace terms may be is impossible to say definitely, but they might be on the terms of the following:

'1. A patched-up peace, i.e., one which would be little more than an armistice and in which the nations would continue to develop preparations for possible future hostilities.

'2. Peace terms which, though apparently lasting, would not bind entirely, any or all of the opposing nations to a definite demobilization of their armed forces, or which would entail only a partial reduction in the preparations for war.

'It is not therefore possible at the present time to base a reconstruction policy on the future terms of peace but it may be assumed that economic considerations will govern this policy. Whatever the peace negotiations may determine, there can be little doubt that all the belligerent nations will, from the financial point of view, do their best to reduce expenditure and cut down their armaments to avoid involving themselves in further expenditure on war requirements.

'Great Britain with other nations will have to reduce expenditure on the navy to the lowest possible point compatible with retaining it in such a state of efficiency and superiority as will enable it to meet the German Navy in case of further war.'

On 21 June 1919 the German Navy ceased to be a problem when it scuttled its huge fleet while at anchor in Scapa Flow, but this was not entirely to the satisfaction of the Admiralty because the German ships could have been put to good use in the Royal Navy by using materials, or by scrapping them and using the funds towards fresh construction. But the High Seas Fleet had gone.

During the second post-war year (1920), however, a situation came about to prompt consideration of new construction at an unprecedented level so far as a battleship size was concerned. It seemed that the war had done little to end the struggle for naval supremacy, but merely substituted Japan for Germany. Moreover, America was preparing to rebuild its battlefleet completely to meet any challenge world-wide. On the drawing-board were: America: six battleships (*Indiana* class, 43,000 tons); six battlecruisers (*Constellation* class 43,000 tons); Japan: two battleships (*Kaga* and *Tosa* 40,000 tons); two battlecruisers (*Amagi* and *Akagi* 43,000 tons); two battleships completing with 16in guns (*Nagato* and *Mutsau* 33,000 tons). It was impossible for Great Britain to ignore such a threat and preparations were made to meet the new ships.

Early in 1921 orders were given to scrap dozens of the 1914 – 18 veterans to make way for new construction. The original *Dreadnought* plus all battleships and battlecruisers built from 1907 to 1910 were sold – the largest scrapping programme up to that date.

At a stroke the Royal Navy had reduced its power of sea supremacy to an all-time low. Gone was the 'Two Power Standard' of the late 1900s and the struggle was on to maintain a suitable level to meet different requirements. By the end of 1921 the DNC and staff had produced designs for what were probably the finest and most powerful warship to date. The 1921 battleships and battlecruisers matched anything (in most cases completely outmatched) in foreign navies and moves were made to lay down four of them simultaneously (see *Nelson* class and G3 designs).

When the figures for these ships were released, both America and Japan were less than pleased because it meant that they would have to build even larger ships than envisaged. The only solution was to call a meeting to consider a disarmament policy that would considerably reduce what was perceived as a future war programme, with Great Britain, America, Japan, France and Italy all invited. The delegates met in Washington on 12 November 1921 to discuss a suitable treaty and without going into the very difficult negotiations that took place and the fact that Great Britain conceded much more than any other nation, it will suffice to show the actual results. The treaty made provision for the scrapping of a very large amount of tonnage: America to retain eighteen capital ships with an aggregate of 500,650 tons; Great Britain to retain 22 with an aggregate of 580,450 tons (America to retain a smaller number of capital ships because the American ships were, in general, later and larger than those of Britain. Japan retained ten capital ships aggregating 301,320 tons. The maximum for any replacement tonnage was fixed at 525,000 tons for America and Great Britain and 315,000 tons for Japan. France retained ten ships for a total tonnage of 221,170 tons and Italy ten aggregating 182,800 tons. Each nation was permitted to lay down new tonnage in 1927, 1929 and 1931.

Each nation was allowed a replacement allotment of 175,000 tons. It was agreed that none of the powers should build a replacement capital ship displacing more than 35,000 tons and armed with greater than 16in guns, and the age limit for capital ships was fixed at twenty years. It was also agreed that no power should build more ships than the minimum required. After a heated debate, and as a concession to Great Britain, the Royal Navy was permitted to construct two ships of 35,000 tons armed with 16in guns (*Nelson* and *Rodney*) because the American ships under construction (*Colorado*, *Maryland*, *West Virginia*) and the Japanese pair armed with 16in guns (*Nagato* and *Mutsu*). The agreement was signed on 6 February 1922.

There were many in Great Britain who saw the Washington Naval Treaty as the end of the

Royal Navy as the supreme power in the world's oceans, and in a strict sense this was true. The DNC, Sir Eustace Tennyson D'Eyncourt, wrote:

'Dear Mr Lloyd George,

'I wish to place before you my views on the subject of the present Conference at Washington, more particularly regarding the proposal for a Naval Holiday. There appears to be a tendency to set on one side the opinion of naval and technical men on the subject.

'This is very dangerous, and as Chief Technical Adviser to the Admiralty, I feel it my duty to give you my definite opinion.

'A ten-year naval holiday would result in a complete débâcle in the matter of efficient naval material. It would take us many years to recover the ground lost and we should absolutely cease to retain the lead we have held for so long in the matter of thorough efficiency of our ships.

'I need not weary you with all the details and arguments on the subject, but it is in my very carefully weighed opinion that our present ships would be altogether obsolete in a few years. Some of them are nearly so now, and we should be unable to produce the best ships to replace them after a long period of inactivity such as proposed. We have had practically four years' "Holiday" already.

'You will never produce A1 material if you stop constructing; without an A1 Navy we are finished.

'The French are logical in asking the great powers if they can give assurance and guarantees against aggression from Germany. If not the French say they must have the army they consider necessary. We should be equally logical in saying "can you give us a guarantee at securing our communications our food, etc., in case of war? If not, we must have the Navy we consider necessary."

'Insistence upon a thoroughly efficient if not large navy should be our equivalent cry to the American Monroe doctrine, and it is far more vital to us. A ten-year Naval Holiday would render this impossible.

'There are those who wish deliberately to wreck our capacity for producing efficient war material. That cannot be permitted, as we should be at the mercy of other European powers – perhaps Germany and Russia or a latin combination in the future.

'These "peace at any price" people may argue that we can restore the Navy at any future time; that is a delusion. When once it has been allowed to go down, it will take years to restore; this applies to both material and personnel. It is therefore absolutely necessary to continue building at a reduced rate, but not to stop. The Navy is the sole life-assurance of the nation.

'The careful householder may effect economies in many directions, but he never allows his insurance premiums to lapse.

'Possibly the old saying *Si vis pacem para bellum* requires qualification, but the converse *si vis bellum para pacem* is certainly true.'

During the years following the Washington Treaty there were constant talks aimed at further reducing any show of naval strength:

League Preparatory Commission, 1925
At the end of 1925 the Council of the League of Nations brought into being a Preparatory Commission to take over the work which had been going on since 1921. It stated that the maintenance of peace required further reduction of national armaments to the lowest point of consistency. Although a good idea in principle, it was found that it did not do away with the 'germ' of renewed naval competition. It became a simple case that the great maritime powers could not agree on a suitable limit to tonnage and just how many warships of different types should be scrapped and what should remain.

Geneva Conference, 1927
On 20 June 1927 Britain, America and Japan met again for renewed talks on the further reduction of the armed forces of each nation. Italy and France did not attend in their full capacity but sent observers instead. The failure of the meeting lay in the inability to agree on cruiser strength because of each nation's different requirements. The British suggestion that cruisers be divided into two classes: 10,000 tons and 8in guns, and smaller cruisers with 6in guns did not go down well with the Americans.

Pact of Paris, 1928
A pact by which 56 nations agreed to renounce war as an instrument of policy was signed on 27 August 1928.

Anglo-American conversations, 1929
Talks between Ramsay MacDonald (Prime Minister) and President Hoover took place during June 1929 when the President stated: 'We must find a yardstick with which to make reasonable comparisons' of naval units. During most of the talks since 1921 it had become increasingly difficult to get all the parties to agree on anything. Each country still insisted on doing what was best for its own navy. There was much talk of constructing smaller battleships than were really needed and scrapping larger battleships that were not yet obsolete. Britain saw America as being particularly awkward and America felt the same of Britain. Japan, on the other hand, was seen to be becoming more distant from all parties concerned.

Naval Treaty, 1930
Talks finally evolved into action during the 1930 discussions when Britain, America, Japan, France and Italy all primarily agreed to limit warship construction.
1. The five powers agreed not to build any new battleships before 1936, but France and Italy could use up their unused tonnage allotted to them from 1927 and 1929.
2. America would scrap the battleships *Utah* and *Arkansas*. Britain would scrap the battleships *Iron Duke*, *Benbow*, *Marlborough*, *Emperor of India* and the battlecruiser *Tiger* (*Iron Duke* and *Arkansas* to be retained as training ships). Japan would scrap the battlecruiser *Hiei* (she was, in fact, retained as a training ship).

Further scrapping would take place over the next few years after the conference. Aircraft carriers were limited in size to 10,000 tons (new construction) and an even tighter limitation was proposed on cruiser construction.

From that date the naval side of British affairs was left to decay and many of the skilled workers, draughtsmen and shipbuilders left the service. Battleships themselves were thought to be completely obsolete and there were renewed calls to scrap the lot, but the situation in Germany, where the military element was on the move once more, led to disquiet throughout Europe and among the Pacific powers.

There was to be no more new construction until January 1937 by which time Germany was becoming a real threat and Japan had long gone her own way and was most secretive about her

Below: Port quarter view of *Iron Duke* in Weymouth Bay, 1929.

intentions. When the long capital ship holiday ended it had been agreed to limit new construction to 35,000 tons and 16in guns. This agreement was not at first favoured by the British who had instigated a move towards a smaller battleship which would have only 12in guns (see design notes) and displace about 25,000 tons.

America however, would not agree to this and a compromise was reached. No limit to the number of new ships was fixed, but it would be governed by financial restrictions imposed by individual nations.

Freed from the treaties that had so hampered it during the twenties, and thirties, the Royal

Navy began a panic construction programme in January 1937, but was never ever again on a par numerically with America whose large resources easily outmatched all the other maritime powers. Thus Great Britain's battleships entered the Second World War ill equipped, under powered and at a stage of mid construction.

INTRODUCTION

DESIGN

Although there were basic ideas regarding design that had been formulated in the light of war experience, it became necessary to re-evaluate the entire issue when preparing new ships, given the financial restrictions imposed after the war. Before and during the war types of ships were developed for certain basic roles, but it was found that they needed many additions and alterations if they were to be efficient in multiple roles. Many new types were built for special purposes (*Renown* class, etc.), but as British capital ships had to be all things and carry weapons of all types, it was seen as unnecessary to load a ship down with all sorts of fittings it really did not need. It was argued that if a ship had a main role the designer would have a clearer idea of what was required. The question arose as to whether the differing qualities and functions of the battleship and the battlecruiser could be combined in one ship as a compromise. It seemed that there was no reason why such a type should not be more efficient than the two specialist types – the heavily armoured slow ship and the lightly armoured fast ship. The devastating outcome at Jutland, where lightly armoured ships came into contact with the enemy fleet before the slower, heavily armoured ships, made the prospect of a fast, heavily armoured ship an appealing one.

After the war there was no shortage of personal opinions and the DNC's Department was often bombarded with sketch designs from serving officers as well as from the private sector. One such sketch design came from Rear-Admiral Sir Richard Phillimore, KCMG, CB, MVO (President of the Post-War Questions Committee, 10 October 1919): 'Is there any intention of radically altering the system on which our ships have hitherto been armoured and placing the bulk of the armour in a horizontal deck covering the ships' vitals instead of on the side of the ship? If not, please state what reasons are considered to make this impossible as the main idea in capital ship construction or to make the placing of armour at 20 degrees to the normal preferable to placing it at 70 degrees. What conclusions were drawn by the DNC Department from the trials recently carried out on HMS *Swiftsure* and a target representing armoured protection of *Hood* abreast certain magazines?

'10 x 6in; 16 x 5.5in; 4 x TT; 6,000 miles radius; speed 25 knots maximum; armour 6in horizontal; splinterproof control structures; no conning tower.'

In the Admiralty corridors there was much talk of subermersibles carrying large guns, super ships showing ridiculous features and, as always, the school of thought that was inclined to 'scrap the lot!'. After many months of post-war debate it was concluded with great clarity that if the big gun was still to be the primary weapon (which it was) the ship should be designed accordingly. 1. Make battleships as strong as possible. 2. Do away with torpedo tubes in large ships (they were dangerous in case of direct hit). 3. Give priority to special-purpose ships – cruisers, destroyers, etc. The argument against having two different weapons of offence requiring different tactics and making life difficult for the operators was a sound one that was heeded during those post-war years. Torpedo attacks were better made from specialist vessels: torpedo-boat destroyers, submarines or torpedo-cruisers. Any weight saved by deleting this weapon from capital ships could be better used in protection qualities.

The influence of the Washington Treaty on design in the Royal Navy was profound, but Britain accepted the proposals, admitting that with regret she was no longer able to maintain the 'two power standard' she had enjoyed before the war. Since 1919 the Admiralty had been engaged in the wholesale scrapping of older vessels, but many were good ships that need not have been scrapped. The Washington Treaty only made matters worse; a letter in the German *Gazette* said it all: 'The Washington Conference may prove to be a milestone in the next war.'

The outstanding feature of the Washington Treaty was that naval strength was still classed in terms of capital ships, in complete disregard of the strong opposition that maintained that the day of the battleship was past. The ever-forceful Sir Percy Scott wrote in March 1922: 'Naval strength is no longer measured by the number of battleships a country has but by the number of aeroplane carriers and aeroplanes.' Clearly, however, it had been proved that although the submarines and aircraft were an essential part of the modern fleet, they were certainly by no means a substitute and future designs were prepared accordingly. Although no official sketches of a hybrid battleship/carrier were prepared, many

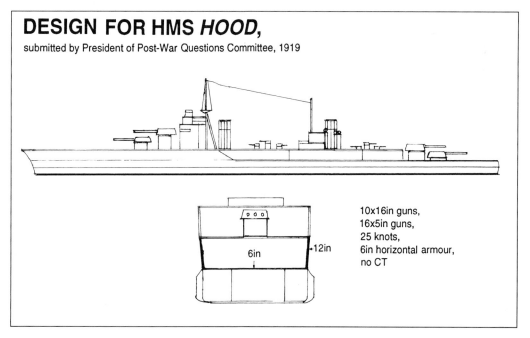

DESIGN FOR HMS *HOOD*,
submitted by President of Post-War Questions Committee, 1919

6in

12in

6in

10x16in guns,
16x5in guns,
25 knots,
6in horizontal armour,
no CT

unofficial sketches were put forward and make interesting reading.

Official sketches drawn up during 1920/21 before the Washington Treaty took effect, show ships of massive proportions. The first few were merely developments of *Hood*, but later culminated in a completely new type (G3) with 18in guns. There was obviously a need for a fast battleship and a slower, heavier armoured battleship, and these early sketches reflected just that. The battlecruiser type had in fact evolved into a fast battleship and the battleship into a huge, well-armed, heavily armoured and capable warship. Most of the sketches sported 18in guns at the largest and 16in at the smallest. To reach final layouts by November 1921 (N3-G3) proved quite complex and the designs had moved through more than eighteen stages (full development of type is described in Raven and Roberts' *Battleships of World War Two*. They came to nothing, however, and naval treaties were expedited to stop the very expensive, over the top, programme which no country could sustain financially. Some of the designs prepared for the G3 group and others that followed are shown in the *Nelson* class chapter, but there were also masses of designs produced in an endeavour to get round the Washington Treaty limitations and they seem to have been produced merely speculatively and to go on record for future use.

When one considers the policy and strength of the Royal Navy during the Washington Treaty discussions, one concludes that there was little realization at that time that the proposals as finally agreed would seriously restrict the decisions of those who were responsible for the design and construction of major fighting units. In fact the limitations, although feasible on paper, were just not practicable. As *Nelson* and *Rodney* completed (1927) and with a construction gloom for many years during and after their construction, it was only natural that new designs should be proposed. Those that were, however, were a compromise still based on severe weight and size restrictions and the sketches show this most clearly. Unofficially the battleship/carrier (see sketch) idea was being debated and in theory and practice it was actually feasible, but unfortunately it was never seriously considered.

After debate, staff requirements in 1928 for new battleships showed an improved *Nelson* type,

but a return to four twin turrets mounted fore and aft as was usual standard Admiralty practice before *Nelson*. Twelve 6in guns remained as secondary armament but were more widely spaced than in *Nelson* (40 feet centre of turrets as opposed to *Nelson*'s 30 feet). The tertiary battery was eight 4.7in guns, and general fire control was a repeat of *Nelson*. To save weight the aft DCT was omitted and control was to be from 'X' turret. In the past the principal objections to the directing turret were: 1. The directing gun had to cease fire, since the loading operation interfered too much with the director layer. 2. A human link was introduced into the elevation and training transmission which introduced lag and errors into the system. Both these objections were largely discounted by modern methods of sighting turret guns and high-speed direct electrical transmission. The system was admittedly not so good as an independent director position, but was good enough for a rarely used alternative and certainly saved the use of personnel and officers.

Protection was similar to that of *Nelson*'s, but the serious threat posed by diving APC shells *vis-à-vis*, for example, *Nelson*'s shallow belt was now realized. *Nelson*'s arrangement of side armour had its advantages, but it was considered that placing the belt inboard from the waterline could result in projectiles glancing down to explode inside the ship and possibly passing under the

armoured belt (see drawings). *Nelson*'s belt was severely criticized officially in 1927 and this fault was at last given serious consideration. The weakness, however, was never officially acknowledged. A meeting was held on 20 November 1928 to discuss Design 545-A+B and most items on the agenda were primarily agreed.

During those doldrum years it was necessary for Britain to watch foreign trends closely and strongly resist any commitment to single types (such as *Deutschland* and *Dunkerque*) being laid down. Certainly no group of ships was planned until it was certain that the design could match any foreign adversary. Displacement and gun calibre were fixed; the two remaining factors being speed and armour. In this respect it was considered sound policy to give any new ships normal battleship speeds and good protective qualities rather than strain the design for a high speed which, it was thought, usually fell off with age. One particular point in all the designs forwarded was that the main armament strongly favoured the standard twin mountings as in the *Queen Elizabeth* and *Royal Sovereign* groups.

A meeting was called by the First Sea Lord on 10 January 1934 to discuss the question of size of future battleships in the light of the approaching 1935 Naval Conference. The following factors governed the situation: 1. A proposal made at Geneva by Britain to reduce the size of future battleships to 25,000 tons with

Tables for various battleship designs 1928 to 1934

	'12A'	'12B'	'12C'
Length (ft/in)	610	610	620
Beam (ft/in)	96	100	100
Draught (ft/in)	27	26	26ft 8in
Displacement (tons)	25,040	25,430	26,700
SHP	37,000	40,000	53,200
Fuel (tons)	2,700	2,700	3,000
Complement	1,264	1,266	1,286
Main armament	4 twin 12in	4 x 12in	4 x 12in
rpg	80	80	80
Secondary	6 twin 6in	6 x 6in	6 x 6in
High-angle	4 twin 4.7in	4 x 4.7in	4 x 4.7in
TT	none	none	none
Catapult and seaplane	1 of each	1 of each	1 of each
Speed (knots)	23	23	25
Armour:		As '12A'	As '12A'
Main belt	10–3in		
Bulkheads	8–3in		
Turrets	12–8½–5¾in		
Barbettes	11–9in		
Conning tower	10–7–4½in		
Decks:			
Over magazines	6in		
Machinery	4in		
Steering gear	4in		
Conning tower	10–7–4½in		
DCT	2in		
Torpedo bulkhead	1½in		
Weights (tons):			
Hull	10,510	10,600	11,100
Armour/protection	7,230	7,400	7,530
Armament	4,190	4,190	4,190
Machinery	2,050	2,180	2,800
General equipment	1,060	1,060	1,080

	'12D'	'12E'	'12F'	'12G', '12H' and '12J'
Length (ft/in)	620	610	610	all similar to
Beam (ft/in)	102	100	104	'12A' except in
Draught (ft/in)	26ft 2in	25ft 5in	25	displacement and
Displacement (tons)	26,800	24,690	24,930	'12J' had 3 triple
SHP	55,000	39,000	48,000	12in turrets.
Fuel (tons)	3,000	2,700	2,700	
Complement	1,286	1,166	1,264	
Main armament	4 x 12in	4 x 12in	2 triple, 1 twin 12in	
rpg	80	80		
Secondary	6 x 6in	6 x 6in	As '12A'	
High-angle	4 x 4.7in	4 x 4.7in		
TT	none	none		
Catapult and Seaplane	1 of each	1 of each		
Speed (knots)	25	23		
Armour	As '12A'	As '12A'	As '12A'	
Weights (tons):				
Hull	11,090	10,475	10,670	
Armour/protection	7,600	7,240	7,090	
Armament	4,190	3,810	4,020	
Machinery	2,840	2,150	2,090	
General equipment	1,080	1,015	1,060	

12in guns, or alternatively ships of 22,000 tons with 11in guns. 2. The proposal by Japan for a ship of 25,000 tons with 14in guns. 3. The American wish to preserve the present size of ship and gun, namely 35,000 tons and 16in guns. 4. The recent construction by the French of a battlecruiser of 26,000 tons and 13.5in guns (*Dunkerque*). 5. The expressed wish of the Germans to build a larger battleship than *Deutschland*.

With severe financial restrictions in force and an unwillingness to build a fleet of gigantic battleships when the treaties allowed new construction again, it was thought that the US Navy might be willing to agree, under gentle pressure that is, to a reduced size of capital ship – about 28,000 tons with 12in guns. They were to be built to stand up against 16in gun fire, attack from 2,000lb bombs and 750lb torpedoes. The Controller was asked to investigate designs of a ship carrying eight, nine or ten 12in guns with a speed of 23 knots. Sketch designs were prepared (see table) accordingly and after some debate suitable arrangements were agreed. Unfortunately, however, no other maritime power showed the slightest interest in conforming to such moderate dimensions.

The sketches for these ships were well laid out and some of the features deserve to be highlighted:

1. Armour and protection. The belt armour was placed on the outside of the hull and not, as in *Nelson* and *Rodney*, slightly inboard. Experiments had shown that the vents provided in the upper portion of the bulges of *Nelson* and *Rodney* could be omitted without disadvantages. The outside position of the armour belt necessitated a different form of bulge from that in *Nelson*, but experiments showed that it was as effective as that in the latter ships.

2. A lower and thinner belt was proposed to be placed below the main belt to meet the impact and explosion of long-range projectiles falling short as in number four round against the target *Emperor of India* and afford protection to the magazines against such plunging shellfire hitting below the main belt.

3. Main armament. Very similar to that in the *Queen Elizabeth* and *Royal Sovereign* classes but better location arrangements were made.

4. Secondary armament. In most cases this was protected in turrets but some provision was

made for armouring the turrets and barbettes.

The small battleship proposals having been dispensed with, the Admiralty returned to the main characteristics of the standard battleship which had been thoroughly worked out by November 1933. (For main dimensions see *King George V* class, 1937.) Designs on paper, although of great importance for theory and the historical record, do not in fact mean a great deal. It is comparatively simple to outline requirements in a sketch design, but to put these into practice, which means financial support and the solving of conflicting design requirements, is another matter. As can be seen from these notes designs took many directions and in fact the 1933 capital ship designs were very different from those planned during the 1920s when the Admiralty was looking ahead to the time when Great Britain could renew her battlefleet. The governing factor in designs although not straightforward are in fact easy to understand: 1. Financial considerations have priority. 2. Information about development abroad. 3. Fleet and staff requirements. 4. Balanced design (well armed, protected and good speed). 5. Unrestricted displacement.

Without a free hand on all these requirements no maritime power in the world could have built the ships that it needed at that time, and the result was that those ships that were built shortly before the Second World War were untried and, if the truth be told, generally left much to be desired.

Table for various battleship designs 1928 to 1934				
	14A	10A	16A	14B
Length (ft/in)	660	620	692	620
Beam (ft/in)	104	96	106	104
Draught (ft/in)	27ft 6in	25	30	27
Displacement (tons)	30,700	21,670	35,000	29,070
SHP	60,500	54,000	45,000	43,500
Fuel (tons)	3,500	2,700	3,000	3,000
Complement	1,320	1,050	1,342	1,300
Main armament	4 twin 14in	4 twin 10in	4 twin 16in	4 twin 14in
rpg	100	80	80	100
Secondary	6 x 6in	4 x 6in	6 x 6in	6 x 6in
High-angle	4 x 4.7in	4 x 4.7in	4 x 4.7in	4 x 4.7in
TT	none	none	none	none
Catapult and seaplane	2 of each	1 of each	2 of each	2 of each
Speed (knots)	25	25	23	23
Armour:				
Main belt	11–3½in	8–2½in	13–4in	11–3½in
Bulkheads	10–7in	8–4in	11–7in	10–7in
Turrets	14–9–7in	11–8–5¼in	15–6in	14–6in
Barbettes	12–11–10in	9–8–7in	13–10in	12–10in
Conning tower	11–8–4in	9–6–4in	12–6in	11–4¼in
Decks:				
Over magazines	6¼in	5½in	6¼in	6¼in
Machinery	4¼in	3½in	4¼in	4¼in
Steering gear	4in	3½in	4in	4in
DCT	2in	2in	2in	2in
Torpedo bulkhead	1½in	1½in	1½in	1½in
General equipment:	1,100	900	1,100	1,090
Weights (tons):				
Hull	12,000	9,460	13,400	11,250
Armour/protection	8,970	5,500	11,150	8,700
Armament	5,680	3,010	6,900	5,680
Machinery	2,950	2,800	2,450	2,350
General equipment	1,100	900	1,100	1,090

ARMOUR

With the cessation of hostilities in November 1918 some of the longest and most important debates concerning standards in capital ship design began. Looking back at certain disasters during the war it was considered at some length (since 1916) that views regarding protection were over-influenced by the losses of the battle-cruisers at Jutland. Apart from those tragic losses the war in general had highlighted the fact that modern battleships' (both British and German) armour had withstood gunfire very well. In fact even ships with pre-war standards of protection, which on paper did not have complete immunity from existing attack, still stood up very well to severe punishment and in most cases had made it back to port under their own steam.

It was considered that this capacity to take heavy punishment was the criterion of a good design, and all protection beyond the requirement of being able to withstand heavy hits was thought to amount to wasted weight. What the required protection ratio should be, however, varied a great deal from ship to ship. So far as armoured plating was concerned the Royal Navy entered the war believing that, at the fighting ranges favoured in 1914, 9in side armour and 4¼in turret roof plating was immune against 12in guns which the German battleships possessed in great numbers. In 1920, however, the Post-War Questions Committee dismissed these thicknesses, and although some favour was given to medium-range armour it was questionable whether the present-day thicknesses (13in in *Queen Elizabeth* and *Royal Sovereign*) would be impervious to the ever-increasing power of the latest APC shells being developed.

Because it had stood up so well to British shelling, the perception of German armour as being superior had been exaggerated, the truth being that the old British APC shells were incapable of penetrating the magazines and other vital areas of German heavy ships in a fit state for bursting, so not too much importance should be attached to the fact that the ships were able to return to harbour after having been hit. Defects in pre-1917 APC shells of 12in and greater calibres were: 1. they broke up on oblique impact having only been proved at normal; 2. the burster was too sensitive to be carried through a thick armour plate; 3. some failed at proof. The German ships never faced the APC shells that were developed after Jutland.

Luckily for British ships it was found that the German shells were not always up to much either; for example in 1915 an 11in shell hit the battlecruiser *Lion* at Dogger Bank and, although having pierced the armour plate, the shell was found lying on the crown of one of the turret magazines, the fuses having failed to detonate.

The latest ship at the end of the war was the mighty *Hood* but her protection had fuelled controversy from the outset, and it was proposed that a series of tests be held with a view to improving her if possible, and any other capital ship that followed. The Royal Navy was well aware of deficiencies in horizontal armour and as early as 1921 made the following statement: 'We can lay down the important axiom that it must be made impossible for the enemy to destroy your ship by one fortunate hit, i.e., it must be impossible for him to ignite your store of explosives. Nothing else is of such vital importance as this. Hits which damage some of the engines and boiler rooms or turrets are of secondary importance. Accepting this principle it can probably be asserted that it is impossible to armour all the important parts of a ship completely against the gun you carry and which it must be presumed the enemy will also carry, but if your design and material are superior to the enemy's you will take correspondingly less risk.'

The form of protection to date (1920) was based on the principle that amour fulfilled its requirements if it remained unholed after attack by shells, and to this end the plates were so designed that their restance to being holed was measurable. The measurement of imperviousness to particular shells was called the 'limit of resistance' of the plate against the shell. The power of attack up to 1917 made it possible to armour capital ships suffciently well to render them capable of resisting shell attack (in most cases) at the ranges then envisaged. The introduction of the new APC shell greatly modified the values of shell and armour and the subject of relative strength came under great scrutiny. It was found that if new construction to be immune against heavy APC shells of 15in calibre and greater, maximum armour thickness would have to be applied. These findings, however, did not quite coincide with a quote from the DNC; 'If such protection as will give, on paper, complete immunity against 18in attack be adopted, there are bound to be methods of defeating the ship and it is not difficult to picture a huge, superbly armoured vessel with its superstructure and control positions obliterated and its machinery personnel gassed, drifting at the mercy of the submarines or aircraft attending the enemy fleet. Such however is likely to be the fate of a ship in which offensive powers have been sacrificed to defence against a vessel in which superiority in offence has been the first consideration.'

After tests had shown just how good the APC shells were, the entire design of the Navy's new ships was open to question, and the Construction Department was constantly engaged in design development. The new shells would govern new standards of protection because it was obvious that other maritime powers would soon (if they had not done so already) reach adequate levels of shell ability. Trials showed that a large proportion of any target was represented by the deck, and making a ship invulnerable to shell hits in this area was exceedingly difficult within the limitations of capital ship design. Various modifications were tried, but the general conclusion was that unless some new radical form of armour were developed it was impossible to improve arrangements in heavy ships other than by increasing armour thicknesses far beyond the present level (1920 = 3in average) which would involve unacceptable weight addition.

It is impossible to deal with a single design feature, such as protection, in isolation. The designer has to consider the ship as a whole, all features depending upon one another. At that time (1920–21) speed was considered a most important factor in relation to other features of a ship, as it affected the other elements of the layout, with the exception of the armament. If machinery were reduced the length of the

Table for various battleship designs 1928 to 1934

	'11A'	'10G'	'12K'	'12L'
Length (ft/in)	600	600	630	620
Beam (ft/in)	98	98	102	102
Draught (ft/in)	26	25	27	27
Displacement (tons)	23,300	22,000	28,150	27,750
SHP	48,000	48,000	80,000	80,000
Fuel (tons)	2,700	3,000	3,000	3,000
Complement	1,030	1,030	1,030	1,030
Main armament	4 twin 11in	4 twin 10in	4 twin 12in	3 triple 12in
rpg	80	80		
Secondary	4 x 6in	4 x 6in	12 x 4.7in	12 twin 4.7in
High-angle	4 x 4.7in	4 x 4.7in		
TT	none	none	none	none
Catapult and seaplane	1 of each	1 of each	1 of each	1 of each
Speed (knots)	24	24	27	27
Armour:				
Main belt	9–3in	8–2½in	10–5in	otherwise as
Bulkheads	9–5in	8–4in	10–7in	'12K'
Turrets	12–5¾in	11–5¾in	12–5¾in	
Barbettes	10–8in	9–7in	10–7in	
Conning tower	10–4½in	9–4in	10–4½in	
Decks:				
Over magazines	5¾in	5½in	6in	
Machinery:	3¾in	3½in	4in	
Steering gear	3¾in	3½in	4in	
DCT	2in	2in	2in	
Torpedo bulkhead	1½in	1½in	1½in	
Weights (tons):				
Hull	10,000	9,800	11,500	11,320
Armour/protection	6,250	5,700	8,470	8,100
Armament	3,550	3,350	4,250	4,400
Machinery	2,500	2,500	2,880	2,880
General equipment	1,000	950	1,050	1,050

Table for various battleship designs 1928 to 1934

	'12N'	'12O'	'12P'	'12Q' Same
Length (ft/in)	614	614	634	as '12N' except
Beam (ft/in)	102	102	103ft 6in	12 x 12in guns
				in triple turrets
Draught	29	29	28ft 6in	
Displacement (tons)	28,500	28,130	28,500	
SHP	45,000	45,000	45,000	
Fuel (tons)	3,500	3,500	3,500	
Complement	1,378	1,400	1,425	
Main armament	8 x 12in	9 x 12in	10 x 12in	
rpg	80			
Secondary:	12 x 6in		otherwise	
High-angle	12 x 4.7in	all same	same as	
TT	10 above water	as '12N'	'12N'	
Catapult and seaplane	1 on turret			
Speed (knots)	23			
Armour:				
Main belt	9–6in			
Bulkheads	10–4in			
Turrets	11–5½in			
Barbettes	11½in			
Decks:				
Over magazines	5½in			
Machinery	3½in			
Steering gear	3½in			
Torpedo bulkhead:	2in			

machinery space, the length of the armoured citadel, the amount of fuel, the amount of deck protection were also reduced, leading to finally, a smaller hull with fewer fittings and less equipment. This was immediately apparent when the design of a battleship of say 22 or 23 knots was compared to that of a battlecruiser of say 30 knots and it was at once found impossible to give the same thickness of protection to the faster ship as to the slower. In HMS *Hood* it was found possible to provide the protection and even increase it over that of the *Royal Sovereign* class battleships while maintaining the same armament and giving the speed of 31 knots, plus a very heavy weight of underwater protection. This result, however, was only achieved by making a very big ship of great length and going to the extreme dimensions that the largest docks could accommodate, and it was here that British constructors came up against a difficult problem since the existing docks precluded ships of even a slightly larger size. Until larger docks were built (which they were not) the Admiralty would have to content itself with vessels of no greater dimensions than those of *Hood*.

It had long been known that the deck protection of the latest giant battlecruiser *Hood* left a lot to be desired, and as she neared completion the Post-War Questions Committee called for a series of trials relating to her deck strength. It was decided to use the new APC shell, which was capable of carrying through and bursting about 40 feet beyond the first plate struck, to determine any critical weaknesses, the main question being, was she adequate against the Navy's 15in APC shell? During the autumn of 1919 plates arranged to simulate *Hood*'s armour were tested. Test 1. Shell perforated and burst 40 feet behind 7in armour in the magazine. Test 2. With magazine roof thickened from 1in to 2in. Shell perforated and burst 34 feet in rear of 7in armour. Roof plate blown to pieces. Test 3. (See page 32). Target: 2in HT plate, 3in HT plate and 2in HC plate (magazine roof). Projectile 15in APC (weighted). Angle of descent 32 degrees striking at 1,350 feet per second. Corresponding range 25,000 yards. A weighted shell was used and the 3in HT plating representing the main deck was wrecked, but the shell did not penetrate and glanced off. Thus the modifi-

cation to the main deck (as seen in the drawing) gave fairly good protection to magazines from shells hitting the side armour.

At the conclusion of the trials it was seen that the weight available to protect *Hood*'s magazines was inadequate against plunging fire unless the ship were re-built with a new deck of thick homogeneous plate. Later, however, it was proposed that more trials be carried out on the *Hood* deck target, with the main deck being reinforced by 4¾in roof plate quality armour. No approval for this was sanctioned, however, and although the matter was not dropped, it was seen to be impossible to modify a ship that had been designed to 1916 standards.

Further tests were carried out against armour in the captured German battleship *Baden* in 1921 and HMS *Superb* in 1922 (see *Nelson* chapter), and these yielded an amazing amount of data for future use. It was concluded in 1921–2 that a main belt of 14in and decks of 7½–8in were necessary to keep out 16in and 18in APC shells at modern battle ranges and it was these thicknesses that were envisaged for the G3 design. By 1937, however, it had been decided that thicknesses would have to be greatly increased if they were to keep out modern bombs and shells, and the protection of the later *King George V* class (1936) was designed accordingly but within the limits of a maximum displacement of 35,000 tons.

Some comfort was offered in a note by DNC Tennyson D'Eyncourt: 'Looked at broadly it is considered that the action of the shell will not be quite so serious as the trials hitherto made would seem to indicate. The conditions of actual warfare do not in general test so severely the armour and protection of ships as do the trials specially made on the material. This is partly due to the angle incidence of the shell being frequently less than that taken, and partly to the fact that in addition to the vertical or deck armour which is erected for special trials, there is always the structure of the ship which adds very considerably to the protection afforded in practice and the chance of the shells hitting some of the very substantial structure of our capital ships is a very great one, and therefore the thickness of the protection given on paper is considerably augmented by the structure which is met with in the passage of the projectile.'

In general this applied to ships that served

MODEL TESTS FOR 1928 BATTLESHIP DESIGN:

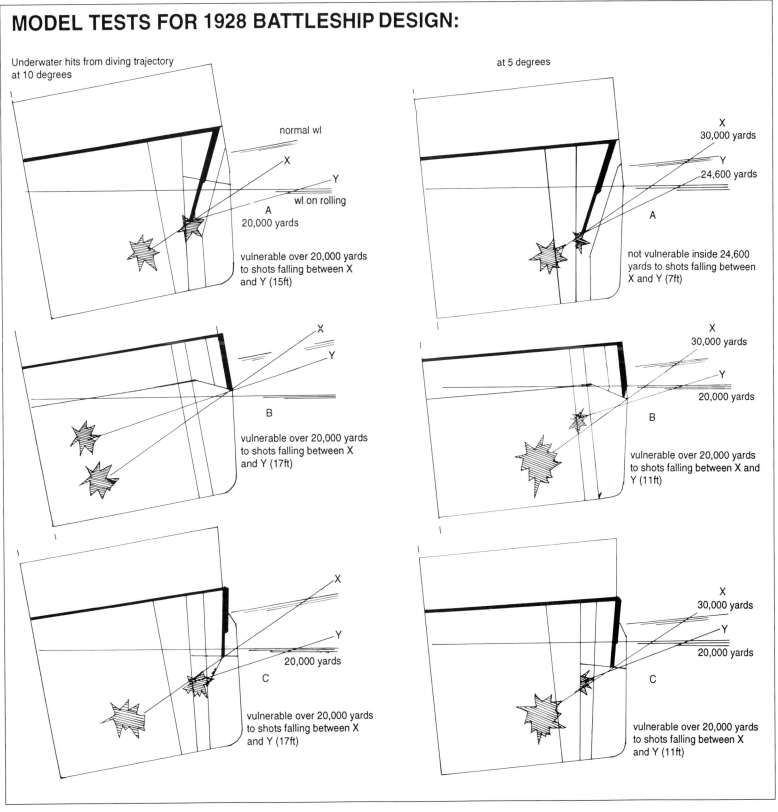

Underwater hits from diving trajectory at 10 degrees

at 5 degrees

normal wl

X

Y

wl on rolling

A
20,000 yards

vulnerable over 20,000 yards to shots falling between X and Y (15ft)

X
30,000 yards

Y
24,600 yards

A

not vulnerable inside 24,600 yards to shots falling between X and Y (7ft)

X

Y

B

vulnerable over 20,000 yards to shots falling between X and Y (17ft)

X
30,000 yards

Y
20,000 yards

B

vulnerable over 20,000 yards to shots falling between X and Y (11ft)

X

Y

20,000 yards

C

vulnerable over 20,000 yards to shots falling between X and Y (17ft)

X
30,000 yards

Y
20,000 yards

C

vulnerable over 20,000 yards to shots falling between X and Y (11ft)

DIVING SHELL TESTS, *HOOD* AND *MALAYA*

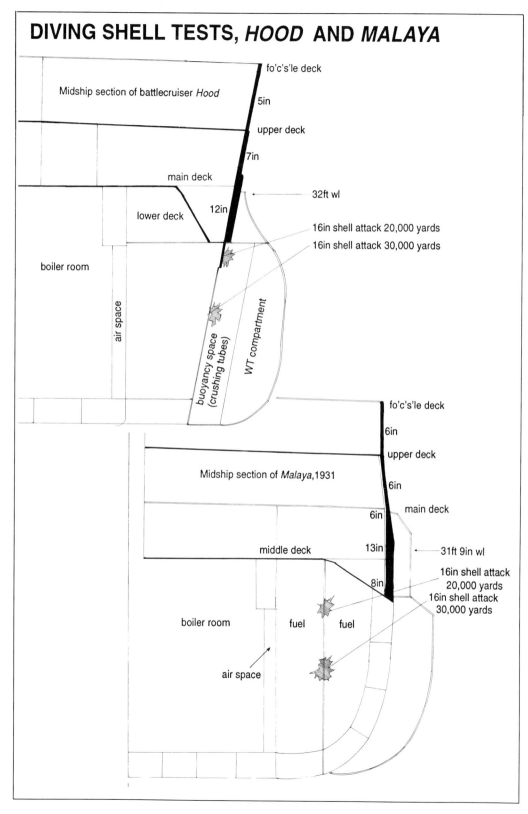

Midship section of battlecruiser *Hood*

fo'c's'le deck

5in

upper deck

7in

main deck

32ft wl

lower deck

12in

16in shell attack 20,000 yards

16in shell attack 30,000 yards

boiler room

air space

buoyancy space (crushing tubes)

WT compartment

fo'c's'le deck

6in

upper deck

Midship section of *Malaya*, 1931

6in

6in main deck

middle deck

13in

31ft 9in wl

8in

16in shell attack 20,000 yards

16in shell attack 30,000 yards

boiler room

fuel   fuel

air space

during the Second World War. It was to prove that shellfire was not the most important threat but aerial and underwater attack proved the most fatal of all. The new *Prince of Wales*'s 6in armoured deck was not pierced nor was her 14in or 15in belt, but she was most effectively sunk beyond the armour limitations. (For further tests against armour plates see Operation 'Bronte' in *Nelson* class chapter.)

CHEMICAL WARFARE

Gas and chemical warfare had shown their deadly possibilities for the first time during the Great War. The mustard and respiratory gases, that could burn, blind or choke men to death, were obviously seen to pose a major threat in any future conflict. Although never used at sea during the Great War, it had become possible to attack ships at sea with gas dropped from an aircraft, and the problem of anti-gas defence was much debated during the inter-war years.

The Admiralty set up a Chemical Warfare Committee which held its first meeting on 7 July 1920. One of the first battleships to undergo gas-attack tests was *Ramillies* (*Royal Sovereign* class) during the winter of 1920 but results showed that with her open bridge work and conning arrangements it was practically impossible to keep out poisonous fumes, and it would be an absolute nightmare if personnel faced such attack. More tests were carried out during the next few years – the most notable being in the aircraft carrier *Courageous* in 1922, but again, because of her numerous openings it was quickly realized that it would be extremely difficult to render many compartments gas tight. In August 1923 their Lordships received an article entitled 'Protection of Capital Ships against Poison Gas' which highlighted tests and trials in which the US Navy had been engaged. The article had three headings:

1. Methods of producing a gas cloud
2. Individual protection
3. Collective protection

METHODS OF PRODUCING A GAS CLOUD:
1. A time-fused smoke float.
2. Liquid gas sprayed on the surface of the water from aircraft out of gun range.

INDIVIDUAL PROTECTION:

The writer advocated the use of four different types of masks for the personnel:

1. Manual labour mask – container carried on the head so as not to impede the arms or body
2. Diaphragm mask – for use of telephone operators etc
3. Optical mask – for use of range-takers gun-layers, etc
4. A combination of b and c – for fire control officers

The British Admiralty favoured the use of a single mask for all ranks and ratings and provided that this universal type proved efficient (a new version was being developed at that time) the question of special masks for special duties would not arise. It was suggested that an optical mask be built in to range-finders and telescopes, one advantage being that the user would be better accustomed to action conditions than would obtain from intermittent use of a personal mask. Serious consideration would be given to this proposal should difficulties arise with the new version of the individual mask. Protective clothing against mustard gas was considered and it was suggested that special overalls be issued in wartime for action only.

COLLECTIVE PROTECTION:

The writer dealt with this subject exhaustively, various suggestions being made as to how to prevent gas entering a ship. The opinion was that the whole ship below the upper deck should be made gas tight including turrets, ammunition passages, secondary batteries, etc., and even engine and boiler rooms. Briefly, compartments were termed either semi-closed or fully-closed. For the first, the idea was to make the compartment as gas tight as possible with regard to fighting efficiency and to prevent gas from entering by keeping the spaces under air pressure. To keep the air pressure up and at the same time filter the air, use of the 'seco spray' machine was suggested. With regard to the fully-closed compartments, the idea seems to have been for an agent for absorbing CO_2 and to replenish the oxygen from tanks or cylinders in the compartment. There was emphasis on the need for collective protection everywhere to avoid the loss of efficiency resulting from the wearing of respirators by personnel. At the same time it was advocated that permanent gas masks be fitted as part of range-finders, gun-laying telescopes, etc.,

which should be used at all times, thus accepting a reduction in efficiency of the users of these instruments.

The Admiralty took the view that the writer had lost sight of the fact that a ship may be hit during an action and that in almost any compartment that was not well protected collective protection would disappear. It was also thought that the writer in his efforts to bring the gas menace to the notice of the US Navy had rather overstated the case. Such conditions as he postulated might be possible in the future, but not at the present time and the first requirement was to examine the means whereby gas could be got into a ship and only then determine practical methods of dealing with it.

In the Director of Naval Ordnance's opinion, the correct line to take was:

1. Stake everything on a good gas mask, and regard this for the time being as the primary and most effective defence.
2. Carry out further research on methods of getting gas into a ship in order to ascertain just how great a danger the new threat might pose during a war.
3. Investigate systematically the means of making some of the more important stations gas tight.

It was thought that any proposals to make the engine and boiler rooms gas tight were somewhat fantastic.

The spraying of gas from aircraft was considered worthy of investigation, not only from the point of view of possible use in a naval action, but also as means of defending beaches from hostile landings.

With regard to the proposals to provide anti-gas apparatus of different types to suit specific duties, Admiralty experience to date suggested that it was possible, but it was highly improbable that any definitive apparatus could be devised. It was realized that the chances of a ship's personnel being gassed were probably greater in harbour than during any fleet action. It was therefore essential that each man be provided with personal anti-gas equipment in the first place; special types for specific duties could be considered when experience had been gained in the use of the new type of respirator being developed.

The emphasis on the need of protective clothing against mustard gas and the proposals to introduce an overall of protective material for use in action was sound in principle and indi-

cated the lines on which issue should be made as soon as suitable material could be developed. It was understood that this was engaging the serious attention of the Chemical Warfare Committee.

US proposals followed generally the lines along which the Admiralty was proceeding. The air purifier, the air filter and the use of compressed air for overcoming small leaks were all at this time under consideration for use in HM ships. The loss of efficiency resulting from closing-in might be as great as, or greater than that resulting from the wearing of gas masks, especially at times of low visibility, a condition that would frequently prevail during a gas attack. For items such as turrets, secondary batteries etc., it was considered that in view of the great practical difficulties in making such spaces even reasonably gas tight, the policy to rely on in respect of these spaces was that of individual protection. It was clear that the main questions regarding collective protection that confronted the US Navy were the same as those with which the Admiralty was faced. In conclusion the Board considered that progress in protecting the personnel of ships against gas should be made along the following lines:

To stake everything at this time on a good gas mask and to regard this as the primary and most effective defence. The Board suggested that the sooner the fleet was completely equipped and had gained sufficient experience in the use of the personal gas mask, the better. Orders were given to carry out research and experiments to ascertain how to get gas into a ship, and to investigate the means of making the more important stations gas tight. The investigations which were then in progress were considered to be on sound and practical lines, but would probably require modification or amplification in the light of experience gained.

Strict procedural training was carried out during the 1920s, the outcome seems to have been that individual safety was favoured, rather than trying to make large areas gas tight. *Nelson* and *Rodney* (and *King George V* class 1937) were fitted with limited gas filter arrangements in their large superstructures, which would at least ensure that most of the bridge personnel would be protected from serious harm, but that seems to have been as far as it went in the days of battleships.

Below: *Monarch* after shell tests and in a mutilated condition. Her funnel has collapsed, the bridgework is wrecked and the forecastle deck has a large hole in it.

THE ARRIVAL OF AIRCRAFT

During the Great War *The Times* newspaper was always noted for its lively reviews on military matters and this of course continued into peace time. In December 1920, however, a series of letters regarding capital ships and the extent of their usefulness sparked off a debate in which practically everyone who was anyone in naval circles joined. The controversy quickly spread to official circles and became the great discussion of the period.

A first article had appeared on 29 November 1920 under the title 'The Navy – A Question for the Nation' and although it is too long to recapitulate here, suffice to say that it pointed out that, as a consequence of the enormous construction programme being undertaken by the USA and Japan, the British Battle Fleet would soon be relegated to third place rather than her usual prime position. It asked 'are battleships really the capital ships for the future or are submersibles and aircraft really the new weapons to conquer all?'

At the end of the war even Sir John (Jackie) Fisher himself stated: 'The greatest possible speed with the biggest practicable gun was, up to the time of aircraft, the acme of sea fighting. Now there is only one word – submersibles.' One of the most prominent naval officers of the day, the gunnery expert, Sir Percy Scott, was quick to reply to the letter to add weight to the doom of the battleship and in fact had, as far back as 1914, been saying that submarines had entirely revolutionized naval warfare. Many famous names were seen on letters which flooded into the columns of *The Times*. Admiral Sir Cyprian Bridge, Sir Herbert King Hall, Lord Sydenham, Admiral W. H. Henderson and Admiral R. H. Bacon to name a few. The most formidable antagonist to the battleship was of course Sir Percy Scott who then came up with an article 'What Use is a Battleship?' (13 December 1920), and to this there were literally dozens of answers, of which he took no notice whatsoever. Sir Percy's article read:

'Sir – Will you help me in my ignorance? I cannot get an answer to my question "What is the use of a battleship?" She must be of some use or the United States and Japan would not be building battleships. A lot of naval officers have written to me but they only tell me what she is

not useful for, they will not answer my question. Is her use a secret that only a few know and will not disclose? Will it be disclosed by the Committee of Imperial Defence who are going to tell what the weapons of the new navy are to be? Admiral Hall, a young and vigorous officer, who had wide experience during the war, will not enlighten my ignorance; he is only telling the public what the battleship is not useful for. What is the good of that? Before we spend 109 millions on battleships and another 100 millions in making safe harbours for them, we ought to know what use they are. Now, Sir, do try and enlighten my ignorance. Ask Lord Sydenham or someone else who knows all about naval affairs.'

As can be imagined the political cacophony that followed was unprecedented, but one of the best replies came from someone who signed himself simply as 'naval officer': (15 December) 'Sir, – In reply to Sir Percy Scott, on the lines of the well-known nursery rhyme I would say the capital ship is: The ship that sinks the enemy's capital ship, that protects the cruisers that sink the cruisers which protect destroyers, that sink the submarines that attack the merchant ships that bring the food that feeds the people who build the ships that transport the army that defends the house that Jack built – the British Empire.'

The columns of *The Times* were ablaze for more than ten weeks, but after that the editor

decided to end the debate as it seemed to be going nowhere. In fact it had got out of hand. There was certainly no easy answer to be had by the written word – practical tests, trials and lengthy experiments were needed to give any degree of truth to the question of how much use was the present-day battleship in the light of four years' wartime experience.

Ships had been set aside after the war, there being no shortage of surplus vessels. The Admiralty at first put forward a few of the pre-dreadnoughts to see how they would stand up against modern technology (*Swiftsure* and *Agamemnon*), but ultimately experience was needed in the dreadnought type and as a result *Monarch* (*Orion* class) was used from 1923 to 1925; *Centurion* (*King George V* class) became Remote Control Target Ship (1927–37) and *Emperor of India* and *Marlborough* (*Iron Duke* class) were used extensively as test ships against shells and explosives of all types.

Probably the most experimental battleship during the 1920s was *Monarch*. She was used extensively for tests to see how armour strength in British battleships would stand up against light, medium and heavy shells (see *British Battleships of World War One*). She was also used in gas and chemical attacks, and later for special tests to see how machinery in the Royal Navy's capital ships would take a knock to its vitals.

On 1 August 1923 she was anchored in

Below: After *Centurion*, *Monarch* was the battleship most used for experimental purposes. Her test results furbished much needed information towards capital ship construction. Shown here shortly before being shelled, she is listing to starboard to expose her armour strake. Note the white bands around the hull (range taking aids). 1925.

eleven fathoms of water and a charge of 2,081 pounds of TNT was hung from a boom fitted 40 feet below the waterline and 7 feet 6 inches from the side superstructure. Her machinery had been prepared in accordance with Admiralty instructions and steam was raised in numbers A1, A2, A3, A5, B1, B2, B4 and B5 boilers. Auxiliary steam pipes were at working pressure throughout the ship. Oil fuel tanks in use were in 'A' Boiler Room (keel to second longitudinal port) and 'B' Boiler Room (second to fourth longitudinal port). Because of bad weather the test was post-poned until 4 August when the charge was ignited at 09.06. After the explosion the vessel was boarded and the following notes were compiled:

At the moment of explosion boiler pressure was evidenced by the lifting of safety valves immediately prior to the charge being fired. After the explosion, as far as could be seen from outside the ship, the machinery was continuing to run satisfactorily, the pilot light on the aft superstructure showed that the dynamo engine was functioning and the funnel discharge appeared normal. As soon as personnel were allowed on board and prior to permission being given for the Engine Room staff to open up compartments and go below, listening at the various ventilating trunks, seemed to show that normal running of the auxiliary engines was continuing. Soon after they returned on board they observed that the funnel discharge from 'A' Boiler Room was diminishing and, suspecting loss of suction of the oil fuel pump because the ship was listing about 11 degrees, shut off the oil fuel pump and oil filter discharges of 'A' Boiler Room. The boilers in 'B', as far as could be ascertained, continued to function satisfactorily. At about 09.40 the hydraulic pumping engine ceased to work and a thick vapour from burning oil fuel was rising from the port after fan intake to 'B' Boiler Room, the dynamo engine had stopped and steam was issuing to a considerable extent from the centre Engine Room ventilating trunk into the after superstructure. Because of the risk of fire in 'B' Boiler Room the oil fuel was shut off at 10.00. At 10.10 the centre Engine Room was entered but the steam vapour was too dense to locate the cause. As the air cleared it was seen that the starboard main condenser inboard door was split and sea water was spurting freely through the fissure. All sea connections were shut as quickly as possible, but it was found that the bilge had already flooded to a depth of just over three feet. All sea valves were still working freely.

The steam pressure in 'A' Boiler Room had remained at 10psi, fans were still running, main feed pumps still moving and all water gauge glasses intact; a few boilers were short of water but A1 boiler was leaking badly at the starboard and blowdown valve. All floor plates were displaced, but ladders and gratings were still in place and slight leaks had occurred here and there. The oil fuel had caught fire in the drip pans of A5 boiler, but this burnt out shortly after the entry of the examination party. 'B' Boiler Room pressure was the same as that in 'A' and the only damage here was confined to a few leaks on the main steam expansion gland; a small oil fire was in progress in the front of B5 boiler but this was easily extinguished. 'C' Boiler Room appeared to have suffered more from shock than either 'A' or 'B', nearly all the glass fronts of the gauges being shattered, floor plates dislodged and much dust shaken down. The boilers them-

selves, however, did not appear to have suffered. Most of the auxiliary machinery in the area remained in fact except for a few fractures to some of the sea water pumps, but on the whole there was no discernible damage.

All engines in use during the test were tried by hand and still moved freely and appeared undamaged.

The damage as a whole was minimal, the only failure being a reduction in water pressure. It was considered that all auxiliary machinery in those compartments not destroyed or flooded at the moment of explosion, could still have been kept in use had immediate access been allowed. With regard to the main propelling machinery, the leakage from the starboard main condenser cover would possibly have been diminished by pads and shores to such an extent as to allow the use of the starboard engines with main circulator bilge suctions in operation. Had the turbines been in running condition it was considered the lift would have been much diminished so that if the blading had fouled the resulting damage would have been slight and the turbines would have remained usable. It was submitted that if any further trials of a similar nature were carried out if would be an advantage to fit gauges and equipment on the upper deck so that it would be easy to see what was going on down below.

This trial was just one of the hundreds carefully carried out by the Royal Navy to try to ascertain how capital ships would fare when damaged. While these and many other extremely valuable tests were taking place during the period of the 'What use is a Battleship?' debate (although published in 1920 it certainly never lost its appeal for the general press), tests were being carried out in the USA on an old German war prize, the battleship *Ostfriesland* by the USAAF (United States Army Air Service). The debate over the ship became a fiasco after the pilot 'Billy' Mitchell (Brigadier General William Mitchell) claimed after he had bombed the ship that the day of the battleship was truly past. The saga was long, but briefly what happened was this:

Mitchell had set his sights on what he saw as magniloquent Admirals and Sea Lords on both sides of the Atlantic, and after attacking all of them verbally in articles appearing in journals, periodicals and newspapers, went on to test his theories in a practical manner. After knocking the old coastal defence battleship *Indiana* to bits, he made moves to get *Ostfriesland* allocated as a sitting target to be destroyed by aircraft. Trials started on 20 July 1921 when the ship was attacked with 230lb bombs, but of 33 bombs dropped only eight hits were scored on the main deck and did little damage. Later, 600lb and 1,000lb bombs were used but none seemed to affect the water integrity of the old battleship. Next day, however, six more 1,000lb bombs were dropped, but only two made contact. One caused no damage whatsoever, but the other was a near miss on the port side which caused the hull to cave in from the 'water hammer' effect – it opened her up to the sea and she began to sink. Disappearing beneath the waves in about forty minutes, it looked like a victory for the arrogant Mitchell and the anti-battleship brigade. In fact the test had proved little so far as the British Admiralty was concerned – a matter of an old, unmanned, sitting target sunk as a result of constant bombing. Would not a crew aboard have saved her by isolating the area of damage? Would she not have been a more difficult target if under way and yet more difficult if firing at the attacking aircraft? The Admiralty, although taking note of the 'interesting' trial, concerned itself with more methodical tests which would furbish them with sound information regarding the real strength of modern battleships. Even the committee set up in the USA had registered its verdict: 'It cannot be said that the battleship has become superfluous because of the possibility of bombing attacks by aircraft. The battleship represents the highest and ultimate fighting strength of the fleet.'

In 1923 more debates took place in the House of Lords regarding the capabilities of capital ships to defend themselves against attacking aircraft, and it was asked whether the wings of sea power had been clipped? It was pointed out as usual that new naval weapons had been developed (namely submarines and aircraft) which greatly weakened the offence in modern sea power. Forces could not, as before, be carried across the seas. A weak power without a navy could, in theory, challenge the strongest sea power simply by having a strong minefield, an adequate aircraft and a handful of submarines.

Even the great Admiral Von Scheer, who commanded the German High Seas Fleet, a staunch believer in battleships, was forced to concede that by the time the Great War ended the submarine had proved its worth and could, in theory, hold off a fleet of capital ships. It was a known fact that had there been a fleet of submersibles present in the Dardanelles in 1915 it would have been almost impossible for any surface ship to approach the beaches for bombardment, as was so often accomplished during that campaign. What more could be said to prophesy and haste the demise and ultimate doom of the world's battleships?

It is obvious that there was more than a degree of truth in the arguments of the anti-battleship lobby, but during the decade from 1920 to 1930 there was more to the affair than just questions of what use were battleships, or what if they were faced with a fleet of submarines, or indeed could they defend themselves against a squadron of high-level bombing aircraft? The entire subject of defence had to be addressed, and the Admiralty was only too aware that some of the questions were almost impossible to answer. The main question of course was what would replace battleships if they were all deleted from the world's battlefleets? Submarines and aircraft carriers at that time were not yet developed to their full potential – there was still much to be done in that area. Moreover there was still a need of a strong, fast, heavily armed type of warship which was and would always be needed to protect smaller ships – especially merchant vessels which could not be looked after by submarines or indeed aircraft at that time. Although the Second World War proved to be the final frontier for the big battleship, the type never lost favour with many of the world's navies and it continued to serve until well after the conflict.

Today (1990s) battleships as a species are extinct except the four US reactivated *Iowa* class. It is obvious that even with all the modern technology, missiles, aircraft and submarines, the 'big gun' still has a place in any war. There was much speculation when during the Gulf War a 'Silk Worm' missile was heading for the battleship *Missouri*, and an uninformed press declared: 'She would have been completely wrecked. Her fate would have been sealed.' Alarming statements and riveting reading, but in fact these statements were made by people who obviously did not know the facts. Of course it would be foolish to say that the ship would not have suffered severe superficial damage, but it is very doubtful that she would have been sunk. Like all battleships, she was designed to take (and deliver) a tremendous pounding – and that is why they survived the barrage of opinion during the inter-war years and that is the reason why they remain in service today.

AIRCRAFT IN BATTLESHIPS

After countless trials from 1920 to 1930, there was general agreement by the early 1930s that aircraft had a definite role within the fleet at sea, and many of the older battleships were given hangars and catapults during their modernization. There was a strong lobby of official opinion, however, that held that such aircraft should be confined to aircraft carriers. The late 1920s

witnessed many debates on the subject and the Commander-in-Chief, Directors of War, Staff Colleges and Tactical School, Director of Naval Ordnance and the Air Ministry featured prominently in the discussions. In about 1933–4 the general opinion was that fighters were the best defence against attacking aircraft – a view which often changed from month to month. What was fully agreed was that the expansion of the Fleet Air Arm was of paramount importance and the use of aircraft in conjunction with battleships and cruisers for trade protection was worthy of serious investigation. The following points outlining the needs to be considered were placed before the Board.
1. Operational, including the types of operation for which aircraft are essential, the frequency of

such operations, and the scale of requirements of aircraft in relation to the strength of the forces engaged.
2. Technical, including the effects on the ship's design of carrying aircraft in capital ships and cruisers, and the limitations inherent upon the operation of aircraft from such ships imposed either by weather or by the ship herself.
3. Financial, to determine the most economical method of carrying the aircraft required for the operation envisaged.

Operational. It was obvious that aircraft were required in practically every operation likely to be undertaken by the fleet as a whole or by detached forces. Moreover aircraft were viewed as essential for the effective control of sea communications.

Technical. The technical aspect of carrying aircraft on catapults was dominated by two main factors:
1. The technical limitations of the aircraft itself with especial reference to its ability to land and be recovered at sea.
2. The limitations imposed upon the ship herself by reason of the inclusion of the catapult and the space and weight taken up thereby. It had also to be borne in mind that catapult-launched aircraft depended to a great extent on calm sea and weather for recovery, which precluded their deployment on a high percentage of days in the year.

The limitations imposed upon the ship by carrying aircraft on a catapult were discussed in 1936. The main technical effects were:
1. The catapult and hangars occupied approximately one-sixth of the upper deck space between the forward and after gun mountings in any class of ship. The remaining space was therefore congested and limitations were imposed upon the arrangement of the secondary or HA armament which was already difficult to site satisfactorily clear of blast.
2. The weight of the equipment was considerable (approximately 160 tons in the 1936 battleship). It was thought that with qualitative limitation of total displacement, to use this weight in ships with the fleet on 'one shot' aircraft was uneconomical and would detract from other important characteristics such as protection or offensive power.

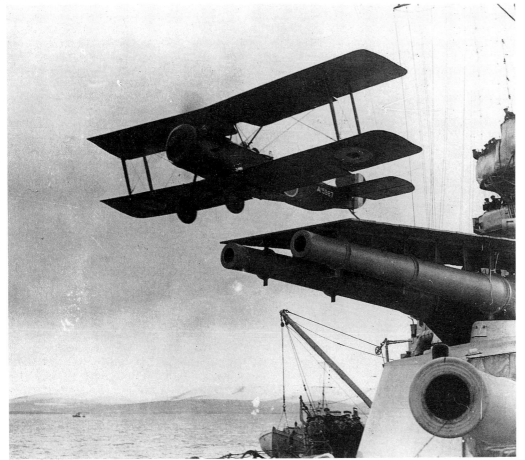

3. The modern type of fixed catapult, necessitating operating machinery between decks affected accommodation.

4. The aircraft on the catapult could not be arranged satisfactorily to be clear of blast from the high-angle or secondary armament (it was assumed that the aircraft would be flown off before the armament was fired). It was considered extremely likely that the anti-aircraft guns would be fired before the aircraft was required to be flown off, in which case it could not be guaranteed that the aircraft on the catapult would still be serviceable after an air attack.

Financial. It was difficult to assess the relative annual cost of catapult-borne and carrier-borne aircraft, but it was thought that the former were more expensive. The initial cost of a catapult was approximately £17,000.

The arguments for and against catapult-borne aircraft were:

FOR

1. They provided an increase in the required number of fighters and/or fighter spotters carried in the fleet since as much as possible of the existing carrier space was required for reconnaissance and strike aircraft.

2. The battleship or cruiser flagship carrying a fighter spotter could be self-contained as regards air spotting (with its attendant increase in hitting power and the ability to carry out indirect fire).

3. It was held by some officers that improved results were obtained by the closer co-operation made possible between ships and aircraft's personnel.

4. The offensive power of ships for subsidiary operations would be increased.

5. There were more baskets for the eggs.

AGAINST

1. Aircraft on catapults were 'one shot' aircraft and must be re-fuelled or re-ammunitioned aboard a carrier on expiry of their endurance or ammunition. Carrier-borne aircraft were capable of continuous operation. Catapult aircraft could not be recovered in weather that would not preclude flying from carriers.

2. Inclusion of fixed catapults rendered the arrangement of the upper deck and secondary and HA armament (for long or close-range defence) unsatisfactory. The efficiency of the AA armament was therefore impaired.

3. Aircraft on catapults were liable to blast from AA guns and arrangements were very difficult to circumvent this.

4. The weight of catapults was considerable and would need to be met by limited displacement from other services.

5. Air spotting entailed a large organization for reliefs etc., and these could only be arranged from carriers.

6. Training of observers was better carried out and more easily co-ordinated from carriers.

In 1933 the Commander-in-Chief of the Home Fleet made a strong plea for more aircraft in the fleet, especially of fighter and reconnaissance types, and requested a statement of policy. The following are extracts from remarks prompted by his letter:

1. 'In general stowage for fighters is not provided in capital ships owing to space restriction and difficulty of launching, a spotting aircraft being the primary consideration. It is therefore considered that the provision of additional carrier tonnage is the proper policy for increasing the number of fleet fighters.' (DNAD)

2. 'As a general rule battleships do not work singly or in pairs but in squadrons or fleets and the right place for aircraft is in aircraft carriers attached to the squadron or fleet controller.

3. 'My conclusion is that it is unwise to neglect any opportunity of providing for the transport of a limited number of aircraft in capital ships provided their main characteristics are not thereby impaired.' (ACNS)

4. 'I agree with the general view that we must have as many aircraft available as is practicable, especially in view of the vulnerability of carriers, and the small number of ships we have.' (DCNS)

5. 'It is essential that we make every reasonable use of such aircraft carrying power as we can in vessels other than carriers to strengthen our air defences.' (CNS)

A staff meeting was held on 26 May 1936 to further discuss the policy of carrying aircraft in capital ships and cruisers even though the new programme of British battleships laid down in 1936 was showing hangars and aircraft within the design (*King George V* class). The subject was still under discussion at some length. It was agreed that the aircraft were better off in carrier types, but the fleet did not possess enough of the type. Moreover, it could be argued that aircraft in battleships and cruisers would be capable of reconnaissance on a scale not possible by other ships of the fleet (i.e., destroyers and scouts etc.). The conclusive results of the meeting saw the staff recommending the following:

1. That battleships and cruisers with the fleet should not carry aircraft on catapults but that all fleet aircraft should be carried in carriers.

2. That the carrier building programme be accelerated to provide an adequate number of efficiently borne aircraft with the fleet and for trade protection duties.

3. That the carrier building programme required immediate review in the light of the above and that after arrears had been made up it should be correlated to the programme of other categories.

4. The development of the autogiro type of aircraft should be treated as urgent and money devoted to the necessary experiments for this purpose.

The general summary implied that when sufficient numbers of armoured carriers had been built, other light carriers should be built which would enable the battleships and cruisers to have their aircraft equipment removed. This policy had two great advantages: 1. More efficient use of aircraft with the fleet. 2. More efficient use of weight and space in ships for offensive and defensive weapons.

It was considered, however, that until this time arrived the policy of carrying catapults in other ships would continue. The Controller, R. G. H. Henderson, on hearing of this general consensus was not happy with it:

'I find myself in entire disagreement with the general policy outlined in this paper. Although I have no wish to be unjust to the appreciation prepared by the naval staff, I do think that the disadvantages of carrying aircraft in ships have been very much stressed, while the advantages therefrom have been treated in the opposite way.

'Firstly, I do not think it should be argued too strongly that the existence of aircraft in battleships and cruisers is due to limitations hitherto imposed by treaty, although no doubt the treaty rules hastened the development of sea-borne aircraft. Further, though there may now be no limitation by treaty as to the number of carriers, we

Below: A full broadside view of *Revenge* in 1940, showing a one-off unofficial camouflage. It consisted of about four shades, the layout being very similar to those used in First World War dazzle, but it was basically an experiment and not carried for long.

have it in another form, namely cost, if the number of aircraft for fleet use is maintained at a high level. It must be remembered that, with the design of armoured deck carrier, the maximum number of aircraft to be carried is 36, and, assuming we have ten of these carriers then broadly speaking, the Fleet Air Arm would consist of only 360 aircraft, and these might well be distributed all over the world for commerce protection, diversions and other operations which must necessarily be away from the main theatre of the war. I should think that in a war the aircraft carriers will be kept busy and that even subsidiary movements and periodical sweeps will necessitate operations by such ships; when they get back to their base they will want to rest and yet the Commander-in-Chief in his base will probably require daily reconnaissance flights, which I suggest should be done by the shipborne aircraft.'

Only experience during the following conflict (1939–45) was to settle the debate when it was seen that the battleship had moved aside as the capital ship to give pride of place to the aircraft carrier with its aircraft and their deadly bombs and torpedoes. Aircraft equipment in battleships was of some value for reconnaissance at the beginning of the war, but the weight and space involved and the personnel – who could more practically be used elsewhere – showed the inef-

fective value of this type of fitting in anything but the proper vessel. From 1942 all aircraft equipment and catapults were removed from battleships and the space was taken up by stores, boat stowage and anti-aircraft batteries.

CAMOUFLAGE

Although this book is intended to cover the period 1919 to 1939 and not merely war history, it has proved impossible to stop short of the 1939–45 conflict (as can be seen in the main chapters). Camouflage is a wartime subject and one of the most popular and interesting items by far for serious warship enthusiasts and modellers alike, and to that end it is therefore worthy of some discussion. Camouflage was first used in warships during the Great War although in 1915 it was applied in a somewhat haphazard fashion so that no two ships were alike. There were no hard and fast rules as to how a ship should be painted, or indeed, as to the type of colours that should be used. Some official interest was shown during 1916–17 and observation units were set up after certain vessels had been given different paint applications. In the beginning only a few colours were used – usually variations of grey and black, but later blues and greens could be seen. Camouflage in big ships virtually disappeared at the end of 1917 and did not appear

again until Lieutenant-Commander Norman Wilkinson, RNVR developed his dazzle painting methods and the Admiralty set up a proper Camouflage School at Burlington House in London where many tests using models were carried out under controlled conditions.

The result of this, so far as capital ships were concerned, was that only a few ships were given the treatment: *Revenge*, *Ramillies* and the aircraft-carrying cruiser *Furious* all received fully fledged schemes. *Ramillies* was very different from *Revenge* as was *Furious*, as can be seen from the paint schemes. The battlecruiser *Repulse* was painted up in a two-tone grey at the end of the war as an experiment, and the effect was not unlike that applied to that ship in 1941 only in lighter shades.

At the end of the war camouflage took a back seat, but was picked up again during the early 1930s and a thorough investigation was made into the matter of how to apply suitable war paint to different types of ship. The subject proved extremely complex and exhausting and although the schemes applied were in most cases rather spectacular in the battleships, the achievement of satisfactory schemes and patterns was not accomplished easily. At the outbreak of the Second World War a few big ships were given 'one off' examples of camouflage which tended to emulate the earlier dazzle types but with fewer colours (*Ramillies* seven colours *Revenge* five – 1918) (see endpapers). Although there are a few photographs of these ships taken during 1939–40, little information was collated about the patterns or colours because in some cases the schemes were only evident for a few months (certainly in the case of *Revenge*, *Ramillies* and *Royal Sovereign*) and therefore were never recorded officially, which leaves some doubt as to the actual colours used.

When examining the official accounts of the use of camouflage it is essential to be sure of the real meaning of the word. When discussing camouflage the actual terms of description used are: 'invisible', 'visible', 'conspicuous' and 'inconspicuous'.

Invisible in plain terms means something that cannot be seen with the naked eye because of its nature and position. Visible objects are capable of being seen – usually without aid; but some complication arises here because one can have good visibility, moderate visibility and poor visibility. When dealing with camouflage this description is best avoided in referring to how visible a ship is. Conspicuous means easy to see, obvious or striking to the eye. Inconspicuous means not readily seen, not bold or prominent in appearance.

These two last descriptions are best when describing camouflage because it is easier to explain how something becomes less conspicuous than to describe how the painting of a ship in strong disruptive colours makes the ship seem invisible or of doubtful visibility. A ship can be very inconspicuous if painted in one colour, but only in certain conditions – in either bright or dull conditions she will be most conspicuous. On the other hand in many conditions a colourful pattern tends to scramble the outline, and the characteristics that identify a ship are affected to some extent. The tremendous difference in illumination between sunlight and overcast conditions can affect the appearance of a camouflaged

ship in many ways, as can a moonlit or moonless night. Moreover, light differs greatly from ocean to ocean; the extreme haze to be encountered in some tropical waters calls for yet more alteration to colour tones.

Although early camouflage (1939–40) underwent many forms in battleships, it was clearly understood that the function of a pattern in sea camouflage was to reduce the range of visibility of the ship from aerial observation and from surface observation including the submarine periscope. At certain long ranges, however, the patterns ceased to be apparent and the ship became a uniform tone. The Admiralty endeavoured to achieve an overall tone to blend in with existing conditions where possible – hence the many colours for home waters and greys and blues in many foreign waters. Additionally, it was decided that an enemy observer or lookout would have no data against which to check a moving target, and his difficulties could be com-

pounded if the ship were badly angled from his point of view. So anything that might blur his image would be more than beneficial in rendering a ship less conspicuous. Once a ship had been spotted, however, a good, coloured pattern could achieve two important results:
1. Cause confusion of identity.
2. Cause confusion of inclination.

So pattern had these useful features: 1. Reduction of visiblity caused by at least one tone harmonizing with its background and reducing the apparent size of the object and the psychological effect of the shapes left possibly visible. 2. The obliteration of the violently arrestive shapes of the 'natural' pattern of the ship resulting from the hard core of unavoidable shadows.

From June 1940 the big ships sported many weird and wonderful patterns in various colours, but the most used tones were light and dark grey (507b and 507c – see drawings and photographs).

Queen Elizabeth
At the end of her reconstruction she left the docks sporting an early Admiralty disruptive type scheme of five different shades. This was worn until her refit after being damaged in Alexandria in December 1942.

Barham
Dark Home Fleet grey until the summer of 1940 when she was painted up in an unofficial two-tone scheme (black and white). Repainted all grey for a short period then repainted in black and white again under the direction of Peter Scott. Lost in this condition. (See photographs.)

Malaya
Dark Home Fleet grey until the summer of 1940, then painted in two-tone unofficial pattern (grey 507a and 507c). Repainted medium grey after leaving the Mediterranean in the spring of 1941.

Warspite
Dark Home Fleet grey until the winter of 1941, then painted in two-tone grey (as *Malaya*) but with different scheme (unofficial).

Valiant
Dark Home Fleet grey until early 1941 when painted up in two-tone grey (507b and 507c or possibly B5). Worn until Christmas 1942.

Royal Sovereign
Entered the war in medium grey tone. Summer 1940 painted in unofficial five-colour 'dazzle' type scheme. Altered during this period to another 'dazzle' scheme but with fewer colours. Repainted in two-tone grey by November 1940.

Royal Oak
Medium grey until sunk (1939).

Revenge
Dark Home Fleet grey at beginning of war until repainted in unofficial four-colour 'dazzle' type scheme by October 1940. Repainted in early 1941 in another 'dazzle' scheme with fewer colours.

Ramillies
Entered war in medium grey until repainted in 'dazzle' in November 1940 (two shades of grey and white). Repainted all grey in early 1941.

Resolution
Dark Home Fleet grey from the beginning of the war until the winter of 1941 when she was repainted in early Admiralty Disruptive type.

Nelson
Dark Home Fleet grey from the beginning of the war until mid 1940 when she appeared in a darker shade. Lighter grey during the summer of 1941.

Rodney
Dark Home Fleet grey from the beginning of the war until late 1940 when she appeared a shade lighter (colour unknown – probably grey).

Renown
Medium grey at beginning of war. Darker grey during Force 'H' period. Repainted in early Admiralty Disruptive type in the winter of 1941.

Repulse
Medium grey from beginning of war until early 1941 when she was repainted in black and white 'contrast' scheme. Uncertain if this was still worn when lost (see drawings).

Glorious
From the beginning of the war in medium grey. Lost in this condition.

Courageous
Dark Home Fleet grey. Lost in this condition.

Furious
Dark Home Fleet grey throughout the early years of war. Admiralty Disruptive 1942.

CAPITAL SHIPS: CAMOUFLAGE, 1941 CONTRAST PAINTING

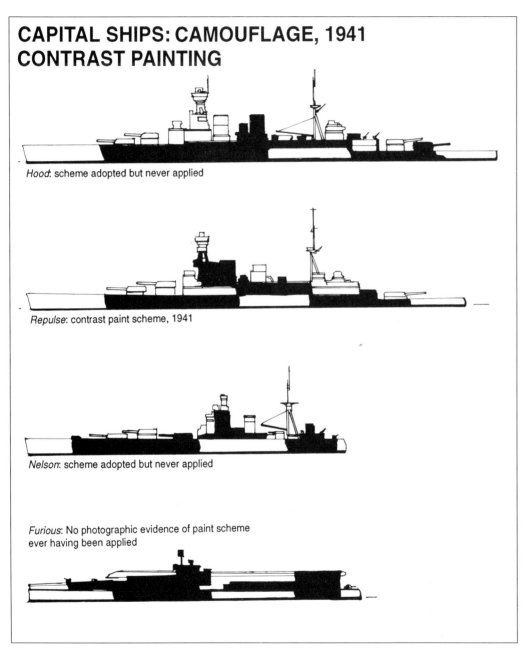

Hood: scheme adopted but never applied

Repulse: contrast paint scheme, 1941

Nelson: scheme adopted but never applied

Furious: No photographic evidence of paint scheme ever having been applied

King George V

From the beginning of the war in two-tone grey (possibly 507 variation) until the spring of 1941 when she returned to overall medium grey.

Prince of Wales

Medium grey until August 1941 when repainted in early Admiralty Disruptive type. Sunk in this condition.

Duke of York

Two-tone Admiralty disruptive type (experimental) until the winter of 1941 when repainted dark grey.

During late 1940 there was some confusion regarding camouflage methods and the Admiralty ordered that all schemes be painted out with a view to further investigations. In December 1940, however, the commanding officer of *Repulse* (Captain W. Tennant) sent a report on the subject of camouflage to the Vice-Admiral commanding the Battlecruiser Squadron, pointing out these salient features:

'1. HTM288 orders that capital ships are not to be camouflaged. I suggest that if controlled and carefully worked out by those who have studied camouflage and not left to the whim of individual captains and executive officers there are certain occasions when considerable benefit may be obtained from it.

2. Capital ships are too big to attempt concealment by camouflage except possibly under certain conditions of light and when against the land; which conditions are unlikely to apply in a Fleet action.

3. On the other hand, it is considered possible that by means of efficient camouflage it is possible to make a ship a much more difficult target on which to obtain an accurate inclination.

4. The gunnery officer of this ship reports to me that recently when carrying out an inclination exercise on the ex-USA destroyers it was exceedingly difficult to obtain their inclination due to their contrasts in painting.

5. I suggest that in the case of battlecruisers much could be done merely by contrast of two shades of grey.

6. Commander E. B. Clark, RN (retired) of this ship, who has studied the subject, has independently produced the attached drawings of this ship giving some idea of what might be done with two shades of grey.

7. I would suggest that if it is decided to give reconsideration to contrast painting of capital ships, his ideas, in greater detail, might be of service.'

In answer to this it was concluded that although a variety of designs had been tired and rejected since the beginning of war, it would be an advantage to camouflage the battlecruisers, but before proceeding with the proposal it would

Right: *Ramillies*, November 1940, showing her three-tone grey, dazzle-type (unofficial) paintwork .
Centre right: *Royal Sovereign* at Gibraltar, November 1940, showing a two-tone grey paintwork scheme.
Bottom right: *Royal Sovereign* in March 1941, just off Bermuda, showing a modified camouflage scheme. The colours are simply light and dark grey.

be necessary for the subject to be officially studied in detail with due regard to previous evidence. The following observations on dazzle painting were offered:

1. It called attention to the presence of a ship.

2. It made a ship more visible from the air. This occurred when HMS *Naiad* (camouflaged) was seen by Skuas whereas HMS *Hood* and destroyers (not camouflaged) in company at the time were not seen.

3. At short and medium ranges it caused temporary confusion regarding the type and class of ship until she was examined through glasses.

4. Could only be said to huff the inclinator under certain conditions of light and range favourable to the particular scheme of camouflage in use.

5. Contravened the wartime policy of darkening all surfaces so as to avoid giving aircraft an aiming mark.

6. Consideration given to visibility at night.

It had been established over the past twelve months (1939–40) that dazzle painting was of value only against a land background and that the present suggestion was not for dazzle but for 'contrast painting' which it was hoped would render inclination difficult by contrasting large masses of light and dark. The principles put forward were:

1. Only very large masses of contrast were of any value.

2. 'Cut in' lines do not tell and should be avoided. The entire constructional features of the ship needed to be contrasted.

3. A bow and stern painted comparatively light did, in fact, confuse the inclinator and the hull line needed to be broken if possible.

To test these theories, two models, of *Repulse* and *Furious*, were painted as stipulated. It was found difficult to approximate to sea-going conditions but the experiment established that inclination was more difficult on them than on the same models painted dark grey, particularly in certain conditions of light. A land background rendered them almost unrecognizable.

Repulse was painted up in a very dark and a very light grey – almost white; both colours were similar to 507b and 507c but were extreme. After tests – although when sailing with destroyers it was said that *Repulse* was difficult to spot at night during certain conditions – this type of contrast paintwork had disappeared by late 1941 (see drawings).

During 1941 the Admiralty introduced the Disruptive type of camouflage on a suggestion from the Experimental Camouflage School, but not content with limited success further observation trials were carried out at Scapa Flow in 1941. The object of the trials was:

1. To observe any effects that might be at variance with Admiralty camouflage policy.

2. To observe whether full-scale trials confirmed model-scale trials.

3. To determine the advisability of employing camouflage designs similar in principle to Western Approaches designs for general-purpose ships, particularly cruisers, capital ships and aircraft carriers.

4. To determine the effect of pattern on concealment.

5. To obtain telephotometric readings for summer conditions in the area observed so that correlations between natural and artificial conditions as produced in the experimental tank could be checked and, if necessary, developed.

6. To give designers further experience of the effects of camouflage as seen under full-scale conditions.

Many different types of vessel were used but the following observations were made on *King George V*, *Duke of York* and *Anson* from the shore:

'*King George V* at a 3-mile range had a slightly better concealment value than *Anson*. The Commander-in-Chief, Home Fleet, had earlier requested that the colour MS1 should be substituted by 507A which gave a difference of 9 per cent reflection factor and it seemed to work. It needed to be seen, however, how far the stronger contrasting pattern of *Anson* would produce the same effect at, say, three or four times this range. In sunlight and diffused sunlight both ships, by reason of their broken-up silhouettes and certainly in diffused sunlight because of their lighter mean tones, were markedly less conspicuous than *Duke of York*. Only in one particular intensity of sunlight was *Duke of York* observed to be definitely less conspicuous than the other two ships.'

In general the trials were very satisfactory and produced some data which was considered to be of considerable value. It was felt that the results proved beneficial to designers who were enabled on several instances to see their designs working satisfactorily, and in cases where designs were not so satisfactory the reason why was usually pretty obvious and the lessons learnt would bear fruit. Observers felt encouraged by the general improvement in camouflage designs. Although there was still much to be learned and faults to be remedied the general trend suggested a definite advance. It was felt that this was due in no small measure to the fact that designers had been able to view their models under conditions that generally represented natural conditions very closely. Although it was felt that some slight improvement was probably possible and even desirable in the tank, the close resemblance to natural conditions would only serve to give designers confidence in the tank's general performance. The high degree of co-operation afforded to the trials by the Commander-in-Chief, Home Fleet, was most satisfactory, indicating as it did, the keen interest the administrative authorities were showing in the question of sea camouflage and its complex problems. Moreover, it was considered that camouflage observation trials were now established as a recognized element of the weekly programme of fleet exercises and it was felt that there would be little difficulty in co-operating further trials.

Further research work was carried out at the Paint Research Station in Teddington during 1942 and finally brought about a standardization of Admiralty camouflage colours. This work was concerned with a series of nine shades of grey chosen as standards for Admiralty use. It had the following main purposes:

1. To establish as a standard of reference the colour and brightness values of the nine standard colours supplied.

2. To establish the tolerance in brightness value allowable in the practical production of these colours.

3. To prepare a number of sets of standard colours for future use.

The grey shades were divided into a bluish grey series: B15, B30, B45 and B55. The greenish grey series were: G5, G10, G20, G30 and G55 – the number of colours indicating the approximate brightness value (these numbers replaced the original designations MS1, 2 and 3, etc.). In setting up this range of colour standards special attention was paid to the correct choice of brightness levels. From late 1942 the battleships carried the following types of camouflage:

Queen Elizabeth
Repainted in Admiralty Intermediate disruptive scheme on re-entering service after Alexandria damage. Slight variations to this scheme by May 1943. Repainted Admiralty Standard type during 1944 (blue panel on hull; light grey on upper works). (Dark grey upperworks by 1945).

Malaya
Admiralty Disruptive type (see painting) until late 1944. All grey by spring of 1945.

Warspite
Same scheme as in 1941 except variation in shades. Scrapped in this scheme.

Valiant
Unofficial Disruptive scheme painted up in late 1942/early 1943. Repainted Admiralty Disruptive type in May 1943. Repainted Admiralty Standard type in 1945. All grey by end of 1945.

Royal Sovereign
Still two-tone grey. Repainted Admiralty Intermediate type in September 1943. Left for Russia in this condition. Repainted two-tone grey (dark hull, light upper works) 1944 until scrapping (1949).

Revenge
Repainted early 1942 with unofficial two-tone grey which she kept until 1943 when she was repainted dark grey.

Ramillies
No photographic evidence during 1942, but repainted in Admiralty Intermediate type during the summer of 1943. Repainted Admiralty Standard type 1944 (dark grey panel amidships). All grey again by mid 1945.

Resolution
Early Admiralty Disruptive type during 1942–3. Repainted all grey in 1944.

Nelson
Two variations of Admiralty Disruptive type from 1942–4 (green type). Repainted Admiralty Standard type (blue panel). All grey again in about March 1946.

VARIOUS EARLY TYPES OF RADAR AERIAL

By 1940 sets had been developed from RAF equipment for air warning and AA gun control, and attention now centred on long-range gun control.

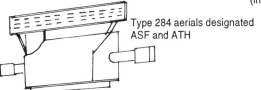

Type 284 aerials designated ASF and ATH

Type 286MY (introduced Apr 1941) A rather odd arrangement of dipoles to give some indication of dead-ahead targets. The ship had to be swung for the set to be used. Max. range was only 3 miles.

This was the range of pure Radar aerials available to the Royal Navy during the period when Britain stood alone and when Radar was seen as essential for sea and aerial warfare. In 1939 only aircraft could be detected and then only rather approximately. By 1941, however, any target could be detected to an accuracy of about 50 yards.

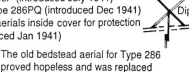

Type 286P (introduced July 1941) also Type 286PQ (introduced Dec 1941) Dipole aerials inside cover for protection (introduced Jan 1941)

Dipole

The old bedstead aerial for Type 286 proved hopeless and was replaced as soon as possible by the above compact arrangement which was a clever way of combining two miniature masthead arrangements on one mast. Range was limited but performance proved reliable.

Type 273 (below)
Type 272
Aerial types AUE, AUG and AUH
These were sets using H/F which was achieved by the cavity magnetron.

They were intended for very precise detection at low level:
273 for large ships
272 for smaller ships
(introduced Dec 1941).
The particularly delicate sets were housed in lanterns of various patterns to protect them from the elements.

Type 273 upper part glazed with Perspex to enable equipment to be examined from outside. Frequently fitted on mast but this was not essential.

Rodney
Early Admiralty Disruptive type from 1942 until scrapping.

Renown
Repainted in early Admiralty Disruptive type in late 1941. Variation of scheme in 1942 until 1944. Admiralty Standard type (blue panel) 1945. All grey again shortly after war.

Furious
Repainted in Admiralty Disruptive type in 1942 until 1943–4 then all grey again.

King George V
Medium grey until mid 1942 when repainted Admiralty Intermediate type. Repainted in 1944 with Admiralty Standard type. Repainted in Pacific colours (dark blue hull, light uppers) 1945.

Duke of York
Medium to dark grey in 1942, then repainted with dark grey hull and light upper works (1943). Repainted Admiralty Standard type 1944. Repainted Pacific colours (dark blue hull, light upper works) 1945.

Anson
Entered service with Admiralty Intermediate type 1942. Repainted Admiralty Standard type late 1944.

Howe
Entered service with Admiralty Intermediate type 1942. Repainted in Admiralty Standard type 1944. Repainted in Pacific colours during spring of 1945.

By 1943 in ships as large as battlecruisers and aircraft carriers it had become obvious that only strongly contrasted designs had been really effective because complete concealment of the ships was out of the question. The experiments continued throughout the war and in 1945 most big ships were still wearing camouflage of some sort, but although the final conclusion was on the whole unfavourable to camouflage, it was noted that some of the schemes had shown some limited success.

RADAR

Radio direction-finding (or Finders) was not a product of war, but rather a development of W/T transmissions, although the Second World War certainly pushed the idea forward to a remarkable degree. In about 1933 the policy was to pick up approaching aircraft before they could be heard or seen and a naval RDF experimental works was set up later in the 30s. The work was directed towards two main themes:

1. Long-range warning of aircraft using a wavelength of a few metres. This was achieved using a wavelength of about four metres and ranges up to 40 miles were obtained using moderate power. Then during 1937/8 the wavelength was changed to about seven metres which led to the Type 79X.. During 1939 the wavelength was again reduced to three to four metres, leading to Type 281. This set could also detect surface craft at ranges of the order of 10 to 20 miles. At that time aircraft could be detected at about 70 to 100 miles at a ceiling of 10,000 to 15,000 feet.

2. Detection of surface ships using a 50cm wavelength. At first the only valves available were of the ACORD type but later valve development, notably the GEC series, led to the introduction of the Type 282 series for gunnery, ship and low-level aircraft detection.

After the war started there began a period of valve development which eventually enabled higher power to be obtained on a wavelength of 10cm. Hence by 1942 there were sets available for long-range warning of aircraft and shorter range for surface ships (Types 279 and 281); short-range warning and gunnery (Type 282, etc.); short-range on surface ships and a few miles on aircraft (Type 271 series).

On the W/T side rapid advances in interception and DF enabled a technique to be developed whereby wavelength of a few metres could be intercepted at very long ranges and their direction found. The development was not regarded as vital, partly because attention was focused on longer HF wavelengths for the Atlantic battle. Research indicated the line to be pursued if wavelengths of a few metres were to become vital from the interception and DF aspects.

The first of many sets produced from 1938 were experimental, but by 1942 the Royal Navy's ships had possibly the best RDF equipment in the world. Each type had its own function and had been designed accordingly. Battleships and aircraft carriers had a variety of aerials and strange-shaped objects to house the equipment within. Space precludes mention of the huge number of radar types and their func-

VARIOUS EARLY TYPES OF RADAR AERIAL

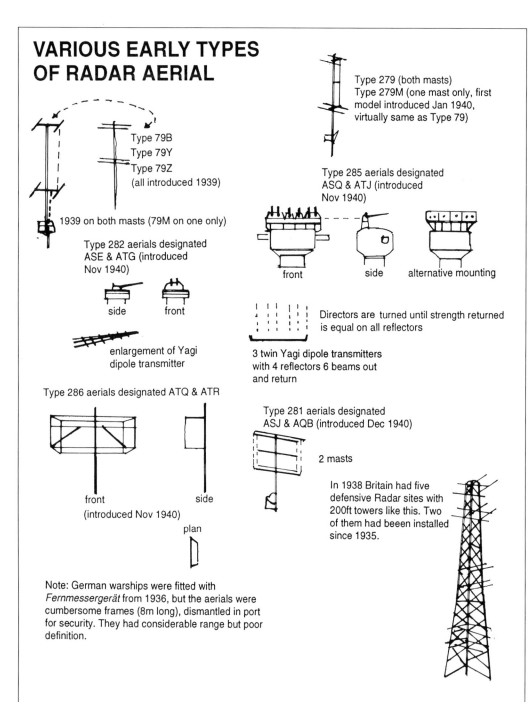

Type 79B
Type 79Y
Type 79Z
(all introduced 1939)

1939 on both masts (79M on one only)

Type 282 aerials designated ASE & ATG (introduced Nov 1940)

side   front

enlargement of Yagi dipole transmitter

Type 286 aerials designated ATQ & ATR

front   side
(introduced Nov 1940)

plan

Note: German warships were fitted with *Fernmessergerät* from 1936, but the aerials were cumbersome frames (8m long), dismantled in port for security. They had considerable range but poor definition.

Type 279 (both masts)
Type 279M (one mast only, first model introduced Jan 1940, virtually same as Type 79)

Type 285 aerials designated ASQ & ATJ (introduced Nov 1940)

front   side   alternative mounting

Directors are turned until strength returned is equal on all reflectors

3 twin Yagi dipole transmitters with 4 reflectors 6 beams out and return

Type 281 aerials designated ASJ & AQB (introduced Dec 1940)

2 masts

In 1938 Britain had five defensive Radar sites with 200ft towers like this. Two of them had beeen installed since 1935.

tion that was developed, but the most important ones (certainly for battleships) are given below.

The first naval sets were developed for air warning. The numbers in sets were not in sequence (e.g., 281, 285) but in most cases sets developed for the same purpose had similar numbers. Numbers started at relatively high figures, probably because of the many early sets being numbered in sequence with normal W/T sets. At first the early heavy aerials could only be fitted at the masthead (to obtain adequate height), and both mastheads had to be used – one for sending and one for receiving.

In November 1940 orders were issued for operational fitting of an improved type of AW radar. Most of the earlier research had been directed towards continual improvement of means of detecting hostile aircraft (particularly at low level). The new air warning set was designated Type 281. It was an SWG (ship warning and gunnery) set and could give ranges of surface targets accurate enough for gunnery. Wavelength was three metres and frequency 85 to 94 MHz. An intermediate set – Type 280 – did not come into general use. This outfit, having a wavelength of 3.66 metres and a frequency of 82 MHz. The object was continually to shorten the wavelength with increasing frequency. Ranges were as follows: Type 280 – six miles against battleship target, five miles against a cruiser target, three miles against a destroyer target, five miles against aircraft at 100 feet, sixteen miles against aircraft at 1,000 feet, 65 miles against aircraft at 16,000 feet. Type 281 – twelve miles against a battleship target, eight miles against a cruiser target, five miles against a destroyer target, two miles against a surfaced submarine, seven to nine miles against aircraft at 100 feet, 38–50 miles against aircraft at 3,000 feet, 88–115 miles against aircraft at 16,000ft. Accuracy: Type 280 – plus 50 yards between ranges 2,000–14,000 yards; Type 281 – plus 100 yards between ranges 14,000–28,000 yards. These high-powered sets had remotely controlled rotating aerials at the masthead to enable all-round sweeping. Singled rod reflectors were used. The aerials required tall, well-supported masts, and fitting took at least five weeks; if masts required strengthening or alteration, however, this period could be ten weeks. In 1940–1 both masts were used (one for transmitting and one for receiving), but the aerials were combined on one mast by the end of 1942.

These sets were first installed in cruisers; indeed the Royal Navy's policy regarding radar concentrated primarily on equipping cruisers as they came in for refit because in all essentials they were the 'eyes of the fleet'. Types 79X, 79Y, 279 and 281 were all early types and all required very tall masts which in most cases involved considerable top weight. The first set for big guns was Type 284 and it was only used for the main armament in capital ships. The aerial was mounted on the director (also doubled up and surface warning equipment). Method of operation was: Permanent watch was maintained on long-range warning sets (79X, 79Y, 281 and 286). On detecting a target Type 285 would be trained in the required direction in an endeavour to pick it up. If surface action were expected Type 284 would also be employed. If aircraft attack developed Type 285 would engage at long range and 282 at short range.

A summary of early RDF procedure was:
1. Masthead search sets picked up target at long range and all AA guns were directed to bearing of target.
2. Type 275 or 285 picked up target and transmitted to Radar Office. Guns (5.25in and 4.5in) followed director and fired when within range.
3. For aircraft making direct dive or torpedo attack, Types 282, 283 and 262 picked up target for 40mm or 2-pdrs, while larger HA directors (Types 285 and 275) indicated target bearing initially to LA. Once latter had picked up target they worked quite independently.

Radar sets installed in *Queen Elizabeth* class (other vessels similarly fitted):
November Type 792–1 *Valiant*; 1940 Type 28 *Malaya*, *Warspite*, *Barham*; 1941 Types 297 (January *QE*), 285 (four sets), RB unit L10, Type 282 production delay, four sets fitted by June, Type 284 *Valiant* at Alexandria, *Warspite* towards end of year; 1943 Type 285P *Malaya*; 1945 from January Type 274 on fore DCT *QE*, *Valiant*, *Warspite*, Types 277, 293 added later.

Interesting experiments were carried out at the beginning of the war, using one aerial with another. Tests were made in *Nelson* during June 1940 to determine the range that could be obtained on surface targets using the standard Type 282 transmitter and receiver with aerials situated on the main armament director control tower. The aerials were large parabolic cylinders with an aperture of 11 feet 4 inches x 4 feet 1½ inches each having a power gain of about one hundred times, i.e., about ten times the gain of the Type 282 aerials. Being fixed to the director tower and rotating with it, the aerials were kept on the target optically or by instructions from the Admiral's bridge by means of flexible voice pipes. On searching for a convoy at sea one ship was picked up at 36,000 yards and three other ships were first detected at 33,000 yards.

Although these were experimental tests they served to show that if one aerial broke down the other could be used in its place. *Hood* was fitted with Types 282, 284 and 285 in Scapa Flow, but in such haste that many of the installations were incorrectly wired. Tests were carried out ranging on *King George V* with the following results:
Outward Run. 11,000 yards ... saturation of target; 14,000 yards ... 10 times the signal; 16,000 yards ... 6 to 8 times the signal; 27,000 yards ... 1½ times the signal; 27,300 yards ... the signal was lost. The echo was very spasmodic from 25,000 yards, but the plot of the run taken from RDF ranges and bearings was a very good one. Inward run. *King George V* came in on an unknown bearing and was picked up at 24,700 yards; it was thought that it would have been possible to pick up the target earlier but for the fact that she came in on the same bearing as land echoes. The destroyers escorting *King George V* were picked up at 16,300 yards.

Typical faults found with Type 284 were:
1. The transmitter and the receiver needed to be properly tuned.
2. The brilliancy control on the ranging unit frequently burnt out.
3. Bad joints caused operation to be spasmodic.
4. Switch panels were often faulty.
5. Voltage control boards often malfunctioned.
6. Aerials were often connected the wrong way round, i.e., the transmitter was connected to the lower array and the receiver connected to the upper array.

Revenge was fitted with Type 279 and tests carried out on 28 April 1941 gave the following results: Aerial height – 160 feet above waterline (both aerials); distance of separation between aerials – 116 feet; working frequency – 42KHz. Type of craft: small fishing vessel – 4,700 yards; average size merchant ship – 8,000–10,000 yards; convoy of 41 ships – 13,900 yards. A certain degree of success was achieved when using the set for navigational purposes.

As war progressed the RDF systems became more and more complex and by 1944–5 capital ships' masts were literally covered with many different sets, some single-purpose, some multi-purpose and IFF and TBS aerials were also integrated with the SW and AW sets. In just four short years radar had become one of the most important features of a ship.

Throughout the lives of the battleships, their crews almost always had affectionate names for their own vessels. Some of them were obvious, others not so, as can be seen. Not all ships' nicknames were recorded, but perhaps this could be rectified at a later date?

Thunderer (*Orion* Class)	'Thunder Guts'
Tiger	'Tigs'
Iron Duke	'The Dook' or 'Iron Duck'
King George V (1913)	'HMS Never-budge'
Ajax	'The Queen of Hearts'
Centurion	'Century' or 'Cento'
Royal Sovereign	'Royal Quid' or 'Tiddly Quid'
Resolution	'Rolling Ressie' or 'Reso'
Royal Oak	'Old Oak'
Ramillies	'Mutton Chop'
Queen Elizabeth	'Bessie', 'Lizzie' or 'Nessie'
Warspite	'Warspider' or 'Old Lady'
Repulse	'Beecham'
Hood	'The Mighty 'ood' or the 'ood have thought it'
Nelson	'Nellie' or 'Nelsing'
Rodney	'Rodo'
Duke of York	'Duck of York'
Howe	'Anyhow'
Anson	'Andsome'
Furious	'Curious'
Glorious	'Laborious'
Courageous	'Outrageous'

EARLY CLASSES THAT SURVIVED THE GREAT WAR

After compliance with the Washington Treaty in 1921, the Royal Navy was left with the smallest battle fleet it had had for hundreds of years. British battleships left in service by 1922 were:

Orion class: one ship (four built) *Thunderer*.
King George V class: (four built) three ships *King George V*, *Ajax*, *Centurion* (*Audacious* sunk 1914).
Iron Duke class: (four built) *Iron Duke*, *Benbow*, *Marlborough*, *Emperor of India*.
Queen Elizabeth class: (five built) *Queen Elizabeth*, *Barham*, *Warspite*, *Malaya*, *Valiant*. *Royal Sovereign* class: (five built) *Royal Sovereign*,

Royal Oak, *Revenge*, *Ramillies*, *Resolution*.

Battlecruisers suffered severely, with the type becoming almost extinct. There remained *Tiger*, *Renown*, *Repulse*, *Glorious*, *Courageous*, *Hood*. With *Glorious* and *Courageous* looking towards full conversion to aircraft carriers, just four of the type remained in service.

The oldest unit to survive (with the exception of *Colossus* as non-seagoing Training Ship) was *Thunderer* from the 1909 estimates. The outstanding feature of the *Orion* class was that they were the first to carry 13.5in guns and on completion were the most powerfully armed British battleships in the Royal Navy. The weakest feature of the *Orion*s and many of those that went before her was the location of the foremast in front of the aftermost funnel. The whole class served with the Grand Fleet from 1914 to 1919.

Conqueror, *Monarch* and *Orion* were placed on the disposal list in 1922 under the terms of the Washington Treaty, *Conqueror* and *Orion* being sold in 1922. *Monarch* was sunk as a target in 1925 (see notes). *Thunderer* continued to serve as a seagoing Training Ship for cadets from 1921 until 1926 when she was sold.

The four *King Georges* followed the *Orion*s and only just survived the 1921 scrapping campaign. They were modified and slightly larger versions of the *Orion* group, but with the faults of the foremast/funnel being rectified. All served with the Grand Fleet from 1914 to 1919. *Audacious* was sunk by a mine on 14 October 1914. Surviving ships were placed on the disposal list or rendered non-effective in 1926 under terms of the Washington Treaty. *Ajax* and *King George V* were sold in 1926. *Centurion* was converted for service as Fleet Target Ship in

TIGER, 1926

Seen here towards the end of her career. Often said to have been the most graceful-looking warship — irrespective of the later *Hood* — she was the final development of the *Lion* class and as such was a distinct improvement over those ships, but she was a battlecruiser and inherited the defects of that type. Note: massive compass platform housing, large control top, three equal funnels, stump pole mainmast and rather odd SL arrangements.

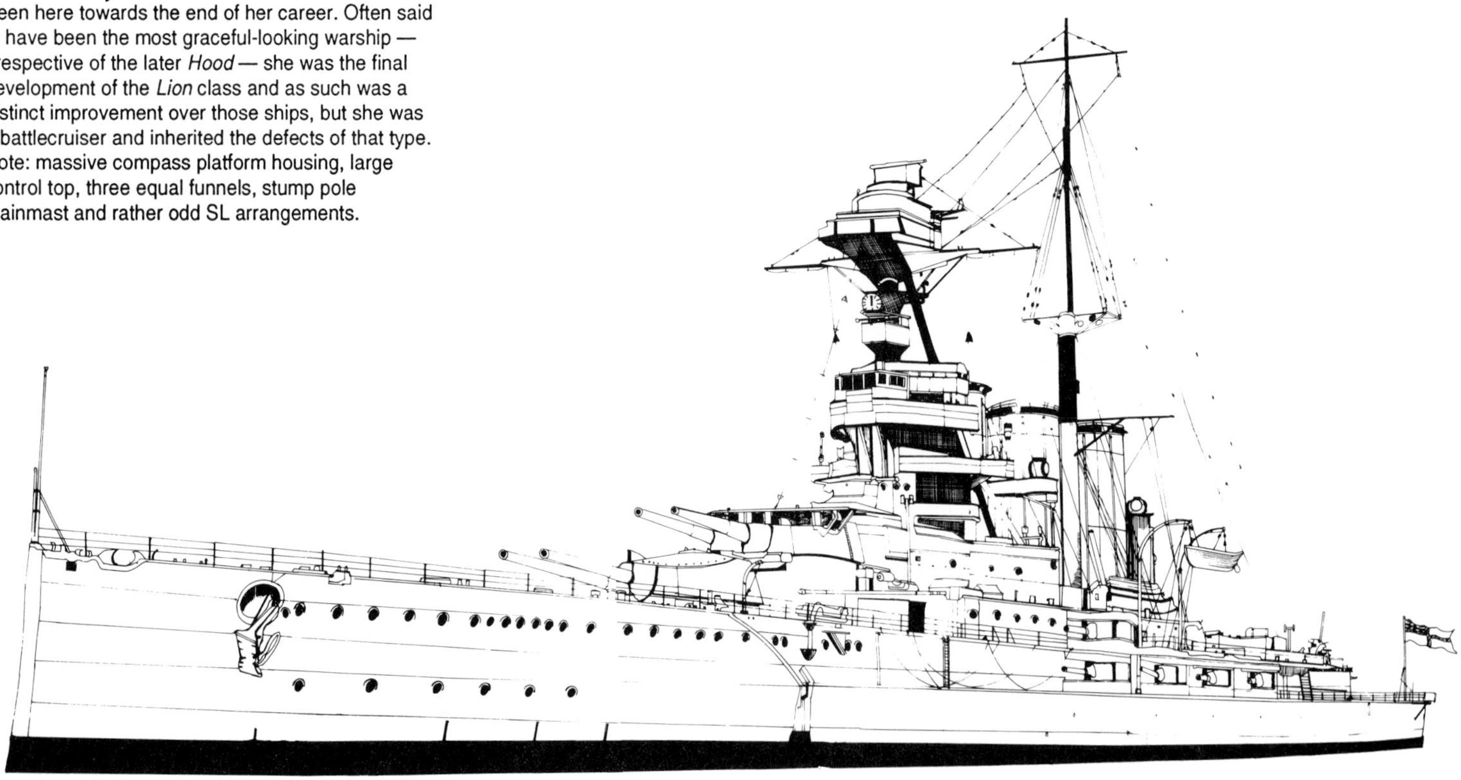

Bottom: The only surviving member of the *Orion* class after the Great War, *Thunderer*, seen here in 1923 in Vik, Norway, was used as a Boys Training Ship for many years up to 1926.

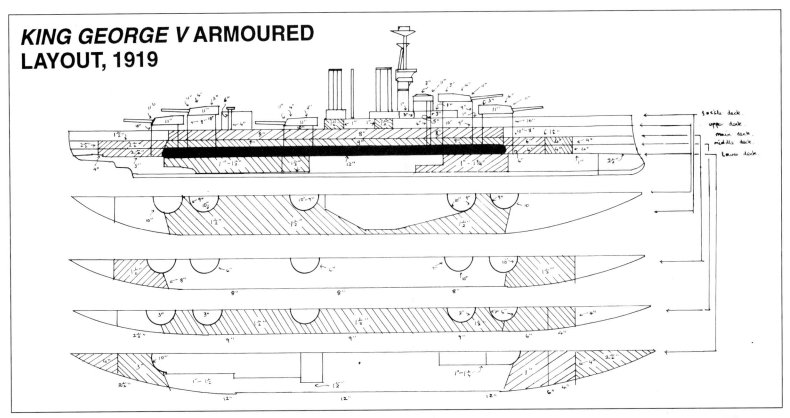

KING GEORGE V ARMOURED LAYOUT, 1919

1926–7 (see notes). Re-rated as Escort Ship in 1940, she saw miscellaneous service in the Mediterranean and the East Indies and Red Sea stations from 1940 to 1944. She was sunk as a breakwater for the Normandy Invasion in 1944.

The battlecruiser *Tiger* was the last ship for which Sir Philip Watts, as DNC, was responsible. The original design was basically a modifed *Queen Mary* with slightly better features all round. While a distinct improvement over *Queen Mary* and the *Lion*s, overall protection was still inadequate to withstand heavy calibre shellfire and on the basis of Jutland experience *Tiger* was not generally regarded as having been equal to the German *Derfflinger* in all-round fighting efficiency despite a heavier armament. She served with the Battle Cruiser force from 1914 to 1918 and was paid off into Reserve status in August 1921. She served as Gunnery Training Ship at Portsmouth from February 1924 until June 1929. After a year with the Atlantic Fleet she was

Bottom: *Tiger* in Weymouth Bay circa 1924. She was a frequent visitor to Portland and became a favourite sight there during the 1920s. Her passing caused an outburst of regret in the press, but it was too late to save her from the Washington Treaty cuts.

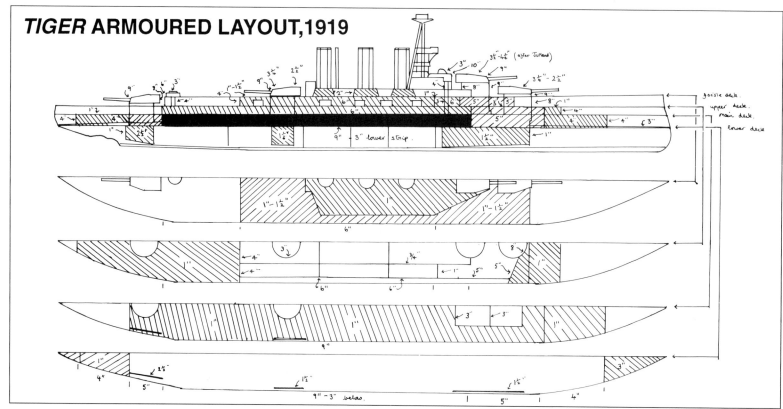

TIGER ARMOURED LAYOUT, 1919

again paid off into Reserve in 1931 under a clause of the naval treaties (see notes on treaties) and was finally scrapped at Rosyth and Inverkeithing from February 1932. Her departure from service was seen as the passing of the most graceful and handsome ship in the Royal Navy, regardless of what was said of *Hood*.

With the scrapping of *Tiger*, *Emperor of India*, *Benbow* and *Marlborough* (see *Iron Duke* class for notes of these three), the Royal Navy's capital ships were at an all time low of just fifteen vessels.

CENTURION AS RADIO CONTROLLED TARGET SHIP

By 1927 the only unit of the class left was *Centurion* which had been selected for Radio Controlled Target Ship to replace the ageing *Agamemnon*. Paid off into dockyard hands for

conversion on 14 April 1926 she reappeared stripped of all small fittings in July 1927 (see table). As she was only to be used for fleet firing against shells up to 8in calibre her general appearance was not drastically altered, but later (1933) her rig was further reduced to prepare her for high-level bombing by the Royal Air Force and Fleet Air Arm in a 'Navy versus Aircraft' competition which would furnish information for the 'Vulnerability of Capital Ships' debate. Many tests were carried out on the old ship which was controlled by radio from the destroyer *Shikari* which from a safe distance took a series of photographs of the fall of shot and of bombs from aircraft.

Continuing in this role for about four years, she served her purpose well but by 1937 was looking like a patchwork quilt after the many hits on her hull and upperworks. Although the tests did not give conclusive evidence of the demise of

the battleship, it did highlight the fact that ships were becoming increasingly vulnerable to aerial attack.

In September 1937 a series of bombing tests were witnessed by the cruiser *Curacoa*. The outstanding impression of the five days' bombing

Particulars of Surviving Classes after First World War

Orion class: one ship, *Thunderer*
Displacement: 27,416 tons deep load.
Length: 581ft (oa), Beam: 88ft 6in, Draught: 31ft 4in (deep).
Armament: 10 x 13.5in, 8 x 4in, 1 x 3in AA.
Armour: Main belt 12–6–4in, upper belt 8in, barbettes 10–9–7in, decks 4–3–2–1in, CT 11–4in.
Machinery
Parsons Marine turbines driving 4 propellers.
SHP: 27,000 for 21 knots.
Fuel: 900/3, 300 tons coal.
Complement: 900/1,040.

King George V class
Displacement: 28,422 tons (deep).
Length: 594/597ft (oa). Beam: 89ft. Draught: 30ft 6in (deep).
Armament: 10 x 13.5in, 12 x 4in, 2 x 3in AA.
Armour: Main belt: 12in. upper belt: 9–8in, barbettes: 10–9–7in, decks 4–3–2–1in, CT: 11–3in.
Machinery
Parsons direct drive turbines driving 4 propellers.
SHP: 27,000 for 20/21 knots.
Fuel: 900/3, 100 tons coal.
Complement: 877.

Tiger
Displacement: 34,100 tons (deep).
Length: 704ft (oa).
Beam: 90ft 6in.
Draught: 32ft 10in (deep).
Armament 8 x 13.5in, 12 x 6in, 2 x 3in AA.
Armour
Main belt 9in, ends 6–5–4in, bulkheads 5–4in, decks 3–2–1in, CT 10in.
Additional armour on roofs of 13.5in turrets, crowns of magazines, ammunition hoists, upper deck, main deck (over magazines) and additional anti-flash protection added.
Machinery
Brown-Curtis impulse-type turbines driving 4 propellers.
SHP: 85,000 for 28 knots (slightly reduced owing to additions).
Fuel: Coal/oil combination. 4,900 tons max combination.
Complement: 1,400

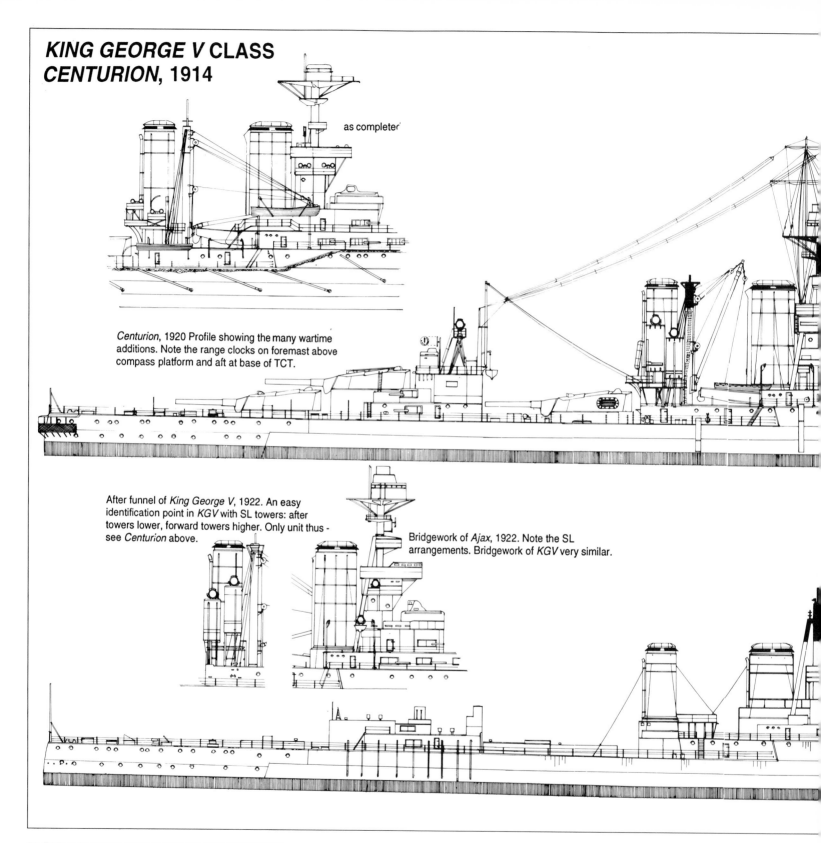

KING GEORGE V CLASS
CENTURION, 1914

as completed

Centurion, 1920 Profile showing the many wartime additions. Note the range clocks on foremast above compass platform and aft at base of TCT.

After funnel of King George V, 1922. An easy identification point in KGV with SL towers: after towers lower, forward towers higher. Only unit thus - see Centurion above.

Bridgework of Ajax, 1922. Note the SL arrangements. Bridgework of KGV very similar.

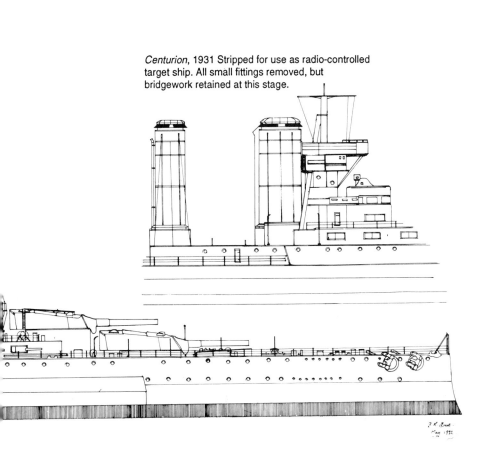

Centurion, 1931 Stripped for use as radio-controlled
target ship. All small fittings removed, but
bridgework retained at this stage.

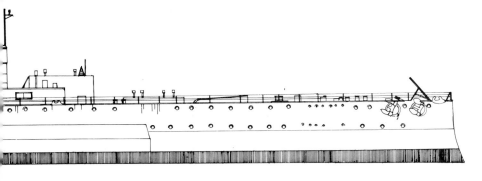

Centurion, 1935 as radio-controlled target for fleet
firing. Note: funnels reduced in height, scarcely any
bridgework, marking strips (ranging) aft, and
extensive aerials for radio control (on bridge, mast,
after structure and barbette tops).

was the dependence of all bombing operations
upon favourable weather. The weather at the
time was described by holiday makers as ideal,
yet a perfect day for bombing was never to be
had and on the most successful day little more
than half the programme was carried out. It was
found that high-level bombers required a clear
sky and good visibility up to the height selected.
A reasonable horizon was also a requirement.
Aircraft had to assess the wind from the height at
which they were flying, dodging clouds when
necessary, and any error in wind estimation, as
was only too frequent and probable on a gusty
day, had a considerable effect on accuracy, given
that the duration of the bombs' fall was in the
order of 25 to 30 seconds. In fact, it was seen
that precision bombing in gusty weather was
almost impossible. Too fine weather on the other
hand, with extreme visibility, laid the attackers
open to accurate anti-aircraft fire throughout the
approach.

In this connection, the first day's bombing
was most interesting. It took place under ideal
conditions. (There was no question of tactics
during the trials.) The hazy weather introduced
a not inconsiderable navigation problem and
two aircraft failed to find the target at all! The
aircraft that did find *Centurion* were able to
bomb from 10,000 feet in safety because they
were almost invisible from the ship. Of the 21
bombs dropped, however, only one hit the target. On the last afternoon, however, when
bombing from 10,000 feet several crews estimated the wind from that height by means of a
sea marker and then found themselves forced
down to about 8,000 feet in order to make their
attack. The error in wind setting caused by this
was sufficient to annul any chance of successful
bombing. It was also found that dive-bombing
was less dependent on visibility conditions, but
it was noteworthy that good results were not
achieved in strong winds. Tests were carried out
at 2,000 feet and as expected the results
improved greatly.

The conclusions drawn were that although
the dive-bombers achieved the best results, and
high-level bombing was limited in its use at sea,
attacking aircraft would pay a heavy price when
approaching a fully manned and fighting battleship – but it was considered to be a price worth
paying if the ship could be slowed down or crippled.

Opposite page, top: Close-up of *Centurion* after the Great War, *c.*1921, showing the culmination of wartime additions. Note the tripod legs on the foremast – low down connection with single pole once above the charthouse.

Opposite page, bottom: One of *Centurion's* last appearances in her original condition before being altered as Target Ship. Shown here at Fleet Review, Spithead 26 July 1924.

Below: *Centurion* now partially stripped for use as Target Ship: no searchlight towers on second funnel, all 13.5in guns and turrets out, no stump derrick and no upper works or masts. 22 September 1930.

Bottom left: Testing the waterline armoured belt and being saturated by medium-calibre shell fire while being manoeuvred by the destroyer *Shikari*.

Bottom right: Another hole to repair after being hit in the after funnel. A shell has passed straight through the funnel without exploding, leaving a large gaping hole. *Centurion*, 1930

IRON DUKE CLASS

DESIGN.

The original design was for a modified *King George V* 21-knot battleship with four broadside torpedo tubes and no stern tube.

Five layouts were submitted to the Admiralty by the DNC Phillip Watts, all featuring a main armoured belt of 12in thickness and running for 360 feet of the hull. Although following the lines of *King George V* in general – including main armament, a distinctive retrograde step was seen in the sketch proposal which featured a reverse in the mast/funnel arrangement as in the earlier *Orion* class of 1909 (see sketch). During preparation, however, the disadvantages were forcibly pointed out and the idea was not pursued any further. Of the five layouts (see table) M1V was approved and funds were allocated for four of the type without question, a war with Germany seeming very likely — and sooner rather than later.

Enlarged dimensions over the *King George V*s and *Iron Duke* (so named later during construction) represented the ultimate development of the basic *Orion* type from which the design was evolved through the intervening *KGV*s. They were the first British dreadnought type with a 6in secondary battery and the first to be given any type of anti-aircraft guns.

As completed they were nominally 2,000 tons heavier than *King George V* with increases of 25–26 feet overall in length, 1 foot in beam and 6 inches on the designed draught. The marked rise in displacement was necessitated by the heavier and better protected secondary armament, augmented torpedo armament and slightly increased fuel capacity.

Legend of Designs

	'LII'	'LIII'	'MIII'	'MIV'
Length	560ft	575ft	580ft	580ft
Beam	90ft	90ft	90ft 6in	90ft
Draught	27¼ft	28ft	28ft	28ft
Displacement (tons)	23,750	24,500	25,000	24,750
SHP	28,500	30,000	30,000	30,000
Armament	10x13.5in	10x13.5in	10x3.5in	10x13.5in
Secondary	16x4in	16x5in	16x6in	12x6in
Main belt	12–9–8in	12–9–8in	12–9–7in	12–9–7in
Costs (£)	2,050,000	2,100,000	2,150,000	2,300,000

There was a design called 'MV' which was the same as 'MIV' but with an armoured belt reduced to 8in and 7in, but it does not appear to have been given any further consideration.

The additional length in this class was allocated over the forecastle and quarterdeck, in the former case to provide some buoyancy against the weight of the 6in battery and set it back from the bows, and in the latter to accommodate the two main deck 6in guns aft. The freeboard was considerably lower than in many of the previous British dreadnoughts and, in fact, was not equalled until the arrival of the *Royal Sovereign* class in 1913. The main armament layout was practically identical with that of *King George V* but with director control in all of the class as completed.

The 6in gun had last appeared in the *King Edward VII* class (1906–7), but as an auxiliary to the main armament rather than for anti-torpedo purposes for which 12pdrs and 3pdrs were provided and, in conformity with the ideas of the First Sea Lord (Admiral Fisher), none of the intervening classes had carried anything heavier than a 4in anti-torpedo armament despite repeated criticism of its ineffectiveness against contemporary destroyers.

As shown in the tables one of the original designs had featured a 4in secondary armament, but a report prepared by Admiral Mark Kerr in 1909 suggesting the change and noting the majority of service opinion favoured the 6in gun for any torpedo work as well as general use against heavy ships during close-range action, made the 6in battery almost the principal feature of the design.

They were the first British dreadnoughts to be given a ratio of protection to displacement equal to the German *Kaiser* class which, in fact, had been designed some three years earlier. They were excellent ships as completed, and almost unequalled until the arrival of the 15in gunned *Queen Elizabeth* class in 1915.

RIG

Full tripod foremast close before fore funnel.
Tall topmast stepped abaft control top.
Short topgallantmast stepped before, except in *Emperor of India* which completed with short flagpole only.
Heavy forward strut at starfish below control top.
No mainmast as completed.
W/T aerials carried direct to the stern or after superstructure.
Tall derrick stump for main derrick fitted close behind second funnel. Very short stumps abeam this (P&S).
Long derrick slung from each forward corner of after superstructure. These could be topped up vertically or crossed against forward face of superstructure.

The rig was very similar to that of *King George V* except that this class were completed with full tripod foremast. They were the last battleships built for the Royal Navy with the distinctive single masted rig which had been a feature of the three preceding classes.

Very simple bridgework as completed which remained more or less unchanged

PROPOSED M4 DESIGN-*IRON DUKE*

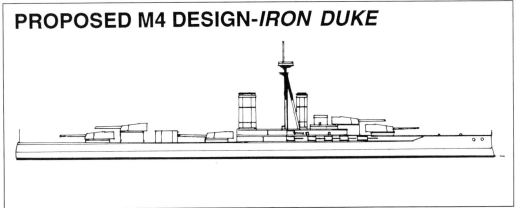

Iron Duke class: General particulars, 1919

Displacement (tons): 26,300 (load) 31,620 (deep),
(average for class).

Length: 580ft 4in (pp), 623ft 9in (oa) (average for
class).

Beam: 90ft 1in.

Draught: 28ft 10in (load), 32ft 6in (deep).

Armament

10 x 13.5in 45cal Mk V, 12 x 6in Mk VII, 4 x 3pdr,
5 x MG, 2 x 3in AA, 4 x 21in (submerged).

Armour

Main belt 12–9–8in, bulkheads 6–4in, upper side
bulkheads 8in, barbettes 10–9–8–4–3in, turrets
11–5$\frac{1}{2}$–4in, CT 11–6–3in, decks: forecastle 1in;
upper 2–1$\frac{1}{4}$in, main 1$\frac{1}{2}$in, middle 2$\frac{1}{2}$in–1in, lower
2$\frac{1}{2}$, magazine screens 1$\frac{1}{2}$in. Searchlights: 8 x 36in,
2 x 24in signalling. Improved control arrangement
fitted.

Aircraft

Runways on 13.5in turret tops ('B' and 'Q'). *Emperor
of India* fitted for towing kite (balloons). During
post-war period aircraft not normally carried, but
embarked when required for exercises.

Machinery

Parsons direct-drive turbines driving 4 propellers.

Boilers: 18 Yarrow (Babcock & Wilcox in *ID* and
Benbow).

SHP: 29,000 for 21 knots.

Radius of action: 8,100 nm at 12 knots.

Fuel (tons): 900 coal normal load, 1,050 oil, 3,250
coal max. Max. speed slightly less than 20 knots
due to extra weights added.

Rig: Short topmast and no topgallant. Very long forward strut at starfish in *Emperor of India* and *Iron
Duke*. Twin W/T spreaders on after superstructure
(short in *Emperor of India*, tall in other three).

Appearance:

Considerably altered and generally heavier-looking
than in 1914 owing to wartime modifications. SL
towers added, enlarged control top, aircraft platforms, reduced rig, turret scales painted up at end
of war (painted out by early 1919), range clocks on
face of control tops and at rear of after superstructure in *Iron Duke* only. Clinker screen to fore funnel
in *Emperor of India* but removed by early 1919.

Individual differences

Benbow: Small hood over director tower (only ship
thus, removed 1921, shallow triangular strut to derrick stump (deep in others).

Marlborough: Long middle bridge wings (from 1916).

Emperor of India: Clinker screen to fore funnel. No
sternwalk. Short W/T spreaders on after superstructure (tall in others).

Iron Duke: 6in director towers on lower bridge (upper
in others).

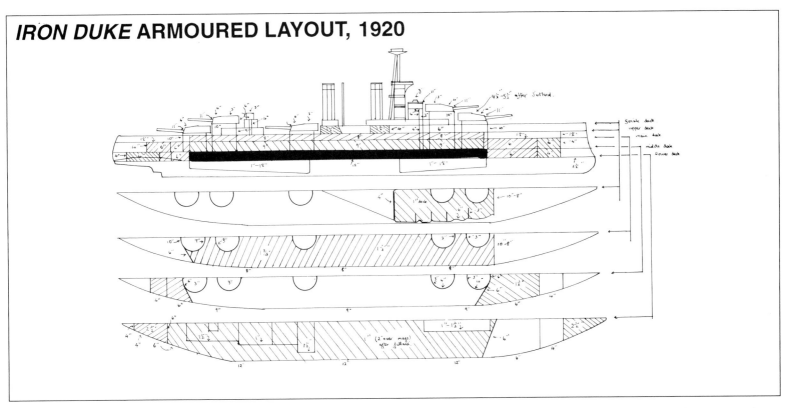

IRON DUKE ARMOURED LAYOUT, 1920

throughout the Great War (see author's *British Battleships of World War One*).

APPEARANCE

Considered not such good-looking ships as *King George V* mainly because of the small round funnels. Sternwalk fitted in all except *Emperor of India*.
Distinguishable from *King George V* by:
1. Forecastle battery and 6in gun on each side of main deck aft.
2. Small round equal-sized funnels.
3. Full-length tripod legs (KGV similar from 1917).
Individual differences (as completed):
Iron Duke: Small rangefinder over bridge.
Marlborough: No rangefinder over bridge (1914 only).
Benbow: Shallow triangular strut to derrick stump.
Emperor of India: No sternwalk; no strut to main derrick stump (added 1915–16).

After the Naval Treaty of 1930 it was concluded that the *Iron Duke* class would be scrapped with the exception of *Iron Duke* herself which would be demilitarized and put to use as a Gunnery Training Ship. The relevant clause in the treaty stated that *Iron Duke* was to be refitted as soon as possible, in fact the work was to be commenced within twelve months of ratification of the treaty and had to be completed within eighteen months. A great deal of thought was given to her demilitarization and the question arose as to what smaller guns could replace the 13.5in which were to be removed.

Twin 8in were very much favoured at the time, but these would involve a great deal of re-arrangement of the barbettes and supports, so 6in and 4.7in were fitted, but some experimental fittings were tested throughout the thirties with an eye to refitting other battleships with a suitable secondary armament when their time came for reconstruction. A total of 4,258 tons was

removed from *Iron Duke* and 202 tons of new equipment were added.

Benbow was placed on the disposal list in 1930; *Emperor of India* and *Marlborough* in 1931 and 1932 respectively. From 1932 only *Iron Duke* was left in service. She was demilitarized from November 1931 until September 1932.

'B' and 'Y' turrets removed (barbettes retained). 6in secondary armament retained. Two 4.7in AA added on quarterdeck, both on centre line on and abaft 'Y' barbette. 4in AA on after superstructure was removed. Small AA gun mounted on crown of 'B' barbette. Rangefinder on after superstructure was replaced by HA director. TT removed. Belt and side armour between 'B' and 'Y' barbettes was removed. Conning tower was removed. Battery armour, deck and internal protection was retained. The forward group of boilers were mutilated and the remaining boilers converted to burn oil only. Speed was reduced to about 18 knots.
1933–5: 4in AA replaced on after superstructure;

IRON DUKE CLASS: *MARLBOROUGH*, AS COMPLETED 1914

4.7in AA on quarterdeck was removed (autumn 1935).

1939: Twin 5.25in dual-purpose turret mounted abaft 'Y' barbette for experimental purposes.

1939–45: More or less unchanged except that some of the 6in guns were removed and many AA guns were added while serving as Depot and Base AA Ship at Scapa.

Although the Naval Treaty of 1930 dealt the death blow to the other three ships of the class, it was advantageous to the Royal Navy in that these ships could be used experimentally to determine the degree to which a modern battleship would stand up to battle damage and retain her structural integrity. To this end, it was agreed to place *Emperor of India* and *Marlborough* in the hands of HMS *Excellent*, the Gunnery Training School. The following tests were made in the two ships during the next eighteen months (from 1931):

1. Effect of gunfire from destroyers on bridgework during night fighting.
2. Flashtight arrangements.
3. Attack by 13.5in shells.
4. Aerial attack.
5. Bridge and control personnel protection, etc.
6. Anti-torpedo tests.
7. Pressure tests on hull and internal bulkheads.

In 1931 *Emperor of India* underwent firing tests at sea when she was hit twelve times and severely damaged. After practically sinking and being raised, she managed to return and was scrapped shortly afterwards.

Marlborough underwent a very different set of trials, mostly internal, and thorough blast ventilation and bulkhead strength comparisons were carried out in her. A small crew was left on board to photograph and make notes of the procedures. Trial 1 was carried out on 21 July, Trial 2 on 24 July 1931, the purpose being to determine how the explosion of an entire magazine – and possible loss of the ship – could be prevented should one or more cartridges ignite no matter what the cause.

Some internal alterations were effected in *Marlborough* in that Trial 1 represented the smallest 16in magazine in *Nelson*. Trial 2 represented the 8in magazine in the cruiser *Norfolk*. In both trials, one 16in charge of 498lb of size 45 MC cordite plus three 16in cartridges in open cases (total 249lb) was placed up against a bulkhead of chosen value.

Some slight alteration to after CT platform: TCT removed and additional housing fitted at rear with rangefinder above

1929

July 1926 CT platform

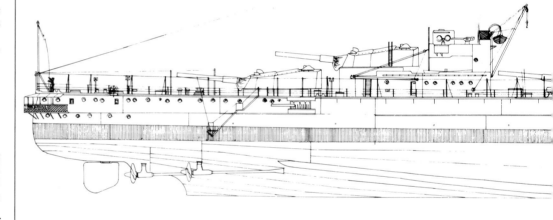

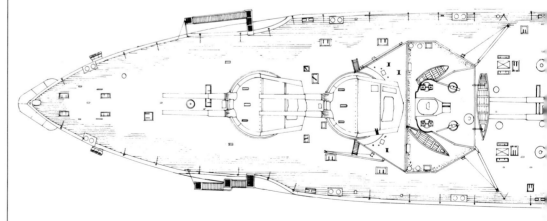

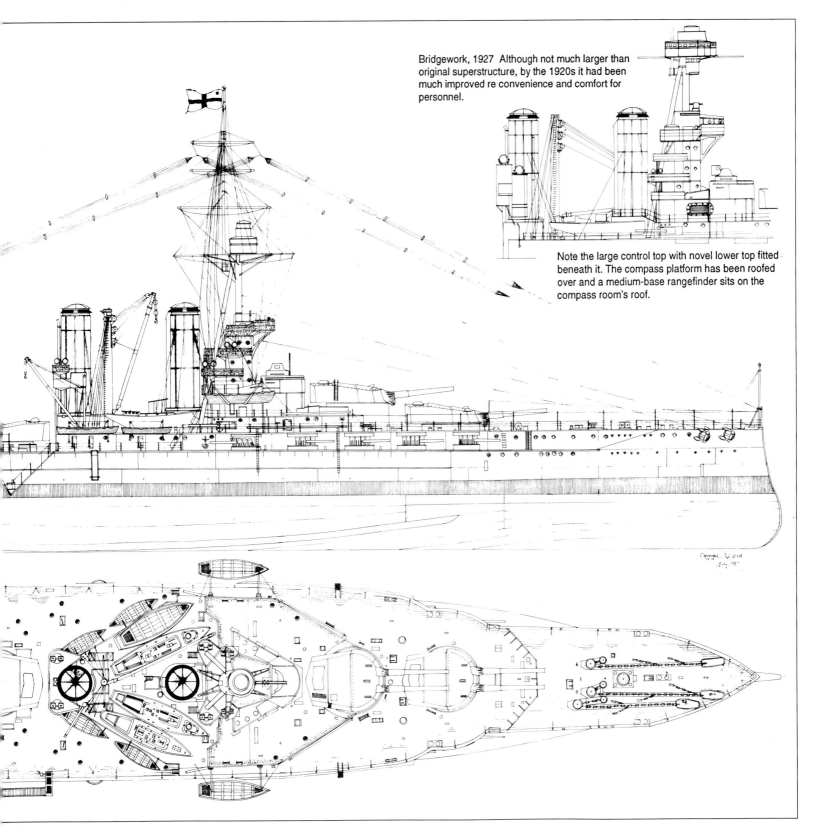

Bridgework, 1927 Although not much larger than
original superstructure, by the 1920s it had been
much improved re convenience and comfort for
personnel.

Note the large control top with novel lower top fitted
beneath it. The compass platform has been roofed
over and a medium-base rangefinder sits on the
compass room's roof.

Below: Two on-deck views of *Iron Duke* – the boat deck looking aft and the shelter deck looking down from the control top, 1926.

Both trials were extremely successful in that the explosion vented itsef out of the ship by the designed route and caused no fatal damage by re-routing and setting off other magazines had they been in location. The tests were recorded on film, but the film has yet to be found! The explosions were heard (from the quarterdeck observers) as a faint rumble followed one second later by jets of smoke from 'B' 13.5in gun muzzles. A half-second later high-pressure smoke issued from 'B' gunhouse including the turret aprons. After about nineteen seconds the smoke had ceased. No flame was observed, but examination of the bulkheads later indicated that there had been flame and great heat in the area which was sprayed with water for eight minutes. On entering the area about 1½ hours later it was evident that there had been much damage, particularly to the bulkheads, but the main explosion had vented itself from the handing room through the vent plates provided. (see drawings for location).

In March 1939, with the increasing likelihood of war, the question was raised of restoring *Iron Duke* to her former glory and strength, proponents of the idea pointing out that the Japanese had worked wonders in modernizing to a remarkable degree their old battlecruiser *Hiei*.

Iron Duke's armour was the first consideration and it was proposed that an 11in main belt be run between her upper and main decks (KC armour, 1,750 tons or non-cemented, 1,200 tons); hull to bulged similarly to the *Royal Sovereign* class, and 4in armour to be laid over the main deck. The 13.5in turrets would be replaced and the secondary armament completely renewed with four to eight 4.5in or 5.25in guns.

The main argument against the project was the question of speed; the entire boiler/-engine/machinery arrangements would have to be renewed to achieve the desired increase, and with outside estimates ranging from £920,000 to £1,200,000, which could be better spent on a new ship, it is not surprising that the idea was dropped.

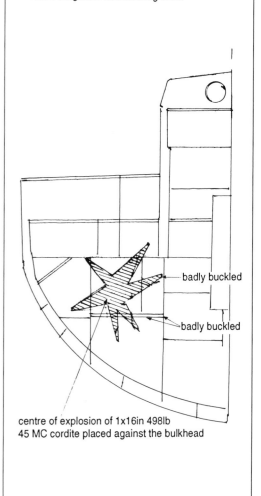

IRON DUKE CLASS

Marlborough: Magazine Tests, 21-24 July 1931

'B' 13.5in magazine and handing room

badly buckled

badly buckled

centre of explosion of 1x16in 498lb 45 MC cordite placed against the bulkhead

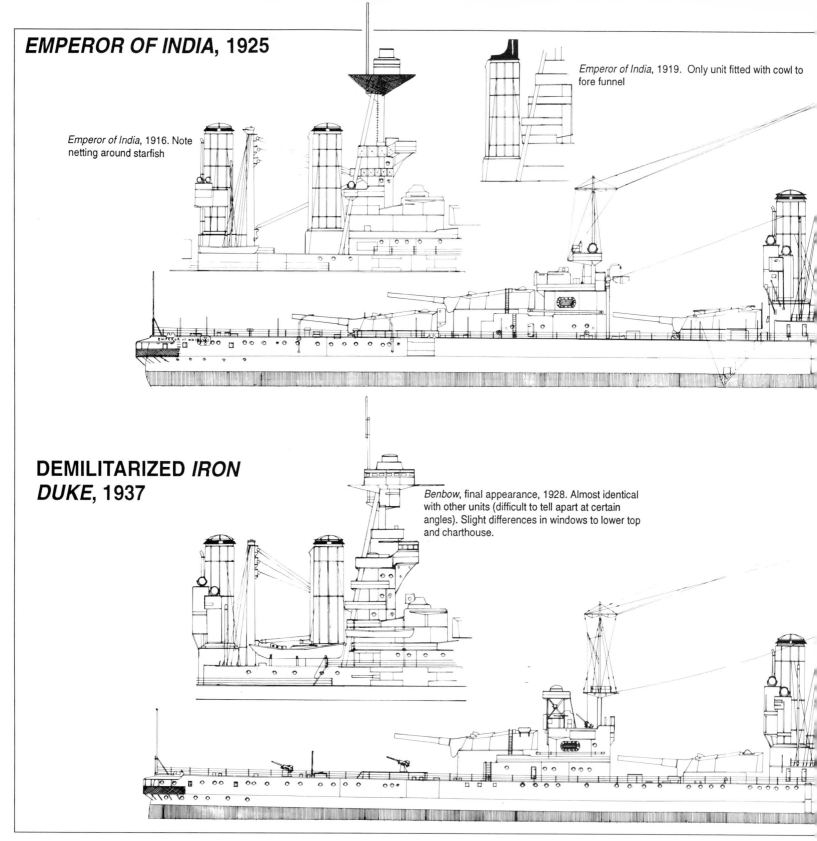

EMPEROR OF INDIA, 1925

Emperor of India, 1916. Note netting around starfish

Emperor of India, 1919. Only unit fitted with cowl to fore funnel

DEMILITARIZED *IRON DUKE*, 1937

Benbow, final appearance, 1928. Almost identical with other units (difficult to tell apart at certain angles). Slight differences in windows to lower top and charthouse.

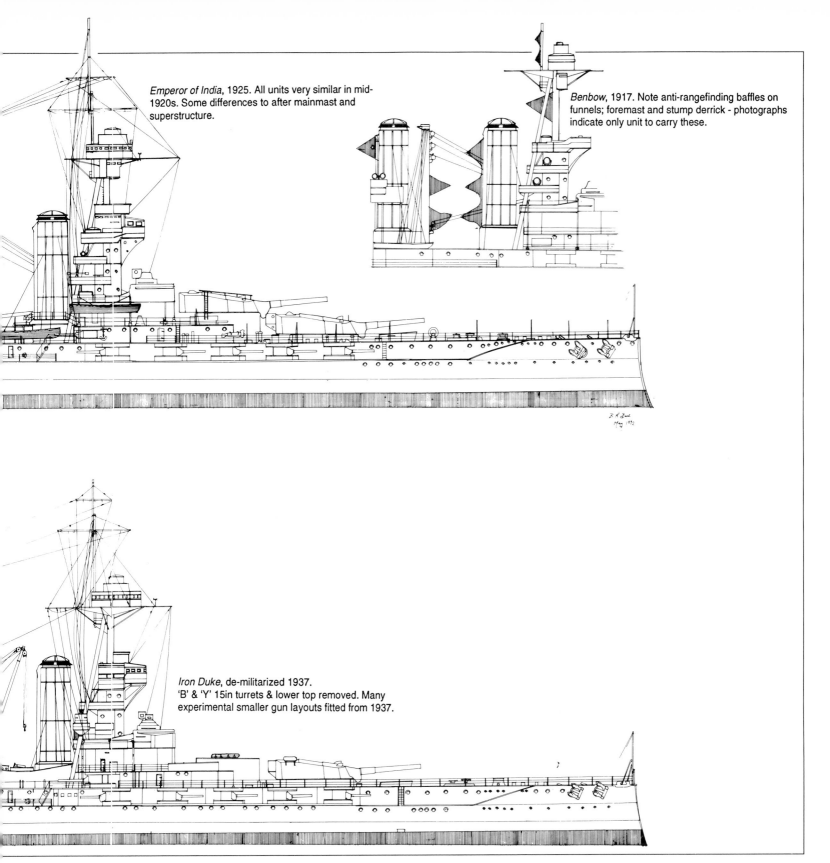

Emperor of India, 1925. All units very similar in mid-1920s. Some differences to after mainmast and superstructure.

Benbow, 1917. Note anti-rangefinding baffles on funnels; foremast and stump derrick - photographs indicate only unit to carry these.

Iron Duke, de-militarized 1937.
'B' & 'Y' 15in turrets & lower top removed. Many experimental smaller gun layouts fitted from 1937.

Iron Duke class: General particulars, 1930
Displacement (tons): 25,850 (light), 27,190 (load), 31,410 (deep) (*Emperor of India*).
Length and beam unchanged.
Armament: Original main and secondary unchanged. 4 x 4in AA in *Iron Duke* and *Marlborough*, 2 x 4in in *Emperor of India*.
Searchlights: 6 x 36in *Benbow* and *Emperor of India*. 4 x 36in *Iron Duke* and *Marlborough*.
Aircraft platform still in *Benbow* and *Emperor of India*.
Rig: Topgallant to foremast. Long forward strut at starfish below control top in *EOI*. Short mainmast with SL platform. Tall main topmast in *Benbow* and *Iron Duke*, shorter in others.
Original appearance further modified by addition of mainmast which detracted considerably from former symmetry of outline.
Individual differences
Benbow, Emperor of India: Aircraft platforms over 'B' and 'Q'. Short mainmast with SL platform carried lower down. Very long strut forward from starfish below control top (*Emperor of India* only).
Iron Duke, Marlborough: No aircraft platforms. No SL on mainmast. AA guns on forward superstructure, abeam bridge. Raised platform on after bridge.
Iron Duke: Lattice support to RF platform on after superstructure.
Marlborough: Solid base (deckhouse) below RF on after superstructure.
See notes for *Iron Duke* after this period.

Masts (*Iron Duke*, 9 September 1929).

Foremast:	height	diameter	weight (tons)
Steel			
Lowermast:	80ft	36in	11.6
struts:		24in	35
Wood			
topmast:	52ft	16–10in	
topgallant:	39ft 9in	10–7in	
yards (2):	27ft	8–4in	
topgallant yard for W/T:	27ft 6in		
Mainmast:			
lowermast:	30ft	30in	2
topmast:	60ft	13in	
SL platform:	15ft		
gaff:	22ft		
yard for W/T:	25ft		
derricks:	60ft		
stumpmast			
for derrick:	33ft		
ensign:	27ft		
jackstaff:	21ft		

Total weight of all including all booms: 101.11 tons.

HISTORY: *IRON DUKE*

After the Great War the *Iron Duke* class formed the 4th Battle Squadron and as such were very effective. (For their service history 1914–19 see author's *British Battleships of World War One*)
21 November 1918 Present in the southern line at surrender of the German High Seas Fleet off the Firth of Forth.
21 March 1919 Commissioned for service as flagship of newly reconstituted Mediterranean Fleet (4th BS) on abolition of Grand Fleet.
April 1919 Relieved *Superb* as flagship, Mediterranean.
April–June 1919 Operations against Bolshevik in Black Sea.
11 August 1919 Left Alexandria for Malta.
April 1920 Small refit at Malta, flag temporarily flown in *Ajax*.
June–July 1920 Operations against Turkish Nationalists in Sea of Marmora and at Constantinople.

Below: A unique view of *Emperor of India* laying just off Portsmouth after being severely damaged and bottomed by shelling tests, 1931. Note that all small fittings have been removed. Soon after the photograph was taken she was towed away to be scrapped.

July 1920 Shelled Turkish Nationalist forces at Beicos.
9 March 1921 Recommissioned at Portsmouth for further service as flagship, C-in-C Mediterranean Fleet (4th BS).
5 April 1922 Reached Bosphorus from Malta with Admiral Sir John de Robeck on his farewell visit.
14 April 1922 Left Constantinople for Malta visiting Chanak, Mitylene, Smyrna, Limassol, Haifa, Port Said and Alexandria.

28 April 1922 Arrived Malta.
12 May 1922 Left Malta for Marseilles.
15 May 1922 Arrived Marseilles where flag of Admiral Sir John de Robeck was replaced by that of Admiral Sir Osmond Brock.
May 1922 returned to Malta and left to visit Alexandria and Port Said.
23 May 1922 Reached Jaffa where the following day one of her signal men was drowned while bathing from the beach.
July 1922 Visited Haifa, Cyprus and Smyrna.

12 July 1922 Reached Constantinople.
31 July 1922 With the Fleet left Constantinople after Greek threat to city during Graeco–Turkish War.
20 August 1922 Visited Tuzla Bay (where *Sultan Selim Yavuz* was lying) and Kilia Liman before returning to Constantinople.
31 August 1922 Left Bosphorus for round of visits in Adriatic.
2 September 1922 In Doro Channel when she received urgent instructions to proceed to

Smyrna to protect British interests during the rout of the Greek army. Reached Smyrna the next day.

9–13 September 1922 During the massacre and fire at Smyrna she was endeavouring to maintain order and assist the victims with *Ajax*.

3 October 1922 Carried Allied representatives to the Mudania Conference.

5 October 1922 Carried delegates to Constantinople from Mudania.

6–8 October 1922 Lying at Mudania.

17 November 1922 Landed an armed guard at Constantinople to escort the deposed Sultan Mahommed VI to the harbour for passage into exile in *Malaya*.

23 December 1922 Reached Malta.

27 December 1922 Left Malta for Dardanelles.

September 1924 Relieved as fleet flagship by *Queen Elizabeth* and became private ship in 4th BS.

1 November 1924 4th BS became 3rd BS.

9 March 1926 After combined exercises in Mediterranean transferred with her class to Atlantic Fleet as flagship of newly formed 3rd (Special Boys' Training) BS. Relieved in Mediterranean by *Resolution* and *Royal Oak*.

15 May 1928 Relieved as flagship, 3rd BS by *Benbow*.

30 May 1928 Paid off into Dockyard Control at Devonport for extensive refit; transferred into independent service as seagoing gunnery firing ship.

7 June 1929 Commissioned for service as seagoing gunnery firing ship at Portland, relieving *Tiger*.

11 June 1931 Carried out firing tests at her sister ship *Emperor of India* off Bognor Regis, damaging her and causing her to settle on the bottom in shallow water.

27 July 1831 Arrived at Rosyth to prepare for demilitarization under terms of London Treaty.

10 November 1931. Paid off into Dockyard Control at Devonport.

6 September 1932 Commissioned Devonport for further service as seagoing gunnery training ship and other training duties (attached to Portsmouth).

20 February 1935 Recommissioned for same service at Portsmouth.

16 July 1935 Took part in Jubilee Naval Review of HM King George V at Spithead and afterwards visited Torbay.

21 May 1936 Recommissioned at Portsmouth for further service as seagoing gunnery firing and training ship.

20 May 1937 Present at Coronation Review of HM King George VI at Spithead.

12 August 1939 Present at Review of Reserve Fleet at Weymouth.

August 1939 (later part) Visited Falmouth and left three days before she was due to reach Scapa Flow.

September 1939–December 1945 Served as Base Ship at Scapa Flow and as Flagship of the Admiral commanding Orkney and Shetlands.

Battle Damage While in Scapa Flow 17 October 1939:

'*Iron Duke*' was lying at 'C' Buoy in about 10 fathoms of water when a power-dive attack was made from 1,000 to 1,500 feet by four bombers at 10.33 hours. One bomb (probably 500lb) which struck the water some distance out on the port bow shook the ship and threw mud and water to a considerable height; a second bomb fell some distance out on the port quarter.

The major damage against 'C' boiler room appears to have been caused by two bombs (probably 500lb) which were observed to be released simultaneously and struck the water not far out from the ship's side. It is possible that these bombs contacted ship's side near the turn of bilge before exploding. They were released from a plane which power-dived down some 1,000 feet in a direction slightly inclined to the fore and aft line of ship travelling from bow to stern. A third bomb was observed to be released immediately after the two released simultaneously. There is no record where the third bomb struck but it probably caused the further damage aft.

Ship heeled to port quickly, reading a maximum angle of probably 20–25° and appeared to steady at that angle. Main deck scuttles were open and these came awash when the ship heeled. Estimates of the time to reach this heel vary from 2–5 minutes, when raiders had passed cable was slipped and ship towed to shallow water in Ore Bay by tugs. She was beached forward about 40 minutes after the attack and about an hour before high water, with damaged side towards the shore. Tugs were kept until about one hour after high water hauling in the

BOMBING OF *IRON DUKE* IN SCAPA FLOW, 17 OCTOBER 1939

port side

Two near misses by 500lb bombs exploding very near hull

path of bombs

'C' BR

inner bunkers

outer bunkers

area of damage

hull badly corrugated

Below: *Iron Duke* after being badly damaged by bombs in 1939 (see report). She became Tender Ship in Scapa Flow and remained in this position throughout the war. She is seen here in 1943. Note AA batteries on 'X' and 'Y' positions and on the quarterdeck.

Bottom: Jellicoe's once proud flagship *Iron Duke* on her last voyage to the scrapyard. 1946.

stern to get ship approximately parallel to the shore to ground her fore and aft. With fall of tide she slowly righted, vibrating noticeably, and finally took up a heel of 3–4⁰ to starboard (the undamaged side), presumably in conformity with the slope of the bank on which she grounded. Ship was secured by two 7½ ton anchors supplied by Metal Industries. Further efforts were made at the next high water to get the stern further in. Bottom in sand and shingle. Divers reported 17.10.39 ship grounded forward to about after end of engine room and 18 inch to 2 foot clear at the after cut up.'

She remained in that position until the end of the war.

February 1946 Sold to Metal Industries to be raised and broken up.

19 April 1946 Refloated at Scapa Flow.
15 August 1946 Left Scapa Flow bound for Faslane (Gareloch), a wartime port acquired by Metal Industries for shipbreaking (taking possession on 15th).
19 August 1946 Reached Faslane after being delayed for twenty hours by rough seas and high winds.

QUEEN ELIZABETH CLASS

DESIGN

The design of the ships of the *Queen Elizabeth* class caused a hiatus in the general development of 'Standard Admiralty battleship practice'. Instead of merely enlarging and improving the *Iron Duke* design, the ships of the 1912–13 estimates departed from the norm and featured many revolutionary ideas. From the outset it had been intended to produce something that would' constitute a 'fast battleship division. Although official documents do not state that the new ships might have followed the *Iron Duke* layout in having five turrets, it was obvious that a ship that sported ten 15in guns would be highly desirable and there is a general feeling within the Admiralty papers that this was so.

Despite the unusually high speed, about four knots above existing battleship average, these ships were by no means a compromise featuring reduced protection, as were the contemporary battlecruisers, but represented a bona-fide, well-armoured fast battleship type, and their unique combination of fighting qualities and speed, on very moderate dimensions (the designers would have liked another 5–6,000 tons incorporated) placed them, on completion, in a class apart.

From the three sketch designs (RIII, RIII★, RIV) RIII★ was chosen as being the most suitable, and by November 1912 had become known as the *Queen Elizabeth* class. Four ships had been planned, but the gift of a battleship from the Federated Malay States was quickly and gratefully accepted.

The essential features of the design, compared with the *Iron Duke*s, were:
1. Nominal displacement at normal load was increased by approximately 2,500 tons with an increase of 20 feet (oa), 6in beam, and 9in designed mean draught.
2. Main armament was eight 15in guns against ten 13.5in with an increase of 1,369lb in weight of broadside
3. Secondary armament (as designed) was increased from twelve to sixteen guns.
4. Armour protection differed mainly in increasing thickness at waterline, turrets and anti-torpedo bulkheads, with reduction on the middle and upper side.
5. Designed speed was increased from 21 to 25 knots.
6. Fuel capacity of 3,400 tons oil in *QE* com-

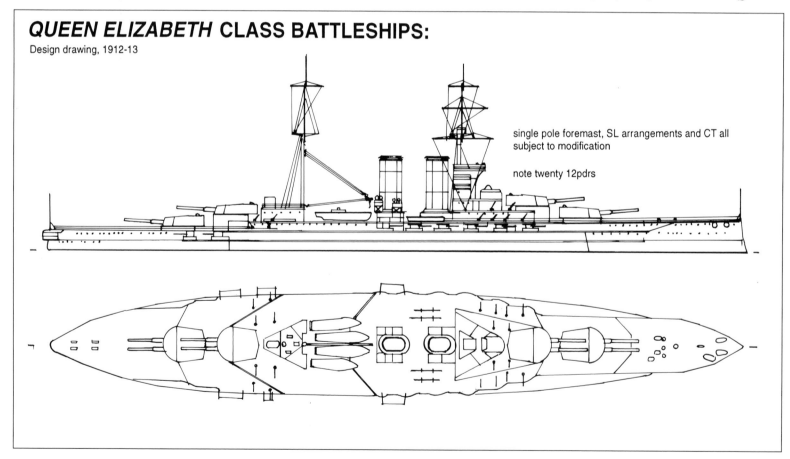

QUEEN ELIZABETH CLASS BATTLESHIPS:
Design drawing, 1912-13

single pole foremast, SL arrangements and CT all subject to modification

note twenty 12pdrs

Below: On completion, great things were expected of the *Queen Elizabeth* with her 15in guns when she was sent to the Dardanelles in 1915. Unfortunately, however, her indirect fire, although spectacular, proved a failure because of the lack of suitable spotting and range finding. She is shown here leaving for the Dardanelles at full speed.

pared to 3,250 tons coal and 1,600 tons oil in *Iron Duke*, giving approximately the same nominal radius.

The outstanding features of the *Queen Elizabeth* design and the innovations to which its success was mainly due, were the adoption of the 15in gun and oil fuel; the former providing a substantial increase in offensive power on practically the same armament weight as in the immediately preceding *Iron Duke* class; the latter enabling the requisite high speed to be achieved on moderate dimensions and without undue sacrifice in fighting qualities. In the absence of a midships turret, the forecastle deck could be carried aft to 'X' turret by a light unarmoured structure abaft the battery, freeboard amidships being about 8 feet higher than in the *Iron Dukes*. The forecastle sides were recessed before the battery to allow direct ahead fire for the first three pairs of 6in guns. The sides amidships between main and upper decks were slightly tumblehome, reverting to normal above the upper deck. The increase in dimensions and displacement over the *Iron Duke* class was almost entirely due to the additional boiler room space required for the higher speed. Weight of armament was practically the same, but the length required for this was actually somewhat less because of the reduced number of turrets.

In accordance wth the 1921 Washington Treaty restrictions on new capital ship construction, all were modernized in varying degrees from 1934 to 1941, *Queen Elizabeth*, *Valiant* and *Warspite* being more extensively reconstructed than any other British battleships. The following principal alterations carried out from 1924 to 1933 were:
1. AA armament increased and after pair of torpedo tubes removed.
2. Aircraft catapult fitted in *Barham* and *Valiant*.
3. Anti-torpedo bulges added (*Barham* the last to be fitted).
4. Fore funnel trunked into the second to reduce some interference to control top (*Barham* the last to be fitted).

Malaya was again modified from 1934 to 1936, AA armament being further increased and hangar accommodation provided for aircraft with an improved catapult fitted. *Warspite*, *Valiant* and *Queen Elizabeth* underwent a second and more extensive reconstruction from 1936 to 1941 with a view to bringing their offensive and defensive qualities as far as possible into line with modern requirements.
1. Elevation and range of 15in guns increased. The 6in secondary armament in *Warspite* was reduced to eight guns. New dual-purpose 4.5in secondary armament was fitted in *Valiant* and *Queen Elizabeth*. AA armament was further increased in all.
2. Hangars and catapult fitted as in *Malaya*.
3. Geared turbines and new high-pressure boilers installed.
4. Fuel capacity slightly increased, but steaming radius was increased by 75 per cent as a result of the greater economy of the new machinery and boilers, especially the latter.
5. The former bridgework, conning tower and heavy tripod foremast were replaced by a large control tower.

Warspite completed in 1937, *Valiant* in 1939 and *Queen Elizabeth* in 1941.

During the Great War the class had been famous for forming the 5th Battle Squadron in the Grand Fleet from 1915 to 1919, being attached to the battlecruisers at Jutland in 1916. *Queen Elizabeth* was withdrawn from the squadron in January 1917 to replace *Iron Duke* as Fleet Flagship. They were all employed from 1939 to 1945, mainly for bombardment and escort duties in home waters, Atlantic, Mediterranean and Indian Ocean. *Queen Elizabeth* and *Valiant* also took part in operations against the Japanese in the East Indies and Pacific during 1944 and 1945.

After the Great War, when the time came for their first reconstruction it was not without some opposition from their designer Sir Philip Watts who pulled no punches when dealing with the DNC, Sir Eustace Tennyson d'Eyncourt. In a letter to the Admiralty Watts stated his case (29 November 1923):

'Dear Sir,

I am now informed that as the ships of the *Royal Sovereign* class have now all been fitted with bulges, it is intended to fit the ships of the *Queen Elizabeth* class with similar bulges in accordance with a decision recently come to and that the *Warspite* would be shortly taken in hand for this purpose. It was necessary to fit bulges to the *Royal Sovereign*s as their deficient instability would have caused them to capsize when damaged at or below the water line which would have resulted in flooding of adjacent compartments, but the *Queen Elizabeth*s in common with previous dreadnoughts had and have ample stability.

This was proved in the war: *Marlborough* and *Inflexible* were badly hit by a torpedo and adjacent compartments flooded, but they remained afloat and in no danger of sinking from the attack. If bulges were added to the *QE*s they would be scarcely less liable to damage from underwater or above water attack. Moreover, their speed, which is already on the low side, would be considerably reduced and I submit there would be no advantage in making the change.'

Having received no reply by December, Watts sent a letter to the DNC (29 December 1923):

'I saw a newspaper report some time back to the effect that the *Warspite* was to follow the *Royal Oak* at Portsmouth and be fitted with bulges which I assumed was incorrect but visiting Sir Oswyn Murray shortly afterwards I was very much surprised to learn from him that it was correct. I then wrote Mr. Amery a letter. Mr. Amery has been a great deal away from his office, but I understand he will see the letter on his return in a few days. I still think there must be some mistake about the matter.'

Tennyson D'Eyncourt seemed to tire of Watts' constant heckling which had prevailed over the last few years. Nevertheless he kept calm and wrote to the ex-DNC on 1 January 1924:

'Thank you for your letter of the 29th.

It was decided a long time ago and has since been confirmed to fit bulges to the *Queen Elizabeth* class whenever opportunity offers itself, and I should think it is very doubtful whether they would go back on their decision. The fact is that the weight of the charge of modern torpedoes has increased three- or four-fold since the design of *Queen Elizabeth* and experience has shown that the underwater protection as originally designed is insufficient defence against a modern torpedo. By adding bulges this defence can be increased sufficiently to be effective against a modern torpedo. I do not therefore see that there can be much objection to this addition to the protection and it is no reflection whatever on the original design. There is a certain loss of speed amounting to about $3/4$ kt, on the other hand there is the advantage that as the buoyancy added by the bulges is greater than the weight, the draught of the ships will be reduced by over 1 foot. The vessels were rather deep from the very start and by various additions have become deeper and at low tide they sometimes ground at Portsmouth.'

In the face of these technical details, Watts had no alternative but to withdraw his criticism.

ARMAMENT

When design work began utmost secrecy was paramount; one of the assistant DNCs, E. N. Mooney writing on 4 May 1912: 'This design is to be regarded as *secret* and neither the design as a whole nor any features of it should be mentioned, either inside or outside of the office to anyone whatever except people actually engaged on the design.' Moreover, the guns themselves were regarded as top secret for some time after the design had been completed. Mooney, 20 June 1912: 'Every effort is to be made to keep the nature of armament *secret*, the large gun must be spoken of and written about as the 14in experimental.'

The adoption of the 15in gun was the outstanding feature, and one of the factors primarily responsible for the success of the design. The advance in calibre from 13.5in of the preceding classes is said to have been influenced by the introduction of the 14in gun in the latest American and Japanese battleships. At this stage in the design work, however, a 15in gun was not available, but to get the design under way

quickly it was decided to accept the 15in gun in principle, a departure from all previous Admiralty practice; if the gun proved a failure it would be the fault and responsibility of the Admiralty alone.

A test gun was produced and tested and the results soon dispersed any doubts and fears that had prevailed during its construction. The gun proved remarkably accurate and its performance in general was unequalled by any other British heavy gun to date. Shortly after completion the guns proved their worth at Jutland in May 1916 and scored hits at 19,500 yards, a record in naval gunnery at that date, especially at high-speed targets. With a broadside 1,360 pounds heavier than *Iron Duke*'s and a plus 50 per cent increase in destructive effect, they were without doubt the most capable heavy gun at sea during the Great War.

The main armament as fitted consisted of eight 15in guns located in four twin-mounted turrets, all on the centre line, two on the forecastle and two on the upper deck aft, the inner pair superfiring over the outer mountings. Turret arcs were: 'A' and 'B' turrets 300⁰ bearing direct ahead to 60⁰ abaft the beam on each side; 'X' turret 310⁰ bearing direct astern to 65⁰ before the beam on each side; 'Y' turret 300⁰ bearing direct astern to 60⁰ before the beam on each side.

The original secondary armament was for sixteen 6in guns and twenty 12pdrs (see sketch). The 6in were all located on the main deck level, but the 12pdrs were to be placed on the forecastle and shelter decks forward and aft. After some debate, however, it was decided, because of the weight factor, and the unsuitable shell weight of the 12pdr gun that the entire 12pdr armament should be eliminated. The 6in guns were an increase of four over that of *Iron Duke*, the extra guns being located on the main deck aft (pair each beam). *Queen Elizabeth* and *Barham* were completed like this, but after trials in December 1914 the guns were found to be practically useless and were frequently washed out even in moderate seas. By May 1915 two of the guns had been removed and the other two remounted behind shields on the forecastle deck abaft the second funnel where they had an exceptionally high command and good arcs of fire. All other units of the class were modified accordingly. These remounted guns were removed in 1916 because the gun crews were inadequately protected and there was an inadequate supply of shells to the new position.

ARMOUR

The basic armour layout was an improvement over the *Iron Duke* design, but in general was not fully adequate against the 15in gun. The 13in strake, although being thick enough, was inadequate in its coverage and was reduced to 8in on the lower edge and 6in at the upper level. It must be borne in mind, however, that sacrifices had been made to secure a high speed and together with the heavier armament it was obvious that on the given original displacement it would be impossible to apply a thicker armour on a greater displacement. Internal protection was very fine and more complete than in any British battleships to date, the longitudinal anti-torpedo bulkheads being continuous between forward and after magazines for the first time since *Neptune* (1911). Despite the exceptionally high speed, all-round protection was very strong and quite equal

to existing average battleship standards, although armouring was generally lighter than in the contemporary German battleship *König*, especially on the middle and upper side, while the greater beam (96ft 9in against 90ft 6in) of the German ships allowed for a more effective underwater protection.

The ability of the *Queen Elizabeth* class to withstand severe punishment without significant loss of fighting efficiency was strikingly demonstrated at Jutland where four of the class (5th BS) were for some time heavily engaged with German battlecruisers and the van of the High Seas Fleet battleships. Although subjected to a heavy and concentrated fire, their efficiency was in no case appreciably impaired, main armament and machinery remaining intact in all four ships. Later in the action *Warspite*, as a result of a jammed helm, became again heavily engaged at a range of about 12,000 yards and was hit seven times by 12in shells which caused much structural damage although no turret was permanently disabled and machinery still remained

intact. The principal weak points in the protection were: 1. Inadequate height of heavy armour above waterline. 2. Absence of rear screens to 6in battery guns and insufficient inboard depth (only 15 feet) of traverses between these, deficiencies which were largely responsible for nearly 100 casualties in *Malaya* at Jutland when the flash from ignited cordite charges, stowed in the passage behind the shallow gun bays, swept the entire starboard battery and put all its guns out of action.

MACHINERY

The ships were intended to form a special fast battleship division and the designed speed was 2 or 3 knots higher than in any contemporary battleship and not equalled in the British Navy until after the war. The horsepower required for the increase of nearly 4 knots over the *Iron Duke* class was more than 2½ times that in those ships, an unprecedented class-to-class increase for battleships, and was obtained on a very moderate

QUEEN ELIZABETH ARMOURED LAYOUT, 1919

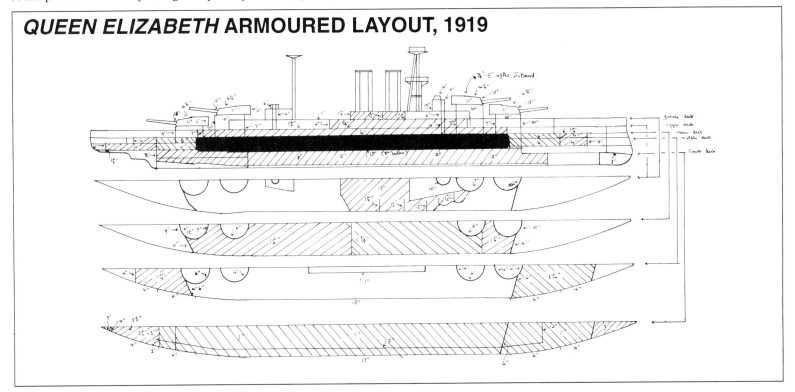

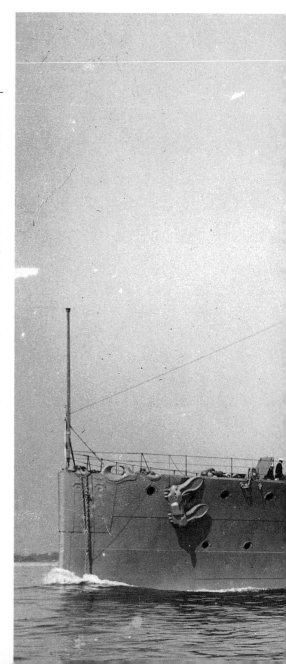

Below: The general overall appearance of the *Queen Elizabeth* class, except for minor details, is shown here as *Queen Elizabeth* herself passes by in 1922. Note the improved compass platform, range clocks and control tops.

Steam Trials 19 May 1922
Type of trial: 2 hours full power.

	Draught (mean)	Mean Revs	HP	Bottom	Speed
Malaya:	32ft 5in	301	79,844	foul	24.1kts
Warspite:	32ft 8in	296	75,200	clean	24kts
Valiant:	32ft 7½in	292	69,140	clean	23.9kts

Barham inclined. 4th November 1933 (Stability and GM) and compared with rest of class

	Warspite	*QE*	*Valiant*	*Malaya*	*Barham*
Displacement (tons):	35,060	35,480	35,710	35,380	35,970
Mean Draught:	32ft 6in	32ft 2in	32ft 2in	31ft 11in	32ft 6in
GM:	7.01ft	6.92ft	6.9ft	6.9ft	6.78ft
Maximum stability:	40°	37°	37°	37°	33°
Stability vanishes:	73°	69°	69°	69°	69°

Valiant, as inclined 11 November 1940
Displacement: 29,696 tons (light ship); 33,903 tons (half oil fuel on board), draught 30ft 7¾in; 35,698 tons (deep load), draught 32ft 1⅛in; 36,513 tons (deep plus water protection), draught 32ft 9½in.
GM: 6.93ft in deep load; 6.10ft with half oil.
Stability range: 61.1° with half oil and 68.5° in deep load.

Steam Trials: 1926 to 1933 (maximum speeds attained)
Warspite: 26 March 1926. 76,742shp = 24 knots.
Queen Elizabeth: 14 September 1927. 71,753shp = 23.45 knots.
Malaya: 26 January 1929. 75,784shp = 24.45 knots.
Valiant: 7 November 1930. 67,555shp = 23.3 knots.
Barham: 20 November 1933. 65,644shp = 22.5 knots.

rise in displacement largely by the adoption of oil fuel only. It was estimated that with mixed firing (coal and oil) not more than about 22 knots could have been obtained on the displacement while 25 knots would have necessitated either: 1. Undesirable sacrifice in offensive and/or defensive qualities. 2. Substantially increased size and costs.

They were the first battleships to have oil fuel only. Apart from the ability to produce increased power on a given boiler weight, oil fuel also offered the following additional advantages as compared to coal:
1. Speed could be increased more rapidly and maintained more easily.
2. Steaming radius increased about 40 per cent on a given weight of fuel.
3. Simplified and fast refuelling with no strain on personnel.
4. Absence of smoke.

Despite these very considerable advantages the decision to adopt oil only was not finally taken without considerable apprehension regarding maintenance of supply in wartime and was subjected to some criticism on the grounds that it was highly undesirable to build ships whose mobility was entirely dependent on overseas fuel supplies. Although intended to be a fast division when joining the Fleet, it was found that their extra speed was not as advantageous as was first envisaged. As they were completed in wartime none of the class ran proper speed trials, but if official documents are studied it can be seen that none of the group ever reached the high of 25 knots.

REPLACEMENT PLANS IN 1933

Standard Admiralty practice held that the average life of a battleship was about twenty years which meant that the *Queen Elizabeth* class was due for replacement in or around 1935. This would also apply to the slightly newer *Royal Sovereign* class, and there were discussions about this during the early 1930s. As there was no question of building new ships because of the naval treaties in force, it was agreed that something had to be done about the two groups of existing battleships if they were to remain frontline units.

In a paper presented to their Lordships by the DNC, A. W. Johns, it was pointed out that the *Queen Elizabeth* class had all been built during 1915–16 and therefore had pre-war experience worked into their design. They had, however, undergone limited modernization and had later and better bulges than the *Royal Sovereign* class.

Armour protection was practically the same in both groups, that for *Royal Sovereign* being slightly superior in the way of the main belt. There was, however, less space between 'B and 'X' turrets in *Royal Sovereign* and this left little room for additional AA guns and similar fittings. The stability of *Queen Elizabeth* was slightly superior to that of *Royal Sovereign*. Radii were: *Queen Elizabeth* 18 knots giving 3,650; *Royal Sovereign* 18 knots giving 2,950; *Queen Elizabeth* 20 knots giving 3,000; *Royal Sovereign* 20 knots giving 2,150 nautical miles. The bridges were given some modernization during early refits and were therefore roomier and more handy than those in the *Royal Sovereign* class. *Queen Elizabeth* was easier to handle and the full speed of the class was much greater: 23.9 knots (*Barham*) against 21.9 knots (*Revenge*). After considering the DNC's points it was provisionally agreed that the *Royal Sovereign* class would be scrapped before the *Queen Elizabeth* class, and a table was prepared the replacement programme was as follows:

Two *Royal Sovereign*s (*Royal Oak* and *Revenge*) 1940

Two *Royal Sovereign*s (*Resolution* and *Royal Sovereign*) 1941

Ramillies and *Queen Elizabeth* 1942.

Two *Queen Elizabeth* class 1943.
Remaining *Queen Elizabeth* class and *Repulse* 1944.
One *Queen Elizabeth* class and *Renown* 1945.
Rodney 1947.
Nelson 1948.

It was considered that if the treaty situation altered to allow fresh construction sooner than had been envisaged, replacement could begin more quickly than the table implied, but at the time that it was drawn up the only thing possible was seriously to consider a massive reconstruction programme which would inject new life into the rapidly ageing vessels. It was agreed that this, to some extent, would bring the battlefleet into the new age and prepare it for combat against all other capital ships except those of completely new construction.

BRIDGEWORK ALTERATIONS AND THEIR EFFECT

As completed in 1915–16 the *Queen Elizabeth* class featured the simplest of bridges consisting of very basic platforms fitted up and around the foremast tripod legs.

During the Great War, however, experience showed that there was a growing need of a better layout within the group. Practical evidence was forthcoming and there was no shortage of criticism from officers serving in the vessels, who made it quite clear that there were inadequate fittings aboard. Lack of space for requisite equipment to control the guns, searchlight facilities, overcrowding of staff in confined areas and protection for personnel when exposed on the compass platform were just a few of the grumbles that found their way to the corridors of the Admiralty.

The Admiralty, in turn, was not oblivious of these shortcomings, and measures were being prepared to alleviate some of the problems as the ships came in for refit during hostilities. During the refits, bridgework was built up and platforms were extended in length and width. In some ships a small roll-back roof was placed over the charthouse platform to protect personnel from rain at least. Possibly because of a lack of a suitable type of glass, no windows were fitted in this position until after the war because it had been suggested that it would impair good all-round vision which was paramount for look-out person-

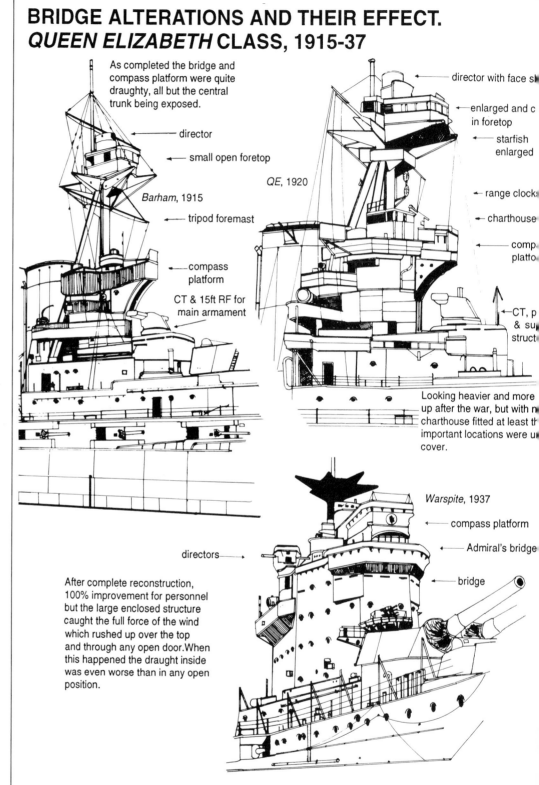

BRIDGE ALTERATIONS AND THEIR EFFECT.
QUEEN ELIZABETH CLASS, 1915-37

As completed the bridge and compass platform were quite draughty, all but the central trunk being exposed.

director

small open foretop

Barham, 1915

tripod foremast

compass platform

CT & 15ft RF for main armament

QE, 1920

director with face s▮

enlarged and c in foretop

starfish enlarged

range clock▮

charthouse

comp▮ platfo▮

CT, p▮ & su▮ struct▮

Looking heavier and more ▮ up after the war, but with n▮ charthouse fitted at least th▮ important locations were u▮ cover.

Warspite, 1937

compass platform

Admiral's bridge▮

directors

bridge

After complete reconstruction, 100% improvement for personnel but the large enclosed structure caught the full force of the wind which rushed up over the top and through any open door. When this happened the draught inside was even worse than in any open position.

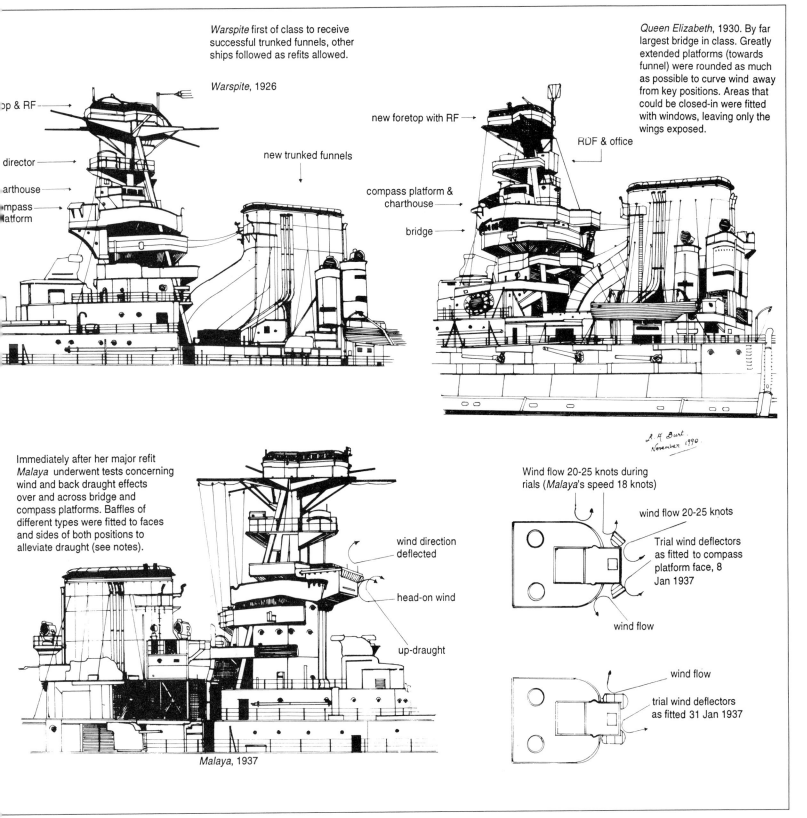

Warspite first of class to receive successful trunked funnels, other ships followed as refits allowed.

Warspite, 1926

op & RF

director

arthouse

mpass latform

new trunked funnels

Queen Elizabeth, 1930. By far largest bridge in class. Greatly extended platforms (towards funnel) were rounded as much as possible to curve wind away from key positions. Areas that could be closed-in were fitted with windows, leaving only the wings exposed.

new foretop with RF

RDF & office

compass platform & charthouse

bridge

Immediately after her major refit *Malaya* underwent tests concerning wind and back draught effects over and across bridge and compass platforms. Baffles of different types were fitted to faces and sides of both positions to alleviate draught (see notes).

wind direction deflected

head-on wind

up-draught

Malaya, 1937

Wind flow 20-25 knots during rials (*Malaya*'s speed 18 knots)

wind flow 20-25 knots

Trial wind deflectors as fitted to compass platform face, 8 Jan 1937

wind flow

wind flow

trial wind deflectors as fitted 31 Jan 1937

Below: After the Great War, most of the big ships went through a series of small refits and the *Queen Elizabeth*s were no exception. *Valiant* is shown in dry dock having had her bottom cleaned and a general overhaul, Rosyth, 1920.

nel in the bridgework. The personnel, it seems did not like being closed in. Although drawing on practical experience when altering the ships, the finished result was not always up to expectations and it became a case of trial and error when adding to the upper works in capital ships in general.

By 1919–20 the bridgework had almost doubled in size and had a very cluttered appearance. There were searchlights, rangefinders and a mixture of canvas and sheet metal covers around the bridgework during the early years, but the first successful methods were really applied during the refits from 1924 to 1930 when the funnels were trunked together and the bridgework was given a facelift in general. Levels were extended around the tripod legs now that they were free from smoke interference, and additional shelter was provided for charthouse staff. There was also the provision of a large charthouse at the back of the charthouse platform which was built around the foremast. The problems of the staff were not altogether solved, however, and they are highlighted in the following reports: In *Valiant* on 12 November 1930, the opportunity was taken to observe the ship: 'The weather was cold and windy and the raised compass platform was uncomfortable especially with a wind on the bow. The screen around the platform is about 5ft 6in high and the flare of this screen throws up the wind so that a portion of the platform immediately behind the screen is sheltered from the wind. The draught descends at a point 5ft 6in abaft the screen at the height of the pelorus so that it is extremely difficult to take a sight from the instrument under these conditions. The forcing down of the wind is probably due to the existence of the torpedo control position above and slightly abaft the round compass platform. The down-coming draught is divided by the charthouse and platform office abaft the raised charthouse platform, and sweeps along the two sides of the charthouse proper with such force that standing is made difficult without hanging on, and involves considerable difficulty in working instruments. Some mitigation of discomfort could be by increasing flare of screen. It is thought that the only way to eliminate this wind is to fully cover the platform.'

A more conclusive set of trials were carried out in *Malaya* after she had been partially reconstructed in 1936. On 4 November during sea trials at a speed of 15 knots, the following observations were made 'There is an unpleasant back draught around the charthouse platform especially around the floor. There are no windows around the platform but space has been provided for them. Wind speeds reached 30 to 40 knots when the ship increased speed to 20 knots. An experiment was carried out and a flat screen was placed over the charthouse on a light framework. It was tilted at various angles and things did improve. Owing to the extreme wind, however, the canvas ripped and it is recommended that windows be fitted all round, and the after part of the charthouse closed in.'

Further tests in *Malaya* were carried out on 8 January 1937 (see drawings) after windows had been fitted, and experimental small screens positioned at the corners to deflect the wind upwards away from the charthouse area. The screens fitted in the first trials proved of limited success, but when modified the tests carried out on 31 January 1937 proved much better, and the general feeling was that the best had been accomplished with what was available. The conclusion was that the windows around the charthouse needed to be kept shut if draught was to be excluded completely, but on a moderate day some of the windows could remain open with little or no back draught.

The question of back draught was a particular point in the trials of *Barham* in 1934 after she had been given a new bridge and compass platform which was completely closed in. Comments made by staff who first tested the ship on 25 September 1934 referred to the compass platform and that it was draughty and generally uncomfortable. 'If the windows were left open around the compass platform it was not too bad, but if a back door were open at the same time, the condition became almost intolerable if there were any sort of tail wind following the ship. The new bridge, which was now fully closed in, was

considered only partially successful because its defensive qualities hindered its offensive measures.'

The bridge had to be habitable in all weathers and provide the best all-round vision, but as fitted *Barham* and others of the class, with their roofed-in bridges, proved extremely difficult to reflect this feature and still be tenable when windows were opened. The windows definitely had to be open at certain times and caused all sorts of problems inside. Requirements for better conditions in bridgework and compass platforms were recorded as follows: Captain's bridge: armouring was desired and the control office should also be armoured to give some sort of protection against aircraft attack; searchlight control, star shell control and torpedo control should all be within reach. It was felt that the bridge should be free from serious draughts. The shape was not always correct and instead of being square it should be rounded off so as to cheat the wind from all angles. Moreover, it would be advantageous to be able to see both the bows and stern of the vessel from this platform. Obviously there was much to be done by way of improvements, but in practice, no matter how well layouts were designed, the results were not always acceptable.

Even when *Warpsite* was fitted with her new bridge structure after reconstruction in 1937 the problems were not over. On 23 September 1937 the C-in-C was invited to inspect the mock-up bridge for the reconstructed battlecruiser *Renown*, and at the same time look over the new bridge of *Warspite*. After a thorough inspection at Portsmouth he wrote to the DNC to say that the conning tower (within the superstructure housing) was too lightly armoured and that it should be capable of withstanding close-range attack from medium calibre shells.

In *Warspite*, the front and sides of the new conning tower were only 3in with a 2in back, $1\frac{1}{2}$in roof and 1in floor. Similar protection was intended for *Renown*, *Queen Elizabeth* and *King George V*. The protection in *Warspite* was intended to give immunity against shells and bombs bursting in the near vicinity, but it was not intended to give protection against direct hits. To keep out shells of 4.7in calibre at 2,000 yards would require 4in NC armour; 6in shells at 4,000 yards would require $6\frac{1}{2}$in cemented armour, and 8in shells at 4,000 yards would need $9\frac{3}{4}$in cemented armour.

At this stage, of course, progressive demands for extra armour could not affect *Warspite*, but in any future reconstruction it would be most

General Particulars, 1919

Displacement (tons): 30,430 (load), 33,625 deep (*Valiant*, others similar).

Length: As completed (639ft 9in to 643ft 9in) unchanged.

Beam: 90ft 6in as completed, unchanged.

Draught: 33ft average at deep load.

Armament: main guns unchanged (8 x 15in)

Secondary 12 x 6in unchanged.

Original 3in guns changed for larger, 50 calibre.

Searchlights

Malaya, Queen Elizabeth, Warspite: 8 x 36in

Barham: 7 x 36in.

Valiant: 6 x 36in.

2 x 24in signalling lamps in all.

Aircraft

Airplane platforms on 'B' and 'X' turret in all except *Queen Elizabeth*.

Barham and *Queen Elizabeth* fitted for towing kite balloons.

In peacetime turret aircraft were not usually carried, but embarked specifically for exercises. Runways were removed from one or both turrets from end of 1919.

Platform removed from 'X' turret in *Queen Elizabeth* 1924, *Valiant* 1930, removed from both turrets in all 1933–4.

Armour: unchanged except for some additional protection to turret roofs and magazines, etc.

Machinery unchanged.

General appearance was rather heavier than original owing to wartime additions to bridgework, including SL towers around second funnel. The removal of the main topmast detracted considerably from their former symmetrical profile. Deflection scales painted out after war. Range clocks fitted in various positions in class. Main deck casemates (6in) not yet plated over.

Armour and Machinery, 1919

Main belt 13in reducing to 8in at lower edge, ends 6–4in, bulkheads 6–4in, barbettes 10–9–7–6–4in, turrets 11–13–5in, decks: forecastle 1in, upper 2–1$\frac{1}{2}$–1$\frac{1}{4}$in, main 1in, lower 3–2–1in, CT 11–6–3in, anti-torpedo screens 2in, CT tubes 4in, secondary battery 6in, secondary gunshields, 3in, tunnel uptakes 1$\frac{1}{2}$–1in.

Armour protection unchanged by 1919 except for additional 1in plating around the magazine area after Jutland in 1916 and, as opportunity arose, turret tops were increased from 4$\frac{1}{4}$in to 5in.

Machinery:

Parsons reaction turbines fitted in *Queen Elizabeth*, *Warspite* and *Malaya*; other two had direct turbines.

4 shafts, 4 propellers.

Boilers: 24 Babcock & Wilcox in first three; Yarrow in *Warspite* and *Barham*.

Working pressure: 235psi.

Pressure at turbines: 175psi.

Length of boiler rooms: 144ft.

Length of engine rooms: 83ft 11$\frac{1}{4}$in (each)

Designed SHP: 56,000 from 23 knots; 75,000 for 25 knots (overload).

Fuel (tons): 650 oil normal, 100 coal. 3,400 oil maximum.

Radius of action: 5,000 nm at 12 knots; 3,800 nm at 18 knots; 1,600 nm at full speed.

Machinery unchanged from 1915, but speed reported to have dropped slightly owing to increased weights during the war.

Extra signal yard fitted on main topmast (lower yard carried close above starfish)

Wide W/T yard fitted low on topgallantmast.

---

advantageous. Nevertheless, to make the increases mentioned above would require 4,9$\frac{1}{2}$ and 18 tons in weight respectively, and would require additional framework. This extra weight would not be significant in *Renown, Warspite* and *Queen Elizabeth*, but it would be in the new *King George V*. As regards the draught factor in *Warspite*, the new large structure as fitted was a vast improvement over previous layouts but still not absolutely free from back winds if any doors were open.

Valiant's bridge as reconstructed in 1939 received a slightly better review: 'The CO was very pleased with the bridge which was free from vibration and unpleasant draught. The draught at the searchlight sights was slight. The CO did, however, complain that the chart table was too large resulting in the compass platform being too cramped. Considerable draught was experienced by the lookouts through openings, with wind on all bearings. The doors to these positions had, however, been taken off for gun trials, and when these are fitted and closed it is anticipated that things will be better. In general, the Captain and staff were pleased with the ship's splendid behaviour.'

FUNNEL EXHAUST PROBLEMS

When the ships were being reconstructed during the 1920s the twin funnels were trunked and smoke problems to the bridge were more or less corrected. During 1938, however, it was brought to the DNC's attention that complaints were being voiced about gases from the funnel entering the main boiler intake and the two aircraft hangars on either side. Experiments were conducted at the National Physical Laboratory's Aerodynamics Department with a model built to a scale of $\frac{1}{8}$in = 1 foot. The same model was used to represent each of the four ships, only the funnel being altered as necessary. There was some initial difficulty in establishing a suitable procedural method. The first necessity was to introduce an identifiable substance whose rout after leaving the funnel could be traced and quantified. To this end a measured quantity of finely powdered cork was projected into the funnel discharge for four seconds during each test. Subsequently it was necessary to modify the model so that heated air could be discharged at scale velocities, and a boiler intake was constructed into which air could be drawn at appropriate rates. Any particles of cork drawn into the boiler intake passed along a tube and were discharged outside the wind tunnel on to a small sticky detector to which they adhered. Whenever possible the particles were counted so as to form a table of comparison for the various conditions tested.

The experiments established the existence of a large eddying region caused by the mast and neighbouring structure, and indicated that gas from the funnel would be drawn into this eddying region and into the main boiler intake.

Malaya

An analysis of the flow in the region of the funnel and hangars is shown in drawings 1 and 2. This analysis, of a test where the air was heated by hot wires, showed an extensive eddy caused by the mast and nearby structure which gave rise to a considerable back flow in the first few feet above the deck, some distance aft of the funnel. Drawing No. 2 was based on observations made by placing $\frac{1}{4}$in strips of gummed paper one at a time across the model ship at a point 5.2 inches behind the after edge of the funnel. For the first 2 inches above the deck the strips were mounted with the sticky side facing aft, while in the top 3 inches the sticky side faced forward. The cork dust deposit on the top 3 inches therefore came directly from the lower fringe of the funnel stream on to the detectors, whereas that on the lower 2 inches turned in the eddy and travelled in the direction of motion of the ship.

As a worst possible condition, the equivalent of a wind speed of 17 feet per second and a boiler intake of 8.5 cubic feet per minute were selected, and tests were made as described. It was found that from each charge introduced into the funnel stream some 300 to 370 particles were found on the detector at the exits of the boiler intake. An experiment was then conducted with

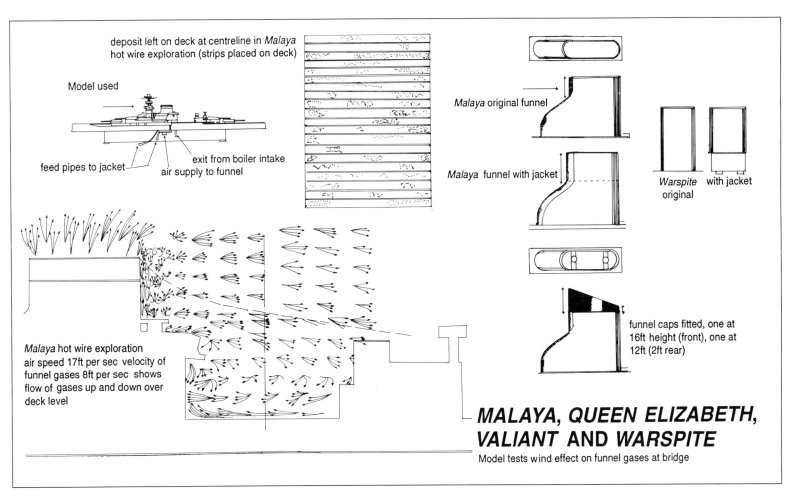

deposit left on deck at centreline in *Malaya*
hot wire exploration (strips placed on deck)

Model used

feed pipes to jacket

exit from boiler intake
air supply to funnel

Malaya original funnel

Malaya funnel with jacket

Warspite original with jacket

funnel caps fitted, one at
16ft height (front), one at
12ft (2ft rear)

Malaya hot wire exploration
air speed 17ft per sec velocity of
funnel gases 8ft per sec shows
flow of gases up and down over
deck level

MALAYA, QUEEN ELIZABETH, VALIANT AND WARSPITE
Model tests wind effect on funnel gases at bridge

the mast and surrounding structure removed. With the ship in this condition no deposit whatever was collected.

A number of tests was made in the course of which the funnel height was progressively increased. The results of these tests are shown below, and it will be seen that the addition of some 5 inches (40 feet) would be required to the funnel before all gas was carried safely away.

Tests were also made of two sloping funnel tops, but the amount of cork deposited was not noticeably reduced.

From the manner in which cork particles were deposited on detectors placed near the funnel, it was strongly suspected that the troublesome gas was coming from the edges of the funnel, where

Height of Funnel		Deposit at boiler intake (percentage of original)
Original		100
Lengthened	1in (8ft)	82
"	2in (16ft)	3
"	3in (24ft)	23
"	4in (32ft)	10½
"	5in (40ft)	1½

elements were probably discharged at low velocity and carried round into the boiler intake. It was considered that if these edge conditions could be modifed and the offending particles forced up into the main funnel stream an

improvement might be effected. Some attempts at bringing this about by means of baffles and deflectors were unproductive, chiefly because the influence of the mast and other structures made it impossible to collect enough air to influence conditions at the funnel without drawing it from the main stream, which would entail the use of baffles or guides of an unacceptable size. It was decided, therefore, to endeavour to blow the edges of the funnel clean by means of a current of air obtained mechanically. Accordingly, an outer casing or jacket 0.1in (9.6in) in width was constructed round the top portion of the funnel, and the bottom of the casing was sealed so as to form an annular chamber. Into this a supply of air was fed from the inside by a blower, and was

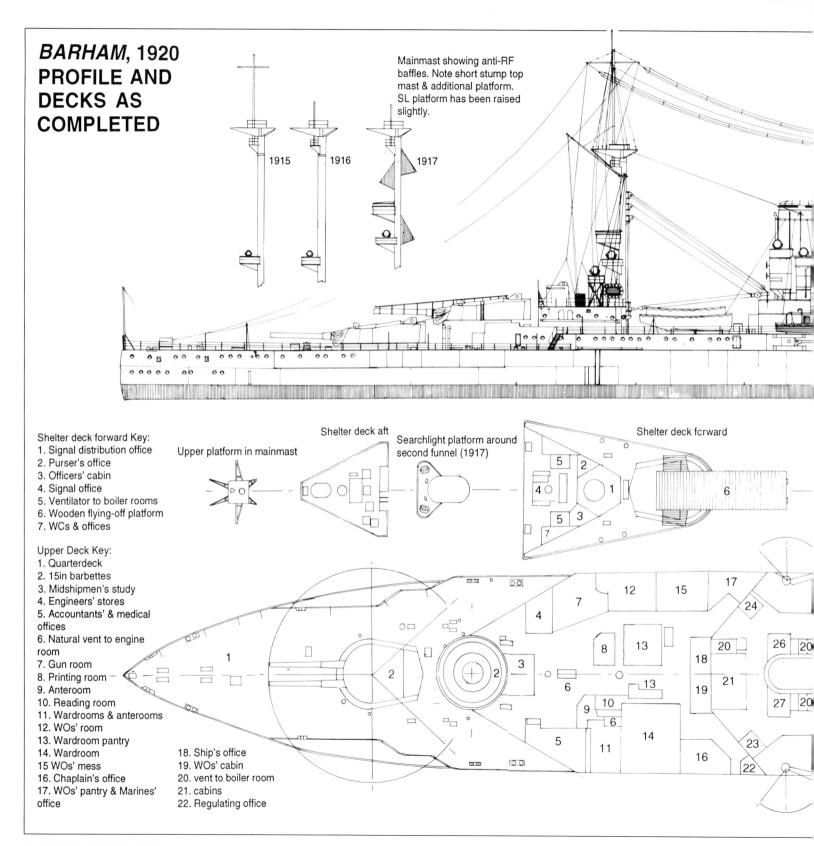

**BARHAM, 1920
PROFILE AND
DECKS AS
COMPLETED**

1915   1916   1917

Mainmast showing anti-RF
baffles. Note short stump top
mast & additional platform.
SL platform has been raised
slightly.

Shelter deck forward Key:
1. Signal distribution office
2. Purser's office
3. Officers' cabin
4. Signal office
5. Ventilator to boiler rooms
6. Wooden flying-off platform
7. WCs & offices

Upper Deck Key:
1. Quarterdeck
2. 15in barbettes
3. Midshipmen's study
4. Engineers' stores
5. Accountants' & medical
offices
6. Natural vent to engine
room
7. Gun room
8. Printing room
9. Anteroom
10. Reading room
11. Wardrooms & anterooms
12. WOs' room
13. Wardroom pantry
14. Wardroom
15 WOs' mess
16. Chaplain's office
17. WOs' pantry & Marines'
office

18. Ship's office
19. WOs' cabin
20. vent to boiler room
21. cabins
22. Regulating office

Upper platform in mainmast

Shelter deck aft

Searchlight platform around
second funnel (1917)

Shelter deck forward

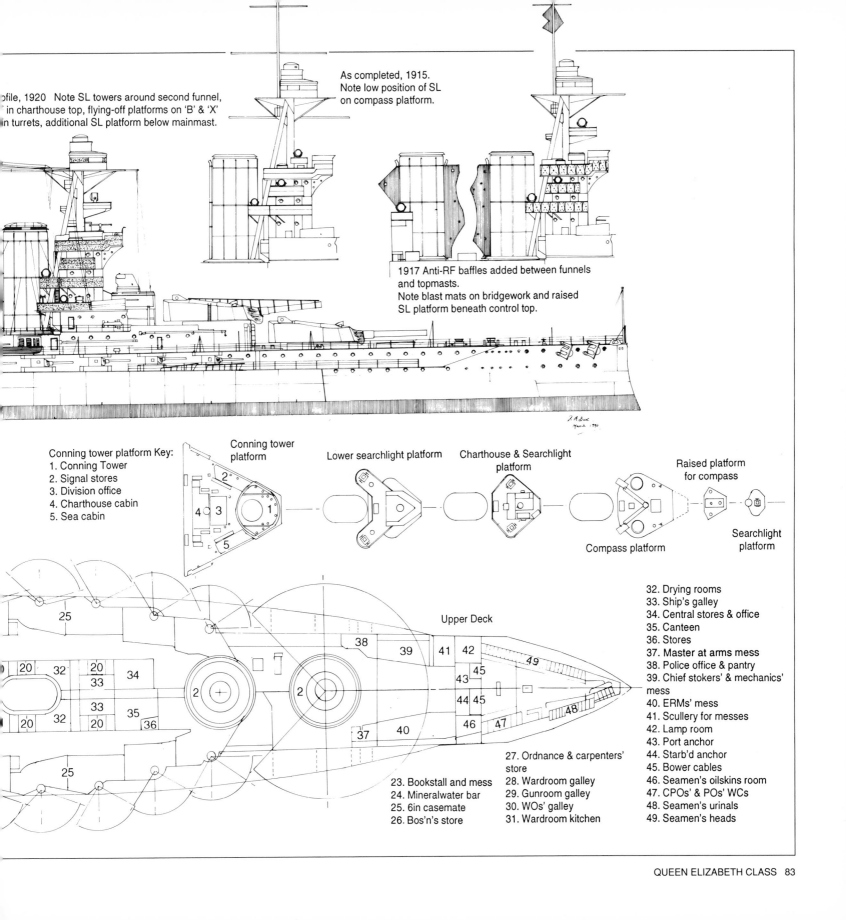

ofile, 1920   Note SL towers around second funnel,
' in charthouse top, flying-off platforms on 'B' & 'X'
in turrets, additional SL platform below mainmast.

As completed, 1915.
Note low position of SL
on compass platform.

1917 Anti-RF baffles added between funnels
and topmasts.
Note blast mats on bridgework and raised
SL platform beneath control top.

Conning tower platform Key:
1. Conning Tower
2. Signal stores
3. Division office
4. Charthouse cabin
5. Sea cabin

Conning tower
platform

Lower searchlight platform

Charthouse & Searchlight
platform

Raised platform
for compass

Compass platform

Searchlight
platform

Upper Deck

32. Drying rooms
33. Ship's galley
34. Central stores & office
35. Canteen
36. Stores
37. Master at arms mess
38. Police office & pantry
39. Chief stokers' & mechanics'
mess
40. ERMs' mess
41. Scullery for messes
42. Lamp room
43. Port anchor
44. Starb'd anchor
45. Bower cables
46. Seamen's oilskins room
47. CPOs' & POs' WCs
48. Seamen's urinals
49. Seamen's heads

27. Ordnance & carpenters'
store
28. Wardroom galley
29. Gunroom galley
30. WOs' galley
31. Wardroom kitchen

23. Bookstall and mess
24. Mineralwater bar
25. 6in casemate
26. Bos'n's store

discharged from the top of the funnel, completely encircling the normal funnel discharge.

Warspite
Tests similar to those described above were made on the funnel of *Warspite*. This funnel, which was divided vertically into three sections, was tested with and without jacket, and in each case the front and rear compartments were alternately in use.

Queen Elizabeth and Valiant
The funnel was divided into two compartments only, and tests were made with these alternately in use. With the original funnel the experiments showed that when the rear half of the funnel was in use relatively no trouble was experienced, but that with the forward half in use a heavy deposit was recorded. The same deposit was obtained

when both sections were working simultaneously.

Warspite, Queen Elizabeth (and Valiant)
A comparison of the results obtained on the *Queen Elizabeth* (and *Valiant*) funnel with those obtained for *Warspite* shows that while in the former case the forward section of the funnel gave trouble, in the latter case it was the rear portion which provided the heavy deposit. This result is almost certainly to be attributed to the different placing of the funnels with respect to the mast, the *Warspite* funnel being much further forward.

The conclusion of the experiments were forwarded to the DNC but whether or not anything was ever done to right the situation is not evident – certainly not from records or even photographs.

APPEARANCE CHANGES, MODIFICATIONS AND REFITS

Queen Elizabeth
No other British class of battleships changed their appearance more than the *Queen Elizabeth*s. At the end of the Great War they were considered to be the best-looking battleships in the Royal Navy. Their twin amidships funnels, heavily built-up tripod foremast and four twin 15in-gunned turrets gave them a symmetrical look unequalled by most others in the heavyweight group. In 1918 the bridgework was similar in all five, but there were many small differences, and it was quite easy to tell them apart and identify the individual ships. *Queen Elizabeth* and *Barham* were more easily identifiable than the other three.

Queen Elizabeth: No aircraft platforms on turrets

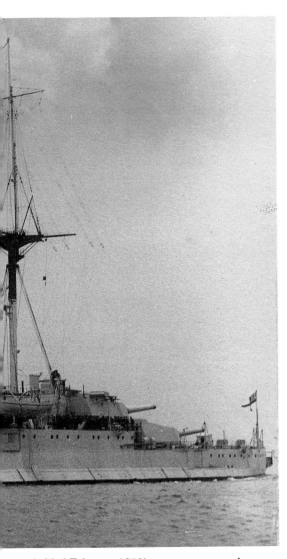

Left: *Warspite* was the first of the class to undergo major reconstruction. During 1926 she re-appeared looking much heavier, with the massive trunked funnel. The photograph shows her in April 1926 leaving Portsmouth for trials.

(added February 1919); a topmast to each mast.
Barham: Searchlight fitted on small platform close below control top; small platform close below control top (abaft mast); lower yard on foremast at starfish level; Gaff below starfish (on main).
Malaya: Lower yard on fore below starfish; Gaff well below starfish.
Valiant: Struts at starfish in place of yards; gaff below starfish; navigating light on main starfish was below mast.
Warspite: Lower yard on fore at starfish; gaff well below starfish; navigating light abaft mast.
Queen Elizabeth: 1919–20: Foretop enlarged; large base rangefinder fitted at rear of 'B' and 'X' turrets; deflection scales on turrets deleted; two rangefinder clocks fitted below forward control top and over 'X' turrets; high-angle rangefinder fitted on fore control top (original, small rangefinder). Original small rangefinder on tor-

pedo tower replaced by medium base rangefinder; aircraft platforms on 'B' and 'X' turrets in place by February 1919; 1921–22: topgallant fitted to mainmast; 1922–3: searchlights removed from main and after superstructures (platform retained); 1924–6: range clocks removed; 3in guns replaced by 4in (two fitted August/September 1924 (£2,000); aircraft platform removed from 'X' turret; after superstructure built up at rear, and sternwalk replaced; refit June 1926–October 1927: (cost of bulges and bridgework, £195,000); underwater bulges added which increased beam; control top enlarged and modified; two extra 4in fitted; after control top removed; range clocks retained over 'X' turret only; high-angle rangefinder retained on control top, extra high-angle rangefinder added in small tower over bridge; torpedo control tower removed and rangefinder remounted on small platform; RDF equipment fitted; DF cabinet fitted at rear of director platform with aerial over control top; 36in SL removed from

bridge; bridgework greatly modified and funnels trunked into one unit; flag signalling transferred from fore to mainmast, after superstructure built up to accommodate signal staff and equipment; fore topmast, together with signal yard and signal struts at starfish removed, taller topgallant fitted to mainmast.

RECONSTRUCTION OF BARHAM DEC 1930 TO OCT 1933

1. Beam and Displacement changes as *Queen Elizabeth*.
2. Range clocks over 'X' turret removed. Multiple 2pdr AA (eight barrels) added port and starboard on raised platform abeam funnel. Multiple 0.5in AA (four barrels) added port and starboard on superstructure abeam conning tower. HA-RF on control top replaced by HA director and remounted in small tower over bridge. HA director fitted on platform on main tripod legs. AA lookout position added port and

Queen Elizabeth: Legend, 1927 after refit
Displacement (tons): 31,300 (standard), 35,480 (deep) (without water protection).
Length: 644ft 3in (oa). protection 36,295 (with water).
Beam: 104ft.
Draught: 28ft 4in forward, 29ft aft (standard), 31ft 8in (deep).
Freeboard: 26ft 1in forward, 16ft 3in amidships, 17ft 10in aft.
Height of 15in guns from water: 'A', 31ft; 'B', 40ft 11in; 'X', 33ft 1in; 'Y', 23ft.
Speed: (estimated) 23½ knots.
Total oil capacity: 3,500 tons.
Armour:
16ft above water line at load displacement, 4ft below. Main belt unchanged. Bulkheads and barbettes unchanged. Turrets 11in faces, roofs increased to

5in. Decks: forecastle 1in, upper 2–1¼in, main 1¼in, middle 1in (2in over magazines, lower 3-1in.
General weights before and after refit (tons):

	1918	1927
Armour	17,500	21,110
Armament	4,550	4,950
Machinery	3,950	3,890
General equipment	750	700
Fuel (min.)	650	650

1930: Range clocks removed from over 'X' turret. High-angle rangefinder replaced by high-angle director. Improved type DF aerial fitted (early in 1930).
1933–4: aircraft platforms removed from 'B' turret.
Other of the class were all very similar during this period (see *British Battleships of World War One*).

Warspite: Refit, 18 July 1924–April 1926
Weight added (tons):

Bulge platings	575 (total weight of bulge 1,140 tons)
Transverse framing	280
Longitudinal framing	125
Bulkheads	55
Wood filling	15
Bilge keels	50
Rubber	17
Piping and valves	5
Paint, etc.	18
Additional dynamos	30
4 x 4in guns and ammunition	60
2 pom-poms	35

Increase in displacement from 1919 to 1924 was approximately 200 tons. 33,625 tons (deep) 1919.
Displacement (tons) after bulging (1926): 30,380 (light), 31,300 (legend), 34,970 (deep), 35,770 tons with water protection in bulges.

Typical refit for the whole class during this period. *Warspite* as follows:
Control top enlarged and modified.
After control top removed.
Range clocks retained over 'X' turret only.
HA RP retained on control top with extra pair added in small tower over bridge.
36in SL removed from bridge and SL platforms from mainmast and after superstructure.
For smaller refits see *Battleships of World War One*

MALAYA, 1919

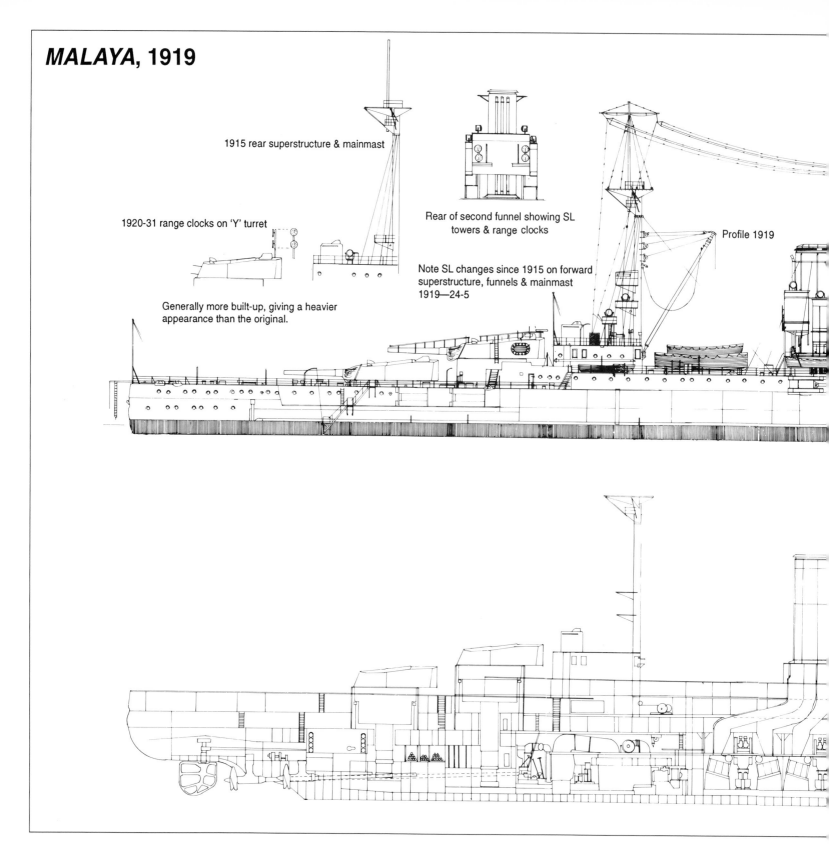

1915 rear superstructure & mainmast

1920-31 range clocks on 'Y' turret

Rear of second funnel showing SL towers & range clocks

Note SL changes since 1915 on forward superstructure, funnels & mainmast 1919—24-5

Generally more built-up, giving a heavier appearance than the original.

Profile 1919

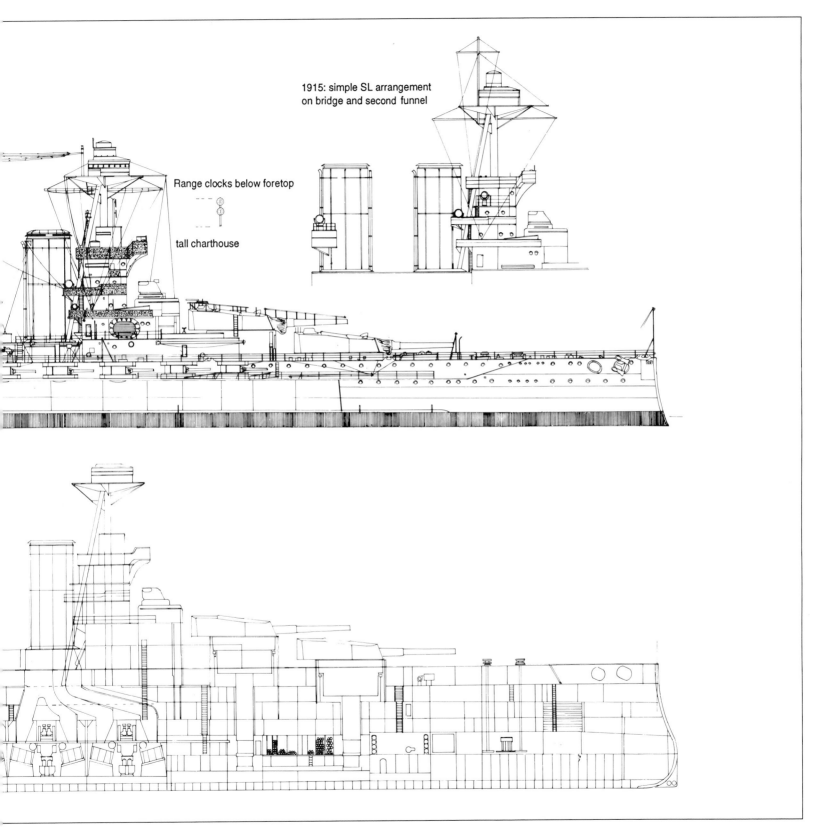

1915: simple SL arrangement
on bridge and second funnel

Range clocks below foretop

tall charthouse

Below: Close-up of *Queen Elizabeth* showing improved bridgework and trunked funnel after refit, November 1927. Note the heat shield on the base of the funnel.

General Particulars for Class 1934
Displacement (tons): *Queen Elizabeth* 36,295 (deep) (as inclined August 1927).
Length: 634ft 6in (wl), 643ft 9in (oa) (*Warspite*).
Beam: 104ft over rubbers.
Draught: 29ft to 34ft max. (varied in all).
Armament
Original main guns unchanged, secondary guns as in 1918.
4 x 4in AA
16 x 2pdrs (2 x 8 barrels) in *Barham*.
8 x 2pdrs (1 x 8 barrels) in *Valiant*.
8 x 0.5 AA (2 x 4 barrels) in *Barham*.
Original saluting guns and MGs.
2 x 21in TT (forward).
Radio directional finders in *Barham*, *Queen Elizabeth* and *Valiant*.
Searchlights: 4 x 36in on funnel towers, 2 or 4 x 24in signalling.
Aircraft
Training catapult in *Barham* and *Valiant*. One Fairey III reconnaissance seaplane. Barham carried a Walrus amphibian for a short period in 1934.
Protection: As original except for bulges added and some additional armour on turret tops and around magazines (see revised legend of *QE* 1927 after refit).
Machinery and boilers as built.
Speed reduced slightly to approx. 23.6 average.
General Appearance
Enlarged and modified bridgework in all, which extended right round tripod legs. Upper bridge completely enclosed in *Barham* and *Valiant*. Fore funnel trunked into second. Anti-heat plate fitted on lower part of funnel. Tripod mainmast in *Barham* only. Sternwalk in *Queen Elizabeth*, *Barham* and *Warspite*. Signal struts at starfish below control top (very short in *QE*) and no yard on foremast. Yard at starfish on main in *Malaya*, *Queen Elizabeth* and *Warspite*, with extra signal yard on topmast above this in *Queen Elizabeth*. As reconstructed, they were very distinctive and notably heavier and more

starboard below control top. After pair of torpedo tubes removed. Torpedo rangefinder removed from after superstructure.
3. RDF equipment fitted as in *Queen Elizabeth* (1930 type aerial).
4. SL towers around funnel modified but arrangement of SL unchanged. Two 24in signalling SL remounted on lower bridge (ex forward superstructure).
5. Training type catapult fitted on starboard side of 'X' turret roof with straight arm crane abeam main mast on starboard side. Aircraft platforms removed from turrets.
6. Anti-torpedo bulges fitted as in *Queen Elizabeth*.
7. Bridge enlarged and modified and funnels trunked as in *Queen Elizabeth*. Upper bridge completely enclosed in addition and lower bridge extended further aft than in the other ships; entire bridge structure now merging with tripod legs.
8. Tripod legs fitted to main mast to support HA director. Arrangement of signal struts below control top modified.

Modifications, *Barham* March to June 1938
1. Single 4in AA replaced by twin enlarged shields. HA-RF over bridge removed.
2. 36in SL replaced by 44in.

SECOND RECONSTRUCTION PERIOD, 1934–41

In 1934 a second modernization programme for the class was initiated with a view to bringing the ships in line with existing requirements, especially in respect to increased horizontal protection against plunging fire and aerial attack by the powerful modern guns and bombs to which all older battleships were very vulnerable. The menace of aircraft attack and the necessity for improved defence against this, both by guns and armour, had by this date become a particularly vital factor in battleship design. Underwater protection against increasingly efficient torpedoes and mines was also considered to require strengthening as far as possible. *Malaya* and *Warspite* were taken in hand in 1934 and completed in 1936 and 1937 respectively. *Valiant*

and *Queen Elizabeth* followed in 1937, *Valiant* being completed in 1939 and *Queen Elizabeth* in 1941.

Modifications in *Malaya*, however, were limited, being confined mainly to increased AA armament and provision of hangar accommodation for aircraft and an improved type of catapult; protection, machinery and boilers remained unchanged. But the additional top weight imposed, and for which no real compensation was made, resulted in some loss of stability associated with a substantial increase in displacement, deeper draught, reduced freeboard, dryness and speed. Displacement increased by approximately 1,000 tons and maximum speed reduced to just over 22 knots.

piled up than in 1918. The unbalanced rig (low on foremast and high on main) detracted from their original symmetry, although with a reversed arrangement to that in 1918 and a considerably more marked disparity between relative height on the fore and mainmasts.

The principal features were:

Large trunked funnel. Enlarged bridgework, extended completely around tripod legs. Heavy control top and director platform below. Prominent waterline bulges. Catapult on 'X' turret in *Barham* and on quarterdeck right aft in *Valiant*. Low rig on foremast and high on main. Tripod mainmast with director tower on legs in *Barham*. DF aerial abaft control top in *Barham*, *Queen Elizabeth* and *Valiant*.

The trunking of the funnels had been well arranged, and the resultant enormous flat-sided fittings constituted a most imposing feature, being less unsightly than might have been the case. Mainmast, with topmast and topgallant, was very tall, and the height was accentuated by the absence of any foretopmast.

Easily distinguished from the *Royal Sovereign* class by trunked funnel, no shelterdeck amidships. Shorter 6in battery, not carried abaft amidships. Director platform on foremast was noticeably lower.

Individual differences in 1934

Barham: (1) Tripod mainmast with director tower halfway up tripod legs. (2) Catapult on 'X' turret and crane abeam mainmast (port side). (3) Lower bridge extended farther aft than in the others. (4) Projecting lips to SL towers around funnel. (5) Sternwalk.

Queen Elizabeth: (1) Enlarged after superstructure. (2) Extra yard on main topmast. (3) Sternwalk.

Valiant: (1) Catapult and crane on quarterdeck right aft. (2) Strongly projecting lip to forward pair of SL towers. (3) No sternwalk.

Warspite: (1) Sternwalk. (2) Flagpole to top main mast.

Malaya: (1) No sternwalk. (2) No flagpole.

The reconstruction of *Warspite* was considerably more drastic, the primary object being to secure a substantial advance in offensive and defensive qualities without additional displacement and further loss of speed, maintenance of the existing 24 knots being considered essential in view of rising battleship standards in this respect. In addition to the modifications in AA armament and aircraft accommodation as carried out in *Malaya*, elevation and range of main armament was increased, secondary armament was reduced, AA armament was further increased, horizontal protection materially strengthened, internal sub-division improved, speed maintained and steaming radius extended by 75 per cent. This was accomplished on an

estimated reduction of 500 tons in displacement (see table), mainly by the adoption of improved and lighter machinery in boilers which constituted the governing factor in the whole scheme of reconstruction.

The modernization of *Valiant* and *Queen Elizabeth* followed similar lines to that of *Warspite*, but was even more extensive, incorporating an entirely new dual-purpose (HALA) secondary armament and some modifications in detail. Estimated displacement increased by 420 tons in *Valiant* and 1,600 tons in *Queen Elizabeth* with correspondingly increased draught and reduced freeboard as compared to *Warspite*. Although it had been planned to maintain the speed of 24 knots, it was reduced to about 22/23 knots as a consequence of the substantial rise in displacement. Bridge work, superstructure, general layout and rig in all three ships was drastically altered, the new design representing in this respect a prototype for the *King George V* class.

Although all-round efficiency in these three ships was officially considered to have increased by 50 per cent, subsequent war experience indicated that horizontal and underwater protection was still below modern requirements. *Barham* was to have been modernized after *Valiant* and *Queen Elizabeth*, but the outbreak of war in 1939 precluded this. It had been intended to re-modify *Malaya* as in *Valiant* and *Queen Elizabeth*, but here again the war intervened.

Queen Elizabeth 1935, July to October modifications. Two multiple 2pdr AA (eight barrels) added on superstructure abeam bridge; two multiple 0.5in AA (four barrels) added on after superstructure; aircraft spotting position fitted port and starboard below control top.

RECONSTRUCTION OF MALAYA OCT 1934 TO DEC 1936

Reconstruction involved 60 per cent of structure.
(1) Draft and displacement increased by 8in and 944 tons respectively by additional weights imposed. The considerable extra and uncompensated top weight, especially the heavy hangar structure, involved a slight loss of stability which was accepted because of the increase in original stability resulting from the addition of bulges on the first reconstruction. The degree of stability was quite low, however, and would not have been approved under later standards. As a con-

sequence of reduced freeboard the ship was very wet in any seaway after reconstruction.
(2) The 6in director towers were re-located port and starboard on extensions of the 15in director platform abaft the tripod legs. The single 4in AA were replaced by twin 4in in large shields, the after pair being sponsoned out at sides. Multiple 2pdr AA (eight barrels) were added port and starboard on a high platform abeam the funnel. Multiple 0.5in AA (four barrels) were added port and starboard on 'X' turret. HA RF on control top was replaced by HA director (raised well clear of top) and a second director was added on the after superstructure. HA RF over bridge was removed. Remaining torpedo tubes (forward pair) were removed together with torpedo control tower and RF, torpedo armament being reported as not worth the space and personnel it absorbed.
(3) MD/DF equipment was fitted, a modified type of DF aerial being fitted on main top mast.
(4) The 36in SL were replaced by 44in and their distribution modified, two (port and starboard) on superstructure before funnel and two (port and starboard) on platform abaft funnel. Former control towers around the funnel were removed.
(5) Two aircraft hangars were provided (port and starboard) in superstructure abaft funnel, opening at the rear. A straight arm electric crane was fitted on top of each hangar and a fixed athwartships catapult on the upper deck abaft hangars. Accommodation for four aircraft (maximum): two stowed in hangars, one on deck outside and one on catapult. Swordfish T/S/R and/or Walrus Amphibians carried. First battleship to have hangar accommodation for aircraft.
(6) Original machinery and boilers retained. Speed was reduced as a result of extra weights added in reconstruction (ship unable to maintain

station with *Valiant* and *Warspite* in 1940/41.
(7) New type, completely open, upper bridge fitted, this design being otherwise only adopted in *Royal Oak* (see notes on bridges). After superstructure abaft mainmast was enlarged. Boat stowage rearranged to accommodate hangars and catapult, the majority of boats being stowed on top of hangars and handled by aircraft cranes. The original main boat derrick was removed. Accommodation, ventilation and general equipment was modernized but habitability at sea suffered from the reduced freeboard.
(8) Main topgallant mast replaced by flagpole. Forward and after struts removed from main starfish and yard raised well above this.

RECONSTRUCTION OF WARSPITE MARCH 1934 TO JUNE 1937

(1) The estimated draught and displacement was reduced by 4in and 500 tons respectively, mainly because of the reduced weight of new machinery and boilers together with the removal of four 6in guns and their armour and the original heavy conning tower. Original stability was adequately maintained. Forecastle flare was extended aft almost to 'A' turret and the deck was widened so that the side flushed with what was formerly the second 6in gun port. The side was plated up over main deck casemates aft and decked over. Hull strength was satisfactorily maintained and although the removal of heavy weights amidships during reconstruction caused the hull to be permanently hogged to the extent of 4½in the ship stood up well under very severe tests. The extension of forecastle flare and plating up to the forward pair of battery gun ports tended to assist dryness in head seas.

Masts: *Malaya*, 1937			
Foremast	Length	Diameter	Weight (tons)
Lower mast	87ft 10¾in	36in	32.54
struts	91ft 0¾in	24in	17.94
outriggers (4)	16ft	6 x 3in	
Mainmast			
Lower mast	102ft 10¾in	36in	31.3
Topmast	47ft	16–10in	1.25
D/F yards (4)	10ft	5 x 4in	
Jack	21ft 6in		
Ensign	25ft 6in		
Height of spotting top	121ft 3¾in		
Highest point above WL	157ft 7¾in		
All above measurements with ship at mean draught of 28ft 8in.			

Warspite after reconstruction, 1937

	Before	After
Armament	4,970 tons	5,264 tons
Machinery	3,691 tons	2,300 tons
Equipment	1,287 tons	1,420 tons
Armour	5,431 tons	5,980 tons
Hull & Protective Plating	16,250 tons	17,130 tons
Oil fuel	3,431 tons	3,735 tons
Reserve Feed Water	497 tons	267 tons
Draught Forward		33ft 2in mean
Draught Aft		32ft 1in
GM		6.63ft normal load, 6.82ft deep load
Displacement		33,842 tons half oil condition, 34,228 tons ordinary deep condition, 31,446 tons standard, 36,911 tons deep (including water protection)
Boiler weights	1,461 tons	900 tons
Engine Room	1,737 tons	967 tons
Conning Tower	339 tons	102 tons
Battery Protection	339 tons	105 tons
Deck over (protective) magazines forward		260 tons
Deck over (protective) magazines aft		189 tons
Deck over (protective) Engine Rooms		253 tons
Deck over (protective) Boiler Room		456 tons
Hull weights	16,250 tons	17,130 tons

(2) Elevation of the 15in guns increased to 30°, the maximum provided in any capital ship to that date for guns of 12in or higher calibre. Range substantially increased from approximately 23,400 yards to 32,200 yards. New fire control and range-finding equipment was fitted, with a 15ft and 9ft rangefinder. New and much larger (15in) director was fitted on top of a new bridge tower. The armoured RF position formerly over the conning tower was transferred to the after superstructure. The forward and after pairs of 6in guns removed to accommodate additional AA armament, and the hull side was plated up flush over the vacant gun positions. This was not considered to involve any loss in actual fighting qualities because secondary guns that were unavailable for use against air as well as surface targets had become virtually obsolete.

BARHAM: PROFILES, 1928 AND 1937

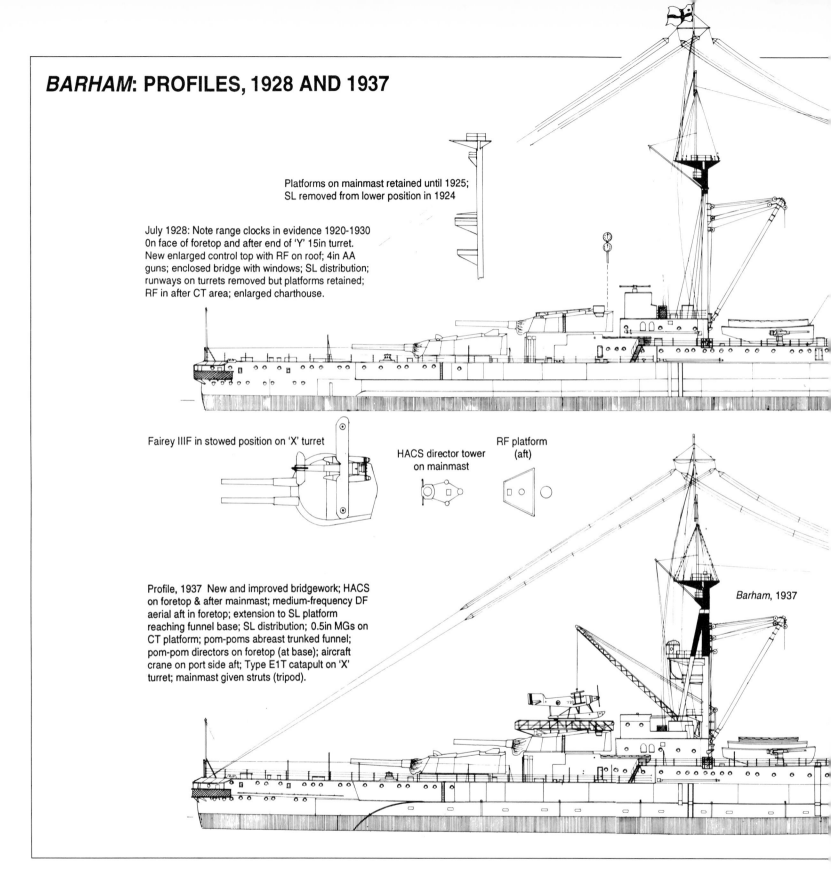

Platforms on mainmast retained until 1925;
SL removed from lower position in 1924

July 1928: Note range clocks in evidence 1920-1930
0n face of foretop and after end of 'Y' 15in turret.
New enlarged control top with RF on roof; 4in AA
guns; enclosed bridge with windows; SL distribution;
runways on turrets removed but platforms retained;
RF in after CT area; enlarged charthouse.

Fairey IIIF in stowed position on 'X' turret

HACS director tower
on mainmast

RF platform
(aft)

Profile, 1937 New and improved bridgework; HACS
on foretop & after mainmast; medium-frequency DF
aerial aft in foretop; extension to SL platform
reaching funnel base; SL distribution; 0.5in MGs on
CT platform; pom-poms abreast trunked funnel;
pom-pom directors on foretop (at base); aircraft
crane on port side aft; Type E1T catapult on 'X'
turret; mainmast given struts (tripod).

Barham, 1937

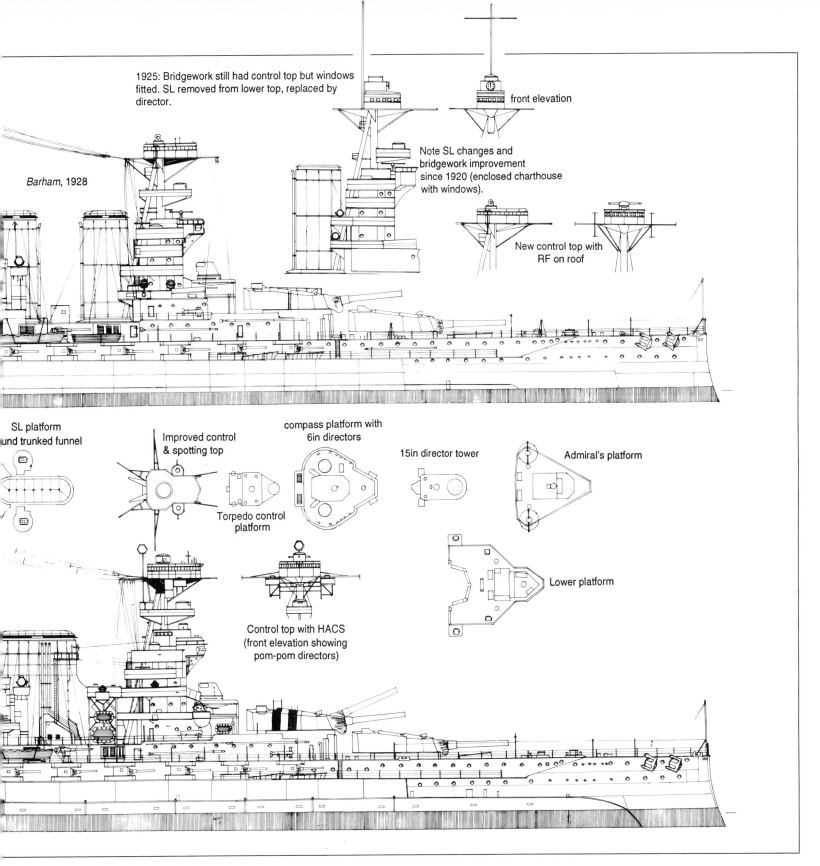

1925: Bridgework still had control top but windows fitted. SL removed from lower top, replaced by director.

front elevation

Note SL changes and bridgework improvement since 1920 (enclosed charthouse with windows).

Barham, 1928

New control top with RF on roof

SL platform und trunked funnel

Improved control & spotting top

Torpedo control platform

compass platform with 6in directors

15in director tower

Admiral's platform

Lower platform

Control top with HACS (front elevation showing pom-pom directors)

Right: *Valiant* leaving Gibraltar in April 1931. Over against the mole, *Renown*, *Tiger* and *Repulse* can be seen.

***Warspite*: General Particulars in 1939**
Displacement (tons): 36,911 (deep) as inclined.
Length and beam as in 1934.
Forecastle flare lengthened giving increased dryness.
Side plated up over original main deck casemates aft.
Armament:
Main armament as original.
8 x 4in AA (twin).
32 x 2pdr (4 x 8 barrels).
16 x 0.5in AA (4 x 4 barrels).
Original saluting guns and MGs.
No torpedo armament.
Radar: MF/DF equipment fitted.
Searchlights: 4 x 44in, 2 x 24in signalling.
Armour
As original, plus increased horizontal and internal protection and minus original conning towers. New bridge protection: 3in plates (NC) on front and sides, 2in back, 1½in roof, 1in floor. New bridge tower also made gas and chemical proof as far as possible.
Total deck armour: 6¾in over magazines, 5¾in over machinery.
Eight watertight compartments in machinery and six in boiler spaces.
Machinery
Parsons geared turbines.
6 Admiralty type 3-drum boilers.
Fuel: 3,730 tons.
General: Large tower structure replacing former bridgework and conning tower. Boat stowage rearranged, accommodation, ventilation and equipment all modernised.
Rig: Light pole foremast with topmast and topgallant. Short pole mainmast. No control top. DF aerial on pole at each masthead.
Reconstruction costs: £2,800,000.
Complement: average 1,183.

The 6in director towers were relocated port and starboard on the new bridge tower below and abeam the 15in director. The single 4in AA was replaced by twin 4in in large shields. Four multiple 2pdr AA (eight barrels) were added. Two enlarged sponsons were fitted on top of the superstructure amidships abeam and abaft the funnel, the after pair being carried noticeably higher than the forward pair. Four multiple 0.5in AA were added, two port and starboard on 'B' and 'X' turrets. HA director for 4in AA was located port and starboard at rear of bridge tower below and abaft the 15in director. The remaining torpedo tubes were removed together with the torpedo control tower and RF; the torpedo flats were used for extra ammunition stowage

(3) MF/DF equipment fitted, DF aerial at each masthead.

(4) The 36in SL were replaced by 44in and distribution was modified: two port and starboard on sponsons at sides of bridge tower, two port and starboard on platform against fore side of funnel. The former control towers around the funnels were removed.

(5) Aircraft hangars and catapult were installed as in *Malaya*.

(6) The 6in battery was removed from vacant gun positions and the after battery bulkhead was shifted forward of the original after pair of guns. The original main deck casemates aft were plated up, but casemate armour was retained to form an irregular-shaped bulkhead between ship's sides and 'Y' barbette. Horizontal protection was considerably improved, but war experience showed this to be still inadequate against modern high-powered bombs, the ship being badly damaged by a 500lb bomb off Crete on 22 May 1941 and completely disabled by a 3,000lb glider bomb at Salerno on 16 September 1943 (see battle damage). On the first occasion one boiler room had to be temporarily evacuated while on the second the bomb penetrated six decks and burst in No. 4 boiler room, completely demolishing this and flooding all the others armour modifications comprised: main deck from 'A' barbette to forward bulkhead increased from 1¼in to 3in. Middle deck increased from 1in uniform to 5½in over magazines and 3½in over machinery and boilers. Total horizontal protection over magazines 6¾in (1¼in upper deck and 5½in middle deck). Total over machinery and boilers 5¾in (1in forecastle, 1¼in upper and 3½in middle decks). Armour on boiler room uptakes increased from 1½in to 4in. Original conning tower and lower navigating position was removed and a new armoured position placed high up in the bridge tower at the forward end of No. 3 platform, this being fitted as a new lower navigating position with armoured communication tube to the base of the tower. Splinter protection was provided for bridge personnel and at 2pdr AA positions. Internal sub-division was extensively modified and improved. Existing bulge protection was retained, but sub-division inside the longitudinal anti-torpedo bulkheads was substantially increased. A centre line bulkhead was fitted in machinery and boiler spaces with eight watertight compartments in machinery and six in boiler space. In the event of heavy damage port and starboard engine rooms could be completely isolated from one another and the pumping capacity was increased from 950 to 9,050 tons per hour.

(7) The ship was re-engined and re-boilered by Parsons with Parsons geared turbines and six Admiralty three-drum high-pressure boilers arranged in three compartments, grouped together. The original arrangements of turbines and propeller shafts were retained. Horse power increased to approximately 80,000shp for 24 knots. Separate diesel driven generators were provided, these being entirely independent of the

main steam system. Generating capacity increased from 700kW to 2,400kW. Because of the reduced number of boilers (six against original 24) the original forward boiler room was no longer required and became available for other purposes, including diesel oil tanks, bomb and sub-calibre magazines, secondary wireless and telegraphy office, telephone exchange and HACP, turbo-generator rooms, SL stabilizing room and stores. Total saving in weight and space on machinery and boilers was approximately 1,480 tons and 4,540 square feet (see

table). Concentration of all three boiler rooms in one group was a weak point as all steam power was cut off when these were flooded by bomb damage at Salerno in September 1943. Fuel capacity increased by 300 tons and nominal radius increased from 7,670 miles to 13,500 miles at 10 knots by the greater economy of the new geared turbines and more efficient boilers, especially the latter.

(8) The former bridge work and conning tower was replaced by a large splinter and gas proof tower, a modification of the type first introduced

in the *Nelson* class (1925), designed to meet the requirements of a fleet flagship and accommodating the fire control top and director position formerly located on the tripod foremast. Arrangement of tower from base upwards: shelter deck – general reading room and oilskin store; No. 1 platform – Officers' sea cabins. CPOs' reading room, midshipmens' study; No. 2 platform – sea cabins for Admiral, Chief of Staff and Captain, Master of Fleet and Navigating Officer, two bathrooms; No. 3 platform – lowered armoured navigating position in face. Signal office DF and cipher office, signal officer's cabin, SL and lookout position at sides; Admiral's Bridge – Admiral's shelter and charthouse at forward end, remote control office, plotting office, 6in and HA directors at rear; the roof – 15in director. The trunked funnel was replaced by a single much smaller funnel, affording space for additional AA armament with clear arcs of fire. Boat stowage and handling arrangements were modified as in *Malaya*. Accommodation, ventilation and general equipment was completely modernized.

(9) Rig modified. Original heavy tripod foremast was replaced by light pole stepped at the rear of control tower with short topmast and topgallant and tall DF aerial pole (actual light pole was part of original mainmast). No control top. Short pole main mast with DF aerial at head. Signal and WT yard on foremast. WT yard on main.

RECONSTRUCTION OF VALIANT MAR 1937 TO NOV 1939

Reconstruction involved 90 per cent of structure.
1. Nominal draught and displacement increased by approximately 3½in and 420 tons by additional weights imposed on reconstruction, which were not entirely offset by the lighter machinery and boilers and weight of items removed as had been the case in *Warspite*. Nominal displacement as reconstructed about 920 tons heavier than *Warspite*. Compared to pre-construction figures, the estimated weight of hull and armour increased by 1,163 tons, armament by 596 tons and equipment by 87 tons. Machinery and boiler weights reduced by 1,485 tons giving an estimated net increase of 361 tons. As a consequence of the removal of the entire 6in battery, the forecastle side modifications were considerably more extensive than in *Warspite*. The original recessed forecastle was built out into a normal curve extending to a point abaft amidships where it angled in to the centre line of 'X' turret as before. The side was plated up over main deck casemates aft and decked over as in *Warspite*. Special measures were taken in this ship (and *Queen Elizabeth*) to prevent any hull distortion (hogging) as had occurred in *Warspite* during reconstruction as a result of the removal of heavy weights (machinery and boilers) amidships.
2. Main armament and fire control modifications were practically the same as in *Warspite*. The 6in

Valiant: **Particulars as in 1939**
Displacement (tons): 35,698 ordinary deep condition, 36,513 (including water protection).
Length and beam as in 1934.
Original recessed forecastle and flare as in *Warspite*.
Armament
Main guns as original.
20 x 4.5in dual-purpose (10 twin turrets).
Light AA as in *Warspite*.
Original saluting and MGs.
No torpedo armament.
Radar: AW type 79Z, MF/DF aerial.
Searchlights: 6 x 44in, 2 x 24in signalling.
Armour
Main belt as original. As refitted same as reconstructed *Warspite* except: 4in special 'D' armour on upper sides amidships in place of original 6in battery. Main deck armour increased to 4¼in around outer face of 'Y' barbette. Increased subdivision in boiler and machinery spaces.
Machinery
Parsons geared turbines.
8 Admiralty type 3-drum boilers.
Fuel: as *Warspite*.
General
Same as *Warspite* except for bridge slightly different in shape.
Rig: Same as *Warspite* except light tripod legs to foremast.
Reconstruction costs: £3,000,000 (approx).
Appearance: Similar to *Warspite* except: Secondary turrets port and starboard, no 6in battery, upper part of bridgetower extended farther aft, tripod foremast, no sternwalk.

Queen Elizabeth: **Particulars 1941**
Displacement (tons): 37,696 (deep) (includes 699 tons water protection), 35,930 average action condition.
Length and beam as 1934.

Armament as *Valiant*.
Radar: AW Type 279 fitted January 1941, improved MF/DF as *Valiant*.
All other features almost identical with *Valiant* and difficult to tell them apart at certain angles.

General Particulars for Class in 1944
Malaya in Reserve from October 1944 owing to relatively unmodernized condition compared to *Queen Elizabeth*, *Valiant* and *Warspite*.
Displacement (tons) *QE*: 37,385 (deep) June 1944; 38,450 (deep) 1945. *Valiant* 35,647 (deep) 1944; 38,908 (deep) 1946. *Malaya* 37,710 (deep) 1945.
Length and beam as 1939.
Armament
Main and secondary as 1939.
Malaya: 48 x 20mm AA (singles) (plus 32 x 2pdrs).
Warspite: 35 x 20mm AA (plus 32 x 2pdrs).
Queen Elizabeth: 32 x 2pdrs. 54 x 20mm AA.
Valiant: 32 x 2pdr. 47 x 20mm AA.
Radar
Type 284 for main guns. Type 285 for 4in AA. Type 282 for light AA. AW Type 281. SW Type 273 (Type 284 replaced by 275). Various IFF aerials plus Type 650 anti-missile aerials seen in *Malaya* and *Warspite*.
Searchlights: as in 1939.
Aircraft: all removed and area used for other equipment. Catapults removed.
Protection as in 1939.
Machinery: as in 1939.
Speed: Greatly reduced owing to many wartime additions and doubtful if any of the surviving vessels could sustain more than 22 knots for long periods. *Warspite* reduced in speed even more after hitting mine in 1944 (about 16 knots).
All HACS equipment greatly improved from 1939 to 1944.
All vessels overweight by 1944 and very wet in a seaway.

secondary battery was replaced by twenty 4.5in DP HA/LA guns in ten light twin turrets of a special gas-tight pattern with mushroom crowns armoured against aerial attack. The turrets were arranged five port and starboard amidships in two groups, three on forecastle deck abeam bridge tower and funnel and two further aft on upper deck abeam after superstructure. Rate of fire was about 18 rounds per minute under good conditions. The turrets revolved on weather deck with tween deck mountings travelling on roller paths on deck below and permitting both flat and high trajectory fire. Blast effects between turrets was often reported as severe and special arrangements were made to prevent catapult from being damaged by blast from the after pair of turrets when trained ahead. The guns were controlled from four directors, two port and star-

board on bridge tower abaft 15in director and two port and starboard on after superstructure. Ammunition was supplied by endless chain hoists. The 4in AA armament was removed.

The change to dual-purpose guns marked the beginning of a new cycle of capital ship secondary armament in the Royal Navy in which defence against air attack was to take precedence over surface torpedo attack. Medium calibre guns, which could not be used against both air and surface targets, were no longer considered worth the weight and space they absorbed, and screening cruisers and destroyers were relied upon to break up enemy destroyer attacks; 4in–5in guns being considered adequate against smaller torpedo craft, these guns being also well adapted for high-angle fire. The guns selected for *Valiant* and *Queen Elizabeth* were 4.5in instead of

Below: *Queen Elizabeth*. Fleet Reviews were a favourite public gathering and none more so than when the big ships were present. *Queen Elizabeth* is shown here during the 1935 Review (the last for His Majesty King George V).

the 5.25in of the *King George V* class because the larger gun could not have been carried in adequate numbers on their length and displacement. Light AA armament was increasd to thirty-two 2pdr in 4–8-barrel mountings, two port and starboard on superstructure amidships around funnel, plus sixteen 0.5in in four 4-barrel mountings, two each on 'B' and 'X' turrets. Light AA directors were fitted port and starboard at the sides of the bridge tower abaft funnel and on the after superstructure. The diameter of these directors was only about 2in less than that of the 8ft platforms on which they were mounted and the fittings were reported to be very complicated. Additional space for the considerably increased light ammunition supply required was obtained by removal of the remaining torpedo tubes and a reduction in boiler room space.

3. Air warning radar (Type 79Z) was fitted (November 1939), with an aerial on each mainmast. She was the second British capital ship to have operational radar (fitted in *Rodney* 1938).
4. The 36in SL were replaced by 44in and the number was increased from four to six, two part and starboard low on face of bridge tower; two port and starboard on platform against rear of funnel; two port and starboard on after superstructure before mainmast.
5. Aircraft equipment added as in *Warspite* except bent instead of straight arm cranes.
6. The 6in battery and casemate armour was removed, partially offsetting increased weight of new secondary armament and ammunition supply. Special very high-tensile 'D'-type steel armour was fitted on sides in place of battery armour below forward group of secondary tur-

rets. Improvements in horizontal and boiler uptake protection was as in *Warspite* with the following additions: main deck increased from $1\frac{1}{4}$in to $4\frac{1}{4}$in around outer face of 'Y' barbette; lower deck increased from 3in to $31\frac{1}{2}$in outside forward bulkhead; total horizontal protection over magazines, machinery and boiler spaces as *Warspite* plus the extra 3in on main deck around 'Y' barbette; conning tower modifications as in *Warspite*; existing bulge protection retained, but internal subdivision and pumping capacity improved and extended as in *Warspite*, internal subdivision in boiler spaces being further increased.
7. Re-engined and re-boilered by Fairfield with Parsons geared turbines and eight Admiralty three-drum boilers in four compartments. The original arrangement of turbines and propeller

MALAYA: PROFILES, 1926 AND 1930

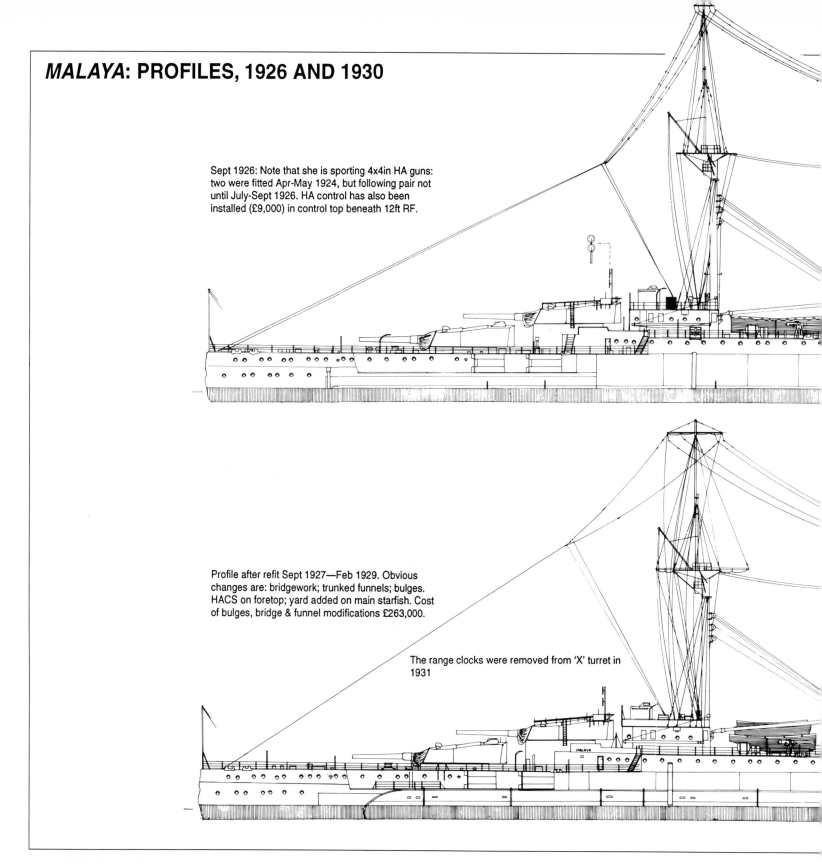

Sept 1926: Note that she is sporting 4x4in HA guns:
two were fitted Apr-May 1924, but following pair not
until July-Sept 1926. HA control has also been
installed (£9,000) in control top beneath 12ft RF.

Profile after refit Sept 1927—Feb 1929. Obvious
changes are: bridgework; trunked funnels; bulges.
HACS on foretop; yard added on main starfish. Cost
of bulges, bridge & funnel modifications £263,000.

The range clocks were removed from 'X' turret in
1931

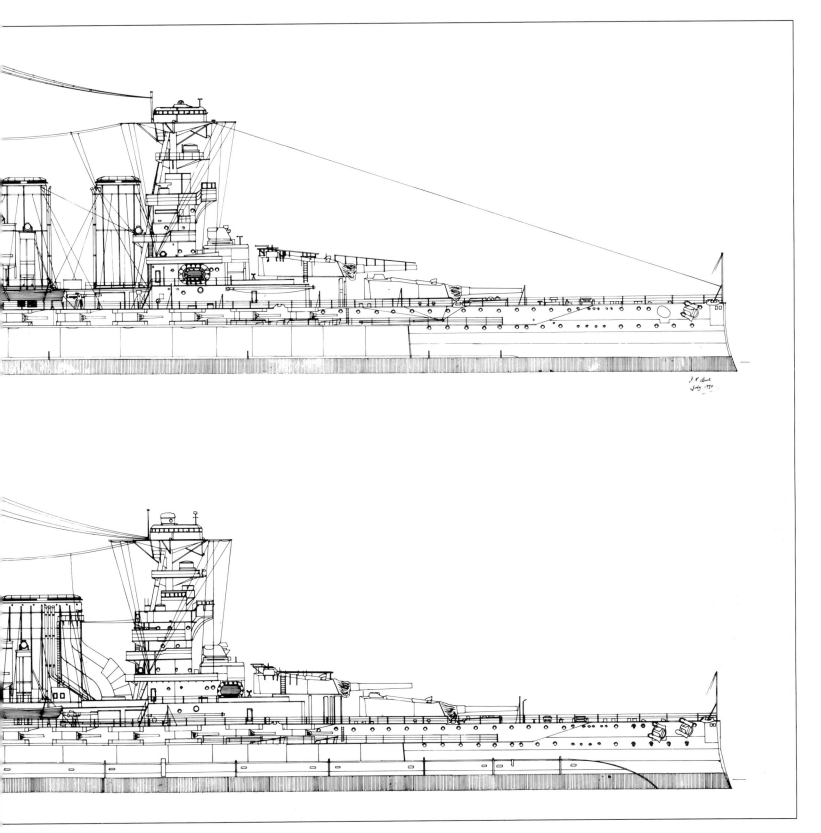

shafts was retained. The number of boilers increased by two as compared to *Warspite* and the arrangement extended to four compartments instead of three to provide greater subdivision. Horse power increased to 80,000shp for provisional 24 knots. Separate diesel driven generators were fitted as in *Warspite*.

8. Bridge, conning tower, funnel, boat stowage and handling modifications were as in *Warspite* except that the upper part of the bridge tower extended further aft. Accommodation, ventilation and general equipment were brought up to date.

9. Rig modified to light tripod foremast with topmast only and short pole mainmast without topmast. A radar aerial on a short pole was fitted at each masthead.

RECONSTRUCTION OF QUEEN ELIZABETH, AUG 1937 – JAN 1941

Reconstruction involved 90 per cent of structure.
1. Nominal draught and displacement increased by 14in and 1,600 tons by additional weights imposed on reconstruction which, as in *Valiant*, were only partially offset by the lighter machinery and boiler weights. Hull modifications were as in *Valiant*. The lengthened bow flare and built out forecastle side tended to assist dryness in head seas although in *Queen Elizabeth* this was offset to some extent by the considerable increase in draft and displacement with a corresponding loss of freeboard and stability. Armament modifications were as in *Valiant*.
2. Air warning radar was fitted in January 1941 (Type 279), with an aerial at each masthead. Improved MF/DF as in *Valiant*.
3. Searchlight modifications as in *Valiant*.
4. Aircraft equipment as in *Valiant* except straight instead of bent arm cranes.
5. Protection modifications as in *Valiant*.
6. New machinery and boilers as in *Valiant*.
7. Rig modified as in *Valiant* except that tripod legs (raked forward) were added to mainmast. Hull superstructure and funnel were camouflaged.

MODIFICATIONS TO OTHER SHIPS OF THE CLASS

Type 79Z air warning radar in *Valiant* replaced by Type 279 (by March 1940).

QUEEN ELIZABETH

Armoured deck as reconstructed, 1940

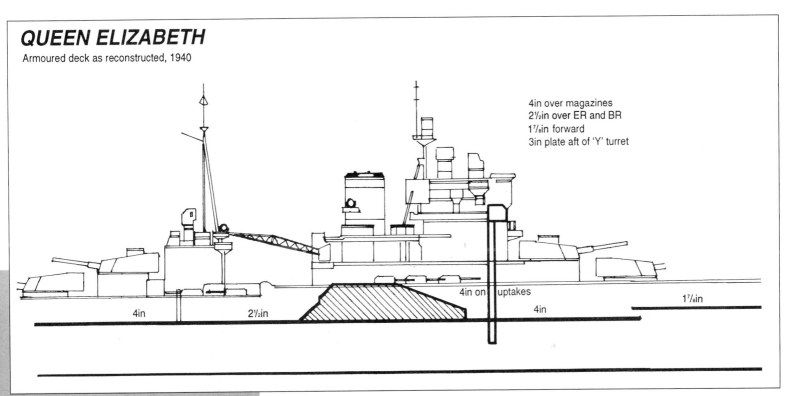

4in over magazines
2½in over ER and BR
1⅞in forward
3in plate aft of 'Y' turret

4in on uptakes

4in   2½in   4in   1⅞in

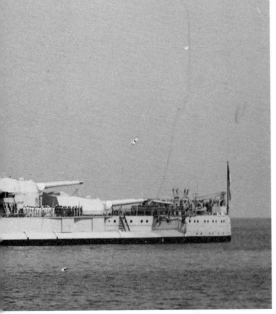

Main topgallant removed in *Malaya* and short topmast fitted to foremast.

Camouflage painted up in *Malaya* (1940), deleted in June 1941.

1941–3:

1. Radar control (Type 284) fitted for main armament in all except *Barham* (1941). In *Queen Elizabeth* Type 285 (high angle) aerial used in conjunction with the 284 set. *Valiant* and *Warspite* did not have this in the Matapan action, 28 March 1941 (fitted at Alexandria later). Radar control Type 285 fitted for 4.5in and 4in AA in all except *Barham*. Fitting in *Queen Elizabeth* commenced February 1941, others later. Fitted in *Malaya* by July 1941. Bridge work added around 4in AA in *Malaya*. Light AA generally increased. Multiple 2pdr (four barrels) added on 'B' turret in *Barham* (1941). Multiple 2pdr (eight barrels) added port and starboard on after superstructure in *Malaya* (1942–3). 0.5in removed and varying numbers of twin and single 20mm AA added on superstructures, turrets and quarterdeck, right aft. Quarterdeck 20mm in *Queen Elizabeth* replaced by DF aerial (1943). *Valiant* and *Warspite* carried 20mm on all turrets in 1943, *Malaya* and *Queen Elizabeth* on 'B' and 'X' only.

Radar control (Type 282) for close-range barrage fire fitted for 2pdrs and twin 20mm. Fitted in *Queen Elizabeth* June 1941. LAA directors added in *Warspite* as for *Queen Elizabeth* and *Valiant*. In *Malaya* these were located in cupolas port and starboard over bridge.

2. Air warning radar (Type 281) added in *Barham*, *Malaya* and *Warspite* aerial at each masthead. Surface warning radar (Type 273) added 1942–3. Aerial on maintop in *Malaya*, on foretop in others. Improved MF/DF equipment fitted in *Malaya* and *Warspite* (as *Queen Elizabeth* and *Valiant*). Aerial and after superstructure in *Malaya* and on face of bridge tower in *Warspite*. Additional DF aerial fitted on quarterdeck right aft in *Queen Elizabeth*, replaced 20mm AA.

3. Prominent ventilating trunks added at base of mainmast in *Malaya* (1942–3). Stern walk removed in *Queen Elizabeth* 1943.

VALIANT: PROFILES, 1924 AND 1940

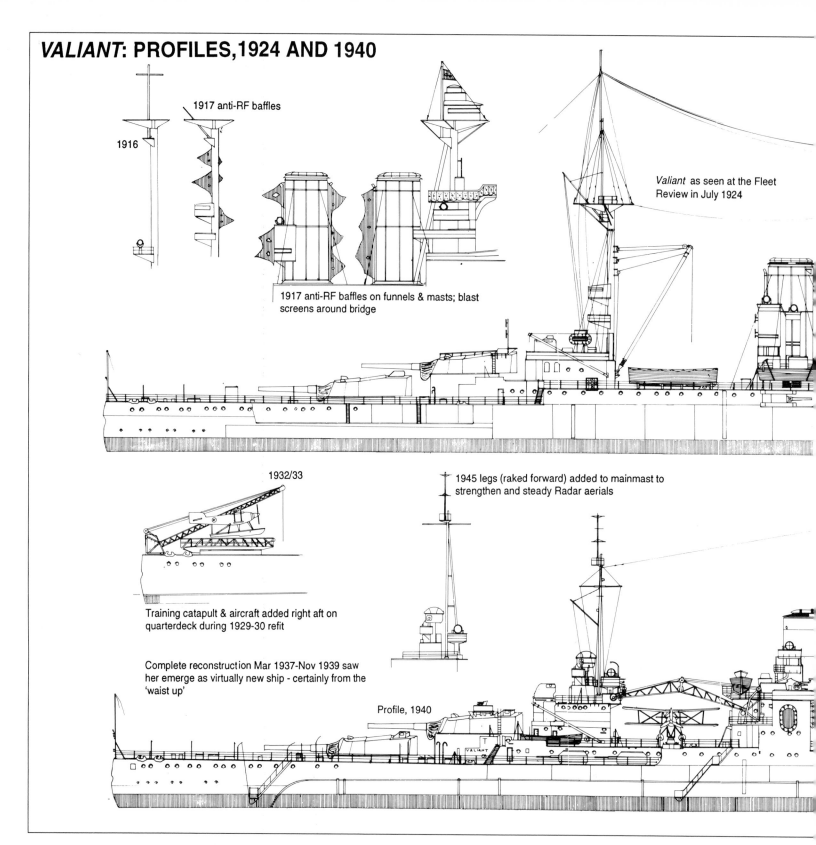

1916

1917 anti-RF baffles

1917 anti-RF baffles on funnels & masts; blast screens around bridge

Valiant as seen at the Fleet Review in July 1924

1932/33

Training catapult & aircraft added right aft on quarterdeck during 1929-30 refit

1945 legs (raked forward) added to mainmast to strengthen and steady Radar aerials

Complete reconstruction Mar 1937-Nov 1939 saw her emerge as virtually new ship - certainly from the 'waist up'

Profile, 1940

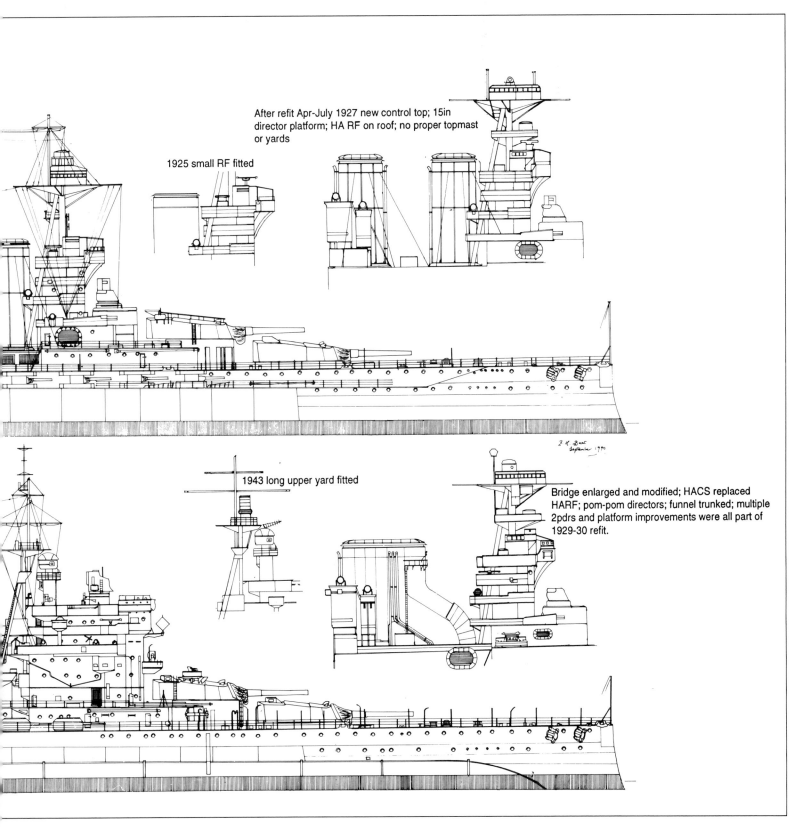

After refit Apr-July 1927 new control top; 15in director platform; HA RF on roof; no proper topmast or yards

1925 small RF fitted

1943 long upper yard fitted

Bridge enlarged and modified; HACS replaced HARF; pom-pom directors; funnel trunked; multiple 2pdrs and platform improvements were all part of 1929-30 refit.

4. Camouflage painted up in *Malaya*, *Valiant* and *Warspite* (see camouflage chapter).

1944:

1. Aircraft not carried after 1944. Hangars and cranes retained.

2. Pacific-pattern camouflage painted up in *Queen Elizabeth* and *Valiant* (in Eastern Fleet).

1945:

Proposed in January 1945 to fit improved radar in *Queen Elizabeth* and *Valiant* as opportunity occurred. Gunnery Type 284 to be replaced by Type 274. Surface warning Type 273 by 277. Surface warning Type 268 (navigational) and air-surface warning Type 293 added. These

modifications actually carried out only in *Valiant* during a refit in 1945–6.

BATTLE DAMAGE

Barham, torpedoed 28 December 1939

While on a zigzag course at 19 knots off the west coast of Scotland in position 58° 47' N, 8° 05' W, *Barham* was torpedoed on the port side abreast 'A' and 'B' shell rooms (48 station) at a depth of about 18–20 feet. A column of spray shot up to about 150–200 feet and fell back on the vessel, inundating the bridge, boats and personnel in the vicinity. All water protection compartments were full at the time of the explosion which occurred at the forward end of the bulge

where the protection offered was necessarily less because of the 'run in' of the bulge structure. Generally all compartments abreast 'A' and 'B' shell rooms on the port side flooded immediately. 'A' shell room and 'A' magazine filled quickly, but six of the ten occupants escaped. 'B' shell room and 'B' magazine filled up slowly. At the time of the explosion watertight doors were in the cruising state, i.e., 'X' and 'Y' doors were closed and clipped except a few that had been left open by special permission of DCO of the Watch. Damage control worked perfectly.

Immediately after the explosion *Barham* took a heel of 7° to port which was quickly arrested by transfer of oil fuel. No water was admitted into the ship for correction of heel and trim until she

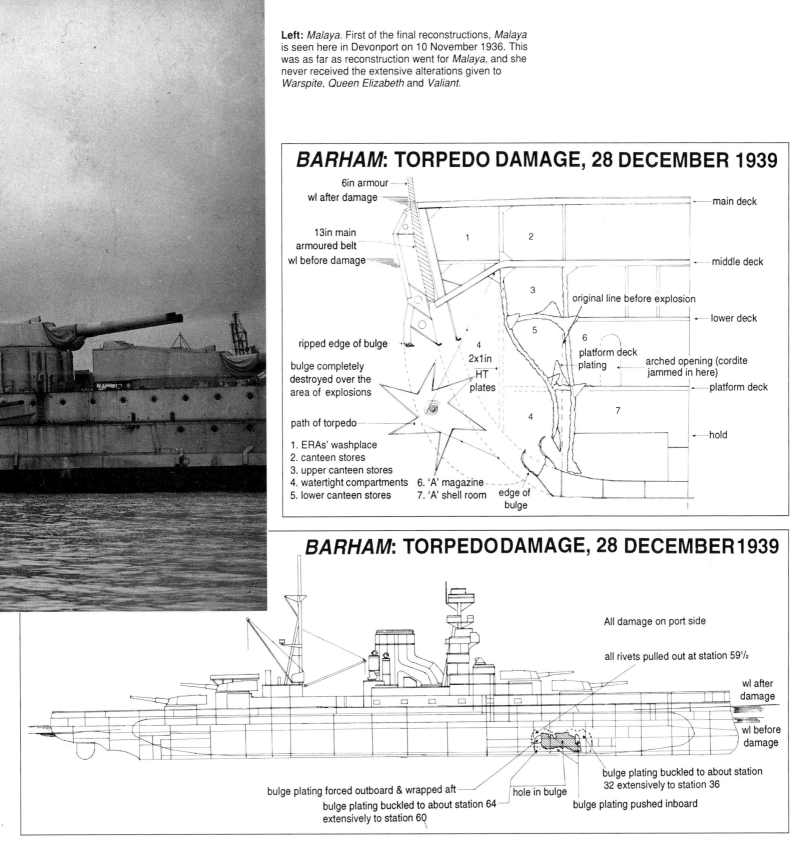

Left: *Malaya*. First of the final reconstructions, *Malaya* is seen here in Devonport on 10 November 1936. This was as far as reconstruction went for *Malaya*, and she never received the extensive alterations given to *Warspite*, *Queen Elizabeth* and *Valiant*.

BARHAM: TORPEDO DAMAGE, 28 DECEMBER 1939

6in armour
wl after damage
main deck

13in main
armoured belt
wl before damage
middle deck

original line before explosion
lower deck

ripped edge of bulge

bulge completely destroyed over the area of explosions

path of torpedo

4
2x1in
HT
plates

5
6
platform deck plating

arched opening (cordite jammed in here)

platform deck

4
7

hold

edge of bulge

1. ERAs' washplace
2. canteen stores
3. upper canteen stores
4. watertight compartments
5. lower canteen stores
6. 'A' magazine
7. 'A' shell room

BARHAM: TORPEDO DAMAGE, 28 DECEMBER 1939

All damage on port side

all rivets pulled out at station 59½

wl after damage

wl before damage

bulge plating forced outboard & wrapped aft
bulge plating buckled to about station 64 extensively to station 60
hole in bulge
bulge plating buckled to about station 32 extensively to station 36
bulge plating pushed inboard

QUEEN ELIZABETH, MALAYA AND WARSPITE: MODIFICATIONS, 1920-37

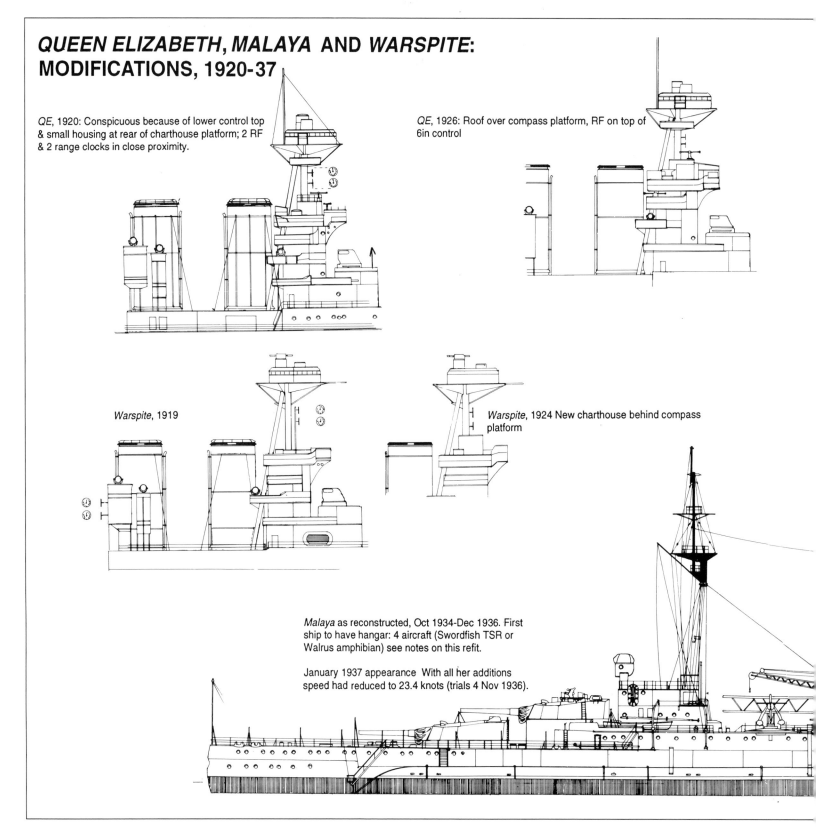

QE, 1920: Conspicuous because of lower control top & small housing at rear of charthouse platform; 2 RF & 2 range clocks in close proximity.

QE, 1926: Roof over compass platform, RF on top of 6in control

Warspite, 1919

Warspite, 1924 New charthouse behind compass platform

Malaya as reconstructed, Oct 1934-Dec 1936. First ship to have hangar: 4 aircraft (Swordfish TSR or Walrus amphibian) see notes on this refit.

January 1937 appearance With all her additions speed had reduced to 23.4 knots (trials 4 Nov 1936).

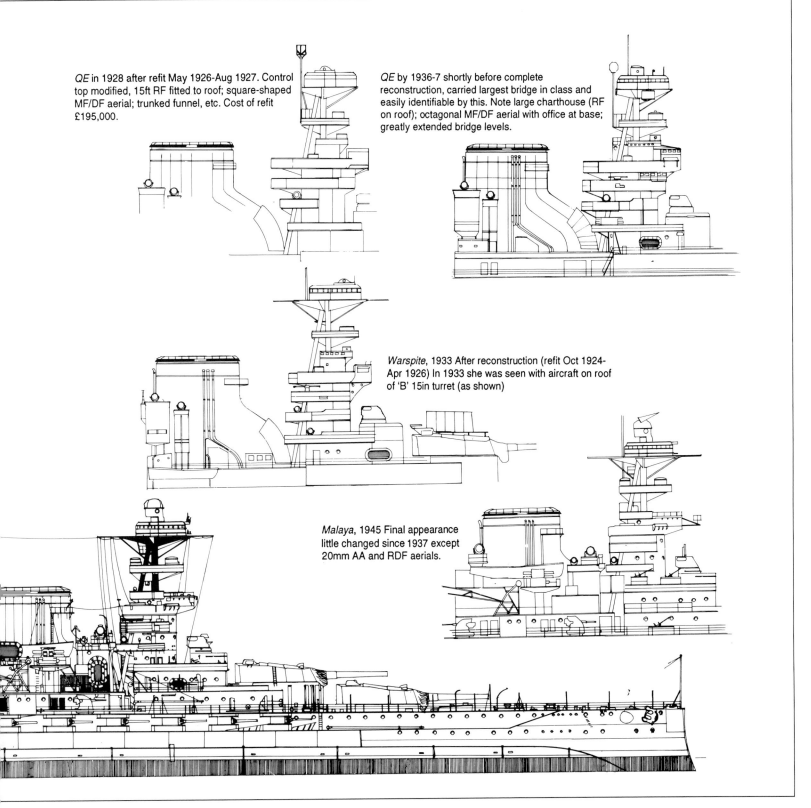

QE in 1928 after refit May 1926-Aug 1927. Control top modified, 15ft RF fitted to roof; square-shaped MF/DF aerial; trunked funnel, etc. Cost of refit £195,000.

QE by 1936-7 shortly before complete reconstruction, carried largest bridge in class and easily identifiable by this. Note large charthouse (RF on roof); octagonal MF/DF aerial with office at base; greatly extended bridge levels.

Warspite, 1933 After reconstruction (refit Oct 1924-Apr 1926) In 1933 she was seen with aircraft on roof of 'B' 15in turret (as shown)

Malaya, 1945 Final appearance little changed since 1937 except 20mm AA and RDF aerials.

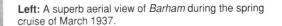

Left: A superb aerial view of *Barham* during the spring cruise of March 1937.

returned to dock. The main engines were still working satisfactorily and she made off at 10 knots increasing to 16 knots later. Distance to port was about 380 nautical miles zigzagging. There was no failure of primary lighting and the secondary lighting was generally satisfactory. The explosion caused no damage to the primary or secondary high-angle armament except that of flooding. There was no fire on board and no secondary explosion. None of the vent plates on the bulge in the vicinity of the explosion were blown off or strained.

STRUCTURAL DAMAGE:

In general the bulge plating was ruptured and thrown away from 39 station to $55^{1}/_{2}$ station – a length of 32 feet. Vertically the main rupture extended from the lower edge of the bulge to the lower edge of the sixth strake of bulge plating – a vertical distance of about 17 feet. The approximate centre of the damage was at 48 station. Here the outer bottom was turned up and forced inboard above the third longitudinal, and heavily corrugated below the third longitudinal as far as the middle line. The damage faded out at about stations 36 and 60. Inboard of the rupture in the bulge plating the ship's outer bottom (40lb) and inner bottom (14lb) plating (and framing) was missing or turned inboard over an area almost identical with that of the rupture in the outer bulge plating. The thick bulkhead (two in number, 40lb HT) was forced inboard and torn away at its bottom connection. At the point of maximum deflection it was forced back sufficiently far to have touched the magazine shellroom longitudinal bulkhead (port), but was later made about 12 inches clear of that bulkhead. The maximum deflection at 48 station was about 78 inches.

The thick bulkhead had two major ruptures, one almost exactly opposite the centre of the damage running the full depth of the bulkhead and with a maximum opening of about 12 inches; the second started at the bottom edge at a butt at 42 station. The third longitudinal bulkhead, inboard of the thick bulkhead, was also set in and ruptured. Generally tranverse bulkheads between 36 station and 68 station were buckled.

Casualties: four killed and two wounded.

The general effect of the explosion was localized to a remarkable extent and the damage in no way affected the fighting efficiency of the ship. The damage control officer of the watch had kept a pegged record of the doors which

WARSPITE: PROFILE AND INBOARD AS RECONSTRUCTED, 1937-8

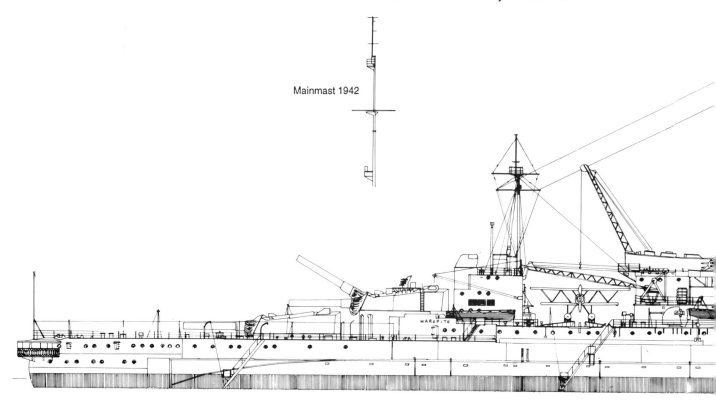

Mainmast 1942

Inboard profile
1. Shell rooms
2. Boiler rooms
3. Engine & machinery rooms
4. Hangars
5. Steering compartments
6. Catapult area

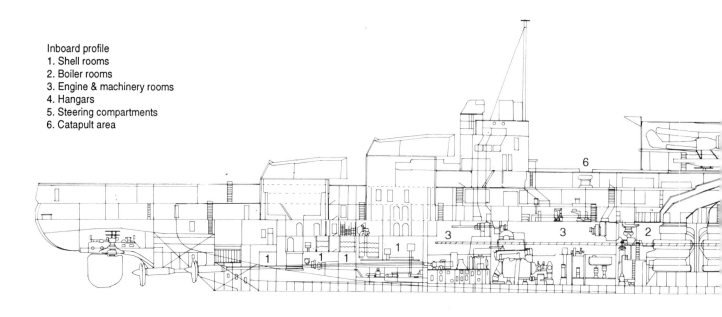

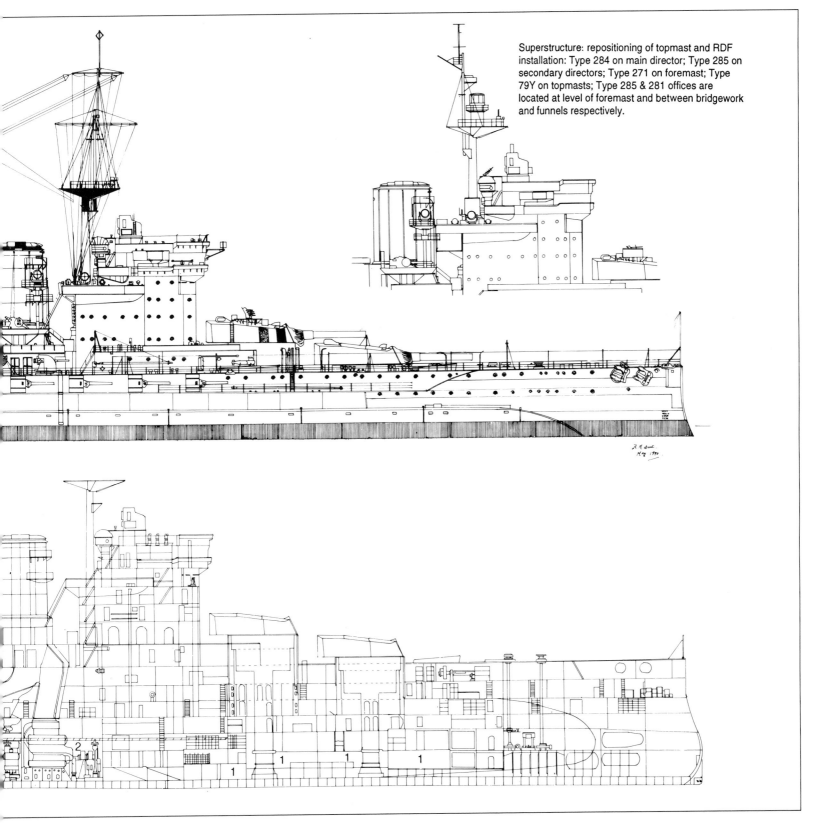

Superstructure: repositioning of topmast and RDF installation: Type 284 on main director; Type 285 on secondary directors; Type 271 on foremast; Type 79Y on topmasts; Type 285 & 281 offices are located at level of foremast and between bridgework and funnels respectively.

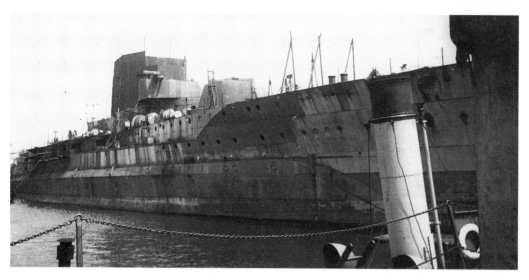

voy from long range and not specifically aimed at *Malaya* which at the time was making only 7 knots.

On reaching Trinidad divers were put over to inspect the damage although conditions were not good for a thorough survey at that time. The following damage was noted however: 1. Three armour plates had been forced in above turtle back, and ship's side immediately below had a horizontal split approximately 14 feet long and 4 inches wide. 2. Ship's side was badly dented below split. 3. All adjacent upper and lower bulges had been blown away.

No major damage was done to any of the armament. 15 inch: The flooding of No. 2 hydraulic room necessitated changing over to duplicate pressure in 'B' turret, and meant that only three pumps were available for the four turrets. No machinery in the turrets was in any way affected. 6in: P.4 mounting was jammed for director training by the shock of the explosion, and this was rectified after two hours' work by the ship's crew. The remaining mountings were quite undamaged but P.2 and P.3 jumped teeth on the director elevating drive and black pointer adjustments were necessary. The entire battery could have been used at any time in Gunlayer's firing. 4in and close range: No damage of any kind sustained.

Engine Room: small leaks and drips were noted in many of the compartments forward of 82 Station and below armoured deck (middle). These leaks were present where pipes, ventilation shafts, etc., passed through the armoured deck. It appeared that as the armoured deck was laid on top of the original middle deck, water could circulate in the space between and thus cause leaks.

Leaks were noted in: forward dressing station; lower conning tower flat; 'A' space; 'B' space; searchlight stabilizing room; gunner's store.

After temporary repairs *Malaya* sailed for the USA where permanent repairs kept her out of action for four months.

were open and had men standing by to shut them as soon as the order to do so was given. Damage control arrangements not only worked perfectly, but an engineer officer had been detailed especially for this task and for three months prior to this incident had had no other duties except watch-keeping.

One particularly interesting fact was that none of the vent plates in the bulge had blown off or even showed signs of strain. The fact that they were specifically designed to blow out on such an occasion indicates that the theory of vent plates did not necessarily hold up in practice.

Draught of ship before explosion 31ft mean; after explosion, 41ft 6in forward, 27ft aft. On entering dock, 35ft 2½in forward, 32ft 11in aft.

Malaya Torpedoed by U81 off Cape Verde Islands, 20 March 1941

While on convoy duties *Malaya* was hit by a torpedo on the port side just abaft 82 bulkhead abreast the forebridge, and sustained considerable damage. Draught before the explosion was 33ft forward and 32 ft aft, but one hour after the hit this increased to 35ft and 33ft respectively. The ship listed 1½° to port. The torpedo track was seen from the upper conning tower deck at about 50 yards, approaching from Red 70°. The track was visible for about two seconds and appeared almost to have reached the ship when the explosion occurred. It was concluded that the torpedo had been running at a shallow depth setting and therefore had been fired at the con-

Warspite and Valiant Damaged By Enemy Air Attack off Crete, 22 May 1941

Warspite and *Valiant* were bombed by Messerschmitt Bf 109s and both ships sustained more than superficial damage. *Warspite* was flying the flag of Rear-Admiral H. B. Rawlings, OBE, and

Below: *Warspite* starboard bow view, March 1937.

was in company with *Valiant, Gloucester, Fiji* and seven destroyers (*Napier, Hero, Hereward, Isis, Decoy, Greyhound* and *Griffin*). In response to a request for assistance from Rear-Admiral, 15th Cruiser Squadron in HMS *Naiad*, the ships were steaming on a north-easterly course at 20 knots, and had just passed through the Kithera Channel. Considerable air opposition had been met during the forenoon, and as many hostile aircraft were in sight at varying distances, the ship's company was at Retire Stations, with all HA Armament and supply manned.

Three Messerschmitt Bf 109s were sighted right ahead coming out of the haze at about 2,000 yards, having already commenced their dive on the ship. Each aircraft dropped one bomb estimated to be of at least 500lb calibre. The bombs were dropped within a few seconds of one another from a height of approximately 800 feet, almost immediately after the aircraft had been sighted. About 120 rounds were fired

from the machine-guns, but the pom-poms did not fire. Before avoiding action had become effective a hit was received on the starboard side next to the foremost 4in gun mounting. The second bomb fell 50 yards clear of the starboard side, the third fell about 100 yards right ahead.

The first bomb passed through the forecastle deck about 6 inches from the ship's side just before the starboard forward twin 4in HA gun mounting, then passed through 112 battery bulkhead under the beam, hit the upper deck at 116 station 1 inch from ship's side, shot slightly inboard (not piercing the deck) and burst either on 125 battery bulkhead or upper deck at approximately 124 station 12 inches from ship's side. Angle of descent 44° to 45°. Distance of point of strike to point of burst approximately 29 feet. Thickness of plates through which the bomb passed, and particulars of other obstructions between point of strike and point of burst: 1. Forecastle deck, 1in HT and ½in double plat-

ing for forward 4in HA mounting; 2. Battery bulkhead, 1½in HT; 3. Upper deck, 1¼in and ¾ HT.

Major damage sustained: forecastle deck, holed in stringer and two adjacent strakes of plating between stations 114 and 137, with beams under blown up with deck (destroyed over an area of 90ft x 30ft); bent up between stations 98 and 140, approximate maximum 1ft 4in; between stations 112 and 125 the fore and aft girder under deck distorted and partly blown away; upper deck, hole in strake adjacent to stringer plate between stations 120 and 126 (upper deck bulged downwards over an area 130ft long x 30ft wide); blown down between stations 86 and 146, approximate maximum 2 feet; beams broken at stations 122 and 124; fore and aft girder distorted from stations 106 to 118; pillars, main to upper decks distorted at stations 100, 106, 112, 124 and 134; No. 3 boiler room intake between forecastle and fan casings blown

WARSPITE: AS RECONSTRUCTED 1937, GENERAL ARRANGEMENTS AND RIG PROFILE

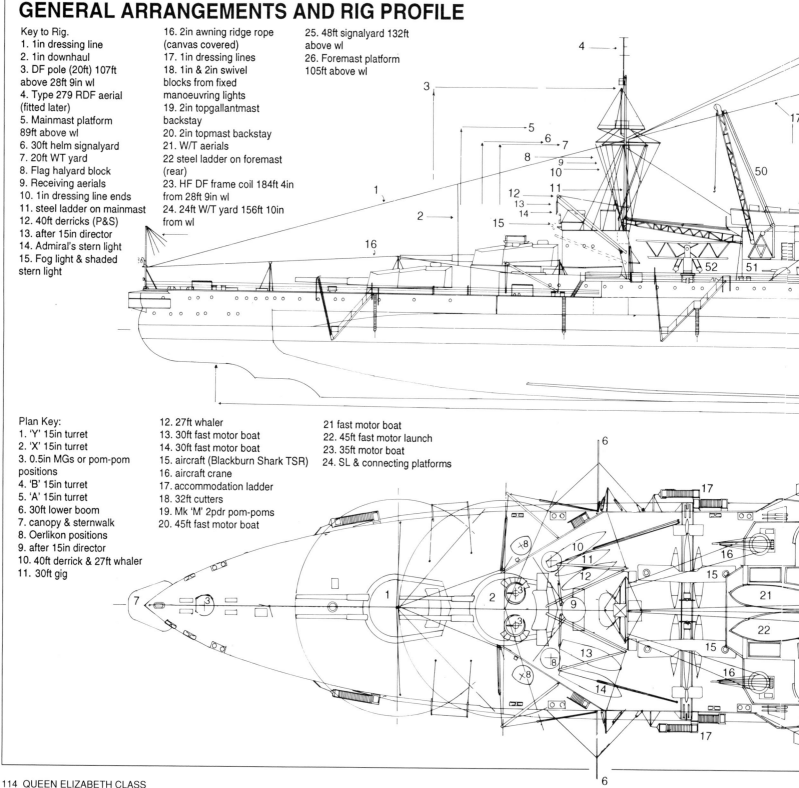

Key to Rig.
1. 1in dressing line
2. 1in downhaul
3. DF pole (20ft) 107ft above 28ft 9in wl
4. Type 279 RDF aerial (fitted later)
5. Mainmast platform 89ft above wl
6. 30ft helm signalyard
7. 20ft WT yard
8. Flag halyard block
9. Receiving aerials
10. 1in dressing line ends
11. steel ladder on mainmast
12. 40ft derricks (P&S)
13. after 15in director
14. Admiral's stern light
15. Fog light & shaded stern light
16. 2in awning ridge rope (canvas covered)
17. 1in dressing lines
18. 1in & 2in swivel blocks from fixed manoeuvring lights
19. 2in topgallantmast backstay
20. 2in topmast backstay
21. W/T aerials
22 steel ladder on foremast (rear)
23. HF DF frame coil 184ft 4in from 28ft 9in wl
24. 24ft W/T yard 156ft 10in from wl
25. 48ft signalyard 132ft above wl
26. Foremast platform 105ft above wl

Plan Key:
1. 'Y' 15in turret
2. 'X' 15in turret
3. 0.5in MGs or pom-pom positions
4. 'B' 15in turret
5. 'A' 15in turret
6. 30ft lower boom
7. canopy & sternwalk
8. Oerlikon positions
9. after 15in director
10. 40ft derrick & 27ft whaler
11. 30ft gig
12. 27ft whaler
13. 30ft fast motor boat
14. 30ft fast motor boat
15. aircraft (Blackburn Shark TSR)
16. aircraft crane
17. accommodation ladder
18. 32ft cutters
19. Mk 'M' 2pdr pom-poms
20. 45ft fast motor boat
21 fast motor boat
22. 45ft fast motor launch
23. 35ft motor boat
24. SL & connecting platforms

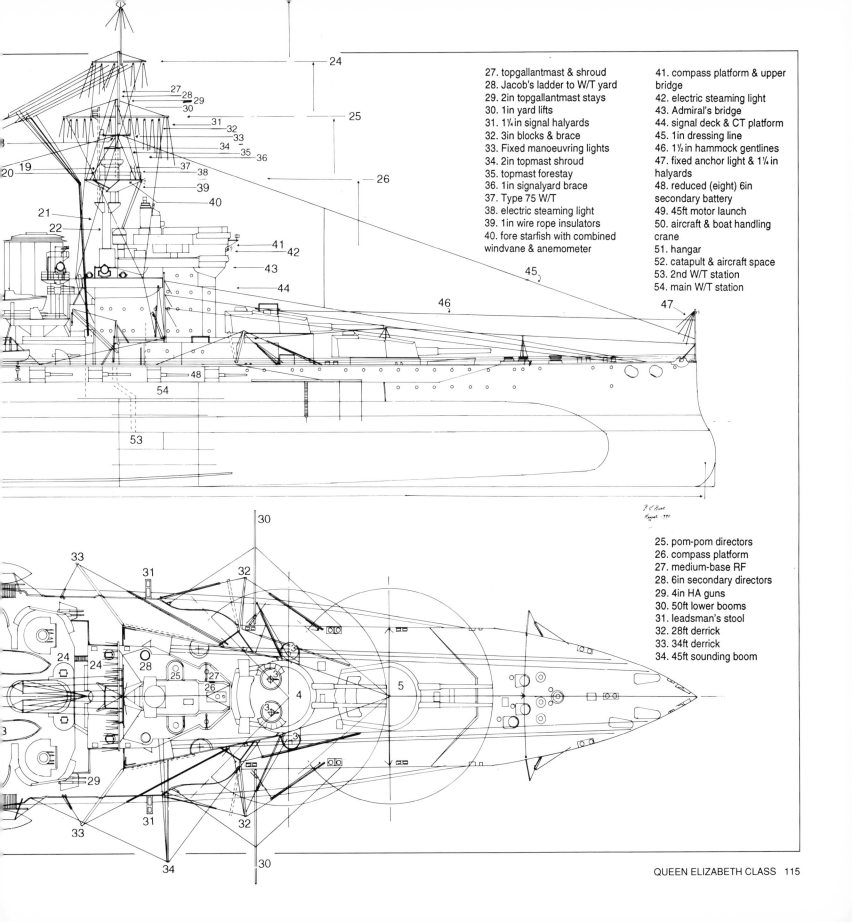

27. topgallantmast & shroud
28. Jacob's ladder to W/T yard
29. 2in topgallantmast stays
30. 1in yard lifts
31. 1¼in signal halyards
32. 3in blocks & brace
33. Fixed manoeuvring lights
34. 2in topmast shroud
35. topmast forestay
36. 1in signalyard brace
37. Type 75 W/T
38. electric steaming light
39. 1in wire rope insulators
40. fore starfish with combined windvane & anemometer

41. compass platform & upper bridge
42. electric steaming light
43. Admiral's bridge
44. signal deck & CT platform
45. 1in dressing line
46. 1½in hammock gentlines
47. fixed anchor light & 1¼in halyards
48. reduced (eight) 6in secondary battery
49. 45ft motor launch
50. aircraft & boat handling crane
51. hangar
52. catapult & aircraft space
53. 2nd W/T station
54. main W/T station

25. pom-pom directors
26. compass platform
27. medium-base RF
28. 6in secondary directors
29. 4in HA guns
30. 50ft lower booms
31. leadsman's stool
32. 28ft derrick
33. 34ft derrick
34. 45ft sounding boom

WARSPITE: BOMB DAMAGE, MAY 1941

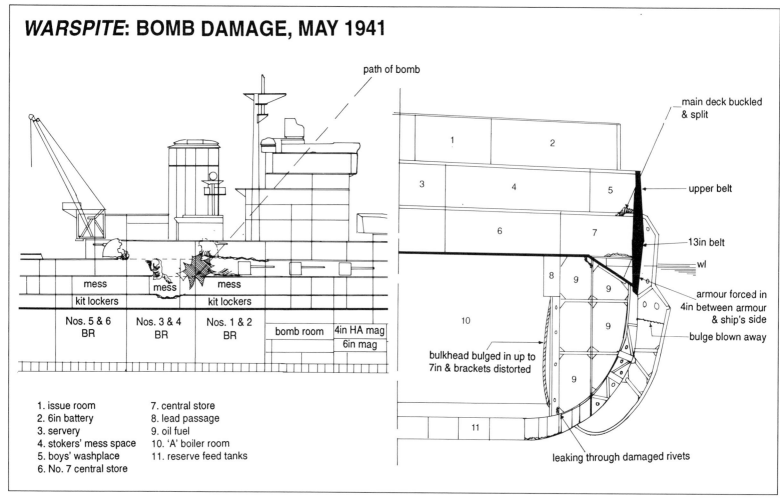

1. issue room
2. 6in battery
3. servery
4. stokers' mess space
5. boys' washplace
6. No. 7 central store
7. central store
8. lead passage
9. oil fuel
10. 'A' boiler room
11. reserve feed tanks

path of bomb

main deck buckled & split

upper belt

13in belt

wl

armour forced in

4in between armour & ship's side

bulge blown away

leaking through damaged rivets

bulkhead bulged in up to 7in & brackets distorted

mess

kit lockers

mess

mess

kit lockers

Nos. 5 & 6 BR

Nos. 3 & 4 BR

Nos. 1 & 2 BR

bomb room

4in HA mag

6in mag

---

in; ship's side plating, forecastle to upper decks, stations 103 to 118, plating hinged from forecastle deck and blown outboard; stations 118 to 127, plating blown out from fore end; 118 bulkhead between main and upper decks compressed; starboard after 4in HA guns support – plating holed and stiffeners distorted (size of hole approximately 1 foot x 10 inches); battery bulkhead, 112 station, distorted and inboard end blown forward approximately 5ft 6in; battery bulkhead, 115 station, shattered from ship's side to vertical welded butt, 18 inches away from doorway and blown aft. Door to bulkhead blown aft, weld round hinges on bulkhead sheared. 6in gun plate bracket supports under upper deck at stations 105 and 118 distorted. Starboard forward pom-pom gun support and deck lifted approximately 12 inches.

Minor damage: main deck bent down between 120 and 126 stations for a diameter of 5 feet to a depth of 5 inches and pierced in three places by holes of 1ft x 3in, 6in x 2in and 3in x 1¹/₂in; bulwark splinter protection blown off from forward

face of forward 4in HA gun to 130 station. Shelter deck bent up approximately 1 foot on each side of pom-pom ready use magazine and holed at 124 station. Superstructure bulkheads above point of burst, split and distorted. Pom-pom platform blast screens holed and distorted. Deck of forward pom pom ready use magazine holed, size 1 foot x 4 inches. Divisional bulkheads of warrant officers' and gun room messes, pantrys, galleys and drying room severely damaged. Warrant officers' mess wrecked. Gunroom mess severely damaged and galley-fittings smashed (ovens remained in quite good state). Note: The damage abaft 125 bulkhead was mostly caused by fragments from that bulkhead when it was shattered. Bakery bulkhead distorted, ovens torn out and fittings damaged. Scupper pipe fractured, main to upper deck at 124 station. Fire main, fresh and salt water services, heating steam and other small pipes fractured and damaged in vicinity of explosion. Large amount of ventilation trunking including that of No. 3 dynamo destroyed in vicinity.

Extent of damage caused by blast effect: ship's side, 103 to 127 stations, blown out (forecastle to upper deck); forecastle deck bent up between 98 and 140 stations approximately maximum 1 foot 4 inches; upper deck bent down between 86 and 146 stations approximate maximum 2 feet, distorting beams, etc. and S.3 and S.4 plate bracket supports; 118 bulkhead between upper and main decks compressed; 112 battery bulkhead blown forward and inboard approximately 5 feet 6 inches; divisional bulkheads of warrant Officers' mess, galleys, drying room and bakery distorted; shelter deck, superstructure bulkheads, pom-pom gun decks and blast screens distorted; No. 125 battery bulkhead on fragmenting, pierced after 4in HA gun support and divisional bulkheads at 141¹/₂ and 158 stations, also cutting ship's side from 154 station; fresh and salt water services damaged in vicinity of explosion and by upper deck being bent down; No. 3 boiler room fan downtake casing blown out from forecastle deck to fan casings.

Extent of damage caused by splinter effect (bomb appears to have fragmented thoroughly): On 112 and 125 battery bulkheads, inside ship's side and on deck plating and beams under forecastle deck were numerous pit-marks of sizes varying from ¹/₂in to 2in diameter approximately. Splinters round edges of forecastle and upper decks holed plating. 112 Battery bulkhead holed in three places, sizes 3in x 1in, 2in x 1¹/₂in and ³/₄in diameter. Ship's side plating (forecastle to upper deck) one hole of 4in diameter at 123 station, 4 feet from deck. Beams at 112–144 stations were pierced in several places. Pom-pom gun blast screens pierced with about eight holes of approximately 1¹/₂in diameter. Superstructure, several pit-marks and three holes of 2¹/₂in diameter.

Effect on fighting efficiency of armament: Starboard 6in battery, two of the four guns completely out of action. Two remaining guns in action with primary control and improvised telephones.

The Squadron was turned to the southward and all further attacks on *Warspite* were made by high-level bombers only. The damage to the fan supply of No. 3 boiler caused very thick black smoke to emerge from the funnel, but this was stopped in about ten minutes. Down below, the fire and repair parties, assisted by extra hands from the mess decks, put out the few small fires that occurred in the battery, and then started removing the dead and wounded and clearing up. The dead were buried at sea at about 20.00 hours. The wounded were distributed among the boys' mess deck, the church and office flats near the marines' mess decks, and a part of the marines' mess deck itself.

Damage to structure: The large expanse of forecastle deck and ship's side which were blown away provided a good venting which saved further damage downwards. The thick forecastle deck, coupled with the oblique angle of impact, the low vertical velocity, and the thick upper deck also prevented further downward damage. It is interesting to compare the large expanse of

upper deck dished downwards (130 feet x 30 feet) with the small hole (6in x 8in) in that deck immediately under the burst.

Temporary repairs were completed in one month, but full repair of damage undertaken in USA from August to December 1941.

Valiant was the target of a stick of four bombs, estimated weight 50kg, fuzed direct action and released from about 15,000 feet. The direct hits were scored on the upper deck port side, one just abaft 196 station and the other just abaft 210 station. One near miss bomb burst about 4 feet below water and close to the bulge plating on the port side abreast 126¹/₂ station. Another near miss bomb burst off the port side between 50 to 60 stations and caused no damage. Detonation was complete, only a few small fragments being found.

First hit, structural damage: The bomb struck the upper deck (30lb HT on 30lb HT) port side just abaft 196 station about 12 feet from the ship's side and burst on impact. It made a hole about 4 feet square in the deck and splinters perforated the 20lb superstructure side plating and fittings in the vicinity. The 10lb WT bulkhead 196 between the main and upper decks was fractured and distorted and the top boundary angle was torn away and fractured. A number of rivets connecting the angle stiffener to the bulkhead were sheared. The 14lb main deck was perforated in four places and dented in numerous other places. The mess tables and stools on the main deck in the vicinity of the burst were smashed and the 7lb pantry bulkhead at 192 station was perforated. A 15lb hatch coaming about 15 feet from the point of burst was perforated by splinters and the drum of the port after deck winch was fractured and distorted.

Electrical damage: The shore leads to No. 8 dynamo used to supply degaussing 'M' coil, supply and control wiring cables for Nos. 6 and 8 deck winches, permanent emergency leads from the port after breaker compartment to main deck and a number of smaller cables were damaged by splinters.

Incendiary effects: There were no incendiary effects, but thick pungent smoke and fumes on the mess deck abaft 196 bulkhead, port, were cleared rapidly by opening the upper deck hatch.

Effect on fighting efficiency – nil.

Second hit, structural damage: The bomb struck the upper deck port side at the junction of the 30lb deck stringer plate and the 25lb sheer strake of the shell plating just abaft 210 station, and burst on impact. It made a hole about 3 feet x 1 feet 6 inches in the deck and 3 feet x 1 foot in the ship's side and destroyed the $3^{1}/_{2}$in x $3^{1}/_{2}$in x 10lb deck boundary angle in way of hole. The 'Z' bar frame and bulb beam at 210 station were distorted. The rivets in the flanged connectcion were sheared and the bracket distorted. A 15lb hatch coaming about 30 feet from the point of burst was perforated by splinters. The guard rail stanchions in the vicinity of the burst were fractured and a part of one was blown a distance of about 150 feet to the hangar top where it pierced the side of the 45ft motor launch. The barbette armour of 'Y' turret was scored in numerous places, in some cases to a depth of half an inch. The degaussing 'Q' coil, which was laid on the deck inboard of the guard stanchions, was severed.

Effect on fighting efficiency – nil.

Near miss, structural damage: The bomb burst about 4 feet below the water close to the bulge

plating port side abreast $126^{1}/_{2}$ station and caused a hole about 4 feet wide x 7 feet deep in the 30lb 'H' strake of the upper bulge plating between $125^{1}/_{2}$ and $127^{1}/_{2}$ stations. Between $127^{1}/_{2}$ and $129^{1}/_{2}$ stations the plating was forced inwards and the rivets in the top and bottom laps were sheared. In the upper bulge the 20lb WT bulkhead at $125^{1}/_{2}$ station was distorted and leaked; the rivets through the outer boundary angle connection were sheared and the angle distorted. The channel bar frame at $127^{1}/_{2}$ station was destroyed. The channel bar frame at $129^{1}/_{2}$ station was distorted, three rivets were sheared and the flanged bracket at the bottom of the frame was distorted. The ship's side armour was unmarked except for one small indentation. In the lower bulge the 22.5lb top strake of plating forming the crown of the bulge was dished to a maximum of about 3 inches between $125^{1}/_{2}$ to $127^{1}/_{2}$ stations and the butt at $126^{1}/_{2}$ station was opened to a maximum of about $2^{1}/_{2}$ inches at the centre. The rivets through the double riveted butt strap were sheared on the fire side while those on the aft side remained intact.

Damage was repaired in two months.

LOSS OF BARHAM

While cruising in single line with *Queen Elizabeth* and *Valiant* at a speed of 17 knots and zigzagging, *Barham* was torpedoed by *U331* off the Libyan coast 32° 29' N, 26° 27' E at 1630 on 25 November 1941. The following report is from *Valiant* which was at a distance of just under three cables. At 1625 the Officer of the Watch, Sub-Lieutenant D. F. Trench, RN, was taking the distance of *Barham* with the Stewart's Distance Meter, when he observed a large explosion on the port side of *Barham* abreast the mainmast. He realized immediately that *Barham* had been struck by a torpedo fired from somewhere on the port side, and quite correctly ordered 'hard-a-port'.

'1. I was not on the compass platform at the moment of the explosion but on reaching the front of it ten seconds later, I observed a very large column of water and smoke alongside *Barham*, only the after end of the quarterdeck being then visible.

2. I immediately ordered "Full speed ahead together"; at the same time the Officer of the Watch informed me that the wheel was hard-a-

port, and I observed that the ship was just beginning to swing to port under the influence of full port rudder.

3. About fifteen seconds later a submarine broke surface between 5° and 10° on the port bow at a distance of approximately 150 yards and moving from left to right. By then *Valiant* had swung 8° to port, and was therefore heading approximately 260°. The submarine was steering between 050° and 060°; her speed appeared to be about 4 knots.

4. Immediately on sighting the submarine I ordered "Amidships", and then "Hard-a-starboard" in an endeavour to ram her, but before the rudder was hard over it was obvious that it would not be possible to check the swing to port before she was across the bow. Actually the swing was just about checked when the submarine passed down the starboard side, and she submerged again when abreast *Valiant*'s bridge at a distance of about 50 yards. As she appeared on the starboard side S.1 pom-pom fired 19 rounds at her with maximum depression, but all rounds appeared to pass over her. The wheel was then again reversed so as to keep clear of *Barham*.

5. The only portion of the submarine which appeared above water was the periscope and about 2 or 3 feet of the conning tower, which was flat topped. A certain amount of disturbed water before and abaft the conning tower indicated the fore and after ends of the hull, and enabled an accurate estimate of her course to be made.

6. As soon as the smoke and spray had cleared away and *Barham* became visible again, it was seen that she had developed a very heavy list to port, probably about 20° to 30°, as it was observed that the water was level with the after screen door into the lobby at the fore end of the quarterdeck. She appeared to hang in this position for about a minute, when she began to roll over on approximately an even keel.

7. She continued to roll over and sink deeper in the water until the water was seen to be entering the funnel. A moment or two after this there was a loud explosion amidships, and a very large column of black and brown smoke with flame from the explosion in the middle of it shot into the air. This explosion occurred at 1630, or 5 minutes approximately after the torpedoes hit, when *Barham* was just abaft the beam from *Valiant*'s bridge.

Below: *Barham* sinking in November 1941. Two of the most dramatic shots taken during the Second World War show *Barham* mortally wounded after taking three torpedoes in her port side. The first shows her about one minute after the hits and already heeling; the second shows her heeling more and passing the point of maximum stability. Note that she is still steaming at speed.

8. All observers are agreed that, as the torpedoes hit, there were three explosions, a first one, followed about one or two seconds later by two in quick succession, and that the explosions all occurred amidships between the funnel and the mainmast. It was not certain what caused the final explosion but the general opinion was that it was the 6in magazine, and it was certainly not "A" or "B" magazine, as the centre of the explosion was abaft the bridge, and I am of the opinion that it was not as far aft as "X" magazine.

[Signed] C. E. Morgan. Captain'

REPORT BY LIEUTENANT-COMMANDER HMS BARHAM:

'1. At 1610 hours 25th November, 1941, I took over the watch as P.C.O. and A.D.O. Having received reports from all the armament closed up, I entered the chart house to see the cyphers and to acquaint myself with the general situation.

2. Soon after I entered the chart house I heard and felt a violent explosion. I was just outside the chart house on the port side of the bridge when I felt two more explosions about half a second apart. I was looking up for aircraft so did not see where the explosions took place (6in director fouled by view aft). I continued my course to the A.D.P. and reached the after end of the bridge when I felt the fourth explosion and saw a column of water and wreckage thrown up abreast the mainmast on the port side. When I reached the A.D.P. I observed from the mainmast that the ship had a list of 7° or 8° to port. Then a submarine broke surface bearing red 120 about 150–200 yards away pointing towards our stern. I could not communicate with the 6in armament from the A.D.P. and before I could get through to the 4in armament the submarine had dived. (*Valiant* was also foul of the range.) *Valiant* fired a burst of pom-pom at the swirl where the submarine dived and made good shooting but the overs reached *Barham*'s side.

3. I looked aft again and saw that the list had increased slightly in spite of the fact that the ship was altering course rapidly to Port. I then gave the order "On lifebelts" and this was passed by S.P. telephone to all quarters although we could not know whether the orders were received. I then told the director's crew to come down and sent the A.D.P.'s crew down to the starboard

side. At this time, the port side of the boat deck aft was under water and the ship was slowly turning over.

4. All traffic from aloft had ceased and I was left in the A.D.P. with Midshipman D.N.A Cox and one rating. We were not able to go down so hauled ourselves up to the starboard side and waited for the sea to take us out. Our lifebelts were on and inflated.

5. We watched the water swirling over the port side of the A.D.P. and come up to us in about one second. I had no control over my movements in this swirling water and expected soon to be clear. Soon I felt three or four ropes foul me round my stomach and I was drawn down. Whilst I was trying to decide the best means of escape these ropes, which must have been the signal halyards, parted and I started swimming for the surface. I could see that I was going towards the light but it looked a long way. I touched two or three others bound in the same direction but do not know who they were. After some time I thought of taking off my clothes but decided not to as I should have to take off the lifebelt first. I still seemed to have a very long way to go when I took my first mouthful of water and spat it out. Then came complete darkness and silence. I couldn't remember anything of this type in the various stories I have read so I opened my mouth and took in three good deep breaths of air. I had no time to think any further before I was in water again and could see the light a long way above. I went towards the light.

Eventually I came to a mass of feet – it was quite dark and I had great difficulty in finding a space to get through. However, I broke surface in time and was seized by the left arm by a rating who tried to hold me up. I persuaded him to let me go and find my own wreckage.

6. The general behaviour of the men was of the highest standard. In the ship they were cheerful, quiet and tried to help each other and in the water this was so too. They talked to each other quietly and waited patiently for the rescuing boats.

There was no rushing the whaler from *Hotspur* which was nearest to me but an orderly queue of men waiting their turn. When the boat was filled a number of us held on to the lifelines at the sides and were towed to *Hotspur* where we were welcomed with every possible attention and kindness.

7. Officers and men of *Hotspur* gave up blankets and clothes for our benefit and provided cigarettes and refreshment.

8. Since the number rescued in *Hotspur* was nearly twice the complement of the ship the supply of blankets was short. It is suggested that destroyers and craft used in rescue work should carry a stock of blankets for use in such an emergency.

9. On arrival in Alexandria the unwounded went to *Resource* where we bathed and were fed and given shipwreck bags (Red Cross). As far as possible the men were kitted up in the clothing store and all received a very welcome £E.2 with which to buy such little necessities and comforts as could be obtained from the canteen. This was greatly appreciated.

[Signed] Lieut. Commander R.N.'

ACCOUNT BY LIEUTENANT G. M. WOLFE, RN
'At the time of the first explosion, I was just outside my office which was on the port side of the A.D.O. Flat, – that is the first deck above the boat deck on the bridge structure.

Since I was leaving the office, I was facing aft, and saw the flash of the explosion which appeared to be immediately abaft the funnel.

After a slight pause, two further explosions occurred, both slightly further aft.

I crossed immediately to the starboard side, where a crowd was already gathering on the upper deck, and gave my pocket knife to a P.O. who was trying to unlash two Carley Floats which were secured at the bottom of the ladder up to the pom-pom deck.

I went rapidly back to my office for my Burberry, and then returned to the starboard side with some difficulty as there was already an appreciable list. I descended to the upper deck, where the ship's company was already going over the side. I shouted to all near me to follow their example – rather unnecessarily as there was little panic and the men were not wasting any time.

The list was steadily increasing and as everyone about me was over the guard rail, I went over also at a point level with the forward end of the bridge, and slid down to the bilge keel.

By now she was going over fast, and I reached the bottom of the ship, now an almost vertical wall. Here I hesitated, owing to the difficulty of keeping my balance because the final jump

appeared hazardous with the bottom coming up to meet me.

It was then that a big explosion took place aft, and the ship plunged over so rapidly that I was flung backwards into the water with many others.

After being sucked down, we eventually surfaced and I swam over to a Carley Float which appeared close at hand. All trace of the ship had vanished.

I discarded my Burberry, blew up my life belt, and held on to the side of the float with many more until picked up by H.M.S. *Hotspur* one hour later.

[Signed] G. M. Wolfe'

DAMAGE TO QUEEN ELIZABETH AND VALIANT AT ALEXANDRIA

While lying at anchor in Alexandria on 19 December 1941, both *Queen Elizabeth* and *Valiant* were successfully attacked and seriously damaged by Italian 'human torpedoes'.

Queen Elizabeth was anchored in 'S' berth in a depth of about eight fathoms. At approximately 0615 on 19 December 1941 there was an extremely violent explosion under the area of 'B' boiler room. Two Italian frogmen had managed to break through defences and place torpedoes against the hull of the ship. The charge was estimated to be about 500 pounds and had been slung between the keels of the vessel. 'B' boiler room flooded immediately and 'A' boiler room flooded within 30 seconds. 'X' boiler room, Nos. 1 and 2 dynamo rooms, 'A' and 'B' hydraulic rooms and a few other compartments in the area also filled very rapidly, and the ship took a list of $4\frac{1}{2}$ degrees starboard and settled by the bow to about eight feet. Although every effort was made to countermeasure the flooding, it slowly spread to 'Y' boiler room and into compartments before number 82 bulkhead. The lower steering position had also flooded completely by the evening of the 19th.

The condition of the ship before the explosion was: draught: 33ft 5in forward, 32ft 7in aft; after the explosion: draught: 41ft 10in forward, 33ft 10in aft. Damage to hull: The outer 1in plating and the inner bottom including the vertical keel, longitudinals and frames were badly dis-

QUEEN ELIZABETH PROFILE AND PLAN: AS RECONSTRUCTED, 1940

As seen in 1941 after total reconstruction: brand-new from 'B' 15in turret through to 'X' turret (see refit notes)

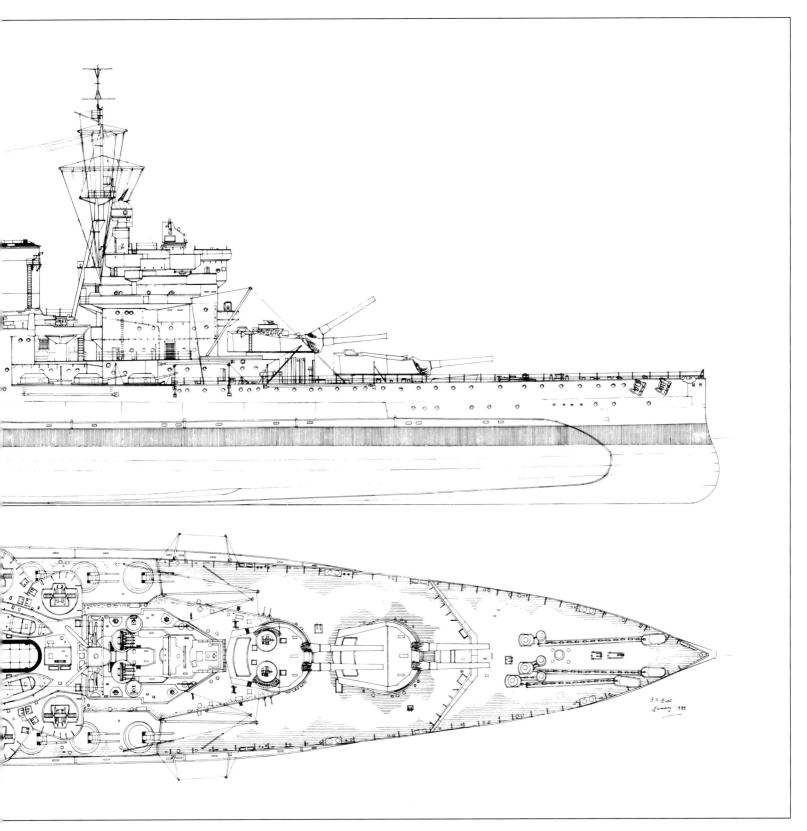

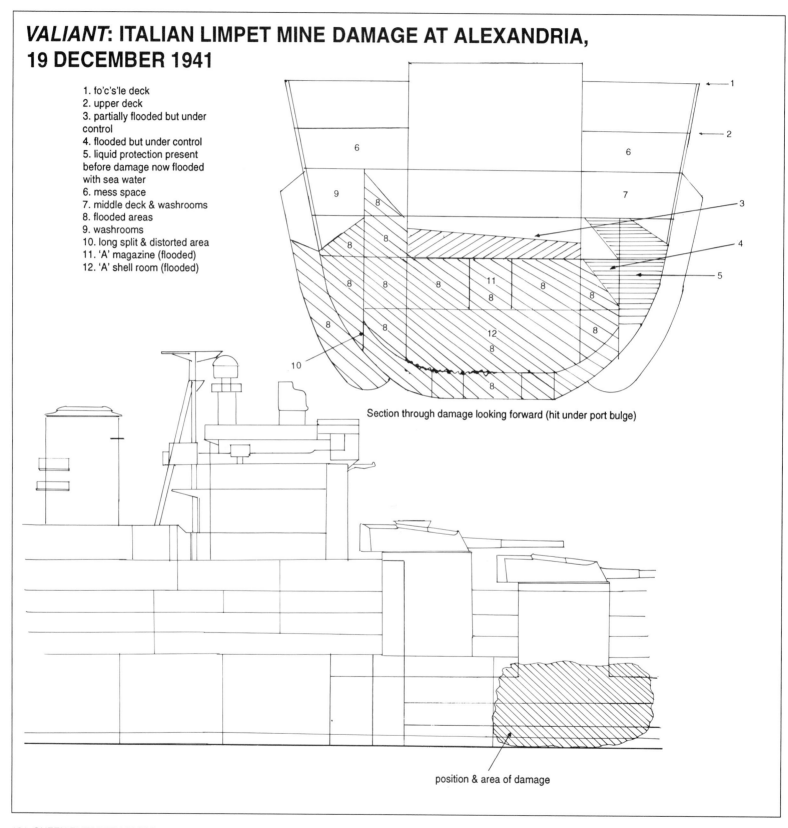

VALIANT: ITALIAN LIMPET MINE DAMAGE AT ALEXANDRIA, 19 DECEMBER 1941

1. fo'c's'le deck
2. upper deck
3. partially flooded but under control
4. flooded but under control
5. liquid protection present before damage now flooded with sea water
6. mess space
7. middle deck & washrooms
8. flooded areas
9. washrooms
10. long split & distorted area
11. 'A' magazine (flooded)
12. 'A' shell room (flooded)

Section through damage looking forward (hit under port bulge)

position & area of damage

torted and fractured between 82 and 120 stations, from 'D' strake port to 'F' strake starboard. The greatest damage was between 100 and 118 stations from 'C' strake port to 'C' strake starboard, both inner and outer bottoms being badly upturned and set up for distances of approximately 22 feet and 16 feet respectively at 112 stations. Between 65 and 132 stations the outer bottom was buckled from 'E' strake port to 'H' strake starboard. The framing between 81 and 82 bulkheads and the pitometer log compartment was distorted between the inner bottom and middle deck between the third longitudinal bulkheads.

100 bulkhead was distorted and fractured to a height of 7 feet above inner bottom, between fifth starboard longitudinal and third port longitudinal. The stiffeners and brackets are distorted. 118 bulkhead was distorted and fractured between third longitudinal port and starboard to a height of six feet above the inner bottom. The third longitudinal bulkhead from 82 to 118 stations port side was slightly buckled between the inner bottom and platform deck and broken away from the bottom boundary angle between 100 and 118 stations. The fifth longitudinal port and starboard sides were distorted between the inner bottom and the platform deck from 82 to 116 stations. The starboard bulkhead was badly buckled between 100 and 118 stations near the bottom.

The following compartments flooded immediately or very rapidly: 'A', 'B' and 'X' boiler rooms; air space 81–82; 'B' hydraulic room; Nos. 1 & 2 dynamo rooms; pitometer log compartment; oil fuel tanks B1-8, C1 and 3, C5 and 8, D1 and 3, D5 and 8; DBCs (68-154) third longitudinal (P) to third longitudinal (S). Bulges 79½–109½ starboard, 109½–119½ port; Wing DBCs 91–118 port, 109–118 starboard.
The following compartments flooded slowly and, in some cases, only partially: Nos. 3, 4 and 5 dynamo rooms; Cable lead passages abreast 'A', 'B' and 'X' boiler rooms; 'A' hydraulic room and searchlight stabilizing room; boiler store; Forward 4.5in magazines port and starboard, and centreline upper and lower 4.5in magazines; DBC (68-82) third longitudinal to sixth longitudinal port and starboard; oil fuel tanks C2, 4, 9, 12, D2, 4, 9, 12; oil fuel working spaces Nos. 1, 3 and 7; hammock and kit locker rooms Nos. 2, 3, 4, 5, 6, 7; builders coaming round boiler

QUEEN ELIZABETH: ITALIAN LIMPET MINE DAMAGE AT ALEXANDRIA, 19 DECEMBER 1941

Section 110
1. mess space
2. washplace 4.5in gun compartments
4. uptakes
5. cable passage
6. reserve feed tank
7. Gear store
8. 9. 10. oil fuel tanks

11. watertight compartments
12. turbo-gen room
13. HP air compressor room

Section 98
1. mess space
2. washplace
3. 4.5in gun compartments
4. dressing-room

5. oil tanks
6. cable passage
7. lobby
8. 9. oil tanks
10. LP air compressor room
11. No. 1 turbo-gen room
12. watertight compartments

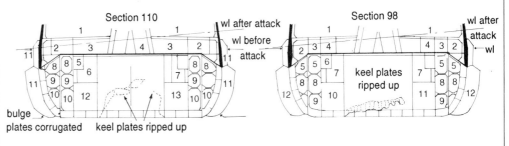

uptakes; lower steering position; low power machine room; protected navigation plot; main switchboard room; fore medical distributing station; No. 2 W/T office; medical store.
On docking the following main items of damage affecting fighting efficiency were found:
(a) Ship unseaworthy.
(b) 'A', 'B' and 'X' boiler rooms out of action.
(c) All evaporators out of action.
(d) Two hydraulic pumps out of action.
(e) All LP compressors out of action.
(f) Nos. 1, 2 and 3 HP compressors out of action.
(g) All oil fuel tanks abreast 'A', 'B' and 'X' boiler rooms out of action.
(h) Main engine room telegraphs out of action.
(i) Forward 4.5in turrets except S.3 out of action through flooded pumps and distorted roller bearing paths.
(j) Only 40 per cent stowage available in lower centre 4.5in magazine.
(k) Forward sections of ring main out of action.
(l) Nos. 1, 2, 3 and 5 dynamos out of action.
(m) No. 2 transmitting room out of action.
(n) Only one set of machinery available for each transmitting room.
(o) Both automatic plots out of action
DAMAGE CONTROL:
No. 82 bulkhead was shored where possible on the fore side. No. 136 bulkhead was shored from inside 'Y' boiler room. 'A' and 'B' boiler room hatches 'A' and 'B' hydraulic room hatches, Nos. 3 and 5 kit locker room hatches and

hatches to escape trunks in Nos. 3, 5 and 7 kit locker rooms were all shored down. All portable pumps were employed in keeping down the water in compartments adjacent to those that were fully flooded by the damage. Heel was corrected by flooding four bulges between 139 and 179 stations. The ship was lightened by every possible means such as de-ammunitioning, de-fuelling from sound tanks, de-petrolling, disembarking all spare anchors and cables, etc.

The ship was docked for temporary repairs to fit her for passage to a refitting yard. It was estimated that she would be able to steam on 'X' and 'Y' boiler rooms. Main armament would be usable in an emergency. The after 4.5in armament would be 100 per cent efficient and a proportion of the forward 4.5in guns would be available.

Valiant

On that fateful day Valiant was moored at Buoy B2 in eight fathoms of water. The explosion took place at 06.06 and caused severe damage to the ship's bottom. Draught before the explosion was 33ft 1in forward, 33ft 1in aft; after the explosion it was 38ft forward and 31ft 6in aft. Heel 4°.

The port 4.5in supply magazine flooded through a split in No. 36 bulkhead and the electricity store immediately above the magazine began to flood through the electric cable gland which blew out of the deck. These compartments were pumped out and 36 bulkhead was shored. Eleven further splits in 36 bulkhead

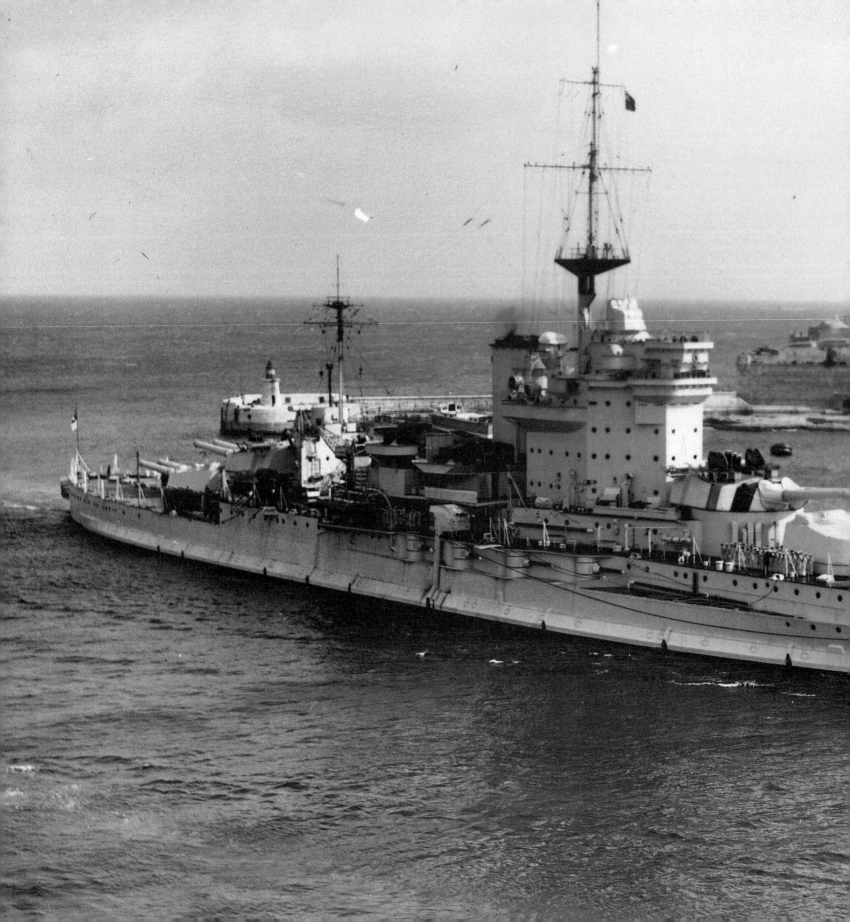

Left: *Warspite* entering Malta in January 1938. Although looking a much 'stumpier' ship than before reconstruction, her masts were still 150ft 6in above the waterline (fore) and 127ft 8in (main).

made it necessary to abandon the 4.5in magazine, but pumping was continued and water was kept to a minimum in these compartments. 'A' turret space was flooded to a depth of 4 feet through splits in the lower deck caused by the head of a pillar protruding through the magazine. This compartment was pumped out. The postmaster's store was flooded to the main deck. The gunners Store (36 to 52 stations, lower and platform decks) were flooded through a vent that had not been fully closed. Small quantities of water seeped through between the armour in the plating of the middle deck into various compartments adjacent to No. 52 bulkhead. All pipes and fittings in the area were badly distorted and pumps were jammed. Plating on the port lower bulge compartment was holed and an area of approximately 60 feet x 30 feet between 29 and 52 stations was damaged. The outer bottom plating (25lb) between 29 and 52 stations was split in many places and pierced by the plate frames. Above the turn of the bilge the bottom plating was crushed into contact with the longitudinal protective bulkhead. The inner bottom was bulged upwards 3 to 4 feet and there were 18in and 16in splits. The keel was arched to an average of 8 inches between 29 and 52 stations. No. 36 bulkhead was buckled. No. 29 was bulged. The platform deck in 'A' magazine was bulged upwards. Deck beams in the area were badly distorted. The lower deck in 'A' turret was also split. There was movement in joints of armour at 'A' barbette and the forecastle deck, 'A' turret shield, 'B' barbette on middle deck. There was no machinery damage. Armament damage: lower part of 'A' turret was distorted.

Damage to Warspite from anti-ship missiles (Type SK1400), 14 Sept 1943

On 14 September 1943 *Warspite* proceeded to Salerno in company with *Valiant* and a destroyer flotilla to support Fifth Army landings by bombarding the beaches. After steaming at 23 knots throughout the night, Salerno Bay was reached next day and enemy positions were attacked during the evening of the 15th despite air attacks. After daybreak on the 16th *Warspite* was detailed to proceed to the area of operations of the previous day, but at 1410, after one shoot, she steamed past the southern swept channel to take part in a further bombardment at position 'Avalanche North'.

Left: Completely reconstructed, *Warspite* underwent a full set of trials. She made 23.84 knots during speed trials, only half a knot slower than when originally built. She is seen here in the Mediterranean on her way to Malta in 1938.

Below left: *Warspite* entering Malta, January 1938.

Below: *Warspite*'s hull, showing some of the damage she received at Salerno.

At 1425 *Warspite* was attacked by twelve Fw 190s which dived on the ship out of the sun. Three bombs were seen overhead close together at 6,000–8,000 yards on the port beam. The parent aircraft were then above the ship at a height of 20,000 feet. When directly overhead the bombs turned and dived at great speed towards the ship. One hit *Warspite* and after penetrating various decks burst in the reserve feed tank below No. 4 boiler room. The other two were near misses on the starboard side. One abreast the bulge midships was the cause of considerable near-miss damage (water hammer), the other caused no apparent damage. At the time of attack the ship was making 10 knots in approximately 177 fathoms. Avoiding action was impossible in the congested area and would, moreover, have been ineffective since the time from sighting the bombs to the hit was only about ten seconds. From the size of the hole of penetration the weapon used was adjudged to be a radio-controlled Type FX1400 weighing about 3,000 pounds with a 600lb charge. The shock was very violent and it was thought at first that the ship's back was broken and that the masts would crash to the deck. Numbers 2, 3, 4 and 6 boiler rooms flooded almost immediately and No. 5 flooded shortly afterwards. The ship was able to proceed slowly under her own steam, main steering being available until 1500 when No. 1 boiler room became contaminated with sea water and all steam failed.

Warspite was in a serious situation. Unable to steam, she had drifted into an unswept area and had shipped about 5,000 tons of water. In addition, she was only a few miles from Salerno and liable to further air attacks at any moment, the RDF was out of action and it was not known whether hostile submarines were in the area. The AA armament was intact, good weather prevailed and some counter-flooding had brought the main deck (starboard side) above the water-line. Air protection was required, but none was available until next morning. US salvage tugs (*Hope* and *Marino*) had *Warspite* in tow by 1700. With HMS *Delhi* acting as RDF ship, *Warspite* proceeded to Malta at speeds of up to 4 knots. At 1930 *Euryalus* and *Scylla* joined and the former took *Warspite* in tow, but the line parted. At 1800 next day the only change was that the list to starboard had increased to 4½ degrees, but the spread of flooding had been curtailed by the pumps.

The bomb that hit that ship had approached at about 20 degrees to the vertical and 15 degrees to the centre-line plane. It struck the boat deck, passed through the port hangar, wardroom, galley, stokers' after mess deck, kit locker flat, and No. 4 boiler room before bursting in a double bottom reserve feed tank. Thicknesses were 10lb (MS) plus 40lb (HT), 50lb (HT), 14lb (MS), 100lb (NC), 40lb (HT), 20lb (MS), a total of 6¾ inches. The hole in the boat deck was roughly 5ft 6in square and centred about 11 feet from the centre-line to port and extending from 128 to 130 stations. The Forecastle, upper and main decks were holed (2ft 9in diameter) on the port side, stations 126 to 128, 18–19 feet from centre-line respectively. The middle deck (100lb NC on 40lb HT) was holed (2ft 9in diameter). The outer bottom was holed over A, B and C strakes, port side between 123 and 133 stations, the aperture being 20 feet long by 7–14 feet wide. The inner bottom was blown upwards over the same areas. The main transverse bulkheads 100 to 154 (20lb (MS)) both leaked. The main transverse bulkhead 136 was holed. Other bulkheads were badly damaged in the area of the blast. The near miss hit the water close to the ship's side and burst near the bottom of the bulge at station 140, starboard side. The bulge plating (22½lb MS) was ruptured and bulges themselves between 111 and 159 stations. Splits in seams were evident. The outer and inner battery platform was corrugated (maximum 6 inches) over the area under No. 5 boiler room and both were holed. The bilge had been fractured. The compartments on the mid-

WARSPITE: DAMAGE SUSTAINED AT SALERNO, 16 SEPTEMBER 1943

Section 140 key:
1. mess space
2. oil fuel tanks
3. No.6 BR
4. No.5 BR
5. reserve feed tanks

Section 128 Key:
1. hangar
2. workplace
3. dressing-room
4. kit locker space
5. oil fuel
6. No.4 BR
7. No.3 BR
8. lower bulge compartments

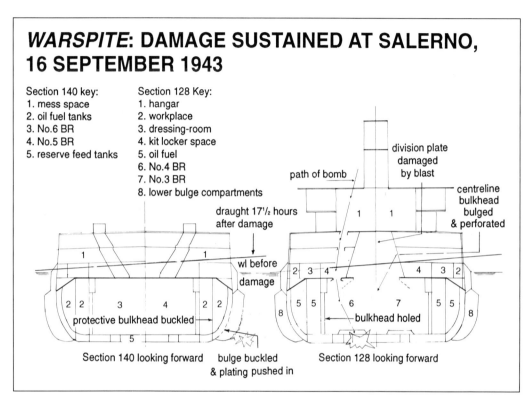

Section 140 looking forward

bulge buckled & plating pushed in

Section 128 looking forward

dle deck from 118 to 154 stations were flooded.

Before the attack draughts were 33ft 9in forward, 32ft 6in aft, no list; one hour later, 36ft 6in forward, 35ft 6in aft, slight list; after 3½ hours, 38ft forward, 36ft 6in aft, 3 degrees list; 17½ hours after the attack, 39ft forward, 37ft 6in aft, 4 degrees list. On arrival at Malta on 19 September draught was 38ft 6in forward, 36ft 11in aft.

Before the ship was hit all doors had been closed and damage control stations were at second degree readiness. No. 4 boiler room had been completely wrecked, the main armament was out of action by the loss of hydraulic power and WT and RDF were also out of action.

The Captain's (Captain Packer) report on the incident makes interesting reading:

'As we were threading our way slowly through the shipping to communicate with the HQ ship *Biscayene* and to Avalanche North for a further bombardment our old friends the Fw 190s roared in out of the sun and attacked us with bombs – no hits.

'Just as they finished dead overhead we suddenly sighted three new objects – glider bombs – I realized at once what they were. They were flying horizontally in formation for a couple of seconds at about 8,000ft, and then down they came absolutely vertically at terrific speed. It was clear they were going to hit us. It took two seconds. There was nothing to be done and I watched carefully. The first to arrive missed us starboard side amidships by a few feet – a fraction of a second later one hit us just abaft the funnel. The third near missed the starboard side. I was not thrown off my feet but for a fraction of a second I had a kind of "blackout" like when you take a hard toss at football or off a horse. I could see and think perfectly clearly all the time. Black smoke and then dirt from the funnels and the hell of a noise. I thought the whole mast was coming down as it rocked and bent and whipped. I must say that for a moment I thought we were probably sunk and was quite prepared for the ship to break in two. No-one lost their heads or shouted or anything on the bridge –

they were all first class and the AA guns which had opened fire kept on firing. That was good. Then there was a calm after the storm. I found the ship could steer, the engines were going ahead. I began to think that we had not been hit after all, only near misses. A fire was reported in the hangar, "Put it out" I said. Then to guns, more for effect than anything, "If we can steam and shoot we will carry out our final bombardment after all." I set course up the channel and then reports began to come in all very calm and accurate. Four boiler rooms out of six flooded–steam for slow speed on starboard engines only – I kept going at 6 knots. Then the ship would not steer, we were in the swept channel and we steered round in a circle. I stopped engines. We were heading straight into the mines. A minesweeper sent violent signals to get out of it. I could not for helm was hard over and finally the starboard engine room died out too. So there we were once again going round in circles with our way carrying us and quite helpless. Steam joints had bust and the engine room was untenable. The 5th boiler room flooded leaving only one. Got shifted over to steering from the tiller flat by electric. The tug, the *Orpi*, a Yank, came roaring up and soon had me in tow and straightened out and I made up my mind to set off to Malta at once – speed 3 knots. The prospect was unattractive. Outside were at least 6 submarines reported in the area. I had only 4 destroyers with me, further air attacks were obviously on the cards. The extent of the damage was unknown, the ship was beginning to list and we were already two or three feet deeper in the water. But off we set. I called *Delhi* as AA protection and asked for special fighter protection from N.C.W.N.F.F., Admiral Hewitt, USN and for tugs. Another tug came up but would not stay but I told him I had orders from Admiral Hewitt that he was to. Now we had two tugs towing us in tandem. We were making 3½ knots and 300 miles to go.

'Casualties 6 killed and about 20 wounded.

'Received message from N.C.W.N.J. To *Warspite*, "Deeply regret the casualties and damage you sustained. Am grateful for your efficient support which has aided so much the force ashore. When they are relieved please send Hopi and Marina to me here. Best of luck, Hewitt."

'Friday 17th September – I said a few words to the sailors over the broadcaster. A common

hazard of war – we had done what we set out to do and had been hit – we had scared the hell out of the German Army and braced up our own soldiers and shouldn't be surprised if we hadn't turned the scale. Admired their good humour and hard work. We would get the "old lady" back to Malta.'

Warspite mined, 13 June 1944

On 13 June 1944 *Warspite* was on passage from Portsmouth to Rosyth, accompanied by the destroyers *Southdown* and *Holmes* at a speed of 16 knots. The weather was slightly overcast with a sea of 3.1. *Warspite*'s draught was 33ft 10in forward, 32ft 10in aft. The degaussing equipment was working at the correct settings and the SA gear was operating. At 0748, when the Force

was in position 51° 52' N, 1° 41' E, that is, just off Harwich, a heavy explosion occurred off the port side abreast *Warspite*'s 'X' and 'Y' 15in turrets. The depth of water in this position was about 17 fathoms. Eye-witnesses reported an area of violently disturbed water close to the ship's side and stated that water was thrown up generally to upper-deck level, but that there was a thin column in the centre rising some distance above this level. There were numerous gas bubbles. They estimated that the centre of the explosion was about 20 feet from the port side. *Warspite* was very severely shaken by the explosion which was caused by the detonation of an acoustic or 'Sammy' ground mine, Type GC, containing a charge of 1,500 pounds of aluminized hexanite.

Immediately after the explosion there was a partial loss of electric power which caused many lighting failures; all W/T and radar sets were put out of action through loss of power, or by shock damage; the port outer shaft seized up, and extensive flooding of the after portion of the port lower bulge compartments caused the ship to list $3\frac{1}{2}$ degrees to port within five minutes. The list later increased to a maximum of $4\frac{1}{2}°$.

The main machinery was shut down for half an hour for examination, during which period the necessary damage control measures were put into effect. When the machinery was re-started neither the port outer nor the port inner shafts could be turned and the ship was forced to proceed to Rosyth using her starboard shafts only. The maximum speed attained was 10 knots and

WARSPITE: MINE DAMAGE, 13 JUNE 1944

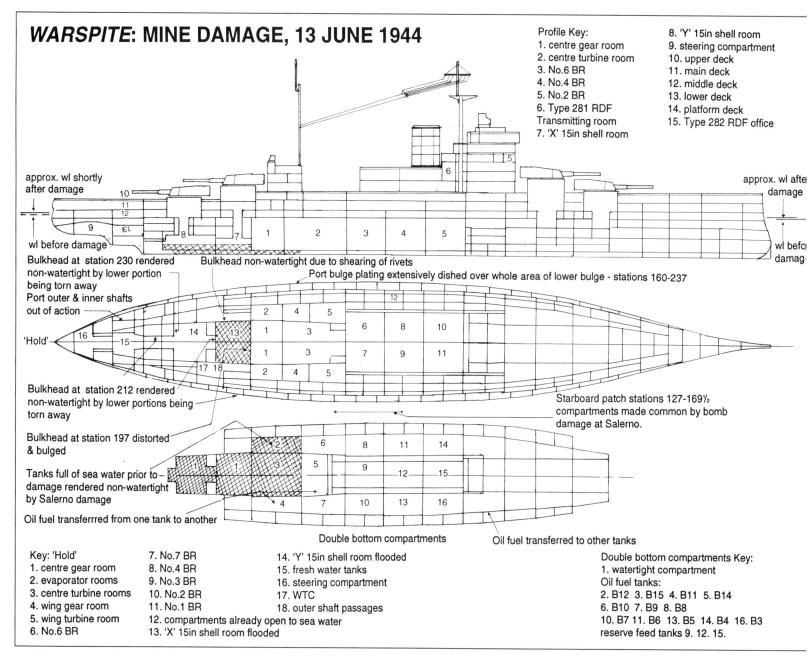

Profile Key:
1. centre gear room
2. centre turbine room
3. No.6 BR
4. No.4 BR
5. No.2 BR
6. Type 281 RDF Transmitting room
7. 'X' 15in shell room
8. 'Y' 15in shell room
9. steering compartment
10. upper deck
11. main deck
12. middle deck
13. lower deck
14. platform deck
15. Type 282 RDF office

approx. wl shortly after damage

wl before damage

approx. wl after damage

wl before damage

Bulkhead at station 230 rendered non-watertight by lower portion being torn away

Port outer & inner shafts out of action

'Hold'

Bulkhead non-watertight due to shearing of rivets

Port bulge plating extensively dished over whole area of lower bulge - stations 160-237

Bulkhead at station 212 rendered non-watertight by lower portions being torn away

Bulkhead at station 197 distorted & bulged

Starboard patch stations 127-169½ compartments made common by bomb damage at Salerno.

Tanks full of sea water prior to damage rendered non-watertight by Salerno damage

Oil fuel transferrred from one tank to another

Double bottom compartments

Oil fuel transferred to other tanks

Key: 'Hold'
1. centre gear room
2. evaporator rooms
3. centre turbine rooms
4. wing gear room
5. wing turbine room
6. No.6 BR

7. No.7 BR
8. No.4 BR
9. No.3 BR
10. No.2 BR
11. No.1 BR
12. compartments already open to sea water
13. 'X' 15in shell room flooded

14. 'Y' 15in shell room flooded
15. fresh water tanks
16. steering compartment
17. WTC
18. outer shaft passages

Double bottom compartments Key:
1. watertight compartment
Oil fuel tanks:
2. B12 3. B15 4. B11 5. B14
6. B10 7. B9 8. B8
10. B7 11. B6 13. B5 14. B4 16. B3
reserve feed tanks 9. 12. 15.

Rosyth was reached at about 2130 on 14 June.

Structural damage: Outer bottom plating (25 to 40lb MS):
Although no rupture occurred there was extensive dishing between frames, of maximum depression 3 inches, within the area bounded by stations 160 and 230, and the port 6th and starboard 5th longitudinals. The intensity of the dishing was much greater on the port side and some of the plating seams on that side were leaking. A few rivets were missing from the connec-

tion to the outer bottom of the bulge portions of inlet tubes passing through the outer bottom of the bulge.

Port bulge (22½lb and 30lb MS):
A few small ruptures of the bulge plating were caused by its being forced inwards against the bulge framing; the largest of these ruptures measured 2 feet x 5 inches. In addition there was extensive dishing of this plating over the whole area of the lower bulge between stations 160 and 237, that is over a length of 145 feet and a depth

of 36 feet. The damage was particularly severe over the 44-foot length between stations 202 and 223½; in this area plating was forced in to a maximum distance of 2 feet and bulge framing and divisional bulkheads were wrecked. Between the same frame stations, inlet tubes were left standing proud from the bulge plating. Plating seams over the whole of the damaged area were badly strained and numerous rivets were missing.

Starboard Bulge (22½lb and 30lb MS):
There were no ruptures in the starboard bulge

Section at station 202 Key:
1. 'X' turret
2. cabins
3. deck spaces
4. bathrooms
5. dressing-room
6. store
7. No.6 turbo-dynamo room
8. No.5 turbo-dynamo room
9. 'X' 15in magazine
10. handing room
11. 'X' 15in shell rooms
12. watertight compartments

Section at station 214 key:
1. deck space
2. church
3. store
4. deck space
5. hydraulic room
6. SA magazine
7. 4in HA magazine
8. 'Y' 15in magazine
9. plummer block spaces
10. 'Y' 15in shell room
11. watertight compartment
12. bathroom

Section at station 202

wl after damage

section at station 202

Inner bottom plating distorted between stations 160 & 230

Port bulge plating extensively dished over whole area of lower bulge between stations 160 & 237. 6in to 24in ruptures also in evidence. Dishing severe between stations 202 & 223½, max. of 2ft inwards.

approx. Depth of water 100ft

Section at station 214 looking forward

wl after damage

wl before damage list 4½ degrees port

Lower bulge (flooded)

Damage to lower bulge

Outer bottom plating extensively dished between frames 160 & 220

Section at station 231 looking forward

wl after damage
wl before damage

lower bulge (flooded)

damage to lower bulge

Section at station 231 key:
1. 'Y' 15in turret
2. cabin
3. deck space
4. mine-sweeping store
5. awning store
6. paymaster's store
7. plummer block compartments
8. 'Y' 15in shell room
9. watertight compartments

J. L. Burt
October 1991

plating, but there was slight dishing between frames, of maximum depression 1 inch at the bottom of the bulge from stations 189½ to 220, that is over a longitudinal distance of 60 feet.

Inner bottom plating (20lb MS):
No rupture of the inner bottom plating occurred, but there was slight distortion in places within the area bounded by stations 160 and 230, and between the port and starboard 3rd longitudinals, due to the upward movement of the bottom framing in this area.

Transverse bulkheads:
The 10lb MS cofferdam bulkhead at station 197 was distorted and bulged aft a maximum distance of 2 feet.

Over a short distance on the port side the 14lb MS bulkhead at station 212 and the watertight frame beneath it were strained and made non-watertight by the lower portions being torn away from the boundary angles connecting them to the inner and outer bottom plating. The water-tightness of the after bulkhead of the port plum-

mer block space at station 216 was destroyed by the bulkhead gland of the port inner shaft being torn from it by the eccentricity of the shaft. The forward bulkhead of the port plummer block compartment at station 230 was also rendered non-watertight by the lower portion being torn away about 2 feet from the boundary angles connecting it to the inner and outer bottoms.

After an hour *Warspite* was under way again at about 10 knots, and reached port next day. She was out of action for two months.

HISTORY: QUEEN ELIZABETH

Naval terms of armistice with Germany arranged on board at Rosyth 15 November 1918.
Became flag new Atlantic Fleet on post-war reorganization April 1919 (see *Barham*).
Beatty promoted Admiral of the Fleet and hoisted Union Flag in *Queen Elizabeth* 4 April 1919.
Grand fleet officially abolished and Beatty's flag hauled down 7 April 1919.

ATLANTIC FLEET (fleet flag) April 1919 to November 1924.
Spithead Review 26 July 1924.
Transferred to Mediterranean Fleet with rest of class 1 November 1924, replacing *Iron Duke* as fleet flag (see *Barham*).

MEDITERRANEAN FLEET (fleet flag) November 1924 to May 1926.
Relieved by *Warspite* May 1926 and paid off at Portsmouth for reconstruction 26 May after nearly ten years as flag of the principal British fleet.

Reconstructed at Portsmouth May 1926 to December 1927.
Commissioned for trials 16 August 1927.
Commissioned at Portsmouth 2 January 1928 for further service as flag Mediterranean Fleet.

MEDITERRANEAN FLEET January 1928 to August 1937 (flag to June 1937).
Visited Constantinople October 1929 as flag of the first British squadron to enter Turkish waters since the signing of the Peace Treaty.
Squadron comprised *Queen Elizabeth* (flag),

QUEEN ELIZABETH, 1941: CROSS-SECTIONS

Section 249 looking aft
1. admiral's dining room
2. cabin
3. awning room
4. steering gear compartment
5. rudder

Section 245 looking aft
1. admiral's dining room
2. cabin
3. awning room
4. steering gear
5. inner shaft

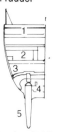

Section 158 looking aft
1. 10ton motor boat & seaplane crane
2. hangar & Walrus aircraft
3. 4.5in turret
4. 4.5in casemate
5. passage
6. comunications office
7. fresh water tank
8. and 9. hammock & kit locker rooms
10. 'A' turbine rooms
11. 'X' turbine rooms
12. oil fuel tanks
13. bulge & W/T compartments

Fo'c's'le deck
upper deck
main deck
middle deck
wl

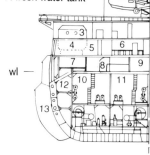

'B' turret looking forward
1. 'B' turret
2. revolving hoist
3. ERs' mess
4. mess space
5. provisions room
6. hose store
7. torpedo gunners' store
8. 15in magazine
9. upper pom-pom magazine
10. W/T compartment
11. 15in shell room
12. lower pom-pom magazin

Courageous, Wanderer, Wild Swan, Veteran and *Bryony.*

Refit Portsmouth November 1929 to May 1930; temporarily replaced as flag by *Warspite* during this period.

Flag rehoisted at Portsmouth 27 May 1930.

Sent to Alexandria, with *Ramillies,* July 1930 to support local forces during riots.

Refit Portsmouth November 1932 to March 1933; temporarily replaced as flag by *Resolution* during this period.

Senior flagship at Jubilee Review, Spithead, 16 July 1935.

Stationed at Alexandria October 1935 to summer 1936 during Italo-Ethiopian crisis.

Coronation Review, Spithead, 19 May 1937.

Relieved by *Barham* 9 June and paid off at Portsmouth for reconstruction 1 August 1937.

Reconstructed at Portsmouth and Rosyth August 1937 to January 1941; transferred from Portsmouth to Rosyth for completion in December 1940 because of risk of aircraft attack at Portsmouth.

Recommissioned at Rosyth 31 January 1941 for 2nd BS Home Fleet.

Joined Fleet at Scapa 21 February for working up.

HOME FLEET (2nd BS) January to May 1941.

Transferred to Mediterranean Fleet May 1941.

Left Gibraltar for Alexandria 6 May, making first part of passage through Mediterranean in company with Force H and convoy for Malta.

MEDITERRANEAN FLEET (1st BS) May 1941 to June 1942 (flag 1st BS and 2nd fleet flag

Above: *Queen Elizabeth* June 1943 showing mid-war appearance.

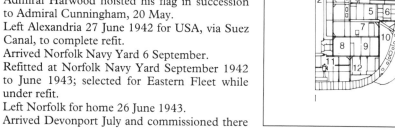

May to August 1941; fleet flag from August 1941).

Took part in defence and evacuation of Crete, May 1941.

With *Barham* and destroyers, supported air attack on enemy airfield on Scarpante Island by aircraft from *Formidable* 26 May.

Became flag 1st BS and 2nd fleet flag 27 May, replacing *Barham* for repairs to bomb damage sustained during this operation.

Became fleet flag in August 1941 on return of *Barham* from refit.

Flag C-in-C had been flown ashore at Alexandria from 24 June when *Warspite* left for refit in USA.

Badly damaged by Italian limpet mine at Alexandria 19 December 1941 (see full report).

Temporarily repaired at Alexandria December 1941 to June 1942, continuing to serve as fleet flag during this period, being relieved by *Valiant* for a short time in April.

Admiral Harwood hoisted his flag in succession to Admiral Cunningham, 20 May.

Left Alexandria 27 June 1942 for USA, via Suez Canal, to complete refit.

Arrived Norfolk Navy Yard 6 September.

Refitted at Norfolk Navy Yard September 1942 to June 1943; selected for Eastern Fleet while under refit.

Left Norfolk for home 26 June 1943.

Arrived Devonport July and commissioned there

Section 239 looking aft
1. Admiral's spare cabin
2. and 3. cabins
4. admiral's store drawer
5. lobby
6. W/T compartment
7. and 8. fresh water tanks

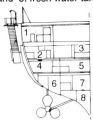

Section 234 looking aft
1. officers' day cabin
2. cabin
3. paymaster's store
4. W/T compartment
5. steering shaft

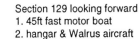

Centre of 'Y' turret looking aft
1. officers' day cabins
2. 'Y' barbette
3. Wardroom store
4. Cabin
5. W/T compartment
6. Spirits room
7. sub-calibre magazine
8. 15in magazine
9. 15in shell room

Centre of 'X' turret looking aft
1. cabin
2. 'X' turret
3. senior officers' bathroom
4. medical distribution station
5. W/T space
6. breaker room
7. engineers' store
8. shaft
9. 15in magazine
10. 15in shell room

Section 185 looking aft
1. Marine officers' room
2. oil fuel working space
3. fitting shop
4. main MC workshop
5. oil fuel
6. HA magazine
7. 4.5in magazine
8. oil fuel tank
9. shaft passage
10. auxiliary machine compartment

Section 129 looking forward
1. 45ft fast motor boat
2. hangar & Walrus aircraft
3. pom-pom magazine
4. & 6. passages
5. galley
7. gunroom pantry
8. crew space
9. drying room
10. washplace
11. reserve feed tank
12. oil fuel
13. tanks
14. turbo-generator room
15. 'X' boiler room

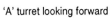

Section 94 looking forward
1. DCT
2. RDF office
3. signal officers' cabin
4. remote control office
5. and 6. cabin
7. reading room
8. ship's galley
9. 4.5in HA/LA casemate
10. locker room
11. HA/LA gun machinery
12. drying room
13. washplace
14. reserve feed tank
15. oil fuel
16. tanks
17. turbo-gen room
18. 'A' boiler room

Section 80 looking forward
1. compass platform
2. Navigating position
3. CT   4. Admiral's sea cabin
5. POs' recreation space
6. oilskins room
7. and 8. passages

9. Bookstall
10. crew mess space
11. medical distribution station
12. medical stores
13. washroom
14. lower steering CT
15. switchboard room
16. LP machinery room
17. WT space
18. HA magazine
19. 4.5in magazine

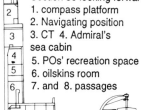

'A' turret looking forward
1. 'A' turret
2. sickbay
3. handwheels
4. awners store
5. washplace
6. gunners' store
7. gunsight gear
8. 15in magazine
9 15in shell room

Section 31 looking forward
1. Dispensary
2. POs' mess
3. central store
4. flour store
5. cold room
6. central store
7. W/T compartment

Section 21 looking forward
1. deck piping
2. sand store
3. bower cables
4. cables
5. cables (sheet)
6. capstan engine room
7. W/T pillar compartment

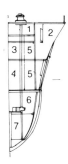

QUEEN ELIZABETH, 1941:
INBOARD PROFILE AND UPPER DECK PLAN

Inboard Profile
1. capstan machinery
2. 15in magazines
3. lower CT and tube
4. vents from boiler & engine rooms
5. uptakes
6. boilers
7. engine rooms
8. after 15in magazines
9. steering gear compartment
10. tiller room flat
11. CT
12. charthouse & compass platform

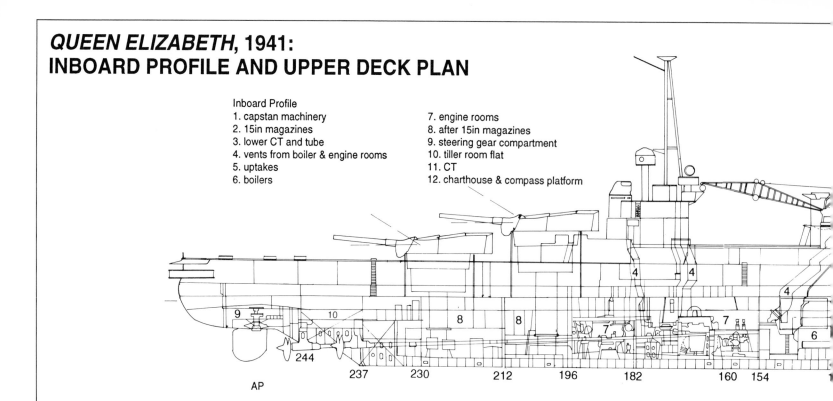

Upper deck key:
1. seamen's heads
2. CPOs' heads
3. handwheels pillar
4. greatcoat room
5. cable lockers
6. cool rooms
7. oilskins room
8. lamp room
9. tables & mess space
10. mess area
11. Bos'n's mates' room
12. annexe
13. dispensary
14. bathroom
15. isolation ward
16. 'A' barbette
17. 'B' barbette
18. cable machinery compartment
19. hammock space
20. operating theatre
21. pantry
22. ECA's mess
23. sickbay
24. surgery
25. Chief stokers & mechanics' mess
26. 4.5in HA/LA casemates
27. flour store
28. issue room
29. bakery
30. bread cooling room
31. canteen
32. naval store
33. hand conveyor
34. parachute office & store
35. Master at arms mail room

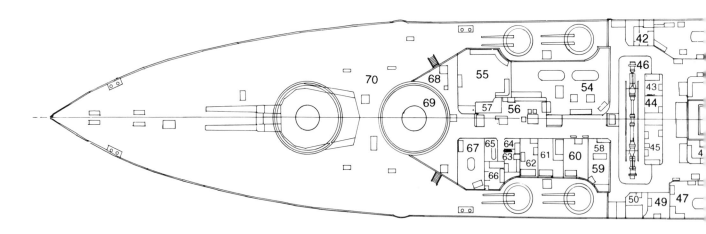

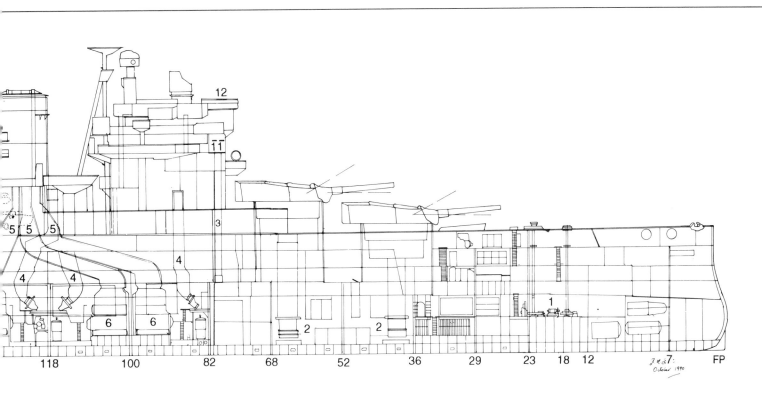

36. funnel uptakes	47 gunroom
37. WOs' pantry	48. gunroom pantry
38. WOs' mess	49. cabin
39. wardroom galley	50. captain's office
40. gunroom galley	51. and 53. drying rooms
41. WOs' galley	52. vent to boiler rooms
42. cabin and bed berth	54. wardroom
43., 44., 45. & 58. cabins	55. wardroom ante-room
46. machinery compartment	56. wardroom pantry

57. wine bar	67. captain's day cabin
59. paymaster's cabin	68. correspondence office
60. commander's cabin	69. 'X' barbette
61. Chief engineer's cabin	70. quarterdeck & 'Y' turret
62. surgeon-commander's cabin	
63. captain's spare cabin	
64. captain's pantry	
65. bathroom	
66. captain's sleeping cabin	

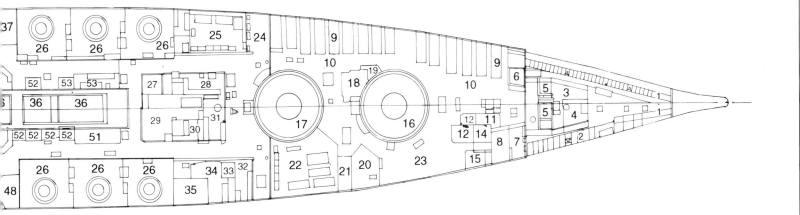

25 July for Eastern Fleet, being temporarily attached to Home Fleet for working up.

HOME FLEET (2nd BS) July to December 1943.
Working up at Scapa.
Left Portsmouth 23 December 1943 to join Eastern Fleet, via Mediterranean and Suez Canal.
Arrived Trincomalee 28 January 1944 and hoisted flag C-in-C (Admiral Somerville).

EASTERN FLEET (flag 1st BS and fleet flag) January to November 1944.
Unit of force supporting carrier attacks on Sabang, Sumatra 19 April 1944 by aircraft from *Illustrious* and the USS *Saratoga*.
Took part in bombardment of Car Nicobar and Port Blair in the Andaman Islands 30 April and 1 May.
Supported carrier attack on Sourabaya by aircraft from *Illustrious* and *Saratoga* 17 May.
Supported carrier attack on Sabang by aircraft from *Illustrious* and *Victorious* 25 July and, with *Valiant*, *Renown*, the French *Richelieu* and destroyers, carried out surface bombardment following this.
Refit Durham October to November 1914.
On 22 November 1944 ships selected to remain in the South East Asia area after the formation of a Pacific Fleet, which was commenced on that date, were redesignated as the East Indies Fleet, the battle squadron for this comprising *Queen Elizabeth*, *Valiant* and *Renown* and becoming the 3rd BS, the 1st BS being allocated to the Pacific.
Queen Elizabeth flag (VA) 3rd BS and fleet flag East Indies Fleet.

EAST INDIES FLEET (flag) November 1944 to July 1945.
Took part in further bombardment of Sabang January 1945.
Burma operations January to May 1945.
Supported landings on Ramree Island 21 January.
Landed marines on Cheduba Island 26 January.
Took part in operations against Rangoon April to May 1945.
Relieved by *Nelson* 12 July 1945 and returned home.
Arrived Portsmouth 7 August 1945 and paid off to reserve to Rosyth on the 10th.

RESERVE (Rosyth) August to October 1945.
Attached to Home Fleet 22 October as Accommodation Ship.

HOME FLEET (2nd BS) October 1945 to March 1946.
Employed as Accommodation Ship at Portland and Portsmouth.
Reverted to reserve, Portsmouth March 1946.

RESERVE (Portsmouth) March 1946 to May 1948.
Decision to scrap announced in Parliament January 1948.
Sale to British Iron & Steel Corporation arranged 19 March 1948.
Ship finally paid off 15 May 1948.
Allocated to Arnott Young, Dalmuir for scrapping.
Arrived Dalmuir 7 July 1948.
Hulk subsequently towed to Troon for demolition.

HISTORY: WARSPITE

ATLANTIC FLEET April 1919 to October 1925 (2nd BS to May 1921; 1st BS subsequently). See *Barham*.
Spithead Review 26 July 1924.
Paid off at Portsmouth 31 October 1924 for reconstruction.
Reconstructed at Portsmouth October 1924 to April 1926.
Recommissioned at Portsmouth 6 April 1926 to relieve *Queen Elizabeth* as flag Mediterranean Fleet (see *Barham*).

MEDITERRANEAN FLEET April 1926 to May 1930 (fleet flag to January 1928. Flag 1st BS and 2nd fleet flag January to September 1928. (1st BS March to November 1929; fleet flag subsequently).
Relieved as fleet flag by *Queen Elizabeth* January 1928 and replaced *Barham* as flag 1st BS and 2nd fleet flag.
Damaged by grounding in the Aegean 12 July 1928.
Returned home September 1928 for repairs, flag 1st BS being transferred to *Barham*.
Refit Portsmouth September 1928 to January 1929.
Recommissioned at Portsmouth 22 January 1929

as private ship 1st BS. Left for Mediterranean 14 March.
Fleet flag Mediterranean November 1929 to May 1930, relieving *Queen Elizabeth* for refit.
Flag struck at Portsmouth 26 May and *Warspite* transferred to Atlantic Fleet (see *Barham*).

ATLANTIC FLEET (flag 2nd BS) May 1930 to March 1932.
Atlantic Fleet redesignated Home Fleet March 1932.

HOME FLEET (flag 2nd BS) to December 1933.
Rammed by Roumanian SS *Peleus* in mouth of Tagus 21 March 1933.
Repaired at Portsmouth and rejoined fleet 5 June.
Relieved by *Barham* and paid off at Portsmouth for second reconstruction 23 December 1933.
Reconstructed at Portsmouth March 1934 to June 1937.
Commissioned at Portsmouth 29 June 1937 as flag Mediterranean Fleet, but departure for station delayed by steering defects and ship not ready for service until January 1938.
Left Portsmouth for Mediterranean 5 January 1938.

MEDITERRANEAN FLEET January 1938 to October 1939 (fleet flag from February 1938).
Relieved *Barham* as fleet flag 8 February 1938.
Transferred to Home Fleet October 1939.
Left Alexandria for home 28 October, via Malta and Gibraltar.
Arrived Gibraltar 6 November and diverted to Halifax for escort duty.
Arrived Halifax 14 November and left on 18th with convoy for United Kingdom.
Detached from convoy 24th to take part in search for *Scharnhorst* following sinking of *Rawalpindi* by that ship on the 23rd.
Searched in Denmark and Iceland–Faroes area until end of month.
Arrived Clyde 4 December and hoisted flag C-in-C Home Fleet at Greenock on 6th, relieving *Nelson* for repairs to mine damage sustained on the 4th, and pending return of *Rodney* from refit.

HOME FLEET (2nd BS Clyde and Scapa) December 1939 to April 1940 (temporary fleet flag to January 1940).

Home fleet base transferred from Scapa to Clyde October 1939, pending completion of adequate defences at Scapa.

Reverted to Scapa March 1940.

Unit of covering force for first Canadian troop convoy December 1939.

Flag C-in-C Home Fleet transferred to *Rodney* 1 January 1940.

Took part in Norwegian operations April 1940; on 13 April, a Swordfish aircraft from *Warspite*, while on reconnaissance prior to second battle of Narvik, sank *U64* in Herjangsfiord (Narvik).

As flag (VA) led force of nine destroyers (*Kimberley, Bedouin, Foxhound, Cossack, Eskimo, Punjabi, Icarus, Hero* and *Forester*) for second attack on German destroyers in Narvik Fiord 13 April and assisted in sinking destroyer *Koellner*.

For this operation, *Warspite* flying flag Vice-Admiral Battlecruiser Squadron Home Fleet, transferred from *Renown* on the 12th and which was retained in the ship during subsequent operations against Narvik until 24 April.

Took part in bombardment of the port of Narvik and defences on that date.

Ordered back to Mediterranean on same day because of increasing threat of war with Italy.

Left Clyde 30 April, arrived Alexandria 10 May and hoisted flag C-in-C Mediterranean on the 11th.

MEDITERRANEAN FLEET (flag) May 1940 to June 1941.

Flag of squadron (*Warspite, Malaya* and *Royal Sovereign*) in action with Italian battle squadron off Calabria 9 July 1940, while covering Malta to Alexandria convoy, and was only British ship able to get within range of the enemy.

Scored hit on Italian flagship *Giulio Cesare* at 26,400 yards which caused 115 casualties and severe damage which kept *Cesare* out of action for four months.

Took part in various bombardments in 1940–1, mainly in support of the army in the Western Desert.

With *Malaya, Ramillies* and *Kent* bombarded Bardia and Fort Capuzzo 15 August 1940.

Flag of supporting force (*Warspite, Valiant, Malaya, Ramillies* and destroyers) covering attack on Italian fleet at Taranto by aircraft from *Illustrious* 11 November 1940.

With *Valiant* bombarded Valona 18 December 1940.

With *Barham* and *Valiant* took part in bombardment and capture of Bardia 3 January 1941.

Malta convoy 7–11 January 1941; starboard anchor hit by bomb on 10th during this operation. No material damage.

Matapan action 28 March 1941.

Assisted in the sinking of Italian cruisers *Fiume* and *Zara*; five, if not all six shells of first broadside were direct hits.

With *Barham* and *Valiant* bombarded Tripoli 21 April 1941.

Flag (RA) special force organized for defence and evacuation of Crete May 1941.

Flag C-in-C flown ashore at Alexandria during these operations.

Damaged by bomb off Crete 22 May while covering evacuation; starboard 6in battery and 4in AA knocked out – speed reduced.

Temporarily repaired at Alexandria June 1941, reverting to fleet flag during this period.

Further damaged by near miss bomb while under repair in dock.

Left Alexandria 26 June for Bremerton Navy Yard USA to complete refit, proceeded via Singapore, Honolulu and Esquimalt.

Arrived Bremerton 11 August 1941.

Refit Bremerton August to December 1941.

Recommissioned at Seattle 28 December 1941

as flag Eastern Fleet, based at Ceylon.

Left Seattle 7 January 1942 for Trincomalee, via Sydney.

Arrived Trincomalee 22 March 1942 and hoisted flag C-in-C Eastern Fleet there on 27th.

EASTERN FLEET (flag 1st BS as fleet flag) March 1942 to March 1943.

Fleet based at Colombo until April 1942, then transferred to Kilindini (East Africa). Returned to Ceylon (Trincomalee) January 1944.

Warspite only unit of 1st BS actually with Eastern Fleet during 1942–3. *Queen Elizabeth* and *Valiant* earmarked for this in 1942 but did not join until January 1944.

3rd BS Eastern Fleet in March 1942 comprised four *Royal Sovereign* class.

Conveyed General Wavell from Bombay to Colombo to confer with Admiral Layton (C-in-C Ceylon) following Japanese attacks on Ceylon on 5 and 8 April.

With other units of fleet, covered passage through Indian Ocean of troop convoy carrying Australian Division home from Middle East in February 1943.

Ordered home in March 1943 and returned via Durban and Freetown.

Arrived in the Clyde 10 May 1943 and attached

to Home Fleet to work up bombardment practice at Scapa prior to joining Force H for invasion of Sicily.

HOME FLEET (2nd BS) May to June 1943; working up at Scapa.
Left Scapa 17 June 1943 for Gibraltar with *Nelson*, *Rodney* and *Valiant*.
Joined Force H at Gibraltar 23rd and hoisted flag RA 2nd in command.

FORCE H (Gibraltar) June to September 1943 (2nd flag until 12 September).
Took part in invasion of Sicily and Italy July to September 1943.
Bombarded batteries defending Catania (Sicily) 17 July.
With *Valiant*, bombarded coastal defences at Reggio (Italy) 2 September prior to landings.
Unit of covering force for Salerno landings 9 September.
Flag of force (*Warspite*, *Valiant* and seven destroyers) escorting surrendered Italian battleships *Vittorio Veneto* and *Italia*, six cruisers and eight destroyers to Malta 10 September, following Italian Armistice.
Relieved as 2nd flag Force H by *Howe* 12 September.
Escorted second group of surrendered Italian warships, including battleship *Giulio Cesare*, to Malta on same day.
Left Malta for home, with *Valiant*, 14 September but diverted to Salerno to support army.
Bombarded enemy positions at Salerno 15 and 16 September; 62 rounds of 15in fired on both days, at long range, 35 fell exactly on target and eight fell within one hundred yards.
Badly damaged by glider bombs on the 16th (see report).
Near missed by one bomb and hit abreast funnel by two others which penetrated boiler rooms and blew out bottom, flooding all boiler rooms. All power lost, ship unable to steer and all armament temporarily out of action.
Towed to Malta by two British and two American tugs and salvage vessel *Salveda*, reaching there on the 19th.
Temporary repairs carried out at Malta September to November 1943.
Left 1 November 1943 in tow for Gibraltar and arrived there on the 8th.

Further repairs at Gibraltar November 1943 to March 1944.
Left Gibraltar for Rosyth under own steam 9 March 1944 and arrived there 16th to complete refit.
Required for service to prepare for Normandy invasion before refit could be completed and, after working-up in Forth during April, joined Home Fleet at Scapa 2 May with X turret and one boiler room out of action although ship able to make 21 knots.

HOME FLEET (2nd BS) April to November 1944.
Working-up in Forth and at Scapa during April and May.
Unit of heavy bombardment force supporting Normandy invasion June to September 1944.
Initially allocated to Sword Beach (Eastern) area. With *Ramillies* and monitor *Roberts* neutralized German heavy batteries at Benerville, Villerville and Houlgate on 6 and 7 June; fired 73 rounds of 15in at Villerville battery on the 6th, scoring nine direct hits.
Supported US forces in Utah and Gold Beach areas on 10 and 11 June. Left invasion area for Rosyth (via Channel) on 12th to replace worn 15in guns, and was first capital ship to pass through the Straits of Dover since *Scharnhorst* and *Gneisenau* broke through in February 1942.
Mined off Harwich on 13th, while en route, but able to reach Rosyth under own steam on the 14th, drawing 42ft aft.
Repaired at Rosyth June to August sufficiently to resume operations but able to use only three propellers and speed reduced to 15¹/2 knots.
Returned to Normandy 25 August and supported attack on Brest on that date, engaging batteries at 30,000 yards and sustaining some damage from splinters. Supported attacks on Le Havre August to September, bombarding enemy gun positions at about 32,000 yards on 10 September with aircraft spotting. These operations concluded the work of the heavy bombardment force in Normandy.
On 9 September ship ordered to reduce to C Category Reserve in conclusion of the Normandy bombardments, but selected in October with the monitors *Erebus* and *Roberts* for the attack on Walcheren Island in the Scheldt Estuary. Supported Walcheren landings 1 November 1944, this being the ship's last operational service.

Attached to Allied Naval Expeditionary Force Command (ANXF) Portsmouth November 1944. Paid off to Reserve Portsmouth 1 February 1945.

RESERVE (Portsmouth) February 1945 to July 1946.
Laid up on Motherbank.
Placed on Disposal List, Portsmouth 31 July 1946.
Sold to British Iron & Steel Corporation February 1947 and allocated to Metal Industries Ltd., Faslane for scrapping.
Left Portsmouth 18 April 1947 in tow for Clyde.
Broke adrift in heavy weather on 20th and grounded in Mounts Bay on the 23rd, becoming a total wreck.
Wreck sold to Bennet & Brewis, Bristol 28 August 1947.
Refloated July 1950 and beached at Marazion.
Hulk resold to Wolverhampton Metal Co. Ltd., September 1955 and broken up as it lay.

During two wars, 1914–18 and 1939–45 *Warspite* accumulated fourteen Battle Honours, including Jutland May 1916, and by 1945 had more than any other ship in the British Navy.

HISTORY: BARHAM

On post-war reorganization, April 1919, Grand Fleet broken up and new Atlantic, Home and Mediterranean Fleets formed.
Atlantic Fleet comprised two Battle Squadrons, the *Royal Sovereign* class forming the 1st BS and the *Queen Elizabeth* the 2nd BS. *Queen Elizabeth* fleet flag, *Revenge* flag 1st BD and *Barham* flag 2nd BS.

ATLANTIC FLEET April 1919 to November 1924 (flag BS to May 1921; flag 1st BS from May 1921).
Flag (VA) of squadron paying ceremonial visit to Cherbourg April 1919.
In May 1921, 1st and 2nd BS merged into one, 1st BS, the *Royal Sovereign*s forming the 1st Division and *Queen Elizabeth*s the 2nd.
Queen Elizabeth remained as fleet flag, *Barham* became flag (VA) 1st BS and *Revenge* 2nd flag.
Spithead Review 26 July 1924.
On 1 November 1924, the *Queen Elizabeth*s were

transferred to the Mediterranean as the 1st BS, with *Queen Elizabeth* as fleet flag and *Barham* as squadron flag, the *Royal Sovereign* class remaining in the Atlantic Fleet as a new 2nd BS with *Revenge* as fleet flag and *Resolution* squadron flag. This distribution of the *Queen Elizabeth* and *Royal Sovereign* classes remained unchanged until March 1926 when *Resolution* and *Royal Oak* went to the Mediterranean to replace the four *Iron Duke* class (3rd BS), transferred to the Atlantic Fleet.

Mediterranean (1st BS) November 1924 to November 1929 (flag VA 1st BS and 2nd fleet flag to January 1928 and from September 1928 to May 1929. 2nd flag 1st BS June to November 1929.
Sent to Alexandria with *Malaya*, May 1927 during unrest in Egypt.
With *Ramillies*, carried out special 'flag showing' cruise along west coast Africa December 1927 to February 1928, visiting Sierra Leone, Sekondi, Accra and Lagos.
Relieved as flag 1st BS by *Warspite* January 1928.
Refit Portsmouth February to July 1928.
Replaced *Warspite* as flag 1st BS September 1928 when latter came home for refit after grounding in Aegean in July.
Relieved as flag by *Revenge* June 1929.
In November 1929 *Barham*, *Malaya* and *Valiant* transferred to the Atlantic Fleet, forming, with *Rodney*, the 2nd BS.
Warspite temporarily retained in the Mediterranean as fleet flag, pending return of *Queen Elizabeth* from refit, and joined 2nd BS Atlantic Fleet in May 1930.
With exception of *Queen Elizabeth* (fleet flag Mediterranean), all *Queen Elizabeth* class then in Atlantic and all *Royal Sovereign*s in the Mediterranean.

ATLANTIC FLEET (flag 2nd BS and 2nd fleet flag) November 1929 to December 1930.
Paid off at Portsmouth for reconstruction 2 December 1930.
Reconstructed at Portsmouth December 1930 to October 1933.
Recommissioned Portsmouth 11 January 1934 to relieve *Warspite* as flag 2nd BS Home Fleet (ex Atlantic Fleet).
Atlantic Fleet redesignated Home Fleet March 1932.

HOME FLEET (flag 2nd BS and 2nd fleet flag) January 1934 to August 1935.
Early in 1935 it was decided to revert to the 1924 distribution of the *Queen Elizabeth* and *Royal Sovereign* classes and to station all the *Queen Elizabeth*s in the Mediterranean and all the *Royal Sovereign*s in the Home Fleet, as opportunity occurred.
Barham and *Valiant* exchanged with *Royal Sovereign* and *Ramillies* to August 1935;
Malaya and *Warspite* with *Resolution* and *Revenge* September 1936 to June 1937.
Barham commissioned at Devonport for Mediterranean 30 August 1935.

MEDITERRANEAN FLEET August 1935 to December 1939. 1st BS to February 1935. Flag VA 1st BS and 2nd fleet flag February to November 1936.
Flag RA 1st BS November 1936 to May 1937. Fleet flag June 1937 to February 1938. Flag RA 1st BS February 1938 to January 1939. Flag VA 1st BS and 2nd fleet flag from January 1939.
Relieved *Revenge* as flag 1st BS and 2nd fleet flag February 1936.
30 November 1936, flag (VA) 2nd in command Mediterranean transferred from *Barham* to *Hood*, flag BS, *Barham* reducing to flag (RA) 1st BS only.
Coronation Review, Spithead 19 May 1937.
Hoisted flag C-in-C Mediterranean 9 June 1937, replacing *Queen Elizabeth* for reconstruction pending arrival of *Warspite* on the station.
Relieved as fleet flag by *Warspite* 8 February 1938 and reverted to flag 1st BS.
Refit Portsmouth February to May 1938.
Became 2nd flag (VA) Mediterranean January 1939 on withdrawal of *Hood* from Mediterranean.
Transferred to Home Fleet as private ship 2nd BS December 1939.
Rammed and sank destroyer *Duchess* in North Channel 13 December 1939 while en route home.

HOME FLEET (2nd BS) December 1939 to November 1940.
North Atlantic convoy duty December 1939.
Torpedoed in bows by *U30* off Hebrides 28 December 1939. Reached Liverpool under own steam 29th.

Repaired by Cammell Laird, Birkenhead January to April 1940.
Detached 28 August 1940 for Dakar operation as flag Force M (*Barham, Resolution, Ark Royal, Devonshire, Cumberland, Fiji*, ten destroyers and minor craft) and Headquarters Ship for operation.
Arrived Gibraltar 2 September.
Bombardment of Dakar 23–25 September 1940; hit four times by fire from shore batteries on second day of bombardment. Bulges flooded on starboard side amidships. Repeatedly hit on third day, no major damage.
Towed *Resolution* to Freetown after latter damaged by torpedo on 25th.
Transferred to Mediterranean November 1940.
Arrived Gibraltar 7 November and left for Malta and Alexandria same day, being attached to Force H for first part of passage and carrying troops for Malta.

MEDITERRANEAN FLEET (1st BS) November 1940 to November 1941 (flag 1st BS and 2nd fleet flag December 1940 to June 1941 and August to November 1941).
With *Valiant* and *Warspite* took part in bombardment and capture of Bardia 3 January 1941.
Matapan action 28 March 1941; assisted in sinking of Italian cruisers *Fiume* and *Zara* during this engagement.
With *Valiant* and *Warspite*, bombarded Tripoli 2 April 1941.
Use, with a C class cruiser, as block ship at Tripoli proposed by Admiralty 15 April 1941 but idea abandoned following strong objections by C-in-C Mediterranean.
Took part in defence and evacuation of Crete May 1941.
With *Queen Elizabeth* and destroyers, supported carrier attack on enemy airfield on Scarpante Island by aircraft from *Formidable* 26 May.
Damaged by bomb off Crete 7 May when retiring from this operation. 'Y' turret hit and fire started. Also flooded in bulges by near miss.
Refitted at Durban June to July 1941.
Completed refit 30 July and rejoined Mediterranean Fleet in August. Torpedoed and sunk by *U331* off Libyan coast 25 November 1941 while on patrol, with fleet, between Crete and Cyrenaica. Ship hit by three torpedoes and rolled over to port beam ends. An explosion occurred in the 6in magazine amidships and she

sank one minute later. Fifty-six officers (including captain) and 806 ratings lost. Vice-Admiral survived.

HISTORY: VALIANT

Atlantic Fleet April 1919 to November 1924.

MEDITERRANEAN FLEET (1st BS) November 1924 to March 1929.
Refit Devonport February to July 1927.
Paid off at Portsmouth for reconstruction 23 March 1929.
Reconstructed at Portsmouth March 1929 to December 1930.
Recommissioned Portsmouth 2 December 1930 for 2nd BS Atlantic Fleet (see *Barham*).

ATLANTIC FLEET (2nd BS) December 1930 to March 1932; Atlantic Fleet redesignated Home Fleet March 1932.

HOME FLEET (2nd BS) March 1932 to July 1935.
Transferred to Mediterranean July 1935, exchanging stations with *Ramillies* (see *Barham*).

MEDITERRANEAN FLEET (1st BS) July 1935 to March 1937.
Paid off at Devonport for second reconstruction 1 March 1937.

Reconstructed at Devonport March 1937 to November 1939.

Commissioned at Devonport 30 November 1939 and attached to the America and West Indies Station for working-up at Bermuda prior to joining Home Fleet.

Unit of escort for second Canadian troop convoy to United Kingdom December 1939.

Joined Home Fleet (2nd BS) at Scapa 7 January 1940.

HOME FLEET (2nd BS) January to June 1940.

With *Malaya*, escorted third Canadian troop convoy to United Kingdom February 1940 (arrived Clyde 7 February).

Norwegian operations April to June 1940.

With *Repulse* covered troop convoy for Narvik expedition 11–15 April. Escorted troop convoys from Norway to Clyde after evacuation during June.

Transferred to Force H (Gibraltar) on its formation 28 June 1940; joined at Gibraltar 2 July.

Took part, with *Resolution*, *Hood*, *Ark Royal*, *Arethusa*, *Enterprise* and destroyers, in attack on French Fleet at Mers-el-Kebir (Oran) 3 July 1940.

Transferred to Mediterranean Fleet August 1940.

Left Gibraltar for Alexandria on 29th.

MEDITERRANEAN FLEET (1st BS) August 1940 to May 1942 (temporary fleet flag April 1942).

With *Warspite*, bombarded Valena 18 December 1940.

Took part in various bombardment operations during 1941, mainly in support of army in Western Desert.

With *Barham* and *Warspite* took part in bombardment and capture of Bardia 3 January 1941.

Malta Convoy 7-11 January 1941. Sustained splinter damage from aircraft attack on the 10th; one killed and two wounded.

Matapan action 28 March 1941; assisted at sinking of Italian cruisers *Fiume* and *Zara* in this engagement.

With *Barham* and *Warspite* bombarded Tripoli 21 April 1941.

Took part in defence and evacuation of Crete May 1941; damaged by aircraft bombing 22

May during these operations. Hit twice, aft, but without serious damage.

Refitted at Alexandria May to July.

Proposed August 1941 for new Eastern Fleet (see *Prince of Wales*).

Badly damaged by Italian limpet mines at Alexandria 19 December 1941 (see full report).

Repaired at Alexandria December 1941 to May 1942.

Temporarily relieved *Queen Elizabeth* as fleet flag 1 April 1942.

Completed refit at Durban May 1942 and transferred to South Atlantic Command, Freetown.

Arrived Freetown June 1942; employed on Harbour Security Service.

WEST AFRICA COMMAND (Freetown) January to February 1943.

Refit Devonport February to May 1943.

Selected for Eastern Fleet April 1943 but attached to Force H (Gibraltar) for Sicily invasion on completion of refit.

Carried out special work-up at Scapa May to June 1943 for bombardment operations.

Left Scapa 17 June for Gibraltar, with *Nelson*, *Rodney* and *Warspite*.

Joined force H at Gibraltar 23 June.

FORCE H (Gibraltar) June to October 1943.

Took part in invasion of Sicily and Italy July to September 1943.

With *Warspite* bombarded coastal defences at Reggio 2 September prior to the landings.

Unit of covering force for Salerno landings 9 September.

With *Warspite* and seven destroyers, escorted Italian battleships *Vittorio Veneto* and *Italia*, six cruisers and eight destroyers to Malta 10 September following Italian armistice.

Left Malta for home with *Warspite* 14 September but diverted to Salerno later same day to support army following enemy counter-attack.

Bombarded enemy positions at Salerno 15 and 16 September.

Returned home October 1943 for refit prior to transfer to Eastern Fleet.

Refit Devonport October to December 1943 (completed 1 December).

Left Devonport for station 23 December, via Mediterranean and Suez Canal, and joined Eastern Fleet at Trincomalee 27 January 1944.

EASTERN FLEET (1st BS) January to November 1944.

Unit of force supporting carrier attack on Sabang, Sumatra 19 April 1944 by aircraft from *Illustrious* and USS *Saratoga*.

Took part in bombardment of Car Nicobar and Port Blair in the Andaman Islands 30 April and 1 May.

Supported carrier attack on Sourabaya by aircraft from *Illustrious* and *Saratoga* 17 May.

Supported carrier attack on Sabang by aircraft from *Illustrious* and *Victorious* on 25 July and with *Queen Elizabeth*, *Renown*, French *Richelieu* and destroyers, carried out surface bombardment following this.

Badly damaged by buckling of floating dock at Trincomalee 8 August (collapse of dock variously reported as due to damage by Japanese aircraft attack in 1942 and to a mechanical defect not connected with this). Three propeller-shaft A frames bent.

Two damaged propellers removed at Suez and ship returned to duty on remaining two.

Left Trincomalee for home October 1944, via Suez, but draught too deep to enter Canal (grounded off southern entrance 21 October) and ship remained at Suez.

Transferred to East Indies Fleet (3rd BDS) at Suez 22 November 1944 (see *Queen Elizabeth*).

EAST INDIES FLEET (3rd BS) November 1944 to February 1945.

Left Suez for home December 1944 via Cape and Freetown.

Arrived Devonport 1 February 1945 and paid off to reserve for refit.

RESERVE (Devonport) February 1945 to February 1948 (attached to *Imperieuse* from June 1946).

Refit February 1945 to April 1946.

Attached to *Imperieuse* Establishment as Seagoing Training Ship 24 June 1946.

Decision to scrap announced in Parliament January 1948.

Paid off to Disposal List January 1948.

Sold to British Iron & Steel Corporation 19 March 1948.

Allocated to Arnott Young, Dalmuir for scrapping.

Left Devonport for Clyde 11 August 1948.

Arrived Cairnryan 16 August.

Hulk transferred to Troon 10 March 1950 for final demolition.

HISTORY: MALAYA

ATLANTIC FLEET April 1919 to November 1924 (2nd BS to May 1921, 1st BS subsequently). See *Barham*.
Unit of Squadron paying ceremonial visit to Cherbourg April 1919.
Conveyed Inter Allied Naval Commission to Germany January 1920.

Left Portsmouth 14 January flying flags of British (VA), French (RA) and Italian (RA) Admirals representing their respective powers on the Commission which was to inspect the carrying out of the Peace Treaty terms.
At Wilhelmshaven, the German naval ensign hoisted and given a twenty-one gun salute for the first time since 1914.
Returned to Portsmouth 28 January.
Flying flag VA, conveyed Duke of Connaught to India and paid special visit to Malay States December 1920 to March 1921.

Detached in September 1922, with *Ramillies*, *Resolution*, *Revenge* and *Royal Sovereign*, to reinforce Mediterranean Fleet during Near East trouble, and, in March 1923, conveyed deposed Sultan of Turkey to Malta.
Spithead Review 26 July 1924.
Transferred to Mediterranean, with rest of class, 1 November 1924 (see *Barham*).

MEDITERRANEAN FLEET (1st BS) November 1924 to September 1927.
Sent to Alexandria, with *Barham*, May 1927

because of unrest in Egypt.
Paid off at Portsmouth 20 September 1927 for reconstruction.
Reconstructed Portsmouth September 1927 to February 1929.
Recommissioned at Portsmouth for Mediterranean 21 February.

MEDITERRANEAN FLEET (1st BS) February to November 1929.
Transferred to Atlantic Fleet November 1929 with *Barham* and *Valiant*.

ATLANTIC FLEET (2nd BS) November 1929 to March 1932.
Atlantic Fleet redesignated Home Fleet March 1932.

HOME FLEET (2nd BS) March 1932 to October 1934.
Paid off at Devonport for second reconstruction 20 October 1934.
Reconstructed Devonport October 1934 to December 1936.
Transferred to Mediterranean on completion, under 1935 reorganization (see *Barham*).
Commissioned for Mediterranean Fleet at Portsmouth 19 January 1937.

MEDITERRANEAN FLEET (1st BS) January 1937 to October 1939 (squadron flag June 1937 to February 1938).
In collision with Dutch SS *Kertesene* off Oporto February 1937 en route to station and sustained some damage.
Repaired at Devonport and left Portsmouth for Mediterranean 1 July.
Joined Mediterranean Fleet 5 July.
Temporary Flag (VA) 1st BS June 1937 to February 1938, replacing *Barham* (which see).
Flag reverted to *Barham* 8 February 1938.
Sent to Haifa September 1938 (relieving *Repulse*) because Arab-Jewish troubles.
Detached to Indian Ocean, with *Glorious* 6 October 1939 as an additional hunting force (Force J) to search for *Graf Spee*.
Arrived Aden 14 October.

EAST INDIES COMMAND (Force J) October to December 1939.
Left Aden on first patrol 14 October and operated in Socotra area throughout.

Force J broken up 6 December and *Malaya* transferred to North Atlantic Escort Force, leaving Aden for Halifax, via UK, on the 7th.

NORTH ATLANTIC ESCORT FORCE (3rd BS Halifax) December 1939 to May 1940.
In November 1939, a 3rd Battle Squadron had been formed, comprising the four *Royal Sovereign* class battleships engaged on escort duties outside the Home Fleet (2nd BS) and Mediterranean (1st BS) commands. This squadron was organized for administrative, rather than tactical purposes, the ships being independently employed, where required. In 1942, the 3rd BS was allocated to the Eastern Fleet, as a tactical unit, and in November 1944 to the East Indies Fleet (ex Eastern Fleet), by which date the *Royal Sovereign*s had been withdrawn. *Malaya* attached while serving in the North Atlantic Escort Force 1939–40.
Employed on North Atlantic convoy duty.
With *Valiant*, escorted the third Canadian troop convoy to the United Kingdom February 1940 (arrived Clyde 7 February).
Rejoined Mediterranean Fleet May 1940 because of threat of war with Italy.

MEDITERRANEAN FLEET (1st BS) May to December 1940 (temporary fleet flag May 1940. Flag 1st BS and 2nd fleet flag from July 1940).
Flag C-in-C Mediterranean hoisted in *Malaya* at Alexandria 5 May 1940, the ship being the only battleship there at that date; transferred to *Warspite* on arrival 11 May.
Engaged mainly in escort work and bombardment of enemy bases in North Africa.
Unit of squadron (*Warspite* flag, *Malaya* and *Royal Sovereign*) in action with Italian battle squadron off Calabria 9 July 1940 while covering Malta to Alexandria convoy. Only *Warspite* able to get within range of the Italian ships on this occasion.
With *Warspite*, *Ramillies* and *Kent* bombarded Bardia and Fort Capuzzo 15 August.
Unit of supporting force (*Warspite* flag, *Malaya*, *Valiant*, *Ramillies* and destroyers) covering attack on enemy ships at Taranto by aircraft from *Illustrious* 11 November 1940.
Transferred to Force H (Gibraltar) December 1940 following the reduction in Italian battleship strength as the result of the Taranto raid which enabled *Malaya* and *Ramillies* to be withdrawn

from the Mediterranean Fleet for other duties.

FORCE H (Gibraltar) December 1940 to March 1941.
With *Renown* and *Sheffield* bombarded Genoa 9 February 1941 while aircraft from *Ark Royal* attacked Leghorn and La Spezia as part of the same operation.
South Atlantic convoy duty March 1941.
Sighted *Scharnhorst* and *Gneisenau* in Cape Verde Islands area 8 March while escorting Freetown–United Kingdom convoy, her presence saving the convoy from attack.
Torpedoed by *U81* off Cape Verde Islands 20 March.
Repaired at New York Navy Yard March to July 1941.
Transferred to Home Fleet on completion of refit and escorted Halifax-United Kingdon convoy en route.
Arrived Clyde 28 July.

HOME FLEET (2nd BS) July to October 1941.
Rejoined Force H 27 October 1941.

FORCE H (Gibraltar) October 1941 to April 1942 (flag from November 1941).
Replaced *Rodney* as flag Force H November 1941.
Detached April 1942 as flag (RA) Force F for occupation of Madagascar.
Left Gibraltar 1 April 1942 for Durban, via Cape.
Replaced in Force F by *Ramillies* at Durban 22 April and withdrawn from this operation for transfer to North Atlantic Command.
Early in the month *Malaya* had been proposed as a reinforcement for the Eastern Fleet but rejected by the C-in-C as unsuitable because of her relatively small steaming radius.
Arrived at Gibraltar 15 May and attached to Force H.

NORTH ATLANTIC COMMAND (attached Force H Gibraltar) May to October 1942.
Employed on search operations against Vichy French ships latter part of May.
Returned home early June to escort Malta convoy.
Left Clyde with convoy 5 June.
Malta Convoy 6–16 June.
Freetown to Cape convoy July to August.

Refit Clyde October to November 1942; attached to Home Fleet on completion of this.

HOME FLEET (2nd BS) November 1942 to December 1943.
Detached for UK–Freetown convoy February to March 1943.
Because of her relatively unmodernized condition, as compared with *Queen Elizabeth*, *Valiant* and *Warspite*, it was decided, in July 1943, that *Malaya* should be withdrawn from service to release crew for newer ships although she did not actually pay off until December. Used as target for dummy attacks by midget submarines, training Loch Cairnbawn August 1943 for attack on *Tirpitz*; ship moored behind nets in the Loch for these exercises.
Paid off to reserve, in Care & Maintenance, 3 December 1943.

RESERVE (Care & Maintenance Clyde) December 1943 to June 1944.
In Western Approaches Command during this period.
Refit March to May 1944.
Recommissioned 22 June 1944 for operational service in Home Fleet as unit bombardment force for Normandy invasion.

HOME FLEET (Normandy Bombardment Force) June to October 1944.
Carried out various bombardments during Normandy campaign, including bombardment of enemy-held islands off St-Malo 1 September. Reverted to reserve October 1944.

RESERVE (Portsmouth) October 1944 to June 1947 (attached to *Vernon* from May 1945).
Attached to *Vernon* 15 May 1945 as Accommodation Ship and known as *Vernon 11*.
Placed on Disposal List June 1947.
Sold to British Iron & Steel Corporation 20 February 1948 and allocated to Metal Industries Ltd, Faslane, for scrapping.
Arrived Faslane 12 April 1948.

Below: *Malaya*'s final guise, 1944, showing her camouflage, which she kept until the end of the war.

ROYAL SOVEREIGN CLASS

DESIGN

The *Royal Sovereign* class were the first ships for whose design Eustace Tennyson D'Eyncourt was wholly responsible; he had been offered the position of DNC by the Lordship of the Admiralty, and was anxious to show that he was worthy of their confidence. He accepted the job in a letter to the Admiralty dated 9 July 1912.

'With reference to our conversation of yesterday I have the honour to inform you that I have now consulted my directors and they have consented to release me from my engagement at Elswick at such time as you may arrange with me. I am therefore in a position to accept the post of Director of Naval Construction which you have offered me upon the terms that you have mentioned, that is to say the salary is to be £2,000 per annum whilst Sir Philip Watts acts in an advisory capacity to the Admiralty and is to be increased to £3,000 per annum whenever the arrangement with Sir Philip Watts ceases.'

His main problem was that the Board could not make up its mind in which direction to go. Would they be better off with an improved *Queen Elizabeth* type (ten 15in guns, 25 knots) or would a return to a slower, less heavily armed ship be more suitable?

The vessels would have to be at least equal in speed to existing battleships (21 knots) and just as well armed and protected. After much debate which showed that it was almost impossible to come up with a satisfactory design to the Board's limited specification, a few sketches were produced. Because of the greater length and cost there could be no question of increasing the armament to nine or ten guns as first envisaged, but all agreed that the new ship should have 15in

guns, and armour strakes equal to those of *Queen Elizabeth*. Moreover, because of the apprehension regarding maintenance of oil supply in times of war, a lower speed together with other disadvantages attendant on coal was excepted as the price of safety. Later, however the ships were modified to burn oil only (late 1914), the changes being made on the initiative of Lord Fisher immediately on taking up his appointment as First Sea Lord in October 1914.

On 31 March 1913 the Board approved a layout (marked T1) for a vessel carrying eight 15in guns with speeds of up to 21–22 knots, but other

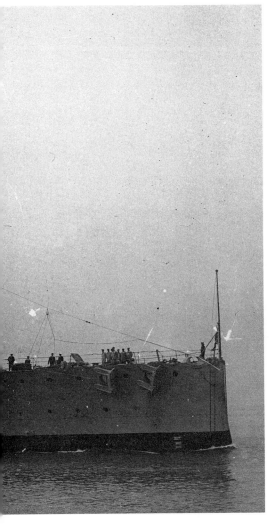

details remained to be worked out. A reduction in dimensions from *Queen Elizabeth* was made possible because the lower speed enabled machinery and boiler spaces to be reduced, but other principal requirements were similar to the *QE*s.

The forecastle extended aft to 'X' turret as in *Queen Elizabeth* but the sides before the battery were less strongly recessed, the flare being unbroken as far aft as 'A' turret in *Revenge* and 'B' turret in the others. Owing to the re-arrangement of the battery, the after end of the forecastle angled in to the centre line from considerably farther forward than in the *Queen Elizabeths*, the quarter-deck, at the sides being about 70 feet longer than in those ships.

A light shelter deck for boat stowage (not provided in the *Queen Elizabeths*) was fitted amidships. Metacentric height and stability were reduced with a view to securing a steadier gun platform than in some of the earlier dreadnought classes which suffered from an irregular motion because of excessive stability. Compared to the *Iron Duke* class, metacentric height was reduced from 5½ feet to 3 feet with 1½ feet less beam on the same length (pp) and 6 inches deeper in the nominal draught. This figure was lower than in any of the preceding British dreadnoughts which had a metacentric height of 5–5½ feet, and special measures were taken to minimize the risk of extensive flooding in the event of waterline damage. These comprised: 1. Raising the height of the strongly protected freeboard by placing the principal armoured deck at main deck level, well above deep load water-line, and carrying a maximum thickness of belt armour up to this. 2. Provision of a longitudinal armoured bulkhead between the middle and main decks on each side amidships.

The addition of bulges (fitted in *Ramillies* while building and in the others later) raised the metacentric height and improved stability but this was again reduced by the extra weights subsequently imposed. Early reports that the bulges being fitted to *Ramillies* were a special stability type intended mainly to reduce rolling were thought to be erroneous, but in fact it was quite true. The bulges fitted in all five ships were specifically for anti-torpedo purposes, but it was calculated that the improvement would enhance stability especially if the bilge keels were retained. To assist manoeuvrability a small auxil-

iary rudder was fitted, but it proved ineffectual and was later remoted from the class.

After the basic design had been released, the former DNC (P. Watts) accused Tennyson D'Eyncourt of stealing one of his designs and claimed that he had in fact been working along the same lines for a new layout before leaving office. No evidence of or reply to this outrageous accusation has been found. It was generally known that Watts did not approve of Tennyson D'Eyncourt's appointment as DNC.

On completion in 1916 (*Ramillies* not until 1917) the class augmented the Grand Fleet with a powerful presence, but the records show that from the beginning they never enjoyed a reputation as good as that of the *Queen Elizabeths* or indeed even the *Iron Dukes*. They were fine ships, though often accused of being wet ships given the reduced freeboard – but then so were the *Queen Elizabeths* and the *Iron Dukes* in anything other than a moderate sea.

After the war (1919) an exhaustive examination of the captured German battleship *Baden* (Germany's final answer to the First World War dreadnoughts) revealed that in many ways *Royal Sovereign* was superior to the German vessel. Protection to waterline amidships and armament was very similar in both ships, weight of vertical armour, excluding turret and conning tower, was 19.8 per cent of displacement in *Royal Sovereign* against 21.8 per cent in *Baden*. Horizontal protection was stronger in *Royal Sovereign* at 9.6 per cent against 7.2 per cent in *Baden*, and underwater protection at 2.3 per cent in *Royal Sovereign* against 2.6 per cent in *Baden*. The stability of underwater strength was slightly less in *Royal Sovereign*, but the fitting of bulges more than compensated any advantages enjoyed by the German vessel.

Much had been said of the German ships' ability to retain a suitable condition when damaged, and they are generally admired for their staying power, but tests carried out in 1921 proved in theory at least that British ships were more or less on a par with contemporary German designs – equal (though sometimes inferior) in some areas, slightly superior in others.

When Admiral John Jellicoe boarded *Revenge* in April 1916 he was not at all impressed with some of her specifications:

'I am enclosing a few criticisms as a result of a short visit to *Revenge* and conversation with her

Captain. She is extraordinarily wet. I prefer to alter her for alternative Fleet Flagship to waiting for *Royal Oak* as the latter will be some time before she is efficient. We can do the work here, I think, quite satisfactorily and certainly at Invergordon.

'It is a very great pity and a very great retrograde step that the vessels have been provided with two masts and the same of course applies to the *Queen Elizabeth* class. I can see no possible reason why the boat derrick should not have been worked from a stump mast, just abaft the funnel. This would meet all requirements and would prevent the two masts being used as they will be now, to enable the enemy to ascertain our course. I suggest that in any ships now building, if it will not delay their completion, this alteration be effected. The conning tower is very cramped and also very difficult of access and egress. Considering the restricted views aft it is essential that the Admiral should be able to get out of the conning tower quickly in order to observe the movements of the Fleet. This is quite impracticable in *Revenge* as he has to crawl

in and out of two holes and when inside, the space available is insufficient for the Flagship of the C-in-C and is considerably less than that in the conning tower of *Iron Duke*. I am of the opinion that a good many of the communications could be placed in the spaces below the conning tower in order to give more room. The bridge arrangements are thoroughly bad compared with *Iron Duke* and *Queen Elizabeth* classes. The ship's charthouse is one deck lower than necessary. There are no facilities for the Admiral on the bridge at all. It is presumably intended that he should work the Fleet from the bridge on which his charthouse is located but it should be obvious that he is much too far away from the Captain and the compass in this position. I am fitting in the *Revenge* an Admiral's charthouse on the bridge below the standard compass platform and placing signalling searchlights on that bridge. It is the position from which the Fleet must be worked. The present Admiral's charthouse is being converted into an Admiral's upper deck cabin leaving the present upper deck cabin for the Chief in Staff or Captain of the Fleet.

'There are many other points in the design which might be enlarged upon but it is perhaps too late to do so now, but there is one point which is certainly wrong and that is that the ship is as usual down by the bows and owing apparently to her not being sufficiently waterborne forward is even wetter in a sea way than her predecessors. It appears from a report of the Captain that when pitching in a head sea she offers no resistance to dipping until the flare of the upper deck level gets under water. Our ships in fact are too fine forward, and this combined with the heavy weight of the two turrets forward renders them unacceptable of keeping their bows above water when pitching.'

It would appear that the class was never fully modernized and there were a number of reasons for this:
1. All documents on the subject show that there was a distinct lack of room from the bridge to the mainmast and any increase in the length would have to be added in this area rather than at the ends. This could not be achieved by simply removing equipment from the upper deck;

extensive internal structural changes would have to be made.

2. The fact that the ships had a very low GM made it difficult to add and subtract items without upsetting the ships' general sea qualities and altering their original stability as a consequence.

3. The main reason seems to have been simply the enormous amount of time and expense involved.

Many papers discussing their modernization were put forward during the inter-war years, but all are marked with a reminder that the ships were due for replacement from 1935.

All were modernized to some extent from 1924 to 1939, but their reduced stability made then unsuitable for reconstruction on the same scale as was possible in the *Queen Elizabeth* class, and the shorter, narrower hull was also more difficult to adopt to modern requirements.

Principal modifications comprised:

1. Increased AA armament with improved control equipment.
2. Removal of torpedo tubes in majority.
3. Addition of aircraft catapult in *Resolution*, *Royal Oak* and *Royal Sovereign* (removed from *Royal Sovereign* in 1936–7).
4. Addition of deep bulges in *Royal Oak* and *Ramillies*. Shallow bulges previously fitted in *Ramillies*, *Resolution*, *Revenge* and *Royal Sovereign* and remained unchanged in the last three ships.
5. Modified and much enlarged bridge work.

In view of their limited modernization and relatively low speed it was proposed, early in 1939, that the ships be discarded, but of course this was dropped on the outbreak of war. In 1941 Churchill proposed converting two or more of the class to super monitors for projected operations in the Baltic and on the enemy's North Sea coast, and for the bombardment of Italian ports. One or two turrets were to be removed, AA armament augmented, deck protection increased and wider bulges fitted. Designs were prepared for this, but the idea was subsequently abandoned on the grounds that the ships might be of greater value in protecting convoys against surface attack by heavy ships, and the work would interfere with other and more urgent requirements elsewhere.

All served in the Grand Fleet from 1916 to 1919. From 1939 to 1945 they were employed mainly on escort duties. With *Warspite* (Flag) *Ramillies*, *Resolution*, *Revenge* and *Royal Sovereign* formed the 3rd Battle Squadron of the Emergency Eastern Fleet organized in the Indian Ocean in March 1942 following the fall of Singapore and based at Colombo and Kilindini.

Royal Oak war loss 1939.

Resolution and *Revenge* reduced to reserve late 1943 and employed on Subsidiary Service.

Ramillies similar, late 1944.

Royal Sovereign transferred to Russia on loan in 1944 and renamed *Archangelsk*. Returned to the Royal Navy 1949. Placed on Disposal List and sold in 1949 (see Histories).

Ramillies, *Resolution* and *Revenge* placed on Disposal List and sold in 1948.

ARMAMENT

Main armament details were the same as those of the *Queen Elizabeth* class with only minor alterations.

During the design stage it was suggested that it might be possible to have ten 15in guns mounted as in *Iron Duke*, but this idea seems to have been dismissed on the grounds that eight guns constituted the ideal number for control purposes and that an extra pair would not provide an increase in offensive power proportionate to the additional size, weight and cost involved. But serious consideration was given to a suggestion that it might be possible to have nine guns if 'Y' turret could be fitted with a triple mount. There would have to be some alteration to the hull shape aft to accommodate the larger turret, but at that time it was considered essential to have as many big guns as possible in any new design. Investigations into this theme revealed that the reasons for rejecting ten guns were equally valid for nine, and to produce a triple turret at such short notice would mean a great delay in construction times. The same thing applied to the secondary armament.

The 6in guns numbered two fewer than in the *Queen Elizabeth*s as designed but were the same as in those ships after the 1915 modifications. At the design stage, however, it had been hoped to fit a more powerful battery than the one

ROYAL SOVEREIGN ARMOURED LAYOUT, 1919

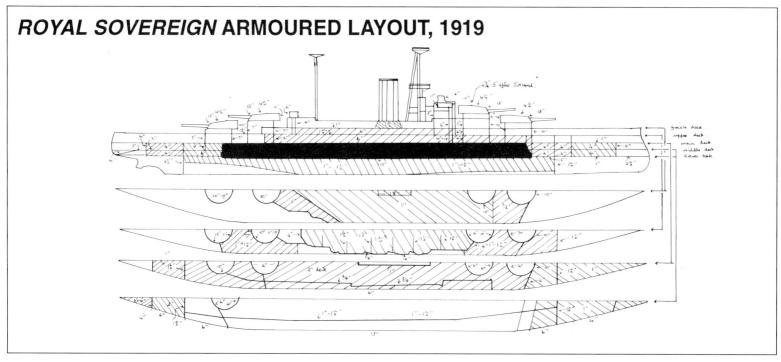

accepted. In the T1 layout, a variation showed a 2-tier 6in battery, shorter in length and placed more amidships.

The design featured some differences from that of the completed *Royal Sovereign*: 1. a 12in main belt; 2. barbette armour increased; 3. hull shape alteration with thicker armoured belt extensions. In the forward battery there were two guns on the upper deck abreast 'A' barbette. The midships 6in were on the upper deck, two firing right ahead, six guns on the forecastle, two on the main deck abreast 'Y' barbette, i.e., eight guns firing right ahead (*RS* only six); six guns right astern (*RS* only four).

The increased dimensions to include these proposals were unfortunately not favoured at the time and a more conventional layout similar to that of *Queen Elizabeth* was approved by the Board. As completed, when firing the aft 15in guns in these ships, it was reported that the wardroom and gunroom were severely shaken up when the muzzles were on a forward bearing and firing full charges. This was never remedied throughout the ships' careers and seems to have been normal in all battleships of the period. The

all-round 6in armament, as completed, was an improvement over the *Iron Duke* and *Queen Elizabeth* classes, but the battery was still very wet and most difficult to fight in a head sea.

These were the last capital ships for the Royal Navy to have a tween deck battery for secondary armament and also the last to carry any guns below the upper deck.

ARMOUR

Following the lines of *Queen Elizabeth*, the *Royal Sovereign* group was very similar in armour qualities. (see WW1 book). Main belt strakes were increased at the lower edge (8in in *Queen Elizabeth*) to make a 13in uniform thickness, and armoured width also increased from 13ft 9in (*QE*) to 15ft 1½in. Elsewhere, on the vertical there was some alteration in plate application as was the case in the deck armour when the protective deck was raised to main deck level to improve armoured freeboard. As completed their vertical protection was second to none. The reduction in thickness of the anti-torpedo bulkheads (from 2in to 1½–1in), and the fact that the

ships were given low stability, proved most advantageous when the fitting of bulges was first discussed. Although *Ramillies* was the experimental ship with regard to bulges for battleships, (see bulges and underwater protection) her bulges were primarily for protection although they did indeed improve stability performance.

Others of the class, however, were given a different type of bulge in the sense that the lower section consisted of single WT chambers without any of the tube compartments or larger chambers as in other bulged vessels. The upper portion was filled with compartments containing cement and wood.

Resolution and *Revenge* were fitted with theirs in 1917–18 as an experiment, and again it was found that stability and rolling had improved. Later (1929) the bulges were fitted with water and air compartments abreast the magazines further to improve their effectiveness against torpedo attack. After completion and the bulge protection had been fitted, no extra protection was given to the class for many years, the ships being completely by-passed in favour of the *Queen Elizabeth* class. During the 1930s, however, it

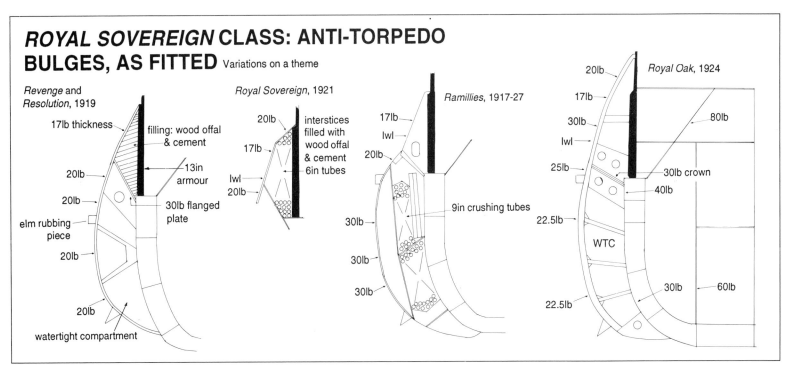

ROYAL SOVEREIGN CLASS: ANTI-TORPEDO BULGES, AS FITTED Variations on a theme

Revenge and Resolution, 1919
- 17lb thickness
- filling: wood offal & cement
- 20lb
- 13in armour
- 20lb
- 30lb flanged plate
- elm rubbing piece
- 20lb
- 20lb
- watertight compartment

Royal Sovereign, 1921
- 20lb
- interstices filled with wood offal & cement 6in tubes
- 17lb
- lwl 20lb

Ramillies, 1917-27
- 17lb
- lwl
- 20lb
- 9in crushing tubes
- 30lb
- 30lb
- 30lb

Royal Oak, 1924
- 20lb
- 17lb
- 30lb
- 80lb
- lwl
- 25lb
- 30lb crown
- 40lb
- 22.5lb
- WTC
- 30lb
- 60lb
- 22.5lb

was considered suitable to fit extra deck protection and in 1934 *Royal Oak* was given 4in NC plates over the main deck around the magazine area and 2¹/₂in NC over the machinery.

In 1939 *Royal Sovereign* and *Ramillies* were considered worthy of modernization, being viewed as the best two of the class (other than *Royal Oak*). Approval was given to fit 4in and 2¹/₂in plates as in *Royal Oak*, but lack of time and suitable materials meant that this was not done. Again, in 1941, the question arose regarding their weak deck protection and forced into the situation, the Admiralty called *Royal Sovereign*, *Resolution* and *Ramillies* into the dockyard (when opportunity arose) to fit 2¹/₂in NC plates over the magazines. From official records, however, it appears that *Resolution* was only partially fitted and *Revenge* not at all (400 tons was fitted in *Ramillies*).

UNDERWATER PROTECTION AND BULGES

From 1906 British battleship construction had progressed fairly rapidly, but in the area of

underwater protection the steps taken were retrograde in the main. There was no standard practice applied to this aspect of a ship's construction and the experimental applications in various ships had been haphazard. Many vessels had only partial internal bulkheads running down from the main deck to the inside of the hull; others had full-length internal bulkheads. All were of various thicknesses.

While *Queen Elizabeth* and *Royal Sovereign* were under construction, however, the matter of underwater protection was addressed seriously. The torpedo had become a very potent weapon and it was realized that it was vital to try to prevent an explosion in the hull proper, and to strengthen the internal bulkheads surrounding the vitals of the ship. Tests were carried out on some of the older ships prior to 1912, but now (1912) Haslar, Chatham and Cambridge test centres were all working on suitable protective measures to be applied not only to ships under construction, but to ships already in service.

The first important tests were carried out on the old pre-dreadnought *Hood* (*Royal Sovereign* class, 1889) which was sent to Portsmouth for

that purpose on 27 February 1913. The experiments were as follows (see also drawings):

1. Explode charge of 280lb wet gun cotton in contact with ship's side at 111 station, twelve feet below the surface. Compartments (111 to 123) to be filled with oil and some other compartments in the area to be left empty (101–111). This experiment was to show the value of *Queen Elizabeth*'s underwater protection (as fitted in design) and the value of oil or empty compartments against explosion.
2. Explode charge of 280lb wet gun cotton against side at station 73, twelve feet below surface. Compartments were to be left empty to show what the effects would be.
3. Place charge of 280lb wet gun cotton at station 91 to test 'A' and 'B' compartments.
4. Fire 21in gun cotton warhead charge in contact with net defence in position of opposite side to experiments 1, 2 and 3. The tests were completed and in June 1914 the following conclusion were reached:

'W. Gard. Portsmouth.
1. A thick bulkhead should be placed at the

ROYAL SOVEREIGN CLASS: BULGES

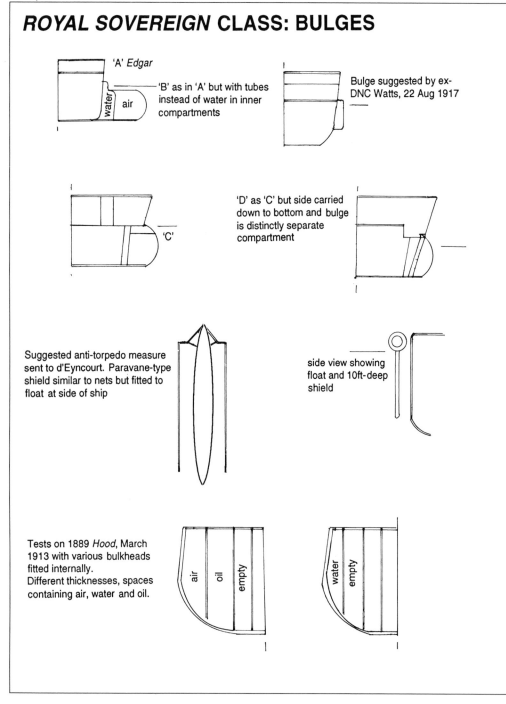

'A' *Edgar*

'B' as in 'A' but with tubes instead of water in inner compartments

Bulge suggested by ex-DNC Watts, 22 Aug 1917

'C'

'D' as 'C' but side carried down to bottom and bulge is distinctly separate compartment

Suggested anti-torpedo measure sent to d'Eyncourt. Paravane-type shield similar to nets but fitted to float at side of ship

side view showing float and 10ft-deep shield

Tests on 1889 *Hood*, March 1913 with various bulkheads fitted internally.
Different thicknesses, spaces containing air, water and oil.

air | oil | empty

water | empty

outer position as in the 1st experiment so that there shall be a greater possible chance of the innermost bulkhead remaining practically intact after the explosion outboard.

2. The inner bulkhead should be connected to the thick bulkhead by ties only so that any deflection on the latter should not be directly communicated to the inner bulkhead.

3. A thick bulkhead constructed in the principle adopted for these experiments can be made sufficiently homogeneous to resist such extensive deformation as would cause the ER or BR to be thrown open to the sea.

The projectile effect noticed in the 1st experiment was absent in the second apparently due to the wings and outer bunkers being filled with water. It seems doubtful, however, whether the water in the wings was an advantage and whether the general result would not have been better if the middle compartments or outer bunker only had been filled.'

Although this and other experiments furnished much data regarding the provision of more suitable internal underwater protective bulkheads in new ships, a letter from J. D. Dick for the DNO indicated that it was not enough to have just an internal bulkhead:

'The two experiments carried out with 280lb wet gun cotton were inconclusive. The modern torpedo carries 400lb of wet gun cotton or TNT which is equivalent to 500lb of wet gun cotton, and presumably the new German 23.6in torpedo reported by the N.I.D. will be much larger.

It is considered that the presence of oil and water in the compartments has a very important bearing on the effect of the explosion and much valuable information would be gained from more tank experiments.'

Taking note of this and other reports that were received from the various departments, attention was turned towards providing not only a good internal bulkhead but an external one in the form of a blister bulge which could be fitted to new ships and older vessels if thought necessary. But it was impossible to rush the experiments, and both *Queen Elizabeth* and *Royal Sovereign* were laid down and completed without external bulges. They did, however, benefit from the *Hood* tests in the way of a thicker and more complete internal protective bulkhead.

By 1915 tests had been carried out using 400lb TNT, not against the hull proper but against various external steel shapes which were so placed as to protect the inner parts of the ship itself. On 30 April the DNC (Tennyson D'Eyncourt) wrote to the DNO explaining some of the methods that had been tried:

'I have made careful inspection of the different small-scale targets and sections of ships with bulge protection, etc., against torpedoes which have recently been experimented with by Professor Hopkinson in conjunction with *Vernon*. The preliminary conclusions are:
1. System of bulge protection, the bulge being kept entirely outside the ship proper, is very much more efficient than similar amounts of protection inside the body of a ship and experiments generally show that the permanent bulges we have put on Monitors and the *Edgar*s (cruisers) and also the temporary attached bulge arrangement on the old *Revenge* will be efficient to prevent serious damage to the ship.
2. A very efficient form of protection has been evolved by means of using layers of tubes – each being sealed at the ends, in conjunction with timber sheathing inside the tubes against the ship's side proper and the sheathing also carried round outside the tubes. This arrangement perhaps involves considerable weight, but a very efficient protection against torpedo attack can be attained by a total thickness of tubes and timber of about 4 to 5 feet which should preferably be in the form of a bulge external to the ship.'

As mentioned in the DNC's letter, a number of ships were fitted with experimental bulges in an endeavour to determine the optimum bulge shape that would inhibit the effects of the explosion of a torpedo, while exacting a minimum loss of ship's speed.

The cruisers *Edgar*, *Endymion*, *Theseus* and *Grafton* were fitted with bulges of enormous proportions (see drawings) which in practice proved very efficient indeed. Because of their size, however, they were of limited value and restricted the ships to slow speeds and affected manoeuvring qualities. *Edgar*, *Grafton* and *Endymion* were all torpedoed but returned safely to port afterwards – proof enough that the work of Professor Hopkins had been successful.

With regard to the fitting of bulges in the battleships, yet another set of experiments had been conducted. The battle-cruisers *Renown* and *Repulse* had been given internal bulges on the drawing-board at the design stage, but these were shallow, much smaller fittings and of course were less effective. Those for the large cruisers *Glorious* and *Courageous* were very similar and had been included in the design. *Furious*'s bulges were larger than those of her two half-sisters but of more or less the same type.

For the *Royal Sovereign* group *Ramillies* was the test ship and she was given the most elaborate bulges fitted to date (1917). As completed, her shallow tube-filled bulges proved very successful and also gave the stability a boost by damping the rolling of the hull to some effect. Approval was given to fit the others of the class, but those for *Revenge* and *Resolution* when fitted in 1918 were, in fact, different from those of *Ramillies* in that they had no tubes. *Royal Sovereign* herself had 6in tubes in the bulges when they were fitted in 1920.

Although visually the bulges appeared the same through the class, the fact is that no two ships were identical and all of them underwent much experimentation and alteration to the underwater protective system (see drawings and *British Battleships of World War One*). As the power of torpedoes increased the effectiveness of bulges and indeed the whole of the underwater protective system in many of the older battleships became less effective. Nevertheless, *Ramillies* and *Resolution* both took serious torpedo hits during the war (see battle damage section) and survived – a tribute indeed to the strength of the internal structure of the ships and the design of the bulges in general. *Royal Oak*, however, was sunk very effectively, having taken at least three hits just below the bulge and armoured belts (see battle damage section). Examination of the holes in her hull show why she sank in about thirteen minutes (see drawing).

MACHINERY

Originally designed as coal-fired ships, following the pattern of the *Iron Duke*s rather than repeating the propulsive system of *Queen Elizabeth*, they were naturally slower ships. SHP was fixed at 31,000 for 21 knots and they were laid down as such.

On Lord Fisher's return to the Admiralty, however, one of his early moves was to instigate the fitting of an oil-fired boilers to new ships on the stocks. This increased their SHP to 40,000 for 23 knots and it was achieved with the minimum of fuss or interruption to the continuity of construction. Having fewer boilers than *Queen Elizabeth* or *Iron Duke*, the ships could be fitted with only a single uptake, the first British dreadnoughts to have this feature. As completed the class all put up a good turn of speed and although the usual full set of trials were not carried out because of wartime conditions, it was reported that they all made in excess of 21–22 knots – not quite up to expectations but certainly as fast as most British capital ships and adequate for Grand Fleet duties. The fastest ship of the class was *Revenge* with *Royal Oak* a close second. Their machinery and boilers were never updated and consequently in 1939 they were sadly lacking in speed; if the hulls were foul, they were lucky to reach 19 knots on full power.

BRIDGEWORK

As completed the class were fitted with a tripod foremast and simple bridgework different in appearance from the *Queen Elizabeth*s but identical in arrangement. The Great War saw many additions to the bridge and upper works in the way of SL towers, extra wing extensions, covers, windows, rangefinders, range clocks and charthouses, etc., so that their appearance became rather unique and they could easily be distinguished from one another by the different bridge fittings.

During the 1920s and 1930s the canvas surrounds were removed and in many cases replaced by light gauge sheet metal; the bridges were given canvas covers and sometimes completely enclosed with similar plating (end of 1930s, not in all). Extra windows were installed around the charthouse and the tripod foremast was almost hidden from view and could be called overcrowded – by 1939 the tripod was in fact hidden except for the section reaching up to the control top.

Although the staff serving these ships were almost always at the mercy of the elements, there was never any general complaint because the simple fact was that although the bridge and charthouse positions were draughty, wet and generally uncomfortable, the all-round view and manning positions at all levels were much preferred to a completely enclosed position. By 1940 many more extras had been added includ-

ROYAL SOVEREIGN CLASS

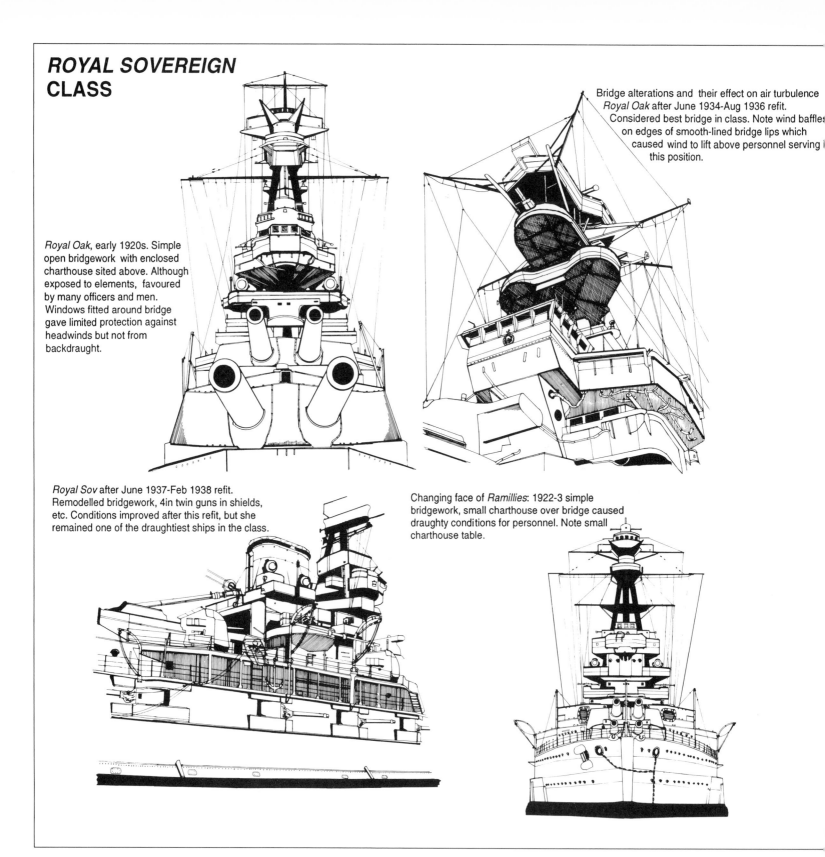

Royal Oak, early 1920s. Simple open bridgework with enclosed charthouse sited above. Although exposed to elements, favoured by many officers and men. Windows fitted around bridge gave limited protection against headwinds but not from backdraught.

Bridge alterations and their effect on air turbulence *Royal Oak* after June 1934-Aug 1936 refit. Considered best bridge in class. Note wind baffles on edges of smooth-lined bridge lips which caused wind to lift above personnel serving this position.

Royal Sov after June 1937-Feb 1938 refit. Remodelled bridgework, 4in twin guns in shields, etc. Conditions improved after this refit, but she remained one of the draughtiest ships in the class.

Changing face of *Ramillies*: 1922-3 simple bridgework, small charthouse over bridge caused draughty conditions for personnel. Note small charthouse table.

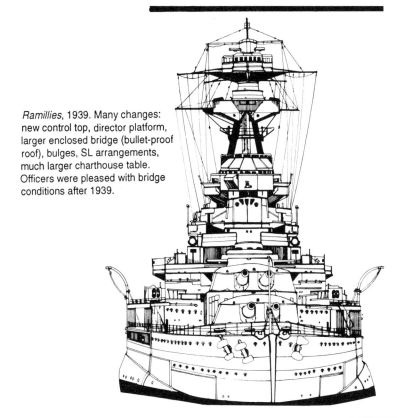

Royal Sov, 1923 Simple narrow bridgework protruding forward away from tripod legs. Note tall charthouse (which had reached a tremendous height by 1935 - see main drawings) and companion-ways at rear of bridge.

Ramillies, 1939. Many changes: new control top, director platform, larger enclosed bridge (bullet-proof roof), bulges, SL arrangements, much larger charthouse table. Officers were pleased with bridge conditions after 1939.

Below: A close up of *Resolution* in 1924 showing clearly how the upper bridge charthouse projected forward of the tripod. Note the searchlight towers incorporated at the rear of the superstructure (upper and lower levels).

ing light AA guns at the base of the bridge and all upperworks becoming overcrowded with RDF aerials of many kinds. The manning of the ship from open bridge work was still preferred, however – one officer commenting: 'We like to see what the Germans are throwing at us'. During this period *Ramillies* and *Royal Oak* had the newest and most spacious bridges with *Resolution* and *RS* following.

Report from the Bridge in Ramillies after her refit in July 1934:

'During the period of the trials the weather was fine and warm. Conditions on the bridge were quite pleasant. The D.N.E and Commander Wadham both visited the ship and were on the bridge during full power runs. Also Commander Tush representing D of N. The CO (Captain R. Leatham) of the ship stated that from a navigational point of view the bridge would be reported upon favourably but from a tactical standpoint

Below: Close up of the *Royal Sovereign*'s bridge after refit May 1938. Note that the underside of the bridge has been enclosed to alleviate the draught, and the bridge has been roofed in.

he would not be able to make a report until the ship had had exercises with attacking aircraft. He opened all the windows on the bridge in demonstration to the DNE and conditions were not unpleasant, the inevitable draught being at about the height of the windows and not low down as was the case in *Valiant* before the compass platform was enclosed.

'With regard to the open corners of the compass platform, the awnings had not yet been fitted and therefore could not be tried. Captain Leatham made the suggestion that the openings would be more effective if stools were provided so that the observer's head could be taken to just above the level of the roof. He also suggested that the openings might be much smaller (just large enough for an observer to place his head through) rectangular in shape and fitted with a bullet-proof shutter

'The view of the forecastle from the bridge is quite good enabling the Captain and Navigating Officer to watch operations on deck.'

HANDLING AND MANOEUVRABILITY

As completed the class did not have a bad reputation in either handling or manoeuvring qualities, although they tended to roll slightly more than had been intended in the design. After being bulged conditions improved to a degree and the subject was practically forgotten. As they became older, however, and many weights had been added, they became rather awkward to handle in certain conditions. Although this could be said of many of the older battleships, it was almost customary to pay lip service to the *Royal Sovereign*s and it is on record that some of them 'played up' especially at slow speeds.

During the early months of the Second World War the Captain of *Ramillies* (H. T. Baille-Grohman) had nothing but praise for the old ship and some of his comments disperse criticism which in many cases were unfounded:

'No difficulty was experienced entering or leaving Fremantle, but immediately after leaving the port at 0630 on Thursday 21st December it was found necessary to anchor owing to overheated condensers. This overheating was caused by immense quantities of particularly stringy weed which had entered the condensers. It would appear that Fremantle as dredged is not

Right: *Ramillies* in July 1934 after extensive refit. Note the large bulges, tripod mainmast and catapult on 'X' turret. After this refit she achieved 22.03 knots on her four-hour trials on the Tolland Mile at 29,540 tons.

Royal Sovereign class: Particulars, as completed

Construction

Royal Sovereign: Portsmouth DY; Laid down 15.1.1914; Launched 29.4.1915; completed 8.4.1916. *Royal Oak*: Devonport DY; Laid down 15.1.1914; Launched 17.11.1914; Completed 1.5.1916.

Revenge: Vickers; Laid down 22.12.1913; Launched 29.5.1915; Completed 24.3.1916. *Resolution*: Palmers; Laid down 29.11.1913; Launched 14.1.1915; Completed 7.12.1916. *Ramillies*: Beardmore; Laid down 12.11.1913; Launched 12.9.1916; Completed 5.5.1917.

Displacement (tons):

27,970 tons load, 31,130 tons average deep load.

Dimensions

Length: 580ft 3in (pp), 614 ft 6in (wl), 620ft 6⅞in (oa). (*Ramillies*)

Beam: 88ft 6in (88ft 7in *Revenge*)

Draught: 30ft load, 33ft 7in deep.

Armament

8 x 15in 42cal Mk I

14 x 6in 45cal Mk XII

2 x 3in AA

4 x 3pdr QF

10 Lewis

4 x 21 TT in submerged tubes (21 torpedoes)

Armour

Main belt 13in amidships; Forward strakes 6–4–1in; Aft strakes 6–4in; Upper side amidships 6in; Barbettes 10–9–7–6in; Turrets 13–11in; Bulkheads 6–4in; Decks: forecastle 1in; upper 1½in; main 2in; middle 4–3–2in; lower 2½in.

Machinery

Parsons reaction turbines driving four 3-bladed propellers (diam inner 10ft, outer 9ft 3in).

18 Babcock & Wilcox boilers in *Revenge*, *Ramillies* and *RS*, Yarrow in other two.

Engine room size 69ft 11in;

Boiler room size. No. 1: 37ft 11¾in, No. 2: 38ft, No. 3: 38ft 1in, 6 boilers each room.

Weight of machinery: 2,550 tons (approx).

Main feed output: (vertical steam reciprocating cylinder) 71.4 tons per hour.

Auxiliary feed pump output: 35.7 tons per hour.

Average designed revs 300rpm.

Designed SHP: 40,000 for 23 knots.

Fuel (tons) oil normal, 3,400 max.

Radius of action: 900 7,000 nm at 10 knots, 3,600 nm at 18 knots, 2,700 nm at full speed.

Searchlights: 8 x 36in in all (11 x 36in *Ramillies* as completed).

Complement: 909 *Royal Oak*; 910 *Resolution*; 938 *Ramillies*.

Costs: £2,570,504 (*Royal Sovereign*), *Ramillies* being the most expensive at £3,295,810.

Royal Sovereign class: Particulars, 1919

Displacement (tons)

Revenge: 29,590 (legend), 32,460 (deep), 32,820 (extra deep); *Ramillies*: 30,400 (legend), 33,200 (deep), 33,570 (extra deep).

Dimensions

Length unchanged. Beam: *Ramillies* (bulged) 101ft 5½in; *Revenge* and *Resolution* (bulged) 101ft 6in; *Royal Sovereign* and *Royal Oak* as completed.

Draught: 29ft 3½in (legend), 31ft 11in (average deep).

Armament: unchanged.

Machinery: unchanged.

Searchlights: 8 x 36in; 2 x 24in signalling. Improved control equipment fitted.

Aircraft

Platform fitted over 'B' and 'X' turrets in all. *Revenge* fitted for towing kite balloon. In post-war period aircraft not normally carried, but embarked only when required for exercises. Runways over 15in guns generally removed from 1920.

Armour

As original with the exception of extra plating over magazines and turret tops as a result of Jutland.

Armoured casemates added to upper pair of 6in guns in *Resolution*, *Revenge* and *Royal Sovereign*.

Machinery and boilers: unchanged.

Speed: About 22 knots full.

Fuel and radius: unchanged.

Rig: As original, plus struts forward from starfish below control top in *Ramillies* and *Royal Sovereign*.

W/T: Type 1–16, 32, 2–34, 9 and 31.

Complement: *Revenge*, 1,240; *Ramillies*, 1,213; *Royal Oak*, 1,215.

suitable for warships of this draught.

Strong head winds were experienced on the first part of the voyage to Melbourne and subsequently a fairly heavy swell on the starboard beam or quarter. This necessitated an increased in revolutions in order to arrive on time as arranged. The ship arrived at Melbourne at 13.45 on Christmas Day, Monday 25th December 1939.

The ship remained in Melbourne for 63 hours which time was not enough to allow boilers to cool down sufficiently for work to be carried out on them.

'The distance steamed by HM Ship under my command in December 1939 is of interest, and likely to be a record up to date for a month's steaming by a battleship of any Navy, with also a possible record for the best day's run.

Distances are as follows:

On patrol to Aden (1st and 2nd December) 500 miles.

Aden to Wellington, calling at Socotra (4th to 31st December) 8,985 miles.

Total distance for month 9,485 miles.

Average speed for whole distance 16.5 knots.

Best day's run: (24th December) 464 miles.

Average speed for best days run 19.3 knots.

Fastest run was from Fremantle to Port Philip Heads, 1,757 miles.

Average speed 19.2 knots.

The distance steamed for the first year of commission will be over 40,000 miles.

A comparison with peace-time steaming is as follows:

Average annual distance steamed for period 1930–1938, 6,861 miles at an average speed of 11.5 knots.

Ramillies was docked 28th October to 6th November 1939 at Alexandria, otherwise she has had no refit since February 1939.

HANDLING:

Although an *R* class battleship is notoriously unsteady at slow speeds and in shallow water, the ship handled very well throughout both passages. Recourse to working the engines to over-

GM and Stability

Royal Sovereign after bulging (figures taken from 1924 inclining tests)

Displacement (tons)	Draught	GM	Max. stability
Condition A (legend)			
29,710	29ft 5in	5.22ft	35°
Condition B (deep)			
32,570	31ft 11in	5.52ft	36°
Condition C (extra deep)			
32,930	32ft 4in	5.66ft	36½°
Condition D (light)			
28,520	28ft 4½in	5.30ft	34½in
Compared to *Royal Oak* with her larger bulges, June 1924.			
Condition A (legend)			
29,160	28ft 3½in	6.3ft	
Condition C (extra deep)			
32,800	31ft 4½in	6.3ft	

come incipient sheers was only necessary on two occasions on the passage South and on one for the passage North. The greatest care was required when entering a restricted portion of the Canal from a wider.

It was found, as intimated, that the rudder has to be used generously and quickly. The wash caused by the ship did not appear to be any more excessive than that caused by a moderate sized vessel.'

This was a wonderful report for an old ship which, according to the Admiralty, was due for scrapping in about 1935 and especialy given that

the design had received little or no reconstruction since 1917.

By the end of the war (1944), however, many more weights had been added (extra bridgework, radar, AA guns, etc.) which proved too much for the old ships as the following report shows:

'By 1944 *Ramillies* had increased her draught from 29½ft to 34½ft and was exceedingly difficult to manage. Coming home through Suez it was impossible to steady ship for a moment. She had to be carried with large rudder and frequent reversals of one engine for hour after hour and despite a tug she took the ground 4 times. 8

knots seemed to be the most manageable but not good at that.'

APPEARANCE CHANGES, REFITS AND MODIFICATIONS

Well-proportioned, fine-looking ships, they were characterized by the single large flat-sided funnel which gave then a most impressive appearance. They were easily distinguishable from the *Queen Elizabeth* class by:
1. Single funnel.
2. Upper bridge not extended back so much.

ROYAL SOVEREIGN CLASS

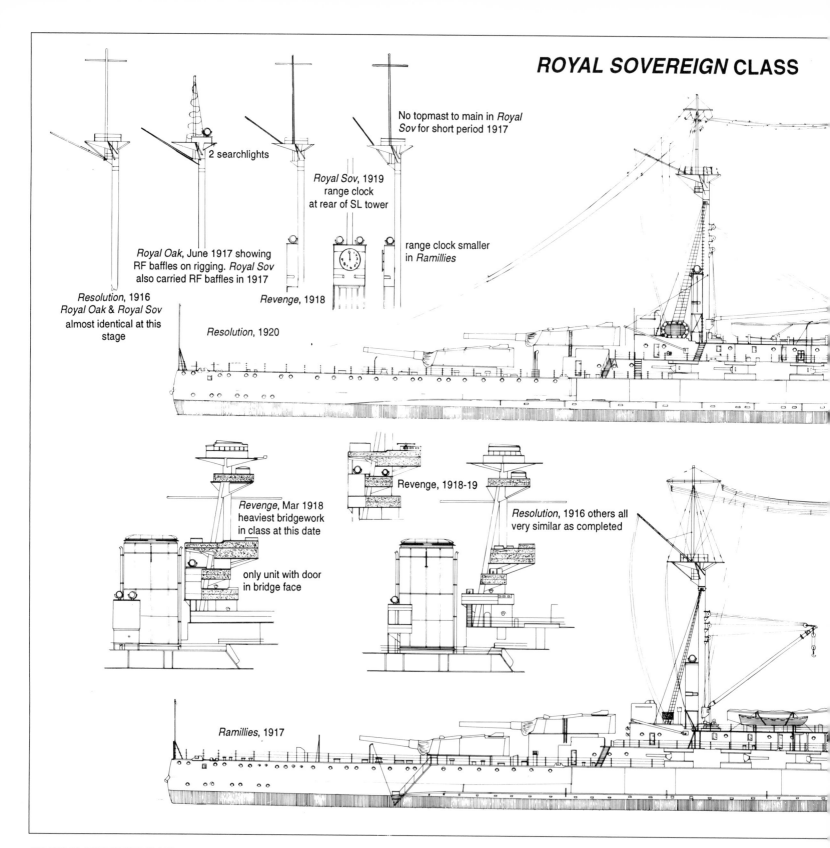

2 searchlights

No topmast to main in *Royal Sov* for short period 1917

Royal Sov, 1919 range clock at rear of SL tower

range clock smaller in *Ramillies*

Royal Oak, June 1917 showing RF baffles on rigging. *Royal Sov* also carried RF baffles in 1917

Revenge, 1918

Resolution, 1916 *Royal Oak* & *Royal Sov* almost identical at this stage

Resolution, 1920

Revenge, Mar 1918 heaviest bridgework in class at this date

Revenge, 1918-19

only unit with door in bridge face

Resolution, 1916 others all very similar as completed

Ramillies, 1917

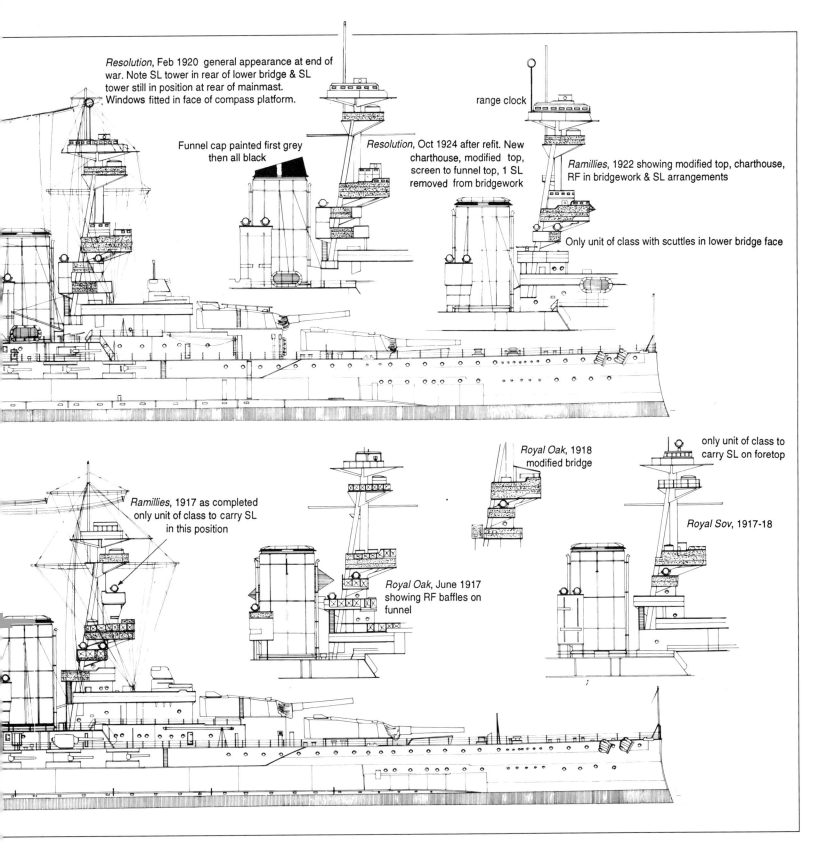

Resolution, Feb 1920 general appearance at end of war. Note SL tower in rear of lower bridge & SL tower still in position at rear of mainmast. Windows fitted in face of compass platform.

Funnel cap painted first grey then all black

Resolution, Oct 1924 after refit. New charthouse, modified top, screen to funnel top, 1 SL removed from bridgework

range clock

Ramillies, 1922 showing modified top, charthouse, RF in bridgework & SL arrangements

Only unit of class with scuttles in lower bridge face

Ramillies, 1917 as completed only unit of class to carry SL in this position

Royal Oak, 1918 modified bridge

only unit of class to carry SL on foretop

Royal Oak, June 1917 showing RF baffles on funnel

Royal Sov, 1917-18

REVENGE: GENERAL ARRANGEMENTS AS COMPLETED, 1916

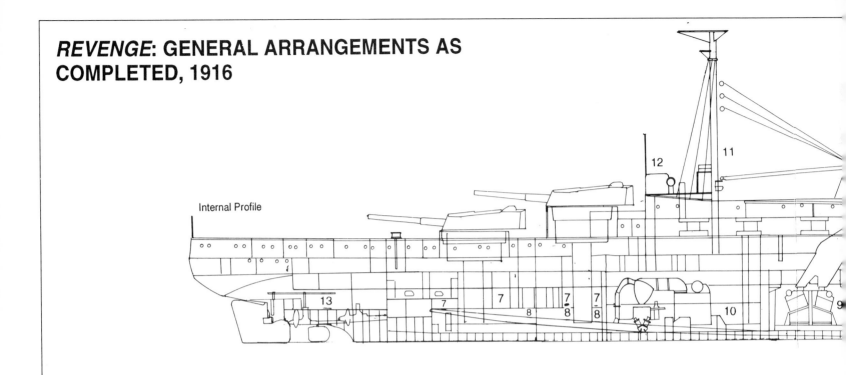

Internal Profile

3. Navigating platform projected noticeably further forward.
4. Longer 6in battery, more amidships.
5. 6in gun (P&S) on forecastle deck over second battery gun.
6. 15in director tower on platform below control top instead of over this.

Their appearance in 1919 was rather heavier than originally as a consequence of the 1916–18 wartime additions, including enlarged control tops, enlarged bridge (*Resolution* and *Revenge*), SL towers and aircraft platforms on turret tops. Anti-torpedo bulges in *Ramillies*, *Revenge* and *Resolution* were not very prominent at this stage.

Individual differences:

Ramillies	Low SL towers abeam funnel. Lower yard on foremast at director platform.
Others:	Taller SL towers at rear of funnel. Lower yard.
Revenge	Forecastle side recessed abaft out face of 'A' barbette (shaft 'B' in other four). Upper bridge extended back to near funnel. Middle and lower bridges extended back and was connected by curved screen.
Resolution	Middle and lower bridges as *Revenge*, only two ships thus. Very long gaff at starfish.

Royal Oak	Flange high up between tripod legs(only ship of class with this). Bridges not extended. Very long gaff from heel of top mast.
Royal Sovereign	Bridges as *Royal Oak*. Signal struts forward from fore starfish. Shorter gaff from heel of topmast.

Royal Sovereign Refit, May 1921 to September 1922:
1. Large base RF fitted at rear of 'B' turret.
2. RF removed from between SL towers at rear of funnel.
3. Range clocks added over 'X' turret and extra one fitted over control top.
4. HA RF fitted on small tower over bridge.
5. SL tower abaft mainmast removed.
6. Anti-torpedo bulge fitted, similar to those in *Revenge* and *Resolution*.

Royal Sovereign 1924–5: 3in AA guns replaced by 4in AA.

Royal Sovereign Refit, October 1927 to June 1928:
1. Control top enlarged and modified.
2. Upper pair of 6in guns and casemates removed.
3. Extra pair of 4in AA added.
4. Foretopmast and yard below director platform removed.

5. Extra signal struts fitted at starfish below control top and at director platform.

Royal Sovereign 1931: HA RF on control top replaced by HA director.

Royal Sovereign Refit, January to November 1932:
1. Range clock over 'X' turret removed.
2. Multiple 2pdr AA added (8 barrels) on raised platform P&S on shelter deck abeam funnel.
3. AA observation platform added each side of 15in director platform.
4. After torpedo tubes removed.
5. New rectangular SL towers fitted around funnel, with after pair of SLs raised above forward pair.
6. 24in signalling SL remounted on small platform (P&S) abeam lower bridge.
7. Training catapult (McTaggert type) fitted on quarterdeck, right aft, with crane (straight arm) abaft this.
8. Aircraft platforms removed from turrets.
9. Bridge modified and enlarged.
10. Deep supporting flanges added below navigating platform.
11. Lower bridge extended back around funnel to meet SL towers.

Royal Sovereign May to July 1935:
1. Multiple 0.5in AA (4 barrels) added P&S abeam conning tower.
2. HA RF over bridge replaced by high open tower.

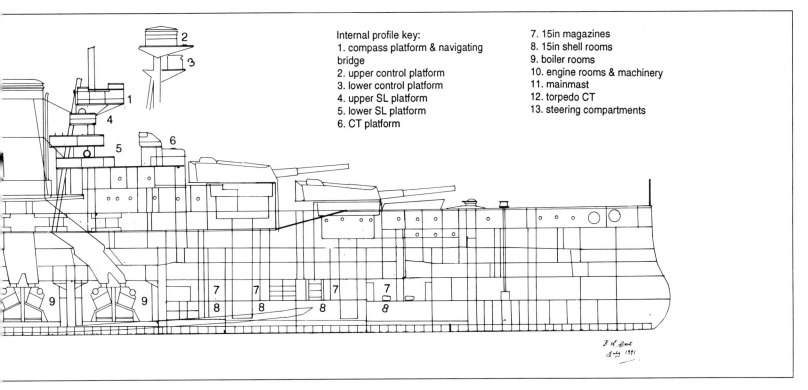

Internal profile key:
1. compass platform & navigating bridge
2. upper control platform
3. lower control platform
4. upper SL platform
5. lower SL platform
6. CT platform
7. 15in magazines
8. 15in shell rooms
9. boiler rooms
10. engine rooms & machinery
11. mainmast
12. torpedo CT
13. steering compartments

Royal Sovereign by March 1937.
Multiple 2pdr temporarily removed (some 2pdrs from *Royal Sovereign* were fitted in the aircraft carriers *Glorious* and *Courageous*). *Royal Sovereign* was given new guns. 36in SL replaced by 44in. Catapult and crane removed. Catapult base on quarterdeck retained.

Royal Sovereign Refit, June 1937 to February 1938:
1. Single 4in AA replaced by twin mount in large shields.
2. HA director on control top raised clear of top.
3. After HA director fitted in place of torpedo control tower.
4. Remaining torpedo tubes removed.
5. RDF equipment fitted (aerial at head of maintopmast).
6. Large open platform added over bridge, extended back around tripod legs.
7. Maintopgallant mast removed.
8. HA RF on bridge removed.

Royal Oak 1922. SL removed from towers abaft mainmast. Towers remained until 1924–5. (SL remounted on middle bridge in *Ramillies* only, others suppressed).

Royal Oak Refit, September 1922 to July 1923:
1. Large base RF fitted at rear of 'B' turret.
2. RF removed between SL towers at rear of funnel.

3. Range clocks added over 'X' turret.
4. HA RF mounted in small tower over bridge.
5. Very prominent anti-torpedo bulges fitted which carried almost to upper deck amidships.
6. Middle bridge level was extended back to funnel.
Legend for *Royal Oak* after refit (1924).
Length: 620ft 6in (oa), Beam over bulges: 102ft 1in, Draught: 26ft 6in forward, 29ft 6in aft
Freeboard to top of deck: 28ft forward, 16ft amidships, 17ft aft.
Height of turrets:
'A' 31ft 9in
'B' 41ft 6in
'X' 32ft 9in
'Y' 22ft 6in
SHP 40,000 and still capable of 21.75 knots.
Complement 1,188.
Armament:
Eight 15in; fourteen 6in; two 4in AA; four 21in torpedo tubes
Weights (tons)
General Equipment	720
Armament	5,020
Machinery	2,710
Fuel	900 oil
Armour and hull	19,650

Royal Oak, 1924–5: 36in SL removed from middle bridge:
Royal Oak, Refit, March 1927 to June 1927:
1. Control top enlarged and modified.

2. Range clocks over control top removed.
3. Upper pair of 6in guns removed (casemate retained).
4. Extra pair 4in AA added.
5. Foretopmast and yard below director platform removed.
6. Extra signal struts fitted to starfish below control top.
7. Topgallant fitted to mainmast.

Royal Oak, by April 1932:
1. Range clock over 'X' turret removed.
2. Forecastle deck 6in casemate removed.
3. HA RF on control top replaced by HA director (April to July 1932).

Royal Oak 1933: After pair of torpedo tubes removed. Aircraft platforms removed from turrets:

Royal Oak Refit, June 1934 to August 1936:
1. 6in director towers relocated P&S on new platforms on foremast beow 15in director.
2. 4in singles replaced by twin mountings in large shields.
3. Multiple 2pdr (8 barrels) AA added P&S on raised platform abeam funnel.
4. Multiple 0.5in AA (4 barrels) AA added P&S abeam conning tower.
5. AA RF removed from control top and over bridge
6. HA director platform fitted on tripod legs

REVENGE: GENERAL ARRANGEMENTS AS COMPLETED, 1916

Shelter deck plan key:
1. 'X' 15in turrets 2. torpedo CT
3. 50ft steam pinnaces
4. 42ft launch & 32ft pinnace
5. boiler room vents
6. funnel uptake
7. 30ft gig
8. 32ft cutter
9. captain & admiral's sea cabins
10. navigating officer's cabin
11. signal distribution office
12. 'B' 15in turret
13. 32ft life cutter

Fo'c's'le deck plan key:
1. 'Y' barbette
2. 'X' 15in turret
3. officers' smoking room
4. wardroom
5. gunroom pantry
6. wardroom pantry
7. boiler room vents
8. gunroom
9. wardroom & ante-room
10. WOs' mess
11. wardroom galley
12. gunroom galley
13. WOs' galley
14. wardroom kitchen
15. gymnastic gear store
16. bakery
17. seamen's reading room
18. funnel uptake
19. officers' drying room
20. ship's galley
21. electrical ready-use store
22. electricians' workshop
23. intelligence office
24. potato store
25. gyro table store
26. lamp room
27. inflammable paint store
28. Bo'sn's ready-use store
29. 'B' barbette
30. 'A' 15in turret

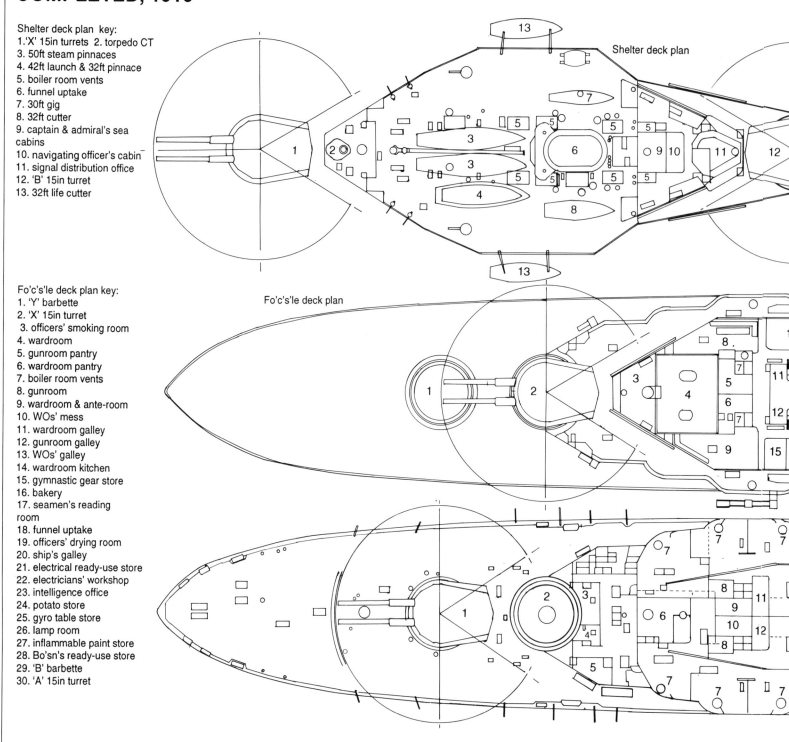

Shelter deck plan

Fo'c's'le deck plan

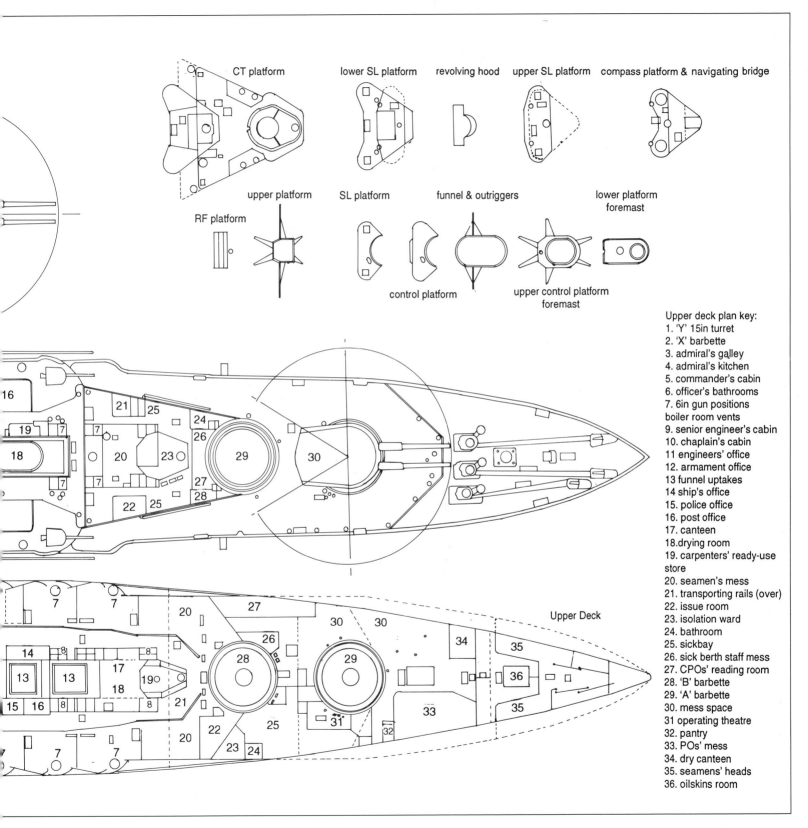

CT platform

lower SL platform

revolving hood

upper SL platform

compass platform & navigating bridge

RF platform

upper platform

SL platform

funnel & outriggers

lower platform
foremast

control platform

upper control platform
foremast

Upper deck plan key:
1. 'Y' 15in turret
2. 'X' barbette
3. admiral's galley
4. admiral's kitchen
5. commander's cabin
6. officer's bathrooms
7. 6in gun positions
boiler room vents
9. senior engineer's cabin
10. chaplain's cabin
11 engineers' office
12. armament office
13 funnel uptakes
14 ship's office
15. police office
16. post office
17. canteen
18. drying room
19. carpenters' ready-use
store
20. seamen's mess
21. transporting rails (over)
22. issue room
23. isolation ward
24. bathroom
25. sickbay
26. sick berth staff mess
27. CPOs' reading room
28. 'B' barbette
29. 'A' barbette
30. mess space
31 operating theatre
32. pantry
33. POs' mess
34. dry canteen
35. seamens' heads
36. oilskins room

Upper Deck

Below: Fleet manoeuvres in the Atlantic, March 1934. Manoeuvres took place quite often, but during those of 1934 HM ships encountered some of the heaviest seas during an exercise. *Royal Oak* is shown almost completely concealed by spray.

Bottom: *Revenge* seen from the air, showing her overall appearance in March 1934 after the stormy manoeuvres of that year.

Right: *Resolution* at anchor in Weymouth Bay *c*.1936. Note the twin 4in HA mounting on the forecastle deck abeam the funnel, fitted for experimental purposes (see drawing).

(director not fitted).
7. Four 21in torpedo tubes fitted (2 P&S) in recessed ports in forecastle before 'A' turret, for experimental purposes.
8. Remaining pair of submerged TT removed.
9. RDF fitted (aerial on main topmast with DF cabinet on starfish).
10. 36in SL replaced by 44in.
11. New SL towers fitted as in *Royal Sovereign*.
12. Training catapult (McTaggart type) and crane (large bent arm) fitted as in *Ramillies*.
13. Bridge enlarged and modified. Upper bridge a new, and completely open design, adopted only in *Royal Oak* and *Malaya*.
14. Lower bridge extended around funnel as in *Royal Sovereign*.
15. Tripod legs fitted to mainmast to support HA director.
16. Maintopgallant removed and topmast reduced.

Royal Oak Refit, by April 1939:
1. Large open platform added over bridge

extended back around tripod legs.
2. Small shield added at lower bridge level.

Revenge 1922:
1. SL removed from towers abaft mainmast.
2. Armoured casemates fitted to upper pair of 6in guns.

Revenge 1924:
1. RF removed from between SL towers
2. 3in AA replaced by 4in AA.

Revenge 1925–6:
1. Range clock added over 'X' turret.
2. 36in SL removed from middle bridge.
3. Two 24in signalling SL ex bridge remounted on forward superstructure and extra 24in SL temporarily mounted on 'B' turret (removed spring 1926).
4. Signal distributing and remote control office added at rear of upper bridge and screen between middle and lower bridges removed.
5. Topgallant fitted.

Revenge 1926–7:
1. 24in signalling SL transferred from forward superstructure to lower bridge.
2. Office at rear of upper bridge considerably enlarged.
3. Taller topgallant to main.

Revenge 1927:
One 24in SL mounted on small platform low down before bridge.

Revenge Refit, January 1928 to January 1929:
1. Control top enlarged and modified.
2. Upper pair of 6in guns and casemates removed.
3. Extra pair of 4in AA added.
4. AA observation position fitted P&S below director platform.
5. RDF equipment fitted. DF cabinet at rear of director platform.
6. Forward section of each SL tower enlarged and forward pair of SL brought further forward from funnel.
After section raised bringing after pair to a higher level.
7. 24in SL and small platform before bridge removed.
8. Aircraft platforms removed from 'X' turret.

9. Bridge enlarged.
10. Flag signalling transferred from fore to mainmast and after superstructure enlarged to accommodate signal staff.
11. Foretopmast and yard below director platform removed.
12. Taller topgallant to main.
13. Signal yard at head main topmast and close above starfish.

Revenge Refit, May to December 1931:
1. Multiple 2pdr (8 barrels) added on raised platform side of shelter deck abeam funnel (starboard only, none on port).
2. After pair of TT removed.
3. Modified type DF fitted.
4. Base of SL tower on starboard side of funnel cut away to accommodate multiple 2pdrs.
5. 24in signalling SL remounted on small platform low on mainmast.
6. Signal struts (raked well aft) fitted at starfish below control top.

Revenge 1933: Aircraft platforms removed from 'B' turret.

Revenge Refit, July 1936 to March 1937:
1. Torpedo control tower and RF removed.

2. 36in SL replaced by 44in SL. Letters 'RE' painted on turret tops.
3. Underwater bulges inspected and reconditioned.

Revenge Refit, winter 1938 to August 1939:
1. Single 4in replaced by twin guns in large shields.
2. Multiple 2pdr added on platform on port side abeam funnel.
3. Multiple 0.5in AA (4 barrels) added P&S on superstructure abeam conning tower.
4. HA director on control top raised well above top.
5. After HA director added in place of torpedo control tower.
6. DF aerial removed from over control top.
7. Modified type of aerial fitted at head of topgallant mast.
8. Base of SL tower on port side cut away to accommodate 2pdrs.
9. Signal distribution office and remote control station at rear of bridge replaced by small open platform built around tripod legs.
10. Clinker screen fitted to funnel top.
11. Signal yard removed from maintopmast.

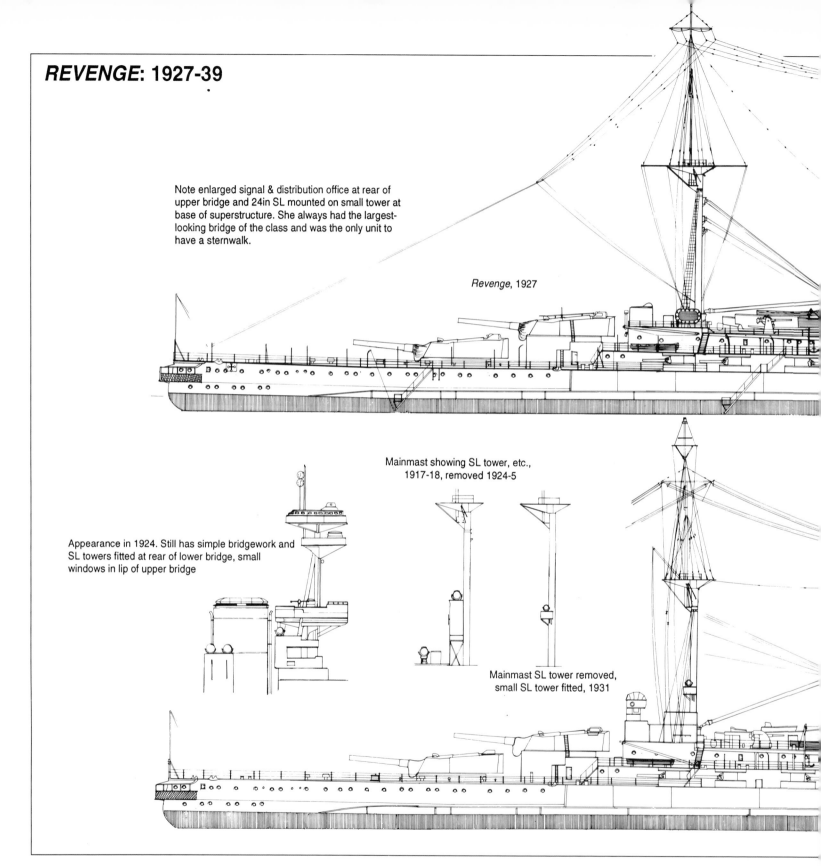

REVENGE: 1927-39

Note enlarged signal & distribution office at rear of
upper bridge and 24in SL mounted on small tower at
base of superstructure. She always had the largest-
looking bridge of the class and was the only unit to
have a sternwalk.

Revenge, 1927

Mainmast showing SL tower, etc.,
1917-18, removed 1924-5

Appearance in 1924. Still has simple bridgework and
SL towers fitted at rear of lower bridge, small
windows in lip of upper bridge

Mainmast SL tower removed,
small SL tower fitted, 1931

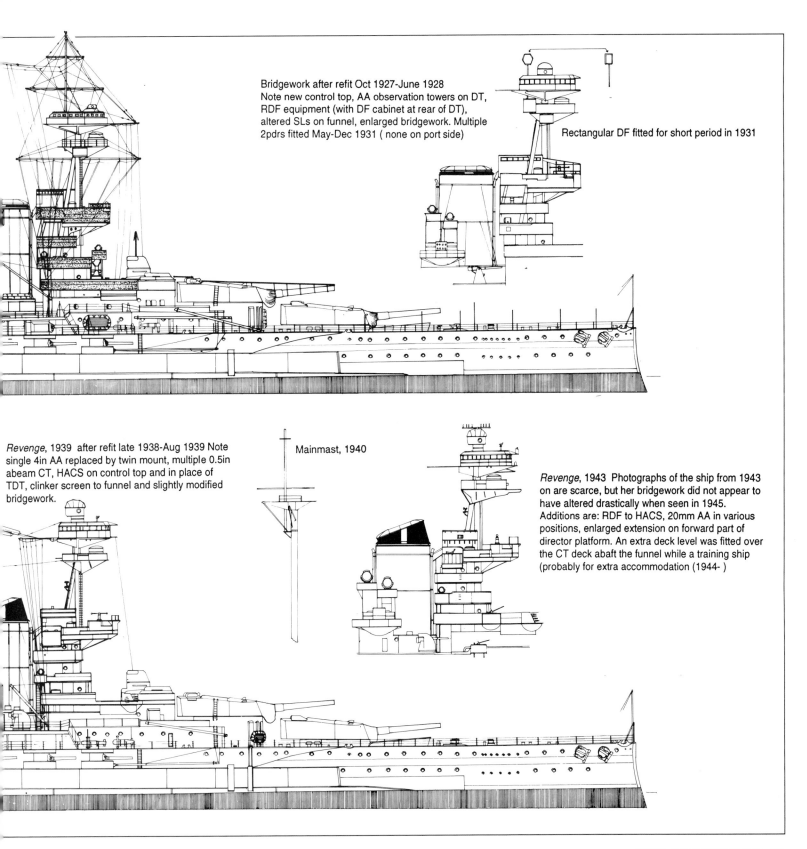

Bridgework after refit Oct 1927-June 1928
Note new control top, AA observation towers on DT,
RDF equipment (with DF cabinet at rear of DT),
altered SLs on funnel, enlarged bridgework. Multiple
2pdrs fitted May-Dec 1931 (none on port side)

Rectangular DF fitted for short period in 1931

Revenge, 1939 after refit late 1938-Aug 1939 Note
single 4in AA replaced by twin mount, multiple 0.5in
abeam CT, HACS on control top and in place of
TDT, clinker screen to funnel and slightly modified
bridgework.

Mainmast, 1940

Revenge, 1943 Photographs of the ship from 1943
on are scarce, but her bridgework did not appear to
have altered drastically when seen in 1945.
Additions are: RDF to HACS, 20mm AA in various
positions, enlarged extension on forward part of
director platform. An extra deck level was fitted over
the CT deck abaft the funnel while a training ship
(probably for extra accommodation (1944-)

Below: *Royal Sovereign*, July 1928, a full-length por-
trait view showing the simplicity of layout. Note the
new control top.

Ramillies 1919–21:
    Large base RF added at rear of 'B' turret and
slightly later in 'X' turret.
    Range clock, ex face of control top, relocated
on pole over top.

Ramillies 1922: SL removed from towers abaft
mainmast. Remounted on middle bridge.

Ramillies 1923–4:   Range clock removed from
over control top and relocated over 'X' turret.
SL removed from middle bridge.
Armoured casemates fitted to upper pair of 6in.
    Short topgallant mast added to main and sig-
nal struts to starfish below control top.

Ramillies Refit, September 1926 to April 1927:
1. Control top enlarged and modified.
2. Upper pair of 6in guns removed (casemates
retained).
3. Extra pair of 4in AA added on shelter deck.
4. HA RF mounted on small tower on bridge.

5. 36in SL removed from middle bridge.
6. 24in SL transferred from forward superstructure to lower bridge.
7. New high-fitting bulges replacing smaller original ones.
8. High sloping roof fitted to upper bridge.
9. Fore topmast and lower yard removed from
foremast.

Ramillies 1931–2:
1. Range clock over 'X' turret removed.
2. Forecastle deck 6in casemates removed (by
August 1932).

Ramillies Refit, January 1933 to August 1934:
1. Multiple 2pdrs AA added P&S on raised platform abeam funnel.
2. Multiple 0.5in AA added abeam conning
tower.
3. HA RF on control top replaced by HA director and after HA director added on platform on
newly fitted tripod legs.

4. AA observation positions fitted at each side of
15in director platform.
5. After pair of TT removed.
6. Torpedo control tower and RF removed.
7. New SL towers as in *Royal Oak*.
8. Training catapult (McTaggart type) fitted on
port side of 'X' turret roof, with crane (straight
arm) on port side of superstructure.
9. Aircraft platforms removed from turret tops.
10. Bridge modified and enlarged.
11. Lower bridge extended aft around funnel
and upper bridge more steeply sloped and
prominent with supporting flanges added below.
Ramillies, 1935:

HA RF over bridge replaced by high open tower
(August to October).

Ramillies: by May 1937.
1. 36in SL replaced by 44in.
2. Tower over bridge replaced by large open
platform extended back around tripod legs.

Royal Sovereign class: Particulars, 1927

Displacement (tons)
Royal Oak 29,160 (legend), 32,800 (extra deep);
   Revenge 30,244 (legend), 33,008 (extra deep);
   Royal Sovereign 29,710 (legend), 32,930 (extra deep).
Dimensions
Length: unchanged except when fitted with sternwalk (625ft). Beam: unchanged except *Royal Oak* (bulged) 102ft 6in; *Royal Sovereign* (bulged) 101ft 11½in.
Draught: *Royal Oak* 28ft 3½in (legend), 31ft 4½in (deep).
Royal Sovereign 29ft 5in (legend), 31ft 11in (deep).
Stability: Angle of maximum stability: 35/36½°, Vanishes at 62/68½° GM: 5.22/5.66ft
Armour: unchanged except water protection added to bulges in 1927 and tubes removed where fitted (*Ramillies*).
Machinery: unchanged.
Trial figures *Ramillies* after refit, July 1934:
4 Hours, Tolland Mile.
Displacement: 29,540 tons load condition.
Draught: 28ft 8in.
Speed: 22.03 knots.

Royal Sovereign class: Particulars, 1939

Displacement (tons): 31,560 (load), 33,200 (deep) (average for class).
Length: unchanged. 620ft (oa) 625ft *Revenge* with sternwalk.
Beam: unchanged. 101ft 11½in *Royal Sovereign*; 102ft 6in *Ramillies*.
Armament: Main guns unchanged
Secondary: 12 x 6in in upper deck battery
8 x 4in AA in twin shields
16 x 2pdr AA (2 x 8 barrels)
8 x 0.5in MG AA (2 x 4 barrels)
4 x 3pdr saluting
4 x 21in TT above water, (*Royal Oak*), 2 x 21in submerged (*Revenge*).
Radar: MF/DF equipment in all.
Searchlights: 4 x 44in; 4 x 24in signalling in *Revenge*, 2 in others.
Aircraft
Catapult (training) on 'X' turret in *Resolution* and *Royal Oak*. One Fairey IIIF reconnaissance seaplane.
Armour
As original except for additions to *Royal Oak* in 1936 refit.
Machinery and boilers: unchanged.
Speed: reduced to about 20 knots. *Ramillies* unable to exceed this by 1940.
Radius of action/(tons per hour):
6,000nm at 10 knots (5.1), 5,500nm at 12 knots (6.7), 4,650nm at 14 knots (9.2), 3,850nm at 16 knots (12.7), 3,050 at 18 knots (18.0), 2,250nm at 20 knots (27.4).
Rig: No foretopmast. Short topmast to main in all.
Topgallant to main in all except *Ramillies* (tall in *Revenge* shorter in others). Tall flagpole to fore in *Resolution*. Short flagpole to each in *Royal Oak*. DF aerial on main topmast or topgallant. Signal struts at starfish below control top in all.
Appearance: Generally notably heavier and more piled up than during 1920s owing to many post-war modifications, mainly from 1927 onwards, including enlarged control top, bridge and searchlight towers,

heavy multiple AA mountings amidships and prominent directors over control top and on mainmast or on after superstructure. Director on control top raised well clear of top in *Resolution*, *Revenge* and *Royal Sovereign*. Clinker screen to funnel in *Revenge* and *Resolution*, *Royal Sovereign* fitted 1940, *Ramillies* fitted 1941. Tripod mainmast in *Resolution*, *Ramillies* and *Royal Oak*. Control top painted very light in all, contrasting noticeably with dark-grey (Home Fleet colours) of hull and superstructure.
Individual differences
Ramillies: Deep flanges below director platform on foremast. High domed roof over upper bridge. Very prominent bulges. Tripod mainmast with director platform on legs.
Resolution: HA director raised well above control top. Original type upper bridge (only ship to retain this). Clinker screen to funnel. Catapult on 'X' turret. Tripod mainmast and director as in *Ramillies*.
Revenge: HA director raised as in *Resolution*. Deep flanges below director platform as in *Ramillies*. HA director on after superstructure. Lower bridge wings not carried back around funnel (only ship thus). Small SL platform low on mainmast (only ship thus). Sternwalk (only ship thus). Topgallant to main noticeably taller than others. DF aerial at head main topgallant (on topmast in others).
Royal Oak: 6in director towers on platform below 15in director (only ship with this). Wide flange between tripod legs close above bridge (only ship with this). Square-faced open upper bridge. Catapult on 'A' turret. Recessed torpedo ports in forecastle side (only ship thus). Very large prominent bulges as *Ramillies*. Large DF cabinet on maintop (only ship thus).
Royal Sovereign: HA director raised as in *Resolution* and *Revenge*. Shallow flanges below main director platform. Prominent vertical strut on each side below director platform (only ship thus). HA director on after superstructure as *Revenge*. Very deep flanges on face of bridge below navigating platform.

Red, white and blue stripes painted up on turrets in all.

Ramillies Refit, by June 1938:
1. Single 4in AA replaced by twins in large shield.
2. Remaining pair of TT removed.
3. RDF fitted.
4. Catapult removed, crane retained.
5. Maintop gallant reduced in length.

Resolution 1919–20:
Large base RF fitted over 'B' turret only.
Small torpedo RF on control tower replaced by larger RF.
Long forward struts fitted to fore starfish.

Very few alterations to *Resolution* except those similar to others of her class (range clocks, SL alterations, etc.) during the early 1920s.

Resolution: Clinker screen fitted to funnel July to October 1924.

Resolution Refit, December 1926 to December 1927:
1. Control top enlarged and modified.
2. Range clock added over 'X' turret.
3. Upper pair of 6in guns removed (casemate retained).
4. Extra pair 4in AA added.
5. Training catapult added to quarterdeck.
6. Foretopmast and yard below removed from

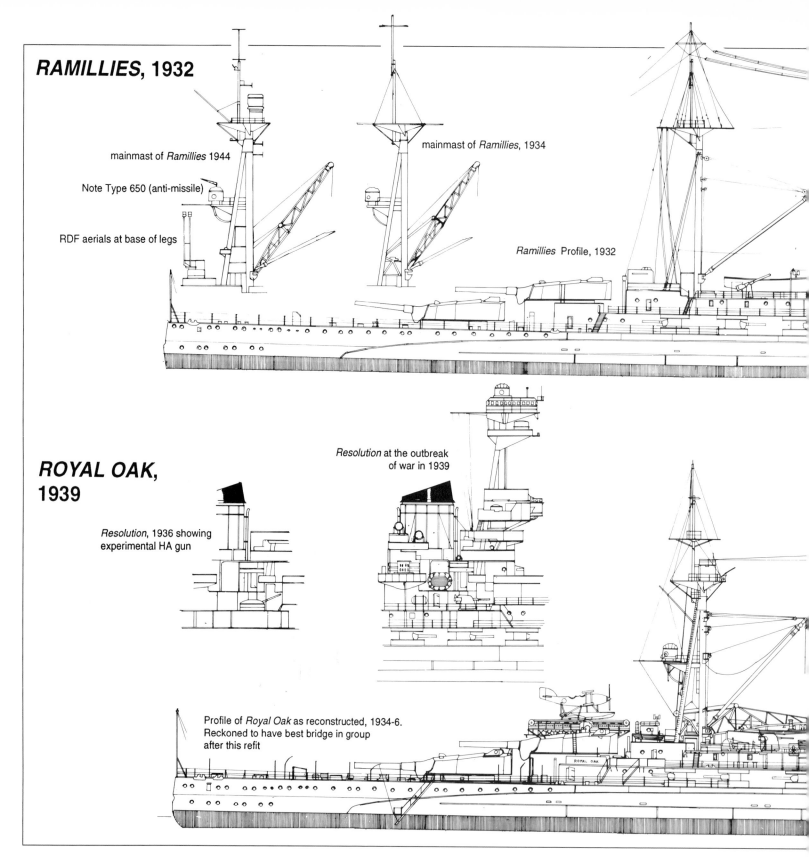

RAMILLIES, 1932

mainmast of *Ramillies* 1944

Note Type 650 (anti-missile)

RDF aerials at base of legs

mainmast of *Ramillies*, 1934

Ramillies Profile, 1932

ROYAL OAK, 1939

Resolution, 1936 showing experimental HA gun

Resolution at the outbreak of war in 1939

Profile of *Royal Oak* as reconstructed, 1934-6. Reckoned to have best bridge in group after this refit

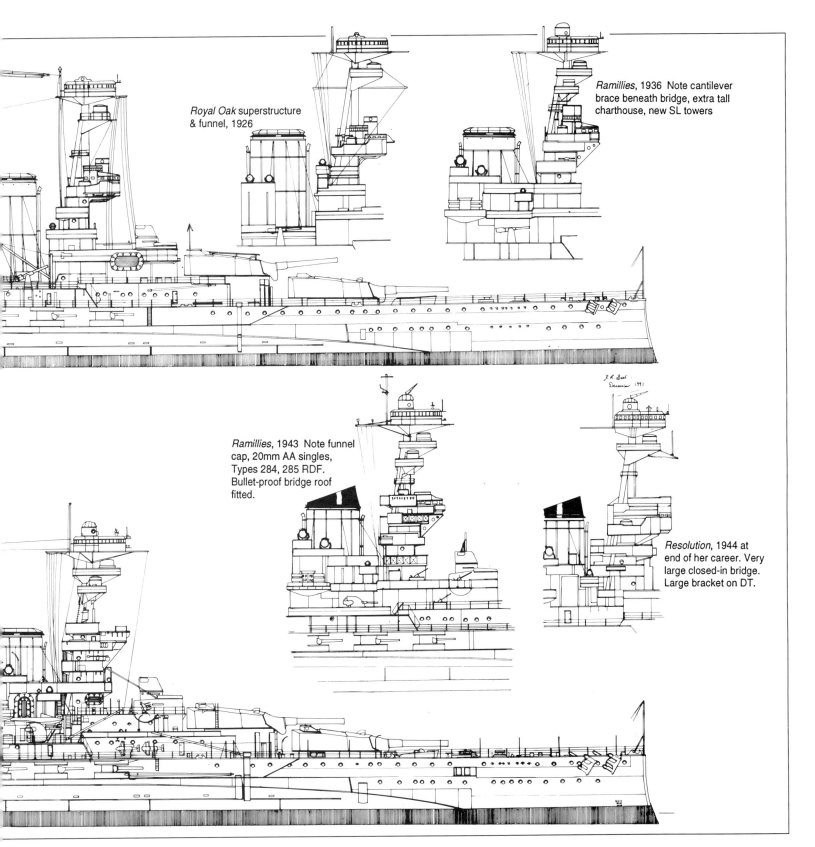

Royal Oak superstructure & funnel, 1926

Ramillies, 1936 Note cantilever brace beneath bridge, extra tall charthouse, new SL towers

Ramillies, 1943 Note funnel cap, 20mm AA singles, Types 284, 285 RDF. Bullet-proof bridge roof fitted.

Resolution, 1944 at end of her career. Very large closed-in bridge. Large bracket on DT.

On board *Royal Oak*, October 1937.
Left: 'A' and 'B' 15in turrets and newly modelled superstructure.
Below left: The rear of the funnel, boat deck and searchlight towers.
Below: Looking aft over the boat deck, showing the tripod and newly fitted crane.
Right: A unique view inside the control top, showing instruments crammed into every corner.
Opposite page, bottom: *Royal Oak* in an acting mood, playing the *El Mirante* in the motion picture on 21 February 1937. She is shown here inclining, to feign sinking.

director level.

7. Extra signalling struts fitted to starfish below control top.

8. Topgallant to mainmast.

Resolution Refit, December 1929 to March 1931:

1. Forecastle deck 6in casemates removed.

2. HA RF on control top removed and replaced by HACS.

3. After pair of TT removed.

4. Starboard forward 4in replaced by 4in LA HA experimental gun in new type mounting. Gun and mounting proved most successful after trials on 20–21 February 1931 off Plymouth.

5. Catapult removed from quarterdeck.

Resolution By September 1933:

1. Range clock over 'X' turret removed.

2. Multiple 0.5in AA added abeam conning tower on shelter deck.

3. Aircraft platforms removed from turrets.

Resolution Refit, December 1935 to September 1936:

1. Platform for multiple 2pdr fitted (no guns).

2. HA director platform fitted on tripod legs of mainmast, no director.

3. HA RF over bridge removed.

4. Torpedo control tower and RF removed.

5. New SL towers fitted around funnel as in *Royal Sovereign*.

6. Training catapult and crane (bent arm) fitted as *Ramillies*.

7. Large open platform extended back around tripod legs added over bridge.

8. Lower bridge carried back around funnel as in *Royal Sovereign*.

9. Tripod legs fitted to mainmast to support HACS.

Resolution January 1938 modifications:

1. Single 4in experimental type replaced by twin 4in AA.

2. Multiple 2pdrs added P&S abreast funnel.

3. After HACS fitted.

4. RDF equipment fitted as in *Royal Sovereign*.

5. Main topgallant reduced.

Resolution Tall flagpole fitted at rear of control top by August 1939.

Wartime Modifications

Ramillies: Two 0.5in AA removed and ten 20mm AA added on superstructure, shelterdeck and

quarterdeck right aft. Clinker screen fitted to funnel 1941. Two quadruple pom-poms fitted on 'B' and 'X' turrets late 1941. Modified type of DF aerial fitted to face of bridge in 1942. Maintopgallant mast removed 1942.

Eight single 20mm AA added on and around superstructure plus four extra fitted on quarterdeck by April 1943. Two 20mm AA added on 'B' and 'X' turret 1944. Total of twenty-two 20mm AA by 1944.
VHF equipment Type 650 RDF added, prominent aerials on after superstructure (*Ramillies* only).

Others fitted very similarly to *Ramillies* through-ut the war.
Resolution: Proposed increase in 15in elevation to 30° never carried out. Two forward pairs 6in guns removed (from all 1942–3). Nine single 20mm AA added 1941. Quadruple pom-poms added to 'B' and 'X' turret 1942.

Royal Sovereign: Eight single 20mm AA plus two on quarterdeck added 1941. Fourteen 20mm AA added 1942. Sixteen twin 20mm AA added in USA refit 1943.

Revenge: Quadruple pom-poms added on 'B' and 'X' turret 1942.
Light AA guns uncertain for *Revenge* after 1941 due to lack of photographic evidence.
Extensive RDF fitted in all ships of class.
Types 284 for main guns, Type 273 SW; Type 285 for 4in AA; Types 79 and 279 got AW. Type 282 for 2pdrs.

Resolution: catapult removed from turret 1944. All light AA guns removed from *Resolution* and *Revenge* 1944.
15in guns removed from *Resolution* only.

PROPOSED SUPER BULGING AND RE-ARMOURING

The original proposal for such a move was brought before the Board in February 1940 at a time when it seemed almost certain that Great Britain would be invaded from across the Channel.

The idea was for two *Royal Sovereign*s and two *Queen Elizabeth* class to be taken in hand for a rough and ready job, using flame cut armour that would be supported in position as well as

could be expected in such circumstances. The whole programme was scheduled to take about twelve months. The situation across the Channel altered throughout 1940, however, and the matter of reconstruction was dropped for the time being.

In October 1940, after *Resolution* had been damaged by a torpedo off Dakar, consideration was again given to a similar scheme on the above lines, but for *Resolution* only. The alterations would take place concurrently with her damage repairs and approval to proceed was given at the Controller's Conference on 8 October 1940. The following plans were forwarded:

1. Sheer draught of new super bulge.
2. General arrangements and rolling sizes of 4in armour.
3. Arrangement of WT bulkheads in upper and lower bulge.
4. Structural sections of new bulge.
5. Body plan showing bulge keel.
6. Pumping arrangements for new bulge.
7. Consideration for protection to upper deck openings.
8. Boiler room uptakes and downtakes.

Protection was proposed by fitting 5in drilled NC plates in uptakes and by extending 4in armour over downtakes. It was planned to

Royal Sovereign class: Particulars, 1945.

Displacement (tons):
Ramillies 34,032 (average action), 35,385 (deep); *Royal Sovereign* 33,491 (average action), 34,836 (deep); *Revenge* 32,200 (average action), 33,500 (deep); *Resolution* 33,159 (average action), 34,520 (deep).

Length and beam unchanged.
Draught: 32ft 4in to 33ft 8in average for class.
Armament: Main guns unchanged.
Ramillies and *Royal Sovereign*:
8 x 6in
8 x 4in twin AA
24 x 2pdr AA (8 barrels, 2 x 4 barrels)
12 to 22 x 20mm AA (twins and singles).
Resolution and *Revenge*:
8 x 6in
8 x 4in twin AA
All smaller guns removed (see changes for details of wartime AA).
Radar
Type 284 for 15in guns, Type 285 for 4in, Type 282 for light AA,
Type 79 AW in *Ramillies* and *Resolution*; Type 279 AW *Revenge*;
Type 273 SW in all.
Type 650 VHF equipment in *Ramillies*.
Searchlights as in 1939. Aircraft: none. Armour as in 1939. Machinery unchanged.
Fuel (tons): 1,875 oil average 3,220 max.
Radius of action/(tons per hour):
4,500nm at 10 knots (6.8), 4,260nm at 12 knots (8.6), 3,960nm at 14 knots (10.8), 3,570nm at 16 knots (13.7), 2,900nm at 18 knots (19.0), 2,280nm at 26.2 knots (26.2).
Speed: Barely managing 19 knots with squadron speed fixed at 18 knots.
GM: 3.90ft average action, 4.15ft deep load.
Rig: Short topmast to fore and main. No topgallants. Radar aerial at head of each mast, and on maintop.
Appearance:
No major changes from 1939, but ships very cluttered with light AA guns on 'B' and 'X' turrets, superstructure and quarterdeck (removal in *Resolution* and *Revenge*) prominent RDF aerials over conning tower, on HA directors, on maintop (lantern screen) and at mastheads. Two forward 6in guns on each side removed from all. Clinker screen to funnel in all.
Ramillies, *Royal Sovereign* still camouflaged, *Resolution* and *Revenge* repainted in all grey after arriving at Devonport as Training Ships.
Individual differences:
Ramillies: Deep flanges below 15in director platform. High domed roof over upper bridge. Small tower at base of mainmast. Prominent aerials at base of mainmast. Tripod mainmast with director platform on legs.
Resolution: No 15in guns in turrets. HA director raised well above control top. Tripod mainmast and director platform.
Revenge: 15in guns in turrets. Deep flanges below 15in director platform. HA director on after superstructure. Lower bridge wings not carried back around funnel. Small SL platform low on mainmast. Sternwalk.
Royal Sovereign (*Arkangelsk*): HA director raised well above control top. Shallow flanges below 15in director platform. Prominent vertical strut each side below director platform. HA director on after superstructure. Very deep flanges on face of bridge below navigating platform.

replace the boiler room forced draught fans by turbine-driven units and renew the boiler fronts and pressure feeds to enable the SHP to be maintained. (Armouring all round the uptakes and in many cases over them would have reduced the SHP by about 10,000).

Proposals to fit 4in protection over all openings of more than 17½ inches were put forward. Armour covers for all hatches, escape manholes and certain hatches in the upper deck were planned.

The estimates of effect of 'super bulging' on speed were given as: speed for 40,000shp as re-bulged 20.3 knots; speed for 30,000shp as re-bulged 18.5 knots. Estimated added weights for 4in armour (leaving upper deck openings unprotected): 1,990 tons. Protection for upper deck openings: 71 tons. New bulge: 930 tons. Estimated deep displacement based on *Royal Sovereign* deep of 33,235 tons, with new bulges, deck armour, vertical protection to uptakes and downtakes was 36,420 tons. Draught: 32ft; GM: 8.69ft.

Finally, however, because of the time involved, cost, material and general age of the ship, the Controller decided on 27 December 1940 that work on *Resolution* be confined to making good the torpedo damage and a minimum of AAs (which did include, however, increasing the two foremost 15in turrets' elevation to 30 degrees, but was never actually carried out). It would appear from official documents that the story did not end in 1940 because another 'suggestion' was made in favour of *Resolution* becoming a 'Super Shore Battery Ship' in October 1942. The following was planned:
1. Reinforced steel platform erected over deck to cover all vital parts. Sufficient thickness – 5in.
2. Heavy torpedo nets (twelve feet from ship's side) to run 40 feet deep (250 tons in weight).
3. All top hamper cut down – bridges, etc. Mainmast shortened and main derrick removed.

Again the plan was dropped.

The final proposal for *Resolution* came in July 1943 when it was decided to renew her bridge completely, remove all 6in guns and remove the conning tower and associated armour. This plan also was recorded for future reference but was never accomplished.

LOSS OF ROYAL OAK

After the sinking of *Royal Oak* a committee was appointed to ascertain the circumstances leading up to her loss (18 to 24 October). A full report covering all aspects of the incident would require a book in itself because there were two main topics of discussion: 1. the actual loss of the ship; 2. the entry of the German submarine into Scapa Flow. The report by Admiral Drax, however, sums up the salient points:

'At 0104 on 14th October 1939 H.M.S. *Royal Oak* was lying at single anchor in Scapa Bay when an explosion occurred right forward on the starboard side below water. Its effect was to break all the slips on both cables which allowed the port cable to run out to a clinch and let go the starboard anchor. The explosion itself and the effect of the cable running out woke most of the officers and some of the ship's company. The Admiral, Captain, Commander, Engineer Commander and others hurried on deck putting on a few clothes. Many officers who were aft thought that the explosion was in or under the after part of the ship, this being accounted for by the vibration effect from the other end of the ship.

'Witnesses in the A.D.P. and on the Flag Deck state that a column of water was shot up the starboard side forward and drenched the fore part of the forecastle. Through the hole in the side a number of shores and other timber may have dropped or been blown out.

'The Captain, on turning out, went on to the W.D. and being informed that the slips on the cable had parted went forward to the forecastle. It was a fine clear night, the sea was calm and the sky was lit up by the Northern Lights. He arrived on the forecastle, looked at the cables, received reports from various Officers, and sent the First Lieutenant down to inspect the forward compartments. He remained on the Forecastle a few moments in order to ascertain whether the ship was in any way affected by what he thought

was an internal explosion in the Inflammable Store. As the ship was neither listing nor settling down by the bows he went down the after forecastle hatch and forward to the cable locker flat. Here he met several Officers, including the Engineer Commander, and received reports that the Inflammable Store was venting through the breather pipe showing that water was entering that compartment and that there was no fire. The compartment immediately abaft it, the CO_2 room, was intact. Up to this time no one had thought that the ship might have been torpedoed, the general impression being that there had been an internal explosion, or possibly a bombing attack by aircraft. Under the Captain's direction orders were given for starting salvage pumps and preparing to open and examine damaged compartments. No orders were given for closing watertight doors or deadlights.

'In the meantime the S.O.O. turned out and went to the Admiral's cabin at 0106. The Admiral had already turned out. S.O.O. made a quick examination of the after part of the ship and returned to report "No damage aft". This was confirmed a few moments later by the Engineer Commander who had also made an inspection of the after compartments. S.O.O. accompanied the Admiral on deck, but the latter then went forward and S.O.O. went on to the Marines' Messdeck. He did not see the Admiral again.

'The ship's company generally were not much disturbed by the first explosion, and there are several records of men having turned out and then turned in again between the first and second explosions. During this interval the launch and picket boat were called away, the Drifter *Daisy II* was ordered to raise steam, and two prisoners were released from the cells.

'At 0116 the Captain was still near the CO_2 room with several officers. In his own words, "I had no thought other than that a local explosion had taken place in the Inflammable Store. This was backed up by the report I received that the CO_2 room was intact. I had not even thought of the ship being torpedoed. I felt no uneasiness about the safety of the ship." Suddenly there was another "shattering" explosion, followed at very short intervals by a third and fourth. These explosions occurred on the starboard side of the ship approximately between "A" and "X" turrets, and had an immediate and catastrophic

effect. The ship at once started to heel to starboard and, with only a slight "hang" for perhaps three or four minutes, heeled over with increasing velocity until she capsized at about 0129.

'From the moment at which the second explosion occurred it was practically impossible to do anything effective to save the ship, nor was it possible to broadcast the order to "Abandon Ship" as the lights went out and power failed. Officers in various parts of the ship told the men near them to save themselves. The Captain was still in the cable locker flat. He told Officers and men to clear out of the flat and walked aft to the Messdeck which was in darkness. He sent the men up to the forecastle and followed them up. On the forecastle he realised that the ship was going over as she was heeling so quickly and felt sure that the only thing left to do was to throw over the side the Carley floats, etc., and as much wood as possible. The Captain and Commander

got to work on this assisted by a few men, but the ship turned over so rapidly that little could be done. In a few minutes they found the deck becoming impossible to stand on so climbed over the port guard rails and up the port side until they slipped or were flung into the sea.

'The ship capsized and finally sank at 0129, twenty-five minutes after the first explosion and thirteen minutes after the second explosion. An Officer who had climbed up the port side, over the bilge keel and on to the bottom checked the time at 0133 before taking to the water.

'The second, third and fourth explosions were observed by men stationed in the A.D.P. These explosions were accompanied by columns of water which fell on the A.D.P., also a flash which was seen round the funnel casing, and a quantity of black smoke which covered the after part of the ship for a short period.

'After the first explosion the Assistant

Torpedo Officer went to the Main Switchboard, then on to the Messdeck, where he reported to the Engineer Commander and met the Warrant Electrician. The Assistant Torpedo Officer and Warrant Electrician again went down to the Switchboard and thence to Nos. 4 and 3 Dynamo Rooms, where everything was normal. While still in No. 3 Dynamo Room the second, third and fourth explosions occurred. The second seemed to be well forward, the third abreast the Boiler Rooms, and the fourth close to No. 3 Dynamo Room, but forward of it, probably at the starboard wing Engine Room. After the second and third explosions orange-coloured flames appeared at the top of the dynamo room hatch. After the fourth explosion the forward bulkhead of the dynamo room, between the dynamo room and the wing engine room, began to bulge inwards and steam began to escape. The two Officers and the Watchkeeper made their way up

ROYAL SOVEREIGN

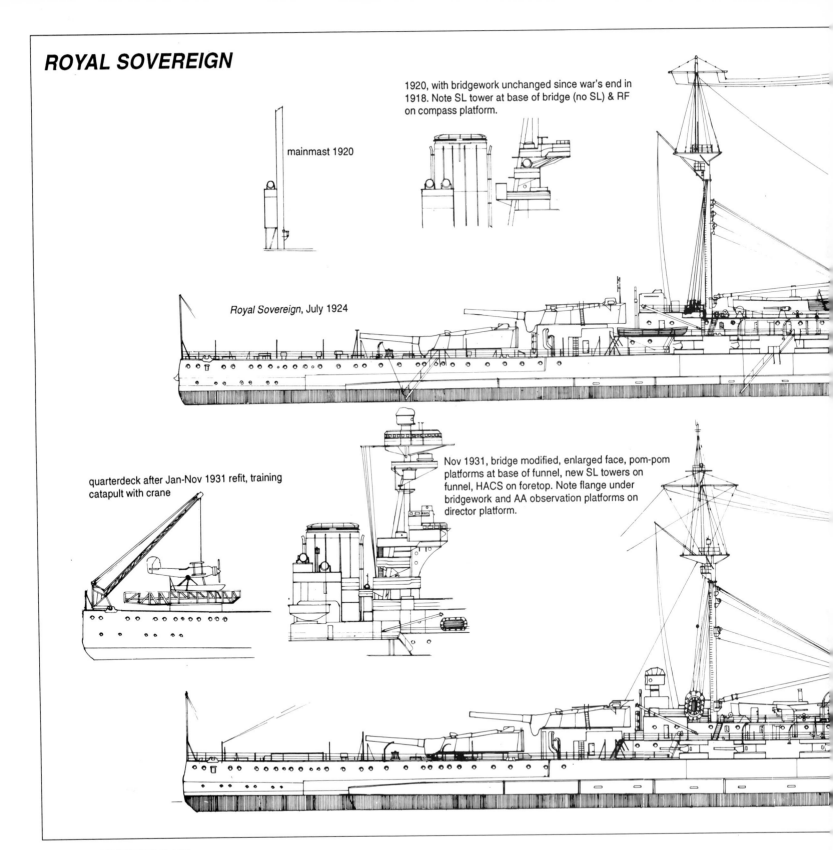

1920, with bridgework unchanged since war's end in 1918. Note SL tower at base of bridge (no SL) & RF on compass platform.

mainmast 1920

Royal Sovereign, July 1924

quarterdeck after Jan-Nov 1931 refit, training catapult with crane

Nov 1931, bridge modified, enlarged face, pom-pom platforms at base of funnel, new SL towers on funnel, HACS on foretop. Note flange under bridgework and AA observation platforms on director platform.

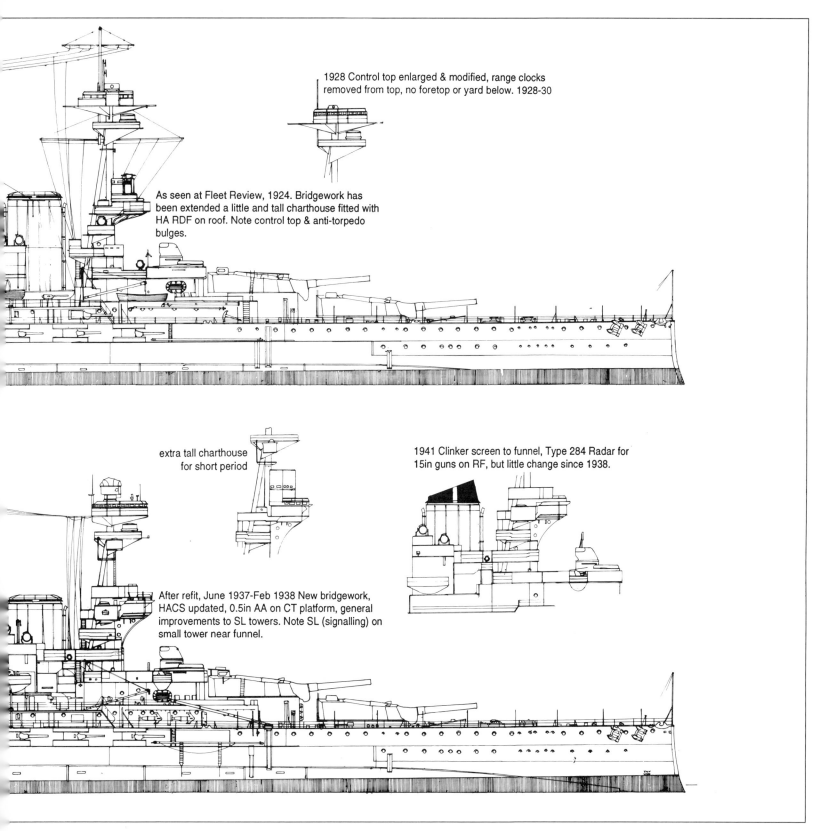

1928 Control top enlarged & modified, range clocks removed from top, no foretop or yard below. 1928-30

As seen at Fleet Review, 1924. Bridgework has been extended a little and tall charthouse fitted with HA RDF on roof. Note control top & anti-torpedo bulges.

extra tall charthouse for short period

1941 Clinker screen to funnel, Type 284 Radar for 15in guns on RF, but little change since 1938.

After refit, June 1937-Feb 1938 New bridgework, HACS updated, 0.5in AA on CT platform, general improvements to SL towers. Note SL (signalling) on small tower near funnel.

ROYAL OAK: TORPEDOED 14 OCTOBER 1939

Divers' report Oct 1939

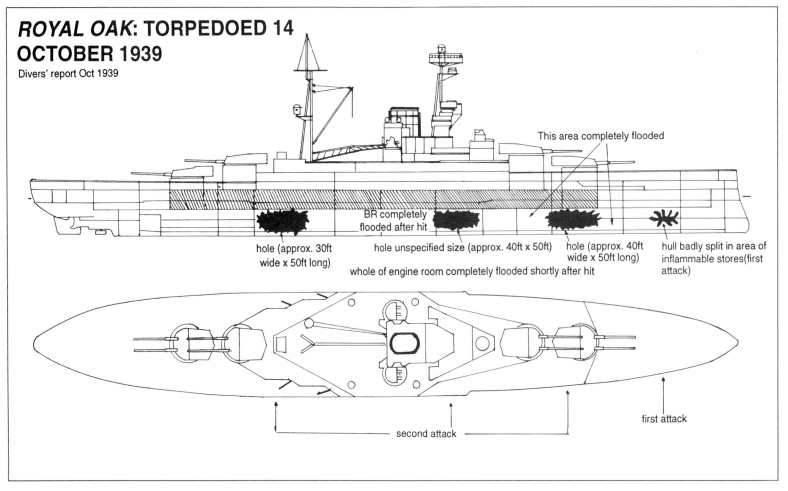

This area completely flooded

BR completely flooded after hit

hole (approx. 30ft wide x 50ft long)

hole unspecified size (approx. 40ft x 50ft)

hole (approx. 40ft wide x 50ft long)

hull badly split in area of inflammable stores(first attack)

whole of engine room completely flooded shortly after hit

second attack

first attack

the ladder. The lights then failed and the flames became less intense. By the time they reached the Marines' Messdeck the ship had listed about 25 degrees to starboard. The Messdeck was full of choking fumes and burning hammocks and other material.

'From other reports it appears that, after the third and fourth explosions, the Marines' Messdeck was swept by flames and full of smoke and fumes. Several hammocks caught fire and were extinguished by men near them. There is also evidence that holes appeared in the decks and that the decks caved in.

'A sliding horizontal hatch abaft "A" turret slid across and jammed in the closed position due to the heel of the ship and to the fact that the wire strop used to hold it open had not been properly secured. Men in this compartment may not have had time to escape by another route. Sliding hatches in other positions may have closed similarly.

'During this period there are several reports of men being blown through doors, up hatches, and out of scuttles. By the time the ship capsized

a large number of men had reached the water via the Forecastle and Quarter Deck. It appears that few men were saved from the Engine and Boiler Rooms.

'The Admiral had been on the Boat Deck where the Engineer Commander, on his way aft, reported to him. Later the Admiral was seen on the Q.D. by the Captain's Maltese steward, who had come up from below and collected a lifebuoy from the starboard guard rails. This steward saw the Admiral amidships calling to the men on the Port side to jump overboard further forward because they were likely to injure themselves by jumping on to the propellers. The steward climbed up towards the Admiral and asked him to come overboard with him as he had a lifebuoy, but the Admiral refused, saying: "Don't worry about me; try to save yourself." He remained there helping the men to save themselves and was not seen again.

'Men who tried to man the launch at the starboard lower boom had a terrifying experience. They could not cast off from the boom and saw the ship turning over on top of them. Metal from

the foretop fell into the launch and sank her, and the funnel came down into the water between the launch and the ship's side. One man from the sunken launch was partially sucked into the funnel and then blown out again. Others saw "A" and "B" turrets swing round and "fall into the sea".

'After the ship capsized she rolled over to about 160 degrees, possibly righted a little, and is now lying bottom up at an angle of 40 degrees from the vertical with a trim of 2 degrees aft.

CONCLUSIONS OF THE BOARD

'Great reliance was placed on the Scapa Air Raid Warning, and if an air raid warning had been received, scuttles and deadlights would have been closed and riding lights extinguished. No such warning was received and it was not until the second, third and fourth explosions occurred in quick succession that anyone realized that an enemy attack had been made. Consequently, no additional precautions were taken after the first explosion; after the other explosions light and power failed and the ship heeled over and sank so quickly that nothing could be done. Individual lifebelts had not been supplied to the ship, so that men had only the limited quantity of floats, wood, etc., which had been thrown or floated over the side to help them. These were very inadequate.

'Considering that the ship was in harbour and that the sea was calm the loss of life appears to have been very heavy. We put this down to the fact that the ship was at Air Defence Stations, so that an abnormally large number of men were stationed below the main deck. Their escape from the ship was probably impeded by the number of watertight doors that were closed. It has also been stated that a number of men probably took shelter under armour and between decks in the belief that an air raid was taking place, as they had been taught to do so.

'We think it probable that the attack was made by a Submarine which got in at one of the seven entrances and worked its way along the East shore of the Flow between Skerry Sound and Scapa Bay, until the Commanding Officer sighted two ships ahead which, from air reconnaissance, he probably considered to be *Royal Oak* nearest and *Repulse* beyond. We think it likely that he fired a salvo at the further ship, actually *Pegasus*, and that one of these torpedoes struck *Royal Oak* in the bows. He then reloaded and fired a salvo of three at *Royal Oak* which all hit.

'There were probably four explosions, one right forward on the starboard side, the remainder extending from "A" to "X" turrets on starboard side. All torpedoes seem to have hit the side, and there is no evidence to suggest a magnetic pistol or any explosion under the bottom.

'We have investigated the suggestion that the presence of baulks of timber floating past the ship may have had something to do with the attack, but believe this may be explained by the fact that recently a number of telegraph poles have been washed up on the shores of the Flow and may have floated off again on the high tide of this night. Also, a certain amount of timber, shores, etc., may have dropped out of, or been blown out of, the ship's forward compartments by the first explosion.

[Signed] G. C. MUIRHEAD GOULD, Captain.
[Signed] R. H. T. RAIKES, Vice-Admiral
[Signed] R. E. E. Drax, Admiral (President).

REPORT OF DIVERS AFTER INSPECTION OF SHIP
'Divers carried out examination of *Royal Oak*. Ship is lying 40° from bottom up. Trim 2° aft. Forward damage starboard side starts 80' to 100' from stem and extends 40' to 45' aft depth of 3 plates starting one plate below water line. Plating is blown inboard and extreme edges bent in. Damage surveyed aft starts 10' abaft after end of bilge keel and extends from water line to bilge keel. Hole about 30' x 50'. Plating bent inboard. Bilge keel is blown away and bent outboard. Midship section of the ship was not surveyed. Divers surveyed vicinity of mast and found no trace of submarine. Nature of bottom soft silt and mud. In addition divers brought up part of what was almost certainly part of the balance chamber or after body of a torpedo and other small fragments of internal parts.'

BATTLE DAMAGE

Resolution Torpedoed 25 September 1940

On 25 September 1940 the *Resolution* was struck abaft the port beam near station 97 by a torpedo. It seems probable that the detonation occurred before the torpedo passed the outer bottom because the armour plates near the striking point were forced inwards. Depth of hit was about 8 feet from the waterline.

1. A very large splash was observed and the Spotting Top's Crew were wetted, large quantities of water fell on the Boat Deck, and the after High Angle Director was filled with water to a depth of two feet. The great height and width of the splash was probably caused by the fact that the bulge was split along the top edge, and this had an effect on the rising water similar to that produced when a thumb is placed over the open end of a garden hose.

2. The torpedo detonated with a heavy thud which was mistaken by people who had not seen the approaching tracks, and who did not appreciate the significance of the sudden list, either as a hit by a heavy shell or even only as the firing of a broadside. There was no subsequent vibration or shaking of the ship. There were no failures in communication or lighting, nor did any breakers come off as a result of the shock of the detonation.

3. On being struck the ship listed very quickly to 12½°, with a momentary partial recovery when

the wheel was put amidships, but the ship then took up and kept a list of 12°. The Turrets could not train owing to the list and the ship therefore withdrew out of action to the southward, maintaining the revolutions at 252 (19 knots) until out of gun range. Speed was later reduced to 12 knots.

4. A.4 Boiler was shut down when the Chief Stoker saw oil fuel spraying near it. Water was also spraying from the port bulkhead on to A.3 Boiler and the resulting steam led to the belief that tubes had gone; A.3 Boiler was therefore next shut down. By this time oil fuel was being scattered round about A.4 Boiler, and oil vapour was rising from the Boiler Casings and it was therefore decided to close down all Boilers and evacuate the Boiler Room.

5. Damage Control Parties soon localised the main damage as being between 87 and 108 Bulkheads. The Main Deck Messdeck between these Bulkheads flooded fast and a submersible pump was brought to try and keep this under control. A second pump was brought later. Surrounding compartments were shored up. A leak was seen high up in the outboard corner of Number 2 Diesel Dynamo Room (87 Bulkhead) but although every endeavour was made to check the flow, it was inaccessible behind the silencer and pipes, and this compartment slowly flooded.

6. Soon after being hit, oil fuel was sluiced from port inner and outer tanks to Double Bottoms, and was pumped over to the Starboard fuel tanks, to correct the list. No counter flooding was carried out. Later, the water protection compartments on the port side were pumped out. Six inch ready use Shell and Cordite and all movable gear was transferred from port battery to starboard. At a later stage, when power became available turrets were trained to port and guns run in, and 15in Shell were transferred from port to starboard bins in "X" and "Y" Turrets. A few (12) 15in A.P.C. Shell were jettisoned from the port bins of "A" by means of the after capstan. The aircraft was moved along the catapult to its extreme starboard position. The wreckage of the Second Cutter (which was completely shattered by the splash of the explosion) was thrown overboard. On Thursday, 26th September five tons of aviation spirit were jettisoned to correct trim.

7. Within an hour of the torpedo hitting, it was certain that "A" Boiler Room was on fire. Boiler Room intakes were all covered with canvas with

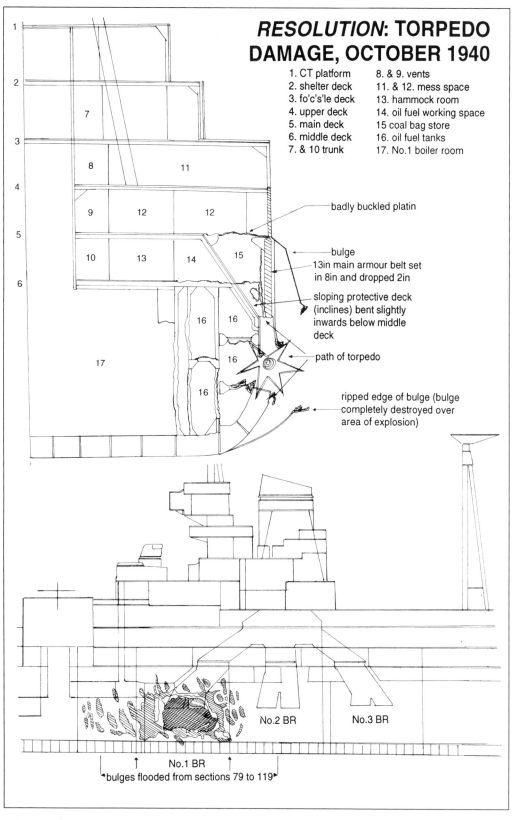

RESOLUTION: TORPEDO DAMAGE, OCTOBER 1940

1. CT platform
2. shelter deck
3. fo'c's'le deck
4. upper deck
5. main deck
6. middle deck
7. & 10 trunk

8. & 9. vents
11. & 12. mess space
13. hammock room
14. oil fuel working space
15 coal bag store
16. oil fuel tanks
17. No.1 boiler room

badly buckled platin

bulge

13in main armour belt set in 8in and dropped 2in

sloping protective deck (inclines) bent slightly inwards below middle deck

path of torpedo

ripped edge of bulge (bulge completely destroyed over area of explosion)

No.1 BR

No.2 BR

No.3 BR

bulges flooded from sections 79 to 119

hoses playing to improve the air seal, but nothing could be done to block the funnel uptake. From 1130 to 1400 "A" Boiler Room safety valve escapes were blowing off and the smoke from the funnel gradually changed from black to grey and then to dirty white: the smoke thinned during the afternoon. At 1230 fire broke out in Number 20 Store and also in the Hammock Compartment, starboard 87 to 108. The temperature of the Six Inch Magazine was rising, but from feeling the heat of adjacent bulkheads it seemed that "A" Boiler Room was flooding up slowly.

8. At 1057/25th September a French aircraft Glen Martin, approached from the port bow at a height of 9,000 feet and dropped one large bomb which fell 300 yards on our starboard beam.

9. At 1345 on 25th September, owing to a failure of the lubrication system due to the list, Main Engines had to be stopped. By 1400 on 25th September Engines were started again except for the port outer which was half stopped. Revolutions at first were for 6 knots, and were increased to 10 knots at 1439 on 25th September. At 1400 "B" Boiler Room had to be

evacuated owing to the heat from "A". At 1915 speed was increased to revolutions for 8 knots.

10. One of the great handicaps was a shortage of power before "A" Boiler Room. Steam was not available owing to the burst pipe which could not be got at owing to fire. Number 2 Dynamo was flooded. Number 1 was short of fuel: the pump for renewing the fuel supply was in "A" and even a supply by bucket was not feasible as access to the shale oil tank was through the Hammock compartment which was on fire. The Ring Main and Emergency Main on the port side were flooded, and the cable passage on the starboard side was in the hottest part of the fire in "A" Boiler Room. Electrical power forward had all to be supplied by emergency leads: secondary lighting and hand torches were invaluable in the shortage of high power lighting.

11. At 0220 on 26th September Main Engines had to be stopped as lubrication had again failed. By 0445 it was possible to proceed at 2 to 3 knots, and at 0615 at 4½ knots, but Engines had again to be stopped at 0624. At 0641 the Engines were moved ahead again, but seemed to be unreliable as long as there was a heavy list.

12. On Thursday morning "A" Boiler Room was opened up, but the fire restarted. It was therefore not possible to investigate damage further, and as there seemed to be no immediate prospect of correcting the list and thereby restoring the reliability of the Main Engines, it seemed best to be taken in tow. HMS *Barham* accordingly took the ship in tow at 1145 on 26th September and went ahead with HMS *Resolution* in tow with Engines stopped. Speed was gradually increased until 7 knots was being made good.

13. During the day of 26th September and the night of 26/27th September buoyancy was maintained and the list was gradually reduced to 8°, partly by pumping out partially flooded compartments or the Main Deck before 87 and abaft 108, partly by pumping out the air space port side of "B" Boiler Room and similar compartments, partly by gradual consumption of fuel from port tanks, partly by the flooding of Hammock compartment starboard side (87 to 108) to put out the fire, and various other measures.

14. At about 0900 on 27th September, tide rips were encountered and steering became difficult.

At 0915 the starboard slip parted, the cable rendered on the brake and shortly afterwards the port 5½" wire parted as it was taking all the strain. After the port tow parted a second 6½" wire was passed and secured by 1140. On going ahead HMS *Barham* worked up to ten knots and HMS *Resolution* (being now more upright) steamed with the inner shafts at revolutions for 5 knots. Before dark it was necessary to change over to a fuel tank which might be contaminated with water, and in order to avoid possibly having to stop suddenly and thereby throw an extra strain on the cables, HMS *Resolution* stopped engines for the night and HMS *Barham* reduced to revolutions for 8 knots.

15. By the morning of 27th September fires in the Hammock compartment and Number 20 Store were out and "A" Boiler Room Bulkheads were less hot. The Boiler Room was entered in the afternoon and the fire was found to be out; the water level (and oil) was half way up the air lock on the starboard side.

16. At 0815 on 28th September HMS *Resolution* went ahead on the two inner shafts and the two ships worked up until HMS *Barham* was doing

Left: *Resolution* limping home listing heavily to port after being hit by a torpedo in 1940.

Below left: *Resolution* listed enough for her aircraft on 'X' turret to be in danger of falling off, and it was decided to fly the machine off the catapult. The view here is from the quarterdeck, with the aircraft already perilously near the end of the catapult.

revolutions for 10 knots and HMS *Resolution* revolutions for 6 knots on the inner shafts; speed made good 7 knots. At 1120 HMS *Resolution* stopped and HMS *Barham* reduced to 8 knots; at 1450 HMS *Barham* reduced speed and at 1554 tow was slipped. Thenceforward speed was maintained at about 4 to 5 knots on all shafts as requisite for making Cape Sierra Leone Light and for entering harbour on the first of the ebb.

17. The tug *Hudson*, which had met the ship the previous evening and had been standing by all night, took the ship in tow at 0530 on 29th September off the Fiarway Buoy, the ship passed the gate at 0615 and anchored off Kissy at 0753, handy to a shelving beach should this be necessary. The list was 5° and maximum draught 38' 6".

18. By Sunday 13th October all compartments before 87 and abaft 108 had been cleared of water except Watertight Compartments 75 to 87. (Water Protection Compartment 74 to 87. + P.3. outer fuel tank.) Divers reported that 87 bulkhead had torn away from the inner bottom at the side and in the absence of any means of pumping out the compartment this was left flooded.

19. The following recommendations arose from experience after the torpedoing:

(i) Easily transportable pumps were invaluable. The best way to deal with a fire is to catch it early; much the same applies to a flood. Several Compartments such as the Stoker Petty Officers' Mess (74 to 87 Bulkhead) and P.1 and P.2 electrical lead passages were flooded and considerable damage done which could have been avoided if small easily transportable pumps had been available. The rate of flooding in these and similar compartments was such that "snorers" or Worthington Simplex's could easily have stemmed the flood while the damage was being repaired.

(ii) Large compartments with only self-contained pumping arrangements should be capable of being pumped from undamaged adjacent compartments.

(iii) Access trunks to compartments such as Dynamo Rooms, etc., should be large enough for a pump and men to pass easily through. If the two trunks to the Dynamo and Hydraulic Rooms (both of which Rooms were flooded and always will flood together until some means is found of making watertight the securing of

Hydraulic pumps) there would have been enough room.

(iv) All electrical fittings which were watertight and which were within reach of flooding from fuel tanks, should be made oiltight by use of some substance other than rubber.

(v) More oxy-acetylene cutting and welding equipment should be supplied to the ship.

(vi) An electric welding plant should be installed.

(vii) Doors such as those to oil fuel working spaces should be open against any flooding from outboard.

(viii) It would have been an advantage to have facilities and necessary tools for operating pneumatic drills and cutting machines throughout the ship.

(ix) Finally, the old story, greater care was necessary to ensure that all electrical needs (and gearing) through bulkheads were made properly tight.

The ship was out of action for eleven months.

Ramillies Torpedoed 30 May 1942

At 2025 on 30th May 1942, while *Ramillies* was at anchor in twelve fathoms off the inner harbour at Antsirano in Diego Suarez Bay, an explosion on the port side forward shook the ship, putting out all lights for a few minutes. She had been hit by a torpedo from a Japanese midget submarine.

'The centre of the explosion was at about 39 station Port. The explosion holed the bulge and bottom plating and the protective plating over an area approximately twenty feet in diameter, extending between 33 and 43 stations from the Lower Deck to the bottom of the Hold Flat.Extensive flooding was caused in the vicinity; the main damage effect being felt by the upper and lower 4in magazines Port.

Draught and Heel of the ship before and after the Explosion:

Before the explosion the draught was 34ft 11in forward and 32ft 3in aft and the ship was on an even keel.

After the hit the trim increased rapidly to about 13ft and the ship listed over to 4½° Port. The Damage Control Officer then flooded s.4 Inner Bulge 177-208S to counteract and heel was reduced to 3° port. At dawn on 31st May draught was 42ft 6in forward and 30ft aft. Heel was reduced to 1° on 31st May by transfer of oil-fuel and was kept between 1° and 2° thereafter.

On 1st June 640 tons of oil fuel were transferred to destroyers and from 31st May onwards cable was fleeted aft to the starboard side of the Quarterdeck and the gear in the forward Boatswain's Store transferred to the after end of the Starboard Battery.

The sheet anchor and "B" shell and cordite were taken out and 6in shell removed to the after end of the batteries. When the ship sailed 3rd June the draught was 39ft 6in forward and 30ft 7in aft and on arrival at Durban on 9th June 38ft forward 29ft 9in aft.

Various compartments were emptied before leaving and during passage and at Durban, and finally air pressure was applied to the Gunsight store, 42-58S Middle, "B" pump space and 27-44P Middle and the water was blown out.

The remaining cable and the two anchors were placed on the Quarterdeck and 6in shell and cordite, Pom-Pom ammunition and "X" and "Y" cordite were landed.

Six compartments aft were flooded, and all bulges and forward W.P.C.s pumped out where possible, and the draught on docking on 15th June was 36ft 2½in forward, 30ft 8in aft.

Temporary repairs to enable the ship to proceed to the United States were carried out; and the ship undocked on Wednesday 29th July draught being 29ft 1in forward, 31ft 8in aft, heel 2° to Port. After completing with fuel, ammunition (except "A" and Port 4) and stores *Ramillies* sailed on Thursday, 6th August, with a draught of 33ft 5in forward, 33ft 11in aft.

Speed of ship:

The ship was at anchor. Speed on passage to Durban 11 to 13 knots.

BULGE:

The hole extended from the top strake of the bulge plating down to C strake between 32 and 47 stations with a tear continuing down to A strake at 38 station (1 & 4). The extremities of the hole were blown in on all sides, carrying the outer bottom plating in wake. Bulge plating, which was 20lb and 30lb plate, between 24½ and 53 stations was corrugated to a varying degree and framing between these limits which was of 9in x 3½ x 23lb bulb angle, was wrecked or distorted. The 9in x 3½in x 3½in x 23lb channel bar forming the top of the bulge was pulled away for about 12ft and the buttstrap at 37 station in the top strake was parted, the rivets shearing, leaving the ends of the plating hanging free. The loose end of the after side was turned over exposing distorted framing (2 and 3).

The intercostal stringer 15in wide of 20lb plate with 3½in x 3½in x 10lb angles was destroyed or distorted within the same limits. The bulge bulkheads of 20lb plate at 39½ and 41½ stations were destroyed. Boundary angles to these bulkheads were 3½in x 3½in x 10lb. The longitudinal bulkhead separating the inner and outer bulge compartments was destroyed or badly distorted to 50 station. It was of 20lb plate. The boundary angle along the lower edge of the bulge of 6in x 6in x 37lb was very distorted.

In the outer bottom plating the hole was bounded by 33 and 45 stations between the Lower deck and "D" strake, being 20ft x 16ft in extent. Distortion of plating and framing occurred between 28-49 stations and the distorted plating was blown against the Longitudinal Protective Bulkhead in the vicinity of the hole. Distortion of plating and framing behind the armour extended to the upper deck and tears in the plating occurred in the wake of certain armour bolts, at 33 station from the Lower Deck extending upwards for 2ft and at 3ft

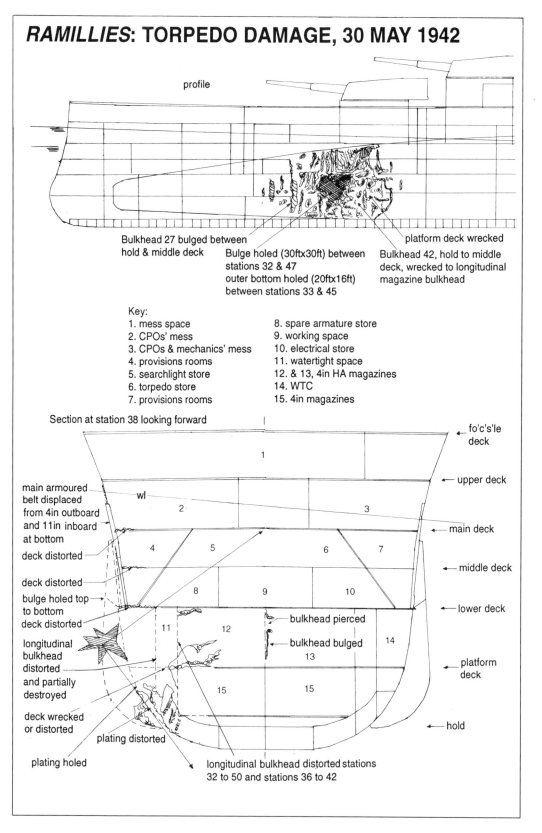

RAMILLIES: TORPEDO DAMAGE, 30 MAY 1942

profile

Bulkhead 27 bulged between hold & middle deck

Bulge holed (30ftx30ft) between stations 32 & 47
outer bottom holed (20ftx16ft) between stations 33 & 45

platform deck wrecked

Bulkhead 42, hold to middle deck, wrecked to longitudinal magazine bulkhead

Key:
1. mess space
2. CPOs' mess
3. CPOs & mechanics' mess
4. provisions rooms
5. searchlight store
6. torpedo store
7. provisions rooms
8. spare armature store
9. working space
10. electrical store
11. watertight space
12. & 13, 4in HA magazines
14. WTC
15. 4in magazines

Section at station 38 looking forward

fo'c's'le deck

upper deck

main armoured belt displaced from 4in outboard and 11in inboard at bottom
deck distorted

wl

main deck

deck distorted

bulge holed top to bottom
deck distorted

longitudinal bulkhead distorted and partially destroyed

deck wrecked or distorted

plating distorted

plating holed

middle deck

lower deck

bulkhead pierced

bulkhead bulged

platform deck

hold

longitudinal bulkhead distorted stations 32 to 50 and stations 36 to 42

190 ROYAL SOVEREIGN CLASS

above the main deck at 43 station. The lower boundary angle behind the armour was of 6in x 6in x 28½lb. The rivets connecting this angle to the Lower deck were sheared between 28 and 44 stations and the side plating and armour were blown in a maximum of 11in. The 15lb plate frames in wake were buckled. Across the bottom of the hole a sloping shelf of damaged plating was formed by blast.

Outer bottom plating in the wake of damage was 20, 25 and 30lb with 25lb H.T. behind armour and the framing was 6in x 3½in x 3in x 14lb Z bar between 31 and 41 stations from the 4th longitudinal to the Lower deck. Below the 4th longitudinal 20lb bracket frames with 5in x 4in x 15lb angles existed. These were distorted between the 1st and 4th longitudinals.

The 14lb inner plating was distorted in wake of the 4th longitudinal between 34 and 42 stations. The distorted boundary angle between those stations was 4in x 4in x 15lb. Abaft 42 station the inner bottom plating, which continued up the Lower deck, was blasted and torn to 47 station with severe distortion to 50 station. The lightened plate frames of 20lb plate were wrecked or distorted, between 42 and 50 stations.

BULKHEADS:
The Port Longitudinal Protective Wing Bulkhead, constructed of two thicknesses of plating, 40lb outboard and 20lb, was destroyed or very badly distorted between 27 and 50 stations and the ragged edges were blown inwards (4, 5). The top boundary angle 6in x 6in x 28½lb was torn away from the deck head (Lower deck) with the bulkhead which was blown to within 8ft of the middle line corrugating and compressing the Platform deck in its wake. Rivets to edge and butt straps were sheared. A jagged hole of about 4ft diameter was blown in the bulkhead in the vicinity of the old torpedo tube. A piece of the 60lb blanking plate to the torpedo tube access measuring 18in x 10in approximately was blown from this section of the bulkhead. It passed through the middle line bulkhead, 2ft below the lower deck at 38 station and damaged gear rods behind. The hole made in this bulkhead was bulged by blast a maximum 5in. The stiffening to the middle line bulkhead was by vertical channel bars of 6in x 3in x 3in x 12lb.
Other bulkheads in the area were damaged also.

DECKS:
The hold of 4in magazine flat of 14lb chequered plate supported on 15lb brackets and 2½in x 5in bulb angles was slightly distorted in wake of protective bulkhead between 34 and 42 stations.

Platform deck of 14lb plate supported by 9in x 3½in x 3½in x 26lb channel bar was wrecked to within 12ft of the middle line and distorted a further 3ft throughout the upper 4in magazine. There was distortion beyond 42 bulkhead for 6ft outboard of the magazine bulkhead. This flat was of 10lb plate supported by 7in x 3in x 16lb bulb angle.

The lower deck of two thicknesses of 20lb plate was distorted along the stringer plates between 28 and 48 stations and the supporting bulb angle beams 9in x 3½in x 23lb were distorted in wake of damaged plating. The deck was lightly bulged in the spare armature room along the edges of the stronger plate and fastenings of brackets to the sloping deck were loose.

Between 29 and 45 stations, four 240lb armour plates were displaced a maximum of 4in

outboard at the top and 11in inboard at the lower edge which rested on the lower deck.

EXTENT OF FLOODING:
As a result of the explosion all compartments below the main deck between 27-58 bulkheads were flooded except 7-58 Starboard Middle and 42-58 Port Middle outside the sloping protective deck.

Forward of 27 bulkhead the Fresh Water tank 24-27 Lower was flooded through a fractured filled pipe and No. 3 Provision Room 22-27 Middle up to 2ft of water through minor leaks which were plugged. In No. 2 CO_2 Room the brine pipe leading to No. 3 CO Room was fractured and room was partially flooded but controlled by "A" 50 Ton pump.

Aft of 58 bulkhead a number of small leaks through cable glands, a ventilation valve from the air purifier to "A" space that was not completely shut, hydraulic pipe glands and the doors between "A" and "B" shell rooms caused some flooding at all decks which was controlled by "D" pump aided by the portable pumps. This was worst in "B" space where the drains on Starboard side led to "A" drain tank – when these were shut the studs were found to have sheared and these valves had to be boxed in cement before the leak was stopped. As a result, with the list to Port some 3ft–4ft of water accumulated on the Port side and caused damage to L.P. generators and the 15in T.S.

The main deck was flooded to about 2ft between 27-42 stations by water leaking through a hole in the Port side in the aft corner where the armour had been displaced and an armour bolt had been torn away and also through the casing of "D4" fan supplying the deck below. These were both plugged with cement and water pumped out.

Engineering:
Main machinery was not affected.

GUNNERY:
The flooding of "A" and "B" spaces had considerable effect on the fighting efficiency of the ship. With the consequent loss of low power, the armaments were reduced to the following degrees of readiness:

15in. Three turrets in quarters firing controlled by means of a Vickers range clock and a Dumaresq in the G.C.T. with communication

Below: *Royal Sovereign*, Cape Town, 20 October 1940, showing early camouflage (two-tone grey and reminiscent of the Great War dazzle schemes.

Right: *Royal Sovereign* leaving Philadelphia Navy Yard, USA, on 14 September 1943 after refit. The Admiralty wanted more refits in America, but US shipyards were so busy with their own war effort that there was little time to consider the ships of Great Britain.

through the emergency telephone in the G.C.T. 6in. All guns in quarters firing, firing by percussion. Controlled from the Tops, orders, ranges and deflections being passed by voice pipe to the cabinets and thence to the guns.

4in. Forward H.A.C.S. in action with either Port or Starboard guns, power being obtained by emergency leads run from the low power batteries to the fuze panels in the forward H.A.T.S. Air Defence: Air defence telephones being all sound powered were not affected.

Effect on fighting efficiency of the ship. Electrical: damage to ring main also occurred with communication and switchboards put out of order by flooding or shock. Armour: four armour plates between 29 and 45 stations were displaced to a maximum of 4in but were not distorted. A small number of armour bolts were sheared.'

Ship was out of action for twelve months.

HISTORY: ROYAL SOVEREIGN

ATLANTIC FLEET (1st BS) April 1919 to January 1921
1st BS detached to Mediterranean January 1920 because of Near East crisis.
Took part in operations against Turkish Nationalists at Constantinople and in the Black Sea March to July 1920.
Rejoined Atlantic Fleet July 1920.
Collision with *Tiger* at Portland autumn 1920. Considerably damaged.
Reduced to reserve at Portsmouth January 1921 for refit.

RESERVE (Portsmouth) January 1921 to September 1922.
Extensive refit Portsmouth May 1921 to September 1922.
Recommissioned at Portsmouth 3 October 1922 for 1st BS Atlantic Fleet.

ATLANTIC FLEET October 1922 to December 1926 (1st BS to November 1924, 2nd BS later).
Again detached to Mediterranean with *Ramillies*, *Resolution* and *Revenge*, September 1922 to reinforce Mediterranean Fleet during further trouble in the Near East.

Stationed at Constantinople and the Sea of Marmara.

Rejoined Atlantic Fleet September 1923, being the last of the Atlantic Fleet ships to return home.
Under reorganization 1 November 1924, became 2nd BS Atlantic Fleet (see *Ramillies*).
Transferred to Mediterranean December 1926.

MEDITERRANEAN FLEET (1st BS) December 1926 to April 1935 (2nd flag 1st BS April to August 1927).
Stationed at Port Said June 1927 during unrest in Egypt.
Extensive refit Portsmouth October 1927 to June 1928 and January to November 1932.
Stationed in Greek waters during rebellion early 1935.
Transferred to Home Fleet 1935, exchanging stations with *Barham* and replacing her as flag 2nd BS (see *Ramillies*).

HOME FLEET (2nd BS) April 1935 to October 1939 (flag 2nd BS to Jubilee Review, Spithead 16 July 1935).
Attached to Portsmouth Training Service

January 1936 as Seagoing Training Ship for boys and RNR Officers (see *Ramillies*).

Refit Devonport June 1937 to February 1938.
Recommissioned 18 February 1938 and relieved *Resolution* as Boys' Training Ship.
Transferred to North Atlantic Escort Force (Halifax) October 1939.

NORTH ATLANTIC ESCORT FORCE (flag RA Halifax) October 1939 to May 1940 (3rd BS from November 1939. See *Ramillies*).
Refit Devonport December 1939.
Transferred to Mediterranean Fleet May 1940 because of threat of war with Italy.

MEDITERRANEAN FLEET (1st BS) May to August 1940.
Unit of squadron (*Warspite* flag, *Malaya*, *Royal Sovereign*) in action with Italian battle squadron off Calabria 9 July 1940, while covering Malta to Alexandria convoy, although only *Warspite* got within range of the Italian ships.
Left Mediterranean August 1940 to rejoin North Atlantic Escort Force, proceeding via Suez

REQUEST 1/3
AIR VIEW, OFF THE BOW.
NAVY YARD, PHILA., PA.
SEPT. 14 1943
1488-43

Canal, Aden, Durban, Capetown and Gibraltar.
Refit Durham September to October 1940.
Arrived Halifax December 1940.

NORTH ATLANTIC ESCORT FORCE (flag
RA 3rd BS Halifax) December 1940 to August
1941.
Escorted Canadian troop convoy to England
February 1941.
Refit Norfolk, Virginia May to June 1941.
Selected in August for Eastern Fleet (see
Ramillies).

Refit Glasgow August to October 1941.
Transferred to Eastern Fleet October 1941.

EASTERN FLEET (3rd BS) October 1941 to
November 1943 (Colombo to April 1942,
Kilindini later).
Eastern Fleet based at Colombo to April 1942.
Transferred to Kilindini April 1942. Returned to
Ceylon (Trincomalee) January 1944.
Employed mainly on Indian Ocean convoy duty.
Detached September 1942 for refit in the USA
and proceeded via Cape and Freetown.

Refit Philadelphia 1942 to October 1943.
Withdrawn from Eastern Fleet on completion of
refit and returned home.
Paid off to Care & Maintenance Reserve at
Rosyth 5 November 1943 to May 1944.

Lent to Russia 30 May 1944 and renamed
Arkangelsk.
This transfer carried out under an agreement
concluded in lieu of the handing over of a proportion of the surrendered Italian Fleet which
had been claimed by Russia.

Other ships transferred on loan were: US cruiser *Milwaukee*, six ex-US destroyers (previously transferred to Britain under Lend Lease) and four British submarines (one sunk in error on passage).

Left Scapa for Murmansk 17 August 1944.

Officially handed back to Royal Navy at Rosyth 9 February 1949 and placed on Disposal List.

Sold to British Iron & Steel Corporation 5 April 1949 and allocated to T. W. Ward & Co. Ltd. for scrapping.

Arrived Inverkeithing 18 May 1949.

Royal Sovereign Loan to Russia, 1944

HMS *Royal Sovereign*, the US cruiser *Milwaukee*, nine British destroyers and four British submarines were lent to Russia in 1944 in lieu of a proportion of the surrendered Italian fleet.

The transfer of Italian ships to Russian ports would have been inconvenient at that time because of impending Allied operations, and would have prevented the useful role the Italians subsequently played during the period of co-belligerency. A spirit of non-cooperation in the Italian Navy at this time might have had an adverse effect on Operations 'Overlord' and 'Anvil'.

Royal Sovereign having just been placed into Reserve on her return from a refit in the USA was more than ready for such a move. After the ceremony of handing her over in Murmansk the British crew left the ship as quickly as possible. Little is known of her service during her stay with the Russian fleet. She remained in Russian hands until 1949, the Russians having frequently intimated that they would like to keep her permanently, and in fact, anything else in the way of foreign warships. On 23 January 1948 Sir Winston Churchill asked the Prime Minister whether or not the ship was in fact to be returned to this country. The question was raised during a debate on Foreign Affairs, and the reply was as might be expected given the public interest concerning the loaned vessels and the severe mistrust of the Russians during the immediate post-war years.

The Prime Minister said: 'I can see no reason why we, in return for such help to Russia and Italy, should leave our ships in Russian hands. We are entitled to get those ships back; and the scrap would be extremely useful to us at the present moment.'

The Admiralty considered that the ships, especially *Royal Sovereign*, would have soon

Left: *Royal Sovereign* passing under the Forth Bridge into Rosyth shortly after being handed back by the Russian Fleet in which she had served since 1944. Note modifications and paintwork (hull dark grey and upper works lighter shade of grey. February 1949.

Below: *Revenge*, 8 August 1939. This superb full-length view of *Revenge* first appeared in *Jane's Fighting Ships* for 1939. It shows all the modifications made during her recent refit.

become ineffectual through lack of suitable replacement equipment; during the period of four years that she had been in Russian hands she had never received the major refit that would be needed if she were to serve on in any fleet. But the prestige of the Royal Navy was at stake and the matter of her recovery was pursued. After much hassle and discontent on the part of the Soviet Navy, *Royal Sovereign* was handed back to the Royal Navy at Rosyth on 9 February 1949. She was immediately placed on the disposal list and finally sold to British Iron and Steel Industries and allocated to T. W. Ward and Co. She arrived at Inverkeithing on 18 May 1949, being the last unit of her class not already under the cutters' torch.

HISTORY: REVENGE

ATLANTIC FLEET

April 1919 to January 1928 (Flag 1st BS and 2nd fleet flag to May 1921. 2nd flag 1st BS May 1921 to November 1924. Fleet flag November 1924 to October 1927. 2nd BS from October 1927.

1st Battle Squadron detached to Mediterranean January 1920 because of Near East crisis. Took part in operations against Turkish Nationalists at Constantinople and in Black Sea March to July 1920.

Rejoined Atlantic Fleet July 1920.

On reorganization May 1921, *Revenge* became 2nd flag 1st BS (see *Ramillies*).

Again detached to Mediterranean, with *Ramillies*, *Resolution* and *Royal Sovereign* September 1922, to reinforce Mediterranean Fleet during further trouble in the Near East. Stationed mainly at Constantinople and in the Dardanelles.

Rejoined Atlantic Fleet March 1923.

Became Fleet Flag Atlantic Fleet 1 November 1924 on transfer of the *Queen Elizabeth* class to the Mediterranean (see *Ramillies*).

Relieved as flag by *Nelson* October 1927 and became private ship in the 2nd BS.

Paid off at Devonport 11 January 1928 for refit until January 1929.

Recommissioned Devonport 2 January 1929 for Mediterranean Fleet.

Below: *Resolution* in Philadelphia after repairs to torpedo damage; the photograph was taken on 11 September 1941.

MEDITERRANEAN FLEET (1st BS) January 1929 to February 1936 (flag 1st BS and 2nd fleet flag from June 1929).
Jubilee Review, Spithead 16 July 1935.
Stationed at Alexandria latter part of 1935 during Italo–Abyssinian crisis.
Paid off at Portsmouth 6 February 1936 for extensive refit until March 1937.
Recommissioned at Portsmouth 1 June 1937 for 2nd BS Home Fleet.

HOME FLEET (2nd BS) June 1937 to August 1939.
Employed as Seagoing Training Ship for Boys and RNR officers, with special complement, for some months during 1937 (see *Ramillies*).
Present at Portland Review of Reserve Fleet by HM the King 9 August 1939.
Assigned to Channel Force (Portland) under War Organization August 1939.

CHANNEL FORCE (Home Fleet Command Portland) August to October 1939.
Ordered to join South Atlantic Command (Freetown) 1 October 1939 following sinking of SS *Clement* by *Graf Spee*. Orders cancelled 5 October and ship transferred to North Atlantic Escort Force (Halifax), with *Resolution*, for convoy duty.
Left England 5 October, carrying bullion to Canada.

NORTH ATLANTIC ESCORT FORCE October 1939 to August 1940 (3rd BS for November 1939). (See *Ramillies*)
Unit of escort for first and second Canadian troop convoys to England December 1939.
Transferred to Plymouth Command August 1940 because of anticipated German invasion.

PLYMOUTH COMMAND (Base Ship Devonport) August to November 1940.
Bombarded Cherbourg from 15,700 yards, October 1940.
Rejoined North Atlantic Escort Force November 1940.

NORTH ATLANTIC ESCORT FORCE (3rd BS Halifax) November 1940 to August 1941.
Took part in search for *Bismarck* 23 to 27 May 1941 (left Halifax for this operation 23 May).

Selected for new Eastern Fleet August 1941 (see *Ramillies*).
Proceeded to Colombo via Freetown and Cape (at Freetown 31 August).

EASTERN FLEET (3rd BS) August 1941 (Colombo to April 1942. Kilindini later).
Eastern Fleet based at Colombo to April 1942.
Transferred to Kilindini April 1942. Returned to Ceylon (Trincomalee) January 1944.
Employed mainly on convoy duty in Indian Ocean.
Unit of escort for large convoy carrying Australian division from Suez to Australia February 1943.
Returned home September 1943.
Arrived Clyde September and reduced to reserve for Subsidiary Service.

RESERVE
September 1943 to March (Clyde to January 1944, Southampton January to December 1944, Devonport later).
Employed as Stokers' Training Ship throughout although, in a memo to the First Lord in November 1943, Sir Winston Churchill commented that the ship should be put to a higher use.
Detached November 1943 to take Churchill to Malta, en route to the Cairo and Tehran Conferences.
Left Clyde 14 November. Arrived Malta 17th.
Transferred to Portsmouth Command at Southampton January 1944.
Main armament removed May 1944 to provide spare guns for *Warspite*, *Ramillies* and monitors of the Normandy Bombardment Force.
Attached to Imperieuse Training Establishment, Devonport 17 December 1944.
Placed on Disposal List 8 March 1948.
Sold to British Iron & Steel Co. Ltd. July 1948 and allocated to T. W. Ward & Co. Inverkeithing for scrapping.
Arrived Inverkeithing 5 September 1948.

HISTORY: RESOLUTION

ATLANTIC FLEET April 1919 to March 1926 (2nd flag 1st BS to April 1921 and September to November 1924. Flag 2nd BS and 2nd fleet flag from November 1924).
Detached to Mediterranean with rest of class

(1st BS January 1920 because of Near East crisis.
Took part in operations against Turkish Nationalists at Constantinople and in the Black Sea March to July 1920.
Rejoined Atlantic Fleet July 1920.
1st and 2nd Battle Squadrons, Atlantic Fleet merged into one, 1st BS, May 1921 (see *Ramillies*).
Again detached to Mediterranean (with *Ramillies*, *Revenge* and *Royal Sovereign*) September 1922 to reinforce Mediterranean Fleet during further trouble in the Near East.
Employed mainly in the Dardanelles and Sea of Marmara.
Flag of British squadron sent to Smyrna February 1923 to demonstrate following Turkish demand for evacuation of that port by Allied warships.
Rejoined Atlantic Fleet August 1923.
Became flag 2nd BS and 2nd fleet flag November 1924 (see *Ramillies*).
Transferred to Mediterranean Fleet (with *Royal Oak*) March 1926 to replace the four *Iron Duke* class, transferred to the Atlantic Fleet.
Became 2nd flag 1st BS on joining Mediterranean Fleet.

MEDITERRANEAN FLEET (1st BS) March 1926 to December 1935 (2nd flag 1st BS March to November 1926. Fleet flag November 1932 to March 1933 and July to September 1935).
Stationed at Alexandria during Egyptian political crisis June 1926.
Refit Portsmouth December 1926 to December 1927.
Recommissioned 30 December 1927.
With destroyers *Keith*, *Basilisk* and *Bulldog*, carried out relief work following earthquake in Macedonia and Thessaly September 1932.
Temporary fleet flag November 1932 to March 1933 while *Queen Elizabeth* refitting.
Jubilee Review, Spithead 16 July 1935.
Again temporary fleet flag July (after Review) to September 1935 while *Queen Elizabeth* refitting.
Stationed at Alexandria latter part 1935 during Italo-Abyssinian crisis.
Paid off at Portsmouth 10 December 1935 for refit to September 1936.
Recommissioned at Portsmouth 15 September for Home Fleet (ex Atlantic Fleet, renamed Home Fleet March 1932).

HOME FLEET (2nd BS) September 1936 to August 1939 (flag 2nd BS August to October 1937).
Temporarily replaced *Royal Oak* as flag 2nd BS and 2nd fleet flag August to October 1937.
Employed as Seagoing Training Ship for Boys and RNR officers 1937 to February 1938 (see *Ramillies*).
Refit Devonport March to July 1938.
Recommissioned 22 July 1938.
Assigned to Channel Force (Portland) under War Organization, August 1939.

CHANNEL FORCE (Home Fleet Command Portland) August to October 1939.
Ordered to join South Atlantic Command (Freetown) 1 October 1939 following sinking of SS *Clement* by *Graf Spee*. Orders cancelled 5 October and ship transferred to North Atlantic Escort Force (Halifax) with *Revenge*.
Left England 5 October, carrying bullion to Canada.

NORTH ATLANTIC ESCORT FORCE (Halifax) October 1939 to April 1940 (3rd BS from November 1939 (see *Ramillies*).
Unit of escort for first and second Canadian troop convoys to England December 1939.
Rejoined Home Fleet April 1940 for Norwegian campaign.

HOME FLEET (2nd BS April to June 1940).
Norwegian operations. Took part in capture of Bjerkvik 12 May during operations against Narvik. Carried tanks and motor landing craft for this attack. Damaged by bomb at Tjeldsundet later in the month. Two killed and 27 wounded.
Transferred to Mediterranean June 1940.
Left Scapa for Gibraltar 4 June and joined Force H (Gibraltar) on its formation 28 June 1940.

FORCE H (Gibraltar) June to September 1940.
Took part (with *Valiant*, *Hood*, *Ark Royal*, *Arethusa*, *Enterprise* and destroyers) in attack on French Fleet at Mers-el-Kebir (Oran) 3 July.
Unit of Force M (*Resolution*, *Barham*, *Ark Royal*, *Devonshire* flag, *Cornwall*, *Cumberland*, *Australia*, ten destroyers and minor craft).
Bombarded Dakar 23 to 25 September.
Engaged by *Richelieu* and shore batteries on 24th, hit four times.

Torpedoed by French submarine *Bévéziers* on 25th and considerably damaged.
Towed to Freetown by *Barham*, arrived there 29th.
Temporary repairs carried out at Freetown and Gibraltar September 1940 to March 1941, ship being transferred to South Atlantic Command while at Freetown.
Left Gibraltar for Portsmouth March 1941.
Attacked by aircraft en route but not hit.
Left Portsmouth for USA April 1941 to complete refit.
Refitted at Philadelphia Navy Yard April to September 1941.
Selected for new Eastern Fleet August 1941, while under refit (see *Ramillies*).
Completed refit 6 September, worked-up at Bermuda and left for Devonport (via Clyde) 27 September.
Temporarily attached to Home Fleet on return.

HOME FLEET (2nd BS) October to December 1941.
Hoisted flag (VA) 3rd BS Eastern Fleet December 1941.
Left Colombo via Cape, January 1942. Arrived Colombo 26 March 1932, being last ship of the class to join.

EASTERN FLEET (flag 3rd BS and 2nd fleet flag) December 1941 to September 1943 (see *Ramillies*).
Unit of escort for large convoy carrying Australian division from Suez to Australia February 1943.
Returned home September 1943.
Refit Rosyth September to October 1943.
Reduced to reserve for Subsidiary Service on completion of refit.
Reserve October 1943 to February 1948 (Southampton to June 1944, attached Imperieuse Establishment Devonport from June 1944).
Employed as Stokers' Training Ship throughout. In a memo to the First Sea Lord in November 1943 the Prime Minister commented that the ship should be put to a higher use than this.
Portsmouth Command, Southampton to June 1944.
Main armament removed May 1944 to provide 15in guns for ships of the Normandy bombardment force.

Transferred to Devonport 30 June 1944 and attached to the Imperieuse Establishment.
Paid off to Disposal List 2 February 1948.
Sold to British Iron & Steel Corporation 5 May 1948 and allocated to Metal Industries Ltd., Faslane, for scrapping. Arrived Faslane 13 May 1948.

HISTORY: ROYAL OAK

ATLANTIC FLEET (1st BS) April 1919 to March 1926.
1st BS detached to the Mediterranean in January 1920 because of Near East crisis.
Took part in operations against Turkish nationalists at Constantinople and in the Black Sea March to July 1920.
Rejoined Atlantic Fleet July 1920.
Extensive refit at Portsmouth September 1922 until April 1924, the first she had received since completion in 1916.
Transferred to Mediterranean Fleet March 1926 until May 1934.
Refit at Devonport March to June 1927.
Returned to Mediterranean Fleet.
Paid off again in May 1934 and transferred to Devonport for extensive refit, June 1934 until August 1936.
Home Fleet August 1936 until lost in October 1939.
Commissioned for Mediterranean Fleet 7 July 1939 but never joined, remaining with Home Fleet on War Organization in August 1939.
Torpedoed and sunk by *U47* while at anchor in Scapa Flow on 14 October 1939, the first British capital ship to be lost in the Second World War.

HISTORY: RAMILLIES

ATLANTIC FLEET April 1919 to August 1927 (1st BS to November 1924, 2nd BS later).
First BS detached to Mediterranean January 1920 because of Near East crisis.
Took part in operations against Turkish Nationalists at Constantinople and in the Black Sea March to July 1920.
Rejoined Atlantic Fleet August 1920.
In May 1921 1st and 2nd BS merged into one, 1st BS, the *Royal Sovereign*s forming the 1st Division and the *Queen Elizabeth*s the 2nd.
Queen Elizabeth remained as fleet flag, *Barham* became flag 1st BS and *Revenge* 2nd flag.

Ramillies again detached to Mediterranean, with *Resolution*, *Revenge* and *Royal Sovereign*, September 1922 to reinforce Mediterranean Fleet during further trouble in the Near East. Employed mainly in the Dardanelles and Sea of Marmara.

Rejoined Atlantic Fleet November 1922.

Refit Rosyth June to September 1924.

On 1 November 1924 the *Queen Elizabeth* class transferred to the Mediterranean as 1st BS with *Queen Elizabeth* fleet flag, the *Royal Sovereign*s remaining in the Atlantic Fleet as a new 2nd BS with *Revenge* as fleet flag and *Resolution* flag 2nd BS and 2nd fleet flag. This distribution of the two classes remained unchanged until 1926.

Underwent extensive refit at Devonport September 1926 to March 1927.

Recommissioned 1 March 1927.

Transferred to Mediterranean Fleet (1st BS) August 1927 to June 1932.

With *Barham* carried out special flag showing cruise along west coast of Africa December 1927 to February 1928.

Stationed at Jaffa October 1929 during trouble in Palestine.

Paid off to reserve at Devonport for refit June 1932 to August 1934.

Extensive refit February 1933, completed 31 August 1934 and recommissioned for Mediterranean 17 September to July 1935.

Early in 1935 it was decided to revert to the distribution of the *Royal Sovereign* and *Queen Elizabeth* classes which had been adopted in 1924 and to station all the *Royal Sovereign*s in the Home Fleet and the *Queen Elizabeth*s in the Mediterranean, as opportunity occurred. *Royal Sovereign* and *Ramillies* exchanged with *Barham* and *Valiant* April to August 1935; *Resolution* and *Revenge* with *Malaya* and *Warspite* September 1936 to June 1937.

HOME FLEET (2nd BS) July 1935 to February 1939.

Jubilee Review, Spithead 16 July 1935.

Collision with German steamer *Eisenach* in gale off Dover 31 August 1935; damage to bows.

During period January 1936 to September 1939, all the *Royal Sovereign* class, with the exception of *Royal Oak*, employed at various times as Seagoing Training Ships for Boys and RNR officers, with special complements, although remaining within the 2nd BS oranization while serving as such.

Ramillies employed thus February 1936 to December 1937.

Coronation Review, Spithead 19 May 1937.

Refit Devonport July 1938 to February 1939.

Recommissioned at Devonport 22 February 1939 for Mediterranean Fleet (1st BS) to July 1939.

Transferred to Home Fleet (2nd BS) July 1939 to October 1939.

Employed as Seagoing Training Ship for Boys and RNR officers July to August.

Present at Portland Review of Reserve Fleet by HM the King 9 August.

Left Clyde for Alexandria, via Gibraltar, 5 September 1939 as Senior Officer of the first troop convoy of the war.

Stationed at Gibraltar September to October.

Ordered to join North Atlantic Escort Force (Halifax) 5 October but recalled on the 6th and joined 1st BS Mediterranean Fleet, replacing *Malaya* detached to Indian Ocean to take part in search for *Graf Spee*.

MEDITERRANEAN FLEET (1st BS) October to November 1939.

Transferred to East Indies Command (3rd BS Aden) for convoy duty November 1939.

In November 1939 a 3rd Battle Squadron was formed, comprising the four *Royal Sovereign* class battleships engaged in escort duties outside the Home Fleet (2nd BS) and Mediterranean Fleet (1st BS) Commands.

Malaya also detached for a short time while in the North Atlantic Escort Force December 1939 to May 1940.

This squadron organized for administrative rather than for tactical purposes, the ships being independently employed, where required.

In 1942 the 3rd BS was allocated to the Eastern Fleet and in November 1944 to the East Indies (ex Eastern) Fleet.

EAST INDIES (3rd BS Aden) November 1939 to May 1940.

Attached to Force J (*Malaya* and *Glorious*) in Indian Ocean November 1939 during search for *Graf Spee*.

Later escorted Australian and New Zealand troop convoys to Aden December 1939 to April 1940.

Transferred to Mediterranean Fleet May 1940 via Suez Canal because of threat of war with Italy.

MEDITERRANEAN FLEET (1st BS) May to November 1940.
With *Malaya*, *Warspite* and *Kent* bombarded Bardia 15 August 1940. Unit of supporting force for attack on enemy ships at Taranto by aircraft from *Illustrious* 11 November 1940.
Transferred to North Atlantic Escort Force November 1940 following reduction in Italian battleship strength as a result of the Taranto raid which permitted *Ramillies* and *Malaya* to be withdrawn from the Mediterranean.
Attached to Force H 27 November while on passage through Mediterranean to Gibraltar and was with this force during convoy action with Italian squadron off Cape Spartivento on same date although not actually engaged.
Refit Devonport December 1940 to January 1941 prior to joining North Atlantic Escort Force at Halifax.
Left Devonport 12 January for Halifax, via Clyde, to escort Middle East convoy on initial stage.
Arrived Halifax late January 1941.
North Atlantic escort force (Flag RA 3rd BS Halifax) January to August 1941.
Employed on Bermuda-Halifax-United Kingdom convoy duty.
Sighted by *Scharnhorst* and *Gneisenau* 8 February 1941 when those ships attempted to attack convoy; presence of *Ramillies* causing them to abandon the attack.
Detached from a convoy 23 May 1941 to take part in operations against *Bismarck*.
Because of the threat of war with Japan, it was proposed in August 1941 that all four *Royal Sovereign*s should be sent to the Indian Ocean by the end of the year as the initial instalment of a new, Eastern Fleet for the defence of that area.
This force was to be based in the first instance at Colombo and would later move to Singapore after it had been brought to full strength which could not be done before March 1942. It was proposed to reinforce them with *Nelson*, *Rodney* and *Renown* in December 1941 or January 1942, but this was never carried out.
In October 1941, as a concession to the views of the Prime Minister, *Prince of Wales*, *Repulse* and *Indomitable* were selected as a fast striking force of the Eastern Fleet, to be based at Singapore for offensive operations against the Japanese in the event of war.
Prince of Wales and *Repulse* arrived there on 2 December but were sunk by Japanese aircraft on the 10th, two days after the outbreak of war. *Indomitable* never joined the force.
Following the loss of these ships, the *Royal Sovereign*s, which arrived at Colombo between October 1941 and March 1942, remained in the Indian Ocean until the summer of 1943, constituting the 3rd BS Eastern Fleet, with *Warspite* as fleet flag from March 1942 to March 1943.
Fleet based at Colombo until April 1942, Kilindi (East Africa) April 1942 to January 1944, Trincomalee from January 1944.
Ramillies refitted at Liverpool August to November 1921.
Hoisted flat (RA) 3rd BS Eastern Fleet in Clyde 2 December 1941 and left for Colombo.

EASTERN FLEET (3rd BS) December 1941 to December 1943 (2nd flag 3rd BS to April 1942)
Attached to Force F April 1942 for occupation of Madagascar.
Arrived Durban 22 April, replacing *Malaya* as flag (VA) Force F.
Took part in bombardment and occupation of Diego Suarez (Madagascar) 7 May 1942 and remained there following the surrender.
Torpedoed and considerably damaged by Japanese midget submarine at Diego Suarez 30 May. Midget was one of two launched from the parent submarines *I 16* and *I 20*.
Left Diego Suarez for Durban for repairs 3 June. Arrived Durban 9th.
Temporarily repaired at Durban June to August 1942. Completed refit at Devonport September 1942 to June 1943.
Rejoined Eastern Fleet at Kilindini (East Africa) July 1943, being then the only battleship remaining on the station.
Left Colombo 28 December 1943 for home to transfer to Home Fleet.
Joined Home Fleet January 1944.

HOME FLEET (2nd BS) January 1944 to January 1945.
Unit of bombardment force for Normandy invasion June 1944.
Bombarded batteries at Villerville, Benerville and Houlgate until 7 June.
Again attacked Houlgate battery on 17 June, putting it out of action.
Unit of bombardment force for invasion of southern France August 1944.
Bombarded batteries at entrance to Toulon 25 to 28 August.
Reduced to reserve at Portsmouth 31 January 1945 to December 1947.
Attached to Vernon Establishment 15 May 1945 as Accommodation Ship (with *Malaya*) and known as Vernon III.
Placed on Disposal List December 1947.
Sold to British Iron & Steel Corporation 20 February 1948 and allocated to Arnott Young Ltd. for scrapping.
Arrived Cairnryan 23 April 1948.

RENOWN AND *REPULSE*

DESIGN

Originally proposed as battleships, *Renown* and *Repulse* were laid down under the 1914 estimates as slightly improved vessels of the *Royal Sovereign* class.

On 19 December 1914, however, the DNC had the first intimation that a new battlecruiser and not a battleship was required; the ship to have a speed of about 32 knots and be armed with at least six 15in guns fitted in pairs.

The basic concept of the design was conceived as a direct result of the Battle of the Falkland Islands in December 1914 and an earlier battle at Heligoland Bight (in August) which showed the immense value of high speed coupled with long-range powerful gunfire and a large radius of action; factors which enabled a ship to run down any enemy ship under almost any circumstances, and accept or decline action at will. These features of course could only be obtained at the expense of good armour protection, and with the battlecruiser type in mind no improvement was demanded beyond that given to the original battlecruisers built in 1906 (*Invincible*). Although this was seen by many to be a dangerous policy, especially as the latest battlecruisers completing were sporting a 9in armoured belt, the move to get the ships approved was given priority.

By 21 December 1914 the dimensions of the new ships had been determined and by Christmas Eve a model had been made and inspected by Admiral John Fisher who was making every effort to see that the ships would materialize. On 28 December the DNC was notified that the model had been approved and that construction should start immediately. It being essential that the ships be completed at the earliest possible date, the DNC suggested that the battlecruiser *Tiger*'s machinery installation be repeated to avoid any delays to the final layout.

At this time, *Renown* and *Repulse* were still on the stocks as battleships, and were in the early stages at the yards of Palmer and Fairfield. Because of the greater length of the new battlecruisers Palmer's could not undertake the work and after compensation for materials used, *Repulse* was passed over to John Brown's Shipyard on Clyde bank.

The rapidity of the design and construction was indeed remarkable as the following table shows:

19 December 1914 First intimation given that battlecruiser was required.
21 December Dimensions established for guns and speed.
24 December Lord Fisher inspects model of proposed ship in DNC's room and asked for certain modifications before showing it to the Board.
26 December Model completed.
28 December DNC informed that model agreed on and ordered to proceed with design.
29 December Contractors interviewed by Fisher himself and orders placed with the clause that the ships were to be built in fifteen months. Action taken by DNCs department regarding the ordering of material and what stock could be used from Palmer's yard that had been put into place for the improved *Royal Sovereign*-type battleship. Material was re-directed to John Brown's almost immediately. Modification of keel plates from battleship to battlecruiser presented no problems.

Legend: As originally designed as battleships, 1914.
Displacement: 27,750 tons.
Length: 580ft
Beam: 88ft 9in
Draught: 28ft 6in
Freeboard: 16ft forward, 18ft aft.
Fuel: 900/3,000 tons coal.
Armament: 8 x 15in; 16 x 6in; 4 x 3in AA; 4 x 21in TT.
Armour main belt 13in, ends 6in, barbettes 10in, turrets 11in, CT 11in, 3–1in. Weights (tons): Hull 8,400; armour 8,600; armament 4,550; machinery 2,550; general equipment 700; BM 50.

Designs proposed after the original legend above. ('C' and 'D' actually worked on when a battlecruiser was given priority).

	'A'	'B'	'C'	'D'
Length (ft)	720	760	760	780
Beam (ft)	90.6	100	90	100
Draught	25	26	24	25
Displacement (tons)	28,500	28,000	27,000	31,500
Speed (knots)	29	25/26	30	28
SHP	90,000	70,000	90,000	90,000
Armament	8 x 15in	8 x 15in	6 x 15in	8 x 15in
	12 x 5.5in	12 x 5.5in	12 x 5.5in	12 x 5.5in
	TT: 2 x 21in	TT: 2 x 21in	TT: 2 x 21in	TT: 2 x 21in
Armour	12–5in	12–5in	12–5in	12–5in

ONE OF THE PROPOSED DESIGNS AFTER *ROYAL SOVEREIGN* CLASS
Design 'C2' and 'C', January 1916

Displacement 26,250 tons
Length 657ft
Beam 100ft
Draught 28ft 3in
Speed 22 knots

Armament
8x15in, 10x5.5in

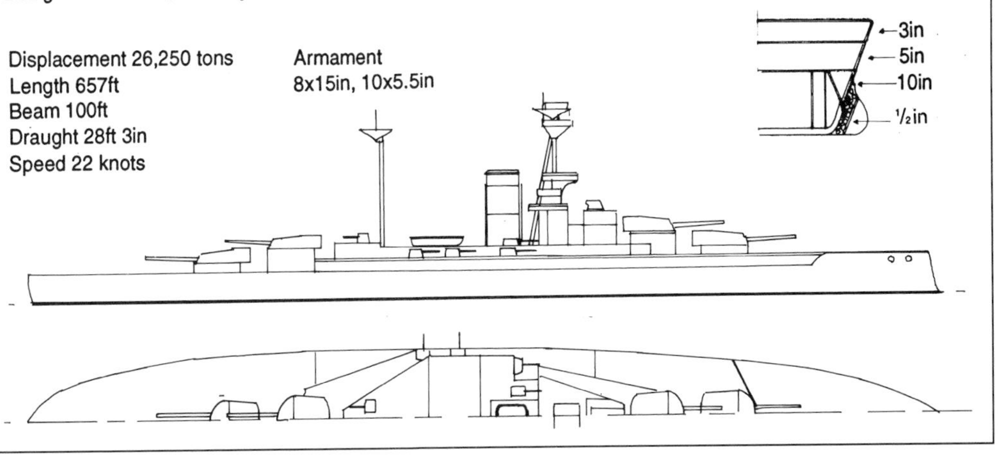

3in
5in
10in
½in

Below: *Renown* , showing details of the bridge and funnels in early 1920, when she was used to convey royalty on trips around the world. Note the housing between funnels and the box on the charthouse roof for royal viewing.

17 January 1915 Fairfield and John Brown's were supplied with complete information to enable them to build midships portion of ship out of the turn of bilge and order much material.
25 January Keels laid down.
31 January Both firms supplied with sufficient data for preparing all main structural drawings: Hull specification; Midships section; Part profile and deck flats; sections of protective deck; Sketch of armoured plating.
15 February 250 feet of the keel on blocks, 4,000 tons of material ordered.
28 February Drawings almost complete.
15 March 375 tons on blocks, 3,000 tons of steel on premises.
30 March Hull specification completed, 800 tons on blocks.
12 April All drawings completed, 1,200 tons on blocks.
8 January 1916 Launch.
15 August Preliminary sea trials.

Thanks to Lord Fisher's drive and a high degree of co-operation between the Constructor's Department and the contractors, both vessels were completed in 19 to 20 months which at that time constituted a world record for ships of this size and novel design.

The ships were the largest and among the most noteworthy laid down and completed during the Great War and can be regarded as the last representatives of the original battlecruiser type built for the Royal Navy.

In the succeeding *Hood*, as redesigned after Jutland, the characteristics of the battleship and battlecruiser were merged into one 'fast battleship' type by substantially increasing displacement to allow for additional protection. Both ships turned out remarkably well, within the limits of the design, and it is reported that the Americans were so impressed that their US *Constellation* class were redesigned along similar lines. But war experience emphasized that, although useful for purely cruiser work against weaker ships, such as performed by *Invincible* at the Falklands, their weak protection rendered them quite unsuitable for employment against other capital ships. In the light of Jutland and the battlecruiser losses, this deficiency was subjected to severe criticism when the ships joined the fleet late in 1916, and at Admiral Jellicoe's instigation they were sent back to the shipyard where another 504 tons of protection was worked into

the decks around the magazine area (carried out at Rosyth by the builders).

As completed they had an average draught of 25ft 9½in, about 3½in deep of the design figure and an extra deep of 29ft 8in with 4,243 tons oil. After alterations (October 1916) the normal draught had increased to 26ft 2in and deep to 30ft 0½in. The commanding officer of *Repulse* reported that the ship behaved very well in a considerable Atlantic sea and had an even motion. With regard to the flare at the bows (which caused considerable comment at first) which exceed that of previous ships, he was of the opinion that *Repulse* would make more progress against a heavy sea than a ship of similar freeboard without the flare.

In service the ships proved very popular even though they were poorly armoured and while on a cruise after the war the correspondent Lionel Halsey sent this report to the DNC on 29 June 1920:
'My Dear d'Eyncourt,
In know you are interested in *Renown*.

The ship is a perfect marvel to me. She steams beautifully and is extraordinarily economical. She only burnt a little over 1 ton of oil per knot at 20 knots and she is perfectly wonderful in heavy weather – in fact, I never knew any ship

could behave as she does and she is not abnormally wet, in fact, in head seas, she is wonderfully dry, but her steadiness is extraordinary.

We had a real gale and heavy seas and she made good weather of it.'

ARMAMENT

Although it is well known that *Renown* and *Repulse* had six 15in guns in twin turrets because of their availability and a directive to complete the ships in fifteen months, the fact is that the number of guns was a compromise and not at all popular in many naval circles. But Lord Fisher had been directly responsible for the ships and their construction, and as he was a very important and powerful man who could move mountains to get what he wanted, nobody was going to be foolhardy enough to criticize him.

Six guns in pairs made for difficulty with fire control and salvo shooting, and the single turret aft took up a lot of space internally whereas for a few feet more another turret could have been worked in to give four guns in two turrets. But only six guns for each ship were immediately available so this layout was given the go-ahead and the dimensions were worked around it. Before the layout had been decided it was suggested that eight 15in guns could be carried on a hull of 780ft (pp) x 92ft x 27½ft, displacing 27,100 tons and having a speed of 31 knots. Six guns in twin mounts reduced the figures of 750ft x 90ft x 26ft, displacing 25,750 tons on a speed of 32 knots. There was much correspondence on the subject with the DNC (D'Eyncourt), but although eight guns were most desirable the increased dimensions also had some sway in the matter and it was easy for Fisher to persuade the Board into voting for no delay.

The secondary armament was also a compromise, the 4in gun having long been discredited as being too small effectively to stop some of the larger destroyers in the German Navy. Fisher did not like heavy guns as a secondary armament, however, and saw the 4in as the maximum size that could possibly be incorporated into the new ships. To make up for this the guns were fitted in triple mounts so as at least to give saturation fire, but in practice the guns proved awkward to work because of the 'bunching' of breeches at the rear of the open turret. And the turrets were not popular because they offered little or no protection to the crews serving them.

During the design stage it had been the intention to fit the ships with mines (July 1915, 25 Vickers Automatic Submerged mines No. 20), but when the construction staff studied the requirements it was found that it would prove difficult to them from the quarterdeck because of the stern anchor and the fact that the mine rails would reach back across the quarterdeck beneath the 15in muzzles and would almost certainly be damaged by the blast from the guns. To fit them internally would have caused immense problems with compartmentation and alteration of the protective plating at the rear of the ship, and having mines inside the ship so near to the conventional gun magazines was potentially dangerous. Although the First Sea Lord favoured the idea, it proved a case of 'too many eggs in one basket' and the matter was dropped.

ARMOUR

As the protection for such large ships was so poor, the actual thickness of the armour (6in) was kept secret for as long as possible – 'Hush Hush' ships they were for more reasons than the sobriquet suggested.

As ships armed with 15in guns it was obvious that in time they would probably face enemy ships with a similar armament, aprospect that caused shudders at the Admiralty. Although the opitome of the battlecruiser type, Jutland in May 1916 had proved that these ships had no place in the battle lineat any distance and the type quickly became obsolete after the battle. More armour was asked for, but it was no easy matter to re-armour a ship in practically all areas without extensive alterations and a serious effect on stability.

During their lifespan the scale of protection was improved to some extent (see tables and drawings), but throughout their existance they remained the weakest of all British capital ships. But until 1940 they could outrun anything powerful enough to sink them, and outshoot anything that was fast enough to catch them- which was exactly what they had been desgned to do.

The following compares their thin scale of armour with various ships (1917), all battlecruisers:

Inflexible:	2,020 tons armour, 1,200 tons plating (decks, etc).
Princess Royal:	3,900 tons armour, 2,300 tons plating.
Tiger:	4,750 tons armour , 2,300tons plating.
Repulse:	2,440 tons armour, 3,300 tons plating.
Hood:	6,750 tons armour, 7,500 tons plating.
Seydlitz:	5,200 tons armour, 2,400 tons plating.

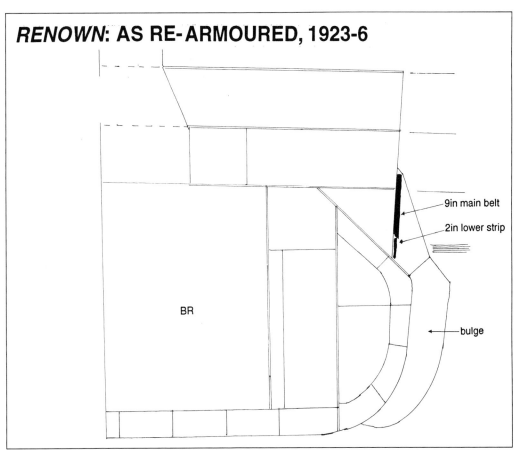

RENOWN: AS RE-ARMOURED, 1923-6

9in main belt

2in lower strip

BR

bulge

REPULSE ARMOURED LAYOUT, 1919

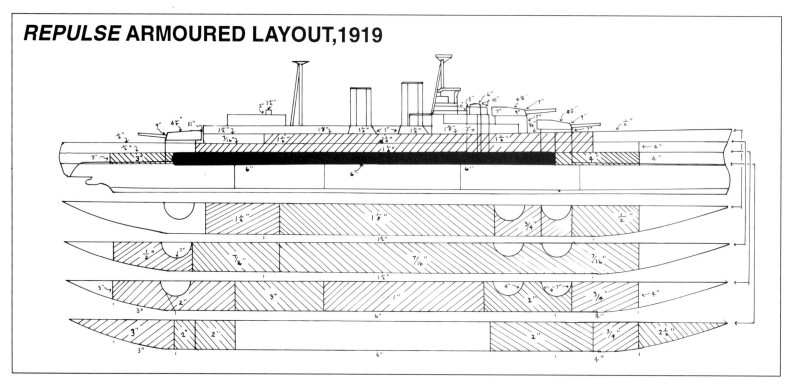

MACHINERY

Because of the speed at which the ships were constructed there was no question of any alteration from 'standard Admiralty practice' regarding machinery, which had been used up to and in the battlecruiser *Tiger* (1911).

The *Tiger* layout was virtually repeated, but with oil-fired boilers instead of coal and the addition of three boilers to attain the required high speed.

Designed as battlecruisers, they were naturally fast ships but being lightly constructed on such a fine hull there were some problems with vibration during full-power steaming. The fault, however, was rectified during the early refits as shown in *Renown* during 1932 when fitted with HACSI and foremast strengthened between the 15in spotting top and 15in defence position:

'On the day of trial the sea was smooth to slight and observations of the vibration of the 15in spotting top and 4in control platform were made.

The structure at the top of the mast vibrated at a frequency of approximately 2/3rds of a second. The vibration was transverse not longitudinal, no oscillation of the mast was observed.

It was constant for all speeds of the ship.

The vibration on a straight course was very slight.

When helm was put over, however, the whole top vibrated much more.

In order to test the sighting instruments I took a seat in the H.A.C.S. and trained and elevated the instruments – landmarks on the Isle of Wight and a small steamer provided suitable targets. It was found that it was reasonably easy to keep the sights on target even when vibration was noticeable. The ship's gunnery officers were satisfied with conditions on the top.'

BRIDGEWORK

Having been completed with open bridgework in much the same way as the *Queen Elizabeth* and *Royal Sovereign* classes, the personnel serving those positions were subject to all weathers.

Levels were added and platforms covered in to varying degrees throughout the years from 1916 to the early 1930s during their refits, but severity of back draught and foul weather always posed problems and occasionally caused difficulties in conning the ship. After reconstruction in 1936 *Repulse* had been given a new, remodelled bridge and compass platform, a more closed in fitting with flat sides in an endeavour to deflect the wind away from staff. Two views were expressed about the ship's upper works during her trials after refit:

'31 January 1936. 1 hour full power trials.

At high speeds, head to wind there was considerable down and back draught over the bridge, especially at the after end. At the fore end, the wind deflectors had some effect but they only extended for 12in or so above the top of the bridge plating. The Watch Officer standing at the Gyro repeater experienced the full force of relative wind in his face. There is troublesome eddying at the position of the revolving chart table. The effects are due partly to the large platform over the bridge. The 4in director platform appears to throw down the wind on to the after end of the bridge.

Full power trials 6 March 1936.

The covered in bridge appeared to be quite comfortable but crowded. Front windows were kept open while doors at back of bridge were kept closed. The plotting house being used as an airlock. With this arrangement there was very little draught on the compass platform. The height of the roof could be lowered.

4in control platform – the conditions here were uncomfortable due to low screen and heavy down draught caused by structure overhead and abaft.

15in director platform – no instruments are fitted except inside director tower.

15in spotting top – conditions quite comfortable – abaft the H.A.C.S. tower, however, conditions were not so good owing to air stream being deflected downwards by H.A.C.S. H.A.C.S. aft complained of vibration but none forward.'

After her complete reconstruction *Renown* sported a brand-new smooth-faced semi-circular bridge which drew the following comments on 25 July 1939:

'The open compass platform was generally satisfactory. With a wind of 65 feet per second, 10 degrees on starboard bow the wind stream passed overhead at a height of about 8–9ft. The H.D.O. and SL sights abaft the compass platform were draughty due to wind striking the 15in DCT and being deflected down.

On turning the DCT on beam, conditions were better. The fairing on the fore side would be better removed. It was found that low bulkheads about 2ft high across compass platform at forward edge of chart table prevented draughts along floor in vicinity of pelorus. Throughout the trials no tendency for funnel smoke to be drawn down in the vicinity of the flying-off space or quarterdeck was observed. The extra height of funnels after experience with *Warspite* appears to have been most effective.'

Research with a view to achieving the optimum design in bridgework for capital ships continued at the National Physical Laboratory throughout the war. Satisfactory reports had been received from several ships fitted with semi-circular bridges, but wind tunnel tests on mock bridgework to different scales showed the superiority of square-faced bridges. The square, open bridge had a serious disadvantage, however, in

Steam Trials

Repulse 23 August 1916
Firth of Clyde. Arran Course.
Displacement: 28,200 tons.
Draught: 26ft 2in forward, 27ft 7in aft.
Diameter of propellers: 13ft 6in; Pitch: 13ft 6in.
Expanded surface: 100 sq ft.
Mean revolutions: 273.5
Mean SHP: 116,992
Speed: 31.31 knots.

Repulse 6 March 1936
Measured Mile.
Tolland Course.
Wind: 4–5
Mean SHP: 112,400
Mean speed: 28.36 knots.

Renown: 10, 11, 24 and 25 July 1939
Tolland Course.
Displacement: 31,424 tons
Draught: 26ft 11⅝in forward, 27ft 6¾in aft.
Diameter of propellers: (3-bladed) 13ft 6in; Pitch: 12ft 11in. 1,250 tons ballast on board plus lower bulges flooded. Designed rpm 275 for 30.1 knots but not actually reached. Best speed with 120,951shp was 29.926 knots.

9 knots	15knots	18 knots	FP:
32,252 tons	32,262 tons	32,272 tons	32,790 tons
27ft 8⅝in	27ft 8¾in	27ft 11⅞in	28ft 2⅜in
Sea: 3	Sea: 3	Sea: 3	Sea: 2
87½rpm	137rpm	162rpm	278rpm
3,742shp	13,061shp	22,128shp	120,951shp
9.877 knots	15:633 knots	18.530 knots	29.926 knots

that the degree of efficiency of its protection was variable; a bridge that was good in head winds sometimes suffered from oblique draughts at angles between 15 and 35 degrees. The determining factor appeared to be the height of the massive superstructure. The semi-circular form of bridge while not as satisfactory as the square could be made more effective by roofing it in or fitting suitable wind baffles as had previously been fitted in many of the older battleships. It was noted that the twin 15in turrets were an obstruction to the smooth flow of air up and around the bridgework.

Renown's bridge was, as already mentioned, a new structure, that had been developed as a result of many tests throughout the 1930s. It stood 56 feet above the forecastle deck and projected slightly forward of the main vertical line of the superstructure. It was twelve feet in diameter at the top and thirteen feet at the floor level. Baffles were fitted during the end of her reconstruction and these were found to give sufficient

wind protection to the bridge personnel. The baffles had 3ft 6in compartments and were fitted around the mouth of the bridge and in fact made conditions over the all-important pelorus position most satisfactory; it was stated that there was no definite deterioration in conditions throughout the whole area, and only slight draughts were felt at the rear of the bridgework when catching the wind at oblique angles or when thrown up from the turrets below.

APPEARANCE CHANGES, REFITS AND MODIFICATIONS

As completed they were exceptionally fine-looking ships with a most graceful hull. With their equal height funnels in the early months they were a designer's delight, and even the raising of the forward funnel did not detract from their good looks. The superstructure was simple, but rather piled-up in appearance and the searchlight arrangement on the funnels was rather unique. Another distinctive feature was the double row of scuttles along the hull – indicating the lack of armour of course – which were very eye-catching.

Principle characteristics of the class were:
1. Marked upward sheer forward and aft with strongly curved stem and deep bow flare.
2. Long double row of scuttles along main and upper deck sides.
3. Unusually high superstructure forward with wings carried aft to abeam fore funnel.
4. Short, equal-height flat-sided funnels (fore funnel raised before entering service).
5. Small, strongly projecting searchlight platforms on funnels.
6. Two 15in turrets forward and one aft.
7. Prominent triple 4in mountings abeam fore funnel and on centreline before and abaft mainmast.
8. Tripod masts with short topmast on each.

During the Great War they both received the usual modifications that other capital ships were given (see *British Battleships of World War One*), but this did not drastically alter their appearance. The superstructure was built up slightly and searchlight towers were added around the second funnel. Both ships were used for experiments with camouflage paint.

Repulse was the first of the two to be considered for refit after the war, plans for this having

been made well in advance of the cessation of hostilities.

Repulse Refit, December 1918 to October 1920:
1. High-tensile plating worked into main deck, adding 1in to the flat and 2in on the slopes. The lower deck received 1in plating over the magazines.
2. The main 6in armoured belt was removed from its original position and placed one deck higher. A new 9in strake was fitted in the old position.
3. New, wider anti-torpedo bulges were fitted, rather like those fitted to *Ramillies* and were filled with crushing tubes. There were 6ft 4in wider than the original fittings.
4. 2½in plates were added around torpedo ports.
5. Submerged torpedo tubes were removed, having been found unsatisfactory at high speeds.
6. Eight 21in above-water torpedo tubes were added in four twin mountings, two P&S in ports on upper deck; forward pair close abaft second funnel, after pair abaft mainmast.
7. Large-base rangefinder added over control positions on conning tower and at rear of 'A' and 'Y' 15in turrets.
8. Single range clocks fitted over control top and at rear of after control position on main tripod legs.
9. Maintopmast replaced with topgallant.
10. Searchlights were removed from after pair of towers but towers were retained.
Armour protection increased by 4,300 tons in weight.

This was the last refit for *Repulse* until her major refit of 1936, but minor changes were made: 1924–5 single 4in anti-torpedo guns on shelter deck abeam conning tower were replaced by 4in AA. Original 3in AA was replaced by 4in increasing AA armament to four 4in. Navigating platform enclosed.
1925 deckhouse accommodating squash court for royal tour by the Prince and Princess of Wales added on starboard side of shelter deck between funnels. 1926 New type control top. Signal distribution office added at rear of upper bridge. Foretopmast removed and signal struts added.

Renown Refit, July 1923 to September 1926:
Following along the lines of the 1918–20 refit that her sister had received, her main 6in belt

Renown and Repulse: Particulars 1919

Construction

Renown: Fairfield; laid down 25.1.1915; launched 4.3.1916; completed Sept 1916. *Repulse*: John Brown; laid down 25.1.1915; launched 8.1.1916; completed Aug 1916.

Displacement (tons)

31,592/32.220 (average), 32,500 (load) as completed. *Repulse* after refit 36,780 (ordinary deep), 37,780 (extra deep).

Length: 750ft (pp), 787ft 9in (w2), 794ft 1½in (oa). Beam: 90ft as completed, *Repulse* after refit 102ft 8in.

Draught: *Renown* 26/30ft (mean); *Repulse* 27ft 11in (load), 31ft 1in (deep).

GM: as completed 3.5ft (load), 6.2ft (deep); *Repulse* after refit 4.95ft (load), 6.5ft (deep).

Armament

6 x 15in 42 cal Mk I 120rpg
17 x 4in 44 cal Mk IX 200rpg
2 x 3in QF HA

1 x 12pdr
4 x 3pdr
5 Maxims
10 Lewis
8 x 21in above water, 2 x 21in submerged TT.

Armour (see *Repulse* refit for her alterations)
Main belt 6in, ends 6-3in; Bulkheads 4–3in; Barbettes 7–4in; Turrets 11–9–7–4¼in; CT 10–6in; Decks: forecastle 1⅛–¾in; main 1in; slopes (over magazines only) 2in; lower 2–1¼in; funnel uptakes 1½–1in.

Machinery:
Brown Curtis Impulse turbines driving 4 propellers. 42 Babcock & Wilcox boilers, 275psi.
Designed SHP: 112,000 for 31.5 knots.
Fuel: 1,000/4,200 tons oil (average).
Radius of action: 4,700nm at 12 knots, 2,700 at 25 knots.
Searchlights: 8 x 36in, 2 x 24in signalling.
Complement: *Repulse* 1,057; *Renown* 1,223.

Aircraft
Flying-off platforms on 'B' and 'Y' turrets. In post-war period aircraft not normally carried on turrets, but embarked when required for exercises. Kite balloon equipment fitted in *Repulse*.

Enlarged bridgework since completion. Otherwise not much change in basic appearance.

Rig: *Renown* short topmast to fore and main (stump only to fore); *Repulse* short foretopmast. No main topmast.

Individual differences since completion:
Renown Range clocks to face of control top. Short topmast to each mast.
Repulse Range clock on director platform below control top. No main topmast.

Renown, legend particulars after refit, 1923-6

Displacement (tons): 37,210 (deep), 32,520 (as inclined).

Beam: 102ft 4in.

Draught: 31ft 3in (deep), 27ft 9in (as inclined).

Freeboard: 29ft 9in forward, 21ft 3in amidships, 16ft 9in aft.

Fuel: 1,000 tons/4,289 tons oil.

Armament

Main guns unaltered
15 x 4in (200rpg)
4 x 4in HA AA (150rpg)
4 x 3pdr (64rpg)
5 Maxims
10 Lewis

Armour
Main belt 9in (over 460ft, 7ft 3in above water, 4ft below at normal draught, 2in strip below this; 4in armour forward, 3in aft; bulkheads 4–4–3in; turrets 9–7in; vertical bulkheads 2in; main deck 4–3in flat (over-magazines), slope 4in, lower deck 4in.

was removed and replaced by a 9in strake. The original 6in belt, however, was not re-installed but the new 9in belt was placed slightly higher than in *Repulse*. This was because of the deepening that *Renown* had already suffered as a consequence of additional topweight since completion in 1916 (see drawing). Protective high-tensile plating was added to the main deck so that the total thickness was 2½in amidships and 4in over the magazines (against 1in and 1–3in in *Repulse*). Plating was also added to the lower deck as protection against end-on fire.

A new type of underwater anti-torpedo bulge was fitted, being much lighter, and was similar to that fitted in *Warspite*. The crushing tubes were omitted along most of the bulge but were retained in wake of the magazines. A small 2in strip of armour was fitted underneath the main 9in armour plates to assist in deflecting diving shells . A new type of square-shaped control top was fitted; it was considerably deeper than the original one. Single range clocks were fitted over 'Y' turret. The after triple 4in mounting was replaced. The single 4in anti-torpedo guns were removed. AA guns as in *Repulse*. Flying-off platform replaced on 'B' turret. Searchlights removed from after pair of towers but towers retained. Upper bridge enlarged and modified. Signal distribution office added at rear of bridge. Foretopmast removed. Short signal struts added below control top. Topgallant fitted to main.

The consequence of these alterations was a net sinkage of about 3in compared with 12in for *Repulse*. This was attained at the expense of the crushing tubes in the bulges and the complete removal of the original 6in armour. It was agreed that although *Repulse* was the better armoured ship of the two, the new position of the 9in belt in *Renown* had its advantages. Weights: 896 tons removed (6in old main belt); 1,050 tons added for bulges; 1,020 tons added in armour plating; 1,430 added in new 9in belt.

The alterations greatly improved the ship's protection against fire at long ranges and in certain circumstances at short ranges. The deck, which always formed the greater part of the target, was stated to be proof against 15in shells because of its ability to deflect them at 15,000 yards and under. Although the new 9in belt was not considered quite equal to that of a 4in armoured deck it was stated that it should either break up a 15in shell during its path of flight or

at least explode the shell at a moderate distance inside the armoured belt so that it would not reach the ship's vitals.

Some of the ex-*Eagle*'s armoured plates were used in this refit as they were in that of *Repulse* during her 1918–20 refit.

Estimate of costs *Renown* refit, 1923–6: labour £404,000, materials £114,000, total £518,000.
January 1927. Short flagpole fitted abaft control top and to main topmast for royal tour (January to June 1927). Deckhouse replaced on port side of shelter deck amidships autumn 1927 (after return of tour).
1929. Fitted as flagship.
1930–1. Range clock over 'Y' turret removed.
September 1931 to June 1932. Refit: midships triple 4in removed to accommodate aircraft catapult (fitted later). Multiple 2pdr AA (8 barrels) added on starboard side of superstructure abeam fore funnel. HA RF on control top replaced by HA director. Flying-off platform removed from 'B' turret. After pair of SL towers abeam funnel removed.
1932–3. Aircraft catapult (McTaggert Training type) fitted abaft second funnel in place of midships 4in triple guns. One Fairey IIID seaplane carried. No special crane provided, aircraft being handled by boat derrick.

Both ships were reconstructed to various degrees during the period 1934 to 1939 with a view of bringing them more nearly in line with modern requirements. The modifications in *Repulse* were in fact quite limited, being confined mainly to increased AA armament and provision of hangar accommodation for aircraft with improved type of catapult. Against this, the additional topweight, for which no compensation was made, resulted in increased draught and displacement with some loss of speed, stability, dryness and freeboard. Reconstruction of *Renown* was considerably more drastic, the primary object being to secure the maximum possible advance in offensive and defensive qualities without additional displacement or any appreciable loss of speed.

It proved impacticable to bring the level of vertical armouring up to modern requirements so such modernization as did take place was mainly in the interests of retaining high speed combined with strong AA defence and ability to withstand aerial and underwater attack. There was still no question of her ever facing ships

Renown and *Repulse* : Particulars, 1934
Displacement (tons): *Renown* 34,540 (load), 37,630 (deep) (after 1926 refit 32,520 (load), 37,210 (deep); *Repulse* 34,880 (load, 38,100 (deep).
Length: unchanged; Beam: both 102ft 8in.
Draught: 26ft 8in/31ft 9in mean (average).
Armament
Original main armament
Secondary 12–15x4 in
Single 4in mountings in both ships.
4 x 4in AA
8 x 2pdr
Original TT in *Renown*; 8 x 21in above water in *Repulse*.
Searchlights: 6 x 36in, 2 x 24in signalling.
Aircraft
Renown: Fairey IIIF reconnaissance seaplane (with catapult); *Repulse*: Still carried flying-off platforms.
Armour: see Alterations for details.
Machinery: unchanged.
Speed: slight reduction owing to additions.
Both fitted as flagships.
Rig: No foretopmast; topmast and topgallant to main.
Average complement: 1,181/1,200.
Appearance: as in 1918 but with modifications.
Renown: Original line of unbroken main deck scuttles. Large aircraft catapult abaft second funnel. Prominent HA director on control top. Large deckhouse on port side of shelterdeck amidships. Bulges carried up to main deck level. Smooth face to bridgework. Two compass tables to bridgeface.
Repulse: Side armour higher in position. (6in upper belt). No upper row of scuttles (between 'A' and 'Y' turrets). No catapult. Small RF on control top. Bulges not visible above waterline. Complicated and messy bridgework with communication pipes running down from compass platform.

armed with larger calibre guns if it could be avoided because of her weak (9in) side armour.

In addition to the modifications in AA armament and aircraft accommodation and equipment carried out in *Repulse*, elevation and range of main armament was increased, an entirely new, dual-purpose (HA/LA) secondary armament was mounted, light AA guns were further improved, horizontal and underwater protection was strengthened, speed was maintained and radius slightly extended. Bridgework, layout, superstructure and rig were all materially altered.

Repulse: Refit, April 1933 to May 1936.
Midships 4in triple mouting taken out to accommodate aircraft catapult.
AA armament increased to eight 4in, sixteen 2pdrs and eight 0.5in MG (the 4in guns were in two twin and four single mountings).

The twin mountings were a prototype turret

Below: *Renown* entering the Panama Canal on 8 November 1921 during the Royal Tour, on her way to Trinidad. Note the crest on the royal viewing platform.

Below: The forward superstructure and 15in guns of *Repulse* (note Etna stripping on deck), during a public open day *c.*1928.

Below: *Repulse,* 1928, looking aft over the second funnel and mainmast.

Below: *Repulse,* looking down from the 30ft rangefinder over the forecastle during a public open day *c.*1928.

Bottom: *Renown c.*1931 during 4in AA gunnery practice. The 4in gun as originally fitted was considered a troublesome mounting, which required too large a crew to serve each triple mount.

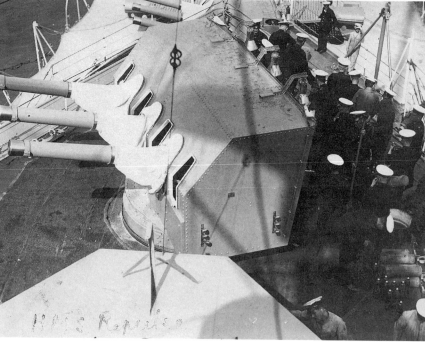

used later in the reconstructed battleships of the *Queen Elizabeth* class and *Renown* (prototype turret also carried in *Resolution*). HA directors added on control top and on high pedestal abaft mainmast. Former HA/RF on control top was removed. MF/DF equipment fitted.

DF cabinet fitted on mainmast.

Searchlights redistributed; 24in signalling lamps retained. Two aircraft hangars provided (P&S) in superstructure abaft second funnel, with opening at rear.

Straight arm electric crane fitted on top of each hangar.

Fixed athwartships catapult fitted on upper deck abaft hangars, shelter deck being cut away to accommodate this.

Accommodation for four aircraft: two in hangars, one on deck outside and one on catapult.

High superstructure containing hangars built up around and abaft second funnel.

Heavy boats stowed on top of hangars, all handled by aircraft cranes.

Seaboats carried in davits P&S amidships as before.

Except for longer signal struts at base of control top, her basic appearance had not changed since 1933. The Bridge face was slightly remodelled, giving smoother-looking finish.

Renown: Refit (major reconstruction), September 1936 to August 1939:

Superstructure razed to upper deck level.

15in turrets removed.

4in secondary armament removed.

Funnels razed to upper deck level.

Foremast (tripod) and mainmast taken out.

Original bridgework and conning tower was replaced by large splinter-proof and gasproof control tower, similar with variations in detail to that fitted in *Warspite* as reconstructed in 1937, and representing a further development of the type first introduced in the *Nelson* class.

Platforms sited within the tower were: 1. Accommodation and recreation spaces. 2. Sea cabins for Admiral and certain senior officers. 3. Armoured lower navigating position, signal, direction-finding and cipher offices. Navigating platform, main and secondary directors were fitted on top of this tower. Searchlight, signalling and lookout platforms were fitted in the sides.

New streamline funnels fitted, slightly thicker and flatter than original pair, and set closer together.

36in searchlights replaced by 44in lamps. Four 24in signalling (2xP&S) on lower platform on control tower. Horizontal armouring was improved over magazines and machinery, but it was a complicated effort with existing plating being removed in some cases and a mixture of high-tensile and non-cemented armour being used to make up certain thicknesses. A certain amount of 'D' type steel was used for the protection of the secondary armament. Basically it amounted to fitting 4in armour over the magazines and 2½in elsewhere. For best results in application see drawing as reconstructed.

Original 4in secondary armament replaced by twenty 4.5in dual-purpose guns in ten turrets (five per side): forward group of turrets on each side abeam fore funnel; after group of two abeam mainmast.

Light AA increased from sixteen to twenty-four 2pdrs in three 8-barrel mountings.

Re-engined and reboilered with Parsons all-geared turbines and eight Admiralty 3-drum boilers. New machinery by Cammell Laird. SHP increased to 120,000 for nominal speed of 29 knots. Fuel capacity slightly increased using outer wing bunkers, and radius of action increased as a consequence of greater economy of new equipment installed.

Other items as fitted (or removed) were:

1. Type 71 W/T removed.

2. Type 511 buzzer outfit installed.

3. Combined HA/LA control and calculating position, each group consisted of one HACS Mk IV, HALA director, AFC clock and one HACS calculating table with new switch installation.

4. New pom-pom director Mk II and wind speed and direction equipment.

5. New Fire control tables fitted where required.

6. Underwater TT removed and flat subdivided to accommodate cooling machinery.

7. New above-water 21in torpedo tubes fitted.

8. Improved pumping arrangements and seven new 350-ton discharge pumps.

9. Wireless offices redistributed.

10. New and improved W/T fitted:
Types 36c; 49c; 52c (2 sets); 75c; and 7d together with rack-mounted receiving gear.

11. New venting arrangements to main armament handing rooms.

12. New anemometer, magslip indicator and other meteorological equipment fitted.

13. New air defence positions fitted.

14. New wire phones fitted.

15. Existing fire systems were updated and renewed in certain areas.

16. Provision for electrical power for motor-driven auxiliary machinery fitted, also modern lighting equipment in many areas.

17. New modern D/F (FT Wa/T Type 405) equipment and back-up system fitted.

18. Old torpedo control positions removed.

19. Bulges coated with bitumastic solution and enamel.

20. Modernization of feedwater systems.

21. Old steam capstan removed and new motor-driven machinery fitted for anchors.

22. New ring main, new cables, release switches, dynamos and new mains control board fitted.

23. Distribution boxes renewed, and regrouping of existing boxes.

24. Removal of 200 tons of steam bilge ejectors.

25. Redistribution of oil fuel.

26. Rudder indicator and supply renewed.

27. Signal deck completely refitted and modernized.

28. Accommodation for crew improved.

29. Six 44in power-controlled searchlights fitted.

30. 15in turrets cut away to give greater elevation (increased from 20° to 30°).

31. New rig modified to light tripod foremast, stepped through rear of control tower, but well clear abaft upper part. Short pole mainmast. No control tops. Topmast to foremast with DF aerial pole at head. No main topmast. DF aerial (starfish type) at head of mainmast. Cost of reconstruction: £3,088,008.

Repulse, Refit, September 1938 to January 1939:
Twin 4in turrets replaced by single 4in in open mountings eight 0.5in AA (4 barrels) added on director platform on main tripod legs. Special accommodation provided internally for royal tour to Canada by the King and Queen, but it was later decided to use CPS *Empress of Australia* with *Repulse* as escort.

Renown, 1939–45:
1941 Radar control fitted for main and secondary armament, Types 284 for main and 285 for 4.5in secondary. Multiple 2pdr (4 barrels) added on 'B' 15in turret top. Radar control (Type 282) fitted for light AA guns (2pdrs);

Repulse: Particulars 1937
Length and beam as original.
Displacement (tons): 34,600 (load), 38,311 (deep).
Armament
Original main
Secondary 12 x 4in
6 x 4in Mk XV AA
16 x 2pdr AA
16 x 0.5in AA
8 x 21in TT
Aircraft
Two hangars with fixed athwartships catapults amidships. Capacity for 4 Swordfish, TSR or Walrus amphibians.
Radar: MF/DF.
Armour: see Appearance notes.
Machinery: as original, but completely overhauled.
Speed: slight reduction from original.
Searchlights: 6 x 36in, 2 x 24in signalling.
General
Boat stowage rearranged to accommodate hangar and catapult. Majority of boats stowed on top of hangars. Accommodation, ventilation and equipment modernized.
Rig: As in 1932 except shorter maintopmast and topgallant. DF aerials on main topmast and at head of maintopgallant.
Appearance:
Generally more piled up and heavier-looking.
Smooth face to bridgework. Height of superstructure accentuated by cutting away of shelter deck abaft it. Light twin turret P&S abeam mainmast.
Large multiple AA mountings P&S on superstructure amidships.
Prominent director over control top and high pedestal abaft mainmast. Prominent DF aerial and cabinet on mainmast.
Other than rig alterations during early years of war, Repulse changed very little in appearance up until the time of her sinking in 1941. According to 16mm official movie film, her contrast camouflage was painted out before she was sunk in December 1941.
Trials after refit, 1936–7:
1 hour Full Power. 31.1.1936.
Wind of 15–20mph and short steep sea, longest waves estimated at 120 x 15ft
Going ahead was very wet forward of breakwater.
Gunnery officer stated that water had penetrated between turrets and barbette armour at 'A' position and reached down to shell rooms.
No speed recorded.
Full power: June 1936.

Wind 4–5
Tolland Mile.
Mean figures: 112,400shp for 28.36 knots.
Repulse was fitted to take 15in supercharged shells 5/10CRH and magazines and shell rooms were modified to accommodate these. (20rpg). Date: 25.6.1941.

Renown: Particulars, 1939
Hull and dimensions unaltered.
Displacement (tons): (average since 1916)
1917 32,220, 1926 37,150, 1936 38,105, 1939 33,725 (average action), 36,080 (deep load).
Armament
Original 15in unchanged (turrets cut away for greater elevation)
Secondary: 20 x 4.5in dual-purpose in twin turrets 400rpg
24 x 2pdr Mk VIII (3 mounts, 8 barrels) 1,800rpg
TT: 8 x 21in Mk IV and IV*
Depth-charges: 24 Type D Mk VII
4 x 0.5in MG AA   2,000rpg
6 x 6pdr   100rpg
2 Vickers MG   5,000rpg
12 x Lewis   2,000rpg
Searchlights: 4 x 44in, 4 x 24in signalling.
Armour: see Appearance, Refit notes and drawing.
Machinery
Parsons geared turbines. 4 propellers
Boilers: 8 Admiralty 3-drum type, 300psi
SHP: 120,000 for 29/30 knots.
Fuel (tons): 1,000/4,860 oil.
Radius of action: 6,580nm at 18 knots.
Alterations since completion: (average)
1916: 32.58 knots. 27,900 tons.
1919: 29.85 knots. 31,820 tons.
1939: 29.93 knots. 32,800 tons.
GM: 5.07ft average action load, 5.76ft deep condition.
Stability vanishes at: average action 70°, deep condition 76°.
General
Large tower structure replacing former bridgework and CT.
Boat stowage and handling as in Repulse.
Accommodation, ventilation and general equipment all modernized.
Rig: Light tripod foremast with topmast. No control top. Short pole mainmast. D/F aerials at each masthead. No main derrick.
Boats: 2 x 50ft steam pinnaces; 1 x 42ft sailing launch; 1 x 36ft pinnace; 2 x 32ft cutters, 2 x 30ft gigs; 2 x 27ft whalers; 1 x 16ft and 1 x 13ft balsa rafts.

on superstructure forward, midships and aft and in catapult space amidships (two twin and two single on each side).

Deck sponsoned out abreast catapult space to accommodate these guns. Additional light AA directors (282 RDF) fitted on superstructure amidships and aft.

February–June 1943 Refit, Catapult removed but cranes were retained. Hangar space converted for use as offices, etc. Aircraft no longer carried. Boat stowage rearranged on catapult deck.

Renown, 1944–5
20mm AA removed from 'B' turret (by March 1945).
Previous camouflage replaced by Admiralty Standard type (Pacific colours).
In Renown this camouflage also featured 15in turrets painted blue and guns grey on top and white and blue beneath. Blue strip of camouflage on hull was repainted dark-grey before returning home from Pacific in April 1945.
Armament reduced in July 1945 after ship passed into Reserve.
Forward group of twelve 4.5in guns were removed.
All light AA landed, mountings retained.

Repulse, 1939–41, additions and alterations.
Radar control (Type 284) fitted for main guns August 1941 (proposed November 1940, approved February 1941).
4in triple mounting on superstructure abaft mainmast removed.
Single 4in AA P&S on forecastle deck amidships remounted on top of hangar (by May 1941).
Multiple 2pdr AA (8 barrels) mounted on after superstructure in place of 4in triple (approved February 1941 fitted by July 1941).
Single 20mm AA added P&S on 'Y' 15in turret.
Unusual camouflage painted up (contrast painting, see camouflage).

The following were proposed for Repulse but it is not certain if they were all done before her loss in December 1941.
May 1940: DG cables following the line of the forecastle deck from the bow to one-third of the length from the bow, and following the lines of the upper and forecastle decks from the stern to one-third of the length from the stern. Internal DG cables also fitted.

directors located P&S on top of control tower and abeam fore funnel.
ASW radar added; AW Type 281 with aerial at each masthead SW Type 271 with aerial in lantern (for protection) on foretop. Original 271 set transferred to corvette Verbena at Rosyth in September 1941, replaced by new set later. Improved D/F equipment fitted, with aerial on

face of control tower. Tripod legs and topmast fitted to mainmast for Type 281 RDF. Elaborate camouflage paintwork scheme evident.

Renown, July 1942–August 1943 modifications:
Seventy-two 20mm AA in 23 twin and 26 single mountings, located on 'B' turret (two twins), on platforms at sides of control tower (four twins),

September 1940: RDF Types 279 or 281 proposed. Gaff for Admiral's flag.

Foretopmast to be fitted when aerial (radar) was shipped. November 1940: Proposed RDF equipment. Type 284 for main guns (completed in 1941); two sets Type 282 forward, one set Type 285 forward, two sets Type 285 aft, one set Type 282 aft.

December 1940. Report on performance at sea:

'In a headwind suction of the funnel gases into the after part of the bridge where the torpedo, SL and starshell control positions are situated is clearly noticeable. I consider that the question of fitting a cowl on the foremost funnel or lengthening it must be thoroughly investigated before further extensions are made to the bridge work.' [Captain]

January 1941. It was reported that with light wind on the bow the opposite wing of the bridge was distinctly affected by funnel fumes. Addition of 3-foot extension to fore funnel was suggested.

February 1941. Alterations and additions approved by the Admiralty:

All 4in mountings to be removed. Proposed to fit seven 4in twin mountings with fourteen 4in Mk XVI* guns. Light AA to comprise of three 2pdr (8 barrels) with directors and four 0.5in MG.

Radar outfit for *Repulse* finally amended:

One Type 281; set three Type 282 sets; one Type 284 set; two Type 285 sets. August 1941:

Type 284 set fitted and operational.

March 1941: Conning tower deck was arranged to accommodate HA rearmament. Type 281 office was built into this deck and two offices for Types 282 and 285 were placed on the flag deck.

May 1941: Zarebas of protective plating to be fitted around 4in mountings. Protective screen proposed, 1ft high, for 0.5in AA MG.

June 1941: Cowl for funnel again suggested.

July 1941: Main topmast redesigned for Type 281 RDF. DF outfit Type FM2 to be fitted. Cowl for funnel finally approved.

September 1941: Armament refit in the USA proposed: Three-cornered control of HA guns. Two HA towers aft, and one forward. Half TT

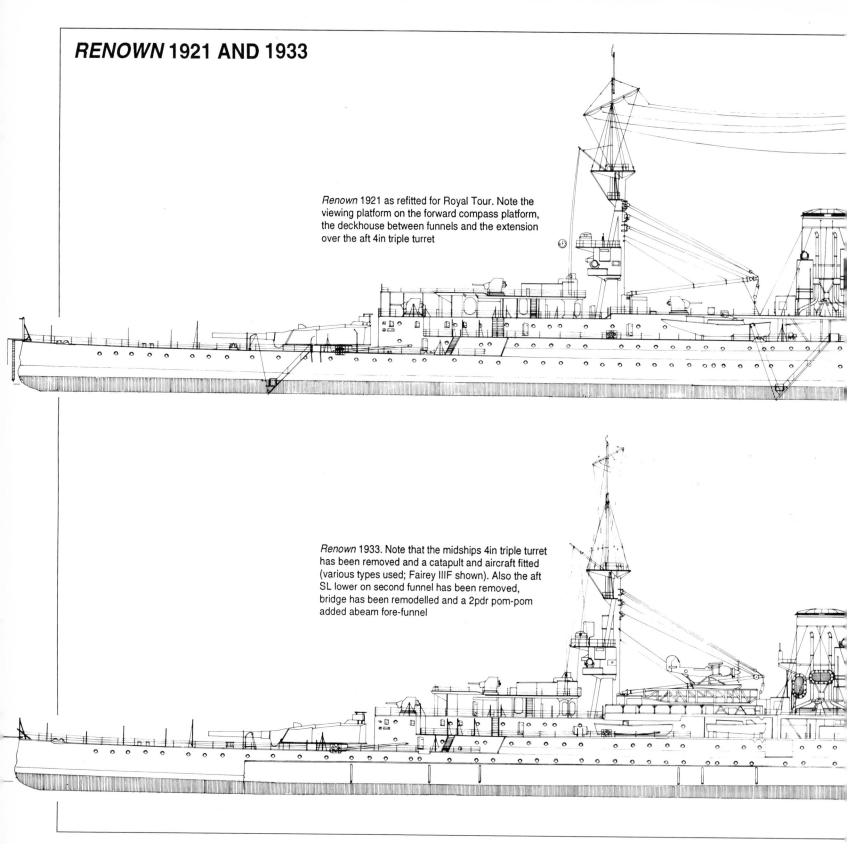

RENOWN 1921 AND 1933

Renown 1921 as refitted for Royal Tour. Note the
viewing platform on the forward compass platform,
the deckhouse between funnels and the extension
over the aft 4in triple turret

Renown 1933. Note that the midships 4in triple turret
has been removed and a catapult and aircraft fitted
(various types used; Fairey IIIF shown). Also the aft
SL lower on second funnel has been removed,
bridge has been remodelled and a 2pdr pom-pom
added abeam fore-funnel

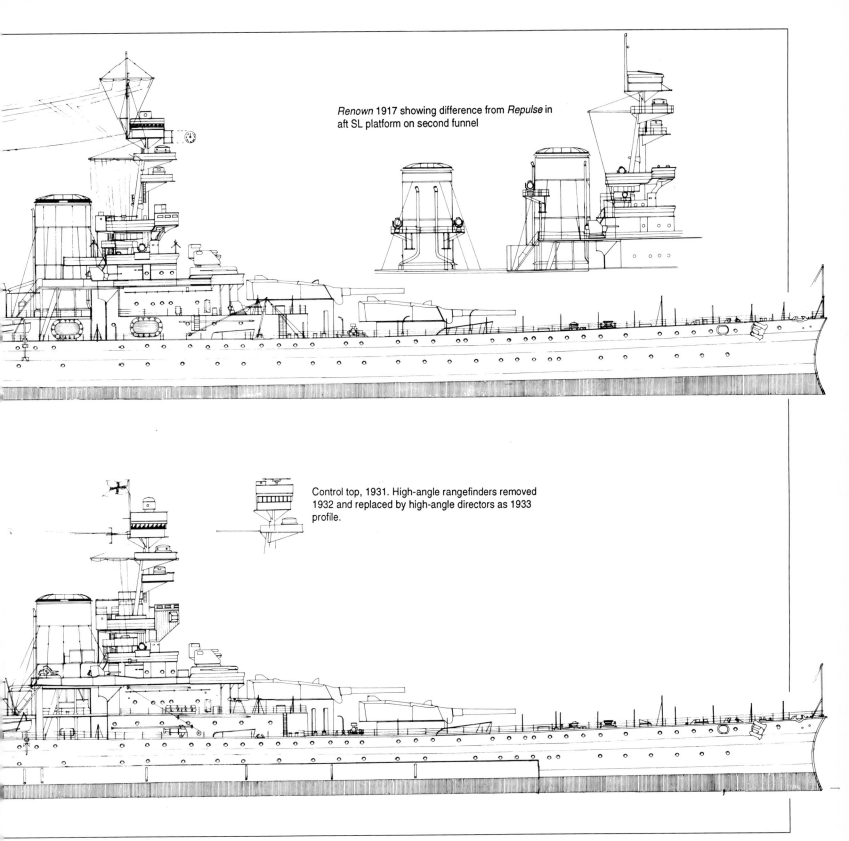

Renown 1917 showing difference from *Repulse* in aft SL platform on second funnel

Control top, 1931. High-angle rangefinders removed 1932 and replaced by high-angle directors as 1933 profile.

Renown: Particulars, 1944

Displacement (tons) 35,240 (average load), 37,600 (deep)
Draught: 29ft 11½in forward, 29ft 9in aft (average).
Hull and dimensions as in 1939.
Armament
Main and secondary unchanged
28 x 2pdr
68 x 20mm AA. All light AA landed by July 1945
Forward group of 4.5in guns removed by May 1945
TT: as in 1939.
All guns except single 20mm AA radar controlled.
Radar: Types 284 for main guns, 285 for 4.5in, 282 or 283 for light AA, AW Type 281, SW Type 271.
Searchlights: as in 1939.
Armour: as in 1939.
Machinery as in 1939.
Speed: slight reduction due to additions.
After the loss of *Hood* in 1941 *Renown* was the fastest capital ship in the Royal Navy.
Aircraft: Approval to remove catapult given 19 January 1943.

armament to be removed. Type 271 to be fitted before refit.

36in SL to be repositioned on mainmast when after HA towers fitted.

Convert guns to fire extremely long (67in) 6CRF shells (termed Mk IIIB) which just fitted in hoist cage.

HISTORY: REPULSE

Alternated with *Renown* as flag (RA) 1st BCS 1917–18.

From September 1917 to March 1918, flag 1st BCS also served as flag Grand Fleet carriers (see *Renown*).

Took part in Heligoland Bight operation 17 November 1917.

On this occasion, 1st BCS & 1st BS supported sweep by *Courageous* and *Glorious*, 1st and 6th LCS and destroyers to attack enemy minesweepers working in Heligoland Bight under battleship protection although, apart from *Repulse*, none of the British battlecruisers of 1st BS actually made contact with enemy forces. Detached from 1st BCS to cover the retirement of the 1st LCS after appearance of the German battleships *Kaiser* and *Kaiserin* and became engaged with these ships and light cruisers. Scored one hit on *Könisberg* which passed through three funnels and upper deck and burst in coal bunker starting bad fire.

RENOWN AND *REPULSE*: BRIDGEWORK

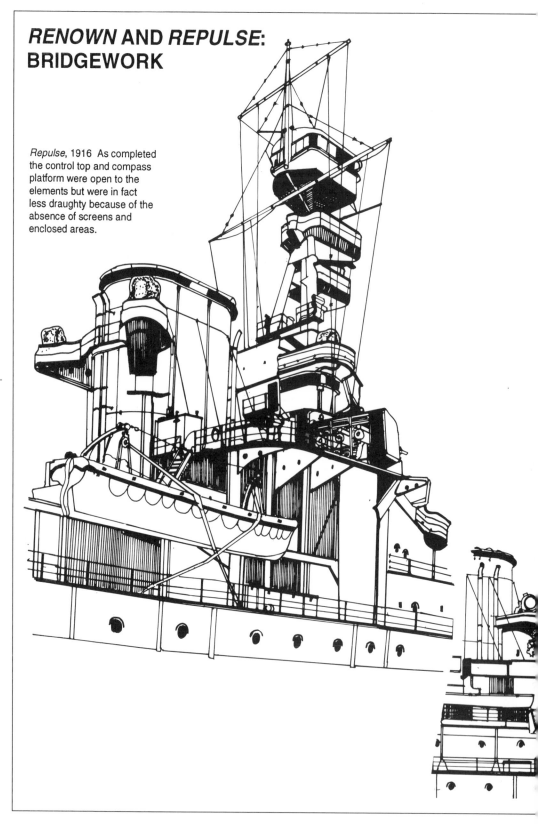

Repulse, 1916 As completed the control top and compass platform were open to the elements but were in fact less draughty because of the absence of screens and enclosed areas.

After her 1927 refit *Renown*'s curved face bridgework had the effect of forcing the wind up over the compass platform which had been given a roof; conditions improved considerably for personnel in the upper positions.

Renown, 1927 From this was developed the wedge-shaped bridge & compass platform. Conditions in the control top improved after it was enclosed.

Repulse, 1939 Partial reconstruction in 1936 brought some improvement with the enclosing of the charthouse and modification to the bridge face. Note wind deflecting baffles fitted beneath window during the refit.

Below: *Renown*, April 1928, on Fleet manoeuvres with the Battlecruiser Squadron off Portland, watched by King Amanullah and carried out in honour of his presence.

Was the last British ship in action with German capital ships during the Great War.
Paid off at Portsmouth for extensive refit, 2 December 1918.
Recommissioned at Portsmouth 1 January 1921 for BCS Atlantic Fleet (see *Renown* re post-war reorganization).

ATLANTIC FLEET (BCS) January 1921 to November 1923.
Detached, with *Hood*, August 1922 to represent Royal Navy at Brazilian Independence Centenary Celebrations in Rio de Janeiro and subsequently carried out flag-showing cruise in the West Indies. Left Devonport 14 August; returned 23 November 1922.
With *Hood* and *Snapdragon* visited Norway and Denmark June to July 1923.
Again detached November 1923 as unit of

Special Service Squadron comprising *Hood* (flag), *Repulse* and 1st LCS *Delhi*, *Danae*, *Dauntless* and *Dragon* for Empire and world cruise.

SPECIAL SERVICE SQUADRON (World Cruise) November 1923 to September 1924.
Squadron left from rendezvous off Plymouth on 27 November, proceeding outwards via Cape and Indian Ocean and returning across the Pacific. Itinerary of the battlecruisers and light cruisers varied in some instances and finally separated after leaving San Francisco on 11 July 1924, on return leg, the former passing through the Panama Canal while the latter proceeded around South America. Squadron reformed again off the Lizard on 28 September 1924, the ships arriving back at home ports on the 28th and 29th.
Hood and *Repulse* visited Sierra Leone,

Capetown, Zanzibar, Trincomalee, Port Swettenham, Singapore, Fremantle, Albany, Adelaide, Melbourne, Hobart, Jervis Bay, Sydney, Wellington, Auckland, Fiji, Honolulu, Vancouver, Victoria, San Francisco, Panama, Colon, Kingston (Jamaica), Halifax, Quebec, St. John's (Newfoundland). *Repulse* arrived Portsmouth 29 September 1924 and rejoined Atlantic Fleet.

ATLANTIC FLEET (BCS) September 1924 to March 1925.
With *Hood* represented the British Navy at Vasco da Gama celebrations at Lisbon February 1925.
Detached March 1925 for Prince of Wales's tour to West and South Africa and South America. Left Portsmouth 25 March, visiting Bathurst (Gambia), Sierra Leone, Takoradi and Lagos. Arrived Capetown 1 May where Prince disem-

barked for inland tour, rejoining ship on 29 July. Proceeded to St. Helena, Montevideo, Buenos Aires and West Indies. Returned Portsmouth 16 October 1925.

ATLANTIC FLEET (BCS) October 1925 to March 1932 (flag BCS April 1929 to July 1931). Refit Portsmouth November 1925 to July 1926 and July to September 1927.
Relieved *Hood* as flag BCS April 1929 (*Hood* to refit).
Flag reverted to Hood 11 July 1931.
Atlantic Fleet redesignated Home Fleet March 1932.

HOME FLEET (BCS) March to June 1932.
Paid off to reserve Portsmouth June 1932 prior to extensive refit.

RESERVE (Portsmouth) June 1932 to April 1933.
Paid off to Dockyard control at Portsmouth for refit 1 April 1933.
Extensive refit Portsmouth April 1933 to April 1936.
Commissioned for trials 14 January 1936.
Completed full crew Portsmouth April 1936 for BCS Mediterranean fleet under 1935 Fleet Reorganization plan (*Renown*).

Left Portsmouth for Mediterranean 8 June 1936.

MEDITERRANEAN FLEET (BCS) April 1936 to September 1938.
Protected British interests in western Mediterranean during Spanish Civil War 1936–8. Embarked five hundred refugees at Palma, Majorca, for Marseilles late 1936.
Coronation Review, Spithead, 20 May 1937.
Sent to Haifa July 1938 because of Arab-Jewish disturbances.
Relieved by *Malaya* August 1938.
Selected to convey King and Queen to Canada and USA in May 1939 and withdrawn from

REPULSE 1922 AND 1933

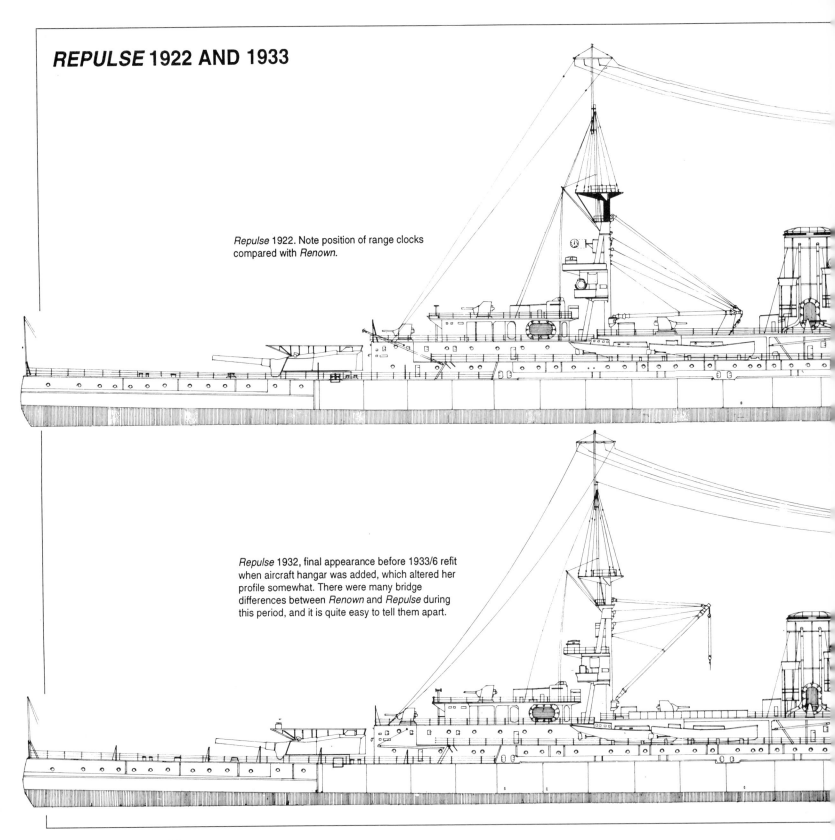

Repulse 1922. Note position of range clocks compared with *Renown*.

Repulse 1932, final appearance before 1933/6 refit when aircraft hangar was added, which altered her profile somewhat. There were many bridge differences between *Renown* and *Repulse* during this period, and it is quite easy to tell them apart.

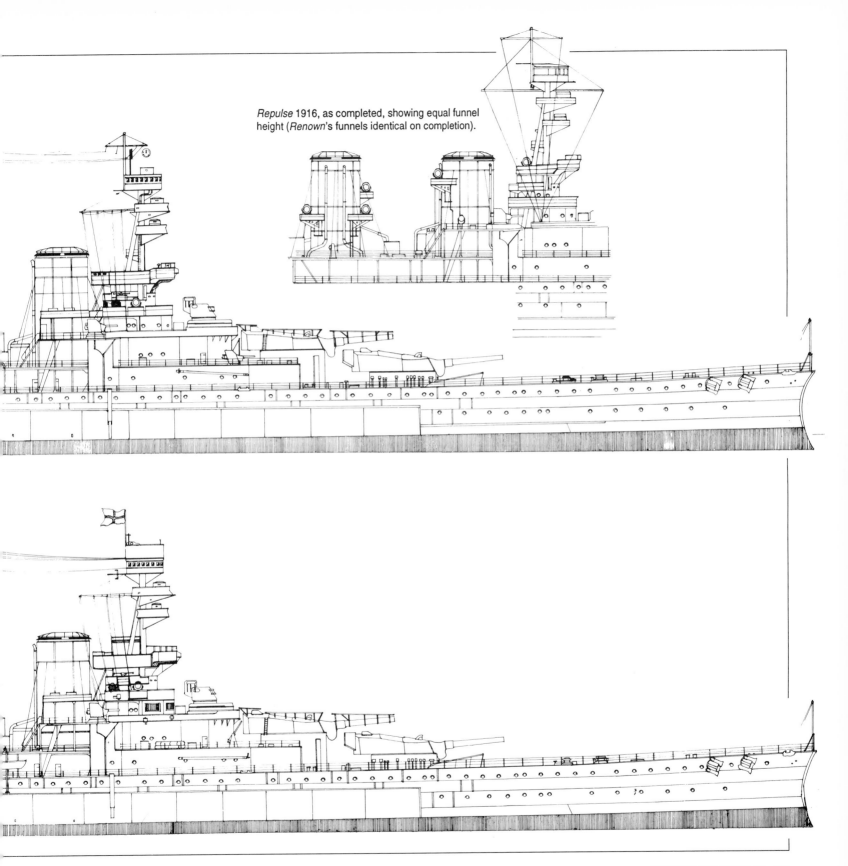

Repulse 1916, as completed, showing equal funnel
height (*Renown*'s funnels identical on completion).

Two views of *Renown* in October 1936, showing her final appearance in the old guise before total reconstruction.
Below: Starboard quarter view (note catapult amidships).
Opposite page: Close-up of bridgework and funnels.

Mediterranean Fleet September 1938 to refit prior to this.
Refit Portsmouth October 1938 to March 1939.
Recommissioned at Portsmouth March 1939 for Home Fleet, BCS having reverted to this in February 1939.

HOME FLEET (BCS) March to October 1939.
Because of the uncertain political situation, original plans for the Royal visit to Canada and the USA were later modified, the Royal party travelling in the CPS liner *Empress of Australia*, *Repulse* acting as escort for first half of the Atlantic crossing. Left Portsmouth 5 May 1939.
With *Nelson*, *Rodney* and *Ark Royal*, carried out patrol off Norwegian coast 7–12 September to intercept enemy shipping and enforce British blockade.
Took part, with *Hood*, *Sheffield*, *Aurora* and four destroyers in search off Stadlandet for *Gneisenau*, *Köln* and destroyers 8–10 October following sortie by the enemy force. No contact established.
Detached, with *Furious*, to America and West

Indies Command 21 October 1939 to cover Halifax–UK convoy and later to patrol area south-east of Newfoundland following reports of enemy heavy ships in the North Atlantic. Arrived Halifax 3 November.

AMERICA AND WEST INDIES COMMAND (Halifax) October to December 1939.
Left Halifax 23 November to take part in search for *Scharnhorst* after sinking of *Rawalpindi*, but damaged by heavy seas and forced to return.
With *Resolution* and *Furious*, escorted first Canadian troop convoy to UK December 1939.

HOME FLEET (BCS) December 1939 to October 1941.
Norwegian operations April to June 1940.
Reinforced *Renown* on patrol off Vestfiord 9 April to intercept enemy ships attempting to reach Narvik.
Escorted cruiser *Suffolk* from Stavanger to Scapa 18 April, *Suffolk* having been heavily damaged by aircraft bombing attack when retiring from bom-

bardment of Stavanger on 17th.
Sent to Faroes–Iceland area, with *Renown*, 5 June to investigate report of enemy heavy ships being sighted off the Faroes, possibly intending raid on Iceland. Report proved erroneous and on the 10th *Repulse* joined covering force for troop convoys returning from Harstad on evacuation of British forces from Norway.
With *Renown*, 1st Cruiser Squadron and eight destroyers, endeavoured to intercept *Gneisenau*, reported en route from Trondheim to Germany 27 July 1940. No contact made.
With *Hood*, three ships of 1st CS and six destroyers, covered approaches to Brest and Lorient during search for *Scheer* after sinking of *Jervis Bay* 5 November 1940.
Unit of covering force for raid on Jan Mayen Islands November 1940 when German scientific mission captured and WT station destroyed.
With *Nigeria*, patrolled Atlantic convoy routes following attack on troop ship off Finisterre by *Hipper* on 25 December 1940.
Took part in search for *Scharnhorst* and

Gneisenau in North Atlantic January to March 1941.

Diverted from sailing with Gibraltar convoy from Clyde 22 May 1941 to take part in search for *Bismarck* and *Prinz Eugen*.

Covered Halifax convoys in Newfoundland area June 1941 after *Bismarck* operation.

Refitted on Clyde June to August 1941.

Detached from Home Fleet on completion of refit to escort Middle East Troop Convoy and left Clyde with convoy 30 August 1941, via Cape.

Arrived Durban 3 October and transferred to East Indies Command.

EAST INDIES COMMAND October to November 1941.

Visited East African ports during October and November.

Transferred to Special Striking Force of new Eastern Fleet 11 November 1941.

Because of the threat of war with Japan, consideration had been given, in August 1941, to the reinforcement of British Naval Forces in the Indian Ocean and East Indies and the eventual formation of a powerful Eastern Fleet. The Chiefs of staff recommended that, by mid September 1941, one battleship from the Mediterranean, either *Barham* or *Valiant*, should be sent to the Far East and that the four *Royal Sovereigns* should follow by the end of the year. One aircraft carrier, probably *Eagle*, was also proposed, but it was not considered that any additional cruisers or fleet destroyers could be spared immediately.

This force was to be initially based at Ceylon to protect the Indian Ocean trade routes, for which purpose it was regarded as adequate, for the time being at least, and was to constitute the first instalment of an Eastern Fleet, comprising seven capital ships, one carrier, ten cruisers and about 24 destroyers, which it was planned to build up in the Indian Ocean by the spring of 1942 when it would be transferred to Singapore.

The First Sea Lord had proposed sending the *Royal Sovereigns* to the Indian Ocean immedi-ately, reinforcing them with *Nelson*, *Rodney* and *Renown* in December 1941 or January 1942.

The Prime Minister (Winston Churchill) did not approve either proposal but urged instead that a small, powerful group of fast modern battleships should be sent to Singapore at the outset; their presence, he suggested would probably deter Japanese aggression. This plan was strongly opposed by the First Sea Lord on the grounds that none of the *King George V* class battleships could be spared from home waters.

The basic difference in the two points of view lay in the fact that the force the Admiralty had in mind would be defensive in character, but well placed strategically, in the centre of the important Simonstown–Aden–Singapore triangle, while that proposed by the Prime Minister was potentially offensive, based far forward in an area which the potential enemy was threatening to dominate. It was found impossible to reconcile these opinions and the matter was dropped for the time being, although, the gradual transfer of the *Royal Sovereigns* only to the Indian Ocean

Below: *Repulse* entering port fully dressed *c.*1937.

was begun with *Royal Sovereign* herself at the end of August, and in September *Repulse* was sent to Durban. In mid October, however, the further deterioration in the political situation *vis-à-vis* Japan led to the question being considered by the Defence Committee at the request of the Foreign Office. The Committee, supported by the Foreign Office, endorsed the Prime Minister's plan in principle and suggested to the Admiralty that one modern battleship (*King George V* class), together with *Repulse* (then in the Indian Ocean) and one aircraft carrier be sent to Singapore as a fast striking force for offensive operations in the event of war with Japan.

The First Sea Lord was still opposed, but agreed to send *Prince of Wales* to Capetown to await a final decision while the new carried *Indomitable* was earmarked to follow when ready. As a consequence of grounding while working-up in the West Indies, *Indomitable* was delayed and never joined the force. On 25 October 1941 *Prince of Wales*, flying the flag of Admiral Phillips (CinC of the proposed Striking Force) left the Clyde for Capetown accompanied by the destroyers *Electra* and *Express*. On 11 November the Admiralty finally accepted the Defence Committee's recommendation and *Prince of Wales* (still en route to Capetown) and *Repulse* were ordered to rendezvous at Colombo prior to going on to Singapore. *Prince of Wales* reached Capetown on 16 November and Colombo on the 28th. *Repulse* also reached Colombo on the 28th and the force was given the code-name Force Z.

Arrived Singapore 2 December 1941.

EASTERN FLEET (Force Z Singapore) November to December 1941. *Repulse* left

Singapore on 5 December with two destroyers for a short visit to Darwin, but was recalled the following day when a Japanese convoy was sighted south of Indo-China, steering west, and obviously intending a landing on the east coast of Malaya, which it accomplished on the night of 7/8th.

On the 8th, Force Z, comprising *Prince of Wales* (flag), *Repulse, Electra, Express, Vampire* and *Tenedos* left Singapore to attack the supply lines of the Japanese invading forces. The remaining two destroyers, *Jupiter* and *Encounter*, were refitting at Singapore and did not take part in the operation.

Captain Tennant's official Report on the sinking of *Repulse*, 10 December 1941.

'We spent October and November on what really amounted to a yachting trip in the South Indian Ocean and during this time had two short visits to Durban when I think the ship's company enjoyed themselves more than at any other port they visited. Toward the end of November we found ourselves rushed off to Ceylon. *Repulse* was lying at Trincomalee and I got a signal from the C in C Eastern Fleet (who had then arrived at Colombo in *Prince of Wales*) telling me that he had to fly on to Singapore to attend a conference there and that I had to take the Eastern Fleet there. This consisted of *Prince of Wales, Repulse*, four destroyers *Electra, Express, Jupiter* and *Encounter*. We arrived by 1st December. There was a great flourish of trumpets and much publicity by the press about our arrival and how we had command of the seas in these waters. Before I go any further many of us are hesitant to attribute blame for the loss of the two capital ships but I would like to tell the inner history of this political move. Japan was getting more troublesome and both the British and US Foreign Offices and also the local government on the spot declared that if we only showed force and sent some capital ships to the Far East Japan would pipe down. There was no time to collect a balanced Fleet of aircraft carriers, cruisers destroyers, etc., and so to a large extent we were bluffing and in this case our bluff was called. The Prime Minister practically admitted this in the House of Commons so do not be tempted to attribute blame hastily to the Air Ministry or the Air Forces on the spot for this would be, I think, unfair. A week after arrival of the Eastern Fleet war was declared and the Japanese started bombing our aerodromes on the north coast of Malaya and also carried out landings there. The question we all asked in the ships lying there at the Naval Base was, what are we going to do about it? How could we remain sitting in Singapore Harbour with the enemy landing on our shores? So the C in C (Admiral Phillips) after asking for such air protection as could be provided did the only possible thing.

'He went to sea and tried to cut their communications between Indo-China and the North East Coast of Malaya along which route convoys of troops were running. Just before dark on Monday 8th December *Prince of Wales, Repulse, Electra, Express, Vampire* and *Tenedos* sailed from the Naval Base with the intention I have just mentioned. It was about 30 hours' run to reach our objective off the North East Coast of Malaya where it was intended to arrive near dawn. The convoys and any shipping we would find and then sweeping down the coast at 26 knots and so home. The next day at sea, except that it was warm, was very much NS weather, low clouds and heavy rainstorms, visibility sometimes down to half a mile. This was a great advantage to us as we did not wish to be located by Japanese aircraft. However, at about 16.45 hours the sky cleared considerably and the Force was very soon being shadowed by at least three aircraft. We were then steaming to the north which the Admiral continued to do until dark where he made a large alteration of course to the west increasing speed to 26 knots with the intention of shaking off our shadowers. At about 8 o'clock I got a signal from him saying that as we were being shadowed he had decided to cancel the operation for if we now persisted and went into the enemy landings the next morning we should probably find out ships heavily attacked by submarines, aircraft and possibly destroyers and so we started to return home. A few hours after we had turned back a report was received saying that a landing was taking place at Kuanton. Now Kuanton is only 150 miles from Singapore whereas Singari and Kata Bahru, where we had intended to be at dawn, are some 400 miles from Singapore. The Admiral decided to investigate this landing at Kuanton on his way back and to arrive off that place at dawn. This we did and found nothing but at about 6.30 hours *Repulse* sighted a reconnaissance aircraft which I reported by flags to the *Prince of Wales*. This I think was the aircraft who put the torpedo-bombers on to us for they arrived some four hours later which would allow for them to come from south Indo-China.

'At about 10.45 we went to first degree HA readiness. *Repulse*'s RDF shortly after picked up formations of enemy aircraft. The first aircraft we sighted about 11.00 hours. I will now describe the various phases of aircraft attack which finally caused the destruction of the *Repulse* and *Prince of Wales*. They are divided in five separate attacks with varying periods between them. The intervals between these periods were between 10 and 20 minutes but the period between the fourth and fifth attack was very short.

'The first attack developed shortly after 11.00 hours when 9 aircraft in close single line abreast formation were seen approaching *Repulse* from just about Green 50 and of a height of about

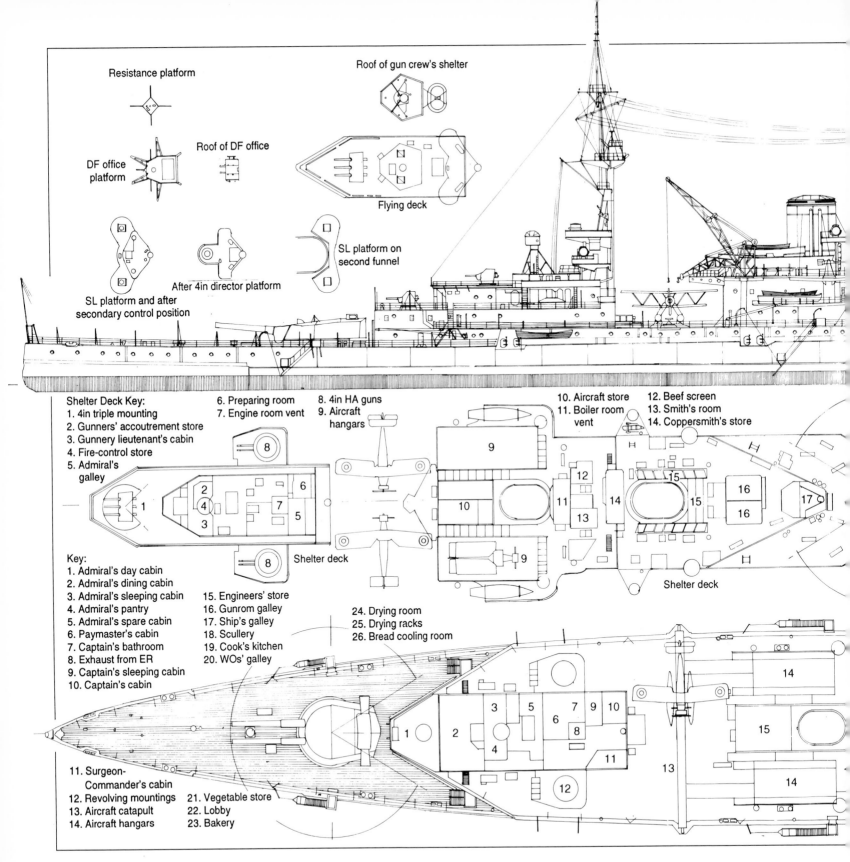

Resistance platform

Roof of gun crew's shelter

DF office platform

Roof of DF office

Flying deck

SL platform on second funnel

After 4in director platform

SL platform and after secondary control position

Shelter Deck Key:
1. 4in triple mounting
2. Gunners' accoutrement store
3. Gunnery lieutenant's cabin
4. Fire-control store
5. Admiral's galley
6. Preparing room
7. Engine room vent
8. 4in HA guns
9. Aircraft hangars
10. Aircraft store
11. Boiler room vent
12. Beef screen
13. Smith's room
14. Coppersmith's store

Shelter deck

Shelter deck

Key:
1. Admiral's day cabin
2. Admiral's dining cabin
3. Admiral's sleeping cabin
4. Admiral's pantry
5. Admiral's spare cabin
6. Paymaster's cabin
7. Captain's bathroom
8. Exhaust from ER
9. Captain's sleeping cabin
10. Captain's cabin
15. Engineers' store
16. Gunrom galley
17. Ship's galley
18. Scullery
19. Cook's kitchen
20. WOs' galley
24. Drying room
25. Drying racks
26. Bread cooling room

11. Surgeon-Commander's cabin
12. Revolving mountings
13. Aircraft catapult
14. Aircraft hangars
21. Vegetable store
22. Lobby
23. Bakery

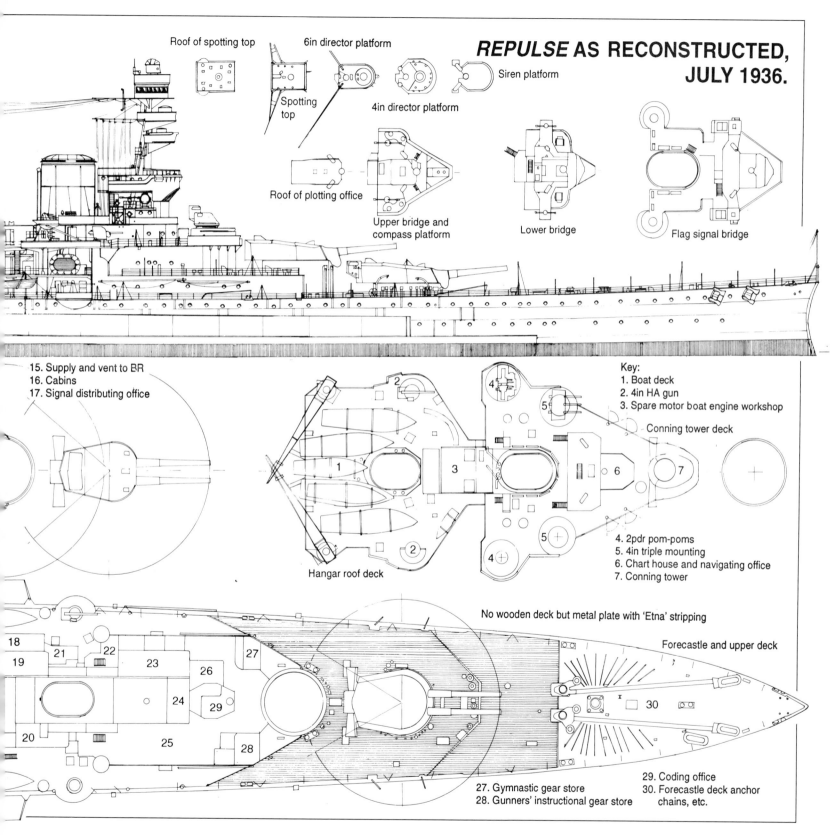

Roof of spotting top

6in director platform

Spotting top

4in director platform

Siren platform

Roof of plotting office

Upper bridge and compass platform

Lower bridge

Flag signal bridge

REPULSE AS RECONSTRUCTED, JULY 1936.

15. Supply and vent to BR
16. Cabins
17. Signal distributing office

Hangar roof deck

Key:
1. Boat deck
2. 4in HA gun
3. Spare motor boat engine workshop

Conning tower deck

4. 2pdr pom-poms
5. 4in triple mounting
6. Chart house and navigating office
7. Conning tower

No wooden deck but metal plate with 'Etna' stripping

Forecastle and upper deck

27. Gymnastic gear store
28. Gunners' instructional gear store

29. Coding office
30. Forecastle deck anchor chains, etc.

10,000 ft. Fire was at once opened on them with the long-range HA by *Prince of Wales* and *Repulse*. It was very soon obvious that the attack was to be entirely concentrated on *Repulse*. The formation was very well kept and bombs were dropped with great accuracy. One near miss on the starboard side abreast 'B' turret and one hit on the port hangars burst on the armour below the marines' mess deck and caused minor damage. The remainder of the salvo, it was thought 7 bombs were dropped altogether, it fell very close to the port side and this concluded this attack. There was now a short lull of about 20 minutes during which the damage control parties carried out their duties in a most efficient manner and fires which had been started by this bomb had all been got under control before the next attack and the bomb having burst on the armour, no damage was suffered below in the engine or boiler rooms. It is thought that the bombs dropped were about 250lb.

'The second attack was shared by *Prince of Wales* and *Repulse* and was made by torpedo-bomber aircraft. They appeared to be the same type of machine believed to be Mitsubishi 86 or 88. I am not prepared to say how many machines took part in this attack but on its conclusion I had the impression that we had succeeded in combing the tracks of a large number of torpedoes – possibly as many as 12. We were steaming at 25 knots at the time. I made a steady course until the aircraft appeared to be committed to the attack when the wheel was put over and the attacks providentially combed. I would like to record here the valuable work done by all bridge personnel at this time in calmly pointing out approaching torpedo-bombers which largely contributed to our good fortune in dodging all these torpedoes. *Prince of Wales* was hit on the port side right aft during this attack and a large column of water appeared to be thrown up, larger than subsequent columns of water which were thrown up when *Repulse* was hit later on.

'The third attack was a high-level bombing attack again concentrated on *Repulse*. Possibly the enemy were aware, and particularly if they were using 250lb bombs, that these bombs would have little chance of penetrating *Prince of Wales*'s horizontal armour. I was manoeuvring at high speed at the time and we were actually under helm when the bombs fell. No hits were received. There was one near miss on the star-

board side and the remainder fell clear of the port side. The attack was carried out in the same determined manner as was the first. At this time *Prince of Wales* appeared to be in trouble and had [not under control] balls hoisted. I made a signal to the C in C about her damage but got no reply and at that time made an emergency report to Singapore that the enemy aircraft were bombing, followed immediately by an amplifying report which was just about to be transmitted at the time the ship sank.

'The fourth attack now started to develop and about 8 aircraft were seen low on the horizon on the starboard bow. Being low down it signified another torpedo attack impending. When about 3 miles away they split into two formations and I estimated that those on the right hand would launch their torpedoes first and I started to swing the ship to starboard. The torpedoes were dropped at a distance of 2,500 yards and it seemed obvious that we should be once more successful in combing their tracks. The left-hand formation appeared to be making straight for *Prince of Wales* who was at the time abaft my port beam. When these aircraft were a little before my port beam at a distance of approximately 2,000 yards they turned straight at me and fired their torpedoes. It now became obvious that if these torpedoes were aimed straight at *Repulse* they would almost certainly hit as any other alteration to course would have caused me to be hit by the tracks of those torpedoes I was in process of combing. One torpedo fired from my port side was obviously going to hit the ship and it was possible to watch its tracks for about 1½ minutes before the act took place. The ship was hit amidships port side. The ship stood this torpedo well and continued to manoeuvre and steam at about 25 knots. There was now only a very short respite before the final and last attack.

'Torpedo-bombers appeared from all directions and a second torpedo hit the ship in the vicinity of the gun room and apparently jammed the rudder and although the ship was still steaming at over 20 knots she was not under control. Shortly after this at least three torpedoes hit the ship, two on the port side and one on the starboard side – I knew she could not survive and at once gave the order for everyone to come on deck and cast off loose Carley floats. When these final two or three torpedoes detonated the ship rapidly took a list to port. Men were now pour-

ing on to the deck. They had all been warned 24 hours before to carry or wear their life-saving gear. When the ship had a 30 degree list I looked over the starboard side of the bridge and saw the Commander and 200 to 300 men collect on the starboard side. I never saw the slightest sign of panic. I told them from the bridge how well they had fought the ship and wished them good luck. The ship hung for at least 1½ to 2 minutes with a list of about 60 to 70 degrees to port and then rolled over.

'Destroyers *Vampire* and *Electra* closed to pick up survivors.

'When I was in the water I first saw our fighters appear. My signal, enemy aircraft bombing, was in the hands of the Air Vice Marshal in about 25 minutes and 6 minutes later the fighters left the ground and they covered the 150 miles to reach our point in another 40 minutes. About 900 survivors were picked up from *Repulse* which was wonderful considering the speed at which the old ship went down at the end – she was 26 years old. About 400 men and officers were lost.

In conclusion, looking back at the action I think that if 50 or 60 well trained torpedo-bombers can be launched to attack capital ships

Below: *Repulse* showing contrast paintwork, 5 July 1941, only five months before she was lost. During 1942/3 there were many unsubstantiated reports that the Japanese had succeeded in raising *Repulse* and putting her in a serviceable condition. The source of this misconception appears to have been of Chinese origin.

Bottom: *Renown* now fully reconstructed, shown here in Gibraltar, November 1940, as flagship of Force H. Earlier on 4 April 1940 she was in action with the German battlecruiser *Scharnhorst* at extreme range (18,000 yards) and actually hit the German ship. The enemy took advantage of a snow storm to break off the action.

who are without adequate aircraft protection and with very few destroyers, capital ships will be seriously up against it. I found dodging the torpedoes quite interesting and entertaining until in the end they started to come in from all directions and they were too much for me. *Prince of Wales* and *Repulse* had both been without serious anti-aircraft practice for some months and I am afraid the shooting was not good – torpedoes were mostly fired outside pom-pom range at about 2,500 yards.

'I am convinced that we have all got to realize that bursts behind the target of short-range AA fire which were missing astern is just a waste of time and might as well be thrown over the side. I believe that 90% of short range stuff that is being fired at any aircraft goes behind them.'

HISTORY: RENOWN

ATLANTIC FLEET (BCS) April to July 1919
Refitted at Portsmouth July 1919.
Detached July 1919 for Prince of Wales's overseas tours until October 1920.

First tour Newfoundland, Canada and USA August to December 1919. Left Portsmouth 5 August 1919, escorted by *Dauntless* and *Dragon*. Arrived Concepcion Bay, Newfoundland 11 August. HRH transferred to *Dragon* for passage to St. John's (Newfoundland) and Halifax.
Renown arrived Halifax 13 August where HRH re-embarked for passage to Quebec. Arrived Quebec 21 August where HRH left ship for rail tour of Canada and the USA August to November. During this period *Renown* visited West Indies, South American ports and New York. HRH rejoined at New York in November for return home, left Halifax 25 November, arrived Portsmouth 1 December.
Renown specially refitted at Portsmouth January to March 1920 as 'yacht' for later tours.

Second tour New Zealand and Australia March to October 1920.
Left Portsmouth 16 March 1920 proceeding via Barbados, Panama Canal, Honolulu and Fiji Islands.
Visited Auckland, New Zealand, various Australian ports, and Hobart, Tasmania. Returned via Panama Canal, West Indies and Bermuda. Arrived Portsmouth 11 October 1920. Paid off to Reserve (Care and Maintenance) at Portsmouth 5 November 1920.

RESERVE (Portsmouth) November 1920 to September 1921.
Refit 1921.
Recommissioned Portsmouth 15 September 1921 for Prince of Wales's third tour. Left Portsmouth 26 October 1921, proceeding to Bombay via Malta, Suez Canal and Aden. Arrived Bombay 17 November 1921. HRH left ship at Bombay for four months' tour of India. During this period, *Renown* visited Persian Gulf ports, Colombo, Bombay and Karachi. HRH re-embarked at Karachi on 17 March 1922. Proceeded to Japan via Colombo, Port Swettenham, Singapore and Hong Kong. HRH left ship at Yokohoma during this period.

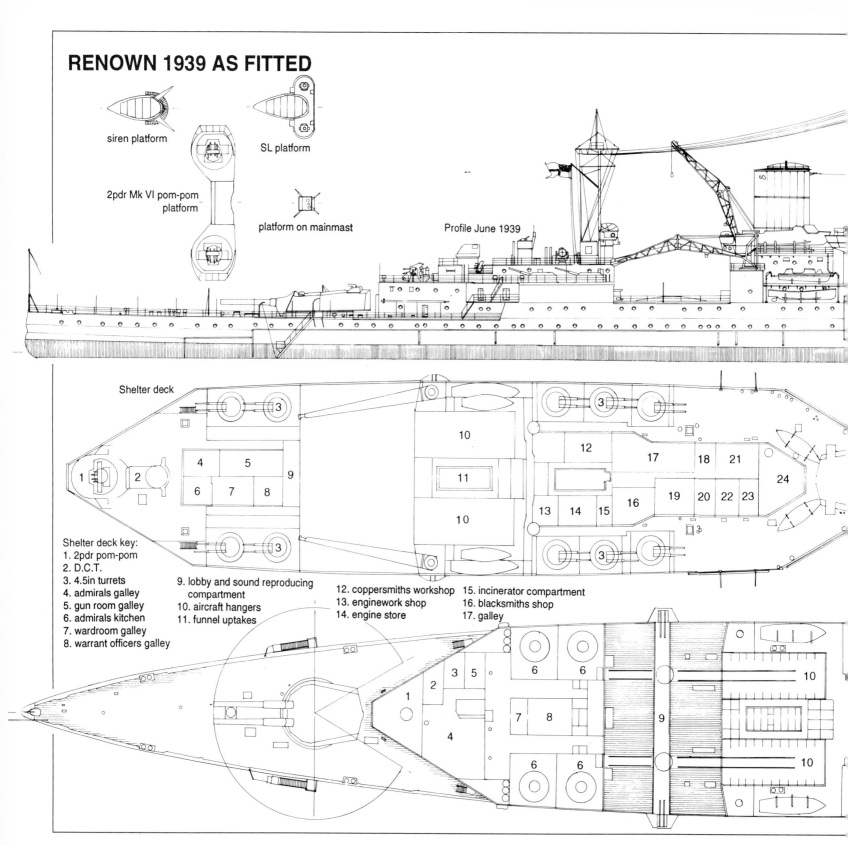

RENOWN 1939 AS FITTED

siren platform

SL platform

2pdr Mk VI pom-pom
platform

platform on mainmast

Profile June 1939

Shelter deck

Shelter deck key:
1. 2pdr pom-pom
2. D.C.T.
3. 4.5in turrets
4. admirals galley
5. gun room galley
6. admirals kitchen
7. wardroom galley
8. warrant officers galley

9. lobby and sound reproducing
   compartment
10. aircraft hangers
11. funnel uptakes

12. coppersmiths workshop
13. enginework shop
14. engine store

15. incinerator compartment
16. blacksmiths shop
17. galley

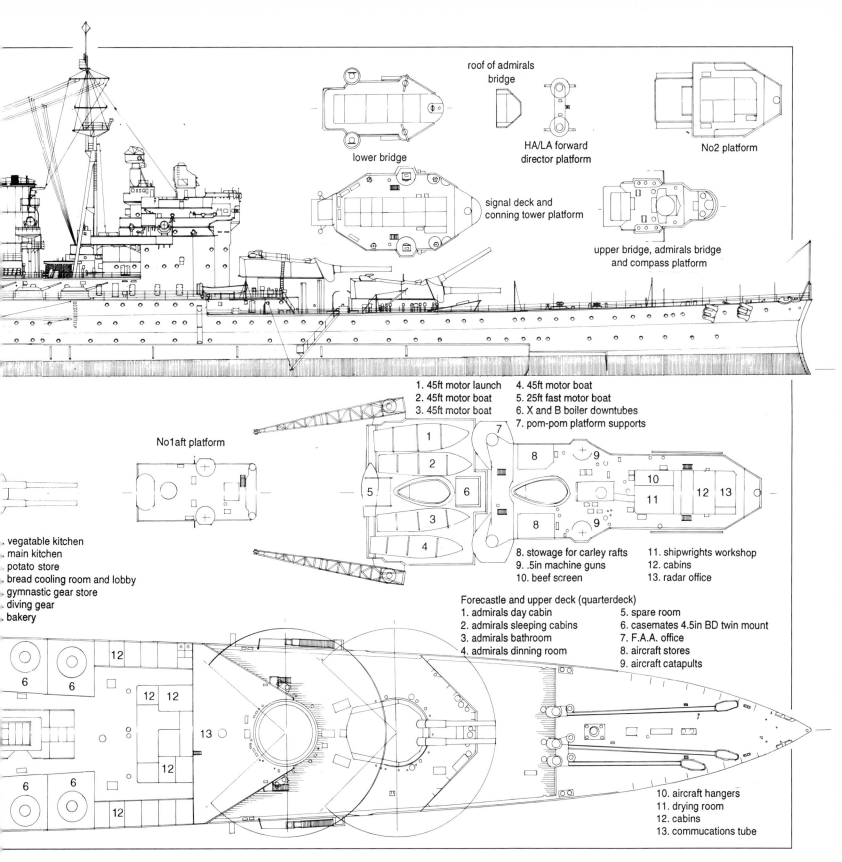

roof of admirals
bridge

HA/LA forward
director platform

No2 platform

lower bridge

signal deck and
conning tower platform

upper bridge, admirals bridge
and compass platform

1. 45ft motor launch
2. 45ft motor boat
3. 45ft motor boat
4. 45ft motor boat
5. 25ft fast motor boat
6. X and B boiler downtubes
7. pom-pom platform supports

No1aft platform

8. stowage for carley rafts
9. .5in machine guns
10. beef screen

11. shipwrights workshop
12. cabins
13. radar office

. vegatable kitchen
. main kitchen
. potato store
. bread cooling room and lobby
. gymnastic gear store
. diving gear
. bakery

Forecastle and upper deck (quarterdeck)
1. admirals day cabin
2. admirals sleeping cabins
3. admirals bathroom
4. admirals dinning room

5. spare room
6. casemates 4.5in BD twin mount
7. F.A.A. office
8. aircraft stores
9. aircraft catapults

10. aircraft hangers
11. drying room
12. cabins
13. commucations tube

Returned home via Manila, Labuan, Penang, Trincomalee, Suez Canal, Malta and Gibraltar. Arrived Portsmouth 20 June 1922.
Paid off to reserve at Portsmouth 28 July 1922 to September 1926.
Extensive refit Portsmouth July to September 1926.
Began refit trials July 1926.
Recommissioned 3 September 1926 for BCS, Atlantic Fleet

ATLANTIC FLEET (BCS) September 1926 to January 1927.
Detached January 1927 for Duke of York's tour to Australia. Left Portsmouth 6 January 1927, proceeding to Australia via Panama Canal. Returned via Suez Canal. Arrived Portsmouth 17 July 1927.
Refit, Portsmouth July to September and rejoined Atlantic Fleet on completion.

ATLANTIC FLEET (BCS) September 1927 to September 1931 (flag July 1929 to July 1931).
Relieved *Hood* as flag (RA) BCS July 1929 (*Hood* to refit).
Flag reverted to *Hood* 11 July 1931 on completion of refit.
Paid off at Portsmouth for refit 11 September 1931.
Refit Portsmouth 1931 to June 1932.
Recommissioned at Portsmouth 2 June 1932 for BCS Home Fleet (ex Atlantic Fleet, renamed Home Fleet March 1932).
From 1932, BCS comprised *Hood*, *Renown* and *Repulse* only.

HOME FLEET (BCS) June 1932 to January 1936.
Collision with *Hood* during exercises off Spanish coast 23 January 1935, struck *Hood*'s starboard quarter. Stem casting fractured with structural damage above and below waterline. Temporary repairs carried out at Gibraltar January to February and ship left for Portsmouth 18 February.
Completed repairs at Portsmouth February to May (completed 18 May).

In March 1935 it was decided for the sake of homogeneity, gradually to separate the *Queen Elizabeth* and *Royal Sovereign* classes, stationing the former in the Mediterranean and the latter in the Home Fleet. Because of the heavy reconstruction programme in the *Queen Elizabeth* class, the Mediterranean Fleet would lose one battleship by the change and the Battlecruiser Squadron was to be transferred to the Mediterranean to offset this. Squadron initially divided between Home and Mediterranean Fleets April to September 1936, and not finally transferred to Mediterranean until September 1936.

Renown present at Jubilee Review, Spithead 16 July 1935.

Because of the Italo-Abyssinian crisis, the Battlecruiser Squadron, comprising *Hood* and *Renown* (*Repulse* reconstructing) was sent to Gibraltar to reinforce the Mediterranean Fleet although remaining as a Home Fleet unit.
Hood remained at Gibraltar until June 1936 when she returned home.
Renown transferred to Alexandria in January 1936 and was attached to 1st Battle Squadron, Mediterranean Fleet until May 1936.

Returned home May 1936 and rejoined BCS Home Fleet. Replaced in Mediterranean by *Repulse* June 1936.

HOME FLEET (BCS) June to September 1936.
Paid off at Portsmouth 2 September 1936 for reconstruction there until August 1939.
Recommissioned at Portsmouth 28 August 1939 for Home Fleet, the Battlecruiser Squadron having reverted to this in February 1939.

HOME FLEET (BCS) August to October 1939.
With *Hood*, two cruisers and four destroyers, carried out patrol between Iceland and the Faroes 7–12 September to intercept enemy merchant shipping and enforce the British blockade.
Detached 2 October as unit of Force K (*Renown* and *Ark Royal*) to take part in search for *Graf Spee*.

FORCE K (South Atlantic Command Freetown) October 1939 to March 1940.
Force operated in the Freetown–Pernambuco area October to November 1939.
Diverted to Cape area to join Force H (*Eagle*, *Cornwall* and *Dorsetshire*) following location of *Graf Spee* in Indian Ocean.

RENOWN: ARMOUR LAYOUT AS RECONSTRUCTED, 1939

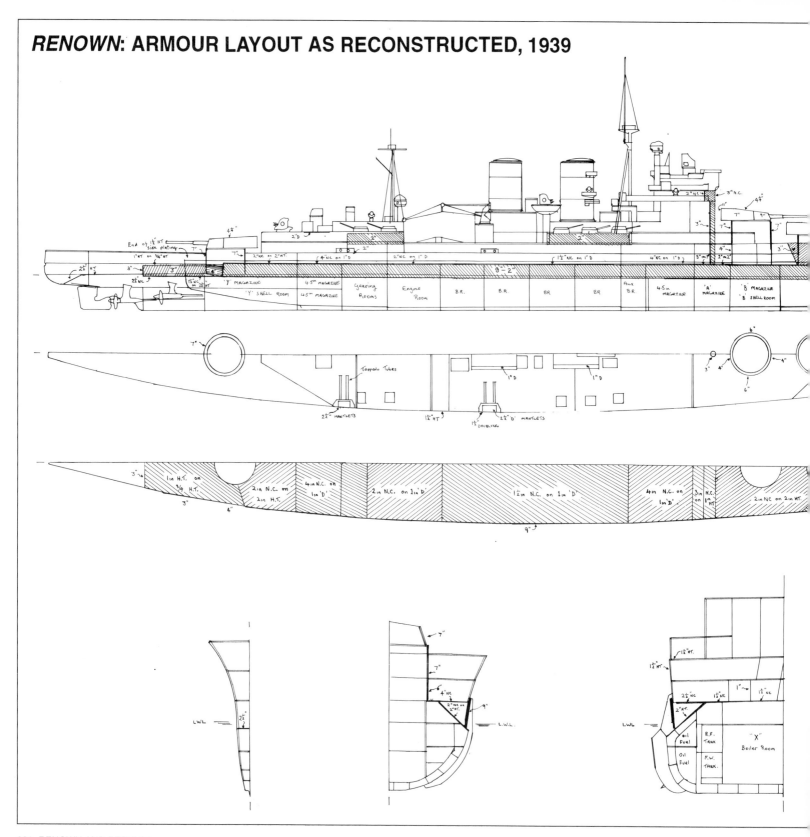

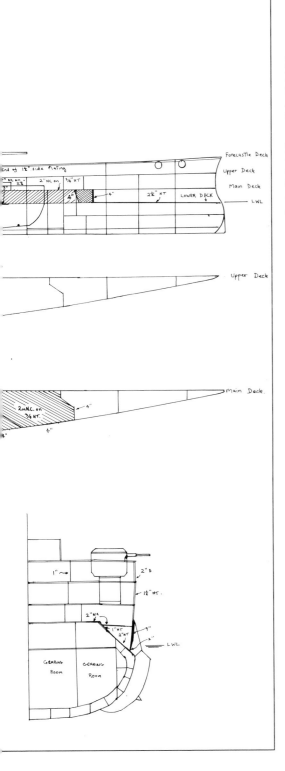

Patrolled area south of Cape of Good Hope 28 November to 2 December in order to intercept the German ship if she broke back into the Atlantic although she did not do so.

Sank German SS *Watussi* off Cape 2 December 1939 after the latter had been intercepted by *Sussex*, set on fire and abandoned by crew.

Force ordered back to Pernambuco–Freetown area on same day, after *Graf Spee* again located in South Atlantic, and was off Pernambuco when *Spee* brought to action by *Exeter*, *Achilles* and *Ajax* off the River Plate on 13 December.

Rejoined Home Fleet 4 March 1940.

HOME FLEET (BCS) March to August 1940 (flag BCS and 2nd fleet flag from late March).

Detached February 1940, with *Ark Royal*, *Galatea* and destroyers, to assist French forces in intercepting six German merchant vessels expected to break out from Vigo. All but two of these captured or scuttled, one wrecked off Norwegian coast and one reached Germany.

Became flag VA BCS and 2nd fleet flag late March, relieving *Hood* for refit.

Norwegian operations April to June 1940; covered minelaying operations by destroyers in Norwegian waters 5–8 April.

Briefly in action with *Scharnhorst* and *Gneisenau* in the Narvik area 9 April in bad weather. Scored three hits on *Gneisenau* at 18,000 yards, disabling fore turret and main armament fire control. Hit twice by enemy fire without any material damage.

Enemy ships broke off action after about ten minutes and contact lost in thick weather. During this engagement, *Renown* reached 29 knots in heavy seas. Flag VA Whitworth temporarily transferred to *Warspite* 10 April for second attack on enemy destroyers at Narvik by that ship and a destroyer group.

Refit Rosyth (repairs to action damage) 20 April to 18 May.

Sent to Faroes–Iceland area, with *Repulse*, 5 June to investigate reports (subsequently found incorrect) of enemy heavy ships being sighted off the Faroes, possibly intending raid on Iceland.

Unit of covering force for Norwegian evacuation convoys June 1940.

With *Repulse*, 1st Cruiser Squadron and destroyers, endeavoured to intercept *Gneisenau*, reported en route from Trondheim to Germany 27 July 1940 but no contact made.

Transferred to Force H (Gibraltar) August 1940, relieving *Hood* as flag. Flag VA transferred at Scapa 10 August. *Renown* joined at Gibraltar 20 August.

FORCE H (Gibraltar, flag) August 1940 to August 1941.

Ordered to intercept French cruisers *Georges Leygues*, *Gloire* and *Montcalm* after they had passed through Straits of Gibraltar 11 September 1940 en route to Dakar, but not despatched in time to do so.

Temporarily detached 6 November to reinforce Home Fleet for operations against *Scheer* in the Atlantic. Rejoined Force H by the 15th.

From 15 to 19 November Force H covered *Argus* carrying the first fighter aircraft reinforcements (Hurricanes) for Malta, these being flown-off from a position south of Sardinia.

As a consequence of inadequate training of pilots, only four of twelve aircraft reached Malta, the others running out of fuel and being lost at sea.

On 27 November 1940 Force H, comprising *Renown* (flag), *Ark Royal*, *Sheffield*, *Despatch* and nine destroyers, reinforced by *Ramillies*, *Berwick*, *Manchester*, *Newcastle*, *Southampton*, *Coventry* and four destroyers from the Mediterranean Fleet, fought an indecisive action off Cape Spartivento (Sardinia) against an Italian squadron comprising two battleships, five cruisers and sixteen destroyers.

The enemy retired following a short engagement between the cruisers, being later unsuccessfully attacked by aircraft from *Ark Royal*. *Renown* briefly engaged with the Italian cruisers at long range before the action was broken off. Convoy reached Malta intact.

Malta convoy 7–9 January 1941.

With *Malaya* and *Sheffield* bombarded Genoa 9 February 1941 while aircraft from *Ark Royal* carried out search for *Scharnhorst* and *Gneisenau* in Atlantic 8–28 March 1941 after the enemy ships had been sighted by aircraft from *Malaya* while latter escorting Freetown to UK convoy. *Renown* and *Ark Royal* joined convoy on the 10th and remained with it until the 19th. Search operations broke off on 28th after *Scharnhorst* and *Gneisenau* located at Brest.

Force H escorted important convoy carrying tanks and supplies to army in Egypt for first leg of passage from Gibraltar to Alexandria 5–9 May

Below: An aerial view of *Renown* on 25 June 1942, showing intermediate disruptive camouflage.

1941 (convoy handed over to Mediterranean Fleet escort south of Malta).

With *Ark Royal* and *Sheffield* took part in search for *Bismarck* 24–27 May 1941. Intercepted German supply ship *Gonzenheim* in Atlantic 4 June 1941. *Gonzenheim*, which had been intended to work with *Bismarck* and *Prinz Eugen*, scuttled and finally sunk by *Neptune*.

Malta convoy 21–23 July 1941.

Returned home for refit August 1941, speed being restricted to 20 knots by torn plating in starboard bulge; left Gibraltar 8 August, arrived Rosyth on 14th. Flag Force H transferred to *Nelson*.

Refit Rosyth August to November 1941.

Proposed, in August 1941, as unit of new Eastern Fleet but not sent out (see *Repulse*).

Transferred to Home Fleet on completion of refit and rejoined at Scapa 22 November 1941.

HOME FLEET (2nd BS) November 1941 to October 1942 (flag VA 2nd BS and 2nd Fleet flag, December 1941 to April 1942).

Replaced *Duke of York* as flag VA 2nd BS and 2nd fleet flag 9 December 1941 when latter detached to take the Prime Minister to the USA.

Second flag of Home Fleet comprising *King George V* (flag), *Renown* (flag VA), *Duke of York*, *Victorious*, *Berwick* and twelve destroyers providing special cover for outward and homeward Russia convoy from 6 to 10 March 1942 during sortie by *Tirpitz*.

Contact with *Tirpitz* established by aircraft from *Victorious* off the Lofoten Islands, but torpedo attack by these failed and *Tirpitz* able to return to base without being brought to action. Convoys not attacked.

Flag reverted to *Duke of York* 3 April 1942.

Left Clyde 14 April as Commodore in Command Force W, comprising *Renown*, *Charybdis*, *Cairo* four British and two US destroyers, escorting the US carrier *Wasp* with fighter reinforcements (Spitfires) for Malta. Fifty-seven aircraft flown-off south of Sardinia on 20 April and all but one reached Malta. Force back at Scapa by 27th. Similar operation carried out by same force on 9 May 1942 when aircraft flown-off from *Eagle* and *Wasp*.

Force rejoined Home Fleet 15 May.

Based at Hvalfiord (Iceland) May to June 1942 as cover for Atlantic convoys against possible attack by enemy heavy ships.

Returned to Force H October 1942 for North Africa invasion.

FORCE H (Gibraltar) October 1942 to February 1943.

Took part in North Africa invasion operations 1942.

Force H employed in covering initial British invasion force and follow-up convoys against attack by Italian or Vichy French forces.

Returned home February 1943. Arrived Rosyth 7 February for refit until June 1943. Transferred to Home Fleet on completion.

HOME FLEET (2nd BS) June to December 1943.

Detached to Halifax August 1943 to bring Prime Minister and Chiefs of Staff home from Quebec Conference. Left Scapa 24 August, arrived Clyde 19 September.

Again detached November 1943 to take Prime Minister, Admiral A. B. Cunningham and US Ambassador to Alexandria for Cairo Conference. Left Plymouth 12 November via Gibraltar, Algiers and Malta.

Weatherly qualities at high speed in heavy

Below: *Renown's* bridgework in May 1943. Note the roundness of the bridge face, designed especially to ward off backdraught.

Below: A historic meeting, on the forecastle of *Renown* as she lay off Plymouth Sound on 2 August 1945, between HM King George VI and President Truman.

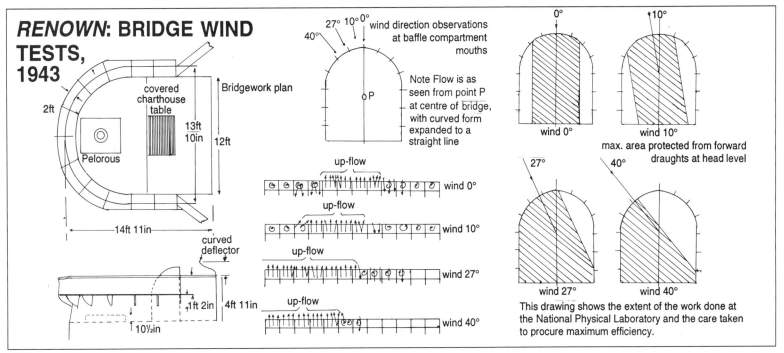

RENOWN: BRIDGE WIND TESTS, 1943

Bridgework plan

covered charthouse table

2ft

Pelorous

13ft 10in

12ft

14ft 11in

curved deflector

1ft 2in

4ft 11in

10½in

27° 10° 0° wind direction observations at baffle compartment mouths

40°

P

Note Flow is as seen from point P at centre of bridge, with curved form expanded to a straight line

up-flow

wind 0°

up-flow

wind 10°

up-flow

wind 27°

up-flow

wind 40°

0°

10°

wind 0°

wind 10°

max. area protected from forward draughts at head level

27°

40°

wind 27°

wind 40°

This drawing shows the extent of the work done at the National Physical Laboratory and the care taken to procure maximum efficiency.

Below: *Renown* in 1942. With *Ark Royal* and the cruiser *Sheffield*, she led the bombardment of Genoa on 9 February 1941, causing considerable damage to the harbour works.

Below: *Renown* leaves Plymouth for the scrapyard in March 1949.

weather in Bay of Biscay, en route, noted by Admiral Cunningham. Rejoined Home Fleet at Rosyth 2 December 1943.
Transferred to Eastern Fleet December 1943 as flag VA 1st BS and 2nd fleet flag. Hoisted flag at Rosyth 18 December, left Scapa 23 December with convoy for Fast East via Mediterranean and Suez Canal. Arrived Colombo 27 January 1944.

EASTERN FLEET (Flag VA 1st BS and 2nd Fleet flag) December 1943 to November 1944.
Unit of force supporting carrier attacks on Sabang (Sumatra) by aircraft from *Illustrious* and USS *Saratoga* 19 April 1944.
Took part in bombardment of Car Nicobar and Port Blair in Andaman Islands 30 April and 1 May 1944.
Unit of force supporting carrier attacks on dockyard and oil refinery at Sourabaya (Java) by aircraft from the same two carriers 17 May 1944 and subsequent air attack on Port Blair on 21 June.
Unit of force supporting carrier attack on Sabang by aircraft from *Illustrious* and *Victorious* 25 July 1944, and with *Queen Elizabeth*, *Valiant*, French battleship *Richelieu* and destroyers, carried out bombardment following this.
Took part in several air strikes and bombardment of the Nicobar Islands from 17 to 19 October 1944.

On 22 November 1944, ships selected to remain in the South East Asia area after formation of a Pacific Fleet, which was commenced on that date, were designated the East Indies Fleet, the Battle Squadron for this comprising *Queen Elizabeth*, *Valiant* and *Renown*, and becoming the 3rd BS, the 1st BS being allocated to the Pacfic Fleet.
On the same date, flag VA transferred from *Renown* to *Queen Elizabeth* as flag 3rd BS and fleet flag, *Renown* becoming a private ship.

EAST INDIES FLEET (3rd BS) November 1944 to March 1945.
Refit Durban December 1944 to February 1945.
Rejoined fleet at Trincomalee 7 March 1945.
Recalled home March 1945 to reinforce the depleted Home Fleet against the possibility of a final sortie into the Atlantic by the remaining German heavy ships, either through the Channel or the Northern passages, although it later became known that the enemy fleet was then in no condition to attempt this even if ordered to do so.
Left Colombo 30 March via Suez Canal, arriving at Scapa on 14 April and Rosyth on the 15th, having steamed 7,642 nautical miles in 306 hours at an average speed of 20 knots.

HOME FLEET (2nd BS) April to May 1945.
Refit Rosyth April to May.
Intended to relieve *Rodney* as flag Home Fleet but this cancelled following end of hostilites in Europe on 8 May.
Conference held on board at Rosyth on 11 May, German Naval delegates bringing details of their minefields, buoys and swept channels.
Reduced to reserve at Portsmouth 15 May 1945.

RESERVE May 1945 to June 1948 (Portsmouth to July 1945, Devonport later, C Category from October 1946).
Partially disarmed at Portsmouth July 1945; six 4.5in turrets removed and all light AA landed.
Transferred to Devonport July 1945.
Meeting between HM the King and President Truman held on board at Plymouth on 3 August 1945 when Truman en route home from Potsdam Conference in the US cruiser *Augusta*.
Reduced to C Category Reserve October 1946.
Decision for disposal announced 21 January 1948.
Placed on Disposal List at Devonport 1 June 1948.
Sold to Metal Industries Ltd. Faslane, August 1948.
Left Devonport in tow for Faslane for scrapping 3 August 1948.

THE GENESIS AND DEVELOPMENT
OF THE AIRCRAFT CARRIER

The use of aircraft concomitant with warships pre-dates the Great War, the US Navy having begun experiments in flying-off aircraft from warships as far back as 1910, and achieved success in USS *Birmingham* while anchored in Hampton Roads. A flight platform had been fitted over the forecastle of the cruiser and the pilot Eugene Ely, can claim the first successful flight from the deck of a warship.

A land aircraft was used throughout most of these tests and arrester gear for landing comprised of wires stretched between sandbags which engaged with hooks on the aircraft's undercarriage. A successful landing was made on the cruiser *Pennsylvania* in the following year (landing deck fitted over the quarterdeck). This demonstrated the practicability of such flights at sea, but the US Navy then dropped all experiments for the time being and further development was left to the Royal Navy.

In January 1912 Lieutenant Samson made a successful flight from the forecastle of the battleship *Africa* at anchor in Sheerness (see Predreadnought book) and then in May of the same year made the first successful flight from the battleship *Hibernia* while under way at about 12 knots (using gear from *Africa*). This was the first occasion when an aircraft took off from a moving warship and a seaplane was used throughout the tests. The craft had wheeled trolleys fitted to the floats which fitted into a pair of elevated rails fitted over the forecastle and fore turret. No arrangements for landings were made and the aircraft came down in the water and was hoisted aboard by derrick. This equipment was then transferred to HMS *London* in May 1912 for further tests. None of these arrangements (US or British) was considered practicable for regular use because the launching gear precluded any use of the forward or after turrets when erected over the top. The equipment was dismantled in all ships after completion of the tests.

In May 1913 the old cruiser *Hermes* was commissioned for service as an experimental seaplane carrier. Canvas hangars were fitted forward and aft and a flying-off rail was fitted forward over the forecastle. No provision was made for landings, the aircraft being lifted from the sea by crane. Successful experiments were conducted in *Hermes* and she joined the fleet as a seaplane carrier at the start of the war; she was torpedoed

and sunk in October 1914. Many independent shipbuilders were keeping abreast of developments and a proposal was put forward by Beardmore for the construction of a genuine seaplane carrier, but no decisions were taken pending the results of the trials in *Hermes*; furthermore construction work was limited to finishing off any capital ship construction then under way.

The first practical and far-sighted specification for an aircraft carrier was made a Dr P. W. Lauchester and appeared in *Engineering* on 20 November 1914. His proposals were for a ship to carry about 50 or 60 aircraft, and guns powerful enough to repel any ship up to light cruiser status. Displacement was to run to about 20,000 tons, speed to be 20 knots and, with a view to smoke problems, diesel oil was suggested.

On the outbreak of war, there was suddenly an urgent demand for seaplane carriers and the quick answer to the problem was conversion. The Admiralty purchased a tanker and converted her into a seaplane carrier and renamed her *Ark Royal*. She was fitted with a hangar and workshops, etc., and was given derricks for handling aircraft. She also had a 160ft flush forecastle from which aircraft could be flown-off by the trolley and rail method. She was completed in December 1914 and sent to the Dardanelles where she was also used as a recovery and workshop ship for crashed aircraft.

She was the first genuine aircraft carrier to be built for the Royal (or in fact any other navy). Given her slow speed, it was not intended that she manoeuvre with the fleet, but be based in an area adjacent to the fleet. She was the first ship to have permanent hangar accommodation built in and the first from which aircraft could be flown-off. She had the 160ft flight deck forward, but there seems to be no record of any flight being made from this deck; the seaplanes were always hoisted out on their own floats to take-off from the water. The hangar was located amidships below the bridge and the aircraft were manhandled through an opening beneath this.

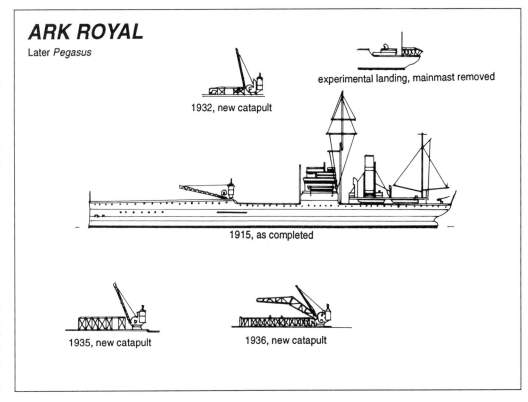

ARK ROYAL

Later *Pegasus*

1932, new catapult

experimental landing, mainmast removed

1915, as completed

1935, new catapult

1936, new catapult

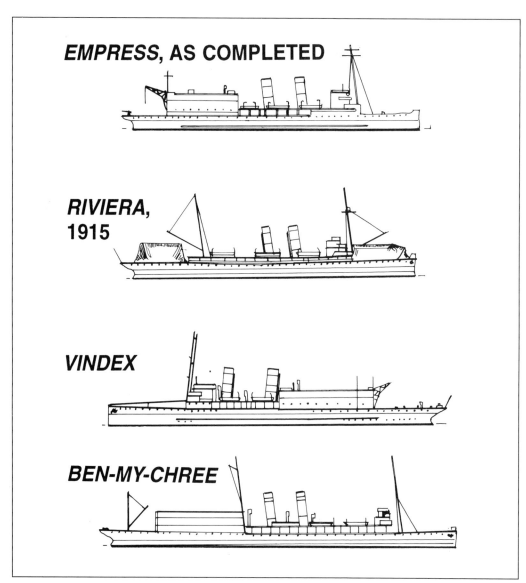

EMPRESS, AS COMPLETED

RIVIERA, 1915

VINDEX

BEN-MY-CHREE

Ark Royal
Laid down by Blyth Shipbuilding Co. 7.11.1913; purchased by the Admiralty in May 1914; launched: 5.9.1914; completed: 10.12.1914.
Displacement (tons): 6,900 (load), 7,450 (deep).
Dimensions: Length 352ft 6in (pp), 366ft (oa). Beam: 50ft 4in. Draught: 17ft 6in mean.
Mercantile hull considerably lengthened in conversion.
Armament: 4 x 12pdr in single open mountings, 2 p&s before bridge, 2 p&s right aft. 2MG.
Aircraft:
8 seaplanes in 1915. Later many types were in use including Sopwith 2-seaters and Sopwith 'Tabloids'.
Machinery
One set of vertical triple expansion engines driving a single propeller.
Cylindrical boilers. Speed: 11 knots on 3,000shp.
Fuel: 500 tons oil.
Complement: 180 RN and RFC as completed. Later reduced to 139 as depot ship.
Cost of conversion: £80,000 (unofficial).
Renamed *Pegasus* in December 1934 to release name for new carrier. Used as Catapult and Repair Ship from 1939 to 1945. Finally sold to Belgian yard for possible conversion to commercial service and renamed *Anita 1*. Work commenced at Cardiff but later towed to Antwerp for completion. Nothing done and later sold to Dutch scrappers (June 1949). Resold to T. W. Ward and arrived in Grays Essex for scrapping on 15 April 1950.

Converted Packet Steamers
Empress, Engadine, Riviera, Ben-My-Chree, Vindex, Manxman, Nairana and *Pegasus*
Empress: Chartered by Admiralty 11.8.1914.
   Commissioned 25.8.1914 for Harwich Force.
Engadine: Chartered by Admiralty 11.8.1914.
   Commissioned 13.8.1914 for Harwich Force.
Riviera: Chartered by Admiralty 11.8.1914.
   Commissioned 13.8.1914 for Harwich Force.
Ben-My-Chree: Chartered by Admiralty early 1915.
   Commissioned May 1915 for Eastern Mediterranean.
Vindex: Taken over by Admiralty March 1915.
   Commissioned 26.3.1915 for Harwich Force.
Manxman: Taken over by Admiralty 1917.
   Commissioned in 1917 for Harwich Force.
Nairana: Taken over by Admiralty 1917.
   Commissioned September 1917 for Grand Fleet.
Pegasus: Laid down by John Brown and purchased

There were eight seaplanes aboard in 1915 when she went to the Dardanelles. She was not employed as an operational carrier after 1920, and from 1928 onwards she was used for trials with catapults and sea landing mats.

The Admiralty was quick to comandeer mercantile ships then completing for convertion to seaplane carriers; they included the small, fast steam packets *Empress, Engadine, Riviera, Ben-My-Chree, Vindex, Manxman, Nairana, Campania* and *Pegasus*. The first three were chartered by the Admiralty, but the rest were purchased outright. In 1914 little was known about the techniques of using aircraft from warships and when the war started it seemed that the adaptation of these steam packets would provide the fleet with an airborne back-up. The equipment in the first three converted (*Empress, Engadine* and *Riviera*) merely comprised of some light removable canvas shelters for the aircraft forward and aft, and the ship itself remained little changed. Following the successful raid on Cuxhaven on 25 December 1914 the aircraft accommodation in these three was improved and two more ships were taken up (*Ben-My-Chree* and *Vindex*). Because of the limitations of seaplanes, however, *Vindex* was given a short flying-by Admiralty on stocks. Commissioned 14.8.1917 for Flying Squadron, Grand Fleet.

Campania: Taken over by Admiralty November 1914. Commissioned April 1915 for Grand Fleet.

Dimensions

Empress: 311ft(pp) x 40ft 1in x 15ft 6in mean. 2,540 tons.

Engadine: 316ft (pp) x 41ft 1in x 15ft 6in mean. 1,670 tons.

Riviera: 316ft (pp) x 41ft 1in x 15ft 6in mean. 1,670 tons.

Ben-My-Chree: 375ft (pp) x 46ft x 18ft 6in mean. 2,550 tons.

Vindex: 350ft (pp) x 42ft x 16ft mean. 2,900 tons

Manxman: 330ft (pp) x 43ft x 18ft mean. 2,030 tons.

Nairana: 315ft (pp) x 45ft 6in x 13ft 3in mean. 3,070 tons.

Pegasus: 330ft (pp) x 43ft x 13ft 6in mean. 3,070 tons.

Campania: 601ft (oa) x 65ft x 27ft mean. 18,000 tons.

Armament

The armament was very variable and difficult to trace especially in the earlier experimental ships, but was usually a combination of 12pdr LA/HA and or 3pdrs.

Empress: 2 x 12pdr plus 2 x 3pdr.

Engadine: 1 x 12pd LA plus 2 x 12pdr HA. 2 x 3in HA added later.

Riviera: As *Empress*. (12pdr were later removed)

Ben-My-Chree: 2 x 12pdr LA plus 2 x 12pdr HA and 2 x 3pdr.

Vindex: As *Ben-My-Chree*.

Manxman: 2 x 12pdr LA and 2 x 12pdr HA.

Nairana: 2 x 12pdr LA and 2 x 12pdr HA.

Pegasus: As *Nairana*:

Campania: 7 x 4.7in.

Aircraft: First eight ships carried various types of aircraft but usually never more than six (all seaplanes).

Campania: carried various types including Sopwith 'Baby' and Sopwith 'Schneider'. Capacity for 13 machines.

Machinery

A mix of boilers and turbines in all.

Speed (knots): *Empress, Engadine, Riviera, Vindex* 22.5.

Manxman 20.5 *Nairana* 19. *Ben-My-Chree* 24.5. *Campania* 22.

Fates: All returned to owners and reconverted. (*Pegasus* kept in aircraft role and finally scrapped in 1931. *Campania* collided with *Royal Oak* and *Glorious* and sank on 5 November 1918.

off deck forward from which small fighter aircraft could take off. The last three ships (*Manxman*, *Nairana* and *Pegasus*) were similarly fitted but with some additional aircraft handling equipment. The aircraft capacity in these three was increased to nine as against the four of five in the earlier ships. Because of their lack of size, carrying capacity, speed and general radius, none of the converted packets ever proved very success-

Aircraft Equipment in British Warships

Ark Royal Conversion completed 1914)		
	1.1.15	1 Short (Canton Unne), 2 Wight, 3 Sopwith 2 seaters, 2 Sopwith 'Tabloid'.
	2.15	1 Short 2-seat seaplane (200 Canton Unne), Wight and Sopwith seaplanes
Ben-My-Chree (Converted 1915)		
	11.5.15.	1 Sopwith 'Schneider'
	21.5.15	2 Short S184 torpedo reconnaissance seaplanes
	12.6.15	2 Short
	17.9.16	Short Canton Unne, Sopwith 'Baby'
	1917	Sopwith seaplanes
Minerva	12–20.4.15	1 Sopwith 'Tabloid'
Doris	25–30.4.15	1 Sopwith 2-seater
	4.15	1 Sopwith 'Schneider'
Roberts	9.15	1 Short S184
Raglan	10.15	1 Short S184
Arethusa	2.6.15	1 Sopwith 'Schneider'
Engadine (Taken over 8/14)		
	1914	3 Short seaplanes (160hp)
	4.7.15	1 Short S184, 3 Sopwith 'Schneider'
	4.5.16	Sopwith 'Baby'.
	31.5.16	2 Short S184, 2 Sopwith 'Baby'
Riviera (Taken over 8/14)		
	1914	3 Short seaplanes (160hp)
	4.7.15	4 Short S184
Vindex (Taken over 1915)		
	3.11.15	2 Bristol Landplane 1-D 'Bullet', 3 Short seaplane S184, 2 Sopwith 'Baby' sea planes
	4.5.16	4 Sopwith 'Baby' only
	24.6.16	All removed
	2.8.16	1 Bristol 1-D 'Bullet' Landplane
	22.10.16	2 Short S184
Campania (Completed conversion 1916		
	30.5.16	3 Short S184, 3 Sopwith 'Baby', 4 Sopwith 'Schneider'
	1917	Fairey 'Campania'
Killingholme	3.16	Sopwith 'Schneider'
Brocklesby	3.16	Sopwith 'Schneider'
Maxman (Entered service 1916)		
	12.16	4 Sopwith 'Baby'
	29.4.17	4 Sopwith 'Pup'
Furious (Converted 1917)		
	7.17	3 Short 225, 5 Sopwith 'Pup' or could carry 10 seaplanes, hoisted in and out
	3.18	14 Sopwith 1½-Strutter, 2 Sopwith 'Pup'
	7.18	7 Sopwith 'Camel'
Slinger	6.18	1 Fairey 3C
Aurora	5.11.15	1 Deperdussin
E22	4.16	1 Sopwith 'Schneider'.
Yarmouth (Modifications to carry aircraft completed 6.17)		
	6.17	1 Sopwith 'Pup'
Repulse	10.17	1 Sopwith 'Pup'
	3.18	1 Sopwith 1½-Strutter
Argus	1918	Sopwith 'Pups', Sopwith 1½-Strutters (49 a/c total)
	19.10.18	1 Sqdn Short Seaplanes (310hp engines)
	1918	Sopwith 'Cuckoo', Blackburn 'Blackbird'
Hermes	1913	Caudron biplane seaplanes
Africa	1912	Short biplane landplane.

STEAM PACKETS CONVERTED TO SEAPLANE CARRIERS

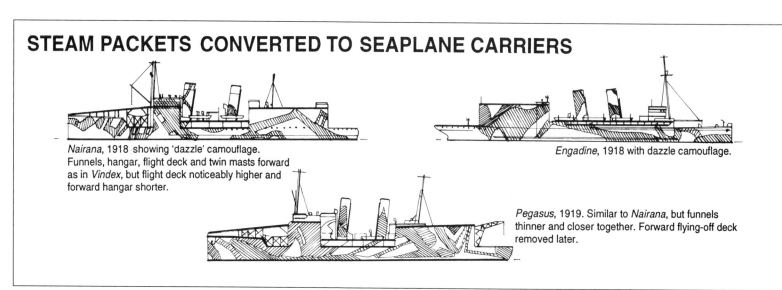

Nairana, 1918 showing 'dazzle' camouflage.
Funnels, hangar, flight deck and twin masts forward
as in *Vindex*, but flight deck noticeably higher and
forward hangar shorter.

Engadine, 1918 with dazzle camouflage.

Pegasus, 1919. Similar to *Nairana*, but funnels
thinner and closer together. Forward flying-off deck
removed later.

CAMPANIA,
showing dazzle camouflage

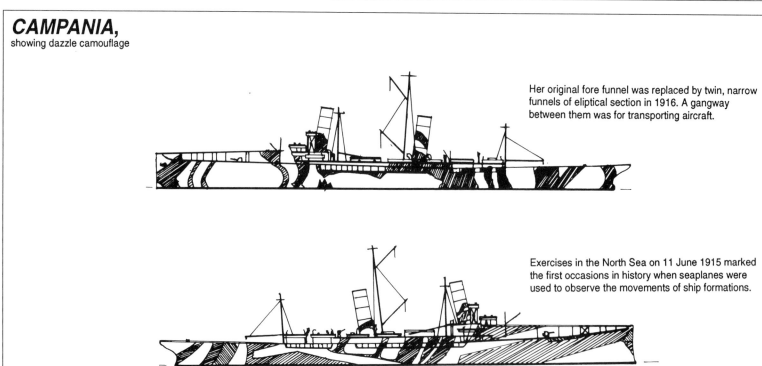

Her original fore funnel was replaced by twin, narrow
funnels of eliptical section in 1916. A gangway
between them was for transporting aircraft.

Exercises in the North Sea on 11 June 1915 marked
the first occasions in history when seaplanes were
used to observe the movements of ship formations.

ful as aircraft carriers and they were, on the whole, unfit for work with the Grand Fleet. On completion, the first three were attached to the Harwich Force, and did not operate as a unit of the Grand Fleet although they did carry out valuable reconnaissance work during the early months of the war. The majority of naval air raids on enemy bases and airship stations from 1914 to 1916 were carried out from *Empress* and *Engadine*, *Riviera* and *Vindex* were also used at times, but repeated failures led to their being abandoned pending the completion of larger aircraft carriers.

The main reasons for the lack of success were: 1. Low performance of seaplanes, difficulty in hoisting them in and out and their inability to take-off in average North Sea weather; 2. Low

speed of the carriers which made it dangerous to keep them standing-by in the vicinity of an enemy coast to pick up the aircraft after a raid. *Ben-My-Chree* performed some useful service at the Dardanelles in 1915 and *Engadine* was actually attached to the Grand Fleet and present at Jutland in 1916, but later, after tests had been carried out in the converted *Furious*, these vessels were used less and less. They were later refitted and returned to their original owners.

During the spring of 1917 the large cruiser *Furious* was completed as a partial aircraft carrier with hangars and a flying-off platform forward in place of a forward turret. Aircraft were successfully flown-off from the platform in the summer of 1917, but attempts at landing proved extremely hazardous. She was modified as a

proper aircraft carrier from November 1917 to March 1918 and fitted with a second hangar and landing deck aft. She had a capacity for twenty aircraft. As modified, however, she retained the original tripod foremast, bridgework and funnel on the centreline, and air eddies caused by these made landing on the after deck extremely difficult. It is reported that only three successful landings were ever made on *Furious* in this condition, so she was not regarded as a satisfactory aircraft carrier at that time and was used mainly for training purposes during the latter part of 1918. Another conversion was the cruiser *Vindictive*, a smaller ship of the *Hawkins* class. The modification took place while she was under construction and she was completed in September 1918 as a cruiser-carrier with a hangar and short flying-off platform forward and landing deck aft. Her capacity was six aircraft. She retained four of her seven guns from the original and continued to be rated officially as a cruiser (see drawings). She was not very successful in the role and during 1925 she was reconverted to a proper cruiser once more.

The first really successful carrier was *Argus*, completed in September 1918 with a capacity for 15 to 20 aircraft. She was originally the Italian liner *Conte Rosso*, building in the UK on the outbreak of war and later purchased by the Admiralty with a view to converting her to a carrier when the opportunity arose. She had a completely unobstructed flight deck which was achieved by siting the navigating bridge etc. forward beneath the deck, the charthouse being raised and lowered by hydraulic power. Furnace smoke was expelled by fans through large horizontal ducts in the side of the hangar, right aft or alternatively at the after extremity of the flight deck, and light collapsible masts were fitted at each side for the WT.

The decision to abandon all masts, funnels and superstructure above the flight deck was a consequence of practical experience with *Furious* (1917–18) and special experiments carried out onshore, both of which emphasized difficulty in landing safely in the face of serious air disturbances caused by hot furnace gases and eddies from upper works. The proposals to fit horizontal ducts instead of funnels originated from Captain Onyon, an engineer on the DNC's technical staff. The Admiralty had little confidence in this system and a normal set of uptakes and funnels were constructed for *Argus* in case it failed. The arrangement as built proved satisfactory on trials, but the various inherent disadvantages (internal complications, extra cost, and excessive heat developed in the after hangar and curtailment in width of this with corresponding reduction in aircraft capacity) led to experiments being carried out in late 1918 with a dummy island superstructure erected on the extreme starboard side of the flight deck to ascertain the possibility of 'landing on' with these present. The trials, which resulted in the adoption of a similar plan in *Eagle* and *Hermes*, then under construction, showed that a narrow superstructure and funnels, set well out on the starboard beam, would leave ample flight deck space and that air eddies from this would not cause interference as had

Argus
Laid down by Beardmore, work stopped on outbreak of war.
Purchased by Admiralty in 1916.
Commissioned for service 14.9.1918.
Displacement (tons): 14,450 (normal), 16,400 (full load).
Dimensions: Length 560ft (wl), 565ft (oa). Beam 75ft 9in. Draught 21ft mean.
Armament: 2 x 4in 50cal MkV, 2 x 4in AA, 4 x 3pdr, 4MG.
Aircraft
First British carrier with flush, entirely unobstructed flight deck, 15 to 20 aircraft carried. (Carried Sopwith 'Cuckoo' torpedo aircraft as completed.)
Machinery
Parsons turbines driving 4 propellers.
12 cylindrical boilers with forced draught.
22,000shp 20.5 knots.
Fuel: 2,000 tons oil.
Complement: 370 (490 RN and RAF as completed).
Cost of conversion: £1,307,615
Fate: Sold for scrap in 1946.

Hermes
Displacement (tons): 10,850 (load), 12,900 (deep).
Laid down by Armstrong 15.1.1918; launched 11.9.1919; commission 19.2.1924.
Dimensions: length 548ft (pp), 598ft (oa). Beam 90ft (flight deck).
Armament: 6 x 5.5in, 3 x 4in AA.
Aircraft: Twenty (carried Flycatchers, Fairey IIIs, Osprey and Swordfish during the late 1920s and 30s)
Armour: sides 2–1½in abreast magazines and

machinery, 1in over flight deck in areas of magazines and machinery, 1in gunshields.
Machinery
Parsons all geared turbines driving 2 propellers.
Boilers: Yarrow small-tube.
SHP: 40,000 for 25 knots.
Fuel (tons): 1,000 minimum, 2,100 max.
Complement: 664.
Fate: Sunk by Japanese aircraft off Ceylon 9 April 1942; 268 men 19 officers lost.

Eagle
Laid down February 1917; launched 8.6.1918; commissioned as carrier 26.2.1924.
Displacement (tons): 22,600 (load). 26,500 (deep).
Dimensions: Length 667ft (oa). Beam 92ft 9in waterline, 100ft flight deck. Draught: 25/27ft mean.
9 x 6in 50cal, 5 x 4in AA, 4 MG.
Aircraft
Capacity 21. Flights carried: 1927–8. Two S One F/F One TB. One SR (Fairey III). One FF (Flycatchers) 1937–9: Two T/B (18 Swordfish).
Machinery
Brown Curtis all geared turbines driving 2 propellers.
Boilers: 32 small-tube Yarrow.
SHP: 50,000 for 24 knots.
Armour
9in main belt was removed on conversion. Belt 4½in, bulkheads 4in, 1½in flight deck. Bulged in 1921.
Complement: 450 RN as completed.
Cost: £4,617,636 by 1927.
Fate: On Malta convoys when she was torpedoed on 11 August 1942 by *U73* and hit four times (port side). Sank in eight minutes taking with her 260 of the crew (900 survivors).

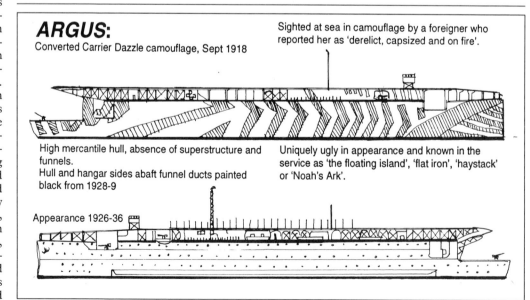

ARGUS:
Converted Carrier Dazzle camouflage, Sept 1918

Sighted at sea in camouflage by a foreigner who reported her as 'derelict, capsized and on fire'.

High mercantile hull, absence of superstructure and funnels.
Hull and hangar sides abaft funnel ducts painted black from 1928-9

Uniquely ugly in appearance and known in the service as 'the floating island', 'flat iron', 'haystack' or 'Noah's Ark'.

Appearance 1926-36

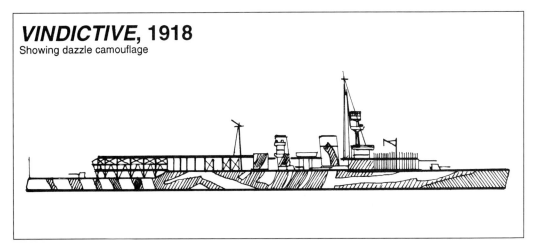

VINDICTIVE, 1918
Showing dazzle camouflage

been the case with the centreline structure in *Furious*. *Argus*'s flight deck was 550 feet long by 62 feet wide and about 60 feet above the waterline at normal load. Windbreaking palisades (14 feet high) were fitted at the sides, to protect the aircraft on deck, and these were lowered flush with the deck when not in use. A landing net (about 200 feet long) was laid over the flight deck and 'dog leash' grabs were fitted to the undercarriages to grip the net on landing, check speed and prevent the aircraft from being blown over the side after losing flying speed. An experimental set of retarding gear originally fitted proved unsuccessful in rough weather landing trials carried out in 1920, but with the modified equipment 80 per cent of 500 subsequent trial landings were entirely satisfactory. Although the clear flight deck was ideal for operating aircraft the arrangement of the uptakes absorbed a great deal of internal space and also caused considerable heating in the hangar spaces, while absence of clear all-round view from the navigating position made handling of the ship a difficult matter at times.

It is perhaps useful at this point to refer briefly to means adopted during the war for operating aircraft from ships other than carriers. In the summer of 1915 some light cruisers of the Harwich Force had large platforms for launching seaplanes fitted over the forecastle along the lines of the 1912 tests. These were very cumbersome and completely masked the forecastle guns and they were removed after a short time. During 1917–18 the majority of capital ships in the

Grand Fleet were fitted with small platforms over one or more turrets with runways extending out over the guns. A Bristol Fighter was carried on these platforms and by steaming the ship fast head to wind it was able to take-off with the length of run provided. It could not of course land on board again and it was frequently necessary for the pilot to crash-land in the sea close alongside where he could be picked up and the engine possibly salved as well. In some cases the importance of the mission was considered sufficient to compensate for the loss of the aircraft.

The platforms and runways formed an integral part of the turret concerned and did not interfere with the guns. Various arrangements for carrying single aircraft were also adopted in certain light cruisers and included forecastle platforms raised well clear of bow guns, hangar below bridge from which aircraft could take-off, standing by, steaming ship fast head to wind and revolving platform amidships.

Some important operations were carried out by British carriers during the Great War, including: the famous raid on Cuxhaven on 25 December 1914 by three packet carriers, three aircraft were recovered of the nine flown off; the raid on Hoyer in March 1916 by *Vindex*, two of five aircraft recovered; the raid on Tondern, May 1916 by two packet carriers, one of the two aircraft recovered. The Short seaplane from *Ben-My-Chree* torpedoed and sank a Turkish minesweeper in the Dardanelles in August 1915, the first ship to be sunk by aerial torpedo. *Engadine*, attached to the battlecruiser fleet,

Grand Fleet, made reconnaissance flights during the early stage of the Battle of Jutland on 31 May 1916 but accomplished nothing because of poor visibility. The raid on the Zeppelin sheds at Tondern by aircraft from *Furious* in July 1918 was the most successful air raid of the war. Losses comprised: *Ben My Chree* sunk by Turkish batteries, January 1917; *Campania* sunk in collision with the battleship *Royal Oak* at Scapa, November 1918.

At the end of 1918 British carrier strength totalled ten ships of which only one, *Argus*, could be regarded as fully satisfactory for all-round aircraft operations, but her speed (20 knots) was too slow for fleet work. Of the others *Ark Royal* was actually nothing more than a seaplane tender, the seven packet carriers had very limited range and capacity and were unable to land their aircraft. *Furious*, however, possessed excellent speed and range and had adequate aircraft-carrying capacity, but the aircraft could only land on her with great difficulty so she was unsuitable for general carrier service. The cruiser *Vindictive* suffered from a similar disability and was in fact not officially rated as a carrier. It should be noted that all these ships were converted types, not designed as a carrier from keel up. During 1919 all the packet carriers with the exception of *Pegasus* reverted to mercantile service.

Prior to 1920 aircraft carrier construction was confined almost entirely to the Royal Navy. The Germans relied on the Zeppelin airships for both military and naval work and the other powers appear to have adopted the policy of 'wait and see'. But there was no doubt by this time that the aircraft carrier represented a perfectly practicable, useful type which had come to stay, and in 1920 carrier construction began in the USA and Japan.

In April 1920 the first British post-war carrier, *Eagle*, began trials. She had been laid down in February 1913 by Armstrong-Whitworth as the Chilean battleship *Almirante Cochrane*. All work ceased on the outbreak of war in August 1914 and the ship lay on the slip until February 1918 when she was purchased by the Admiralty for conversion to aircraft carrier. The conversion began immediately and was completed in September 1923. As a result of the trials that had been carried out in *Argus*, *Eagle* was given an island superstructure, with tripod mast and two funnels on the extreme starboard side of the

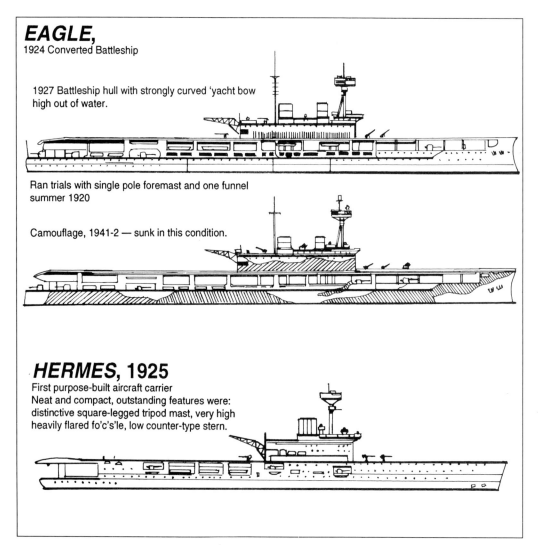

EAGLE,
1924 Converted Battleship

1927 Battleship hull with strongly curved 'yacht bow high out of water.

Ran trials with single pole foremast and one funnel summer 1920

Camouflage, 1941-2 — sunk in this condition.

HERMES, 1925
First purpose-built aircraft carrier
Neat and compact, outstanding features were: distinctive square-legged tripod mast, very high heavily flared fo'c's'le, low counter-type stern.

flight deck, an arrangement which proved quite satisfactory and has since been generally adopted in preference to the *Argus* plan. With a displacement of 22,600 tons, *Eagle* was on completion the largest carrier extant although her capacity (21 aircraft) was relatively small and her speed (25 to 26 knots) was insufficient for fleet work. Her flight deck was 667 feet long by 100 feet wide and extended the full length of hull and was wider than any previous British aircraft carrier.

On her first trials run during the summer of 1920, in a very incomplete condition, without armament or fore funnel, tripod or masts, the ship turned out only a qualified success and, as a carrier, inferior to *Argus*. As a consequence modifications were effected from March 1921 to September 1923 and these considerably enhanced her all-round value and as modified she proved very satisfactory although her speed was still too slow for modern requirements and her aircraft capacity was small in relation to displacement.

One of the most important innovations and improvements in the design was the downward curve at the tail of the flight deck which greatly facilitated safe landing.

Eagle was followed in 1924 by *Hermes*, the first aircraft carrier to be designed and built as such. With a displacement of only 10,850 tons, speed of 25 knots and capacity for fifteen aircraft, this ship embodied the moderate dimensions theory as applied to carriers and, within the limits of the design, turned out very well although again her speed was too low for fleet work under modern conditions, and experience indicated that all essential carrier requirements

could not be fulfilled on this displacement. Full advantage was taken of the experience gained with *Furious* and *Argus* in 1918, and improvements were effected after Hermes was laid down which resulted in considerable delay in completion. Special features of the design included: 1. Exceptionally high forecastle with heavy 'flare' continuous over the whole length and lower counter stern. 2. Novel type of square-legged tripod mast (the exact purpose of this is not clear). 3. Boat stowage inboard with fixed overhead derricks instead of davits. In service the ship proved very satisfactory within the limits of the design, but was found to be too small for efficient handling of aircraft; she was a splendid sea boat and remarkably steady; in fact, she proved a better sea boat than all the other British carriers prior to *Ark Royal* in 1939.

In 1925 *Furious* emerged from her third and final modifications with a clear end-to-end flight deck and arrangements similar to *Argus*, being the last British carrier to have the unobstructed flight deck.

The last of the British conversions were the large cruisers *Courageous* and *Glorious*, half-sisters to *Furious*, which were taken in hand for conversion to carrers in 1923–4 and completed in 1928 and 1930 respectively. Both these ships embodied the island superstructure arrangement as opposed to the clear flight deck in *Furious*. In contrast to the early carriers the armament comprised nothing heavier than 4.7in (large DP) and marked the final abandonment by the Admiralty of any idea that carriers might be capable of engaging surface vessels larger than torpedo-boat destroyers, and the acceptance of the theory that

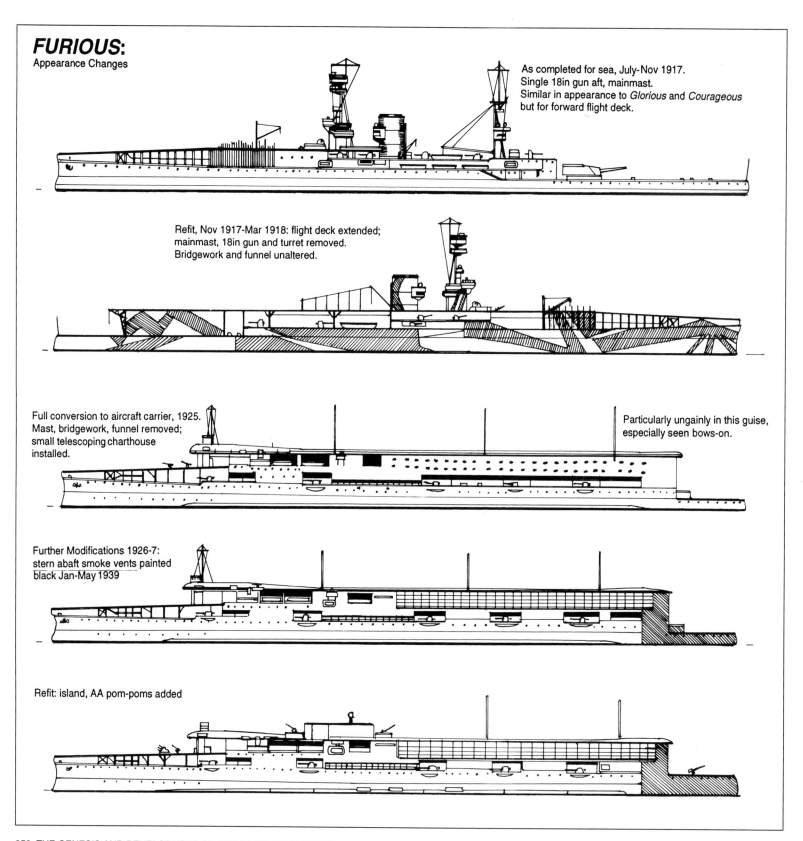

FURIOUS:
Appearance Changes

As completed for sea, July-Nov 1917.
Single 18in gun aft, mainmast.
Similar in appearance to *Glorious* and *Courageous*
but for forward flight deck.

Refit, Nov 1917-Mar 1918: flight deck extended;
mainmast, 18in gun and turret removed.
Bridgework and funnel unaltered.

Full conversion to aircraft carrier, 1925.
Mast, bridgework, funnel removed;
small telescoping charthouse
installed.

Particularly ungainly in this guise,
especially seen bows-on.

Further Modifications 1926-7:
stern abaft smoke vents painted
black Jan-May 1939

Refit: island, AA pom-poms added

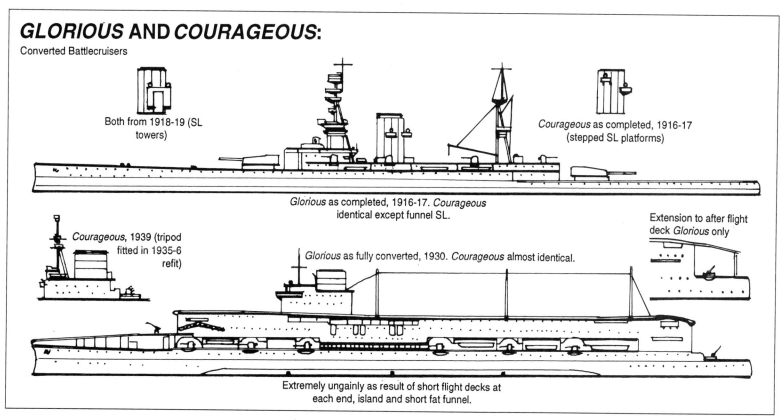

GLORIOUS AND COURAGEOUS:

Converted Battlecruisers

Both from 1918-19 (SL towers)

Courageous as completed, 1916-17 (stepped SL platforms)

Glorious as completed, 1916-17. *Courageous* identical except funnel SL.

Courageous, 1939 (tripod fitted in 1935-6 refit)

Glorious as fully converted, 1930. *Courageous* almost identical.

Extension to after flight deck *Glorious* only

Extremely ungainly as result of short flight decks at each end, island and short fat funnel.

they should rely mainly on their own aircraft and escorting ships for protection against surface attack by cruisers or capital ships. Prior to this there had been considerable confusion of thought both at home and abroad on this question, and calibres up to 8in had been mounted in US and Japanese carriers although the Admiralty had never gone above 6in.

During the immediate post-war period various proposals were put forward for battleship and cruiser carrier types in which the functions of the respective types were combined usually by mounting a 50 per cent normal gun armament forward and devoting the after part of the ship to aircraft (see design notes). The obvious disadvantages of such a type soon became apparent, however, and none ever materialized with the exception of the small Swedish cruiser carrier *Gotland*, completed in 1927 – the only vessel of the type actually designed and built as such, she proved a limited success.

Following the completion of *Courageous* and *Glorious*, British carrier construction was suspended until 1935 when *Ark Royal* was laid down and completed in 1938. The design of this ship, the first large purpose-built British fleet carrier embodied experience gained with the preceding converted ships and formed the basis for development of a new series of fleet carriers of the *Illustrious* and *Indomitable* classes.

The final design was approved on 21 June 1934 and was prepared in close collaboration with the Air Ministry. Alternative plans considered ranged from 12,000 to 24,000 tons which showed that a small ship would be relatively very expensive because of the limited aircraft capacity, and that all major requirements could be satisfied on a displacement of 22,000 tons which was accordingly approved. The Washington Treaty restrictions still in force limited standard carrier displacement of 27,000 tons and total carrier tonnage to 135,000 tons, conditions

which made it desirable that each individual ship have a large aircraft capacity. For some time prior to the expiration of the Washington Treaty the Admiralty had advocated a reduction in the individual displacement limit to 22,000 tons, *Ark Royal*'s design being influenced to some extent by anticipation that this would be the maximum agreed upon if the Treaty were renewed. The London Treaty of 1936, however, which replaced the Washington Treaty, fixed a maximum at 23,000 tons and *Ark Royal* was correspondingly below the permitted limit

The principal features of the design included:
1. Incorporation of flight deck in hull structure and short waterline length, with very long overhang of flight deck aft, combining an easily manoeuvred hull with great length of deck for flying operations.
2. Exceptionally roomy hangars with about 20 per cent greater capacity than in the *Courageous* class, and especially elaborate fire-fighting equip-

ment. Provision of three fast-running double platform lifts ensuring rapid delivery of aircraft from hangars to flight deck with two catapults for launching aircraft if ship were not under way.
3. Location of entire armament high up, at flight deck level, giving wide sky arcs and maximum fighting efficiency in rough weather.
4. Three-shaft machinery arrangement providing economy in weight and space and materially assisting manoeuvrability.

The flight deck was approximately 62 feet above the waterline, 800 feet long x 95 feet, and extended from the stem to 40 feet beyond the

stern. The forward and after extremities were rounded down to improve air flow over the deck and assist flying on and off. Arrester wires were fitted at the after end with the usual longitudinal and transverse windscreens (hinged down flush with deck when not in use) forward to protect aircraft preparing for flight. The funnel was specially designed and stiffened to obviate any necessity for guys which would impede flying space. On trials the smoke was found to come down low over the deck and obscure the landing area, but this was overcome by raising the funnel by eight feet.

The following *Illustrious* class were a slightly enlarged version of *Ark Royal*, but not necessarily an improved version because of the fact that *Ark Royal* was still under construction when the plans for *Illustrious* were being prepared and any failings on the part of the former were not yet manifest. In the older aircraft carriers including *Ark Royal* to some extent, the hangars and flight deck were essentially superstructure in that the hull was structurally a complete unit and the rest was simply added above it. In *Illustrious*, however, the armoured flight deck together with the armoured hangar sides formed an integral part of

Left: Looking down on the converted *Almirante Cochrane* – HMS *Eagle* – in the Mediterranean during the spring of 1930. Note the layout of the flight-deck and position of the aircraft lifts.

the strength of the hull – forming as it were a gigantic girder running longitudinally through the ship.

Designed by Sir Arthur W. Johns and prepared in the spring of 1936, the sketch plans were approved by the Board extremely quickly, in fact, in only three months. The provision of an armoured flight deck had not previously been contemplated, but was adopted at the insistence of the Controller, Admiral Sir Reginald Henderson, who was also mainly responsible for the rapid preparation and approval of the design. The reduced aircraft capacity in the design (36) and provision of single instead of upper and lower hangars as in *Ark Royal* was the result of the increased top weight of the armoured flight deck although there was a maximum capacity of 54 aircraft when the flight deck was fully loaded.

Illustrious and her sisters *Formidable* and *Victorious* proved very successful carriers and stood up exceptionally well under extremely hard and constant war service. From the converted steam packets of the Great War through to the Second World War's *Illustrious* class, the Fleet Air Arm had come a long way and had proved not only that it was a force to be reckoned with, but that in fact the carrier had completely taken over the role of the capital ship.

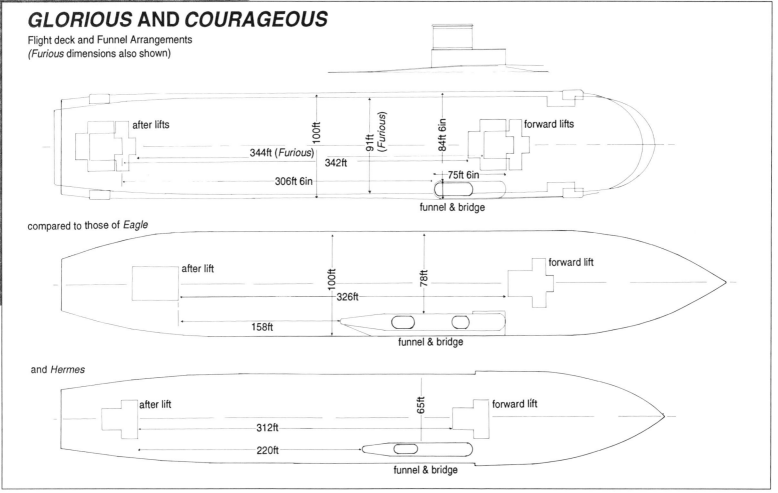

GLORIOUS AND COURAGEOUS

Flight deck and Funnel Arrangements
(*Furious* dimensions also shown)

after lifts / forward lifts
100ft
91ft (*Furious*)
84ft 6in
344ft (*Furious*)
342ft
306ft 6in
75ft 6in
funnel & bridge

compared to those of *Eagle*

after lift / forward lift
100ft
78ft
326ft
158ft
funnel & bridge

and *Hermes*

after lift / forward lift
65ft
312ft
220ft
funnel & bridge

Left: The newest carrier in the Royal Navy at the outbreak of war in 1939. The design of *Ark Royal* was the culmination of many years of experiments on *Furious*, *Courageous* and *Glorious*. This rare shot shows her in Gibraltar, November 1940.

ARK ROYAL, 1937
As completed - note short funnel

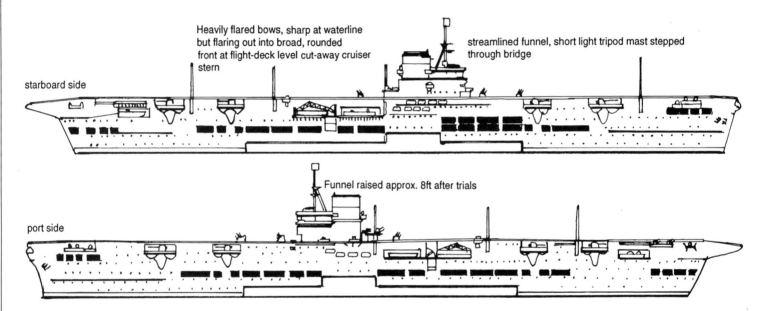

Heavily flared bows, sharp at waterline but flaring out into broad, rounded front at flight-deck level cut-away cruiser stern

streamlined funnel, short light tripod mast stepped through bridge

starboard side

Funnel raised approx. 8ft after trials

port side

Ark Royal
Displacement (tons): 22,000 (load), 27,500 (deep).
Laid down by Cammell Laird 16.9.1935, launched 13.4.1937, commissioned December 1938.
Dimensions: Length 721ft 6in (wl), 800ft (flight deck). Beam 94ft 9in 97ft (flight deck). Draught 23ft (normal), 27ft 6in (deep).
Armament: 16 x 4.5in dual-purpose HA/LA, 32 x 2pdr (as completed), 32 x 0.5in MG.
Aircraft
Capacity 72 (6 Squadrons carried) (4 T/S/R).
Armour
Main belt 4¹/₂in, deck 2¹/₂–3¹/₂in 3¹/₂–2¹/₄in, bulkheads 2¹/₂in.
Machinery
Parsons geared turbines driving 3 propellers.
Boilers: 6 Admiralty 3-drum in three compartments.
SHP: 102,000 for 30¹/₂ knots.
Fuel: 4,620 tons oil
Complement: 860 RN, 770 FAA.
Fate: Torpedoed about 30 miles from Gibraltar by *U81*.

Hit below bridge but only one rating killed.
Started to sink slowly from 15.40 hours on 13 November 1941, but after getting all her crew off (1,540 saved by destroyer *Legion*) did not finally sink until 06.13 hours on 14 November.

Illustrious Class (3 ships)
Construction
Illustrious: Vickers; laid down 27.4.1937; launched 5.4.1939; commissioned 16.4.1940.
Victorious: Vickers: 4.5.1937; launched: 14.9.1939; commissioned March 1941. *Formidable*: Harland & Wolff; laid down 17.6.1937; launched 17.8.1939; commissioned Oct. 1940.
Displacement (tons): 23,100 (as designed) *Illustrious* 27,950 (on trials), 28,210 (deep), 31,190 (deep) by 1946.
Dimensions
Length 673ft (pp), 740–743ft (oa).
Beam 95ft
Draught: 24ft load, 27ft 6in deep.

Armament
16 x 14.5in DP
48 x 2pdr
8 x 20mm AA
Aircraft
Capacity for 36 as designed, later increased to 54, ranging from Swordfish, Albacores, Fulmars to Corsairs, Hellcats and Fireflys throughout their careers. (Many other types carried.)
Armour
Main belt 4¹/₂in; Hangar sides 4¹/₂in; Flight deck 3¹/₂in; Outside hangar was 3–1in 'D' quality steel;
Partial bulkhead at ends 2¹/₂in NC; 3in over steering gear.
Machinery
Parsons geared turbines driving 3 propellers.
Boilers: 6 Admiralty 3-drum, 400psi.
SHP: 110,000 for 31 knots
Fuel: 4,800 tons oil.
Cost: original estimate (official) £4,050,000.

FURIOUS

DESIGN AND CONVERSION

Furious was the first battlecruiser type to be considered for conversion to an aircraft carrier and so she is dealt with before *Glorious* and *Courageous*. Her original design was developed to suit Lord Fisher's requirements for a slightly modified *Glorious* to enhance his projected Baltic operations. *Furious* differed only slightly from *Glorious* and *Courageous* in the way of main armament and was at first fitted with two 18in guns instead of four 15in. The secondary armament was also different with eleven 5.5in as against eighteen 4in in the earlier two. *Furious* was laid down to this design and was practically ready for trials in the spring of 1917. Her unsuitability in the role, however, made her the obvious choice for conversion to a much-needed aircraft carrier and discussions to work this out took place. It became all too obvious that the light unprotected framework and big guns did not make her suitable for battlefleet work and a hangar and forward flight deck were approved after the removal of the forward 18in gun and subsequent equipment. She completed in this guise. The conversion was recommended by a special Board appointed by Admiral David Beatty and the Grand Fleet Aircraft Committee in January 1917 to determine fleet policy, and was approved by the Admiralty in March 1917. The conversion although accepted was at first opposed by Beatty unless the ship could retain her two 18in guns, but this was overruled by the Board.

As a cruiser her value was at best problematical. As a carrier she had the size required, and the fast speed needed for manoeuvres with the Grand Fleet. Her design was otherwise unchanged and she entered service in July 1917. Her forward flying-off deck was approximately 228 feet x 50 feet with a hangar beneath it to accommodate aircraft and although the aircraft took off successfully they came down on the sea and were picked up by the converted packets *Nairana* and *Manxman*.

On 3 August 1917 Squadron Commander E. H. Dunning flying a Sopwith Pup powered by an 80hp le Rhone engine, achieved the first successful deck landing ever made on a ship at sea by side-slipping on to the forward landing deck. As the aircraft passed over the deck officers grabbed the undercarriage in a bid to haul it down in the right direction. At the second attempt, however, a tyre burst and the aircraft went over the side and Dunning was drowned. This mishap coupled with the fact that aircraft accommodation was insufficient, led to the removal of the remaining 18in gun and the fitting of an after flight deck. Gangways were fitted on each side of the funnel and superstructure to connect the landing and flying-off decks and the aircraft complement was more than doubled, the conversion being completed in March 1918. Arrester gear was fitted on the after landing deck comprising longitudinal steel hawsers stretched tight and ending at a ramp at the forward end of the deck. The Sopwith Pups were fitted with skids in place of wheels with hooks at the sides to catch in the wires and prevent the aircraft from going over the side. The hawsers were raised about one foot above the deck to enable the aircraft hooks to pass below and engage if the machine rose again after landing as could happen in a gust of wind. A large net was placed at the rear end of the funnel to prevent aircraft flying into it, but this was later replaced by vertical ropes. Because the funnels and superstructure were retained, however, the landings proved very hazardous as a consequence of serious eddies set up by these fittings, and the hot gases from the funnel. In

Right: *Furious* 1918. Converted to aircraft carrier in 1918 but still limited in practice because of the retention of the funnel and superstructure amidships. Note the small lift doors.

this guise there were a few successful if hazardous landings, but some aircraft broke up on landing or crashed forward and slipped over the side; the pilots had the choice of attempting to land on deck or come down on the water to be picked up later by crane. Not surprisingly many pilots chose the latter. *Furious* continued to serve as a flying-off carrier for the rest of the war and successfully delivered the first attack from a carrier on a land-based target, the Zeppelin sheds at Tondern. Seven Sopwith Camels attacked and destroyed two large sheds and three Zeppelins in July 1918. She was laid up after the war with her future in doubt, but given the great need of aircraft carriers in the Royal Navy it was proposed that she be fully converted to a carrier proper in March 1921.

The job problem fell to the DNC (Eustace Tennyson d'Eyncourt) who assured the Board that a suitable ship would evolve from the conversion. In a memo to the Board he pointed out the salient features:

'23rd March 1921.

The scheme provides for clearing the vessel down to the floor of the present hangar and building a double-decked hangar, with the fun-

nels led fore and aft at the sides of these hangars, eventually discharging at the stern, somewhat as in *Argus*.

The upper hangar can take 33 Sopwith Torpedo Carriers folded, and the lower hangar 28, total 61, or alternatives as shown on sheet 2.

Two lifts are provided to serve these hangars, and in addition machines can be taken out very quickly through the forward end of the upper hangar and flown-off at that level, so that machines may get away from three positions at the same time.

The Navigating Arrangements will be very much better than in *Argus*. A Wheelhouse will be provided on each side of the ship, with a platform outside giving a view right aft. The two houses will be connected by a Bridge or Gangway from which it will also be possible to look aft over the flying deck.

The armament will comprise ten 5.5in and six 4in H.A. guns, with control positions on each side of the ship.

Very much heavier anchors and cables will be supplied, but no alteration will be made in the power of the machinery or the fuel capacity. The present full speed of 31 knots will be maintained.

Accommodation will be arranged as a Flagship.

The flying-on deck with the two hangars will only be about 3 feet higher from the water than in *Argus*.'

GENERAL RECONSTRUCTION AS AN AIRCRAFT CARRIER

It was agreed that arrangements for landing aircraft would embody the results of the latest experience and reports from *Argus*, and such mechanical improvements to the arresting gear as emerged during the course of development. The length of the arresting wires would be approximately 350 feet.

1. The navigating arrangements would be fitted at the fore end of the upper hangar, somewhat as in *Argus*, duplicated on each side of the vessel with a gangway connection between them; these had a much better all-round view than could be obtained from a central position.

2. The siting of the standard magnetic compass was a matter of great difficulty, because of the influence of the ship's magnetic field, and necessitated experimental work before a decision was reached.

Furious, Legend

Displacement: (legend condition) 22,130 tons.
Length: 735ft (pp), 768ft 6in (oa).
Beam: 88ft (waterline), 170ft at navigating bridge.
Draught: 22ft 9in forward,
25ft 3in aft.
Width of flight deck: 92ft; length of flight deck: 576ft; length of upper flying-off deck; 150ft; length of lower flying-off deck: 200ft; area of lower hangar: 23,500 sq ft; area of upper hangar: 25,400 sq ft.
Armament: 10 x 5.5in, 6 x 4in, 4 x 2pdr.
Searchlights: 4 x 36in, 4 x 24in, 4 x 10in.
W/T: Type 36, Type 34, Type 9, DF type.
Endurance: 4,300 nm at 16 knots
Complement: 893 RN officers and men; with 24 aircraft, 251 RAF personnel; with 36 aircraft 325 RAF personnel.

Furious: GM and Stability, as inclined

Light condition: 1925 as carrier. 21,830 tons. GM: 3ft
Deep condition: 1925. 26,800 tons GM: 3.60ft
Light condition: 1932. 22,400 tons GM: 2.30ft
Deep condition: 1932. 27,125 tons GM: 2.91ft

	Stability range	Vanishes at
1925:	Light	52°
	Deep	65°
1932:	Light	50°
	Deep	62°

3. The principal armament proposed was ten 5.5in guns, five on each broadside, and six 4in HA guns, four forward and two aft.

4. No torpedo tubes were to be fitted.

5. The gunnery control positions were to be situated abreast the upper hangar just abaft the navigating positions. The port and starboard control were to be quite separate although the rangefinder in each position could be elevated for use on either side of the ship.

6. The proposed searchlight equipment consisted of four 36in searchlights with Evershed Control and rod control up to 90°; four 24in signalling searchlights and a number of 10in searchlights.

7. The considerable rise in freeboard, offering a much greater exposed wind surface, necessitated, as in *Argus*, much heavier anchors and cables than would be required for the vessel's displacement and this necessitated considerable alterations forward.

8. The machinery and boiler room installations remained below water as before, but in addition to the new horizontal funnel arrangements for discharging gases aft, considerable modifications were required to the arrangement of trunks and fans for supplying air to these spaces, and for engine room exhaust.

9. The matter of boats caused considerable difficulties. It was not possible to carry the complement of boats usually assigned to a vessel of this size and it was necessary to supply a larger proportion of rafts.

Bulk stowage was provided in two separate compartments (one forward and one aft) for 24,000 gallons of petrol and 4,000 gallons of lubricating oil. Steam pumps delivered the petrol to the hangars and to positions on the flight deck. A special room was provided in which to apply dope to aircraft fabric.

Two large hangars were provided, one above the other. The lower hangar was irregular in shape and contained store rooms, workshops and offices, etc. Its internal width varied from 35 feet to 50 feet and it was approximately 550 feet long. The width of the upper hangar was 50 feet and it was approximately 520 feet long. The minimum clear height in each hangar was 15 feet. The hangars were sub-divided for fire purposes by steel roller blinds or curtains. At the forward end of the upper hangar large hinged doors were fitted to enable machines of up to 50ft wing span to fly straight out. This position, together with the two positions on the flight deck in the vicinity of the lifts, gave three flying-off positions. Two lifts, serving both upper and lower hangars, were installed, each able to take a 46ft-long aircraft of 47ft wing span (35ft, wings folded).

The length of deck available for fitting arresting gear was about 340 feet. Safety nets were provided on each side, and although palisading was not indicated on the original design, it was planned for a later date. Cranes were provided at the after end of the ship for the working of seaplanes and amphibians.

The gunnery and searchlight control were centralized and duplicated on each side of the vessel. The navigating arrangements were duplicated on each side with a branch communication to a protected lower conning tower from which the ship would be steered. The chart-house, signal offices, sea cabin, etc., were all arranged in the vicinity of the bridge and adjacent to a cross-gangway connecting the two navigating positions. The nose of the upper flight deck was rounded off, after experiments at the NPL

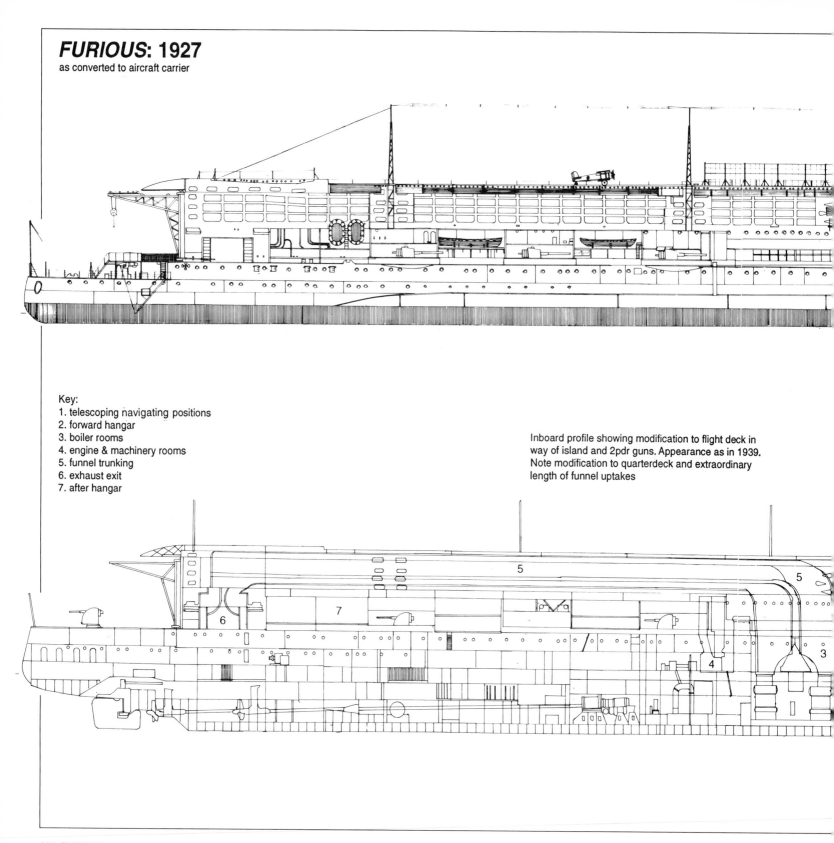

FURIOUS: 1927
as converted to aircraft carrier

Key:
1. telescoping navigating positions
2. forward hangar
3. boiler rooms
4. engine & machinery rooms
5. funnel trunking
6. exhaust exit
7. after hangar

Inboard profile showing modification to flight deck in
way of island and 2pdr guns. Appearance as in 1939.
Note modification to quarterdeck and extraordinary
length of funnel uptakes

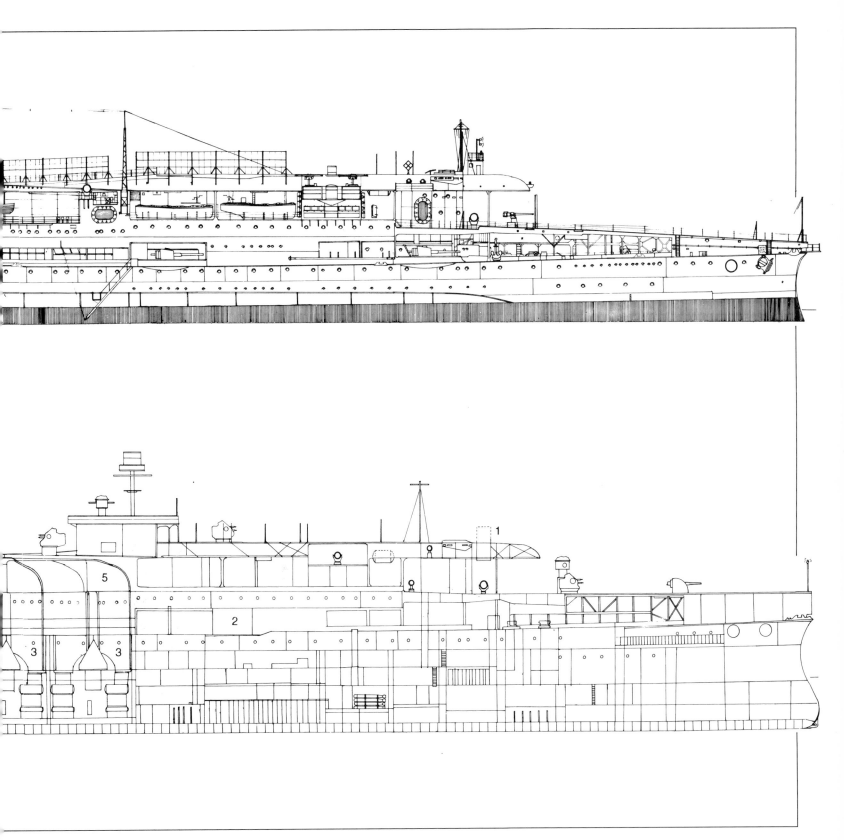

Below: *Furious* at high speed in 1928. Having a fair turn of speed, *Furious* proved successful in her new role and could operate with all the capital ships or cruisers.

showed that there was a tendency for steadier aerodynamic conditions to prevail [with such a form for small angles of yaw of the wind]. Endurance with the existing fuel was 4,300 nautical miles at 16 knots, but it was hoped that this could be increased. Ample accommodation was provided for the aircraft personnel. The entire reconstruction took from June 1921 until September 1925 and she emerged from the dockyard in a very different form indeed. Throughout the next ten years she was in constant use for experiments and tests and much experience was gained towards improving the Royal Navy's wings at sea.

ALTERATIONS IN AIRCRAFT EQUIPMENT

To reach the stage of being a carrier proper was a lengthy process as far as *Furious* was concerned, and the following notes will show that the techniques of using aircraft at sea were a matter of trial and error.

Furious completed in 1917 as a carrier-cruiser with a hangar fitted forward of the bridge and a flying-off deck over this. The flying-off deck was about 220 feet long and sloped downwards, tapering to a point at the stem. Collapsible palisades were fitted along the sides and across the deck to protect the aircraft while they were being prepared for flight. Two derricks (port and starboard) were fitted to handle the aircraft and a single lift was fitted at the after end of the hangar. As completed in this role *Furious* carried three Short seaplanes and five Sopwith Pups (folded wings) which could be brought up from the hangar and flown off in about three minutes apiece.

The seaplanes were easily flown-off by the 'trolley and rail' method in which floats mounted as a trolley running along a slotted tube in the deck were caught at the end of the run by a device which prevented it going overboard. Flying-off operations proved successful during the autumn of 1917 but landing back proved to be disastrous. The first successful landing on the ship was made on 3 August 1917, but it highlighted the unsuitability of landing aircraft on the forward part of the ship. Further conversion made the ship into a carrier proper when a landing-on deck was fitted over the quarterdeck (November 1917 to March 1918). The forward flying-off deck remained the same, but another hangar was fitted aft of the funnel which gave her a capacity for about twenty aircraft. A lift was set slightly to starboard at the after end of the hangar. The landing deck was connected to the flying-off platform by a narrow curved runway on each side of the funnel. The seaplanes were transferred from one deck to the other by means of a trolley on rails.

The first aircraft shipped after these modifications had in place of wheels skids which slid along troughs laid over the flying deck. Primitive 'arrester wires' were laid over the landing deck and a 'stopping net' was fitted across the deck immediately abaft the funnel to stop any aircraft that overran the deck on landing.

Air eddies set up by the superstructure and funnel, however, still tended to make landing difficult when the ship was under way so the carrier was seen as only a qualified success in this respect. It was reported that only a few landings were ever made in this guise and the older method of coming down on the water and being hoisted aboard was reverted to in many cases. With the completion of the carrier *Argus* no more landings were carried out on *Furious*.

The problems with air eddies had been looked into as far back as 1917 when a proposal for securing a clear flight deck by use of telescoping funnels and an elevator for the charthouse had been submitted by Armstrongs, but the Admiralty was not interested in this and none of the usual experiments were approved.

Furious was finally taken in hand for conversion into a full carrier (June 1921 to September 1925) when the funnel, superstructure and masts were removed and she was given a clear flight deck throughout three-quarters the length of the hull. The forward section sloped slightly upwards to slow down the aircraft, which had no brakes at that time. Arrester wires were abandoned. The flight deck was almost as high from the waterline as the original funnel had been, and some 30 feet higher than the original flying-off deck as fitted in 1918. Many steel barricades (known as palisades) were fitted along the sides of the flight deck to prevent aircraft from going over the side. The original flying-off platform forward (considerably below the main flying-off deck) was retained as a 'take-off' platform and was intended to fly off small fighters from the fore end. Aircraft could be flown-off from both deck levels, those from the lower deck turning to starboard and those from the main upper deck going over to port. At the forward end of the flight deck was fitted a telescoping charthouse which could be lowered until the top was flush with the deck level. Collapsible palisades were fitted around the deck over half its length and they folded down into recesses when not in use. Two 15ft-high hangars were provided: upper 520ft x 50ft, lower 550ft x 35–50ft, which were sectioned off by large steel roller shutters (electrically operated and fireproof).

The funnel uptakes from the boilers were carried well out on each beam, but they took up much valuable space which could have otherwise been used for aircraft facilities so the aircraft capacity was not as great as had been envisaged.

As can be seen from the official records (original legend, etc.) provision was made for about 60 aircraft but as completed *Furious* never seems to have carried more than 36.

During reconstruction there had been plans to give her a large funnel at one side of the flying-off deck, like the USS *Lexington* and *Saratoga*, but as *Furious* was too far advanced at the time of submitting the proposal, it was not done; *Glorious* and *Courageous* were later modified to have this form of fume extraction.

Although she was re-rated as an escort carrier in 1942, *Furious* continued to serve until as late as 1947, proving that her conversion had more than justified the contention that she was 'value for money'.

ARMOUR

Practically no protection beyond that given to a large, light cruiser except flight deck (⁵⁄₈in) and underwater bulges similar to those as fitted to the battleship *Royal Oak* (rather large, full-bellied bulges).
Main belt: 2in HT plus 1in MS
Bulkheads: 3in–2in
Protective deck: 1in–³⁄₄in
Flight deck: ⁵⁄₈in
Funnel uptakes: 1in at opening, then mild steel casing.
Longitudinal screens outside bulkheads abreast engine and boiler rooms: 1in.

ARMAMENT

Originally designed to carry two single 18in guns, one forward, one aft, but provision was made to change over to two twin 15in in each turret if required. The single 18in gun, still fitted aft at this time, was not at all successful because, being only lightly framed, the hull of the ship was liable to be badly shaken. Moreover, a single gun was not suitable for modern requirements nor was the rate of fire up to much.

Just prior to her trials it was decided to stiffen the bows of the ship because of weakness found in *Glorious* and *Courageous*. While undergoing

Armament as completed, 1917:
1 x 18in 40cal Mk I
11 x 5.5in
2 x 3in AA (singles)
2 x 3pdr
2 x 21in TT (on part-conversion 1918, 16 x 21in above water tubes added, (two each side on upper deck)

1925:
10 x 5.5in
6 x 4in
4 x 3pdr
4 MG
10 x Lewis.

1939:
12 x 4in HA/LA Mk XVI (400rpg) Mk XIX mountings
4 pom-poms Mark M. Mk VII mountings
2 x 0.5in MG mountings (4 barrels)
4 x 3pdr saluting
4 x MG.
From 1939 onwards the armament remained virtually unaltered except the addition of approximately 22 x 20mm being added.

this refit it was decided to convert her to a 'cruiser-carrier' type. The forward turret and barbette were removed and a flight deck was fitted forward.

Her secondary armament of eleven 5.5in was a new size for the Royal Navy, having first appeared in the cruisers *Chester* and *Birkenhead* which had been taken over from Greece in 1914. Spare guns from these two ships were utilized for *Furious* and later the battlecruiser *Hood*. After conversion her secondary armament still consisted of the 5.5in guns, but various AA guns were added and removed over a period of time (see appearance changes).

During the early thirties it was decided that guns that could not fire at both low- and high-level targets had no place at sea (secondary armament) and it was decided to fit *Furious* with a more suitable AA defence. A meeting was held in the Director of Ordnance's room on 8 June 1936 to discuss this issue. It had long been agreed that the new gun should be the latest 4in HALA piece in twin mounts, but the problem was where to put them so as to give them suitable arcs of fire against both air and surface targets. A method was suggested whereby most of the guns simply replaced the old 5.5in, but the DNO pointed out that this would not be suitable since: 1. The forward guns would severely blast the 2pdr pom-poms and their crews. 2. The mid-

Below: *Furious*'s port bow in Devonport, January 1932. Note the original cruiser bow highlighted in this view.

ships gun (in place of number 2 5.5in) would have very poor arcs of fire in elevation. 3. The after gun on the quarterdeck would be frequently untenable because of smoke.

More discussions followed and it was agreed to mount three guns on the lower flying-off deck: one amidships right forward and two P&S just forward of the present gun positions.

To mount one on the quarterdeck where suitable.

To adopt one of the following pom-pom positions: 1. Mount two pom-poms on the starboard side of the flight deck with a small control platform carrying the director between them. 2. To mount two pom-poms on the flight deck, one each side, each with its director in the position it already occupied. 3. To mount four pom-poms with their directors on the flight deck, two each side.

It was realized that to accept the above would virtually create an island on the side of the flight deck, and flying-off from the lower platform would have to be abandoned. Great consideration was also given to ammunition supply and after more debate the following was finally agreed: 1. Three twin mountings fitted on the lower flying-off deck and one on the quarterdeck. 2. Two 2pdr M pom-poms, with their directors, to be fitted on an island on the starboard side of the flight deck. 3. Two 2pdr M pom-poms fitted at station 32, P&S. The directors for these to be the existing ones outside the wing navigating positions. 4. One HACSI fitted on the island on the starboard side of the flight deck and one on the lower flying-off deck. 5. Chain hoists fitted from the magazines. 6. Stowage provided as follows: 4in guns, 240 rpg (in bottle rack stowage); 2pdrs, 2,780rpg in the magazine and 400rp barrel in ready-use stowage.

The following equipment was removed: 1. Three single 4in HA guns (two from lower flying-off deck and one from the quarterdeck; 2. Two 2pdr from lower flying-off deck; 3. 5.5in guns and their ammunition from No 1 position;

4. Hangar doors from forward end of upper hangar (plated in afterwards); 5. Sponsons to existing single 4in mountings. 6. Wind screens on lower flying-off deck and operating gear.

MACHINERY

Being completed as large, light cruisers they were naturally fitted to give a good turn of high speed. It was stipulated very early in their design that their main function would be to outrun almost anything that floated, large or small, and this was to make them that much more suitable when considering their reconstruction as fully fledged aircraft carriers. They were fitted with small-tube boilers and were the first large warships to have geared turbines (*Furious*, *Glorious* and *Courageous*).

As completed *Furious* never underwent a full set of sea trials because of war restrictions and unfortunately there are no full sets of figures available to show how she performed in her early cruiser carrier role.

On reconstruction in 1925, although trials were carried out, very few speed figures were recorded, the performance of the engines apparently being much more important. Although the ship's cover does not show a speed for full power runs, official data elsewhere states that she made 30.06 knots with 90,600shp on 321 revolutions per minute. After her machinery/boiler installations were refurbished in 1931 further steam trials were carried out in 1932 (see table).

On completion as a carrier in 1925 she was reported to be 'rather light' and prone to roll more than she should (as a consequence of weight removal during refit). Her condition did improve shortly afterwards, but it is unclear whether she was given some sort of ballast or not.

SEA TRIALS AS AIRCRAFT CARRIER, 1925

Her reconstruction as an aircraft carrier completed, she naturally underwent a full set of sea trials:
Monday 31 August: Inspection at 10.00 hours by Admiral Superintendent.
Tuesday 1 September: Commissioned for sea.
Thursday 3 September: Finish fuelling.
Monday 7 September: Move vessel into North Dock from basin.
Wednesday 9 September: Leave Sound and carry out 8-hour full power trials. Gunnery trials and paravane trials also to take place while at sea. Anchor in Sound on completion of trials.
On 7 September the 10-knot trials were carried out:

Run	Speed (knots)	SHP
1:	10.105	3,073
2:	9.527	2,731
3:	10.404	3.243
4:	9.288	2.855

During the trials smoke was ejected through the side openings and the effect on the quarterdeck and hangars was very bad. To prevent smoke getting into the hangars the after fire curtain had to be closed. Observations of deflection of bulkheads and temperature in hangars were taken during the trial, also tests with draughts through the hangars and various arrangements with the fire curtains and lifts, etc. (see table). During full power trials smoke got up through the flight deck but had very little effect on the quarterdeck or hangar. Trials of the hangar doors were successful, and the doors could be opened and closed in about ten seconds. Full power trials took more than two hours to develop and the mean SHP reached was 91,485 on a displacement of 23,900 tons but no speeds were logged (30.03 knots by bearings).

Effect of draught through hangars:

1. Lifts at flight deck. Hangar doors fully open. All fire curtains clear. Wind screens outside hangar doors up.	Slight draught through hangars of about 2–3mph. Sulphur fumes in hangar Quarterdeck clear of smoke.
2. As above except windscreen down.	Wind through upper hangar 15mph (after end). No fumes in hangar. Temperature fell considerably.
3. Forward lift at flight deck and after lift at upper hangar deck. All fire curtains cleared except at 75 upper hangar, which was closed. Windscreens up.	Wind speed at after end off lower hangar. Slight draught about 3mph. Lower hangar and quarterdeck quite clear; upper hangar no fumes or draught. Temperature rising.
4. As above (3) except wind-screen down.	Wind speed in lower hangar 16 mph. Both hangars and decks quite clear of fumes. Temperatures rising in upper hangar. No draught in upper hangar.

It was seen from these trials that so long as there was a slight draught through the hangars the fumes were kept clear of the ship, but when there was no draught at all, the fumes found their way up through the lift well into the upper hangar. When the curtains were closed in some cases the temperature in the hangar rose very rapidly.

ENGINE AND BOILER ROOM REFIT

Propelling machinery:
All turbine rotors lifted, HPs completely rebladed, LPs ahead and astern partially rebladed.
Carbon packing renewed, manoeuvring valves fitted.
Gear wheels and pinions examined and teeth trimmed.
Propeller shafting aligned and stern tubes re-wooded.
Main thrust blocks opened out and pad pieces refitted.
Underwater fittings examined and renewed if necessary.
Main condensers examined and new doors fitted.
New glands, sectional valves, etc., renewed.
All auxiliary machinery checked and renewed where necessary.
Boilers:
Boilers, 18 in number, were re-tubed and new circular water pockets fitted. Boiler casings mod-

Full Power steam trials after complete renewal of machinery parts and boilers re-tubed during 1932 (see list for work done).
Trial: English Channel. 16 February 1932. (4 hour)
Draught: 26ft 4$\frac{1}{2}$in forward, 26ft 1in aft.
Displacement: 24,970 tons.
Bottom of ship: slightly foul.
Wind: 20 kts.
Sea: 4 to 5 slight swell.
Fuel: Consumption per HP per hour: 1.15lb; pressure (oil): 124psi
Propellers: 3-bladed.
11ft 6in diameter
11ft 6in pitch
Total expanded area of each prop: 78ft 6in
Surface: bright
Immersion of upper edge at commencement of trials: inner: 13ft 4$\frac{7}{8}$in, outer: 13ft 0$\frac{1}{8}$in.
Revolutions: inner shaft: port 314.1, starboard 318.4; outer shaft: port 315.2, starboard 319.1.
Mean of all shafts: 316.7
Shaft Horse Power: inner shaft: port 22,841, starboard: 22,813; outer shaft port 22,213, starboard: 21,887.
Total SHP: 45,054 port, 44,700 starboard; 89,754shp.
Speed (taken by bearings, not log): 28.8 knots.

Below: The boiler room of *Furious*. Like all warships with large machinery installations, a close watch was necesssary at high speeds in case of mechanical failure – it was no easy task to keep this lot in good order, as any old stoker will tell you.

ified to suit new water pockets. Brickwork renewed. Uptakes repaired where necessary. New feed valves fitted. Oil fuel heaters re-tubed. New feed heaters fitted. Modification to boiler fronts and new type of oil fuel sprayers fitted. Durability of boilers: steam reservoirs, 5 years; water reservoirs, 10 years; boiler tubes, 7 years.

FLYING-OFF TRIALS

Spithead, 6 April 1925. *Furious*
The Director of Technical Development's deck landing and launching trials of new types of aircraft were begun in April 1925 and continued until the end of October. The following aircraft were tested:
Fairey IIID Seaplane with long V-bottomed wooden floats.
Fairey IIID Seaplane with long flat-bottomed wooden floats.

Fairey IIID Seaplane with short flat-bottomed dural floats.
Flycatcher Seaplane with long flat-bottomed dural floats.
Flycatcher Amphibian with V-bottomed floats and solid tyres.
Flycatcher aeroplane with skids.
Blackburn Seaplane with wooden floats.
Ferret Amphibian with V-bottomed floats and solid tyres.
Ferret Aeroplane (Jaguar).
Ferret Aeroplane (Jupiter).
Hendon Aeroplane.
Dart Aeroplane with overhead rail and axle guides.
Trials were also made with certain types of trollies for moving seaplanes about the deck hangars.
Fairey IIID Seaplane with long V-bottomed wooden floats:

This machine was picked up on the special handling trollies provided. Four trollies were used, two to each float. Each trolley had four wheels which could be adjusted to move in any direction. The trollies had drop axles which could be raised by a ratchet action and thus lift the seaplane. The trollies provided did not fit the particular seaplane and took a long time to adjust. The small wheels of the trollies led to difficulties in passing over the wind-screens, because of holes in the screens and various projections.

The seaplane was flown-off from in front of the wind-screen on the upper hangar deck using a quick release, the deck to the bow being covered with grease. For particulars of runs for launching and landing see table.

In flying-off the machine took the whole available length of run, and the pilot apparently did not pull her off the deck although he stated that he attempted to do so. It was thought that the distance of the step which was some way (about 12 inches) aft of the centre of gravity might make it difficult to tilt the aircraft to obtain the required angle of attack, but another pilot in the Fairey IIID flat-bottomed float experienced no difficulty in pulling the machine off.

In making landings the arresting gear was not used. The length of run when landing proved to be greater than had been anticipated from the trials of the Flycatcher Seaplane with flat-bottomed floats carried out in *Hermes* the previous year, and was actually greater than with wheels. This was possibly because of high speed of approach, and possibly because of the attitude of the machine, the long tail portion of the float preventing the tail coming down and thus limiting the angle of attack of the wings. Other factors that could have influenced the length of run when landing were the grease on the bottom of the floats adhering after flying-off, and approbable reduction in air velocity under the lower wing caused by the rise in the flight deck at the forward end. The wooden floats were protected with steel runners on the forward portion, but were unprotected on the tail portion. Surprisingly little damage was done to the floats despite passing over many projections on the decks. The unprotected tail portion received most of the damage.

After the first launching a second type of trolley, primarily intended as a launching trolley, was tried for moving the seaplane about. This trolley was in one piece and had four small wheels, two for each float. It was found to be quicker to use than the previous trolley, but needed several minutes to fit it, and experienced difficulty in passing over obstacles and the wind-screen. No launchings were made with this trolley. After the first two days, the trollies were no longer used and it was found possible to push the seaplanes about on the bare deck sufficiently quickly without them.

Fairey IIID with long flat-bottomed wooden floats:
This machine was flown off the upper hangar deck, using a greased deck and quick-release slip. For the first flight the entire available length was used, but on the rest of the launchings the

pilot pulled the machine off before the end of the deck. The third landing was a bad one, the machine coming in with drift. The after end of the port float touched the round down of the flight deck right aft and detached the brass tail-piece, and the machine slewed to port. Both floats touched the deck before crossing the step in the deck, well on the port side of the deck and making an angle of about 10° to the fore and aft line. If the aircraft had been an aeroplane (i.e., with a wheeled undercarriage) it would probably have gone over the side. Before reaching the deck edge the machine suddenly swerved to starboard and stopped. The arresting gear was not used, and this was the case, with a few exceptions, throughout the whole series of trials. The floats were more extensively damaged than in the

previous machine. The step of the float was damaged in pushing the machine over one of the stanchions round the lift opening. One of the float runners was detached by a lug on the deck used for bowsing down the arresting gear wires.

Fairey IIID Seaplane with short flat-bottomed dural floats:
This machine was flown-off the after end of the forward lift, without using a quick-release, in a 38½-knot relative wind. The machine lifted before reaching the wind-screen; approximate run 54 feet. No grease was used. The landings were good, and very little damage was done to the floats.
Flycatcher Seaplane with long flat-bottomed dural floats:

This machine made very good landings, and the dural floats stood up extraordinarily well to the rough treatment in passing over obstacles on the deck. The machine was flown-off both with and without using grease and no trouble was experienced in pulling off the greased deck.

Flycatcher Amphibian with V-bottomed floats and solid tyres:
This machine made a number of good landings without the arresting gear, the machine came practically to rest and the pilot then opened up the throttle and flew off again without the aircraft being man-handled. The new feature of this machine was the new shape of wooden V floats and the solid tyres. The deck landing qualities were quite satisfactory but the military load appears to have been reduced to practically nothing.

Flycatcher Aeroplane with skids:
This machine fitted with skids in lieu of wheels behaved perfectly satisfactorily. The intention was to add floats which could be shed during flight if necessary. The design of a float-cum-skid machine was investigated by Messrs. Fairey. The plane was flown-off after each landing except the first without being man-handled.

Blackburn Seaplane with wooden floats:
This machine made successful landings. The step and heel of the floats were damaged by obstacles on the deck. It is understood that this seaplane was unsatisfactory in getting off the water.

Ferrett Amphibian (Jaguar):
This machine made a number of very good landings without the arresting gear. The view from pilot's seat was satisfactory. It is understood that the machine was unsatisfactory in taking off from the water.

Ferret Aeroplane:
This machine behaved satisfactorily, both with the Jaguar and the Jupiter engines. The flexibility of the undercarriage, which in the previous *Argus* trials in September was pronounced, was not so prominent on this occasion, but still observable.

Hendon 2-seater Torpedo Aircraft:
Some trials with this machine were made in *Argus*, but were discontinued as the pilot was not getting the best out of the machine. The landings in *Furious* were more satisfactory. Owing to the high-lift slotted wings the landings are apt to be a bit bouncy.

Dart Torpedo Aircraft:
This machine was launched from the upper hangar deck using an overhead rail to support the tail and axle guides on the deck. The trials were for the purpose of testing the principle of flying-off machines in this manner, so that if successful a number of machines could be flown-off in rapid succession. The tail support was necessary to prevent the propeller striking the hangar roof. The tail dropped after leaving the overhead rail. The trials were successful, and it was considered sufficient to justify altering the hangar

Flying off Trials 1925

Machine	Weight (lbs)	Relative wind speed (knots)	Length of run (ft)	Remarks
Fairey III.D Seaplane, long V-bottom wood floats	4,874	40	70	Flown off U.H.D. using grease and Q.R. Swerved to starboard and hit stanchion stay eyebolt.
	4,862	38	95	Ran straight.
Fairey III.D. Seaplane, long flat-bottom wood floats	4,898	35	90	Flown off U.H.D. using grease and Q.R. Did not pull off deck.
	4,860	36	70	Hangar door shut. Did not pull off deck.
	4,837	37	60	H.D. open. Pulled off deck.
	4,638	35	50	H.D. shut. Pulled off deck.
Fairey III.D Seaplane, short dural flat-bottom floats	–	38½	54	From flight deck, no grease, no Q.R.
Flycatcher Seaplane, long flat-bottom dural floats	3,277	34	39	Pulled off from greased deck.
	3,253	31	30	Pulled off from greased deck.
	3,232	39	27	Pulled off from greased deck. Pulled off from ungreased deck.
Flycatcher Amphibian, with V-bottom flats & solid tyre	3,454	34	48	Using Q.R.
	3,447	35	60	Other launches were without Q.R. from position in which machine stopped.
Flycatcher (Jaguar) Aeroplane with skids.	2,732	31	30	Using Q.R. Other launches were made without manhandling from position machine landed in.
Blackburn Seaplane with wood floats.	6,232	37	98	Took off top of windscreen.
	6,302	32½	77	
Ferret Amphibian (Jaguar)	4,772	38	75	Using Q.R.
	4,761	36	84	Took off windscreen
	4,754	31	78	
	4,744	34	78	
	4,735	34	78	
Ferret Aeroplane (Jupiter)	4,228	28	84	
	4,221	28½	64	
	4,214	29	84	
	4,207	32	55	
	4,198	35	55	
	4,186	32	65	
Hendon Torpedo aircraft	6,866	32	92	With torpedo.
	6,847	38	80	With torpedo.
	6,837	32½	68	With torpedo.
Dart Torpedo aircraft	–	25	109	Ran 21ft between guides.
	–	27	65	Ran 27ft between guides.
	–	24½	85	Ran 27ft between guides.

head room clearance to enable other types of machines to be flown-off in this manner.

Conclusions:

1. The trials showed that any type of aircraft having a low landing velocity and good control at low speed could be landed on and flown-off *Furious*. Seaplanes, Amphibians and Aeroplanes with wheels or skids appeared equally satisfactory in this connection.

2. Throughout the trials the arresting gear was hardly used and it appeared to be established that the improved airflow over the deck of *Furious* together with the high speed of wind rendered the use of arresting gear unnecessary, except possibly in very high natural winds or with rolling and pitching motion on the ship. Since, however, the arresting gear undoubtedly gave confidence to pilots, it was considered that arresting gear should not be omitted until some alternative such as power-operated palisades at the deck edges were fitted in lieu.

3. If seaplanes were to be operated from Carriers it was essential that the deck should be made flush, and all obstructions such as stanchions, eyebolts, fittings at heel of fire curtains etc. removed from the flying deck and hangars. It was for consideration whether seaplanes should be used as long as the arresting gear was retained, although the trials rather suggested that the damage done in passing over the arresting gear hurdles was not very great.

FLIGHTS CARRIED

1927–29: One Fleet Fighter; two Spotter; one Spotter Reconnaissance; two Torpedo. (In 1928 (October) also reported as carrying Six Flights. Single-seat Dart torpedo aircraft and single-seat Flycatcher fighters. 3 or 4-seat Blackburn or Bison for spotting and 3-seat Fairey IIIF reconnaissance.)

1930–32: Two F/F (Flycatchers); three S/R (two Fairey IIIF, one Blackburn); two Torpedo (One Dart, One Ripon II)

1933: One F/F (nine Nimrod or Flycatcher); one S/R (twelve Fairey IIIF); One T/B (twelve Ripon); two Torpedo (one Dart, one Ripon II)

1934: As in 1933 less two Torpedo.

1935: One F/F (six Nimrods); one F/R (three Osprey); one T/3 (twelve Baffin); one S/R (twelve Fairey IIIF)

Furious: Cruiser and Aircraft Carrier, Data as completed

AS CRUISER:

Construction: Armstrong-Whitworth; laid down 8.6.1915; launched 18.8.1916; completed 26.6.1917.

Displacement (tons): 19,513 (load); 22,890 (deep).

Length: 735ft 2¼in (pp), 786ft 9in oa.

Beam: 88ft 0⅝in at waterline.

Draught: 24ft mean.

Armour

Main belt 2in HT plus 1in MS. Bulkheads 3–2in, Barbettes 7–6–3in, Turrets 11–9–7–4¼in, Decks: forecastle 1in, upper 1in, main 1¾–1in, lower 3–1in, CT 10in face 6–3in elsewhere, Funnel uptakes 1½–1in.

Machinery

Brown Curtis geared turbines driving 4 propellers.

Designed SHP: 90,000 for 31.5 knots.

Boilers: 18 Yarrow

Fuel: 750/3,160 tons oil

Radius of action: 6,000nm at 20 knots (design).

Complement: 737 as completed; 890 in 1925 (RN and RAF).

Costs: £1,050,000 for hull.

AS AIRCRAFT CARRIER:

Displacement (tons): 22,500 (normal); 26,500 (deep); 28,430 by 1939.

Length unchanged.

Beam: 107ft over flight deck.

Draught: 27ft 3in mean.

Armour: see notes.

Machinery: unaltered except for renewal of many items (see notes on 1931 machinery/boiler refit) Radius: 4,300 miles at 16 knots.

Armament: see armament notes.

Aircraft: see aircraft list. (carried Barracuda aircraft at end of Second World War)

Complement: 738 RN plus 468 RAF. (1932) Increased later and during the war to accommodate extra AA guns and aircraft as required. No full figure available.

Costs: about £6,000,000 spent on ship up to 1939.

Furious: Mast Dimensions, April 1925

Length:

Signal mast: 27ft 6in

Signal yards: 9ft

Steaming light: 20ft 6in

W/T masts: 38ft 6in

Outriggers for W/T: 8ft

Aircraft signal booms: 17ft

Jack staff: 19ft 10in

Ensign staff: 24ft

Guest warp booms: 50ft

Sounding booms: 30ft

Stern boom: 6ft

Seaplane booms: 50ft

Highest part of signal masts when extended: 84ft 4in

Highest part of W/T masts: forward 90ft 1in, amidships 92ft, aft 92ft.

1936: One F/F (nine Osprey) One T/B (twelve Swordfish) One T/S/R (twelve Swordfish)

1937 to 1939: All types carried for training purposes.

1939 onwards: 18 Swordfish

APPEARANCE CHANGES

In her battlecruiser role *Furious*'s appearance was less than pleasing. Her flight deck forward, large funnel amidships (with superstructure) and single 18in gun aft gave her a rather unsymmetrical profile. As reconstructed to an aircraft carrier proper, although changing drastically her appearance remained rather odd. The superstructure, tripod mast and funnel were removed and a high clear flying deck was fitted over most of the ship. The abrupt termination of the flying deck in a dome-shaped overhang well short of the stern, with sloping flying-off platform lower down forward of this, presented a particularly awkward appearance when seen bows on. As completed for trials the hangar sides from midships to aft over the smoke ducts were plated in with four rows of scuttles for venting, but the plating was removed after trials and before the ship entered service. A small charthouse on the forward end of the flight deck was telescopic and lowered flush with the deck when operating aircraft. Lower deck scuttles forward and aft were extended further midships. Rig: Short, light pole port and starboard on flight deck right forward. Three collapsible lattice W/T poles each side flightdeck spaces well apart. Easily distinguished from *Argus* by a much longer hull, curved stem, flight deck not carried right to stem and stern, and guns in shields along forecastle deck side.

1926–39 period, as refitted September 1930 to February 1932:

AA armament increased to three 4in, sixteen 2pdrs (8 barrels). 4in in single open mountings on afterdeck of flying-off platform and one right aft on quarterdeck. Structure below flying-off platform was more enclosed.

1937–8: Forward end of flying-off platform raised nearly horizontal.

As refitted January to May 1939: 5.5in guns replaced by twelve 4in dual-purpose (HA/LA) with enlarged twin shields.

Below: *Furious* – a rare view of the lower aircraft hangar with the lift about to convey an aircraft up to the flight deck. Note the great height between deck levels.

General details 1939: Hull as in 1925; HA director on flying-off platform on island. Guns increased to thirty-two 2pdrs. Aircraft equipment: As in 1925 except that flying-off platform forward no longer used for this purpose. Machinery and boilers as original. Appearance generally as in 1925 except for the short island superstructure with RDF aerial pole and HA director on starboard side of flying-off deck amidships. Prominent AA guns and HA director on flying-off platform forward. Quarterdeck raised to forecastle deck level. Rear of ship abaft smoke ducts painted black.

1939–45: as refitted in USA September 1942 to April 1943. 20mm AA added port and starboard on forecastle in sponsons at sides of flight deck aft. Type 275 RDF to HA directors. 1943–4: Some multiple 2pdrs removed. Type 281 RDF fitted by November 1943.

HISTORY: FURIOUS

Originally intended as large, light cruiser she was laid down at the Armstrong-Whitworth Yard at Newcastle-on-Tyne but was never actually completed as such. She entered service as a hybrid type, being half cruiser of a very powerful type (18in gun), the forward part of the ship serving as an aircraft take-off platform.

She was subjected to many experiments throughout the Great War and was fitted with an after landing-on deck in 1918. Finally completely reconstructed as a carrier proper when she entered the Royal Dockyard at Devonport in June 1921. The refit was completed in August 1925 and she rejoined the Atlantic Fleet to relieve *Argus*.

Under refit again at Devonport from September 1930 until February 1932 after which

she joined the Home Fleet (ex Atlantic Fleet).

Home Fleet: March 1932 until May 1934.

She was temporarily attached to the Mediterranean Fleet from May to October in 1934.

Rejoined Home Fleet in October 1934 until November 1942.

Employed as Training Carrier 1937 to May 1939.

Refit at Devonport December 1937 to May 1938.

At the outbreak of war she was based at Rosyth.

Halifax Convoy duties October 1939 and escorted Canada convoy to UK in December 1939 (arriving in Clyde on 17th). Norwegian Campaign April–June 1940. Her aircraft attacked a torpedo-boat destroyer on 11 April and it is thought that this was the first time that carrier-borne arcraft had attacked a surface warship at sea.

Underwent turbine repairs during this period.

At the end of June 1940 she crossed the Atlantic carrying £18,000,000 of gold bullion. She left Halifax on 1 July and arrived at Liverpool on the 7th with 49 American aircraft and spares on board.

During September 1940 she took part in anti-shipping strikes at Tromso and Trondheim, Norway, losing six aircraft and suffering casualties during this campaign.

Ferried aircraft to West Africa during November 1940.

Returned to Liverpool on 15 December.

In January 1941 she again took aircraft to Takoradi, West Africa.

Bombed by enemy aircraft while refitting in Belfast on 4 May but sustained no serious damage.

Left for Gibraltar, arriving on 12 May and continued to ferry aircraft to Gibraltar and Malta until September of 1941. At the end of July her aircraft attacked Petsamo, Finland, but found the base empty of shipping. Instead they attacked the quays, oil tanks and shipyard itself; three aircraft lost.

Anti-shipping operations in August 1941 and in October arrived at Philadelphia, USA, achieved for refit.

Returned to UK in April 1942.

Took part in North Africa landings in November after many more trips to Malta from August to October.

Below: *Furious* c.1941 showing Admiralty disruptive camouflage.

Bottom: *Furious* in rough weather. After the loss of *Glorious* and *Courageous* in 1939/40, *Furious* was the oldest carrier serving with the Royal Navy.

In November 1942 became part of Force H and continued operations on North African coast.
Force H November 1942 until February 1943.
Home Fleet February 1943 until September 1944.
July 1943 engaged in campaigns off the coast of Norway.
Refit in Liverpool August 1943 and spent the rest of the year working-up.

During 1944 *Furious* carried out various anti-shipping attacks including two major attacks on the German battleship *Tirpitz* in the Norwegian fiords.
In September took part in mining operations off Norway.
Returned to UK in September and paid off into Reserve.
Reserve Fleet September 1944 to April 1945.

Paid off April 1945.
Berthed at Loch Striven during this period and used for target practice.
Finally sold to British Iron and Steel Co. for scrapping.
Towed to Cairngorm in June 1948 (Arnott Young).
Hull towed to Troon for final demolition which took until 1954.

GLORIOUS AND COURAGEOUS

DESIGN AND CONVERSION

During 1921 and throughout the Washington Treaty months the whole question of aircraft carriers was subject to considerable debate. It was pointed out that at that time the only fleet aircraft carrier was *Argus* – 14,500 tons, 19 knots, which was attached to the Atlantic Fleet. *Pegasus*, 3,000 tons, 20 knots, was in the Mediterranean and carried only a few seaplanes which had to be hoisted aboard at the stern. *Ark Royal*, 7,080 tons, 11 knots, was classed as a Floating Aircraft Depot Ship with a good workshop arrangement, a flying-off deck and a hangar. Three aircraft carriers were under construction and being completed for service as quickly as possible: *Hermes* was in hand at Devonport, the converted *Eagle* at Portsmouth and *Furious* at Rosyth.

It was brought to the attention of the DNC that except for *Hermes* all the others were conversions and the present value of their tonnage did not reflect their value as aircraft carriers. If proper new aircraft carrier designs were allocated to these ships a saving of 4,000 tons for *Furious* and 8,000 for *Eagle* could be achieved. *Furious* – 30 knots, 22,000 tons, a new design – 18,000; *Eagle* 24 knots – 23,000 tons, new design – 15,000 tons. It was also being debated whether or not *Ark Royal* and *Pegasus* could really be classed as aircraft carriers, and be included in the aggregate tonnage for aircraft carriers in the Royal Navy. At that time there was a Board policy that *Glorious* and *Courageous* should be converted to aircraft carriers, which, when completed, would give Great Britain the finest fleet of aircraft carriers in the world. It was considered that if the latter two ships were not converted the Royal Navy would find itself saddled with distinctly inferior carriers as regards speed and numbers of aircraft that could be carried, apart from *Furious*.

It was understood that as soon as *Furious* was completed the data from her trials would influence any decision fully to convert *Glorious* and *Courageous*. Faced with the ever-growing need of fast carriers, and the fact that the US Navy was converting the large, fast *Saratoga* and *Lexington* to fully fledged carriers, the Admiralty issued the following statement on 27 July 1921: 'Their Lordships have decided that HMS *Glorious* is to be taken in hand for reconstruction as an aircraft carrier during the financial year of 1922–3.'

Although the gross tonnage for aircraft carriers in the Royal Navy was 80,580 tons – somewhat in excess of the limit for aircraft carriers as reported to be laid down by the Washington Conference – it was pointed out that all were conversions (except *Hermes*) and therefore inefficient for their displacement and this was accepted. Eager to convert *Glorious* and *Courageous* because of the great saving in expenditure (about £3 million – to build a new carrier £6 million), the DNC was ordered to prepare suitable sketches. Following the lines of *Furious*, the original sketches show superstructure and a funnel (completed as such) on the starboard side of the flight deck instead of the internal ducts for smoke. This was accepted because of the fact that *Furious* had to be completely re-routed internally all for the sake of the funnel trunking. The placing of up-takes on the upper flight deck allowed the hangars to be increased in size to carry extra aircraft and this was considered a vast improvement over *Furious*. (See notes on funnel discharge for *Argus*.)

In October 1923 the Controller gave verbal instructions to go ahead with the complete reconstruction of *Glorious* and *Courageous*. Outline sketches were forwarded showing the amount of cutting away of the main structure and armour required, and these would be easy to follow if *Furious* were anything to go by. Sketches and general descriptions were sent to the dockyards at Devonport and Rosyth, but there was much discussion of the issue in an endeavour to ensure that the work that was about to be undertaken was fully understood.

As *Furious* neared completion she was transferred to Devonport for completing. The portions of the structure and fittings that were altered and cut away to rebuild the two vessels were:

1. Structure above forecastle deck removed generally including: all bulkheads; shelter deck; conning tower; director towers; masts; main derrick; bridges; funnel, uptakes and boiler room vents down to the main deck; all guns and boats.
2. Forecastle Deck: breakwater (39–44½ stations) port and starboard and PU house (37–39) stations; coaling winches; communication tubes forward and aft. Sketches were prepared and submitted for approval showing the filling-in plating in way of the boiler room vents and the funnel hatches in the forecastle deck, this plating being of the same scantlings as the forecastle deck in this area.
3. Upper Deck: longitudinal funnel casing bulkhead 11 feet from the middle line, 81–109 stations port and starboard; bulkhead at 15 feet from the middle line to remain; above water torpedo tubes, ship's side pockets and structure in connection with these torpedo tubes; screen bulkhead 129½–142 stations port and starboard; bollards at 135 stations port and starboard and fairleads at 142 station port and starboard (these were fitted again in other positions); 40lb doubling plates 134–156½ stations and 20lb doubling plates 156½ to 162½ stations.
4. Sections of armour were removed: all holes in the various decks in way of 'A' and 'Y' turrets were filled in with plating of the same thickness as the decks in the area; 'A' turret barbette and guns, ring bulkhead, etc,. removed; ring of armour from upper deck upwards and the horseshoe armour between the main and upper deck were removed; the 240lb armour main to upper deck removed; 60 bulkhead on the upper deck was completed to form a protective bulkhead of the same thickness as the parts now outside the ring and the bulkhead; 'Y' turret: the bulkhead at 154 station on the lower deck remained; the ring armour on the lower deck was taken out and the longitudinal protective bulkheads were extended aft to 154 station; on the main deck the ring was removed and 150 station bulkheads filled in; the barbette, guns, ring bulkhead, etc., and the ring armour on the upper decks were removed.
5. Work below the upper deck: 15in shell rooms and magazines were cleared of all bins, dunnage, etc.; 4in shell rooms and magazines, small-arms blank and gunners' stores were dismantled and a saving was made here by using existing fittings; capstan engine, anchor and cable gear and hawse pipes forward were taken out – the stem pipes remained; submerged torpedo room was dismantled and the compartment cleared; 15in transmitting station was dismantled; lower conning tower was dismantled; the armoured communication tube to the lower conning tower was removed but was utilized in the reconstruction; after capstan gear was removed and re-positioned; boat hoisting winches and gear were

Below: *Courageous* in 1923, shortly before being ear-marked for conversion. Note how much upper work and armament needed to be removed for the conversion.

removed; kite balloon winches on main deck abaft 139 station were removed.

General: Before dismantling the ships the draughts were carefully noted and all removed weights were recorded.

During the summer of 1922 there was some discussion as to what suitable armament could be given to *Courageous*. It had already been decided to give *Glorious* ten 5.5in, six 4in and four pom-poms which corresponded with the armament in *Furious* and *Hermes*. The requisite number of 5.5in guns and mountings were readily available for *Courageous*, but it was argued that a stronger, 6in battery might be a better prospect. There was a glut of 6in guns returning to storage from scrapped cruisers, but it was seen that many of these were worn out (those from *Royalist* had fired more than 1,300 rounds and from *Caroline* more than 900 rounds). They would require considerable servicing and in some cases re-lining before re-issue, and in view of this the 5.5in guns seemed to be the most suitable, and a similar calibre to that of *Furious* seemed advantageous.

Limitations imposed by the Washington Treaty were:

1. Aircraft carriers were not allowed to carry a gun larger than 8in.
2. Not more than ten guns above 6in calibre were allowed.
3. Any number of guns of 6in or less calibre could be carried.
4. Any number of high-angle guns could be carried.

The Naval Air Section pointed out that aircraft carriers would be special targets and there were two forms of attack to which they would be subjected: 1. air attack; 2. attack by cruisers.

AIR ATTACK
It was necessary to be prepared for air attacks to begin long before the main fleets were in contact,

COURAGEOUS: GENERAL AS CONVERTED 1928

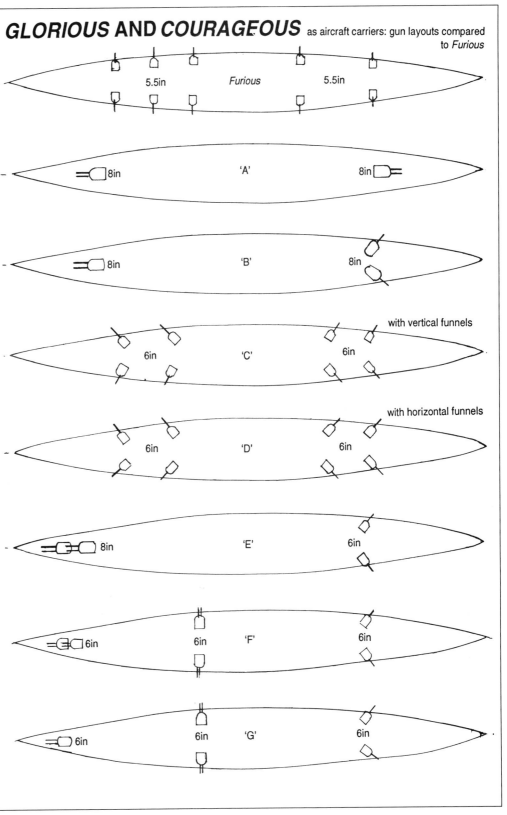

GLORIOUS AND COURAGEOUS as aircraft carriers: gun layouts compared to *Furious*

5.5in   *Furious*   5.5in

8in   'A'   8in

8in   'B'   8in

with vertical funnels

6in   'C'   6in

with horizontal funnels

6in   'D'   6in

8in   'E'   6in

6in   6in   'F'   6in

6in   6in   'G'   6in

i.e., while they were still 70, 80 or even 100 miles apart. Being the first to materialize these attacks are perhaps the most important. In general it could be said that the carriers require considerable sea room to exercise their functions which means that they would be in a comparatively isolated position and would be forced to rely largely on themselves for defence against attacks from hostile aircraft. Assuming that the high-angle armament would engage the aircraft it is very desirable that the main armament should be able to assist in breaking up the more persis-

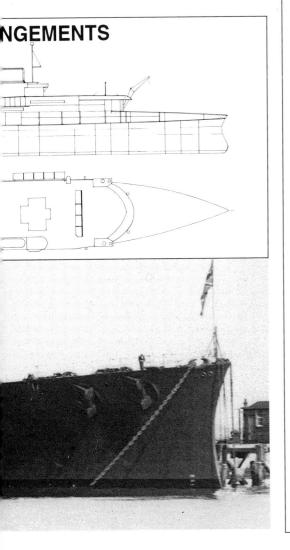

NGEMENTS

tent formations. A high-angle of elevation for the main armament is therefore considered a matter of extreme importance.'

ATTACK BY LIGHT CRUISERS:
'It is thought quite possible that an enemy light cruiser might break through the defence and attack the carriers. Also during an action the carriers might lose their position (due to flying-off and flying-on) to such an extent that they would be liable to attack from single enemy light cruisers without being supported quickly by their own support ships. Under these circumstances it seems essential that a carrier should be able to render a good account of herself against a contemporary light cruiser while working-up her speed to rejoin her own forces. Alternatively, any Commander-in-Chief would be forced to detach a defensive escort for the carriers to the detriment of his offensive powers. Consideration of these forms of attack points to the desirability of an 8in armament for *Glorious* and *Courageous*.'

The possibility of a carrier being able to defend herself against a light cruiser by means of her own aircraft was thoroughly investigated during February and March 1922 and the conclusions reached by the CinC, Atlantic Fleet, were:

'In three cases out of four it is probable that the Aircraft Carrier would have been sunk by the Light Cruiser though in two the Light Cruisers would also have been damaged or sunk by the torpedo planes. Thus the conclusion is that Aircraft Carriers cannot rely on protecting themselves at present from the attack of even a single Light Cruiser by means of torpedo planes and need either a very high speed to escape attack or an adequate escort.'

From the gunnery point of view it was considered that the ideal main armament for the two carriers should consist of 8in guns capable of high angles of elevation. It was realized that the proposal would be more costly than the alternatives, but it was submitted that the extreme importance of these vessels justified its consideration.

A strong body of opinion, however, considered that the carriers should never be exposed in the ordinary course of tactical manoeuvring to attack by light cruisers since the relative importance of recovering aircraft intact would be insufficient to justify such a risk. If the carrier were brought to action, even if her armament were

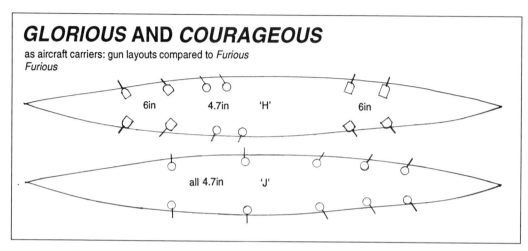

GLORIOUS AND COURAGEOUS
as aircraft carriers: gun layouts compared to *Furious*
Furious

6in   4.7in   'H'   6in

all 4.7in   'J'

superior to that of the enemy ship engaged, it was probable that the deck, hangar lifts, etc., would suffer such damage that she would be unable to continue to work her aircraft. Only in exceptional circumstances of course would carriers be compelled to accept action and therefore the heavier armament was desirable.

When generally considering both air and surface attack it was appreciated that under normal conditions it was better to increase the elevation of the secondary armament rather than increase the calibre because this would enable the main armament to engage approaching aircraft. It was also pointed out that the duties of a carrier were to fly-off her aircraft and avoid getting within range of enemy surface ships. Without entering into any arguments the most important item seen at that time was speed, which was considered to be the main essential of an aircraft carrier; it was also considered that if action could not be avoided by speed alone, then outranging the enemy was of the greatest importance. To achieve this any carrier would have to be provided with the longest-range guns possible provided that her speed were not impaired. Great difficulty had already been witnessed with armament in *Hermes* and *Eagle*, especially high-angle guns. Tests forwarded by *Excellent* showed that interference by blast from the 4in guns in these ships reduced the effective armament virtually to two guns in *Hermes* and four in *Eagle*. As can be seen from the above it was found to be extremely difficult to convert these two ships and give them all the essential qualities of an aircraft carrier: 1.

Suitable armament; 2. High speed; 3. A good aircraft-carrying capacity. The conclusion of these long-winded debates was that neither 8in nor 6in guns with high elevation could be fitted without interfering with the functions of the ship as an aircraft carrier.

Faced with these problems the DNC investigated several alternatives in great detail. Of the nine alternatives submitted (see drawings), 'H and 'J' layouts were the most favoured. The arrangements in 'H' and 'J' were modifications of design 'C', that is, they were generally similar to 'C' as follows:

DESIGN 'H'
The six 4in high-angle guns in 'C' were replaced by six 4.7in high-angle guns. In addition four 4.7in were arranged on the lower hangar deck, two on the port side and two on the starboard side. These guns on the lower deck had a maximum elevation of about 63°. In order to mount the two additional 4.7in guns they were relatively closely spaced and this imposed some restriction in the angle of training.

The four after 6in guns were moved aft relative to the 'C' design which caused the lower hangar in way of the after pair of guns to be restricted as compared with 'C'.

In view of the difficulty of maintaining a direct supply of ammunition to the 4.7in guns on the lower hangar deck without interfering with the working of the 6in guns, ready-use magazines were indicated which would take up a certain amount of hangar space.

DESIGN 'J'

The armament in this arrangement comprised 4.7in guns entirely, eighteen of them being indicated on the upper hangar deck forward, twelve on the lower deck and two on the upper deck aft. The twelve guns on the lower hangar deck showed high angles of elevation. As in design 'H' these broadside guns were sponsored out two feet.

The following table gives the approximate hangar stowage of Designs 'H' and 'J' compared with 'C'.

Design	No. of large aircraft	No. of Flycatchers
'C'	51	67
'H'	51	63
'J'	52	65

The pros and cons of Designs 'H' and 'J' were set out in a letter sent to the DNC by J. C. W. Henley, DNO, pointing out the salient features:

'DESIGN 'J'

(a) A uniform armament; (b) A greatly superior anti-aircraft fire; (c) QF ammunition in brass cartridges alone required, which is an asset in a vessel so vulnerable and liable to serious fires from petrol, aircraft, etc.

The 4.7in guns on the broadside will have a maximum elevation up to 60° on a good arc of training, and the maximum range of the gun as a low-angle weapon on these bearings will be 17,000 yards. On the other hand a 4.7in broadside is considered little use outside about 12,000 yards in stopping TBDs, as the difficulties of spotting these small ships at greater range are insuperable.

Against this must be placed the fact that enemy aircraft at sea or in harbour will undoubtedly be the principal factor against which a carrier must be capable of defending herself.

Whatever guns she may carry, to defend herself against surface aircraft, they will not deter a determined enemy making an effective attack against such a prize. No consideration of gunfire deterred our destroyers in pressing home attacks on the High Seas Fleet at Jutland.

The complete 4.7in armament in Design 'J' has a further advantage in that, with control arrangements fitted at each corner of the flying deck both forward and aft, attacks on 4 separate bearings by aircraft could be dealt with simultaneously.

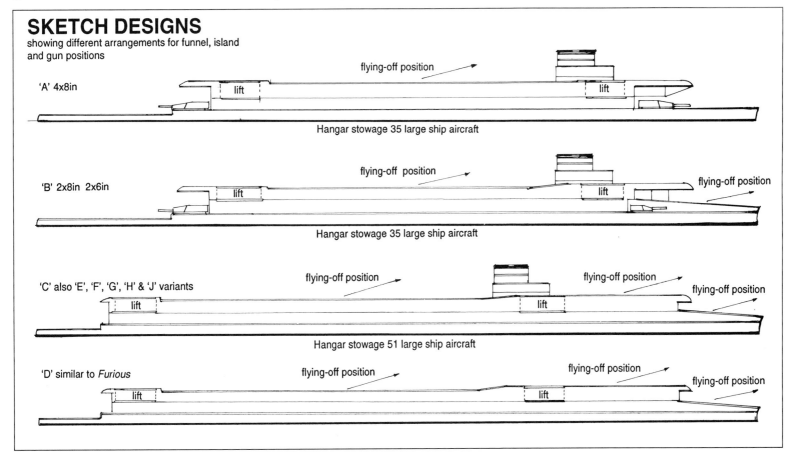

SKETCH DESIGNS

showing different arrangements for funnel, island and gun positions

'A' 4x8in
flying-off position
lift
lift
Hangar stowage 35 large ship aircraft

'B' 2x8in 2x6in
flying-off position
flying-off position
lift
lift
Hangar stowage 35 large ship aircraft

'C' also 'E', 'F', 'G', 'H' & 'J' variants
flying-off position
flying-off position
flying-off position
lift
lift
Hangar stowage 51 large ship aircraft

'D' similar to *Furious*
flying-off position
flying-off position
flying-off position
lift
lift

Below: *Glorious* in January 1930, the first appearance of the newly fitted aircraft carrier, at Devonport. With all her alterations and top weight she still made 29.466 knots on trials.

Glorious and *Courageous*: Particulars, on completion as battlecruisers

Construction
Glorious: Harland & Wolff; laid down 20.4.1915; launched 20.4.1916; completed 14.10.1916.
Courageous: Armstrong; laid down 28.3.1915; launched 5.2.1916; completed 28.10.1916.
Displacement (tons): *Glorious* 19,180 (load), 22,360 (deep); *Courageous* 19,180 (load), 22,560 (deep).
Dimensions
Length: 735ft 1½in (pp), 786ft 9in (oa).
Beam: 81ft (deck).
Draught: 22ft 8in – 25ft 10in.
Armament
4 x 15in 42cal
18 x 4in Mk IX
2 x 3pdr
2 x 21in submerged TT.
Armour
Main belt 3in (2in plus 1in); Bulkheads 3–2in; barbettes 7–6–3in; turrets 11–9–7–4¼in; Decks: Forecastle 1in; upper 1in; Main 1¾-1in; lower 3–1in; CT 10–6–3in; Funnel uptakes 1½in.
Machinery
Parsons geared turbines driving 4 propellers.
Designed SHP: 90,000 for 32 knots.
Boilers: 18 Yarrow small tubed, 235psi.
Fuel: 750/3,160 tons oil.
Radius of action: 6,000nm at 20 knots (designed).
Costs: *Glorious* £1,967,223; *Courageous* £2,038,225.

Glorious and *Courageous*: Particulars, on completion as aircraft carriers

Displacement (tons): *Glorious* (July 1935) 24,970 (load), 27,419 (deep), 27,951 (extra deep); *Courageous* 23,550 (legend), 24,210 (as inclined 13 July 1928), 26,990 (deep), 27,400 (extra deep).
Length: unchanged.
Beam: 90ft 6in waterline over bulges, 104ft flight deck at bridge section.
Armour: (see notes).
Machinery: unchanged. (3,800 tons max. oil).
Armament
16 x 4.7in dual-purpose HA/LA, fitted in single open mountings; eight on each beam, two at end of after flying-off platform forward, twelve spaced along the sides of upper deck amidships, two right aft on quarterdeck.
4 x 3pdr (saluting)
24 x 2pdr (3 x 8 barrels) added in *Glorious* (1935), 12 x 2pdr added in *Courageous* (1936) (3 x 4 barrels ex-battleship *Royal Sovereign*).
Multiple 0.5in AA (4 barrels) added to both.
Searchlights: 5 x 36in: 1 over bridge, 3 in sponsons on port side of flight deck, 1 in sponson on starboard side of flight deck right aft.
Aircraft: see lists.
Complement: *Glorious* (1931) 793 plus 490 FAA; *Courageous* (1938) 814 plus 531 FAA, (1939) 807 plus 403 FAA.
Boats (1936):
2 x 36ft motor pinnaces
2 x 35ft motor boats
1 x 35ft barge (*Courageous* only)
2 x 35ft crash boats (1 in *Courageous*)
1 x 32ft motor cutter
2 x 32ft pulling cutters
1 x 30ft cutter
2 x 30ft gigs
2 x 27ft whalers
2 x 16 skiff dinghies

DESIGN 'H'

The proposal for two 4.7in guns on the broadside is not liked, as it mixes the 6in and 4.7in armament. The alternative of five 6in guns on the broadside is an improvement on Design 'C' and provides a fair TBD armament with 4.7in guns as HA armament.

An angle of fire of 1 degree across the stern is hoped for for the after 6in guns.

For the reasons given under Design 'J' and those in ACNS's minute of 13.2.24, it is considered that 'J' is decidedly preferable and is recommended for approval.

[Signed] J. C. W. Henley'

As completed the ships were the last British fleet carriers not originally designed and built as such, and were more or less similar to *Furious* with the exception of the funnel discharge arrangements. *Courageous* was the first to be completed (May 1928) with *Glorious* commissioning in February 1939.

They proved very successful in their redesigned role and more than fulfilled the Navy's demand for aircraft at sea at that time. As with *Furious*, many experiments were carried out in them and the results all went towards the successful designs of *Ark Royal* (1937) and the later *Illustrious* class (1940).

ARMOUR

With only 2in high-tensile steel covered with 1in mild steel, *Glorious* and *Courageous* were poorly protected indeed. In fact, the scale of protection was barely proof against even the smallest shell. As large light cruisers when completed they were a terrible risk, but as carriers the protection did not seem to matter so much because they would not be called upon to face other ships in the line of battle. As reconstructed into aircraft carriers they were not given any additional protection over their vitals except an extra $5/8$in on the flight deck over the entire length. It was argued that, as with their side armour, this thickness of flight deck protection was totally inadequate against even small bombs – in fact it was little more than bullet-proof. But there was no question of their being classed as armoured ships and they were thought very highly of in their new role as floating airfields.

Main belt: 2in HT plus 1in MS.
Bulkheads: 3–2in HT.
Protective deck was retained: 1–$3/4$in HT.
Uptakes: $1^{1}/_{2}$–1in MS.
4.7in guns: $1/2$in MS.

MACHINERY

As in *Furious*

SEA TRIALS OF GLORIOUS, 27 JANUARY 1930

The ship put to sea on 27 January with the intention of carrying out her 4-hour full-power trials, but because of trouble with the air condenser pumps this could not be done. She returned to Plymouth for repairs and did not attempt trials again until 30 January, although no actual trials were carried out (or certainly recorded) until 1 February. The 4-hour full-power trials were successful although the weather was foul and she was recorded as rolling to 15 degrees maximum with a pitch of 2 degrees each way.

Summary of trial compared with *Courageous* (same trial)

Mean displacement (tons)	*Glorious*	*Courageous*
	24,750	23,460
Mean revolutions of all shafts	316	318.5
Average SHP	92,270	92,065

On the measured mile *Courageous* made 30.507 knots with 90,618shp and 317.75 revolutions.

On 3 February 1930 *Glorious* carried out her turning trials off Plymouth.
Comparison:

		Glorious	*Courageous*
Full speed:	Advance tactical diameter (yds)	1,200	1,070
14 knots	tactical diameter (yds)	1,080	1,090

Aircraft lifts: trials carried out and were most successful.
Hangar doors: Wind speed, 40 knots.
Open by power, 22 seconds.
By hand; (close) 18 men on tackle, 38 seconds.
Wind-screens: up in 8 seconds (down in same time).
Wireless masts: up in 32 seconds, down in 28 seconds.

STOWAGE OF FAA FLIGHTS IN GLORIOUS

In November 1931 it was suggested by the CinC that *Glorious* could not operate 52 aircraft with any efficiency. It was remarked that maintenance was the all-important feature and that to fly more aircraft than could be maintained properly was out of the question. An officer in *Glorious* pointed out that the stowage was for 48 aircraft, but that 52 was definitely not out of the question. The 52 aircraft could be operated (somewhat inefficiently perhaps if nine includes sixteen Flycatchers with small endurance) more freely if fighters (Nimrods and Ospreys) were used. It was noted that since completion as a carrier she had never carried more than 46 aircraft whereas *Courageous* had had (and operated efficiently) 52 aircraft for some time since her completion in 1928. A total of 52 aircraft was undesirable from the training point of view, but when necessary to carry full complement of machines it was thought that this could be accomplished. The Captain of *Glorious* sent a letter to the CinC, Mediterranean Station, dated 8 November 1931:

Flights Carried
1928: *Courageous* 1 F/F. 2 S/R. 2 T/B.
1930: *Courageous* 3 F/F. 4 S/R. 2 T/B. *Glorious* 3 F/F (Flycatchers). 2 S/R (Fairey IIIF). 2 T/B (Ripon).
1931: Both ships. 2 F/F (Flycatchers). 2 S/R (Fairey IIIF). 2 T (Dart).
1932: 2 F/F (Flycatchers or Nimrods). 3 S/R (Fairey IIIF). 2 T (Dart or Ripon).
1933–4: *Courageous* 1 F/F (Nimrod or Osprey). 1 S/R (9 Fairey IIIF). 1 T/B (Ripon). *Glorious* 1 F/F (Nimrod or Osprey). 1 S/R (Fairey IIIF). 1 T/B (Ripon).
1935: *Courageous* 1F/F & F/R (9 Nimrod and 3 Osprey). 1 S/R (12 Seal). 1 T/S/R (12 Shark). 1 T/B (12 Baffin).
1936: Both ships. 1 F/F (9 Nimrod and 3 Osprey). 2 T/S/R (24 Shark). 1 T/B.
1937: Both ships: 36 T/S/R.12 F.D.B.
April 1940: *Glorious* carried 1 Squadron T/B (Skuas) and 1 Squadron F/F (Gladiators).

'1. The problem of operating aircraft from a carrier involves not only the ranging up, flying-off, landing-on and so on, but also the efficient upkeep of the aircraft in the hangars. It is even possible to fly more aircraft than can be maintained in efficient conditions on board.
2. The limiting condition, therefore, is How many aircraft of different types can be stowed so that the work necessary for proper maintenance can be carried out on them?
3. The attached list has been worked out and the various combinations actually tried. The most suitable for ordinary peacetime cruising work seems to be No. 1. This allows of all aircraft belonging to the ship being carried, except one complete flight of Flycatchers.
4. From sea training in peace point of view the single seater fighters can best be spared as the bulk of their training and exercise can well be carried out ashore.
Alternative stowages of *Glorious* which should make it possible to operate them efficiently.

1.

6 new SSF	-	'A' hangar
18 IIIF	-	upper hangar
6 T/B	-	upper hangar
12 TB	-	lower hangar
4 old SSF	-	lower hangar
Total 46		

2.

6 new SSF	-	'A' hangar
18 T/B	-	upper hangar

10 old SSF	–	one side of lower hangar
8 IIIF	–	one side of lower hangar
Total 42		

3.		
6 new SSF	–	'A' hangar
18 IIIF	–	'F' upper hangar
6 old SSF	–	'A' upper hangar
12 T/B	–	'F' lower hangar
4 old SSF	–	lower hangar
Total 46		

4.		
6 new SSF	–	'A' hangar
18 IIIF	–	'F' upper hangar
6 T/B	–	'A' upper hangar
10 old SSF	–	'F' lower hangar
8 T/B	–	'A' lower hangar
Total 42		

5.		
6 new SSF	–	'A' hangar
6 old SSF	–	one side of upper hangar
6 T/B	–	one side of upper hangar
6 T/B	–	'A' hangar (upper)
4 old SSF	–	'F' lower hangar
12 IIIF	–	'A' lower hangar
Total 40		

6.		
6 new SSF	–	'A' hangar
12 IIIF	–	'A' lower hangar
18 T/B	–	upper hangar
6 old SSF	–	'F' lower hangar
Total 42		

[Signed Captain] *Glorious* at Malta, 8 November 1931'

APPEARANCE CHANGES

1928–30:
Appearance (as in *Furious*) particularly unattractive because of abrupt termination of flight deck well short of bows, with separate flying-off platform lower down forward. Leading edge of flight deck rounded steeply down in dome-shaped curve, the effect being especially distinctive seen bows on. Superstructure very short and high. Funnel: flat-sided, very large, occupying about two-thirds the length of superstructure. Bulges: very prominent above waterline amidships. Light pole mast stepped through bridge. Short in *Courageous* as completed (1928), taller in *Glorious* as completed (1930). Collapsible lattice poles (3 port and starboard) for W/T along sides of flight deck. Note that in both ships the mast actually comprised two poles set very close together abreast in *Courageous* and fore and aft in *Glorious*. In *Courageous* seen from abeam and *Glorious* seen end on, the mast appeared as a single pole. The ships were easily identified by a single very large funnel, light pole mast, flight deck not continuous to stern and a low, sloping flying-off platform over the forecastle. The superstructure and funnel separate from *Furious* to which they would otherwise have been very similar.

Individual differences:
Courageous: Short mast with no forward strut. Inconspicuous directors (pre-August 1930 only). Rounded extremity to flying-off platform. Signalling searchlights on port side before funnel. Lower down, small searchlight starboard after corner superstructure. Short searchlight platform before funnel. *Glorious*: Taller mast with prominent forward strut. Conspicuous directors. Pointed extremity to flying-off platform. Signalling searchlight platform. Side before funnel carried higher, taller searchlight platform before funnel. *Glorious*: Taller mast with prominent forward strut. Conspicuous directors. Pointed extremity to flying-off plat-

GLORIOUS AND COURAGEOUS

as converted to aircraft carriers (port & starboard)

Note that funnel takes up about ²⁄₃rds of superstructure

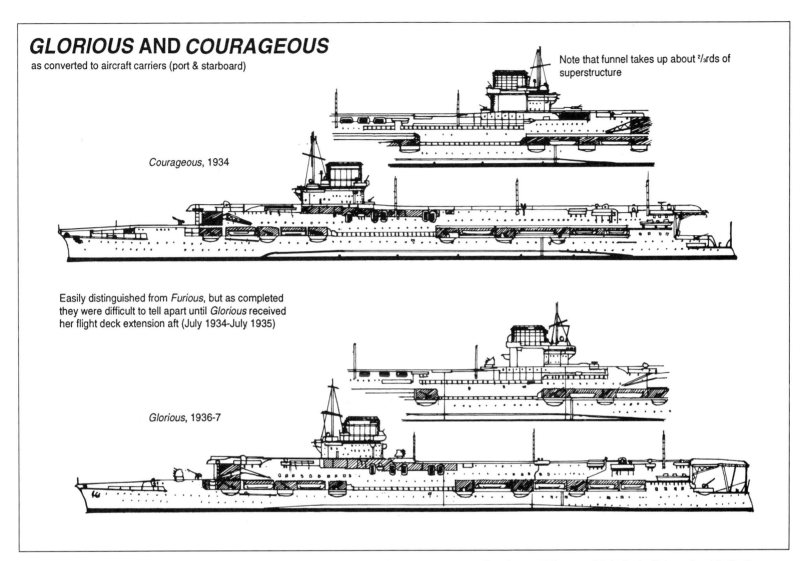

Courageous, 1934

Easily distinguished from *Furious*, but as completed they were difficult to tell apart until *Glorious* received her flight deck extension aft (July 1934–July 1935)

Glorious, 1936-7

form. Signalling searchlight platform. Side before funnel carried higher, taller searchlight platform before funnel.

1928–39:
Light AA added. Aircraft catapults installed and flight deck modified.

1930:
Courageous as refitted June–August 1930.
LA directors for 4.7in replaced by HA/LA (as *Glorious*).
Arrangements of directors and searchlight sponsons at after end of flying deck were reversed, i.e., SL sponsons relocated before instead of abaft directors. Tail of flying deck lengthened and slightly modified. Extra plating added before flying deck forward.
Rig modified as in *Glorious*, i.e., higher mast with

wider yard and prominent struts protruding from this.

Glorious:
Extra plating added below flying deck forward (after trials).

1933:
Courageous
High charthouse added on bridge and 36in searchlights removed (May 1933).

1933–4:
Courageous
Twin catapults fitted in forward flying deck trained fore and aft (before March 1934).

1935:
Glorious
As refitted May 1934 to August 1935

Three multiple 2pdr (8 barrels added). One port and starboard on flying deck forward and one on superstructure abaft funnel. Multiple 0.5in AA (4 barrels) added in sponson port side flying deck right aft.
Catapults fitted as in *Courageous*.
Tail of flight deck extended aft in downward curve.
Midships 36in searchlights on flying deck removed.
Quarterdeck to forecastle deck level.

1936
Courageous as refitted October 1935 to June 1936.
LAA added as in *Glorious* except that multiple 0.5in were on the starboard side instead of port side. 2 pdrs added (4 instead of 8 barrels).
Pole mast replaced by light tripod with aircraft homing beacon aerial at the head.

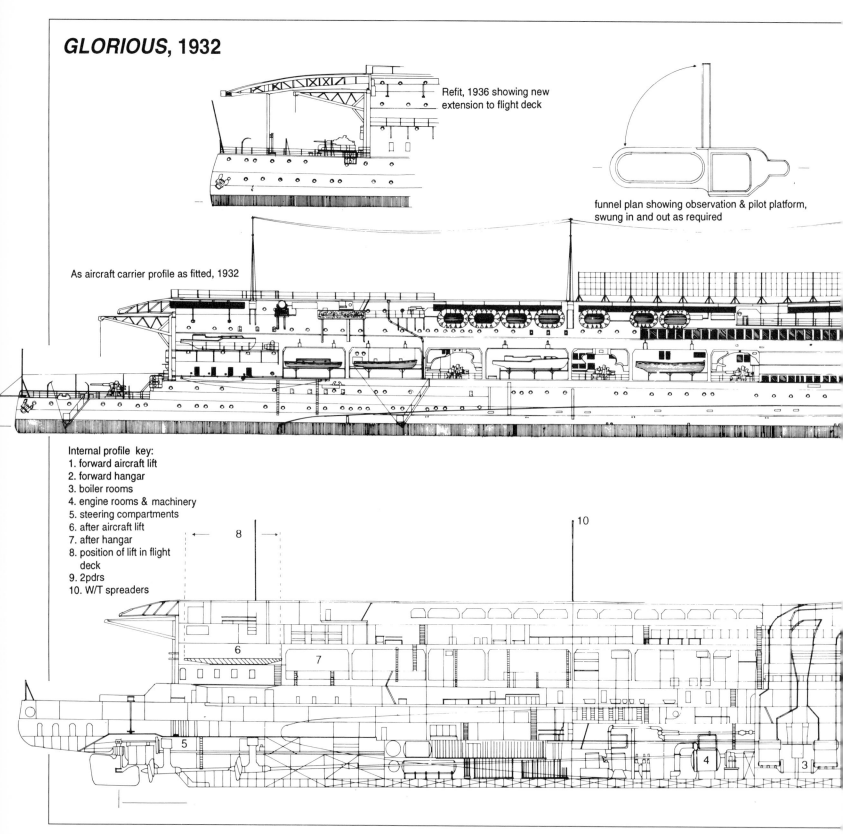

GLORIOUS, 1932

Refit, 1936 showing new
extension to flight deck

funnel plan showing observation & pilot platform,
swung in and out as required

As aircraft carrier profile as fitted, 1932

Internal profile key:
1. forward aircraft lift
2. forward hangar
3. boiler rooms
4. engine rooms & machinery
5. steering compartments
6. after aircraft lift
7. after hangar
8. position of lift in flight
   deck
9. 2pdrs
10. W/T spreaders

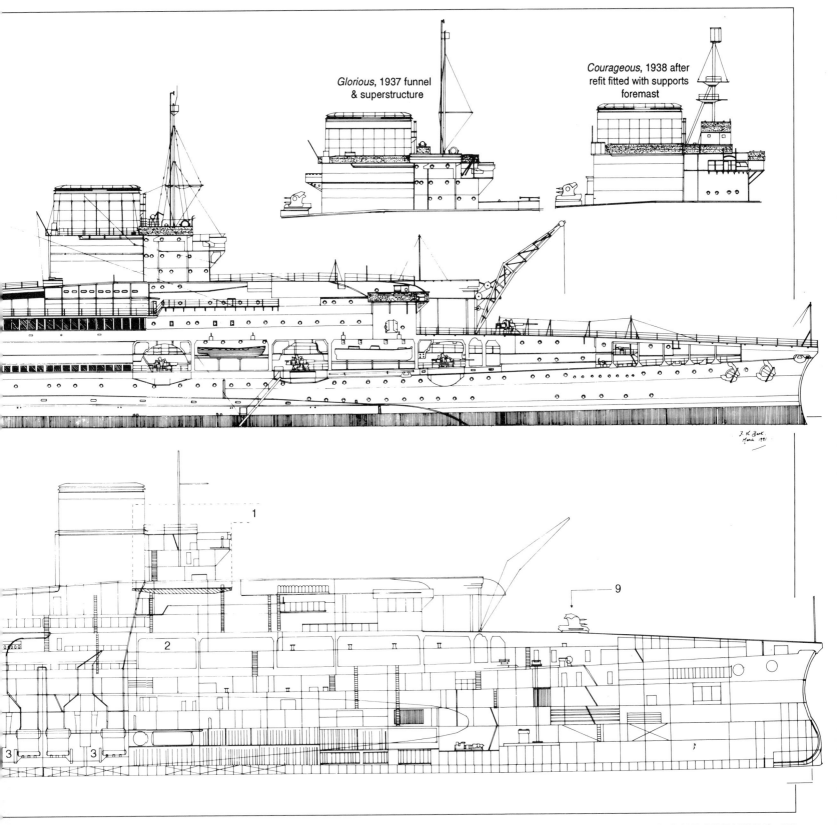

Glorious, 1937 funnel & superstructure

Courageous, 1938 after refit fitted with supports foremast

1939: Apart from tripod mast in *Courageous* and raised quarterdeck in *Glorious*, their original appearance as completed aircraft carriers remained generally unchanged (*Glorious* had 'GL' painted up on flight deck in May 1937, *Courageous* may have been similar.

INDIVIDUAL DIFFERENCES:

Courageous: Tripod mast with extra platform and aircraft homing beacon aerial head. Tall charthouse on bridge and large deckhouse abaft funnel. Low quarterdeck. Short tail to flying deck, rounded extremity to flying-off platform forward.
Glorious: Pole mast. No charthouse. No deckhouse abaft funnel, high quarterdeck, long tail to flying deck and pointed extremity to flying-off platform forward.

1939–40: No outward appearance changes.

EXTENSION TO FLIGHT DECK AFT IN GLORIOUS, 1936

After her after portion of flight deck had been lengthened in 1936, it was found to be a great improvement when landing the aircraft. Tests were made on passage to Suda Bay in October 1936 and the following report ensued:
'Extension to flying deck is a great improvement. The more gradual and extended slope has produced a surface which gives an uninterrupted air flow enabling pilots to land further aft without having to fly through the turbulence set up by the steeper and shorter round-down of *Courageous* type. There is no question of any down when coming into land.

It was noticeable that when we were in company with *Courageous*, aircraft touched down further forward than us which indicated a higher approach taken by the pilots in order to avoid the eddies caused by the abrupt round-down. Although total extension amounts to 41ft, only 3ft 6in of this is level deck so that very little ranging area is gained.

Most aircraft touch down with their hook on the forward end of the after lift and wheels a little ahead. Maximum number of our striking force is 24, i.e., 18 ranged on deck, 1 behind each accelerator and 2 ready each side to take onto trolley.'

Although such a success, and planned for *Courageous* during her next refit, it was never implemented, even in her refit of 1939.

PROPOSED CONVERSION TO SINGLE HANGAR SHIPS, 1938

Towards the end of 1938 the question was raised as to whether to convert both *Glorious* and *Courageous* to single hangar ships.

The apparent advantages – it would be easier to handle the aircraft, protect them with armour plating and perhaps increase capacity – seemed attractive at the time. There were two essentials for single hangar ships: the hangar had to be at least 62ft wide so that aircraft could be stowed three abreast; height had to be sufficient to allow of three gallery decks of reasonable width for accommodation. To achieve these dimensions beam would have to be increased by about 14 feet. To support such an extension of the entire hull, however, would require a great deal of reconstruction which would put the ships out of service for a considerable time (see drawing). As newer aircraft carriers were under construction (*Ark Royal*) and the cost of conversion would be high, the project was shelved and then discarded.

HISTORY: GLORIOUS

Commissioned for trials as a battlecruiser on 14 October 1916, she joined the 2nd LCS in October of that year.

Aircraft Carrier and Battlecruiser data compared

Armour	Carrier	Battlecruiser
Armour	3–2in main belt	3–2in
Protective deck	1in and ³⁄₄in	1in and ³⁄₄in
Flight deck protection ('D1' quality)	⁵⁄₈in	
Weights (tons)		
General equipment	870	650
Armament	760	2,250
Machinery	3,130	2,350
Armour and protective plating	16,680	8,500
Board Margin	100	100
Total displacement	23,250	17,400

Dimensions Compared with *Furious* and *Eagle*

	Courageous Glorious feet	Furious feet	Eagle feet
Length of arresting gear for flying-on (ft):	300	300	320
Space for flying-off (ft approx.)			
(i) after end of flight deck:	300	300	280
(ii) forward end of flight deck:	165	160	185
(iii) forward end of upper hangar deck:	156	156	
Clear distance between lifts (ft):	342	344	326
Total breadth flight deck (ft):	100	91	100
Clear breadth inside island (ft):	84¹⁄₂		78
Length of island (ft):	73¹⁄₂		163

Courageous: GM and Stability, as inclined 28 February 1928

'A' condition (load)	Draught	GM	Max Stability
(1,000 tons oil)			
25ft 10in	3.3ft	30°	
'B' condition	28ft	4.4ft	31°
(3,665 tons oil)			

Stability vanishes in the above conditions at: 'A': 49°, 'B': 55°.

Glorious: Steam Trials as aircraft carrier, 20 March 1930

Displacement (tons)	Revs:	SHP	Speed (knots)
24,165	104	3,466	10.144
24,540	152	9,508	14.685
24,160	208	25,637	19.915
24,435	270	52,948	25.56
24,360	296	72,572	28.104
24,260	318	91,063	29.466

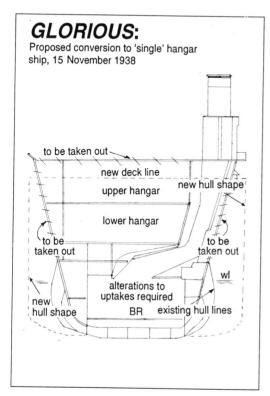

GLORIOUS:
Proposed conversion to 'single' hangar ship, 15 November 1938

to be taken out
new deck line
upper hangar
new hull shape
lower hangar
to be taken out
to be taken out
wl
alterations to uptakes required
new hull shape
BR existing hull lines

Reduced to Reserve at Rosyth on 1 February 1919 and became tender to HMS *Hercules*.
Turret Drill Ship at Devonport, attached to Vivid Training Establishment, December 1920.
1921–22: Flagship of Rear-Admiral Commander the Reserve Fleet at Devonport.
September 1923: Parent Ship in Portsmouth Reserve.
14 February 1924. Paid off to prepare for complete reconstruction to an aircraft carrier at Rosyth. Conversion began at Rosyth but later transferred to Devonport to complete.
Began trials as a carrier January 1930.
Commissioned at Devonport 24 February 1930 to relieve *Courageous* in Mediterranean Fleet, but actually attached to Atlantic Fleet for three months, March 1930 to June 1930.
Mediterranean Fleet: June 1930 to October 1939.
In collision with French liner *Florida* near Malaga 1 April 1931 (see report). Repaired at Gibraltar and Malta April 1931 until September 1931.

Extensive refit Devonport, July 1934 to July 1935.
Present at the Coronation Fleet Review May 1937.
Became unit of Force J (*Glorious* and *Malaya*) organized in October 1939 for operations against the German armoured ship *Graf Spee* in the Indian Ocean.
Left Aden 14 October 1939.
Force J: October to December 1939.
Force J broken up 6 December 1939, *Malaya* to Halifax escort duties, *Glorious* sent to Colombo.
Mediterranean Fleet: December 1939 to April 1940.
Transferred to Home Fleet April 1940 for Norwegian Campaign, arrived off Norwegian coast, flew-off squadron of Gladiators for land use 24 April 1940.
Home Fleet: April to June 1940.
Employed in providing air cover for convoys and troops, landing places, etc., and to attack airfields in Norway.
Flew-off RAF fighters (Gladiators and Hurricanes) for operations against Narvick, 26 May 1940.
Attacked and sunk by German battlecruisers *Scharnhorst* and *Gneisenau* 8 June 1940 (see report). When she was attacked she was largely ineffective because her own aircraft complement had been reduced to make way for the RAF fighters that had been flown off at Narvik. She was also low on fuel, having expended much of it during the operations from which she was just returning, which meant that she was unable to reach the high speeds required for flying-off aircraft.

HISTORY COURAGEOUS

Commissioned for trials as a battlecruiser on 28 October 1916 and joined the 2nd LCS in October 1917.
June 1919. Tender to HMS *Hercules* in Reserve.
March 1920. Flagship of Rear-Admiral Commanding Reserves and attached to Portsmouth Gunnery School.
August 1923. Hoisted the Flag of Rear-Admiral Commanding Reserve Fleet at Portsmouth.
27 June 1924. Taken in hand at Devonport for complete reconstruction to aircraft carrier.
Conversion commenced at Devonport DY June

1924 and commissioned as a carrier 21 February 1928.
Commissioned for service with Mediterranean Fleet May 1928 to June 1930.
Relieved by *Glorious* June 1930.
Refit June to August 1930.
Recommissioned 12 August 1930 for Atlantic Fleet, replacing *Argus*.
Atlantic Fleet: August 1930 to March 1932.
Home Fleet: March 1932 to December 1938.
Paid off at Portsmouth for refit 1 October 1935.
Present at Coronation Fleet Review May 1937.
Temporarily attached to Mediterranean Fleet 1936.
Relieved by *Ark Royal* December 1938 and reduced to Reserve as training carrier December 1938 to August 1939. Relieved as deck training carrier by *Furious* at Rosyth May 1939.
Present at Portland Fleet Review by HM King George VI 9 August 1939.
Channel Force (Devonport and Portland) August 1939.
Sunk by *U29* 17 September 1939 (see report).

COLLISION OF GLORIOUS AND SS FLORIDA

Extract from letter written by Mr. Newnham (Assistant Constructor) to DNC, 5 April 1931:
'At 1630 on 1/4/31 *Glorious* was steaming at about 16 knots in a fog. She came into collision with SS *Florida*, the bows of *Glorious* striking SS *Florida* nearly normally between nos. 1 and 2 holds and penetrating to just beyond the centre line of the ship. The resulting hole was 36ft wide and apparently extended for the whole depth of SS *Florida*.

Damage to *Glorious* was found to be as follows:
(This is a part of a report sent into to the Captain before we arrived at Gibraltar. The under water damage being unknown.)
The lower Flying-Off Deck is buckled for about 60ft from the fore end. The Cable Deck is completely smashed to 10 station, the 2 Bower Hawsepipes being wrenched up with the structure being completely entangled in the wreckage. The port bower pipe is cracked beyond repair. The sheet hawsepipe remains in place, but all its holding down rivets have sheared, and the weight of a long length of cable would probably tear it from the structure. The sheet anchor has

Below: Two views depicting *Glorious* after collision with SS *Florida* on 1 April 1931: the smashed bow head-on and (bottom) the bow from the port side.

Right: *Glorious* enters Malta after temporary repairs to the bow. Complete repairs took until September 1931.

lost one fluke and the starboard bower anchor shank is bent. The fashion plate and adjoining plating has been torn away and bent round to port. Between Cable Deck and Upper Deck everything is smashed as far as and including, 10, bulkhead, Seamen's urinals are damaged. Below Upper Deck no examination has been made on the fore side of 10 bulkhead as manhole was covered with debris. An examination of the after side showed the following state of 10 Bulkhead: Upper – Main Deck – Buckled with some plating torn. Main – Lower Deck – Bulkhead intact. Lower – Platform – A few weeping rivets. Platform – Keel – Intact. The bulkhead was shored up and on arriving at Gibraltar conditions were the same.

The Commander suggests that this would be a good opportunity for giving *Glorious* a narrower lower Flying-Off Deck from before the foremost guns to the fore end. Aircraft flying off do not require so wide a platform as formed by the after part of this deck. There would be less likelihood of its being lifted by heavy seas. Cablework should be facilitated; and incidentally weight should be saved.'

BATTLE DAMAGE

Sinking of Courageous by U29.

On 16 September 1939 *Courageous* sailed from Plymouth for the Atlantic to carry out offensive air operations against enemy submarines off the south-west coast of Ireland escorted by four destroyers. On 17 September *Courageous* had been steaming to the westward at high speed. This course and speed were assumed in order to decrease the distance for the homing of a striking force of four aircraft which had left at 1615 hours for an attack on a submarine which was shelling SS *Kafiristan*. At the same time as the striking force left, the destroyers *Inglefield* and *Intrepid* were detached to follow them up for hunting the submarine. At about 1920 hours *Courageous* turned to the south-eastward into the wind and reduced speed to fly-on the striking force again. At that time the ship was screened by the destroyer *Ivanhoe* on the port bow and *Impulsive* on the starboard bow.

SHIP HIT BY TORPEDO

At about 1955 there were two heavy explosions in rapid succession. All the lights in the ship

went out at once and the ship almost immediately took a heavy list to port. The ship had already been darkened although the sun had not yet quite set when this was done and all deadlights and most of the screen doors were therefore closed. It was estimated that the ship finally sank about 2015 only twenty minutes after being hit. No torpedo tracks had been seen nor had the presence of a submarine been detected by the screen which was regaining station after starting a turn by Red Pendant.

POSITION OF TORPEDO HITS

From statements made by officer and rating survivors it would appear that one torpedo hit the port side approximately abreast the Petty Officers' Flat. The second hit appears to have been at about the after end of 'B' boiler room. Officers and ratings who were on the bridge could give little information in this respect as the bridge, being on the starboard side, any view to port is much restricted by the flight deck. All electric power went off at once after the torpedoes hit and the typhon siren started and could

not be stopped. Immediately after the explosions the Quartermaster reported that the ship would not steer. The Captain then ordered the ship's position to be given to the W/T Office. Meanwhile the signal books had been collected on the signal bridge and the unweighted ones placed in a weighted canvas bag. They were then taken down to the compass platform ready for destruction. About ten minutes after being hit some bulkheads were heard to collapse and the list increased to about 35°. At the same time the Captain ordered the international code signal 'Stand by me' to be hoisted. This was done. He then said that anyone who wished to leave the ship was at liberty to do so.

Lieutenant E. Shenton was on watch in the forward centre engine room and immediately after the double explosion all lights in the engine room went out.

The ship took a heavy list to port immediately and Lieutenant Shenton ordered the starboard engines to be stopped. He then ordered the engine room to be evacuated. In the meantime the steam pressure was falling rapidly and there

was a considerable steam leak on the port side. Lieutenant Shenton therefore operated the emergency bulkhead valve closing lever, and rang the sprayer telegraphs to zero. As he was leaving the engine room the revolution telegraph from the bridge was rung down. A stoker coming up from the boiler room with his overalls on fire could give no information. Other men came up from the boiler rooms later but no statements were taken from them.

ACTION BETWEEN DECKS

This amounted to very little. All the important watertight doors were already closed and due to the heavy list of the ship and the fact that there were no lights or broadcaster working the remainder could not be closed.

Shortly after the explosion the Captain had given the order to flood the starboard bulges. Although the order did not get through, Lieutenant E. Sedgwick and a stoker Petty Officer from the double-bottom party, with the help of a Sub-Lieutenant carrying a torch, had proceeded to 'Z' seacock in order to attempt to

flood the starboard bulge. The cotter pin was removed but in spite of a wheel spanner the valve could not be turned. It was assumed that the rod gearing was distorted and jammed by the explosion.

ACTION TAKEN ON UPPER DECK

All boats except seaboats were turned in and secured. Owing to the heavy list which the ship took to port at once and which finally reached about 35° to 40° it was not possible to lower any boats except the starboard seaboat (cutter). This boat apparently suffered some damage on being lowered and subsequently became completely waterlogged. The fourth motor boat on the port side right aft was, however, traversed out and some ratings were able to unhook the falls as soon as she became waterborne owing to the list of the ship. It was only found possible to cast loose about three of the Carley floats on the starboard side, and these were lowered. Gratings and loose woodwork were also thrown over the side to help men in the water.

HANGARS

Both hangars were evacuated by the few officers and ratings who were there at the time of the torpedoes' hit. Personnel in the lower hangar appear to have had some difficulty in forcing a way through the fire curtains which were jammed down after the explosions.

Immediately after the torpedoes hit, HMS *Ivanhoe* on the port bow turned and attacked the submarine. It is understood that two patterns of depth-charges were dropped. HMS *Impulsive* on the starboard bow dropped astern and commenced picking up survivors who had abandoned ship.

Several officers aft on the Quarter Deck said that they saw a submarine periscope fine on the port quarter showing up against the reflected glow in the water from the western sky. Some of the officers loaded S.8 - 4.7in gun but owing to the list of the ship it could not be trained. They stated that HMS *Ivanhoe* then arrived at the position where the periscope was seen and dropped depth-charges. Several officers and ratings stated afterwards that they saw the stern of the submarine come up out of the water after the depth-charge attack. It is considered that this was quite probably the position of the submarine after her attack, as HMS *Courageous* was still carrying a good deal of way for some minutes after the torpedoes struck.

Captain W. T. Makeig-Jones and 518 of her crew were lost. The destroyers picked up the sur-

Glorious circa 1930/32. **Left:** Plenty of room for Sunday service. **Centre left:** Matelots and Marines gathered on the flight deck. Note the height of funnel and the camber in the deck. During the early years, Glorious and Courageous were practically identical.

Bottom left: Courageous in July 1934 while serving with the Home Fleet.

vivors and U29 was vigorously hunted until midnight. Further attempts to locate the submarine continued for two days afterwards but the U-boat escaped and returned safely to home base.

The Loss of Glorious.

On the morning of 8 June 1940 Glorious, escorted by the destroyers HMS Acasta and HMS Ardent, left the Narvik area bound for Scapa Flow, after participating in the evacuation of British forces from Norway; the carrier had on board some RAF fighters and a few Swordfish. At 1600 on the same day, while off Narvik, two enemy warships were sighted to the north-westward. Ardent was ordered to investigate the contacts which proved to be the German battlecruisers Scharnhorst and Gneisenau, while Glorious turned to the southward, unsuccessfully attempting to fly off her Swordfish aircraft. At 1631 Scharnhorst opened fire at a range of 27,800 yards, closely followed by Gneisenau. Both British destroyers made for the enemy at high speed, laying a smoke-screen, which proved most effective, silencing the battlecruisers' guns for a time. The outcome, however, was already a foregone conclusion. Glorious was completely outranged, her 4.7in guns proving of little use, and shortly after the action began she received a hit in the forward upper hangar which started a fire, destroying the RAF Hurricane fighters stored there, as well as preventing access to the aircraft torpedoes which were also kept there. At 1700 a salvo hit the bridge and at 1715 she received a heavy shell hit aft. Five minutes later the order was given to abandon ship and she sank at 1740, leaving only 43 survivors. Meanwhile Ardent had been sunk at 1728 after firing all eight torpedoes, without success. Acasta steered to the south-east, concealed by smoke, and then fired a salvo of four torpedoes, of which one hit Scharnhorst abreast the after 11in gun turret, causing severe damage and reducing her speed. At 1808 a final salvo devasted Acasta and the order was given to abandon, the ship sinking soon afterwards. Casualties from the three ships were heavy: a total of 1,515 Naval and RAF personnel lost their lives.

A most interesting account of the incident is given in the report written by German staff.

A report on the action fought by the Scharnhorst and Gneisenau with HMS Glorious and her destroyer escort on June 8th, 1940, writ-

ten by Konte-admiral Schubert from memory on 19th July, 1945, and submitted to the Flag Officers Schleswig-Holstein.

'I was Executive Officer of the battleship *Scharnhorst,* which together with the battleship *Gneisenau* sank the Aircraft Carrier *Glorious* and the two destroyers *Ardent* and *Acosta* in the North Sea on June 8th, 1940. My action station as Executive Officer was in the ship's control room. But I was on the bridge at various times to get a picture of how the battle situation was developing. The following statements are therefore based on not only my own observation, but on reports which I received during the course of the battle, or which were subsequently given to me by other officers of the ship. I no longer possess written documents for this report. It is written down from memory.

'After a brief action off Narvik, involving the two battleships and the light naval forces attached to the unit, the battleship sailed northwards on June 8th, 1940 without any escorting vessels, because of news, as far as I can remember, of the presence of an Aircraft Carrier formation in the area of Jan-Mayen. In the afternoon, at about 1700, a cloud of smoke at a distance of about 25 miles to starboard was sighted from the foretop of the *Scharnhorst* through the good lenses of the target indicator. The force of two battleships under the command of the CinC aboard the *Gneisenau,* proceeded at high speed towards this cloud of smoke. The *Scharnhorst* was at this time on the starboard quarter of the *Gneisenau.* On drawing closer, first of all a trellis mast was recognized, later two further masts. At first the impression was gained that there were one battleship and two cruisers. Finally, however, the aircraft carrier *Glorious* was recognized in company with two destroyers.

'One of the two destroyers detached itself from the force, and firing recognition signals, approached the two battleships. The recognition signals were not answered. The battleships opened fire with their for'ard of heavy guns on the aircraft carrier from a distance of about 13 miles. Thereupon one of the escorting destroyers took up a position on the port side of the battleships and from there carried out a torpedo attack, while the second escorting destroyer remained with the carrier. It could be observed that in the aircraft carrier they had immediately begun to bring the aircraft on deck.

'The battleships' first or second salvo had already scored a hit on the aircraft carrier. At that time she was proceeding at a speed of 30 knots. The escorting destroyer in the company of the aircraft carrier laid a smoke-screen between the retreating carrier and the battleships, and thus effectively withdrew the carrier out of sight of the battleships. In carrying out this manoeuvre the destroyer steamed at high speed through the heavy fire of the two battleships. After laying the smoke-screen she took up position on the left edge of the smoke screen (as seen from the battleships), and from there opened fire on the two battleships. The salvos fell very short, as the range was much too great for the destroyer's guns. The salvos from the carrier also fell very short.

The destroyer on the port side of the battleship force again attacked with torpedoes, and endeavoured in an extremely skillful manner to escape the effective defensive fire of the medium guns of the battleships by constant alterations of course. Finally this destroyer also opened fire on the battleships. She fought with a dash which was outstanding in a hopeless situation. The destroyer received numerous hits and finally went down, steaming at high speed with her engines apparently undamaged and firing her for'ard guns (bow chaser) to the last. The last fighting range was about 5 miles. After the battleship force had penetrated the smoke-screen, the *Glorious* was again sighted at a great distance. The heavy guns opened fire from the bows and very quickly the aircraft carrier received further hits. The fighting range quickly narrowed, but still remained comparatively great. The carrier sustained a list to port and was on fire until it finally capsized.

'The destroyer with the carrier closed to attack the battleship force, and at a very close range fired torpedoes at the battleships which took evasive action. At this stage of the battle, at about the time of the carrier capsizing *Scharnhorst* received a torpedo hit on the starboard side by the heavy for'ard turret. As was revealed later the hole torn in the ship's side was of considerable extent. The magazines of the heavy turret were directly penetrated and caught fire. The starboard engine was put out of action, and the starboard shaft with the shaft mountings was torn away from the hull. A large amount of water entered the ship; the ship's situation was

Below: *Courageous* under refit at Portsmouth in 1936, during which she received a tripod foremast.

Bottom: *Glorious* in May 1937, showing the extension to the flight deck aft. This refit, which took from July 1934 to July 1935, was never carried out in *Courageous.*

Left: *Glorious* at the Coronation Fleet Review, 18 May 1937.

becoming difficult, and in particular the middle engine room was gradually filled with water. The ship still continued the action with the destroyer which was not very heavily damaged. The destroyer, with her greatly inferior armament, fought a hopeless fight against the battleships. As far as I can remember, she scored a minor hit with her guns on the middle of the second heavy turret.

'The carrier had meanwhile capsized and sunk far astern of the ship. When the destroyer with her guns out of action ceased fire, the battleships did the same. The situation caused by the severe damage to the *Scharnhorst* made it necessary above all for the damaged ship to return to the nearest Norwegian harbour and for this the necessary steps had to be taken at once. The Narvik area was still in British hands, and the nearest harbour was Trondheim. As far as I can remember, the action took place at about 70 degrees north. The two battleships, leaving the destroyer which was damaged but still afloat, proceeded southwards at a greatly reduced speed.

'It was not clear as to whether the torpedo hit on *Scharnhorst* was really scored by the destroyer in her advanced position or whether it was hit by

Below: *Courageous* in May 1937, showing modifications. Note the bridgework and new tripod.

Bottom: *Courageous* in July 1937. Note the short extension to the flight deck aft, unlike that of *Glorious* during this period.

Right: *Courageous* in July 1937. A good bow view, this shows the extraordinary height of the flight deck, bridge and funnels from the waterline. The photograph also highlights the massive anti-torpedo bulges.

a submarine. At first the latter seemed more probable. To remain longer at the scene of the action was, therefore, not justified.

'Not only the tactical handling, but the audacity and pluck of the destroyers were outstanding. Every officer taking part in the action was of the same opinion. The destroyers put their utmost into the task, although in their hopeless position success was impossible from the start.'

HOOD

DESIGN

The basic concept of *Hood*'s design began on 8 November 1915 when the DNC was asked to prepare a new battleship design along the lines of an improved *Queen Elizabeth*. To this end Tennyson d'Eyncourt forwarded the following data:

Length: 760ft.
Beam: 104ft.
Draught: 23/25ft.
Displacement: 31,000 tons.
Shaft Horse Power: 75,000.
Speed 26/27½ knots.
Fuel: 1,000 tons of oil, 3,500 tons max.
Armament: 8x15in, 12x5in, 2x3in, 4TT.
Armour: main belt 10in, upper and lower 6½–3in ends 5–3½in, barbettes 10in, turrets 11–9in, CT 11in, uptakes 1½in, upper deck 1in, main deck 1½in, middle deck 2–1in, lower 3–2½in.
General equipment: 750 tons, armament: 4,750 tons, armour and backing: 9,150 tons, machinery: 3,550 tons, hull: 11,650 tons, BM: 150 tons.

The initial design, as usual, was modified slightly to give different versions on the same theme, but at this time the primary idea was still to build a superior battleship. The modified figures of January 1916 show:

750ft x 90ft x 25ft 3in.
Displacement 29,500 tons
Shaft Horse Power 60,000
Speed 25kts. Otherwise same as before.

After some discussion two more modified versions were adopted when it was hoped that the best of both worlds would be highly advantageous in perhaps having a very fast battleship rather than a slow battleship and a fast battlecruiser. By 24 January 1916 there were now four designs to discuss, 'A' and 'B', as already mentioned, the other two being designated 'C' and 'C2'. 'C' 660ft x104ft x 23–24ft. Displacement 27,600 tons. Shaft Horse Power 40,000. Speed 22 knots. 'C2' 610ft x 100ft x 24/25ft. Displacement 26,250 tons. Shaft Horse Power 40,000. Speed 22 knots. Otherwise all specifications the same.

Table of Designs 1–6

	Length (pp) (ft)	(oa) (ft)	Beam (ft)	Draught (ft)	Displacement (tons)	SHP	Speed (knots)	Guns	Boilers
Design 1	835	885	104	26/29½	39,000	120,000	30	8 x 15in	large tube
Design 2	790	840	104	25/28	35,500	120,000	30½	8 x 15in	small
Design 3	810	860	104	26/29½	36,500	160,000	32	8 x 15in	small
Design 4	710	757	104	25/29	32,500	120,000	30	4 x 15in	small
Design 5	780	830	104	25/28½	35,500	120,000	30½	6 x 15in	small
Design 6	830	880	104	26/29½	39,500	120,000	30	8 x 15in	small

Design '3': Legend, 27 March 1916
Displacement (tons): 36,250–36,300
Length: 810ft (pp), 860ft (oa).
Beam: 104ft.
Draught: 26/29½ft
Armament
8 x 15in
12 x 5.5in.
Armour
8–5–3in amidships. 5–4in forward, 4in aft, bulkhead 4–3in, barbettes 9in, turrets 11–10in, CT10in, Director Tube 6in, funnel uptakes 1½in, forecastle deck 1½in, upper 1in, main 1½, lower 2–1in.
Weights (tons)
Hull, etc. 14,070
Armour 10,100
Machinery 5,200
General equipment 4,750
Fuel 1,200
BM 180

A conference was held on 26 January 1916 to discuss layouts. The Second Sea Lord pointed out that, '... we are not building battlecruisers in the absence of information on the new German construction and we must act on the assumption that they are keeping up their approved programme'.

Great attention was paid to a series of letters from the Commander-in-Chief, Admiral Jellicoe, who had the advantage of the latest war experience. His guidelines as set out in a letter dated 8 February 1916 reflected the following:

'1. We do not require to build battleships at the moment.
2. Our superiority is very great and gives no cause for uneasiness in regard to this type of ship.
3. Weakness in future will lie in the battlecruiser type especially those possessing high speed. Germany is building at least three very fast battlecruisers, the *Hindenburg*, *Victoria Louise* and *Freya* in addition to *Lützow* and almost certain to approach 30kts, which will be in excess of our battlecruisers.
4. Almost certain that the last three will have 15.2in guns.
5. Any armoured vessel which we are building should be of the battlecruiser type and the need is great.
6. *Glorious* is unable to compete with the German ships owing to inadequate protection and the same applies to the *Repulse*.
7. In some battleship designs forwarded the speed varies from 25 to 27kts. This intermediate speed is to my mind of little use. Either they should be battlecruisers of 30kts or battleships of 22kts.
8. I am attempting to use the *Queen Elizabeth* class as a fast wing but their excess in speed is of very little use and it is questionable whether they can get to head of the line of deployment without blanketing the battle line.
9. Requirements are battlecruisers at 30kts. Not less than 8 guns.
10. None of our armoured decks in battlecruisers are sufficient. Lower decks should be not less than 2½in thick and the funnel casing requires better protection.

Furnished with such advice the First Sea Lord asked the DNC to prepare new designs for a much larger type of battlecruiser.

The Board generally favoured design No. 3 and with some modification it was worked out in detail. The legend appeared on 27 March 1916 showing the same speed as No. 3 for less SHP (144,000) but an armoured belt of only 8 inches maximum. In April the Board approved the design and ordered four of the type which were to be known as the *Admiral* class.

Work on *Hood* commenced in May 1916, but as a result of experience at Jutland it was decided to modify the design to secure increased protection, it having been found possible substantially

Final Legend, 20 August 1917
Displacement: 41,200 tons.
Length: 810ft (pp), 860ft (oa).
Beam: 104ft.
Draught: 28/29ft.
Freeboard: 29ft forward, 21ft 11in amidships, 18ft 9in aft.
Armament
8 x 15in 80rpg
12 x 5.5in 150rpg
4 x 4in 200rpg
2 x 21in submerged TT, 8x 21in above water (changed to 4 at a later date).
SHP: 144,000 for 31 knots
Fuel: 1,200–4,000 tons oil.
Armour
21ft 6in above water line at normal load, 3ft 3in below.
Main belt 12–7–5in, 6–5in forward, 5–4in aft, bulkheads 5–4in aft, 5–4in fore and aft, barbettes 12in max, turrets 15–12–11in, TCT 9–7in, Funnel uptakes 2–1½in, Decks: Forecastle 2–1¼in, Upper 2–1–¾in, Main 3–2–1½-1in, Lower 1½–1in forward, 3–1½–1in aft.
Weight (tons)
Hull, etc. 14,950
Armour 13,550
Machinery 5,300
Armament 5,200
General equipment 800
BM 145

to improve this by accepting deeper draught and slightly reduced speed but without any radical alteration in the design as a whole. Improvements in gunnery and torpedo equipment, bridge and conning tower design, etc., were incorporated at the same time, the details being worked out in collaboration with the CinC Grand Fleet. The modified protection plan was complete by September 1916 and four ships were layed down in the autumn of 1916 although the revised plans were not finally completed and approved in all details until 1917 (see final legend).

Principal modifications on the original design were:

1. Nominal draught and displacement increased by 3 feet and 4,900 tons respectively.
2. Elevation of 15in guns increased from 20 to 30 degrees with corresponding increase in range.
3. Fire control and range-finding equipment for main and secondary guns improved.
4. Four above-water torpedo tubes added with improved torpedo control equipment.
5. Armour on belt, decks (over magazines) and barbettes increased.
6. Hull sides sloped inboard to waterline, offering abnormal angle of impact to projectiles and

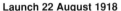

Launch 22 August 1918
Length: 810ft 5in (pp). Beam: 104ft 2in. Beam: 103ft 11½in (as moulded). Depth of keel from forecastle: 50ft 6in.
Breakage: Longitudinally in a distance of 610ft = 2¹⁵/₁₆ths in hog. Transverse in a distance of 88ft = ³/₁₆ths hog.
Displacement: 21,720 tons.
Armament: 74 tons.
Machinery: 1,620 tons.
Armament: 1,184 tons.
Men and equipment on board, etc: 310 tons.
3,188 tons total.

increasing effective armour fitness.
7. Special anti-flash protection fitted to magazines and ammunition hoists.
8. Estimated speed reduced by 1 knot although on trials the original design speed was exceeded by a fraction of a knot.
9. Conning tower and bridge design improved.

The revised design, which represented a merging of battleship and battlecruiser characteristics, constituted what was then a unique combination of offensive power, protection and speed and amounted to a battlecruiser edition of the *Queen Elizabeth* class, the marked rise in displacement (13,700 tons) resulting mainly from the material increase in horsepower (69,000) required to raise speed from 25 to 31 knots.

It also marked the final abandonment in the British Navy of the original battlecruiser concept, embodied to varying degrees in all the preceeding classes, in which protection was sacrificed to an extent which rendered them unfit to engage other capital ships and resulted in the loss of three ships at Jutland. Although benefiting considerably from the lessons learned at Jutland, the design did not fully embody all 1914–18 war experience and was never officially recognized as representing the ideal post-Jutland type. Principal points open to criticism were: 1. Low ratio of offensive power to displacement with only eight guns on 41,200 tons. 2. Retention of relatively light armour on upper sides instead of concentrating protection on belt, deck and gun positions, and absence of any armoured protection to secondary guns.

Early in 1917 the Germans ceased worked on the three *Graf Spee* class, and construction on *Anson*, *Howe* and *Rodney* was suspended in March 1917, the contracts being finally can-

H.M.S. HOOD From the Air
Adamson Photo Copyright

celled in October 1918 after £860,000 had been spent on them. The hulls were dismantled to clear the slips after the armistice.

With a view to bringing her defensive qualities as far as possible into line with modern requirements, *Hood* was earmarked early in 1939 for major reconstruction along similar lines to *Renown*, although the outbreak of war in September 1939 prevented this from being carried out and the ship was never modernized to any sufficient extent. Modifications were to have included:

1. New dual-purpose (HA/LA) secondary armament.
2. Removal of torpedo armament.
3. Addition of aircraft hangars and catapult.
4. Increased protection, especially horizontal.

5. New machinery and new high-pressure boilers (see notes on reconstruction).

Hood served in the Home Fleet 1939–40; Force H (Gibraltar) 1940–1; Home Fleet 1941, lost May 1941.

HULL

The original design, to which work commenced on 27 March 1916, called for a nominal load displacement of 36,300 tons with the same length and beam but with 3 feet less draught. Additional protection worked into the design as revised on the basis of Jutland experience increased nominal draught and displacement by 3 feet. The revised design was nominally 12,700 tons heavier than *Tiger*, previously the heaviest

(although not the longest) ship built for the Royal Navy, with an increase of 156 feet length (oa) and 14ft 9in beam, but with the same designed mean draught. Compared with the *Renown* class displacement increased by 14,700 tons with an increase of 66½ft in length (oa), 15ft 4in beam and 3ft draught. This substantial rise in displacement over earlier ships was necessitated in order to combine all requirements of armament, protection and speed, and for more than twenty years *Hood* retained the disctinction of being the largest warship afloat. The hull lines were perfectly proportioned and exceptionally graceful, careful attention being given to her underwater form so as to avoid any sacrifice in speed because of the provision of anti-torpedo bulges. Her outstanding features were:

1. Strong upward sheer forward and aft, off-setting to some extent the reduced freeboard of the revised design, although the quarterdeck was still very low and liable to be flooded in a seaway.

2. Continuous flare from stem to stern, introduced in the revised design, and intending to augment protection by offering abnormal angles of impact to projectiles. This was considered especially effective against plunging fire. In transverse section the hull sides sloped inwards from weather deck levels right to the keel, where they met the lower edge of the bulge, the flare being such that the outer edge of the bulge was perpendicular to the top side of the hull. The long forecastle carried right through to 'X' turret. Clipper stem without the strong reverse curve of the *Renowns*. Bow flare was considerable but less marked than in those ships.

The fitting of additional armour in the revised design posed special longitudinal strength problems as a consequence of the very considerable bending moment induced by the increased weight of each pair of barbettes, which were located very far apart. Construction was especially stiffened to meet this demand and was exceptionally strong, large areas being covered by thick plating, and heavy framing being an out-

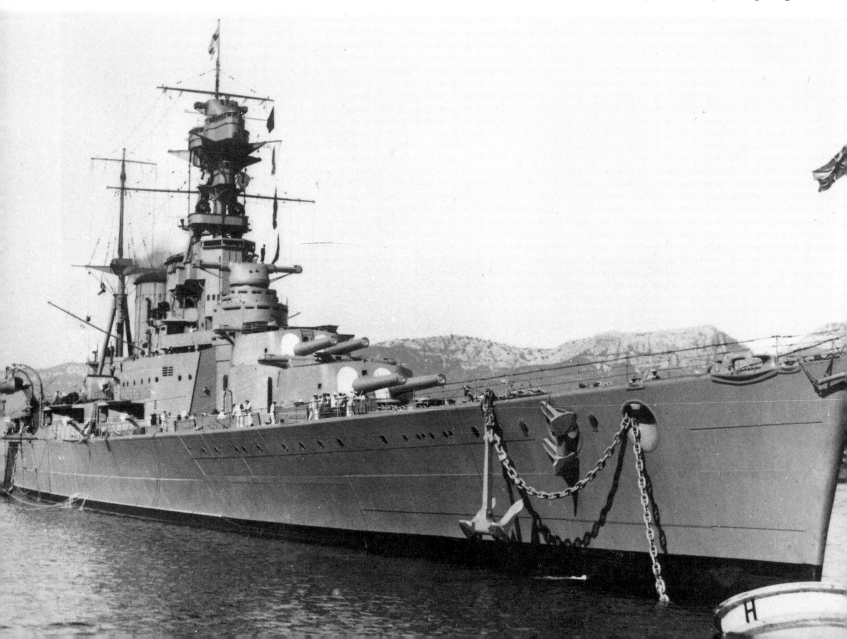

standing feature. Shell plating behind all armour was especially heavy, ranging from 2in HT over the greater portion to 1½in and 1in elsewhere. This materially increased the strength of the entire structure and served as additional armoured protection. The double-bottom was not carried above the turn of the bilge. She proved herself a good sea boat and a steady gun platform. At full speed or in a seaway, however, the deep flare and upward sheer forward kept the forecastle dry although freeboard aft was insufficient to prevent the quarterdeck from being flooded under these conditions.

ARMAMENT

The eight 15in 42cal Mk guns were in four twin turrets all on the centreline, two on the forecastle and two on the quarterdeck, second and third turrets superfiring over first and fourth. Twelve 5.5in 50cal Mk 1 guns for the secondary armament were in single mountings behind open shields, ten pdr (5 P&S) well spaced along the forecastle deck amidships, two (P&S) on shelter deck abeam fore funnel; four 4in anti-aircraft guns in single open mountings at after end of forecastle deck, two on centreline abaft mainmast, two (P&S) abeam this. The 15in guns were the same model as those in the *Queen Elizabeth*, *Royal Sovereign* and *Renown* classes. Director control was fitted: director tower with 15ft rangefinder over the control top, 30ft rangefinder in revolving armoured hood over the conning tower and in rear of each turret. The armoured cases for the turret rangefinders were slightly wider than the rangefinder itself to allow these to be traversed for fine adjustment. Range clocks on foremast, below control top, and at rear of after control platform.

The main armament was equal to that of the latest contemporary battleships, but the ratio of offensive power to displacement was relatively low as a result of the urgent demands for protection and speed, this factor being one of the few points subjected to criticism in the design as a whole. The original design provided 20° elevation for the 15in guns as in *Queen Elizabeth*. In the revised plan, however, this was raised to 30° which increased range by about '7,900 yards. Improved loading gear increased rate of fire from one round in two minutes to one round in about 1 minute 35 seconds. The turrets were a new

design (weighing about 900 tons apiece) with flat crowns and small square sighting ports cut low in the turret face for laying over open sights. This provision of sighting ports in the turret face instead of in hoods on the crown, as in all the earlier classes, allowed direct end-on fire by the superfiring turrets for the first time in the Royal Navy. This had previously been impracticable because of blast effects on personnel at the hoods in the lower turrets. Fire control and rangefinding equipment, which received special attention in the revised design, was unusually elaborate, details being worked out in collaboration with the CinC Grand Fleet. The 30ft rangefinders over the conning tower and in the turrets were the largest afloat to that date. She was the last British capital ship completed with mast location for control and/or director positions. In the later ships these were carried on a large tower structure which replaced the normal bridgework. Gastight arrangements were fitted in the control positions, but the transmitting station was found to become intolerably hot when sealed against the outside air.

The 5.5in secondary armament was a new calibre introduced in the light cruisers *Birkenhead* and *Chester* which were building in England for Greece in 1914 and taken over after the outbreak of war, the spare guns and mountings for these ships being utilized for *Hood*. The shelter deck and first two pairs of forecastle deck guns bore directly ahead to well abaft their beam. Others had wide arcs on their own bow and quarter. They had no direct astern fire. Originally it had been intended to carry four additional guns (making sixteen in all) mounted at the after end of the forecastle deck and bearing directly astern, but these were supressed while building as being unnecessary and entailing extra weight and personnel. Director control was fitted, with director towers (P&S) on the lower bridge. There were control positions each side of the main control top. Official plans show a 9ft rangefinder on each position, but these do not seem to have been fitted until 1924–5 (according to photographs). Battery sighting hoods (P&S) were situated on the shelter deck between the second and third guns and abaft the fifth.

The distribution of secondary guns was well planned and their high command enabled them to be fought in heavy weather although the

absence of any form of protection other than the open splinter shields left the crews very exposed. She was the last British capital ship to have an open secondary battery. The fire control and rangefinding equipment in the revised design received similar attention to that given to the main armament. A torpedo-spotting position was fitted below the main control top. Anti-aircraft armament as completed was double that previously carried in any British capital ship. The design provided for a 6in 'travelling' HA/RF mounted on athwartships rails on the after control position, but this was not actually fitted until after 1926–7. Special arrangements for torpedo control were provided in the revised design, these, as in the case of the gunnery control, being worked out in conjunction with the CinC Grand Fleet. There were three torpedo control towers with a 15ft rangefinder in a revolving hood on each (after hood was armoured): two (P&S) abeam the amidships control tower before the second funnel, one on the centreline abaft the after control position. Directional wireless was fitted, the aerial slung between masts well below the main WT aerials, DF office in the midships control tower before the second funnel. She was the first British warship to complete with D/F equipment.

ARMOUR

The armouring in the original design was very similar to that of *Tiger* with 8in belt and 9in barbettes, but as a result of the loss of *Invincible*, *Indefatigable* and *Queen Mary* at Jutland because of inadequate armouring, it was decided immediately after this engagement to modify the design to secure increased protection, it having been found possible substantially to improve this by accepting deeper draught and slightly reduced nominal speed, but without any radical alteration in the design as a whole. The revised protection plan was completed by September 1916, the principal modifications involving about 5,000 tons additional armour comprising:

1. Increase in maximum thickness of belt armour from 8in to 12in.
2. Materially increased armouring on decks over magazines (extra armour added to crowns of 'X' and 'Y' magazines from 40lb to 80lb). Deck protection increased to a total of 6½in over forward magazines and 7in over after magazines.

Below: *Hood* in 1924 during the World Cruise. Everyone wanted to see the *Hood*, and the ladies were no exception. Note the fashion.

3. Increase in maximum thickness of barbette armour from 9in to 12in.

4. Provision of special anti-flash protection to magazines and ammunition hoists and improved arrangements for isolation and flooding of magazines.

The belt and side armour was backed by special 2in–1½in–1in HT shell plating over the greatest portion, which in effect increased the maximum thickness of belt, lower and upper side to 13½in–9in–7in respectively. One-inch HT plating was carried complete to the stem beyond the ends of the 6in belt armour and over the same height as this. Effective thickness of belt and side armour was further increased by a strong inboard slope of the hull side to the waterline, introduced in the revised design, continuous over the whole length of the ship and offering abnormal angles of impact to projectiles. This feature was of special value against plunging fire. The turrets were a new improved design with flat crowns tending to deflect shells falling at a steep angle and small square sighting ports cut low in the face. Roof plates in the revised design were considerably thicker than in any of the preceding classes. The absence of anything better than open splinter shields for the secondary guns was a weak point and the entire battery was liable to simultaneous disablement by a single hit.

The conning tower, to which particular attention was given in the revised design, was located unusually far ahead of the bridge, affording an unprecedentedly wide range of vision and was the largest, best devised, most elaborate and heaviest ever fitted in any warship to that date. The base carried down to the main deck. The upper stages comprised two shells, 11in outer and 9in inner, with a narrow passage between them. In the middle and lower stages the inner shell (3in) was fitted on the fore side only. The conning tower armour weighed more than 600 tons, the whole structure weighing almost 900 tons.

Provision was made for sealing off the 15in gun turrets, control positions and bridge against gas attack, but during exercises in 1923 conditions in the transmitting station were found to become intolerable when entirely shut off from the outside air.

The anti-torpedo bulges were of an improved type developed by Sir Eustace Tennyson d'Eyncourt (DNC) and Professor B. Hopkinson, from the early pattern fitted in monitors and old cruisers of the *Edgar* class in 1915 as a result of experiments carried out in obsolete battleships shortly before the war (see *Royal Sovereign* class, notes on bulges). The structure comprised an outer section of watertight compartments separated by a $\frac{1}{2}$in HT bulkhead from the inner buoyancy space, also sub-divded and bounded by a $1\frac{1}{2}$in HT longitudinal anti-torpedo bulkhead, sloping inwards to the keel and forming a continuation of the top side plating and inner boundary of the bulge proper. The internal section of the anti-torpedo space behind this bulkhead, instead of comprising part of the bulge as in the *Renown* class, was part of the hull proper and was composed of oil fuel compartments which were separated from working spaces by an air space and an inner $\frac{3}{4}$in HT anti-torpedo bulkhead about 16ft inboard at the waterline rising vertically from keel to main deck. Within the bulge were five rows of crushing tubes over the whole length of the citadel. The width of the bulge for *Hood* had been determined by the weight of the explosive charge carried in torpedoes at that date. The outer edge of the bulge in the perpendicular to top side of hull, the marked flare of the hull side allowing wider bulges than in the *Renown*s. The bulges ran from 'A' and 'Y' barbettes only, hull sides being moulded to flush with these, causing no loss of speed. Complete end to end protection was considered unnecessary because the effect of flooding at the extremities was regarded as being negligible.

As completed it was estimated that *Hood* was capable of withstanding the explosion of four or five torpedoes (1915–18 model) without any material loss of speed or fighting efficiency. Internally she had more than 500 watertight compartments. The independent ventilation in all main transverse compartments eliminated the risk of water passing between them in the event of damage, and there were very elaborate pumping and flooding arrangements. The pumping equipment was capable of discharging about 20,000 tons of water per hour.

The general scheme of protection in the revised design was most comprehensive and similar to that of the latest German battlecruisers, the large areas covered by heavy armour, strong framing and plating, etc., being an outstanding feature. Horizontal and underwater protection was especially strong and on completion (1920) *Hood* was generally conceded to be among the best protected warships afloat, all-round armouring being rather superior to that of the *Queen Elizabeth* class and underwater protection distinctly stronger than in those ships as completed. Percentage of armour weight to displacement 33.5 per cent against 31 per cent in the *Queen Elizabeth*s. Total weight of protection 13,550 tons, which excluded especially heavy HT shell plating. At the same time protection to the main armament, magazines and machinery fell short of the standards afforded by the 'all or nothing' plan adopted by the US Navy in the *Oklahoma* class of 1916, but not accepted by the British Admiralty until after the war when it became universally adopted. As a result light armour was retained over the upper side in *Hood* when it would have been more usefully applied to further strengthening the belt, decks, turrets and barbettes.

During the late 1920s and 1930s it was more than apparent that *Hood*'s protection was vulnerable to modern heavy calibre projectiles, especially at long range when these would fall at steep angles, although the ship would become progressively less liable to vital damage as the range approached 12,000 yards and trajectories flattened. Protection as completed was:

Main Belt: 12in amidships, 562ft long x 9ft 6in wide, extending almost to the outer faces of 'A' and 'Y' barbettes. The upper edge at main deck level was $5\frac{1}{2}$ft above the waterline, the lower edge along the lower deck was 4ft below the waterline; 6in–5in forward extending to within 75 feet of the stem over the same height as the midships section, 6in for 50 feet beyond 'A' barbette, 5in outside this; 6in aft extending to within 80 feet of the stern over the same height as the midships section, 3in lower strip fitted below 12in section.

Middle side: 7in–5in extending from forward extremity of 6in belt armour, 50 feet before 'A' barbette to abeam centre 'Y' barbette between main and upper decks; 7in between outer faces of 'A' and 'Y' barbettes, 5in forward of 'A'.

Upper side: 5in from outer face of 'A' barbette to 65 feet short of 'X' between forecastle and upper decks.

Bulkheads: 5in closing forward extremities of 5in belt armour between lower and main decks. Closing forward extremities of 12in belt armour with 'A' barbette between lower and main decks. Closing forward extremities of middle side armour between main and upper decks. Closing after extremities of 12in belt armour with 'Y' barbette between lower and main decks. Oblique, closing after extremities of 7in middle side armour with 'Y' barbette between main and 'Y' – 12in–9in–6in–5in–2in. Outer face 12in above upper deck, 12in and 9in upper to main, 5in main to lower. Inner face 12in above upper deck, 6in upper to main, 2in main to lower.

Turrets: 15in faces, 12in–11in sides, 11in rears and 5in crowns.

Secondary gun shields: 1in.

Ammunition (5.5in hoists): $\frac{3}{4}$in.

Ammunition passages: $1\frac{1}{2}$in–1in port and starboard between upper and main decks outside engine room casing below 5.5in battery.

Conning tower: 11in–9in–7in–6in–3in sides. Outer shell 11in upper stages, 7in middle, 6in and 3in lower (forecastle to upper deck). Inner shell 9in upper stages, 3in middle and lower (on fore side only), 5in roof, 2in–$\frac{3}{4}$in floor; 2in below upper section, $\frac{3}{4}$in at base on upper deck.

Sighting hood: 10in face, 6in rear over conning tower, 5in crown.

Revolving hood: 6in sides, 3in crown over sighting hood, 2in floor.

Torpedo control tower: 4in face and sides, $1\frac{1}{2}$in rear, 3in roof, 2in floor.

Revolving hood: 4in sides, 3in roof over torpedo control tower.

Uptakes: $1\frac{1}{4}$in (ship's cover states $1\frac{1}{2}$in–$2\frac{1}{2}$in but some plates were removed in revised plan) between shelter and upper decks.

Anti-torpedo bulkheads: $1\frac{1}{2}$in outer, $\frac{3}{4}$in inner. Longitudinal port and starboard over all magazine, machinery and boiler spaces from keel to main deck. Outer bulkheads sloped inboard to keel conforming to angle of hull side. Inner bulkheads vertical. Forward and after extremities closed by $1\frac{1}{2}$in transverse bulkheads.

Anti-torpedo bulges: About $7\frac{1}{2}$ feet wide extending over magazine, machinery and boiler spaces.

MACHINERY

Brown Curtis geared turbines driving four screws. Four separate sets of turbines each comprising: 1. Compound ahead turbines. 2. Cruising turbines in separate casing. Connected with main HP shaft as required and operated in

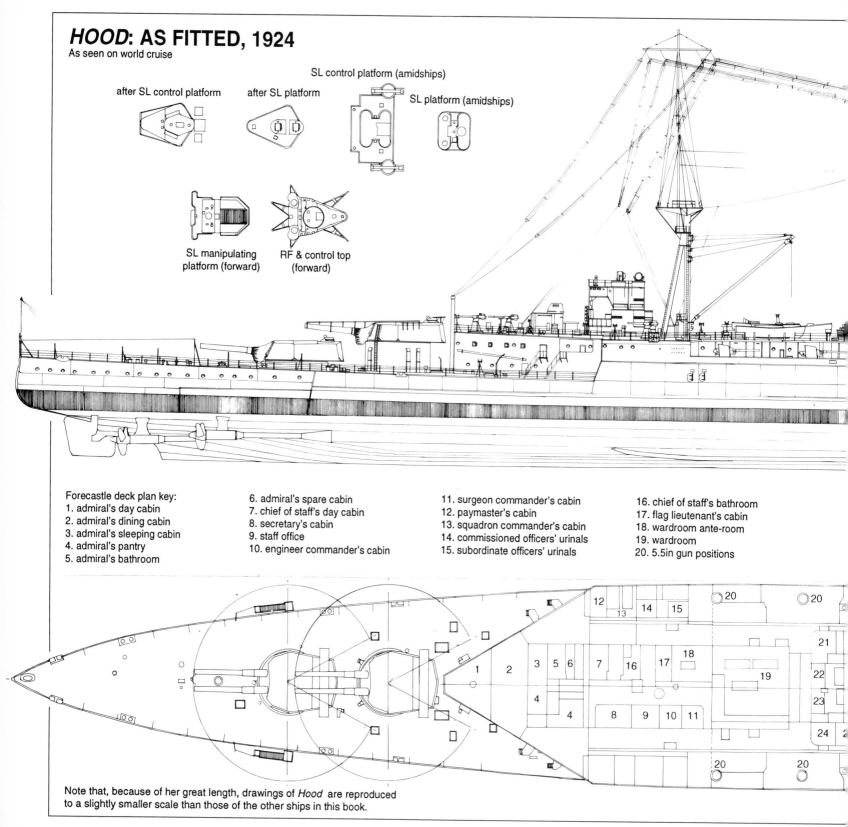

HOOD: AS FITTED, 1924
As seen on world cruise

after SL control platform

after SL platform

SL control platform (amidships)

SL platform (amidships)

SL manipulating
platform (forward)

RF & control top
(forward)

Forecastle deck plan key:
1. admiral's day cabin
2. admiral's dining cabin
3. admiral's sleeping cabin
4. admiral's pantry
5. admiral's bathroom

6. admiral's spare cabin
7. chief of staff's day cabin
8. secretary's cabin
9. staff office
10. engineer commander's cabin

11. surgeon commander's cabin
12. paymaster's cabin
13. squadron commander's cabin
14. commissioned officers' urinals
15. subordinate officers' urinals

16. chief of staff's bathroom
17. flag lieutenant's cabin
18. wardroom ante-room
19. wardroom
20. 5.5in gun positions

Note that, because of her great length, drawings of *Hood* are reproduced
to a slightly smaller scale than those of the other ships in this book.

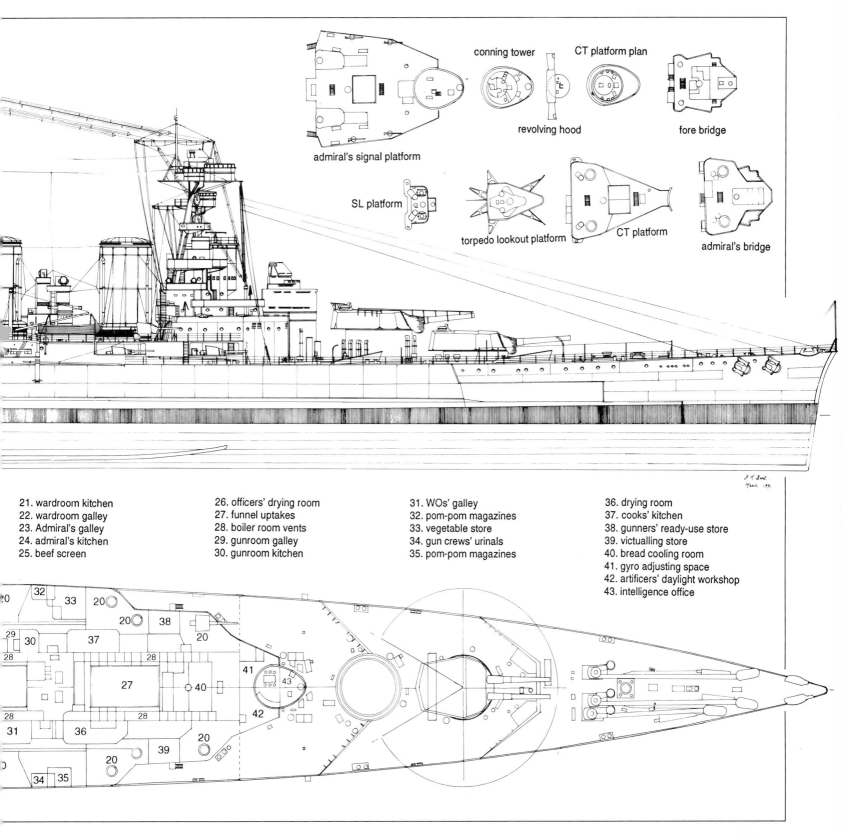

conning tower

CT platform plan

revolving hood

fore bridge

admiral's signal platform

SL platform

torpedo lookout platform

CT platform

admiral's bridge

21. wardroom kitchen
22. wardroom galley
23. Admiral's galley
24. admiral's kitchen
25. beef screen

26. officers' drying room
27. funnel uptakes
28. boiler room vents
29. gunroom galley
30. gunroom kitchen

31. WOs' galley
32. pom-pom magazines
33. vegetable store
34. gun crews' urinals
35. pom-pom magazines

36. drying room
37. cooks' kitchen
38. gunners' ready-use store
39. victualling store
40. bread cooling room
41. gyro adjusting space
42. artificers' daylight workshop
43. intelligence office

Below: *Hood*, Melbourne, Australia, March 1924. One of the her first major tasks was to 'show the flag'. With *Repulse*, cruisers and destroyers, the Squadron went on a World Tour from November 1923 to September 1924 and caused mayhem wherever they went because of the public's wanting to view the largest warship in the world.

completion she was one of the three fastest capital ships in the world (the other two being *Renown* and *Repulse*).

BRIDGEWORK

Although the form of *Hood*'s bridge represented the final development of the older style superstructure, which had been in use since 1912, it was not to everyone's liking, adverse criticisms being:

1. Standard compass platform too small.
2. Impossible to look aft from this position.
3. Necessary communications from this position non-existent.

During preliminary trials the bridge was found rather open and draughty and the following alterations were demanded:

1. Wings fitted at the side of the bridge.
2. Canopy extended to pelorus platform.
3. Canopy given a lip around the opening to deflect air current from opening near the standard compass as far as possible without obstructing view of the instruments.

Even with these modifications and other alterations that took place during the following years, further mild criticism was voiced in 1936.

REPORT OF CAPTAIN'S BRIDGE:
'There is no all-round view. The aft view can only be obtained by going out through the doors to platforms on the wings. When coming alongside the Captain would be on one of these wing platforms which are cut off from essential controls, etc. If bridge is wind down and doors at the back of compass platform are shut conditions are not bad. When doors at the back are open conditions at the compass are difficult.'

ADMIRAL'S BRIDGE:
'From enclosed position in front of charthouse the Admiral cannot see ahead as the view is completely blanked by the armoured hood and rangefinder over the conning tower. From positions in the bridge from which he could see ahead and one side, his view of the other side is blanked. To get a good view aft he has to use the 5.5in director platform on one side and again is cut off from the other side.'

These and other criticisms from officers aboard His Majesty's capital ships led to a completely new type of enclosed structure being

series with HP and LP turbines at cruising speed. 3. Astern turbine fitted in LP casing and rotating in vacuum when steaming ahead. Each set was complete in itself with its own condensers and auxiliaries and could be operated independently. 210 revolutions per minutes at full speed. The turbines were arranged in three compartments: two sets in forward compartment driving wing shafts; one set in midships compartment driving port inner shaft; one set in after compartment driving starboard inner shaft. Reduction in shaft revolutions, as compared with previous ships with direct drive turbines, permitted the adoption of higher efficiency propellers.

The designed horsepower of 36,000 on each shaft was the highest power ever put through gearing to that date, and the total horsepower was higher than in any other ship extant: twenty-four Yarrow small-tube boilers arranged in four compartments (six in each) with an average working pressure of 210psi. Excepting the *Courageous* group as being large cruisers, *Hood* was the first British capital ship to have geared turbines and small-tube boilers. Adoption of small-tube boilers, which had long been advo-

cated by the DNC (d'Eyncourt) and which afforded 30 per cent greater power than the large tube without corresponding increase in weight and space, materially influenced the design as a whole. On a reduction of approximately 185 tons in weight of machinery and boilers, a 30 per cent increase in horsepower was obtained over the *Renown* class, and more than doubled the *Lion*s' horsepower on approximately the same weight; the gain, in this case, being obtained on the same total floor space although substitution of oil fuel for coal was an important contributory factor in this respect. Eight widely separated dynamos provided electric power: two driven by turbines, four by reciprocating engines and two by diesel.

The original design provided for 32 knots at the normal load, rather similar to the *Renown* class. Nominal horsepower was unchanged in the revised design, the estimated speed being reduced by 1 knot as a result of the increased draught in displacement. As completed, however, she proved capable of exceeding the original designed normal load figure.

Careful attention to the hull form meant that the speed was not affected by the bulges, and on developed and this featured for the first time in the *Nelson* pair of 1925.

GENERAL NOTES

The bridge structure, which was a development of the type introduced in the *King George V* class battleships and *Lion* class battlecruisers, comprised a heavy square cut central tower with two wings at each side. The navigating platform was completely enclosed and not projected forward as in the earlier classes. The bridge was set well abaft the conning tower.

Four separate steering positions were fitted: (a) in conning tower; (b) in lower conning tower; (c) in after engine room; (d) in steering compartment (auxiliary only). No hand steering gear was provided, experience having failed to justify retention of this in large, high-speed ships.

Heavy boats were stowed on the shelter deck between second funnel and mainmast and handled by main derrick slung from mainmast. Seaboats were carried in two pairs of fixed davits (port and starboard) on shelter deck between funnels. An extra pair of davits was added further aft, 1926–7.

Accommodation, which embodied recommendations of the special committee appointed shortly before the war, was materially improved in some respects over that in the earlier ships. Berthing and sanitary arrangements were reported as being not inferior to those in contemporary US ships. Officers' accommodation was reported as being excellent, but crew's quarters, located over boiler rooms, not altogether satisfactory. Messes had good headroom but where otherwise cramped and inferior to the preceding classes. Oil-fired cooking appliances, marking a considerable advance over all previous arrangements, were adopted for the first time in the Royal Navy. Special attention was paid to ventilation. Supply and exhaust fans provided fresh air, warmed if necessary, at low velocity to all living spaces, with full natural supply to engine and boiler rooms, a separate supply being provided to each main transverse compartment to avoid openings in bulkheads. The ship was fitted as a flagship but with no sternwalk.

RIG

Tripod fore and mainmasts. Stump topmast to fore and short topmast to main. Top gallantmast to main in early period, when required to increase W/T range, but usually carried housed down abaft topmast; carried throughout world cruise 1923–4 but removed altogether after this. Wide signal struts, raked strongly aft, from lower starfish on foremast. Combined signal and W/T yard at head fore topmast. Main derrick on mainmast. Light derricks port and starboard abeam second funnel and at each side midships control tower before this. According to photographs of the official model, the ship was originally designed without main topmast, after ends of W/T aerials being carried to upward-raking struts at main starfish, and would probably have been rigged thus if completed prior to the end of the war.

APPEARANCE CHANGES AND REFITS

She was much longer and less 'piled up' than the *Renown*s and was generally conceded to have been one of the finest-looking warships ever built.

No previous ship had presented such an embodiment of power and speed combined with beauty and proportion, and her size was not

Metacentic Height and Stability: (As inclined, 21 February 1920
Displacement (tons): 41,125 (light). Draught: 28ft 3in. GM: 4.2ft.
42,670 (legend). Draught: 29ft 3in. GM: 3.25ft.
46,680 (deep). Draught: 32ft. GM:3.2ft.
As inclined, 14 March 1931
Displacement: 41.125 tons (light). Draught: 28ft 3³/₈in forward, 28ft 5¹/₈in amidships, 29ft 5¹/₄in aft.
As inclined, 15 July 1932
Displacement: 45,450 tons (legend). Draught: 30ft 4in forward, 32ft aft

Steam Trials: Held on the Clyde: (Preliminary trials for acceptance) 18 March 1920.

Displacement (tons)	Revolutions	SHP	Speed (knots)
42,090	inner 66.5	inner 655	11.84
	outer 93	outer 3,901	
41,700	inner 61	inner –	15.17
	outer 112	outer 7,480	
41,600	inner 125	inner 7,232	20.37
	outer 123	outer 7,307	
42,190	inner 173	inner 21,229	27.46
	outer 174	outer 22,071	
42,200	inner 203	inner 35,246	31.58
	outer 203½	outer 37,543	
44,600	inner 204.7	inner 40,000	31.88
	outer 204.3	outer 40,900	

Maximum speed attained on this day was 32 knots with 151,600 shp.
The following day *Hood*'s calculations were: 5,000 miles at 18 knots and 4,500 miles at 20 knots based on consumption during trials.

Steam Trials: Measured Mile, April 1920

Displacement (tons)	Speed (knots)	SHP	RPM
42,090	13.53	9,110	80
41,700	15.60	14,630	93
41,700	17.20	20,050	103
41,600	20.37	29,080	124
41,850	25.24	58,020	154
42,100	27.77	89,010	176
42,150	27.71	116,151	191
42,200	32.07	151,280	207
45,000	13.17	8,735	81
45,000	15.78	14,020	96
45,000	19.11	24,720	116
44,600	22.00	40,780	136
44,600	25.73	69,010	161
44,600	28.37	112,480	185
44,600	31.89	150,220	204

HOOD, BRIDGEWORK

1920, superstructure as
completed and during
trials period. Note open
bridge & range clocks
are already fitted.
No RF on control top.
(draughty open bridge)

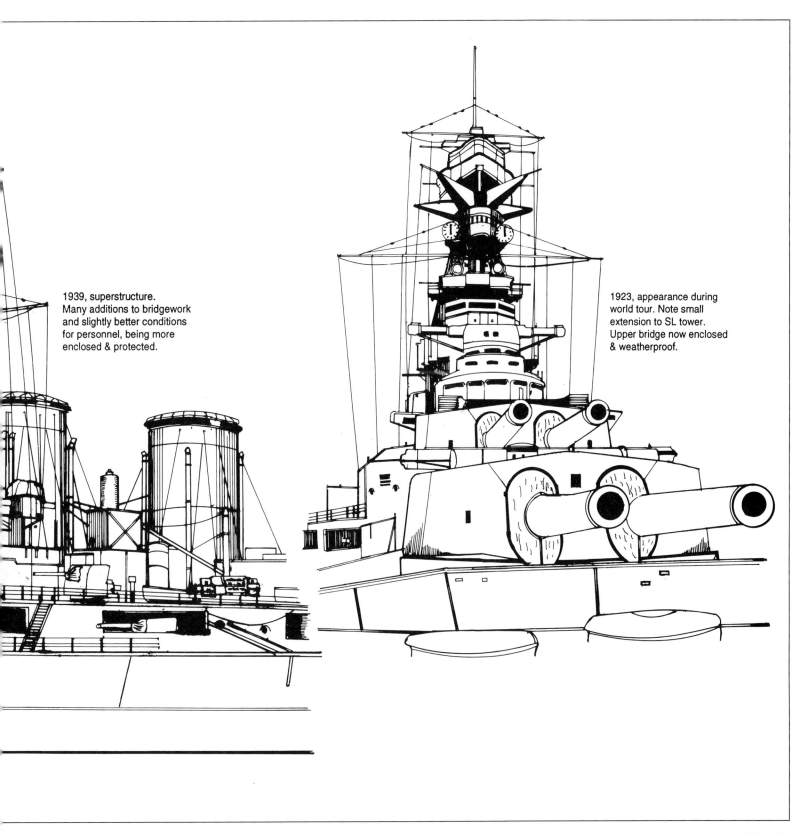

1939, superstructure.
Many additions to bridgework
and slightly better conditions
for personnel, being more
enclosed & protected.

1923, appearance during
world tour. Note small
extension to SL tower.
Upper bridge now enclosed
& weatherproof.

Hood: Particulars, as completed

Construction
John Brown; laid down 1.9.1916; launched 22.8.1918; completed 7.1.1920 (commissioned for trials).
Displacement (tons): 41,125 (light), 42,670 (load), 46,680 (deep).
Dimensions
Length: 810ft 5in (pp), 860ft (oa).
Beam: 104ft 2in (105ft 3in max.).
Draught: 28ft 3in light, 29ft 3in load, 32ft deep.
Armament
8 x 15in 42cal Mk I
12 x 5.5in 50cal Mk I
4 x 4in AA
4 x 3pdr (saluting)
5 MG
10 Lewis
6 x 21in TT (4 above water, 2 submerged).
Armour: (see also armour notes)
Main belt 12in amidships, 6–5in forward, 6in aft, 3in lower strip; Middle side belt 7–5in, Upper side 5in, Bulkheads: 5in, Decks: Forecastle 2–1½–1¼–¾–½in, Upper 2–1–¾in, Main 3–2–1½in, Lower 2–1½–1in forward, 3–2–1½–1in aft; Barbettes 12–10–9–6–5–2½in, Turrets 15–12=11–5in, Secondary gunshields 1in Ammunition hoists (5.5in ¾in, CT 11–9–6–3in, TCT 4–1½in, Anti-torpedo bulkhead 1½) –¾in.
Director control: fitted in tower aloft and also in 'B' and 'X' turrets.
Machinery
Brown Curtis geared turbines driving 4 propellers.
Boilers: 24 Yarrow small-tube in 4 compartments.
Working pressure: 210psi.
Designed shp: 144,000 for 31 knots.
Fuel (tons): 1,200 oil normal, 4,000 max.
Radius of action: 6,400nm at 12 knots.
Searchlights 8 x 36in: 2 on platform low on fore tripod, 4 on midships control tower between funnels; 4 x 24 signalling: 2 on after control position abaft mainmast.
Rangefinders
Five 30ft: 1 in each 15in turret and 1 in director control tower forward.
Ship's boats (see 1939).
Anchors: 3 x 192cwt stockless 1 x 61cwt stern.
Wireless: Types 1–16, Types 1–34, Type 31 (2 offices as completed).
Complement: 1,475 (average).
Cost: published figure: £6,025,000.

apparent unless she was seen in company with other ships. Principal characteristics: (a) Clipper stem. (b) Marked upward sheer forward and aft and inboard slope of hull side to waterline, continuous over whole length. (c) Exceptionally large conning tower, well clear ahead of bridge, with prominent RF over this. (d) Solid, square-cut bridge work. (e) Large control top on foremast with heavy director tower on roof. (f) Large SL and control tower before second funnel. (g)

Large, flat-sided funnels. (h) Secondary guns in shields along forecastle deck amidships.

1920–39
1921: Range clocks removed from sides of after control position; one relocated at rear of this, other suppressed.

1922–3: Lower pair of SL removed from midships control tower. Small tower on light lattice

support temporarily mounted over after control position (removed July 1923).

1924–5: Range clock below fore control top removed. Secondary armament RF (9ft) in shield fitted at each side of main control top. These RF included in original design (vide official plans) but not fitted as completed. Modifications effected by May 1925.

1925–6: After control position enlarged. SL on

after control position remounted abreast with remote control position below each.

1926–7: 6ft traversing HA RF mounted on athwartships rails on after control position. This was included in original design (see official plan) but not fitted as completed.

1931
As refitted May 1929 to March 1931: Multiple 2pdr AA (8 barrels) added port and starboard on shelter deck amidships. HA RF on after control position replaced by HA director. One pair 24in signalling SL remounted on superstructure below bridge. Aircraft catapult (McTaggart training type) fitted on quarterdeck right aft with crane for handling aircraft abaft it. One Fairey IIIF reconnaissance seaplane carried. Flying-off platform removed from 'X' turret. Short wings fitted to upper bridge. Forward pair seaboat davits removed to accommodate multiple 2pdrs.

1932: Range clock removed from after control position. Secondary armament RF at each side of control top removed. Aircraft spotting position added (port and starboard) on after points of starfish below control top. Catapult and crane removed (location reported to have been found inconvenient). Modifications effected May 1932.

1933–4: Multiple 0.5in AA (4 barrels) added

port and starboard on superstructure abeam conning tower. Flying-off platform removed from 'B' turret. Modifications effected by July 1934.

1934–5:
Secondary armament RF remounted port and starboard on forward superstructure abeam bridge. AA spotting positions on starfish below control top enlarged and brought in against rear of top. Modifications effected by July 1935.

1936
As refitted June to September 1936: After control position rebuilt and enlarged. AA spotting positions on foremast removed. SL and platform removed from foremast. Remaining 36in SL replaced by 44in. Upper bridge built up. Middle bridge wings extended aft around tripod legs.

1937–8: Red, white and blue identifiction bands painted up on 'B' turret in Mediterranean during Spanish Civil War.
Refit, February to June 1939: Shelter deck pair of 5.5in removed. Four twin 4in AA in large shields added, 2 P&S on shelter deck abaft sec-

Hood: Particulars, 1939
Displacement (tons): 42,672 (load), 48,650 (deep) (48,360 after removal of 5.5in guns).
Dimensions: unchanged.
Draught greatly increased owing to additions: 33ft 2in forward, 34ft 0¼in aft.
Armament
Main guns as original
Secondary guns as original
8 x 4in (twins)
24 x 2pdr AA (3 x 8 barrels)
8 x 0.5in (2 x quads)
Original field and saluting guns
4 x 21in TT (above water).
Radar: Improved MF/DF (1939).
Searchlights: 6 x 44in.
Aircraft: nil.
Protection: as original.
Machinery and boilers: unchanged.
Speed: Reported as having dropped considerably, 28–29 knots maximum.
Rig: Original plus DF aerial at head of main topmast. D/F cabinet on main starfish.
Complement: 1,341–1,418.
Appearance
Original appearance not materially altered by 1920/39 modifications. Bridgework only slightly modified. Large control tower before second funnel was replaced by small deckhouse well clear of funnel. Twin 4in AA amidships and prominent 2pdr gun mountings. After control position considerably enlarged.

Proposed Modernization, 12 December 1938
1. New machinery.
2. 8 x 5.25in guns in pairs.
3. Short range HA AA increased to 6 Mk VI pompoms, 0.5in guns removed.
4. Fitting D111H Catapult and aircraft hangar as in KGV class.
5. Removal of all above-water TT.
6. Removal of conning tower and reconstruction of bridgework.
7. Modification of underwater protection, removal of crushing tubes and replacement with oil fuel compartments.
8. Increase deck protection (5in over magazines, 4in over machinery).
9. Removal of upper belts (7in and 5in) and replace with 12in plates.
Estimated costs:

Machinery	£1,625,000
Armour protection	750,000
Underwater protection	300,000
Re armament	1,000,000
CT and bridgework	150,000
Extension of forecastle	30,000

Including other small additions and alterations, the total estimated cost was £4,035,000.
After this refit the ship was estimated to be good for another fifteen years.

Masts: August 1931

		length(ft/in)	diameter (in)
Foremast:			
Lower mast	steel	87	36
Struts	steel	100	33
Flagpole	wood	19	6–4
Topmast	wood	30ft 5in	14–6in
Signal yards	wood	30ft 6in	8½–5
Outriggers	wood	9–10	
Mainmast:			
Lower mast	steel	92	36
Struts	steel	72ft 9in	
Topmast	wood	59	
Flagpole	wood	26ft 10in	
Gaff	wood	32ft 10in	
Topgallant yard	for W/T	30	
Derrick	steel	65	
Jackstaff	wood	50	
Ensign staff	wood	21ft 6in	

ond funnel, close to mainmast. After pair of 4in AA remounted in place of shelter deck 5.5in. Multiple 2pdr AA (8 barrels) added on large platform on centreline abaft control position (replacing torpedo control tower). HA directors added (P&S) on forward superstructure abaft bridge. Submerged torpedo tube room utilized for other purposes (TT in this position removed in 1937). Additional DF equipment added. Two 44in lamps added on platform P&S close abaft second funnel and set well out from this. Bridge face slightly modified.

Refit extension, June to August 1939: All single 4in AA removed. Shelter deck 5.5in replaced. Control tower before second funnel removed; original DF position in this was relocated in small deckhouse farther away from funnel. Extension to admiral's bridge. HACS improved.
Refit, March to June 1940: Shelter deck 5.5in removed. All 5.5in equipment removed. Three twin 4in AA (HA/LA Mk XIX) added in large shields. Forward 5.5in openings plated up. Low shields fitted around 2pdr guns. Five UP mountings fitted, one on 'B' 15in turret, four on shelter deck amidships. Degaussing cable fitted outside hull. 5.5in spotting tops converted to 4in control positions.
Refit, January to March 1941 (last modifications received): Type 284 radar fitted for main gunnery. Type 279 AW radar fitted. HF/DF office removed from mainmast. Torpedo lookouts removed from foremast. Foretopmast removed.

HISTORY: HOOD

Ordered April 1916 under Emergency War Programme from H. Brown & Co., Ltd., Clydebank.
Work commenced 31 May 1916 but suspended after Battle of Jutland for modification in design (see General Summary of Design). Laid down to revised design 1 September 1916. Launched 22 August 1918. Commissioned at Clydebank for trials 7 January to March 1920.
Completed full crew at Rosyth 29 March 1920 to relieve Tiger as flag Battlecruiser Squadron, Atlantic Fleet.
Carried out further trials from Devonport March to May 1920.
Officially completed 15 May 1920.
Joined BCS at Portland May 1920. Flag transferred from Tiger 17 May.

ATLANTIC FLEET (flag BCS) May 1920 to November 1923.
Ordered to Reval May 1920, with Tiger and nine destroyers, to reinforce the British Baltic Squadron for proposed summer operations against the Bolsheviks. Squadron left Portland 30 May and proceeded via sweden and Denmark.
Recalled from Copenhagen in June owing to change in policy towards the Red regime, and visited Oslo en route home.

Arrived Scapa 3 July.

Received surrender of German battleships *Helgoland* and *Westfalen* and twelve destroyers in Forth 4 August 1920.

Detached August 1922, with *Repulse*, to represent Royal Navy at Brazilian Independence Centenary Celebrations at Rio de Janeiro and subsequently carried out flag-showing cruise in the West Indies.

Left Devonport 14 August 1922, returned 3 December.

With *Repulse* and *Snapdragon*, visited Norway and Denmark June to July 1923. Hoisted flag King of Norway as Honorary Admiral in Royal Navy during this cruise.

Detached November 1923 as flag Special Service Squadron comprising *Hood* (flag VA), *Repulse* and 1st LCS *Delhi* (flag), *Danae*, *Dauntless* and *Dragon*, for Empire and world cruise.

FLAG SPECIAL SERVICE SQUADRON (world Cruise) November 1923 to September 1924. Squadron left from rendezvous off Plymouth 27 November, proceeding outwards via Cape and Indian Ocean and returning across the Pacific. Itinerary of battlecruisers and light cruisers varied in some instances and finally separated on leaving San Francisco 11 July 1924 on the return leg, the former passing through the Panama Canal while the latter proceeded around South America. Squadron reformed again off the Lizard 28 September, ships arriving back at their home ports on 28th and 29th. *Hood* and *Repulse* visited: Sierra Leone, Capetown, Zanzibar, Trincomalee, Port Swettenham, Singapore, Fremantle, Albany, Adelaide, Melbourne, Hobart, Jervis Bay, Sydney, Wellington, Auckland, Fiji, Honolulu, Vancouver, Victoria, San Francisco, Panama, Colon, Kingston (Jamaica), Halifax, Quebec and St. John's (Newfoundland).

Hood arrived Devonport 29 September and rejoined Atlantic Fleet.

ATLANTIC FLEET (BCS) September 1924 to May 1929 (flag to April 1929).

Refit Rosyth and Devonport September 1924 to January 1925.

With *Repulse*, represented Royal Navy at Vasco da Gama celebrations at Lisbon February 1925.

Flag transferred to *Repulse* April 1929 and *Hood* paid off to Dockyard Control at Portsmouth 17 May 1929 for extensive refit, May 1929 to March 1931.

Recommissioned Portsmouth for BCS 17 May 1931.

ATLANTIC FLEET (BCS) May 1931 to March 1932 (flag from July 1931).

Flag transferred from *Repulse* 11 July 1931.

Atlantic Fleet redesignated Home Fleet March 1932.

HOME FLEET (flag BCS) March 1932 to September 1936.

Refit Portsmouth March to May 1932.

Collision with *Renown* during exercises off Spanish coast 23 January 1935. *Hood* rammed by *Renown* on starboard quarter, damage to stern and propellers. Temporarily repaired at Gibraltar. Repairs completed at Portsmouth February to May 1935.

In March 1935, it was decided, in the interests of homogeneity, gradually to separate the *Queen Elizabeth* and *Royal Sovereign* classes, stationing the former in the Mediterranean and the latter in the Home Fleet. Because of the heavy reconstruction programme in the *Queen Elizabeth* class, the Mediterranean would lose one battleship by the change, and the Battlecruiser Squadron was to be transferred to the Mediterranean Fleet to offset this. Squadron initially divided between the Home and Mediterranean Fleets April to September 1936. Not finally transferred to Mediterranean until 1936, *Repulse* in April, *Hood* in September. *Renown* reconstructing 1936–9.

Hood present at Jubilee Review, Spithead 16 July 1935.

Because of the Italo-Abyssinian crisis, the Battlecruiser Squadron, comprising *Hood* and *Renown* (*Repulse* reconstructing), sent to Gibraltar September 1935 to reinforce the

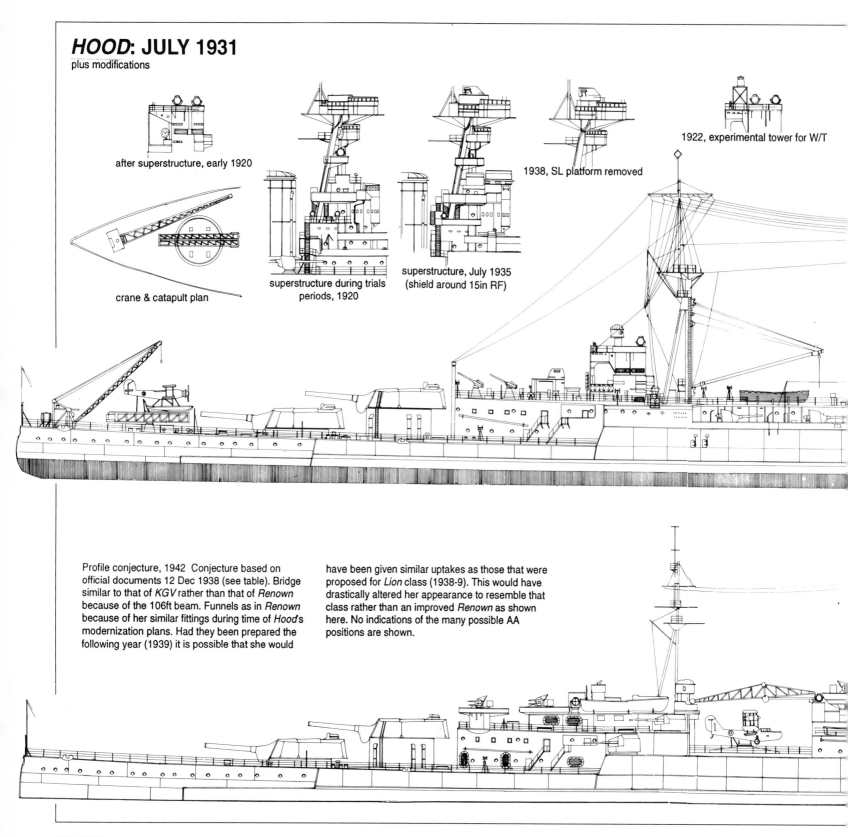

HOOD: JULY 1931
plus modifications

after superstructure, early 1920

crane & catapult plan

superstructure during trials
periods, 1920

superstructure, July 1935
(shield around 15in RF)

1938, SL platform removed

1922, experimental tower for W/T

Profile conjecture, 1942 Conjecture based on official documents 12 Dec 1938 (see table). Bridge similar to that of *KGV* rather than that of *Renown* because of the 106ft beam. Funnels as in *Renown* because of her similar fittings during time of *Hood*'s modernization plans. Had they been prepared the following year (1939) it is possible that she would have been given similar uptakes as those that were proposed for *Lion* class (1938-9). This would have drastically altered her appearance to resemble that class rather than an improved *Renown* as shown here. No indications of the many possible AA positions are shown.

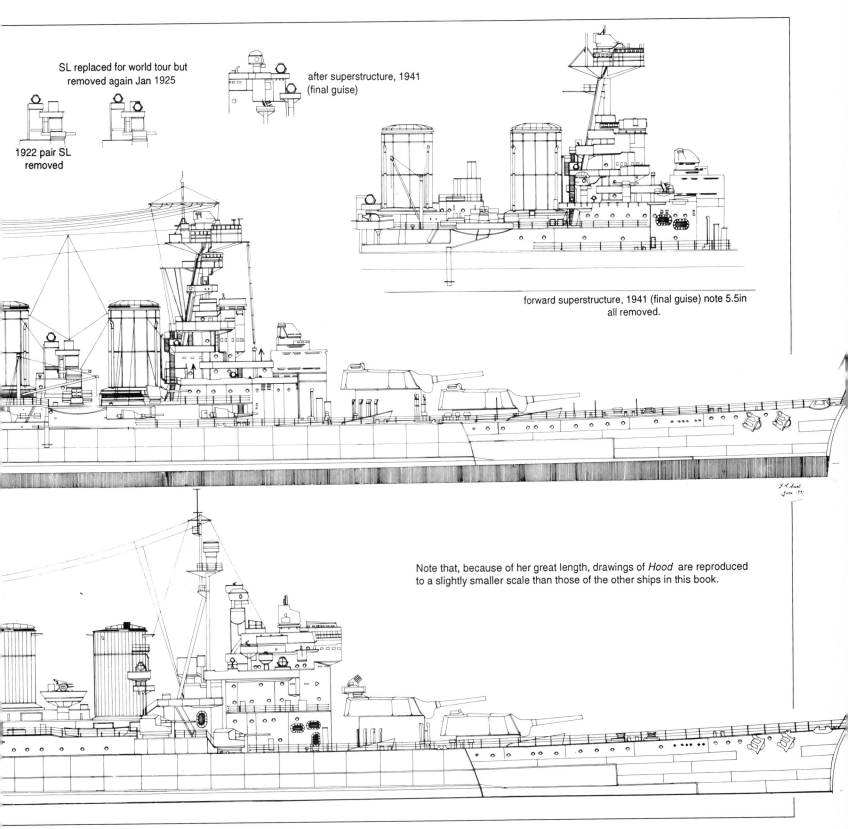

SL replaced for world tour but
removed again Jan 1925

after superstructure, 1941
(final guise)

1922 pair SL
removed

forward superstructure, 1941 (final guise) note 5.5in
all removed.

Note that, because of her great length, drawings of *Hood* are reproduced
to a slightly smaller scale than those of the other ships in this book.

Below: Port-side amidships superstructure.

Mediterranean Fleet although remaining as a Home Fleet unit.

Renown transferred to Alexandria in January 1936 and attached to 1st BS until May 1936 when she rejoined BCS at home.

Hood returned home at Portsmouth until September 1936.

Recommissioned at Portsmouth 8 September 1936 for BCS Mediterranean Fleet under the 1935 Fleet Reorganization plan. Joined at Malta 20 October 1936.

MEDITERRANEAN FLEET (BCS) September 1936 to February 1939 (flag VA BCS and 2nd fleet flag from November 1936).

Flag VA and 2nd fleet flag hoisted at Malta 30 November 1936.

Flag 1st BS (*Barham*) previously 2nd fleet flag.

Employed 1937–8 mainly in protecting British interests (anti-piracy patrols) during Spanish Civil War.

In April 1937 stood by, with *Shropshire*, off Bilbao following interception of British steamer *Thorpehall* by Franco cruiser *Almirante Cervera* outside territorial waters. *Thorpehall* subsequently released following arrival of three British destroyers. Later same month escorted British steamers *Hamsterly*, *MacGregor* and *Stanbrook* carrying relief food supplies from St-Jean de Luz to Bilbao and prevented interference by Spanish warships.

Present at Jubilee Review, Spithead 20 May 1937.

Stationed in western Mediterranean January to November 1938 (Marseilles-Barcelona-Palma area), Vice-Admiral BCS being appointed Senior Officer.

Western Basin Mediterranean from January 1938 in connection with Spanish War operations.

Battlecruiser Squadron reverted to Home Fleet February 1939.

HOME FLEET (BCS) February 1939 to May 1940 (flag BCS to March 1940 and 2nd fleet flag from June 1939).

Refit Portsmouth February to June 1939.

Recommissioned at Portsmouth 1 June 1939, flag VA BCS becoming 2nd fleet flag from that date.

With *Renown*, two cruisers and four destroyers, carried out patrol between Iceland and the Faroes 7–12 September 1939 to intercept enemy merchant shipping and enforce British blockade. Attacked by enemy aircraft in North Sea 26 September 1939 while covering rescue operations for submarine *Spearfish*, damaged off Horns Reef on 25th and unable to dive. Hit glancing blow on quarter by heavy bomb. No damage.

With *Repulse*, *Aurora*, *Sheffield* and four destroyers, searched for German force comprising *Gneisenau*, *Köln* and four destroyers off Stadlandet 8–10 October 1939 following sortie by this group. No contact established.

With *Nelson*, *Rodney* and four destroyers, covered iron ore convoy from Narvik to UK 22–31 October 1939.

Commenced refit at Devonport November 1939 for machinery defects which had reduced speed to 25 knots. Refit interrupted to search for *Scharnhorst* and *Gneisenau* following sinking of *Rawalpindi* 23 November.

Left Devonport 25 November and joined French battleship *Dunkerque* and cruiser *Georges Leygues* and *Montcalm*, with British and French destroyer screen, for search in area south of Iceland.

This was the first Anglo-French naval operation of the war and was under the overall command of the French admiral in *Dunkerque* who was senior to the vice-admiral in *Hood*.

With *Barham* and *Warspite*, covered the first Canadian troop convoy to UK in December 1939. Left Clyde for this operation 12 December.

Resumed refit at Devonport March 1940, flag BCS being transferred to *Renown*. Left Devonport 26 May for Liverpool to complete refit, completed 12 June. While ship under refit, 250 crew mainly Marines, joined Allied Expeditionary Force to Norway.

Escorted first New Zealand troop convoy from Finisterre area to Clyde immediately after completion of refit.

relieving *Renown* as flag BCS. Flag Force H transferred to *Renown* at Scapa 10 August 1940.

HOME FLEET (flag VA BCS and 2nd fleet flag) August 1940 to May 1941.
With *Repulse*, three ships of 1st CS and six destroyers, covered approaches to Brest and Lorient during search for *Scheer* following sinking of *Jervis Bay* 5 November 1940.
Refit Rosyth February to March 1941.
Took part in search for *Scharnhorst* and *Gneisenau* in North Atlantic March 1941.
Based on Hvalfiord (Iceland) with four destroyers early May 1941 to cover convoys passing south of Iceland against possible attack by enemy heavy ships.
Left Scapa 22 May 1941, with *Prince of Wales* and destroyers *Icarus*, *Echo*, *Electra*, *Achates*, *Antelope* and *Anthony*, to cover area south-west of Iceland and support *Norfolk* and *Suffolk* in Denmark Strait following report of sortie by *Bismarck* and *Prinz Eugen*.
German ships sighted early on 24 May off the western end of the Denmark Strait and action opened at 0552 at about 25,000 yards range. Enemy fire initially concentrated on *Hood* although, through to an error in identification, she at first engaged *Prinz Eugen* instead of *Bismarck*.

LOSS OF HOOD

Bismarck had opened fire at about the same time as *Prince of Wales*. At about 0555 *Hood* and *Prince of Wales* executed a turn together of 20° to port in order to bring their after guns into play as only the forward turrets would bear at the angle of early engagement. The third salvo from *Bismarck* had hit *Hood*'s boat deck near the mainmast and started a fierce fire in the area. The masses of evidence show that *Hood* was hit again by the fifth salvo from *Bismarck* and that one or two shells fell in the area of the boat deck and possibly near or below the waterline. This was at the same time as *Hood* and *Prince of Wales* were putting over another 20° (range about 16,300 yards). This move, however, was never executed because at 0600 hours *Hood* exploded in a mass of flames and smoke, and sank in approximately three minutes.

There is some evidence that *Hood*'s after 15in guns actually fired a salvo just before she

Transferred to Force H (Gibraltar) on its formation June 1940.
Left Clyde for Gibraltar 18 June, arrived 23rd.
To offset the loss of the French Fleet in the Mediterranean, following the fall of France in June 1940, it was decided to base a powerful force, designated Force H, at Gibraltar, independent of the existing Gibraltar command, to work in the Western Basin of the Mediterranean and cover the convoy routes from Sierra Leone and Gibraltar.
As organized at Gibraltar on 28 June 1940, Force H comprised *Hood* (flag VA), *Resolution*, *Valiant*, *Ark Royal*, *Arethusa*, *Enterprise* and four destroyers. Flag Vice-Admiral Somerville hoisted in *Hood* on 30 June.

FORCE H (Gibraltar) June to August 1940 (flag).
Took part in attack by Force H (plus seven destroyers from the Gibraltar command) on the French fleet at Oran 3 July 1940.
Slightly damaged by shell splinters from fire of *Dunkerque*.
W/T aerials carried away. One officer and one rating wounded.
Force attacked by Italian high-level bombers in central Mediterranean 8 June 1940 while en route to carry out air attack on Cagliari as a diversionary operation to coincide with passage of convoy from Malta to Alexandria. Operation later abandoned because of risk of further heavy air attack.
On 31 July 1940, Force H left Gibraltar escorting *Argus* with the first fighter aircraft reinforcements for Malta, these being flown-off from a position south of Sardinia. Before returning, aircraft from *Ark Royal* carried out attack on Cagliari airfield. Force later attacked by Italian high-level bombers but no damage sustained.
Hood rejoined Home Fleet in August 1940,

exploded or at least simultaneously with the hit. As might be expected in connection with such a sudden, unexpected and stupendous happening, and the lapse of time from the occurence to recalling the incident, the actual evidence was confused and contradictory.

A Board of Enquiry was set up but it was accepted that no witness to the scene could be

Below: *Hood*, Weymouth Bay, July 1935. One of the most graceful looking warships ever built, the 'Mighty 'Ood' shows her fine lines.

100 per cent certain of what really happened. The only certain fact was that the major explosion was in the area of the mainmast. To try – as many have – to determine exactly how and why *Hood* exploded as she did is fruitless; unless and until her remains are inspected, which might throw some light on the matter, any conclusion is mere speculation. Nevertheless, we can be sure about much that happened on that fateful day and, following official documents closely, the evidence of observers is presented below.

In the vicinity, HMS *Suffolk* (cruiser), 28 miles from *Hood*:

'The plot (Exhibit A) shows that this ship was 28 to 30 miles from *Hood* during the action and it is obvious that little could be seen, although a mirage effect was noticeable (see Captain R. M. Ellis's evidence (Series A.26)). We consider that Commander L. E. Porter's description (A.15) gives an accurate idea of the most that was visible from *Suffolk*. Briefly all he saw was gun flashes from *Hood* and then a very thin parallel-sided pillar of orange flame which went to about 800 to 1,000 feet. This was followed by a cloud of very dark smoke which developed from the bottom of the flame.'

Norfolks's evidence:

'The plot gives *Norfolk*'s distance from *Hood* as 15 miles. A mirage effect was also noticeable from her but it is not considered likely that more than a general effect could be observed. Rear-Admiral Wake-Walker's evidence (A.1) is confident and clear.

The general impression from these two ships was as follows:

A fire in the after part of the ship burnt with a clear, reddish flame, and it appeared to die down and then increase. This was followed shortly by a big explosion which took the form of a high sheet of flame shaped like a fan or inverted cone. Clouds of dark smoke surmounted this flame, and the ship disappeared. One or two witnesses, however, e.g., Captain Phillips (D.6.) and Mids. Summers (C.39) and Buckley (C.40) mentioned a ball or balls of fire showing clearly in the flame of the explosion.

Two witnesses stated they had seen (through glasses) a complete mainmast, and two others what might have been mast or derrick. Although debris could probably be seen, too much reliance cannot be placed on the evidence as to its nature.'

Prince of Wales's evidence:

The very close proximity of *Prince of Wales* and the fact that she was in action at the time prevented many of the observers from getting a clear-cut impression of the occurrence and it was fairly certain that no one observer could record every detail of what happened.

It was clear that a fire had started on the port side of the boat deck of *Hood* by the third or fourth salvo from *Bismarck*, but the opinion was divided as to whether it originated before or abaft the mainmast (evidence shows that it was abaft) but it evidently spread with very great rapidity covering a considerable section of the boat deck. This fact and the inclination of *Hood* from *Prince of Wales* would account for the difference of positions given. The most reliable evidence shows that the colour of the fire was a reddish, orange colour with very little smoke – the latter being a brown or black colour but colours from bright yellow to dull red and even blue are shown in the evidence. Several witnesses who

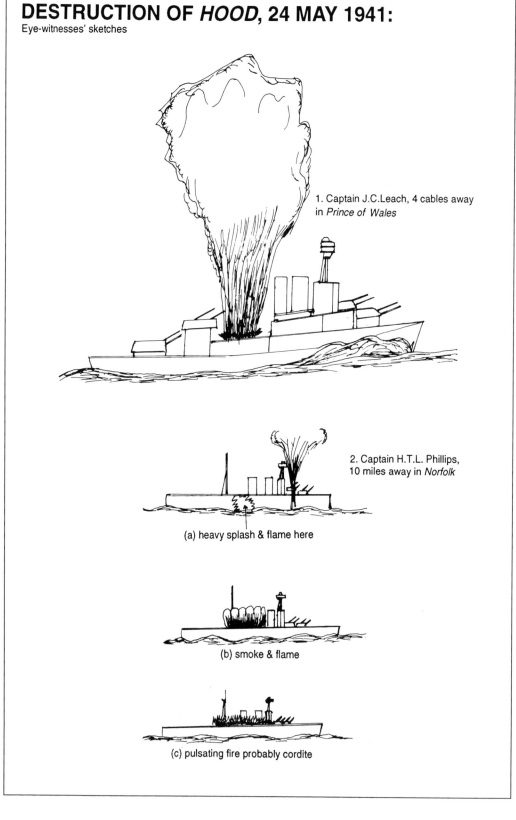

DESTRUCTION OF *HOOD*, 24 MAY 1941:
Eye-witnesses' sketches

1. Captain J.C.Leach, 4 cables away in *Prince of Wales*

2. Captain H.T.L. Phillips, 10 miles away in *Norfolk*

(a) heavy splash & flame here

(b) smoke & flame

(c) pulsating fire probably cordite

DESTRUCTION OF
HOOD Eye witnesses' sketches

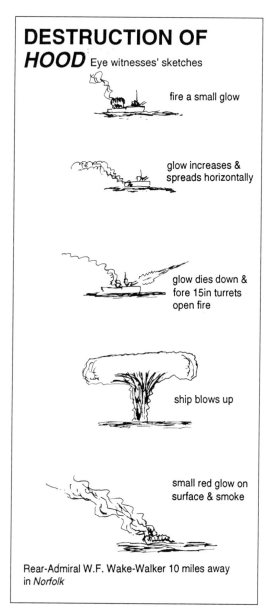

fire a small glow

glow increases & spreads horizontally

glow dies down & fore 15in turrets open fire

ship blows up

small red glow on surface & smoke

Rear-Admiral W.F. Wake-Walker 10 miles away in *Norfolk*

witnesses only recorded a flash of the explosion but others, who showed a keener appreciation of the rapid events, said that the flame of the explosion had definite duration. One of the most reliable witnesses of course was Captain Leach who was impressed by the effect which he described as like a vast blowlamp while Chief Petty Officer French stated that the boat deck appeared to raise in the middle before the mainmast. As can be expected the colour of the explosion under those conditions was difficult to record but it was probably a reddish-orange colour. The smoke ranged from dense white through to having an appearance of rising steam. Other witnesses talked of yellow, brown, white, light-grey and black smoke. Sub-Lieutenant Womersley, who was a chemist in private life, had the impression that the colossal volume of brown smoke had a red glow all the way along the base of it. The Second Gunnery Officer said that it was thick dark yellow smoke which he associated with cordite. The paradox of the whole ordeal was that very few witnesses heard any noise from the explosion, only a rumbling and a few muffled noises – perhaps a dull thud or a roar but not the usual noise associated with such a huge explosion.

Part of the mainmast or main derrick was stated to have been observed by a few witnesses. One witness was positive that he saw a complete 15in turret with two guns and a single gun in the air and five other witnesses claim to have either seen single 15in guns or part of the gunhouse of a turret.

The ship was obviously so enveloped in smoke and disappeared so quickly that it seems that no one witness got a completely clear picture of *Hood* after the explosion. Lieutenant-Commander Rowell stated that he saw her foretop falling backwards and the stern slipping forwards. He said that as *Prince of Wales* drew abreast of *Hood* all that could be seen was what appeared to be three large sections of the hull which were unrecognizable and sinking fast. Other witnesses were certain that they saw the forepart of the ship which was not damaged and several of them saw her forepart sticking out of the water at a very steep angle slipping backwards under water and turning over as it did so. Able Seaman Paton said that he saw her turn to port, roll over and that two funnels were visible lying on the water, he could also see a jagged part of the stern. All evidence agreed that she sank in about three minutes.'

already had experience of cordite fires definitely specified the fire on the boat deck as such and Lieutenant Commander Rowell described it as being similar to a petrol fire. Evidence about the explosion shows that it was divided between before and abaft the mainmast and there was some divulgence of opinion on this point. Other

Two views of *Hood* during the Fleet Review, July 1935.
Below: An aerial view on the day before the King's inspection.
Right: Fully dressed and manned on the day of the King's inspection, depicting the finest traditions of the Royal Navy.

The evidence generally indicated that the first salvo from *Bismarck* fell ahead of *Hood* and the second salvo astern. It was the third that hit, the fourth was close and the fifth hit her again. There were also the 8in salvos from *Prinz Eugen* which made it difficult when recording the fall of shot in the area. To compound the confusion was the fact that witnesses state that *Hood* had just fired 'A', 'B' and possibly 'X' and 'Y' 15in turrets which also caused fierce flame and heavy smoke.

There were only three survivors and their evidence was all-important. Midshipman W. J. Dundas was not available for interrogation at the Board of Enquiry, but he had given evidence shortly after the time of his rescue. He had been employed as Midshipman of the Watch on the upper bridge during the action. The upper bridge was closed in and he had no view aft. His position was amidships at the chart table and he saw very little, but his evidence suggests that the first salvo from *Bismarck* fell on *Hood*'s starboard bow, the second on the port bow. After the third salvo the Torpedo Officer, who was at the starboard after end of the bridge, reported a cordite fire on the starboard side of the boat deck. *Hood* fired at least one salvo after this report and was still steaming fast. On about the fourth or fifth salvo from *Bismarck* everyone on *Hood*'s bridge was thrown off their feet, wreckage started to come down and on getting to his feet Dundas saw a mass of brown smoke drifting to leeward (the port side) the ship was listing heavily to port and he had an uphill scramble to reach one of the windows. He noticed the Officer of the Watch climbing through another window. When Dundas was halfway through the window the water came up beneath him and the next thing he knew he was swimming. He saw *Hood*'s bows at an angle of about 45° with the forefoot, just clear of the water, sliding backwards on an even keel. He was quite sure that the ship received no hits forward and his recollection was that there was complete silence everywhere after the shock and that the ship had stopped and was heeling quickly to port. There was no blast bigger than that of the ship's own guns firing.

The second survivor was R. E. Tilburn, AB. He impressed the Board as being a very intelligent man although inexperienced, and at the time of the Board of Enquiry was still obviously shaken by his ordeal. His was the only firsthand

evidence of what happened on board from an observer who could see aft, but for most of the time he was lying down on the boat deck before the port forward UP mounting so his view was partially restricted. He stated that *Hood* was hit near the port midship UP mounting which caused a fierce fire. The fire did not seem to spread, but he thought that the RU ammunition was affected because he heard noises like 'explosions of a big Chinese cracker'. He thought it was too far forward for a petrol fire – his evidence as regards the petrol stowage was, however, rather shaky. He stated that the 4in ammunition hatch on the boat deck (port side) with which he was familiar was definitely closed during the action. With regard to the explosion, he stated that tremendous vibration resulted from another hit, but he did not see much except a lot of grey smoke. There was a noise as if the guns had fired, then dead silence. One flash of flame came between the control tower and 'B' turret above the forecastle deck just as he was going into the water. A lot of debris and bodies fell over the decks, but apart from the fact that some of those bodies were those of officers, he could identify nothing. One particularly interesting point he stated was that he saw long steel tubes, approximately 15 feet long and 1 foot in diameter, floating in the water, and these were thought to be the crushing tubes from the bulges which confirmed the magnitude of the damage done to the ship. In fact her back had been broken.

The third survivor was A. E. Briggs, Ordinary Signalman, whom the Board also saw as another quite intelligent witness. He was on the compass platform, however, and again did not see much, but he was in a position to overhear the conversation of some officers. Important points were:
1. The SGO said, '... she has been hit on the boat deck and there is a fire in the RU lockers'.
2. The Vice-Admiral said '... leave it 'til the ammunition has gone'.
3. Immediately after the explosion the OOW stated, 'the compass has gone' – this would be the gyro repeater on the compass platform.
4. Briggs stated that there was not a terrific explosion at all as regards noise, and he saw no debris coming down.
5. He testified to the great rapidity of *Hood*'s sinking.

Because of the mish-mash of evidence coming in during the Board of Enquiry, the cause of

Hood's destruction could not be determined, so to clarify certain issues some outstanding pointers in the evidence were emphasized by technical witnesses. It was obvious that she had been sunk by *Bismarck*'s 15in shells which had struck her in or around the area of the mainmast, but what it was that caused the tremendous explosion was uncertain. Whether the 15in shell pierced her upper armour belt, or entered through the decks, and in what area it landed are questions that may never be fully answered. In the after area of the ship there were not only 15in and 4in magazines, but torpedo warheads which could have exploded, starting a chain reaction in other ammunition compartments. Technical evidence, however ruled out the torpedo warhead detonation theory, their evidence being as follows:

1. A warhead would not be detonated by a shell unless it burst inside the mantlet.
2. One warhead detonating in *Hood* would detonate the next one in the horizontal plane. Warheads in one plane would not detonate others in the plane higher or lower owing to the horizontal mantlet. Warheads on one side of the ship would not detonate warheads on the other side. To sum up, one shell would not cause more than two warheads to detonate.
3. If the warheads detonated they would not explode the 4in or 15in magazines.
4. The effect of fire round a warhead would possibly lead to an explosion, but it would have to be a fire of fierceness and duration and the result would probably be comparatively mild.
5. If any of the after 4in magazines, except the forward upper one, exploded it would explode the after 15in magazines.
6. The aural and visual effect of warheads going off would be a noise of a sharp loud crack and a bright flash, which would be instantaneous, and likely to be dull-red, dark-red, reddish-brown or bright-yellow (lighter than cordite).
7. There was no unanimity of opinion about the effect on the ship if two warheads detonated. DTM, DNO and CSRD's representatives considered that although the structure in the immediate vicinity would be shattered and some of the 5in and 7in belt blown away, it would not cause a serious rent in the ship's side below the waterline, and they were convinced that the effect would not be disastrous. DNC's representative on the other hand considered that the strength deck would be destroyed for a considerable

width and the main deck ruptured. There would be a sufficient rupture below the waterline to cause the water to be scooped in and break down the after bulkheads as far as 259 and possibly 280 which would cause the ship to sink very rapidly.

8. The aural and visual effects of a 15in magazine blowing up would be a rumbling noise (unless it detonated, in which case it would be a sharp explosion) accompanied by a spurt of bright-yellow flame of some duration (as opposed to a flash and smoke). The smoke was described variously by the experts as: (a) dark and some white like steam; (b) dense and dirty; (c) black, perhaps grey and; (d) reddish. The first kick of the explosion would take the easiest path, but there might be other effects in other places.
9. The 'balls of fire' seen in the explosion could not be explained, but they might have been partly ignited cordite charges taking fire in the air, or ignition of projected oil fuel.
10. There was general agreement that: (a) The descriptions of the explosion given by Admiral Wake-Walker (A.1), Captain Leach (B.1) and Sub-Lieutenant Wormsley (B.8) pointed to a large cordite explosion. Cordite on the upper deck would not cause the main effect seen. (b) The fire on the boat deck had nothing to do with the explosion, but was probably caused by 4in ready-use or UP ammunition. Ignition of either of these would not produce disastrous effects. (c) It would be impossible for an untrained witness to differentiate between a 4in and a UP ammunition fire.
11. *Bismarck*'s shells probably had a muzzle velocity between 2,721 fps and 3,150 fps.
12. If as low as 2,721, although it could not penetrate the 12in belt, there was a strip on the ship's side about eighteen inches deep and 42 feet long where the shell could enter and pass over the top of the 12in belt and yet get in under the flat portion of the protective main deck. With a fuze delay of about 55 feet it could explode in a vital part.
13. There was a zone a few feet wide the length of the magazine group where a shell could fall short of the ship and enter the ship below the armoured belt. Assuming a fuze delay of about 75 feet, this shell could get to a 15in magazine and with a delay of 55 feet get to a 4in magazine. About half the travel would be under water.

14. German shells probably have longer fuze delays than ours and experience shows that their fuzes are fairly erratic. In the action of the River Plate two German shells burst at 65 and 70 feet respectively.
15. Little is known of underwater trajectory but the general opinion was that if a shell hit below the waterline it would be slowed up so much that a fuze delay of 75 feet under these circumstances would be unlikely.

CAUSE OF THE SHIP'S DESTRUCTION

The very sudden and total disappearance of the ship clearly showed that the explosion which sank her was of great magnitude and, as noted before, much of the evidence was contradictory and inconclusive, and many points in connection with the loss of the *Hood* can never be proved definitely. The first visible evidence of damage which might possibly have led to the destruction of the ship was a fire on the boat deck. There can be no better conclusion than the Board of Enquiry's written report:

1. It is established that this followed immediately on a hit on the boat deck, probably from *Bismarck*'s third salvo.
2. Position and Extent. The exact position of the hit and/or the start of the fire is in doubt, but the bulk of the evidence shows that the fire first appeared on the port side and abaft the mainmast. It is certain that it spread very rapidly until it covered a large part of the port side of the boat deck. It is not certain whether it was confined to the boat deck, but there is very little evidence that it extended below. There was no sign of *Hood*'s speed decreasing before the explosion and it might be inferred that the fire had not, therefore, affected the engine rooms.
3. Appearance. Evidence as to colour of flames, smoke and other phenomena observed in this fire differs very considerably, but analysis of the most reliable evidence indicates that it burned with a reddish-orange flame and comparatively little smoke. Distant observers emphasize the red.
4. Cause.
   1. There are three possible causes of such an immediate and rapidly spreading fire: (a) Petrol, (b) Ready Use ammunition, (c) UP ammuntion.
   2. The exact amount of petrol which was on board at the time cannot be definitely stated, but

Below: *Hood* enters Malta, February 1938. Note the Mediterranean light-grey paintwork and Spanish Civil War recognition bands on 'B' turret (red, white and blue).

if the orders known to be in force in *Hood* a short time previously were carried out – and there is no reason to suppose otherwise – it is unlikely that there was more than 2 gallons. This would have been on the boat deck abreast the mainmast. There is reason to believe that the petrol stowage in *Hood* was carefully supervised and notwithstanding the opinion formed by *Bismarck's* officers which was based on a false assumption the Board consider it unlikely that petrol was the cause or at any rate the sole cause of this fire.

3. Eighty rounds per gun of 4in RU ammunition were stowed in light type lockers on the boat deck. UP ammunition was stowed in lockers on the boat deck and forecastle deck. It is quite possible that either 4in or UP or both could be ignited as the result of a shell bursting in their vicinity and there is definite evidence from the survivors that ammunition was in fact exploding in the fire. One survivor (Briggs) gave evidence that the SGO reported a fire in the RU lockers and Mid. Dundas is stated to have informed the previous Board that the Torpedo Officer had reported a cordite fire on the starboard side of the boat deck. The noises like big Chinese crackers heard by A B Tilburn may have been UP ammunition exploding.

Evidence as to orders which were known to be in force in *Hood* a short time previous to the date in question, regarding the supply of 4in ammunition, makes it practically certain that all the hatches in the train of supply would be definitely closed.

The evidence of expert witnesses also shows that the results of a fire amongst the 4in RU and UP ammunition should not be fatal to the ship.

5. Conclusion. We have made a careful study of the plans showing the stowage of 4in and UP ammunition; the evidence clearly shows that some of this caught fire. After consideration of all the evidence and bearing in mind that *Hood* was certainly hit again after the fire had started, and almost immediately before the explosion, we have come to the conclusion that the fire was not

in itself the cause of, and was distinct from, the explosion which destroyed the ship.

6. Some cause other than the fire must therefore be sought for the explosions, and the three potential dangers are obviously as follows: (1) Torpedo Warheads, (2) 4in Magazines, (3) 15in Magazines.

7. As regards the Torpedo Warheads we put ourselves the following questions:

(a) Could one or more have been caused to explode during the action?

(b) Does the evidence of eyewitnesses correspond to what one might expect to see or hear if one or more warheads had detonated or exploded?

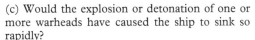

(c) Would the explosion or detonation of one or more warheads have caused the ship to sink so rapidly?

To obtain answers to these questions we consulted the expert witnesses available and draw the following conclusions:

8. With reference to (a). Evidence of eye-witnesses, *Repulse* and an officer who had recently served in *Hood* leaves little room for doubt that the mantlet doors were closed. A warhead could still, however, have been detonated or exploded by a direct hit from *Bismarck*'s shell. There is no direct evidence that such a hit occurred, but it may have done so on either side of the ship. If a single warhead had gone off, one other, but probably not more than one, warhead would also have gone off.

With reference to (b). Expert opinion suggested that the explosion of two warheads would produce an all-round almost instantaneous flash. It would not have produced the very high column of flame of appreciable duration, which was seen by so many witnesses. Nor was the noise, reported as being heard, compatible with that of TNT detonation or explosion. The consensus of expert opinion was definitely against the characteristics of the explosion as given in evidence by eye-witnesses being that of TNT.

With reference to (c). Mr. Offord, our adviser in construction, was of the opinion that this could be the case. Other witnesses, experts in explosions but not in construction, were of the opposite view and the Board is not convinced that such a very rapid sinking could follow from the damage which Mr. Offord considered would result from the explosion of two warheads. Further, there is strong evidence that the widespread and immediate damage actually caused to the after part of the ship was considerably greater than that which Mr. Offord considered would result from two warheads exploding.

We have therefore come to the conclusion that, although the explosion or detonation of two warheads cannot be entirely excluded, this was not the direct cause of the sinking of the ship.

As regards the 4in and 15in Magazines the following questions arise:

(1) Is it likely that enemy gunfire during this action would 'blow up' any or all of the magazines?

(2) Would the blowing up of magazines produce the effects seen and heard by witnesses?

(3) Would the blowing up of any or all of the magazines cause the rapid destruction of the ship?

Here again expert advisers were consulted, and lead us to the following conclusion:

As regards (1). Expert evidence shows that this is quite possible if the muzzle velocity of *Bismarck*'s shell was between 2,721 and 3,050fps (actually 2,790fps).

As regards (2). We consider that what was seen and heard was in accordance with what might be expected if the after group of 4in and/or 15in magazines of *Hood* had blown up.

There is one important point which needed careful consideration and which was remarked on by DNC in his minute on N.L. 9821/41 (Report of previous Board of Enquiry) and by CinC, Home Fleet, namely that the position of the explosion as observed by some competent witnesses was much further forward than would, at first thought, have been expected had the 4in or 15in magazines blown up. This is where we reached the conclusion that not only was a tremendous pillar of flame observed just before the mainmast, but that in addition a very heavy explosion was seen practically simultaneously further aft. Commander Maton and Commander Knight agreed that if the 4in magazines went off first, followed almost instantaneously by the 15in, the first visible sign might well be a large sheet of flame directly above or just before the 4in magazines.

Finally it must be remembered that our peace-time knowledge and practical experience of the results of cordite explosions has been based on experiments with a maximum of about half a ton of cordite. *Hood*'s after magazines contained about 112 tons – over two hundred times as much. The course of the explosion following on the terrific pressures likely to be produced in this case must be difficult to predict. From the last war there are three examples of the effects on battlecruisers of cordite explosions – explosions which both in appearance and effect give very similar results to those experienced in the loss of *Hood*.

As regards (3). There is little room for doubt that the immediate destruction of the after end of the ship followed by the rapid sinking of the remainder would result from the blowing up of the 4in or 15in magazines – in the case of the former because their explosion would cause the 15in also to blow up.

Conclusions – 10 October 1941:

(1) That the sinking of *Hood* was due to a hit from *Bismarck*'s 15in shell in or adjacent to *Hood*'s 4in or 15in magazines, causing them all to explode and wreck the after part of the ship. The probability is that the 4in magazines exploded first.

(2) There is no conclusive evidence that one or two torpedo warheads detonated or exploded simultaneously with the magazines, or at any other time, but the possibility cannot be entirely excluded. We consider that if they had done so their effect would not have been so disastrous as to cause the immediate destruction of the ship, and on the whole we are of the opinion that they did not.

(3) That the fire which was seen on *Hood*'s boat deck, and in which UP and/or 4in ammunition was certainly involved, was not the cause of her loss.

The disaster was broadcast on the BBC at 9 p.m. on 24 May 1941:

'British naval forces intercepted early this morning off the coast of Greenland German naval forces including the battleship *Bismarck*. The enemy were attacked and during the ensuing action HMS *Hood*, wearing the flag of Vice-Admiral L. E. Holland, C. B., received an unlikely hit in the magazine and blew up. The *Bismarck* has received damage and the pursuit of the enemy continues. It is feared there will be few survivors from HMS *Hood*.'

A further official statement was drawn up, but it was thought that the public were not ready to be told the raw truth of the matter. The DNC (S. V. Goodall) said:

'This statement gives the bald facts. If presented to the public as it stands it will be perturbing and although some people may then realize the load of anxiety which has rested upon successive Boards of Admiralty owing to our capital ships being out of date, it appears such a statement would depress our friends and hearten the enemy, giving the latter information which it is hoped they do not at present possess, e.g., we have been bluffing them with the *Royal Sovereign*s for nearly two years. It is for consideration to what extent this statement should be modified on grounds of policy if some publication is essential.'

Left: *Hood* rolls at sea, exposing her underwater bulge, February 1939.

NELSON AND RODNEY

Thursday 17 December 1925 dawned cold and damp, one of those grey mornings when even the most robust and sturdy shipyard worker seemed dejected and miserable. But there was a good reason for high spirits because it was a very special day for the Birkenhead shipyard and a huge crowd had wrapped themselves up in their warmest clothing and gathered in and around the yard to await the arrival of HRH Princess Mary and her husband Viscount Lascelles to perform the naming ceremony of one of the most powerful battleships ever constructed in a British yard. Indeed, the people of Liverpool and the little town of Birkenhead, and Messrs Cammell Laird Shipbuilding and Engineering Works were justly proud of the occasion. Not only had they brought a new concept in warship design to the launching stage, but they were witnessing the construction of one of the few British battleships to be laid down during the inter-war years. The very existence of such a vessel during the depression was something of a miracle; she was being built under the shadow of severe naval restrictions which governed displacements and gun sizes. The general public saw the ship as something of a compromise and hardly knew what to expect because of the continuous agitation in the Press during the last few years since the Washington Naval Treaty of 1921, whereby Britain had agreed to reduce the size of her fleet, abandoning the 'two power standard' and aligning herself numerically with the USA. In 1921 Britain had laid down four giant 48,000-ton battlecruisers of which this ship should have been one, but lengthy negotiations had reduced their size by more than 15,000 tons, and only two instead if four were allowed to compensate for the latest battleships building in Japan and the USA at that time.

At approximately 10.15 a.m. on that December morning HRH Princess Mary and her husband entered the shipyard to be met by The Right Hon Earl of Derby, KG, GCB, GCVO, and a very vociferous crowd. The Royal party were introduced to Mr W. L. Hichens (Chairman) and Mr R. S. Johnson (Managing Director) before making their way to the firm's main offices.

At precisely 10.40 a.m. Her Royal Highness left the offices and made her way to the launching platform where the religious ceremony was then held. At exactly 11.15 a.m., in a moment of hush, a quiet voice called, 'I name this ship *Rodney*, and God bless all who sail in her', and the lever was pulled to release the christening fluid over the bows of the great ship. Thus the mighty *Rodney* slid calmly and majestically down the slipway for about fifty feet before entering the cold water of the River Mersey.

Right: *Rodney* is launched at Liverpool, 17 December 1925. The crowd look on and wonder what her completed appearance will be. Note that part of the tower is already in place.

In the coming months, she and her sister (*Nelson*, which had been launched a few months earlier in September) would be fitting out and taking shape, and the media would get their first look at what had been one of the most controversial designs of the inter-war years. Indeed, they were to wonder whether the two ships would be worth £7,000,000 each, when the latest, and larger, *Hood* had only set them back a little over £6,000,000. With hindsight, however, it can be said that *Nelson* and *Rodney* proved to be two of the most powerful 16in gunned battleships ever built, and the sterling work they were about to do during the coming war (1939–45) would more than justify their building; in fact, at the outbreak of war, they were the latest battleships that the Royal Navy possessed.

DESIGN

During the period 1919 to 1921, a considerable number of alternative capital ship designs, embodying 1914–18 experience, especially the lessons of Jutland and the recommendations of the Post-War Questions Committee, were prepared and considered by the Admiralty, and in 1921, when the large programme in hand in the USA and Japan necessitated a resumption of British capital ship construction, a battlecruiser type of 47,540 tons was chosen. The latest ship to complement the Royal Navy's fleet at that time (1920) was the large battlecruiser *Hood*, and although she had been constructed without regard to the many lessons learnt at Jutland, her general design and layout was naturally followed ('K', 'K2' and 'K3').

Following these sketch designs, there was a serious investigation into the construction of one of the largest and most powerful battleships built to date ('I3'), but although it reached sketch stage and gained some Board approval, the Constructor's department saw it as far too large and radical at that time. In 1920, however, the NID informed their Lordships that both Japan and the USA would probably construct vessels of about 48,000 tons armed with 18in guns in the near future, and it was reluctantly agreed that the Royal Navy would have to follow suit to meet any threat. It was realized, however, that ships of such a size would introduce severe problems not only for designers, but in docking accommodation as well.

During the next few months various designs were prepared (see page 329) for both battleships and battlecruisers, but unfortunately most of the information (ship's covers) concerning the battleships has been mislaid, only the battlecruiser layouts being available (variations of 'K', 'L', 'M' and 'N' Designs were shown). In December 1920 it was decided that the sketches 'G3' and 'H3' (battlecruisers) should be investigated further, but with modifications on 'G3' so as to include extra armour protection to the deck area. After viewing the modified G3 layout, the Board accepted it in principle and in February 1921 asked for confirmation and further preparation on four ships of such a calibre. The DNC (d'Eyncourt) particularly approved of the modified G3 and wrote to the First Sea Lord on 23 March 1921 pointing out the salient features:

'The main armament consists of nine 16in guns in three turrets with 40 degrees elevation. Two pairs forward and one amidships. The latter cannot fire right astern.

'War experience, and our recently acquired knowledge of German and United States turrets have been carefully considered in connection with the main armament; the protection and flashtightness is very complete.

'Secondary armament consists of sixteen 6in in eight turrets, arranged so that supply from magazines and shell rooms is very direct, but is provided with breaks and other safeguards to prevent flash passing down into magazines. AA consists of six 4.7in high-angle guns, and mountings embody the latest high-angle ideas as recommenced by Naval High Angle Gunnery Committee.

'Armament controls are a special feature. An erection forward supports the main director control tower, two secondary directors and the high-angle directors, and calculating positions are free from any smoke interference. Aeroplane hangars may be considered as a permanent feature but a decision is pending.

'Main armament has been concentrated in the centre of the ship in order that the heavy horizontal and vertical armour required to protect it may be a minimum, and also that the magazines may be placed in the widest part of the ship, and the underwater protection be the best that can be afforded. Over this central citadel a 14in belt is arranged, and resting on the belt is a deck of 8in on the flat and 9in on the slopes. These thick-

nesses and angles have been carefully calculated after consideration to oblique attack results with the latest type of shell. Abaft the central citadel a sloping 12in belt and 4in deck are provided over machinery spaces.

'The belt extends over the aft 6in magazine, and here the deck is increased to 7in. Abaft the citadel a thick deck of 5in is provided over the steering gear.

'Barbettes are 14in and turrets and 17in on the face with 8in roofs.

'Underwater experience is based on Chatham Float tests and embodies the principle of the bulge as fitted to the *Hood*. The side underwater protection is designed to withstand a charge of 750lb of explosive.

'Protection against mines is afforded by a double-bottom of 7ft deep.

'By sloping the main belt outwards, not only is the virtual thickness increased, but protection is provided against attack by distant-controlled boats containing large explosives. In order that the stability of the vessel may be adequate, the triangular space between side and armour will be filled with light tubes. Calculations show that the whole of this structure would have to be completely blown away before the ship would lose stability.'

Although never wanting ships with such mastadon proportions, on accepting the 'G3' design and the battleship version 'N3', the Royal Navy had accomplished what it set out to do, and that was completely to outclass any foreign opposition for at least five years ahead. The design was far ahead of its time and showed features which even matched the Japanese giants of the *Yamato* class constructed in 1941. Indeed, it may be that the 'G3' plans were carefully considered by the Japanese when their two ships were under construction because they certainly reflected many qualities of the early 1921 British design.

With all major maritime powers building along the same lines it was only too obvious that it would be but a matter of time before the design was overshadowed by a vessel grossly out of proportion to requirements, with everyone else being forced to follow. The political implications were too complex to be discussed here, but the result ended in a Naval treaty called for by the USA and it would include Great Britain, Japan, Italy and France. An agreement was reached whereby there would be a battleship holiday for the next ten years. New ships could only be constructed after existing ships had reached the age of 20 years, and new construction was limited to 35,000 tons and calibres reduced to 16in guns rather than the 18in being prepared at that time. Dozens of older (in Britain's case not so old) battleships went to the scrapyard.

Contracts for the British 'G3' class (four) had been under way for some time and when in February 1922 letters had to be sent out to the four yards involved, stating that the ships were cancelled, it came as a bitter blow to an already flagging industry during the depression.

To offset the retention of the *West Virginia* and *Nagato* classes by the United States and Japan respectively, which had been too far advanced to scrap, Great Britain authorized under the Treaty two new designs to comply with the severe limitations that had been imposed on construction.

As early as November 1921, when it became probable that the four 'G3' group vessels were to be scrapped, the Constructor's Department was asked to prepare fresh layouts within the limits of

the treaty, but was asked to include any of the G3's features where possible. The first three sketches ('F1', 'F2', 'F3') featured 15in guns because the department thought that no suitable 16in gunned design could be acquired on such a limited displacement, but it would appear that the designs received little consideration because both the USA and Japan now had 16in gunned battleships (see tables). In January 1922 further proposals were forwarded showing a reduced edition of the 'G3' but retaining many of its qualities ('O3', 'P3' and 'Q3') with a speed of 23 knots.

The Controller asked for the designs to be fully worked out, and it was proposed to Constructor E. L. Attwood that dimensions be 710ft by 102ft (waterline) by 30ft, and that SHP sufficient to reach 23/24 knots would be needed. The main armament would be the same as in the G3s (16in), but armour plating would be severely thinned down from that design. In order that the legend weight, as defined by the Washington Treaty, should come within the 35,000 tons limit, the utmost economy was

ARMOUR PROTECTION COMPARISONS

Displacement 43,500 tons
Armament 8x16in, 14x6in
SHP 150,000
main belt 7in, lower edge 5in
anti-torpedo bulkheads ³/₄in-⁵/₈in
main deck 2in-1½in

Lexington

main belt 12in
deck 7in on flat 8in inclines
anti-torpedo bulkhead 1¾in
internal inner bulkhead ³/₄in
outer skin 2in-1³/₈in

British 'I3' layout (battlecruiser)

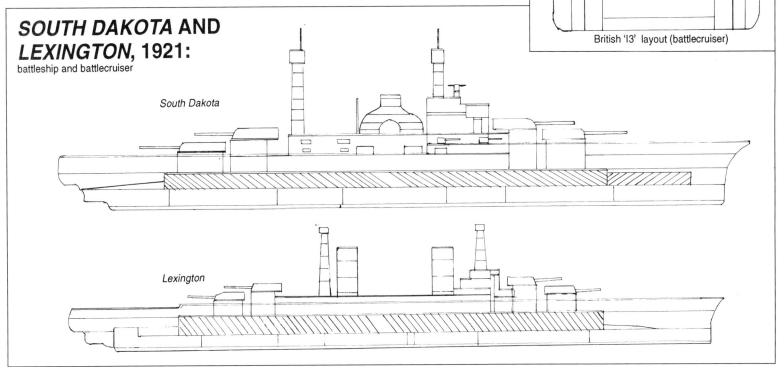

SOUTH DAKOTA AND LEXINGTON, 1921:
battleship and battlecruiser

South Dakota

Lexington

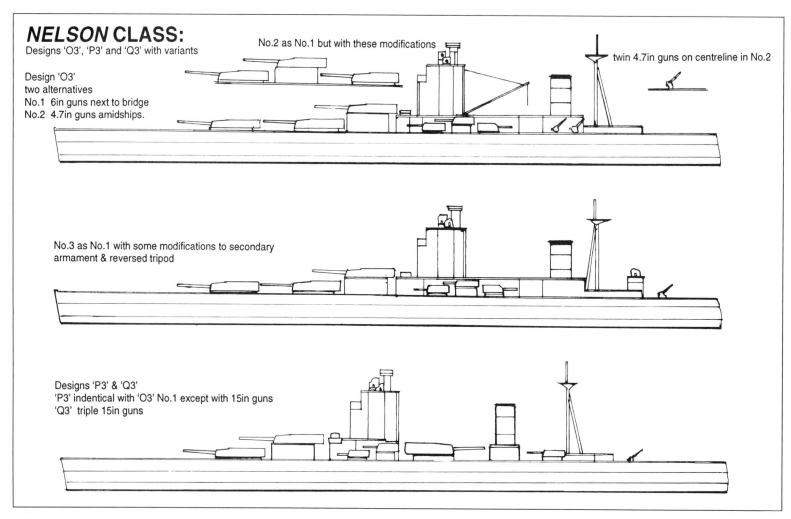

NELSON CLASS:
Designs 'O3', 'P3' and 'Q3' with variants

Design 'O3'
two alternatives
No.1 6in guns next to bridge
No.2 4.7in guns amidships.

No.2 as No.1 but with these modifications

twin 4.7in guns on centreline in No.2

No.3 as No.1 with some modifications to secondary
armament & reversed tripod

Designs 'P3' & 'Q3'
'P3' indentical with 'O3' No.1 except with 15in guns
'Q3' triple 15in guns

called for, and no Board margin was possible for any weights added during construction. In September 1922 the final design was accepted (modified 'O3') and it embodied all the essential features demanded:
1. High freeboard and good seakeeping qualities, these being regarded as essential.
2. Armament as in the cancelled battlecruisers ('G3').
3. Armouring generally similar to that of the battlecruisers, and concentrated over magazines, machinery and gun positions on the 'all or nothing' principle.
4. Speed equal to or higher than contemporary

foreign battleships.

Although having the same main armament and turret arrangement as the cancelled battlecruisers (whose guns and mounts were utilized to a certain extent) and resembling them in certain outward characteristics, *Nelson* and *Rodney* were in no sense merely a reduced edition of those ships, but constituted an entirely distinct 'battleship' type, representing the nearest approach that could be obtained, within the limits, to the 48,000-ton plan previously proposed. The battlecruiser design was stated to have constituted a reply to Naval Staff Requirements for an 'ideal battlecruiser'; *Nelson* and *Rodney*, on the other

hand, represented the best that could be done, within treaty limitations, towards meeting the demand for an 'ideal battleship'.

The influence of the Treaty restrictions on the new ships was considerable, as it was necessary, for the first time, to work to an absolute displacement limit which could not be exceeded, but which had to be approached as closely as possible in order to secure maximum value. The history of these two ships, then, is a complex one, but when laid out in tabular form it seems straightforward:
1: At the conclusion of the 1914–18 war, investigations were conducted into capital ship design

Particulars of sketch designs 'K', 'K2', 'K3', 'L2', 'L3', 'J3', 'I3', 'H3a', 'H3b', 'H3c'

	'K2'	'K3'	'J3'	'I3'
Length (ft) (pp)	850	same except:	810	890
Length (ft) (oa)	885		860	925
Beam (ft)	106		104	108
Draught (ft)	33/34		28/30	32/33
Displacement (tons)	53,100	52,000	43,100	51,750
SHP:	144,000		151,000	180,000
Speed (knots)	30		32	32
Fuel (tons)	5,000 max.		3,895	5,000 max.
Armament	8 x 16in	9 x 16in	9 x 15in	9 x 16in
16 x 6in	16 x 6in	12 x 6in	16 x 6in	
6 x 4.7in		6 x 4.7in	5 x 4.7in	
2 x TT		2 x TT		
Armour (main belt):	12in		12–9in	12in
Weights (tons)				
General Equip.	1,000		910	1,000
Guns	8,770		6,740	8,670
Machinery	5,670		5,670	6,430
Fuel	1,200		1,200	1,200 min.
Armour	17,310	16,060	12,780	14,600
Hull	18,900	19,150	15,640	19,590

	H3a'	'H3b'	'H3c'
Length (ft) (pp)	825	same except	
Length (ft) (oa)	860		
Beam (ft)	105	106	104
Draught (ft)	32/33		
Displacement (tons)	44,500	45,000	46,500
SHP:	180,000		
Speed (knots)	33½	33¼	33
Fuel (tons)	5,000		
Armament	6 x 16in		9 x 16in
6 x 6in		16 x 6in	
5 x 4.7in			
Armour (main belt)	14in		
Weights (tons)			
General Equip.	1,000		
Guns	6,150		7,400
Machinery	6,430		
Fuel			
Armour	13,250	13,600	13,350
Hull	16,400	15,950	16,890

'G3': Final Legend, 12 August 1921

Displacement (tons): 48,000.
Length: 820ft (pp), 856ft (oa).
Beam: 106ft.
Draught: 32ft forward, 33ft aft.
Freeboard: 28ft forward, 21ft amidships, 25ft aft.
SHP: 160,000 = 31/32 knots.
Fuel: 1,200 tons oil min, 5,000 tons max.
Complement: 1,716.
Armament
9 x 16in Mk I (80rpg)
16 x 6in (150rpg)
6 x 4.7in (200rpg)
40 x 2pdr
2 x 24.5in TT

Armour
14in at 72° incline (over magazines), 12in at 72° incline (over machinery and boilers).
Bulkheads forward 12–5in, aft 10–4in, barbettes 14in max., turrets 17–13–8in, CT 12–6in, tube 8in, DT 5–3in, funnel protection 12–9–5in, decks: forecastle 1in, upper 8in, 4in over machinery, lower deck forward 8–7in, aft 5–3in.

Weights (tons)
Hull	17,860
Armour	14,700
Armament	7,030
Machinery	6,000
General equipment	1,000
BM	200

to incorporate the lessons learnt at Jutland in particular.

2: Battlecruiser design with legend displacement of 48,000 tons was approved by the Board of Admiralty on 12 August 1921.

3: Orders were placed for four ships on 26 October 1921, but cancelled on 13 February 1922 under Washington Naval Treaty's directive not to exceed 35,000 tons.

4: Investigations into designs for a 35,000-ton battleship resulted in sketch 'O3' (modified) being accepted by the Board, and became *Nelson* and *Rodney*.

5: The Washington Treaty's 35,000-ton limit led to development of better quality steel.

6: No further capital ships to be built from 12 November 1921 except *Nelson* and *Rodney*.

'F2' and 'F3': Particulars, 30 November 1921

'F2'
Displacement (tons): 35,000.
Length: 720ft (pp), 760ft (oa).
Beam: 106ft.
Draught: 28ft 6in (mean).
SHP: 112,000.
Speed: 30 knots.
Armament: 6 x 15in, 12 x 6in.
Armour: 13in over magazines, etc., 12in over machinery and boilers. turrets 16–12–9in, barbettes 13in, CT 12–6in, 7in upper deck, 3¼in over machinery, 5–3in aft.

'F 3'
Displacement (tons): 35,000.
Length: 700ft (pp), 740ft (oa).
Beam: 106ft.
Draught: 28ft 6in mean.
SHP: 96,000.
Speed: 28½ knots.
Armament: 9 x 15in, 8 x 6in.
Armour: main belt 12in, barbettes 12in, CT 9–5in, otherwise same as 'F2'.

Particulars of 'P3' and 'Q3'

'P3'
Displacement (tons): 48,000.
Length: 717ft (oa).
Beam: 104ft
Draught: 30ft mean.
Armour: 11in Upper belt, amidships 14in, decks 8–7½in, 5–3½in over machinery.
Armament: 9 x 15in (new type), 16 x 6in, 6 x 4.7in, 2 aircraft.
'Q3' same as above except for two main triple turrets forward of bridge instead of all forward of bridge (see drawings).

7: General armour and protection affected (reduction from 'G3') to save weight.

8: The armour citadel was 384ft by 14in abreast 16in magazines, sloped at 70° and was so arranged inside the hull that the slope produced downwards did not meet protection bulkheads. Each belt of armour was keyed, and individual plates were made as large as possible with heavy bars fitted behind the butts. Chock castings housing the lower edge of armour also directed fragments of bursting shells away from the belt.

9: No new construction to be commenced until: United States 1931; Great Britain 1931; France 1927; Japan 1931; Italy 1927.

CONSTRUCTION

The outstanding features, which in respect of the arrangement of armament, were peculiar in being apparently governed more by constructional than tactical principles, included:

1: Exceptionally high freeboard with a flush deck hull.

2: Concentration of entire main armament forward, allowing maximum protection to gun positions and magazines, and grouping of anti-torpedo armament in twin turrets well aft on each quarter for similar considerations, and also to minimize blast interference from the 16in guns.

3: Excellent protection from all forms of attack with main strength formed over the magazines, machinery, boilers and main armament.

4: Designed speed about 2 knots above existing battleship average.

5: Innovatory high structure replacing normal bridgework and tripod.

Both ships were built in great secrecy and it was not until official notification was given that the general public knew anything about the Royal Navy's latest acquisition. Despite its somewhat experimental nature and the hampering Treaty restrictions, the design proved generally satisfactory so far as the Board of Admiralty and Constructor's Department were concerned. The ships were, however, subject to some criticism: 1. Absence of any direct astern fire from the main armament. 2. Insufficient depth of armour belt below the waterline.

The Washington Treaty's dictates meant that economy was more important than ever before,

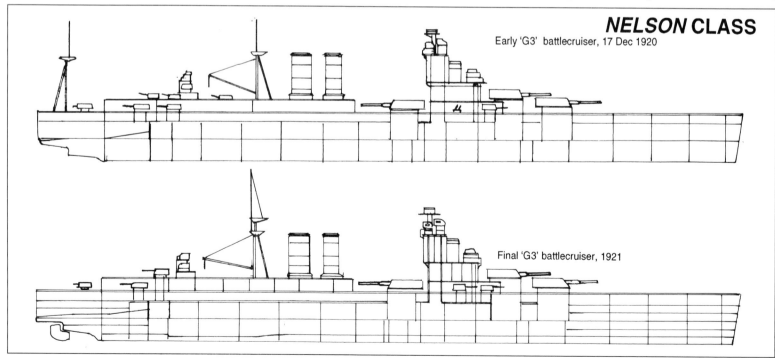

NELSON CLASS

Early 'G3' battlecruiser, 17 Dec 1920

Final 'G3' battlecruiser, 1921

Launch figures
Nelson, 3 September 1925.
Length: 660ft 0⁷/₈in (pp), 709ft 9⁷/₈in (oa).
Beam: 106ft.
Depth from keel to upper deck: 55ft 6in.
Draught at launch: 8ft 5³/₈in forward (10ft abaft pp),
    24ft 10³/₄in aft (42ft abaft AP).
Breakage:
Longitudinally in a distance of 512ft 3in= ¹/₈in hog.
Transverse in a distance of 99ft 9¹/₂in = 0.
Displacement at launch: 19,454 tons.
Equipment on board at time of launch:
94.3tons armament
1,511.5 tons machinery
6,081.9 tons armour
773.5 tons ballast, men, gear, etc.
8,461.2 tons.
Recorded weight of hull: 11,102 tons.

Rodney, 17 December 1925.
Length: 660ft 0¹/₈in (pp), 710ft 2¹/₂in (oa).
Beam: 106ft 0¹¹/₁₆in.
Depth of keel from upper deck amidships: 55ft 3¹/₈in.
Draught at launch: 9ft 7³/₄in forward (8ft 10in abaft
    FP), 25ft 2¹/₄in aft (42ft 2in forward of AP).
Breakage:
Longitudinal in a distance of 438ft = ¹/₄in hog.
Transverse in a distance of 85ft = 0.
Displacement at launch: 20,200 tons.
Equipment on board at launch:
157 tons armament
1483 tons machinery
6107 tons armour
636 tons men, ballast, gear, etc.
Recorded weight of hull at launch: 11,905 tons.

and the general design was so disposed as to give maximum effectiveness to armament and protection within the smallest possible dimensions, while special measures were taken to eliminate all non-essential items and to utilize the lightest practicable materials and methods of construction. These included:

1. The use of special 'D' steel in place of normal high-tensile steel, the superior quality of this enabling higher stresses to be accepted with a consequent substantial reduction in weight of scantlings.

2. Special investigations were made into the strength of the plating and framing of the double-bottom so a to reduce weight to a minimum (7ft double-bottom of 'G3' reduced to 5ft in this class).

3. Modified form of construction for the principal decks, comprising a system of longitudinal girders with widely spaced beams in conjunction with web frames to utilize the maximum amount of material for longitudinal stresses and so reduce thickness of deck plating required for strength purposes, which afforded a considerable saving in weight.

4. The use of Douglas fir instead of the customary teak for the upper deck, the reduction in wearing qualities and appearance being accepted in favour of the reduced weight.

5. Extensive use of aluminium alloys for minor interior fittings (kit lockers, store cupboards, mess racks, etc.) with some plywood for the dwarf and divisional bulkheads that did not require structural strength.

The hull construction was very strong throughout, the unusually concentrated and very heavy weights of armaments necessitating a special provision for adequate longitudinal strength when docking, including the new form of deck construction.

RIG

There was a thick rectangular stump foremast forward at the rear of the bridge tower with an open, diamond-shaped platform carrying the high-angle rangefinder at the head. No topmast and no yards or signal struts. Forward ends of the W/T aerials were carried to prominent struts on rangefinder platform and bridge tower. They were given a tripod mainmast with a tall topmast and topgallant. The main yard was well below the starfish, with another smaller one above the head of the topmast. There was a very wide W/T yard at the head of the topgallantmast.

ARMAMENT

With the exception of the 16.25in gun mounted in the *Benbow* and *Sans Pareil* classes, completed 1888 and 1891 respectively, *Nelson* and *Rodney* were the first and only British battleships to have 16in BL guns in triple-mounted turrets, which made them the most powerfully armed battleships afloat. An experimental mounting had been produced by Messrs Armstrong and Co. and fitted and satisfactorily tested in the monitor *Lord Clive* in February 1921 in anticipation of their being fitted in the 'G3' group. When the 'G3's were cancelled some £500,000 had been spent on them and it was only natural that the money and results of the tests should be used in the new ships of the *Nelson* class. Concentration of the entire main armament forward was unique at the time of their building, and allowed a minimum length of armoured citadel with maximum protection to gun positions and magazines, while the close grouping of the turrets incidentally facilitated fire control. These advantages were considered to outweigh the loss of tactical efficiency caused by the absence of direct astern fire which at first was a much criticized feature; the design, in this respect, subordinating tactical principles to severe pressures in constructional requirements and weight saving. The arrangement was not repeated after the *Nelson* pair, although it was later adopted by the French Navy in the *Dunkerque* and *Richelieu* classes (laid down 1932–7 respectively). Although no direct astern fire was provided, the superstructure was cut away and so arranged as to allow 'A' and 'B' turrets rather large nominal arcs of fire, bearing respectively to within 31° and 15° of the axial line astern.

The 16in gun was a high-velocity/lighter shell weapon, but tests after completion showed that it was much inferior to the low-velocity/heavy shell 15in gun which had proved itself an excellent piece during the Great War. Nevertheless, the heavier weight of broadside did have its compensations (6,790lb heavier than in *Queen Elizabeth*) and was not equalled until 1941 when the US *North Carolina* entered service with a similar armament.

Magazines and shell rooms were grouped together around the revolving hoists, and the boilers were located abaft instead of before the engine rooms so that the uptakes and funnel arrangement could be placed further aft, with a view to minimizing smoke interference to the control positions on top of the bridge structure. She was an improvement over previous designs, but, as completed, the funnel proved to be too short, being appreciably lower than the massive tower and its controls, especially steaming head to wind when the tower produced considerable backdraught and the funnel gases caused severe discomfort.

On trials, and during gunnery tests, it was found that when the guns were fired at considerable angles abaft the beam, the structure and personnel were affected by blast. In particular, 'C' turret, when fired abaft the beam at full elevation was to cause severe problems, and special measures would be needed when firing at these

Two views of *Rodney* being towed, on completion, down the River Mersey.
Right: Port-bow view showing her leaving the fitting-out berth.
Below: Getting up steam and making her way down river, September 1927.

angles (see Captain's report, elsewhere). Many officers thought that the blast was too severe, and that the design was a bad one, but when tests were carried out by HMS *Excellent* during the early gun trials, there was a divergence of opinion.

Gun pressures on the bridge windows were recorded and showed figures of $8\frac{1}{2}$psi when bearing 120 degrees green or red, and it was suggested that bridge personnel might possibly be moved to the conning tower when the guns were firing at these angles. Constructor H. S. Pengelly was aboard *Rodney* on 16 September 1927 and had this to say when making his report for their Lordships:

'During the firing of 'X' and 'B' abaft the beam, I remained on the middle line at the after end of the Admiral's platform. The firing from

'B' was not uncomfortable, but there was considerable shock when 'X' fired at 130 degrees or slightly less, but at 40 degrees of elevation. The shock was aggravated by one not knowing when to expect fire, but apart from this point, it is understood that the blast recorded at the slots on the Admiral's platform were about 9lb psi and on the Captain's platform about 11lb psi. It was noted that 10 degrees more bearing aft made all the difference to the effect experienced on the bridge.

The bridge structure was, in itself, entirely satisfactory, and I was informed by the officers occupying the main DCT forward, that this position was extremely satisfactory, and they would have been ready, throughout the whole of the firing, to fire again in 8 to 10 seconds.

The only damage was on the signal platform –

1 x 18in projector at the fore end – glass smashed, and shutter of another broken.

On the Captain's bridge, four windows broken, a few voice pipes loose. On Admiral's bridge, four windows broken. Number of electric lights put out of action. General damage was little, and the extra stiffening inboard after *Nelson*'s gun trials appear to have functioned well.'

They were the first British battleships to carry anti-torpedo guns in turrets, which afforded, in addition to the better protective area for gun crews, substantially wider horizontal and vertical arcs of fire than the battery system of the preceding classes. On the protection side, however, the secondary armament failed miserably because of the restricted weights allowed in the ships, and the whole of the secondary armament – turrets and barbettes – were practically unarmoured,

with nothing more than 1in high-tensile steel all over as a form of splinter shield.

The turrets were arranged in two compact groups, governed by the same considerations of concentration to allow magazine grouping, as had been the case with the main armament. There was some criticism of the close grouping because a single hit might put the entire battery out of action on any one side. They were located as far aft as practicable so as to minimize blast effect from the after 16in guns when firing abaft the beam. Their higher command (about 23ft against 19ft) meant that the fighting efficiency of these guns in moderate or rough weather was materially better than that of the *Queen Elizabeth* and *Royal Sovereign* classes, an advantage that was demonstrated during fleet manoeuvres in March 1934 when units of all three classes oper-

ated together in some of the worst weather ever experienced during practical battle tests (the secondary guns of the *QE* and *RS* classes were seen to be completely waterlogged and were of no use whatsoever).

The 24.5in torpedo armament was introduced in this class (21in was the largest previously carried) even though there was a body of opinion that expressed a wish to discontinue torpedo tubes in capital ships. The tubes were not trained abeam, but angled forward to within about 10 degrees of the axial line. To eliminate risk of serious flooding, the torpedo compartments were located in a separate flat rather than a single flat as in preceding classes, which was seen a serious fault in those early classes. The torpedo control positions were located on the superstructure close before the funnel.

Below: *Nelson* in 1931. These two sister ships were the first British battleships to be constructed after the Great War and were the last for fourteen years. They were described as the outcome of the gunnery officers' lessons at Jutland regarding protection.

NELSON ARMOUR LAYOUT

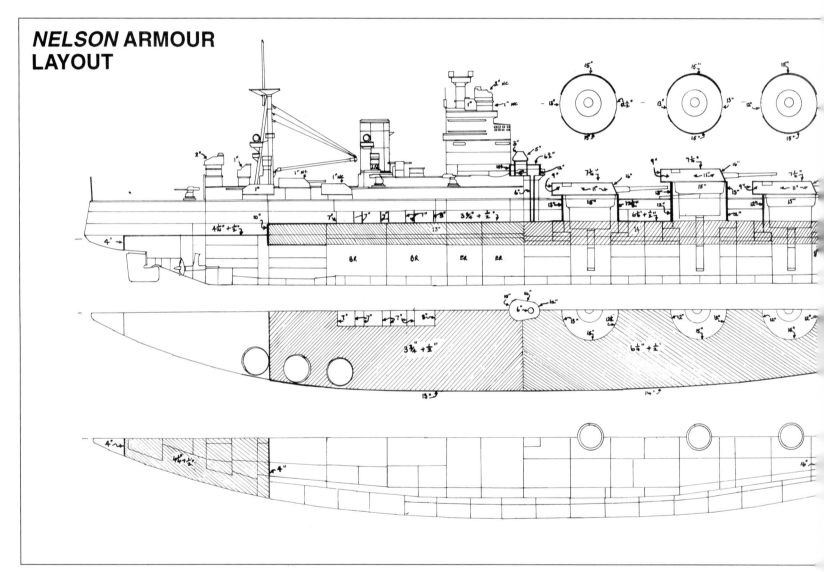

Given that the design had been restricted in displacement, the armament in general was more than adequate, but the triple mounting of the 16in guns was not viewed favourably in the Constructor's Department, which preferred twin mountings as in preceding classes – a well-tried and proven set of equipment. The trouble seems to have been the extreme weight of the entire triple mounting (1,500 tons approx.) which bore down too heavily on the flanges of the roller path

when the turret was being trained. As a result of this and other small teething problems the guns or turrets never achieved the reputation of the twin mounted 15in gun which, in hindsight, has been considered the best combination that ever went to sea in a battleship. After new vertical rollers had been fitted, and much experimentation on the 16in mountings, things did improve, but they were never trouble free during prolonged firing.

ARMOUR

The arrangement of armouring in the 'G3's and *Nelson* and *Rodney* embodied the 'all or nothing' principle, introduced for the first time in the Dreadnought era in the US ships *Nevada* and *Oklahoma* (laid down 1912).

Protection was concentrated over gun positions, magazines, machinery and boiler spaces,

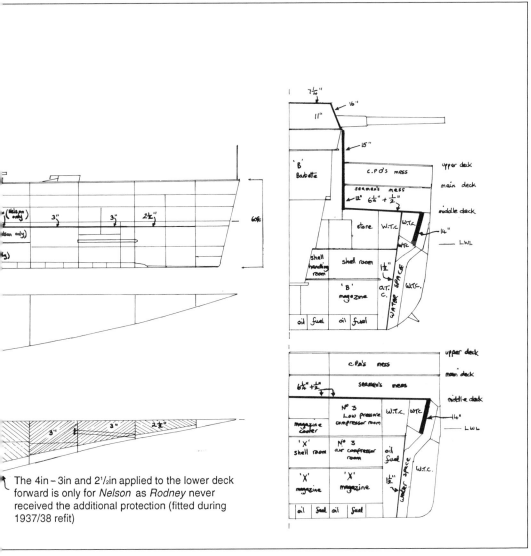

The 4in – 3in and 2½in applied to the lower deck forward is only for *Nelson* as *Rodney* never received the additional protection (fitted during 1937/38 refit)

with the entire hull before and after this being completely unarmoured. To allow minimum length of the citadel, and maximum armour thickness, main armament was located forward, the after turret being located exactly amidships. The adoption of this method of application was a radical departure from British practice, but had been grudgingly accepted in order to secure the great freeboard required, good seakeeping qualities, extremely heavy armament and above aver-

age speed on the 35,000-ton Washington Treaty displacement limit while at the same time meeting strict Admiralty requirements for a very thick belt (14in) to protect the main armament forward.

Extremely valuable information about armour protection was gleaned when the ex-German battleship *Baden* was used as a target for heavy shells on 29 September 1921. Rounds 3, 8 and 14 were of particular interest as they showed

what modern AP shells could do, and the vulnerability of turrets protected by only medium armour thickness. The 7in side armour protecting the secondary armament, and that for the main belt lower edge (6¾in) proved, in fact, almost valueless. These rounds also showed what AP shells could do against medium armour struck at large or oblique angles and proved how relatively ineffectual the armour was. It had long been recognized that armour plate was of the greatest value when worked in large thick masses. Distribution of medium thicknesses over large areas gave a general impression of protection, but this was, in fact, illusory. This was impressively illustrated by rounds 3, 8 and 14 when fired at the 7in plates of *Baden*, which were all pierced by 15in shells of armour-piercing quality, at a velocity of 1,380 fps. Not only was the 7in battery armour pierced, but the 7⅞in armour on the barbettes below the upper deck level was nearly perforated. This would have been accomplished had the range been greater and the shell diving at a steeper angle. The same shells attacking 14in armour under the same conditions would have broken up after considerable damage to the plate, but that thickness would have kept the blast outside.

The policy of the day was to protect any new ship with maximum concentration around vitals and at the maximum thickness that displacement would allow. Horizontal protection requirements were indicated by rounds 2, 4 and 10 which were fired at the unarmoured ends of *Baden* and resulted in explosions between the decks. In round 10(CPC) the upper deck was lifted 4ft 6in and 43 feet of it was torn away from the side of the ship. The shell then pierced the main deck and produced a hole 16ft wide by 4ft 6in long and blew that deck 7ft downwards. It was considered that such severe damage in a strength deck would jeopardize the longitudinal strength of a vessel, especially if the vessel received more than one hit in the same area.

Round 6 was fired to test the tongue-type joints adopted by the Germans for their barbettes. The velocity and angle of attack was so arranged that the attacking shell would just fail to perforate and put maximum pressure on the joint. The result was that the strap behind the armoured joint gave way and the joint split; this was exacerbated by the number of bolt holes in the area.

To complete the tests against modern armour, further firing was conducted against the old battleship *Superb* (*Bellerophon* class, 1907) on May 2 1922. Plates were taken from *Baden* and positioned in *Superb* to take the blast. A number of 15in shells were then fired at the decks (290lb plates) and side armour (560lb plates) from HMS *Terror* from a distance of 500 yards. The results were:

1. The armour quality of the plates from *Baden* stood up to the tests very well.
2. Any electric welding incorporated in the structure broke away.
3. Heavy deck thicknesses of this nature could be supported if necessary.
4. The angle of the 560lb armour was enough to cause the shell to break up on impact, but it was seen that the belt would have to be 'keyed' in properly so as to avoid any damage to the hull proper, or displacement of the armour strakes in question.

The general scheme of armouring in *Nelson* and *Rodney* also embodied all the lessons learned during the Great War, especially at Jutland. New improved 'D' type steel with a tensile strength of 37 to 43psi was used for the first time, in place of normal high-tensile steel, on decks and anti-torpedo bulkheads. The main belt was fitted internally – for the first time in a British battleship – to secure maximum support to the armour against being driven in bodily by a direct hit, as had occurred in *Derfflinger* and *Lion* at Jutland, and it was fitted at an angle of 72 degrees, running away from the waterline at its bottom edge to increase effectiveness against plunging shell fire. The belt was not deep enough, however, and caused great concern among the construction staff. The upper edge of the main strake was supported by a thick armoured deck, but the lower edge rested on an inclined shelf with individual plates 'keyed in' and heavy bars placed behind this. These chock castings which housed the lower edge would also help to direct fragments of a bursting shell upwards and take them away from the lower parts of the ship. The arrangement of internal armouring reduced the armoured water plane, but sufficient resources of buoyancy were available to ensure that the ship would be safe even if the outer hull were opened up by gunfire. The horizontal protection against plunging fire and bombing aircraft was developed to a very high degree, and was considered

at the time to be adequate against anything that could be used against the new ships.

The sloping armoured deck behind the main belt, which had been a feature in all British battleships since the *Majestic* class (1893), was abandoned in *Nelson* in favour of a flat heavy deck across the top of the main strake and covering the magazines, boiler spaces and machinery. An extension aft, at a slightly lower level, ran across to protect the steering gear. The horizontal armouring was concentrated entirely in these two levels, and they were the thickest individual armoured decks ever fitted in a battleship to that date. Their design also received special attention in view of probable developments in aircraft attack.

All openings for ventilation were reduced to a minimum while special hatches, with operating gear under protection below, were fitted to provide a ready means of escape. Protection to the

main armament and magazines was very thorough, special attention having been given to this in view of the high percentage of hits on and around turrets during the war, and the usually disastrous effects of these. Maximum armour thicknesses on barbettes and turrets were respectively 5in and 3in more than in the *Queen Elizabeth* and *Royal Sovereign* classes. The turrets were a new, low design with a flat crown to deflect projectiles falling at a steep angle, and reportedly they afforded a high degree of protection. Anti-flash protection to magazines was materially improved as a result of post-war experiments. They were the first British battleships to carry the anti-torpedo armament in closed turrets, these providing, in addition to other advantages, more complete protection to the gun crews than the battery system. They were the last British battleships to have a separate heavily armoured conning tower, this being

Nelson and *Rodney*: Particulars, as completed

Construction
Nelson: Armstrong; laid down 28.12.1922; launched 3.9.1925; completed April 1927 (began trials).
Rodney: Cammell Laird; laid down 28.12.1922; launched 17.12.1925; completed August 1927 (began trials).
Displacement (tons): *Nelson* (as inclined 19.3.1927) 31,800 (light), 33,300 (standard), 37,780 (deep). *Rodney*: 33,730 (standard), 37,430 (deep).
Dimensions
Length: *Nelson* 660ft (pp), 709ft 9⅞in (oa); *Rodney* 710ft 2½in (oa).
Beam: 106ft.
Draught
Nelson: 28ft 1in (light), 30ft 4in (mean standard); *Rodney*: 30ft 2in (standard), 31ft 8in deep.
Armament
9 x 16in Mk I (100rpg)
12 x 6in Mk XII (150rpg)
6 x 4.7in HA Mk VIII (175rpg)
4 x 3pdr Hotchkiss
8 x 2pdr Single QF
9 x 6pdr
5 x MG
18 Lewis
2 x 24.5in TT submerged.
Armour
Main belt: 14in (KC) thinning to 13in at machinery spaces and after magazines.
Barbettes: 15–12in
Bulkheads: 12–8–10–4in
Turrets: 16–11–9in
Conning tower: 14–12–10–6in
Decks: Protective deck: 6¼in plus ½in plating over whole length of 14in belt, lower deck 4¼in plus ½in plating.

Secondary barbettes: 1in (special 'D' steel)
Secondary turrets 1½–1in (special 'D' steel).
Machinery:
Brown Curtis geared reduction turbines driving 2 propellers. Designed SHP: 45,000 for 23 knots.
8 Admiralty 3-drum small-tubed boilers, 250psi.
Length of engine rooms: 29ft 11⅛in forward, 23ft 11¾in aft.
Length of boiler rooms: 41ft 11¼in forward, 42ft aft.
Fuel: 3,800 tons oil max.
Radius of action: 14,500rpm at 10 knots, 5,500 at full speed (see also 1939 figures).
Ship's boats:
2 x 50ft motor pinnaces, 1 x 35ft motor pinnace, 2 x 45ft motor launches, 2 x 32ft sailing cutters, 2 x 27ft whalers, 1 x 30ft gig, 2 x 16ft skiff dinghies. For private ship add: 1 x 30ft gig, 1 x 50ft admiral's barge, 1 x 13ft 6in balsa raft.
Searchlights
4 x 36in: 2 on platform each side of funnel, 2 on platform on main tripod legs, 6 x 24in signalling lamps.
Complement: 1,361 as flagship, 1,314 as private ship.
Costs: *Nelson* £7,504,055, *Rodney*: £7,617,799.

Nelson: GM and stability, Based on inclining experiments 19 March 1927
'A' condition: Ship fully equipped with 1,000 tons oil in bottom tanks, and 1,000 tons in wing tanks. Draught: 30ft 4in mean. GM: 9.3ft
'B' condition: Ship fully equipped with 95% fuel oil on board (3,900 tons oil). Draught: 31ft 8in mean. GM: 10.2ft
Angles of stability: 'A' condition: 30° max. 'B' condition: 40° max.
Stability vanishes at 'A' condition: 73°, 'B' condition: 77°.

Date	Runs	SHP	Revs (S)	Revs (P)	Speed (knots)
21.5.1927	1. East	6,318	84.7	85	13.01
	2. West	6,224	82	82.25	12.34
	3. East	6,329	83.5	85	12.84
	4. West	6,393	83	82.75	12.29
	1. East	9,463	97.2	96.5	14.89
	2. West	9,332	94.4	96	14.13
	3. East	9,193	96.4	95.6	14.75
	4. West	8,707	91	93.5	13.76
	1. East	14,574	112.2	110.3	17.34
	2. West	14,594	110.6	110	16.38
	3. East	14,633	112.2	111.2	17.211
	4. West	14,583	110.2	110.2	16.47
	1. East	18,331	117.5	120.25	17.9
	2. West	18,777	122.7	121.7	18.85
	3. East	18,624	121.2	120.2	17.70
	4. West	18,763	122	121.3	18.85
23.5.1927	1. West	27,186	136.6	137.3	20.76
	2. East	27,531	137	136.3	20.22
	3. West	27,612	138	137	20.67
	4. East	27,380	136.7	136	20.11
24.5.1927	1. East	37,008	150.6	152	22.53
	2. West	36,992	150.3	151.3	22.19
	3. East	36,936	150.3	151.7	22.67
	4. West	36,569	150.3	147	22.09
26.5.1927	1. East	45,805	161	161	23.14
	2. West	45,878	162	162	23.9
	3. East	45,890	161.5	160.3	23.23
	4. West	45,174	162	162.6	23.84
	5. East	46,212	161.3	161.3	23.32
	6. West	46,089	162	162	23.68

abandoned in the succeeding *King George IV* class and *Vanguard* in which only a light splinter-proof navigating position high up in the face of the bridge tower was provided. *Queen Elizabeth*, *Valiant* and *Warspite* were similarly modified during the final reconstructions. Underwater protection was very complete particularly in the machinery and boiler spaces, where it reached a degree not previously attained in any other British capital ship. The usual external bulges were replaced by an alternative and very efficient system of internal sub-division developed after a long series of experiments and it is reported that this was designed to be capable of withstanding the simultaneous explosion of four torpedoes. A longitudinal bulkhead was fitted throughout the machinery and boiler spaces.

The DNC (Sir William Berry) had favoured inward sloping sides with external bulges as in *Hood*, but this was found to be impracticable because of: 1. Inability of existing docking accommodation to take the increased beam caused by the considerably wider bulges required to resist modern torpedoes. 2. Necessity for maximum armoured beam at waterline to ensure stability in event of heavy flooding.

Pumping and flooding arrangements were very extensive and were designed to deal rapidly with the correction of heel and/or trim resulting from damage. Eleven electrically driven pumps with individual outputs of 350 tons per hour were provided for compartments outside the machinery and boiler spaces.

The main armour protection was as follows: Main Belt: was 14in thick amidships and ran for 384 feet. Angled at 72°, it was fitted internally and extended from the outer face of the forward 16in barbette (about 100 feet from the bow) to the inner face of the after 6in barbette (about 70 feet from the stern) and sloped inwards to the waterline. The 14in plates reduced to 13in abreast machinery and after magazines. Bulkheads were 12in and 8in forward closing forward extremities of belt armour between middle and lower decks, 10in and 4in aft closing after extremities of belt.

Decks: 6¼in armour plates plus ½in plating laid over the top (6¾in) laid flat over the length of the 14in belt armour on middle deck level. Lower deck 4¼in armour plates plus ½in plating laid over the top (4¾in) flat, from after extremity of 14in belt to within about 25 feet of the stern.
Barbettes: 15in carried down to middle deck (see plan for various thicknesses).
Turrets: 16in faces, 7¼in crowns and rear.
Secondary barbettes: 1in.
Conning tower: 14in sides, 12in front, 10in back and 6½in roof.
Tube: 6in.
Conning tower hood: 5in–3in.
Funnel uptakes: 8in–7in.
Anti-torpedo bulkheads: 1½in, longitudinal port and starboard, set well inboard, extending completely between forward and after magazines from keel to middle deck and sloping inwards from top to bottom.

On completion they were probably the best armoured battleships afloat although the shallow 14in belt led to much criticism after completion. During firing experiments in 1931 on *Marlborough* and *Emperor of India* one shell (hit no. 4) burst under the armoured belt, apparently just where it was in contact with skin plating, and caused considerable damage. This hit emphasized the desirability of a deep belt and it was proposed that *Nelson* and *Rodney* be improved in this respect when they came in hand for refitting, but the extension of side armour was never effected and their armour protection remained the same throughout their lives. The only addition was to *Nelson*, which was fitted with 100lb and 120lb NC armour on the lower deck forward between 80 and 84 stations, 160lb armour bulkhead at 80 station from hold to platform deck. *Rodney* was not completely fitted with additional armour forward, but it is understood that she did receive something along these lines although the official records are not clear. Later proposals to modernize the armour protection

Nelson: Steam Trials. Displacement: 37,860/37,748 tons (deep load)
Date: 28 May 1927

Run	SHP	Revs (S)	Revs (P)	Speed (knots)
1st	6,342	80	79	12.33
2nd	6,046	81.2	82.9	12.30
1st	15,238	113.25	113.75	17.48
2nd	15,218	111.25	111.25	16.42
3rd	15,189	113	113.25	17.66
4th	15,115	111.8	112.27	16.36
1st	19,030	121.7	122	19
2nd	18,790	120	120.6	17.31
3rd	18,636	120	120.7	18.33
4th	18,626	119.5	120	17.11
1st	37,027	150.3	150	22.36
2nd	36,554	149	148.3	21.10
3rd	36,920	150	149.3	22.14
4th	36,312	148.6	148.3	21.25
1st	45,876	161.5	161	23.20
2nd	45,685	160	159.7	22.90
3rd	45,844	160.6	161	23.05
4th	45,840	160	160	23.14
5th	45,795	160	161	23.96
6th	45,771	160	160.3	23.35

(1938) were finally abandoned (see notes on reconstruction).

MACHINERY

The arrangement of boilers and machinery was contrary to normal practice, the engines being forward of the boiler rooms. This layout was adopted because: 1. Engine room required more width than the boiler room and in reversing the order of normal practice this was obtained and it was consequently better protected. 2. Large openings for uptakes and boiler room fans were further from the main magazines. 3. Great space for main armament and controls could be provided without smoke interference from the close proximity of the funnels.

They were the first British battleships to have all geared turbines although these had been fitted in the battlecruiser *Hood*, the large cruisers of the *Courageous* class and some smaller cruisers and destroyers. Sub-division in machinery and boiler spaces was developed to a higher degree than in any previous British capital ship. Arrangement of the boilers abaft machinery, contrary to normal practice, brought the engine rooms immediately below the bridge tower and it was adopted to enable the funnel to be placed well abaft the tower with a view to reducing smoke interference to the bridge and control positions. The funnel was located about 40 feet abaft the tower, but in service this distance was found to be still insufficient, especially when steaming head to wind, when the tower created a considerable back-draught to the inconvenience of the bridge and control personnel. On various occasions a funnel extension and cowl were recommended, but this was never fitted.

The *Nelson* arrangement was not repeated, although the practice of disposing engine and boiler rooms alternately for greater security was later adopted in the *King George V* class and *Vanguard* and in some cruisers and destroyers, each group of boilers being placed before the engine room it served. The main machinery was Brown-Curtis single reduction geared turbines driving twin screws, one HP ahead and one LP ahead and astern turbine on each shaft. Cruising stages were fitted to HP turbines for economy at low powers. The machinery was in four compartments forward of the boiler rooms, arranged in pairs abreast, separated by a centreline bulkhead. The turbines were in the two forward compartments, reduction gear, etc., in the two after compartments. There was a complete set of machinery for each shaft, entirely isolated from and independent of the other. Auxiliary machinery was situated in wing compartments farther aft. Boilers were eight Admiralty, 3-drum, small-tube boilers with super-heaters and forced draught, six boilers of 5,600hp and two of 5,100hp. Working pressure was approximately 250psi reducing to 200psi at the turbines, and super-heated to 150° Farenheit. The boilers were in four compartments, two in each, arranged in pairs abreast on each side of the centreline bulkhead abaft the machinery space, with central stokehold spaces. The port and starboard boiler rooms were completely isolated from and independent of one another.

The auxiliary machinery consisted of distilling machinery – four evaporators and two distillery condensers – capable of 320 tons output per 24 hours, arranged in two complete sets, one in each auxiliary compartment (located port and starboard abreast boiler rooms with the turbines in well-separated compartments forward of the engine rooms). This wide distribution minimized the risk of all electric power being lost in the event of damage in any one area. A new type of electro-hydraulic steering gear was introduced in these ships. Rams were operated by oil under pressure from three variable-speed pumps driven by electric motors. Each pump with its motor was placed in a separate watertight compartment. Alternative steam-driven pumps were provided in the after engine room for use in event of complete electric power failure. This gear, which proved very satisfactory in service, was capable of putting the rudder hard over from port to starboard or vice versa in about thirty seconds. Oil fuel was 3,967 tons and was carried in wing tanks and double-bottoms and included 162 tons of diesel oil.

Two sets of trials were carried out in each ship, one at standard displacement and one at deep load. *Nelson*, without forcing, exceeded nominal speed at standard displacement and did very well at deep load, these results representing a mean of eight hours' trial in each case (see steam trial tables).

Both ships proved to be excellent steamers in service and it is said that while chasing *Bismarck* in May 1941 *Rodney* attained a speed in excess of what had been thought possible in view of previous machinery and boiler breakdowns and the long time that had elapsed since her last refit. In relation to displacement *Nelson* and *Rodney* were,

Rodney: Steam trials
Course throughout the trials was about 2 miles from shore at a depth of 25 fathoms. Sea: Smooth.
Displacement: 33,785/33,660 tons.

Date	Runs	SHP	Revs (P)	Revs (S)	Speed (knots)
30.8.1927	1. East	18,162	122	122	18.672
	2. West	18,236	124	123	18.710
	3. East	18,307	124	122	18.367
	4. West	18,399	124	123	18.828
	1. West	14,859	114	114	17.892
	2. East	15,022	116	115	16.901
	3. West	14,803	114	114	18.072
	4. East	14,875	114	115	16.697
	1. West	10,237	101	101	16.514
	2. East	9,623	98	98	14.331
	3. West	9,627	98	97	15,481
	4. East	8,919	97	95	14.074
	1. West	5,760	86	86	13.897
	2. East	6,633	89	89	12.894
	3. West	6,752	87	88	13.667
	4. East	6,809	87	88	12.811
1.8.1927	1. East	27,809	140	140	20.571
	2. West	28.069	140	140	21.277
	3. East	28,167	141	140	20.809
	4. West	27,727	140	139	21.353
2.9.1927	1. East	36,442	154	154	22.670
	2. West	36,626	154	153	22.670
	3. East	37,052	154	153	22.613
	4. West	36,651	153	152	22.785
7.9.1927	1.West	46,477	164	163	23.08
	2. East	45,427	165	163	
	3. West	45,591	163	162	
	4. East	45,365	163	163	
	5. West	46,030	165	161	
	6. East	46,317	165	163	

on completion, probably the most economical steamers in the Royal Navy

GENERAL NOTES

A complete breakaway from the normal bridge-work and heavy tripod foremast, which was relaced by a high tower structure, was considered to be the only satisfactory means of obtaining adequate support and clear vision for the extensive modern fire control equipment, as well as providing the necessary accommodation for the navigating and signalling positions and extra cabins, etc. The controls for the main and secondary armament were located at the top of the tower, and the Admiral's bridge, navigating and lookout platforms were arranged around the upper sides and face of the tower, with signalling searchlights in ports inside and lower down. The sea cabins, plotting offices, etc., were positioned at the base of the tower. All flag signalling was carried out from the foremast (see Captain's report).

The massive tower bridgework, introduced in this class, was retained in the succeeding *King George V* and *Vanguard* classes, and (in modified form) in the reconstructed *Warspite, Valiant, Queen Elizabeth* and *Renown*.

The heavy boats were all stowed abaft the funnel, and handled by the main derrick which was worked from the mainmast base.

Accommodation greatly embodied the recommendations of the Accommodation Committee, which had been appointed by the Admiralty in 1923, and in these two ships it was especially

Nelson: Masts, March 1930
Forward steel spurs on front of bridge: 7ft 6in long, 3–3¹/₂in diameter.
Jack staff: 22ft 6in long, 3–4in diameter.
Ensign staff: 27ft 3in long, 3–5in diameter.
Two sounding booms: 30ft long, 6–4in diameter.
Eight general-purpose derricks (Oregon pine) 40ft long, 11¹/₂–14in diameter.
Mainmast (Oregon pine)

	length (ft/in)	diameter (in)	weight (tons)
Lower mast	90	34	16.89
Struts:	77ft 6in	30	16.28 (two)
Topmast:	60	16–10¹/₄	1.18
Topgallant mast:	49	12³/₄–5	.77
Lower signal yard	19ft 6in	6–4¹/₂	.09
Topgallant yard:	50	9–4¹/₄	.56
Main boat derrick:	59ft 4in	21–16³/₄	.31
(mild steel)			5.36

Highest fixed point: 113ft 5¹/₄in.
Height of topgallant mast from waterline: 190ft 9in.
High-angle control tower: 116ft 7in.
High-angle control platform: 108ft.
Main armament control: 82ft 7in.
Floor of searchlight platform: 61ft 1in.
Pom-pom control platform: 68ft.

good both for officers and ratings – the space available being much greater than usual as a consequence of the high freeboard over the whole length of the ship, which also offered ample headroom between the decks. Natural light was provided in most living spaces, and ventilation was greatly improved over preceding classes. The ships were also provided with such items as reading and recreation rooms, drying rooms for wet clothing, bakery, oil-fired galley, laundry and electric ovens for the first time.

Ventilation received special attention and proved to be generally satisfactory in service. In the crew's galley, however, exhaust fumes were stated to be intolerable during the war when the skylights were often closed to darken ship.

The pair were known affectionately as 'The Queen's Mansions' (because of the massive tower) and by 1930 had become part of the British constitution – the general public loved them and they were always crowded out on 'Navy Days', but a more relevant opinion came from Captain T. H. Binney of *Nelson* when finishing his term of service in her:

'Before relinquishing command of HMS *Nelson*, I have the honour to submit the following

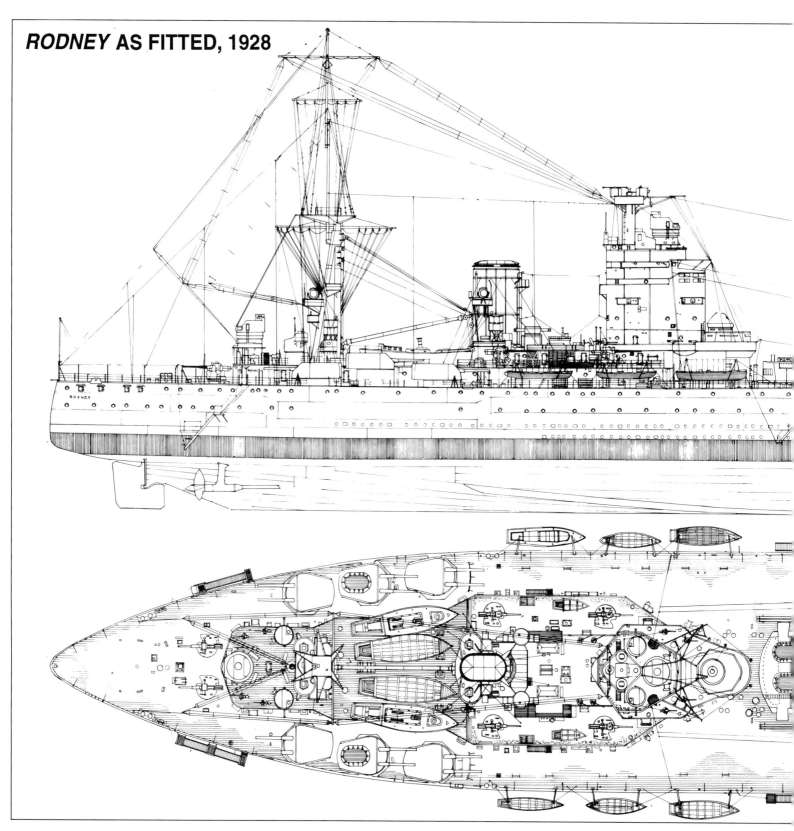

RODNEY AS FITTED, 1928

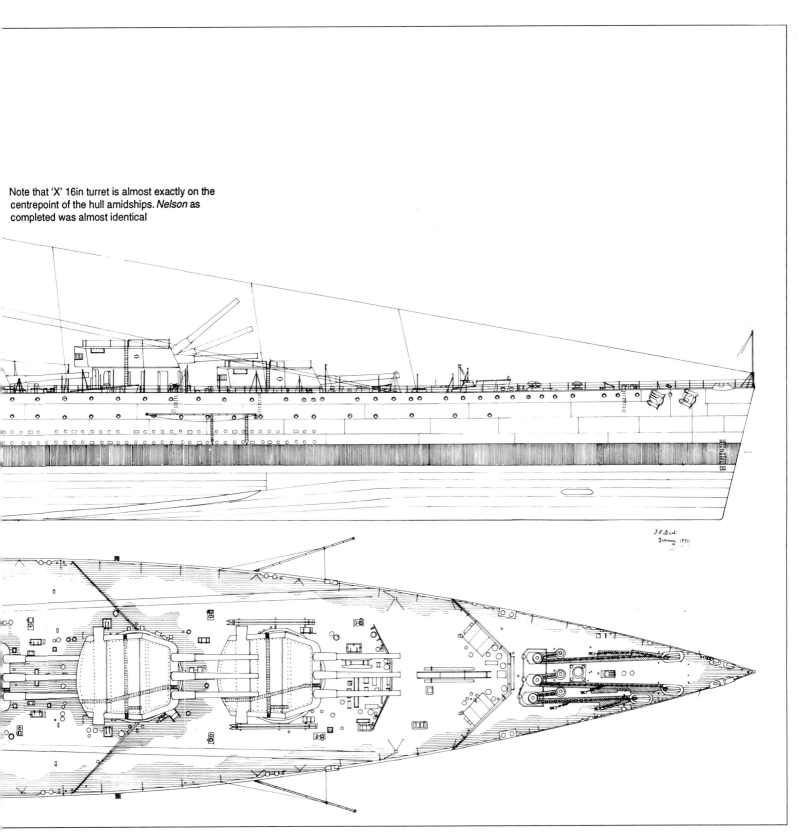

Note that 'X' 16in turret is almost exactly on the centrepoint of the hull amidships. *Nelson* as completed was almost identical

remarks or points of interest relating to this class of ship. I have been fortunate in that I have joined the ship at that moment when she may be said to have got over her initial troubles, and my period of command has included the last twelve months of the first command with a well-trained ship's company, and the first five months of the second command with a new ship's company.

1. Manoeuvring powers.

In the early stages of the ship's first commission, there was a general misconception in the service that the *Nelson* class were unhandy and difficult to manoeuvre. This was probably due to the unaccustomed position of the bridge and the initial inexperience of the personnel of what the ship might do under various conditions. Both my predecessor and myself, however, very soon discovered that this opinion was entirely fallacious. In calm weather, the ship's manoeuvring capabil-

ities are in no way inferior, and in many ways superior to those of *Queen Elizabeth* or *Revenge*. The astern power is much better than that of *Queen Elizabeth*, they steer much better with the engines stopped, and at rest they turn very easily by working the engines. Owing to the high superstructure aft, however, they carry a good deal of weather helm, and for the same reason, their turning circle when turning away from the wind is greatly increased, while when turning into the wind, it is correspondingly decreased.

As an example of the effect of the wind, on one occasion when getting under way with a wind of about 5–6kts on the starboard beam, the ship swung 4 points to starboard against full starboard helm, and it was not until the ship was moving through the water at 9kts that she started to answer her helm.

On another occasion, when anchored with the

fleet, with a wind of about 5 knots on the port beam, the ship's head could not be kept steady with full port helm, and swung to port in spite of starboard screws being reversed. On entering a harbour through a long narrow channel such as Gibraltar a strong head wind is the cause of some anxiety, but the effect seems to be greatly reduced if the wind is a few points abaft the beam or on the bow.

When pointing the ship using the engines, the wind has little effect, except to stop the swing at once.

Generally, the superstructure has the effect of a mizzen sail continuously set, and if this is kept in mind, no real difficulties should be encountered in any circumstances.

ARMAMENT:

I hold the opinion that the low-angle gun equipment as a whole, and particularly the 16in main armament, is a very marked advance on any previous capital ship, and should result in improved rate of hitting at all ranges.

On account of various improvements (rangefinders, control apparatus, etc.) as well as the increased size of splashes, long-range firing from *Nelson* should be more effective in the 25/28,000 yds long-range firing than in *Queen elizabeth* at 21/25,000 yds.

In the case of secondary armament, although the rate of fire is rather low, the increased range at which fire can be opened, and the absence of loss of output due to fatigue, combined with excellent ammunition supply arrangements, will be a very prominent factor in war.

In view of the modern tendering of construction for 'all or nothing' armour protection leaving controls and secondary batteries unprotected, the possibility for using the secondary battery for 'harassing fire' at the main armoured target when the range has been found assumes greater importance, and in *Nelson* the secondary armament can do this efficiently without loss of anti-torpedo boat efficiency.

16IN MOUNTINGS:

The 16in triple mounting has been subjected to considerable criticism from time to time, and there is little doubt, that in some quarters the view is held that a triple mounting for heavy guns is not a good investment.

The great advantage of the triple mounting system from construction point of view (which is that the armament can be concentrated in a much smaller space, and will require less area of armoured protection) has not, perhaps been sufficiently emphasised.

The main disadvantage of *Nelson*'s triple mounting is loss of output on account of the fact that the three guns cannot be fired together owing to ballistic difficulties, whereas they must be loaded together. This, however, is not in itself a reason for condemning the triple mounting in general.

The mounting may be said to have proved itself, when in October 1929, one turret crew with two years' experience, loaded and fired 33 rounds without mishap. The main defects appear to be the roller paths and the rollers.

FIRE CONTROL:

The main armament fire control is very satisfactory, and a marked advance on that of earlier battleships. The efficiency of the rangefinder installation and the Admiralty fire control table are of a high order, and it has been found a comparatively simple matter to train the personnel in their use. In secondary armament apparatus no great advance can be recorded as the installation is essentially the same as in older ships though more automatic in action. The installation, however, fulfils the very requirements of simplicity.

The Captain's bridge is generally satisfactory and a great improvement over previous classes. One small difficulty occurs however, as a Flagship, in that the Captain and officers on the bridge cannot see signals hoisted on the mainmast, and are entirely dependant on the reporting of them by a signalman. The Admiral's bridge is inferior to the Captain's bridge in that the Admiral has no all-round view from any one spot, the bridge itself is unduly crowded with personnel.

I believe that war requirements would very soon lead to a demand to improve the bridge in this respect, and if expense were no object, it could easily be done by extending the fore end of this structure over the compass platform.

ACCOMMODATION:

The accommodation for officers and men is excellent, the men's particularly being in conformity with the spirit of the times and without any kind of pampering and is a great improvement on anything that has gone before.

In conclusion, it may be worth emphasizing the obvious fact of the good moral effect on officers and men of serving in such a ship complete with the most up-to-date material. Serving in such a ship induced a sense of responsibility and consequent thoroughness in quite an exceptional degree.

Men take pride in their ship because she is up to date, and take pride in showing her to their friends because they feel that they have something worth showing. This connection between moral and material factors is not of course in itself a reason for building new ships, but in the post-war navy it is a fact of some importance that should not be neglected.'

BRIDGEWORK

After a long succession of single and tripod foremasts to house the 'eyes and brains' of the battleship, an entirely new concept in bridgework arrived in 1925 with the massive fully enclosed structure fitted to *Nelson* and *Rodney*. This type of structure had never been seen in a capital ship before; gone were the stepped levels of bridgework that had always been open to all weathers and in its place was one large tower with director control equipment located on the top. Within the tower were housed all the essentials to run the ship: Captain's, Admiral's and officer's levels, searchlight platforms, lookout and navigating bridge. The structure was something of a gamble to fit in a £7,000,000 battleship without any proper practical tests, but one that thankfully paid off.

The tower itself, which dominated the appearance of the ship, had some disadvantages, including lack of all-round vision, but its good points, such as being fully enclosed, which offered some degree of protection to everyone serving in there, and all instruments being close to hand, outweighed the disadvantages. A major disadvantage was the fact that the large flat sides of the structure caught the wind at all angles. Tests had shown that the wind when head-on

Nelson and Rodney: Proposed Reconstruction, 1938

Scheme 1. Remove all 4.7in guns and replace with two twin 5.25in turrets. Add deck armour over magazines and machinery. Displacement: 39,470 tons deep load; draught: 32ft 7½in.

Scheme 2. Remove all 6in guns and replace with 4.5in turrets. Amend armour as above, plus modify side armour. Displacement: 40,830 tons

Scheme 3. Fit only 3 x 5.25in turrets. No splinter protection added but modify armour belt.

Costs:

6 x 5.25in	£30,000 each (mountings)
Twelve guns	3,500 each
Sighting and control gear:	20,000
Dockyard work:	60,000
Misc structural work:	30,000
Side armour:	400,000
Removal of old bridge plus new one fitted	13,500
Machinery renewal or modification:	440,000
Chain hoists for 5.25in guns:	60,000
New pom-poms (AA)	13,500

Other work required: Removal of old funnel uptakes. Fit aircraft hangar or position aircraft by side of 'C' 16in turret (2 in number) (catapult on 'C' turret).
Total cost including all work involved: £2,234,500.
All details were agreed in principle before the war, but all work ceased as war approached in 1939.

would flow quickly up over the face of the bridge and then quickly move around to the back of the structure. When the windows were open in the bridge and navigating positions there would be a terrific back draught, which in severe weather would cause discomfort not unlike that experienced in the older, more open bridgework. With all doors and windows closed, the back draught practically ceased.

Throughout the years the structure was subject to criticism, especially in 1934 when *Nelson* ran aground at Portsmouth. (It was argued that the wind caught the structure and pushed the ship off course. See *Nelson* aground notes.) The criticism, however, was certainly less than that levelled at older bridgework. Moreover the design was much favoured abroad and became widely copied in new ships and older vessels being reconstructed. This type of structure continued in the RN in various shapes until the demise of the battleship with *Vanguard* in 1946, so it must have been reasonably successful.

During the Second World War tests were carried out (1943–4) by the National Physical Laboratory to ascertain a degree of habitability for those serving in the uppermost levels of the bridgework. A model was made of *Nelson*'s bridgework at ½ full size, including part of the upper deck and 'X' and 'B' 16in turrets and the funnel.

Various screens were fitted to the original bridge and navigating positions, first 12in in height and then 18in to 24in. It was found that wind pressures and back draught could be eliminated sufficiently by fitting screens and baffles; the small ledge that had been fitted in *Rodney* in the 1930s (below bridge windows) had in fact been a success. *Nelson*, however, was not given this until the tests had been completed. It was probably fitted in late 1943 or early 1944 and can be seen as a small ledge with airflow baffles beneath it fitted just below the lower bridgework windows (see photographs).

NELSON AGROUND, JANUARY 1934

Big ships would often bump into one another during docking and it was no easy task to ensure the safety of about 35,000 tons at low speeds in confined areas. Another regular mishap to ships with large draughts was running aground, and when *Nelson* ran aground in January 1934 a big issue was made of the incident because it hap-

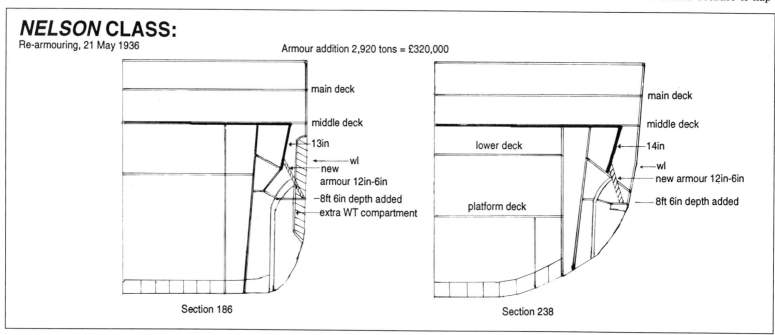

NELSON CLASS:
Re-armouring, 21 May 1936

Armour addition 2,920 tons = £320,000

Section 186

Section 238

Below: *Nelson* aground at Hamilton Bank in January 1934. The tugs are attempting to pull her clear, but to no avail.

pened close to Southsea beach and in full view. On 12 January she was proceeding out of harbour at high tide assisted by three tugs. At the South Railway Jetty the order was given to increase speed to 15½ knots and fixings were taken from the land to attain the correct speed. On passing Marlborough Pier and approaching Hamilton Bank the order was given to reduce to 12 knots. The ship turned against the rudder to starboard and after proceeding about 2½ lengths grounded fast on the Hamilton Bank at a bearing of 10½ degrees starboard. Early efforts to refloat the ship proved unsuccessful and some of the stores and equipment had to be removed. Divers were sent over the side to see what damage had been caused (actually very little) and an inquiry was ordered almost at once to determine whether the grounding had occurred through an error by the officers in charge or had simply been an accident. Was it because of the close proximity of the land, or had the rudder been put over too hard? Abnormal steering was also suggested. The ship was refloated on the next high tide, but by then the Press had more photographs than they needed.

A model of the ship was made and tests were carried out using a simulation of the scene in a test tank. The path of the model was carefully recorded, wind speeds, weather and officer's orders were all taken into consideration. The findings of the Court were variable, but none of the staff in *Nelson* was blamed:

1. Wind effect on such a large structure as carried by the class.
2. Rudder drag in such shallow water.
3. Tug mismanagement.
4. Screw types and sizes.
5. Correct displacement when leaving harbour.
6. *Nelson* class handle badly at slow speeds.

With regard to number one it was concluded that although the structure forward caught the wind this did not in fact have a bad effect on the handling of the ship at sea, but in some cases did affect the vessel at slow speeds.

Number two was dismissed because the rudder did not contribute to the grounding.

Number three. Although one tug had parted the tow during preliminary sailing, the other two performed very well except that at the time it was thought that a greater speed for tugs would have been an advantage.

Number four was dealt with later by Stanley Goodall (Assistant Constructor) who wrote:

'The absence of complaints is the highest reward that the Director of Naval Construction expects, but in this particular case a report was received from a captain relinquishing command (see report elsewhere in chapter) in which it was stated that the ship's manoeuvring capabilities are in no way inferior to those of the *Queen Elizabeth* and *Royal Sovereign* classes. I think this is to be attributed to some extent that *Nelson* and *Rodney* have twin screws of large diameter, whereas the other classes mentioned have four screws of smaller diameter.'

Number five was proved to be correct; the ship was not over weight for her voyage.

Number six, stating that *Nelson* handled badly at slow speeds, did have some foundation (see Captain Binney's report), and when first completed the constructors noted the following: W. J. Berry, 13 December 1927:

'In a beam wind of Force 6 the estimated wind pressure on the ship amounts to more than 38 tons. At a speed of 7 knots the thrust from each screw amounts to about 7 tons and the pressure on the rudder at 20 degrees is about 8½ tons. It will thus be seen that at low speeds a strong wind produces the greater force acting on the ship and could affect her behaviour rendering her less responsive to the action of the rudder.'

All these possibilities were examined, but the conclusion was that the ship's course was too far east of the centre of the channel through which ships leave Portsmouth, probably because the ship was not handling too well at a low speed.

Although it was often stated that the pair did handle well at sea, many reports from 1945 onwards stated that they did not perform at all well at slow speeds as a result of the wind catching the massive superstructure.

APPEARANCE CHANGES, MODIFICATIONS AND REFITS

The unique appearance of *Nelson* and *Rodney* was never equalled in any other contemporary capital ship – British or foreign. Many thought them extremely ugly, and they received derisory nicknames: 'Rodol' and 'Nelsol' (after oil tankers); 'the pair of boots' – the right and left boots of the Second Battle Squadron – 'the ugly sisters' or 'the Cherry Tree class' (i.e., cut-down versions from Washington Naval Treaty). Yet they were generally conceded to be the most impressive-looking British battleships of their day, with a menacing appearance of fighting efficiency seldom, if ever, equalled in any other bat-

Below: An aerial view of *Nelson* at the 1935 Fleet Review.

tleship. One of her officers said of her, 'I challenge anyone to stand on her fo'c's'le and not feel a definite tingle of pride and fear' – certainly a general feeling that was promulgated by the media.

The abnormally long forecastle, with its massive bridge structure located about 60 feet abaft amidships and standing approximately 116 feet above sea level, and the very short quarterdeck made for an extremely unattractive profile and, incidentally, made a true appreciation of their worth somewhat difficult from certain angles. It is often said that they were seen to their best from the quarter, but the author believes that by

far their most impressive appearance was bow-on. Their principal characteristics were:
1. High freeboard, flush deck hull with straight cutaway stem instead of the usual ram or plough-shaped bow.
2. Three triple 16in turrets, all forward with the after turret placed approximately amidships.
3. Three twin 6in turrets closely spaced on each quarter.
4. High massive bridge tower with rangefinders and directors on top, slightly abaft amidships.
5. Rectangular stump foremast at rear of tower.
6. A single rather small funnel set well abaft tower.

As completed they were extremely alike, and from a distance it was almost impossible to distinguish one from the other. Individual differences: *Nelson*, flagpole to main. Second yard on mainmast carried low; *Rodney*, no flagpole. Second yard on main carried higher. Also there were slight variations in the scuttles near anchors and under 6in armament. Pendant numbers (never painted up): *Rodney* 29; *Nelson* 28.
1929–30: High-angle rangefinder on foretop replaced by high-angle director (by March 1930 in *Rodney*, May to June 1930 in *Nelson*). Original diamond-shaped top replaced by circular pattern.

1931–2: *Rodney* by July 1932, multiple 2pdr AA (8 barrels) added in large sponsons on starboard side of superstructure abeam funnel. Original single 2pdr AA removed. Starboard torpedo RF removed.

1933–4: *Nelson* multiple 2pdr AA (8 barrels) added, as *Rodney*, and single 2pdr AA removed (by March 1934). MF DF equipment added May to June 1934. Aerial at head of mainmast. Remote control office fitted at rear of bridge tower.

1934–5: *Nelson*. Multiple 0.5in AA (4 barrels) added P&S on platform low down at the rear of bridge tower. Straight-armed crane for handling aircraft fitted on port side on the upper deck abeam the tower. One Seagull amphibian fitted, mainly for experimentation in connection with the substitution of amphibians for seaplanes in capital ships and cruisers, and for obtaining information regarding their performace in reconnaissance and rough weather operations. The crane was retained for other purposes after the conclusion of trials. No other aircraft equipment ever fitted in *Nelson*. *Rodney*, multiple 2pdr AA added on port side of superstructure abeam funnel. Multiple 0.5in AA added as in *Nelson*. Port torpedo RF removed.

1935–6: 36in SL replaced by 44in in both ships.

1936–7: *Nelson*, multiple 2pdr (8 barrels) added on port side of superstructure abeam the funnel. Shield was temporarily fitted to forward 4.7in AA (removed by March 1938).

1937: Red, white and blue identification bands painted up on 'B' turret in both ships in Spanish waters during Spanish Civil War. Aircraft identification letters painted on crown of 'C' turret in *Nelson* (NE) (painted out by September 1939).

1937–8: *Nelson* as refitted June 1937 to January 1938. Second HA director added on foretop close before the other, and raised well clear of this. Foretop was considerably enlarged. Additional horitzontal armour added in forward part of the ship (see armour drawing). Thicker foremast fitted to support extra weights of second HA director and generally improved stable foundation. *Rodney*, no extra armour fitted, but there were some improvements forward of the main belt internally. Refit September to November 1938, multiple 2pdr added on quarterdeck, right aft. Air warning radar Type 79Y added on each masthead. (First capital ship to have operational radar.) Aircraft catapult (McTaggart) added on crown of 'C' turret. Bent-arm crane fitted on port side of conning tower. Topmast fitted to foremast for RDF (79Y). Maintopgallant removed.

1940–1: UP AA rocket-projectors fitted on 'B' and 'C' turrets (1940). Air warning radar Type 279 fitted in *Nelson* (modifed 79Y). Type 79Y replaced in *Rodney* by Type 279. DF aerial removed from head of mainmast in *Nelson*, with a modified type fitted low on foretopmast. Shields fitted to 4.7in AA guns in *Nelson*. Foretopmast added, and maintopgallant removed in *Nelson*.

1941–2: Radar Type 284 fitted for main armament. Multiple 2pdrs (8 barrels) added P&S on superstructure and 'B' turret, and on quarterdeck, right aft in *Nelson* (*Rodney* already fitted on QD). Seven to nine 20mm AA added in various locations, port and starboard superstructure around and abaft bridge tower in both ships, on 'C' turret in *Nelson* and on 'B' turret and conning tower hood in *Rodney* (removed from 'B' turret in *Rodney* later). 0.5mm AA removed from both ships. Radar fitted for control of 4.7in and 2pdrs (Type 285 for 4.7in; 283 for 2pdrs). AA director platform at head of foremast was considerably enlarged. LAA directors fitted on former 0.5mm AA platforms at rear of bridge tower, on upper pair of main tripod platforms, and before and abaft after 16in director. UP AA rocket-projectors removed from 'B' and 'C' turret in *Rodney*, but still evident in *Nelson* until September 1941. All modifications effected by May 1942. Type 279 radar removed in *Rodney* and replaced by Type 281. Aerials on both mastheads. Surface warning radar Type 271 added in both ship (aerial inside lantern on mainmast). General warning radar Type 291 fitted in *Rodney*, aerial at head of foretopmast above Type 281. D/F aerial removed from foretop in *Nelson*, and a modified type fitted to the face of the bridge tower. MF/DF fitted in *Rodney* with aerials same as in *Nelson*. Heavier foretopmast fitted in *Rodney* to accommodate additional radar. Camouflage painted up in both ships.

1942–3: 13 x 20mm AA singles added (*Nelson*), three P&S on platform at rear angles of bridge tower, replacing former LAA director platform. *Rodney*, 35 x 20mm AA singles added (by August 1943) 'B' and 'C' turret, quarterdeck, etc. Type 271 replaced by Type 273. Extra LAA director added on conning tower. Catapult removed but crane was retained. Shields fitted to 4.7in AA. Modifications to director control platform.

1944: *Rodney*, extra 20mm AA added. Type 650 anti-missile equipment fitted. *Nelson*, 28 x 20mm AA singles added.

1944–5: *Nelson*, as refitted for eastern service, July 1944 to January 1945, main armament director position over conning tower removed. Light AA guns increased by 4 quad mountings 40mm AA, some 2pdr directors removed to make space for extra 20mm AA. LAA directors (283 RDF) were above and abaft forward pair of 40mm AA mountings, port and starboard on

Right: An aerial view of *Nelson* during the spring cruise, March 1937. Note the identification letters on 'C' turret roof.

Below: *Nelson* in 1937. Looking up at the massive superstructure, it is obvious why this class were dubbed 'the Queen's mansions'.

superstructure abeam and abaft mainmast and on platform on main tripod legs. SL removed from main tripod legs to make way for LAA directors. Internal arrangements modified for tropical service. Standard Admiralty camouflage scheme painted up in *Nelson* only. Type 650 anti-missile equipment fitted (late 1944), aerial on face of bridge.

1946: Some 20mm AA removed from both ships. Repainted all grey (*Nelson* only), *Rodney* retained original camouflage to the scrapyard.

1947–8: Stripped of all small guns, aerials and general small fittings, etc.

BATTLE DAMAGE

Nelson, mined 4 December 1939

At 0755 hours as *Nelson* was entering port on 4 December 1939 at a speed of 9–10 knots, she ran over a mine which exploded in the area forward of 'A' 16in turret. The forward part of the ship was pushed up and whipped two or three times before coming to rest. Men on the upper deck forward were thrown down in a forward direction and a splash of about 6 feet above the upper deck was witnessed along with bluish-grey smoke. *Nelson* took a slight list to starboard (about 2°) and trimmed by the bow. Her draught was checked and read 39ft 2in, forward, 31ft 2in aft. The ship was quickly put into port and divers went over the side to examine the damage. From 43 to 74 stations the side plating was slightly buckled and showed a number of cracks, and there was a hole just abaft station 60. Abaft station 60 the plating was dished over a length of about 14 feet. The hole at station 60 was about 10ft x 6ft. The edges of the plating were bent in and out.

FLOODING:

Abaft 80, D.B. tanks under 'A' cordite hanging room were under pressure and oil was leaking slowly into the sump under the false floor in the handing room, and thence through rivet holes in the boundary bar at the bottom of 88 transverse bulkhead into the hold space 84–88. The transverse oil-fuel tank 80–84 was under pressure.

80–86. No. 3 central store hold was flooded at once. CO_2 room S and E.A. room P were flooded slowly to about 6ft and 3ft respectively above the platform deck. Cold and cool rooms on platform deck middle-line remained fairly

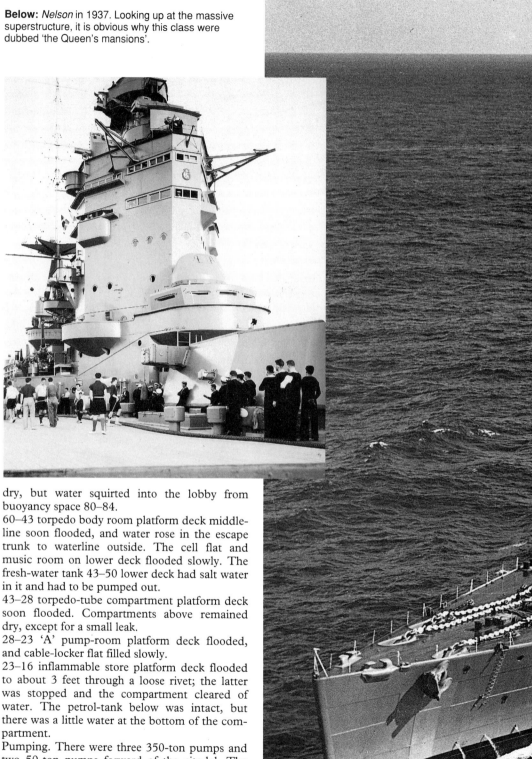

dry, but water squirted into the lobby from buoyancy space 80–84.

60–43 torpedo body room platform deck middle-line soon flooded, and water rose in the escape trunk to waterline outside. The cell flat and music room on lower deck flooded slowly. The fresh-water tank 43–50 lower deck had salt water in it and had to be pumped out.

43–28 torpedo-tube compartment platform deck soon flooded. Compartments above remained dry, except for a small leak.

28–23 'A' pump-room platform deck flooded, and cable-locker flat filled slowly.

23–16 inflammable store platform deck flooded to about 3 feet through a loose rivet; the latter was stopped and the compartment cleared of water. The petrol-tank below was intact, but there was a little water at the bottom of the compartment.

Pumping. There were three 350-ton pumps and two 50-ton pumps forward of the citadel. The

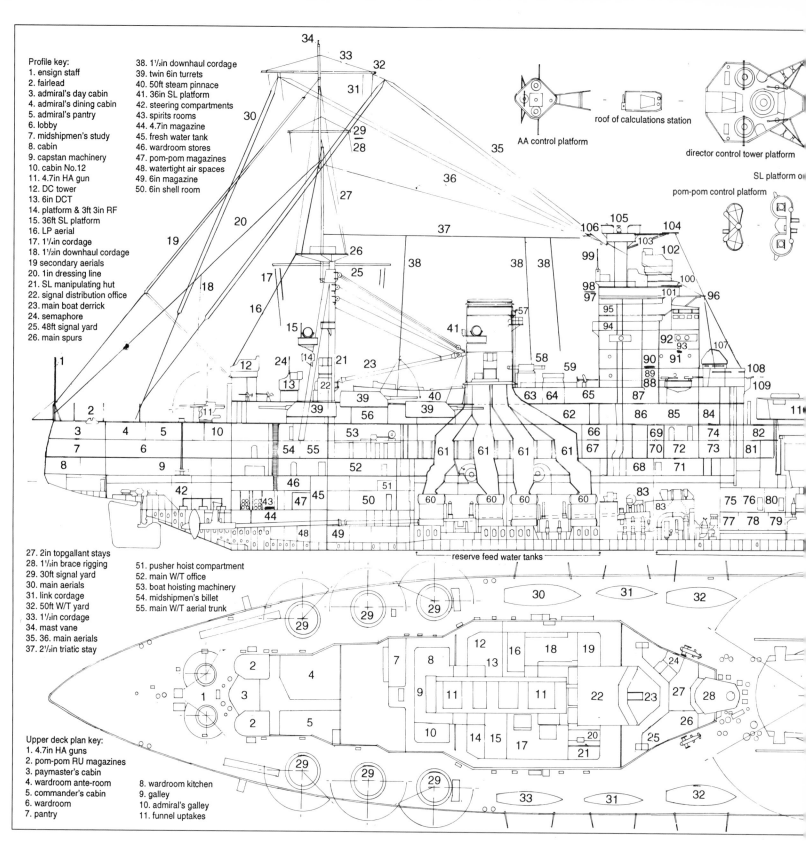

Profile key:
1. ensign staff
2. fairlead
3. admiral's day cabin
4. admiral's dining cabin
5. admiral's pantry
6. lobby
7. midshipmen's study
8. cabin
9. capstan machinery
10. cabin No.12
11. 4.7in HA gun
12. DC tower
13. 6in DCT
14. platform & 3ft 3in RF
15. 36ft SL platform
16. LP aerial
17. 1¼in cordage
18. 1½in downhaul cordage
19. secondary aerials
20. 1in dressing line
21. SL manipulating hut
22. signal distribution office
23. main boat derrick
24. semaphore
25. 48ft signal yard
26. main spurs

38. 1½in downhaul cordage
39. twin 6in turrets
40. 50ft steam pinnace
41. 36in SL platform
42. steering compartments
43. spirits rooms
44. 4.7in magazine
45. fresh water tank
46. wardroom stores
47. pom-pom magazines
48. watertight air spaces
49. 6in magazine
50. 6in shell room

27. 2in topgallant stays
28. 1½in brace rigging
29. 30ft signal yard
30. main aerials
31. link cordage
32. 50ft W/T yard
33. 1½in cordage
34. mast vane
35. 36. main aerials
37. 2½in triatic stay

51. pusher hoist compartment
52. main W/T office
53. boat hoisting machinery
54. midshipmen's billet
55. main W/T aerial trunk

roof of calculations station

AA control platform

director control tower platform

SL platform o

pom-pom control platform

reserve feed water tanks

Upper deck plan key:
1. 4.7in HA guns
2. pom-pom RU magazines
3. paymaster's cabin
4. wardroom ante-room
5. commander's cabin
6. wardroom
7. pantry
8. wardroom kitchen
9. galley
10. admiral's galley
11. funnel uptakes

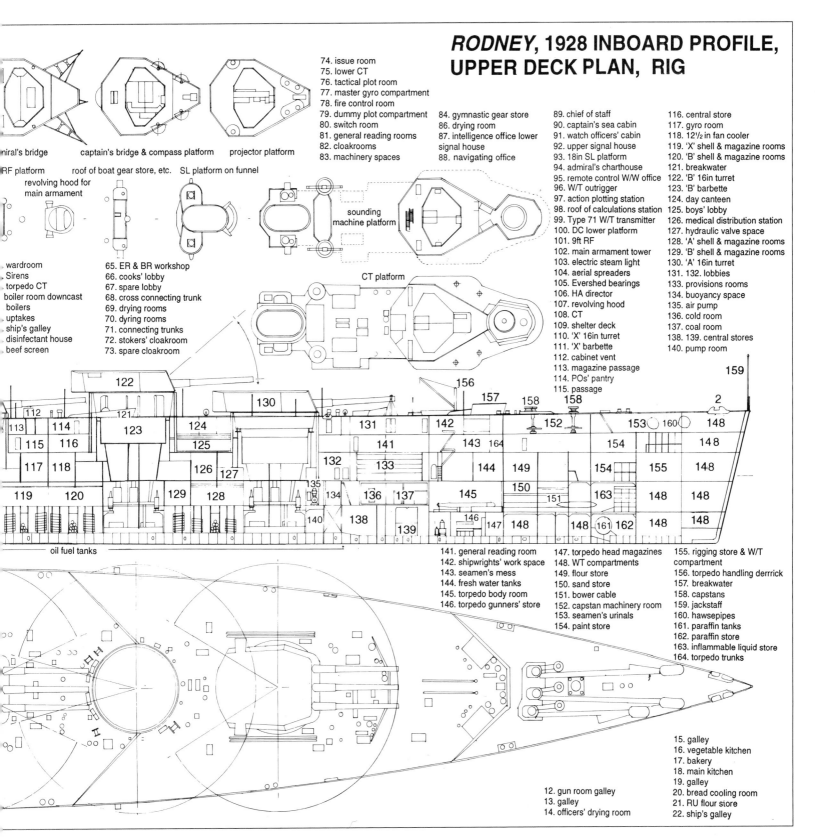

RODNEY, 1928 INBOARD PROFILE, UPPER DECK PLAN, RIG

74. issue room
75. lower CT
76. tactical plot room
77. master gyro compartment
78. fire control room
79. dummy plot compartment
80. switch room
81. general reading rooms
82. cloakrooms
83. machinery spaces
84. gymnastic gear store
86. drying room
87. intelligence office lower signal house
88. navigating office

89. chief of staff
90. captain's sea cabin
91. watch officers' cabin
92. upper signal house
93. 18in SL platform
94. admiral's charthouse
95. remote control W/W office
96. W/T outrigger
97. action plotting station
98. roof of calculations station
99. Type 71 W/T transmitter
100. DC lower platform
101. 9ft RF
102. main armament tower
103. electric steam light
104. aerial spreaders
105. Evershed bearings
106. HA director
107. revolving hood
108. CT
109. shelter deck
110. 'X' 16in turret
111. 'X' barbette
112. cabinet vent
113. magazine passage
114. POs' pantry
115. passage

116. central store
117. gyro room
118. 12½in fan cooler
119. 'X' shell & magazine rooms
120. 'B' shell & magazine rooms
121. breakwater
122. 'B' 16in turret
123. 'B' barbette
124. day canteen
125. boys' lobby
126. medical distribution station
127. hydraulic valve space
128. 'A' shell & magazine rooms
129. 'B' shell & magazine rooms
130. 'A' 16in turret
131. 132. lobbies
133. provisions rooms
134. buoyancy space
135. air pump
136. cold room
137. coal room
138. 139. central stores
140. pump room

admiral's bridge
captain's bridge & compass platform
projector platform

RF platform
roof of boat gear store, etc.
SL platform on funnel

revolving hood for main armament

sounding machine platform

CT platform

wardroom
Sirens
torpedo CT
boiler room downcast
boilers
uptakes
ship's galley
disinfectant house
beef screen

65. ER & BR workshop
66. cooks' lobby
67. spare lobby
68. cross connecting trunk
69. drying rooms
70. dyring rooms
71. connecting trunks
72. stokers' cloakroom
73. spare cloakroom

oil fuel tanks

141. general reading room
142. shipwrights' work space
143. seamen's mess
144. fresh water tanks
145. torpedo body room
146. torpedo gunners' store

147. torpedo head magazines
148. WT compartments
149. flour store
150. sand store
151. bower cable
152. capstan machinery room
153. seamen's urinals
154. paint store

155. rigging store & W/T compartment
156. torpedo handling derrrick
157. breakwater
158. capstans
159. jackstaff
160. hawsepipes
161. paraffin tanks
162. paraffin store
163. inflammable liquid store
164. torpedo trunks

12. gun room galley
13. galley
14. officers' drying room

15. galley
16. vegetable kitchen
17. bakery
18. main kitchen
19. galley
20. bread cooling room
21. RU flour store
22. ship's galley

two 50-ton pumps were out of action, that in 'A' pump-room being flooded and that in the CO_2 room being damaged.

No. 1 350-ton pump in 'A' room, worked on the torpedo drain tank, lowered the water in the torpedo-tube compartment from waterline level to a few feet below the lower deck; the pump then gave out (an electric lead was later found to be parted), and the compartment flooded again. The starter of No. 2 350-ton pump was flooded, and the pump could not be used.

No. 3 350-ton pump in the lobby abaft the cold room dealt with the water in the CO_2 room and in the E.A. room, at first by draining the water into the lobby, and later by wandering suctions.

Two of the ship's 100-ton portable submersible pumps were used in clearing water from 'A' pump room, etc. In addition, the *Englishman* had been alongside, using a 250-ton pump, but the latter did not pump more than 100 tons per hour. Water was cleared from the CO_2 room to platform-deck level, the E.A. room to outer bottom, the lobby of the cold and cool rooms, 'A' pump room, and all spaces above the lower deck. It was possible with the pumps available to lower the water in the torpedo body room and in the torpedo-tube compartment to below the lower deck, but these compartments were still flooded and remained so until damage to the ship's side was made good.

INTERNAL STRUCTURAL DAMAGE:

So far as could be examined (i.e., where not flooded) internal structural damage was slight and much less than would be expected after the forward end of the ship had whipped as described by officers and men. Local damage to fittings, etc., occurred in various places; evidence that the ship was thoroughly shaken is given by minor damage as follows:

(1) Cases in the provision room 60–80 lower deck rose about 2ft and flattened a ventilation trunk.

(2) Store rooms, sick-bay, etc., over the neighbourhood of the explosion had stores, fittings, cots, etc., thrown out of place. The surrounding bulkheads of the sick-bay are undamaged, the paint being uncracked.

(3) A table collapsed in the Admiral's dining cabin.

(4) A few minor bulkheads were buckled, but nothing more than would be expected if the main armament were fired over the deck at moderate elevation.

(5) The fire-main under upper deck fractured at a joint just forward of 43 and stopped supply to the heads.

(6) The wood lining to the cold and cool rooms was practically undamaged, although above the centre of the main external damage.

In all cases damage to structure appeared to be local, and so far as could be seen there was no suspicion of structural breakage, either longitudinal or transverse. The upper deck was sighted as carefully as possible, and, on leaving, the ship was sighted from about 50 yards forward of the bow and appeared to be normal. The upper deck planking was intact and butts and edges of caulking sound.

MACHINERY:

The main machinery suffered no important damage. All bed-plates, glands, etc., were examined and appeared sound. Starboard auxiliary condenser discharge overboard was fractured close to the outboard flange; there was slight buckling of the inner funnel.

AUXILIARY MACHINERY SUFFERED AS FOLLOWS:

(1) Capstan machinery. Control shafting and tilt plate actuating spindle to centre-line capstan

Below and opposite page: A walk around *Nelson* in 1937. **Below:** Looking aft on the superstructure and 'A' and 'B' 16in turrets. **Opposite page:** Looking forward over the forecastle and 16in turrets.

bent and distorted. Pressure joints leaked on all units. The machinery needed re-alignment.

(2) The CO_2 machinery was under water and certain CO_2 bottles cracked.

(3) The E.A. plant was under water.

(4) Hydraulic machinery. One in number suction pipe split in each of Nos. 1 and 2 pumps; the outboard end of the crank-shaft of No. 3 pump distorted. Pressure and exhaust mains were leaking.

ARMAMENT:

(a) Torpedo. This was all flooded.

(b) Gunnery. The secondary, H.A. and D.C.T.s were unaffected. Certain damage was sustained to the main armament, but not serious. 'A' turrets were somewhat affected, but principally 'A'. Items examined were as follows:

(1) Cordite Handing Room. Oil fuel was leaking from D.B. tanks into the sump below the false floor. The floor of the revolving structure was not concentric with the false floor of the fixed structure, nor quite level with the same. With the turret fore and aft there was a gap between the two floors about 1¼in wide at 0 degrees, and at this position the revolving position was 1in below the fixed. The gap reduced to zero and the floors are level at 120° R & G; the gap revolves with the turret. When training, the angle-bar stiffener under the edge of the revolving platform rubbed on brackets supporting the false floor.

(2) All 16in shell hoists were fully loaded at the time of the explosion, but there was no pressure on the turrets. The hoists dropped about ½in, shearing 2 bolts in small brackets connecting the hoists to the main revolving structure. Triangular brackets connecting the hoists to the platform of the training engine compartment depressed the platform slightly.

CASUALTIES:

There were 74 injured, about 45 serious or fairly serious, the remainder minor. The more serious cases comprised three fractured thighbones, two compound fractures of the lower legs, 2 or 3 forearm fractures, kneecap fractures, fractured jaws (one lower), one shoulder-blade, back injuries, and cuts to upper inside leg. The last-mentioned injuries were caused by ratings using the heads falling back on broken pans; one such case was serious. There were also head injuries where heads struck decks. All the injured were in

RODNEY AND *NELSON*, BRIDGE MODIFICATIONS

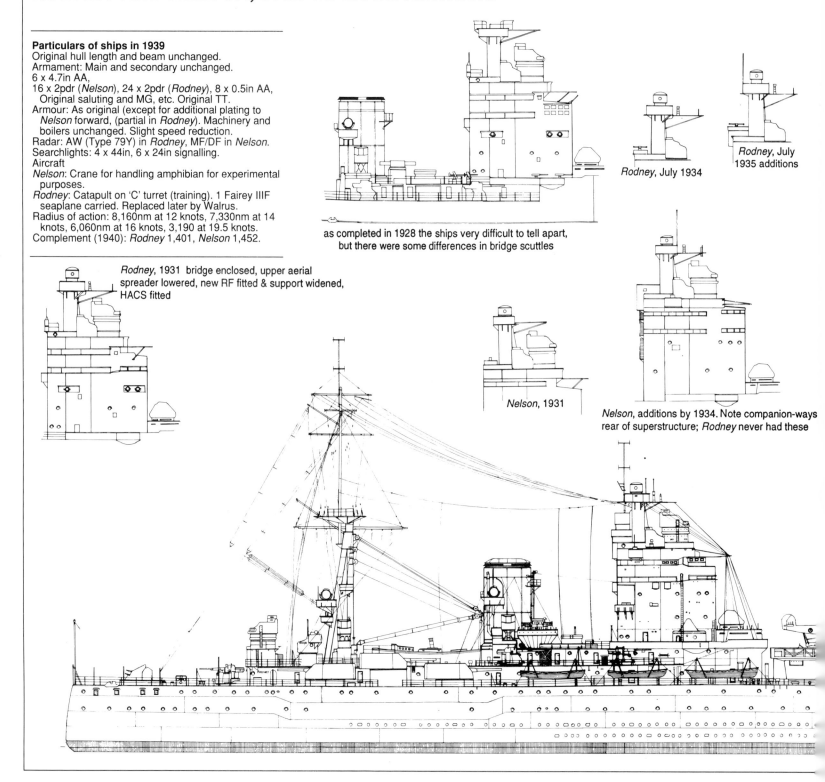

Particulars of ships in 1939
Original hull length and beam unchanged.
Armament: Main and secondary unchanged.
6 x 4.7in AA,
16 x 2pdr (*Nelson*), 24 x 2pdr (*Rodney*), 8 x 0.5in AA,
   Original saluting and MG, etc. Original TT.
Armour: As original (except for additional plating to
   Nelson forward, (partial in *Rodney*). Machinery and
   boilers unchanged. Slight speed reduction.
Radar: AW (Type 79Y) in *Rodney*, MF/DF in *Nelson*.
Searchlights: 4 x 44in, 6 x 24in signalling.
Aircraft
Nelson: Crane for handling amphibian for experimental
   purposes.
Rodney: Catapult on 'C' turret (training). 1 Fairey IIIF
   seaplane carried. Replaced later by Walrus.
Radius of action: 8,160nm at 12 knots, 7,330nm at 14
   knots, 6,060nm at 16 knots, 3,190 at 19.5 knots.
Complement (1940): *Rodney* 1,401, *Nelson* 1,452.

Rodney, July 1934

Rodney, July
1935 additions

as completed in 1928 the ships very difficult to tell apart,
but there were some differences in bridge scuttles

Rodney, 1931 bridge enclosed, upper aerial
spreader lowered, new RF fitted & support widened,
HACS fitted

Nelson, 1931

Nelson, additions by 1934. Note companion-ways
rear of superstructure; *Rodney* never had these

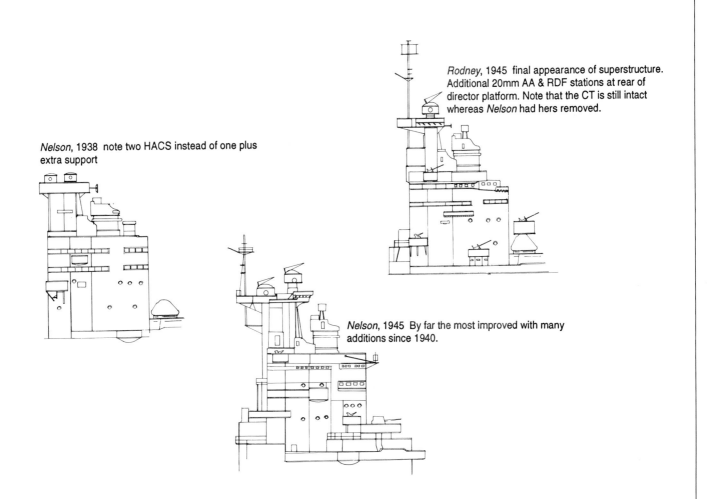

Nelson, 1938 note two HACS instead of one plus extra support

Rodney, 1945 final appearance of superstructure. Additional 20mm AA & RDF stations at rear of director platform. Note that the CT is still intact whereas *Nelson* had hers removed.

Nelson, 1945 By far the most improved with many additions since 1940.

Rodney, appearance Sept 1939. Note the distinguishing feature of a catapult & aircraft on 'X' 16in turret. The Swordfish floatplane was quickly replaced by a Walrus Amphibean. Note 79Y RDF on mast tops.

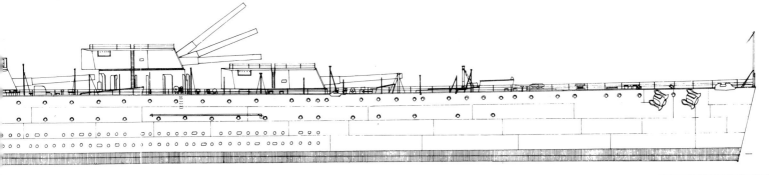

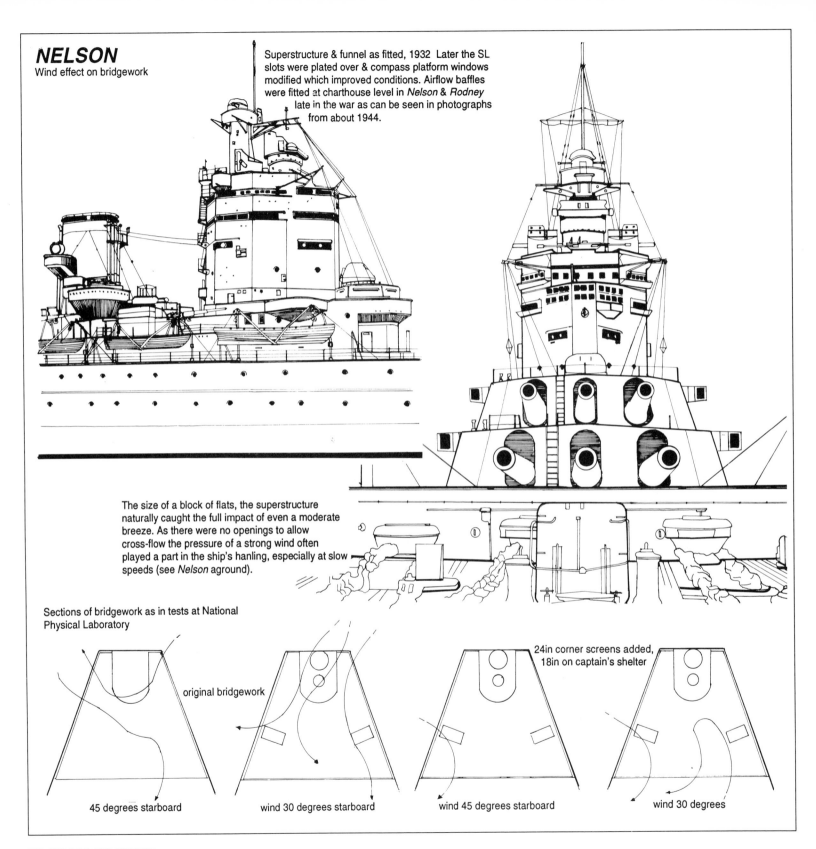

NELSON
Wind effect on bridgework

Superstructure & funnel as fitted, 1932 Later the SL
slots were plated over & compass platform windows
modified which improved conditions. Airflow baffles
were fitted at charthouse level in *Nelson* & *Rodney*
late in the war as can be seen in photographs
from about 1944.

The size of a block of flats, the superstructure
naturally caught the full impact of even a moderate
breeze. As there were no openings to allow
cross-flow the pressure of a strong wind often
played a part in the ship's hanling, especially at slow
speeds (see *Nelson* aground).

Sections of bridgework as in tests at National
Physical Laboratory

original bridgework

24in corner screens added,
18in on captain's shelter

45 degrees starboard

wind 30 degrees starboard

wind 45 degrees starboard

wind 30 degrees

Below: *Nelson*, looking aft from the rear of the tower over funnel and mainmast.

Below: Looking up at the staircase at the rear of *Nelson*'s tower, showing the height of the DCT.

the fore part of the ship at the time of the explosion, either on the upper deck, in the heads or in the cable-lockers.

CONDITION OF SHIP:
Divers attempted to close the various cracks in the ship's side by soft wood wedges, etc., but the hole just abaft 60 could not be closed before docking except by means of a large ship's side patch. It was considered that the ship could pro-

ceed to sea in safety without this patch being fitted.

She was out of service for a total of seven months.

Damage sustained by Rodney during the Bismarck action, 27 May 1941

During the action *Rodney* sustained very little damage from return fire – three minor shrapnel

holes in the side and another small hole which cut the searchlight control leads on the conning tower level. The high-angle director trainer telescope was distorted and put out of action. Much more damage was caused by the firing of her own 16in guns and was as follows:
External. Upper deck was depressed to varying degrees in wake of the turrets. Wood decking was lifted, split and blown out of place. Deck fittings including stowage huts, mushroom heads,

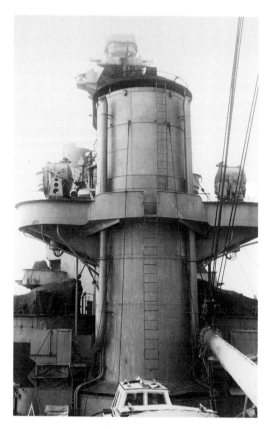

skylights, breakwater and berthing rail stanchions were broken and distorted. Watertight hatches to the sickbay flat were blown open.

Internal. Deck pillars under girders were distorted and shaken, the fore and aft girders themselves being fractured in several places. In the torpedo body room the depression was transmitted to the lower deck and put the torpedo transversing trolley out of action. Partition bulkheads were distorted and split between upper and main decks. Considerable lengths of ventilation trunking were split open and in some cases blown out of place. All the stanchions supporting the sick bay cots came away from the deck fastenings.

Damage by blast. HACS roll corrector glass fractured. The angle support on 16in guns around inside of armoured ring bulkhead for supporting leather apron was damaged. Brass bolts within the turret broke loose leaving some hanging out of place. Periscopes in 'A' turret were pulled from securing bolts by blast from 'B' turret.

Various periscopes in both 16in and 6in turrets had hoods so distorted that they were rendered practically useless. The superstructure stood up quite well to the blast of the 16in guns, but the upper deck and fittings proved to be a problem and there was a need of extra support and additional stiffening which was carried out during refit as opportunity arose.

Nelson, torpedoed 27 September 1941

Operating with Force H in the Mediterranean, *Nelson* was attacked by Italian aircraft and hit by one torpedo on the port side while under way at about 16 knots. Fortunately the torpedo's TNT warhead only weighed about 375lb, but the damage was still extensive. The hit made a hole in the bottom plating approximately 30 feet long x 15 feet deep extending from the lower deck edge to just below the platform deck between stations 50 and 65 and caused extensive flooding to compartments in the area. When flooding had been brought under control there was about 3,700 tons of water inside her hull. Before the hit her draught was 35ft 3in forward and 34ft 6in aft, but after the explosion it increased to 44ft forward and 38ft aft and there was a heel of about 1½°. A course was set for Gibraltar at a high speed of 10 to 17 knots and she arrived at 1045 hours on 30 September. Pumping operations were put into effect immediately after the explosion and continued throughout the passage so that on approaching Gibraltar the draught had been reduced to 39ft 6in forward and 32ft 3in aft. She was docked on 2 October and a full survey of her damage was carried out.

Structural Damage

Outer Bottom. On the port side, the main hole extended from the edge of the lower deck to halfway across 'H' strake and between 50–65 stations, about 15ft in width and 30ft in length. Long, jagged, fractures had occurred upwards across the main strakes between 52 and 54 stations; across 'N' strake between 58 and 60 stations and across 'N', and 12in into 'P' strake between 64 and 66 stations. Fractures occurred diagonally forward across 'H' strake between 50 and 58 stations and to the lower edge of 'C' strake between 60 and 62 stations. The jagged edges of plating were turned in sharply at the forward and after ends along the bottom of the hole and considerable distortion of plating around the

hole was caused over an area extending from the middle deck to the bottom of the strake and from about 48–70 stations, approximately 40ft x 40ft. All outer bottom plating was 20lb 'D' except 'M' strake immediately below the lower deck, which was 20lb 'D' before and 25lb 'D' abaft 61 station. On the starboard side the outer bottom was pierced by three splinters in 'M' and 'L' strakes between 56 and 60 stations.

Framing. The main frames (6in x 3in x 3in x 14lb channel bar) were completely destroyed in way of the hole and were severely distorted and torn from beam arm brackets in way of the damaged bottom plating.

Middle Deck. A hole, approximately 3ft x 2ft situated about 2ft 6in before 60 bulkhead and 20ft to port of middle line, was caused by an armoured manhole cover blown up from the lower deck. The deck plating (12lb 'D' with 14lb stringer) was bulged upwards, maximum 9in over an area extending from 48–60 stations in a fore and aft direction, and from the ship's side to within 4 feet of the middle line athwartships, i.e., approximately 23ft in length by 21ft in width. Abaft 60 bulkhead the deck was bulged upward, slightly between 60½–69 stations and from 17ft to 29ft to port of the middle line, i.e., about 17 feet in length by 12ft in width. Except for the hole referred to above there were no holes or fractures in this deck. Slight leaks occurred along plate edges, boundary angle at side, and through screw-holes to corticene strips which were broken by the bulged plating.

Lower Deck. The deck plating (10lb, 14lb stringer, 100–120lb NC armour) was forced upwards over an area extending from the ship's side to within 6ft of the middle line between 50–60 stations and to about 20ft from the middle line between 60–70 stations. The 10lb and 14lb plating was severely distorted, perforated by splinters, and torn. The 100lb armour plate adjacent to the ship's side, 48–52 stations, was forced upwards, maximum 4½in along the butt at 52 station. This plate was not distorted. The 120lb armour plate, 52–60, was forced upward 9in at the forward butt and 19in at the after butt. The plate was distorted but not fractured. The adjacent armour plate (120lb) abaft 60 station, and also next toward the middle line, 52–60,

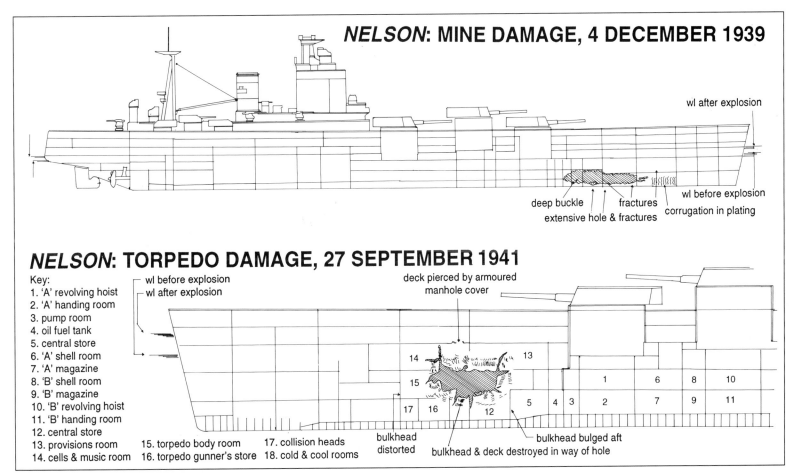

NELSON: MINE DAMAGE, 4 DECEMBER 1939

wl after explosion

deep buckle — fractures
extensive hole & fractures
corrugation in plating
wl before explosion

NELSON: TORPEDO DAMAGE, 27 SEPTEMBER 1941

Key:
1. 'A' revolving hoist
2. 'A' handing room
3. pump room
4. oil fuel tank
5. central store
6. 'A' shell room
7. 'A' magazine
8. 'B' shell room
9. 'B' magazine
10. 'B' revolving hoist
11. 'B' handing room
12. central store
13. provisions room
14. cells & music room
15. torpedo body room
16. torpedo gunner's store
17. collision heads
18. cold & cool rooms

wl before explosion
wl after explosion

deck pierced by armoured manhole cover

bulkhead distorted
bulkhead & deck destroyed in way of hole
bulkhead bulged aft

were disturbed upward maximum 3½in. No distortion occurred. The deck beams (7in x 3in x 14.6lb bulb angle) on the port side in way of the explosion were destroyed and the deep girder at 52 station (14lb x 24in plate, with 9in x 3½in x 3½in x 25lb channel bar to deck and 3½in x 3in x 8lb double angle stiffeners on the lower edge) was severely distorted.

Platform Deck. In the Torpedo Body Room, 43–60, the deck plating 14lb) was distorted over an area extending 12in from ship's side at 43 station to within 6ft of the middle line at 60 station. The plating adjacent to the ship's side was destroyed between 57–62 stations and the jagged edges were turned down over the bottom plating which had been blown inwards. The hatch

between 62–63 stations leading to the Air Compressor Room (under) was destroyed.

Hold. The plating in the Air Compressor Room and Air Bottle Compartment, 52–70, was slightly distorted.

Bulkheads. No. 43 bulkhead was slightly distorted near the ship's side between Lower and Platform Decks. No. 60 Bulkhead. The scantlings of this bulkhead were – 12lb 'D' plating between Main and Platform Decks, 14lb 'D' below the Platform Deck. Stiffeners 4in x 2½in x 6.5lb 'D' bulb angles between Middle and Lower decks; 6in x 3in x 3in x 14lb 'D' channels (continuous) between Lower Deck and Inner Bottom. Below the lower deck the bulkhead was

destroyed from ship's side to the longitudinal bulkhead of the Cold Room, i.e., a distance of 9ft 6in from the ship's side at Platform Deck level. The remainder of the bulkhead was distorted to within 4ft of the middle line. Between the Lower and Middle Decks the bulkhead was distorted over an area extending from the ship's side to the port longitudinal bulkhead of the Provision Room, i.e., about 13ft from the ship's side. Below the Platform Deck to port longitudinal bulkhead to Central Store 60–80 M.L. was distorted between 60–70 stations and torn from the boundary angle at 60 transverse bulkhead. The vertical stiffeners 8in x 3½in x 3½in x 20lb channels at 62–65 and 67 stations were distorted and fractured across the standing flanges. The divisional watertight bulkhead at 70 station

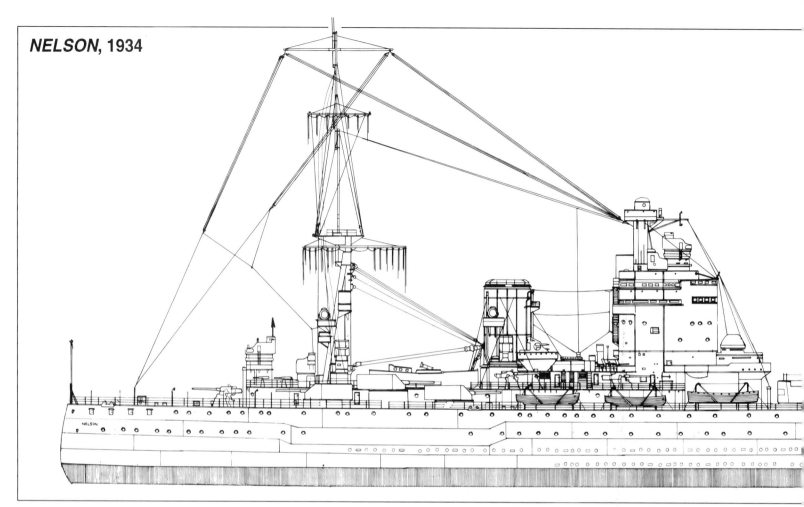

NELSON, 1934

Below: *Nelson* limps back to base, down by the
bows after being torpedoed by Italian aircraft in
September 1941.

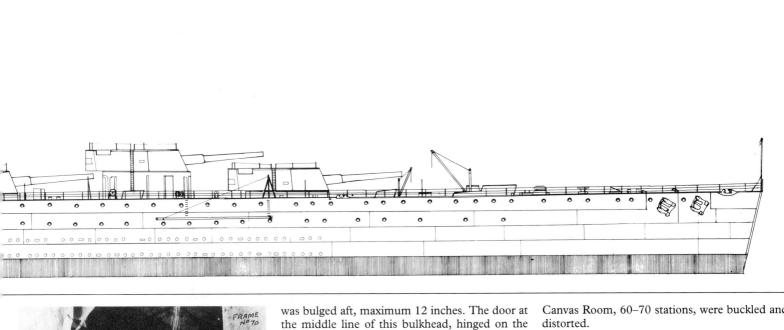

Above: Damage to *Nelson* from the Italian torpedo. When looking at the damage from one torpedo it is not difficult to understand why *Royal Oak*, *Barham*, *Prince of Wales* and *Repulse* succumbed to this weapon.

was bulged aft, maximum 12 inches. The door at the middle line of this bulkhead, hinged on the fore side, remained watertight. Slight distortion occurred to the inner bottom in the vicinity of 60 bulkhead. On the Platform Deck, the port longitudinal bulkhead of the Torpedo Body Room, 43–60 was torn from 60 bulkhead and from its deck connections. The bulkhead was holed by splinters, about 20 No. maximum size 8in x 6in between 50–60 stations. Three of the splinters perforated the outer bottom on the starboard side in 'M' and 'L' strakes, between 50–60 stations. A splinter perforated the cover of the hatch leading to the lobby under. The outer longitudinal bulkhead of the Cold Room, 60–80 Port was severely distorted between 60–72 stations; stiffeners and brackets were torn from the bulkhead and decks. The lower forward portion of the bulkhead was crushed and a hole about 2ft 6in square led directly into the Cold Room. The after bulkhead at 76 station was demolished and blown into the lobby between 76–80 stations. On the Lower Deck the minor bulkheads to Lobby and Prisons, 50–60 stations, and to

Canvas Room, 60–70 stations, were buckled and distorted.

MACHINERY:
Main. No damage was caused to main machinery. The water level in the boilers was not affected.

ARMAMENT:
Gunnery: No damage was caused to gun armament. Torpedo: The torpedo room was wrecked.

FLOODING:
As a result of the explosion all compartments on the Lower Deck between 53–85 bulkheads; on the Platform Deck between 43–84 and below the Platform Deck between 43–80, were flooded. The port Torpedo Tube Room was flooded from the Torpedo Body Room through a multiple electric cable gland in No. 43 bulkhead. The drain valves to the Drain Tank from the Tube Rooms had been left open and resulted in the Drain Tank and Starboard Torpedo Tube Room being flooded. This flooding may have been

NELSON INBOARD PROFILE, 1945

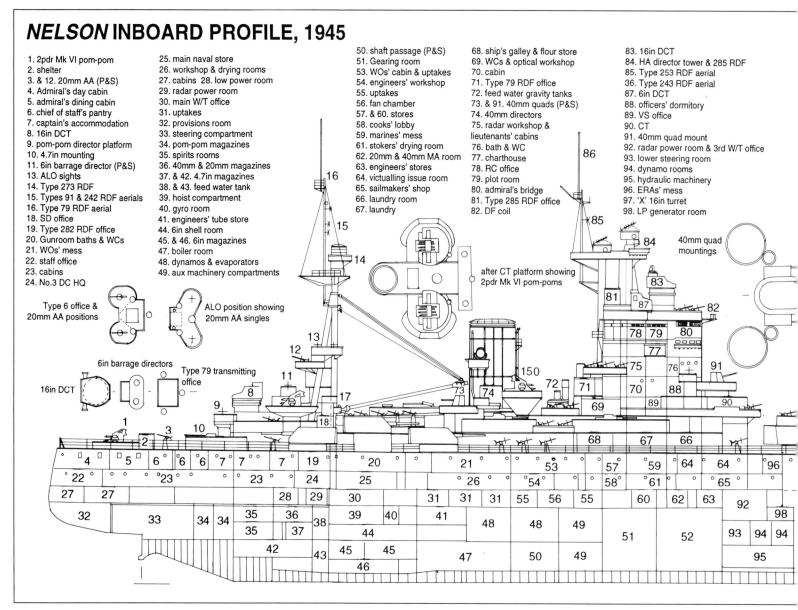

1. 2pdr Mk VI pom-pom
2. shelter
3. & 12. 20mm AA (P&S)
4. Admiral's day cabin
5. admiral's dining cabin
6. chief of staff's pantry
7. captain's accommodation
8. 16in DCT
9. pom-pom director platform
10. 4.7in mounting
11. 6in barrage director (P&S)
13. ALO sights
14. Type 273 RDF
15. Types 91 & 242 RDF aerials
16. Type 79 RDF aerial
18. SD office
19. Type 282 RDF office
20. Gunroom baths & WCs
21. WOs' mess
22. staff office
23. cabins
24. No.3 DC HQ

25. main naval store
26. workshop & drying rooms
27. cabins 28. low power room
29. radar power room
30. main W/T office
31. uptakes
32. provisions room
33. steering compartment
34. pom-pom magazines
35. spirits rooms
36. 40mm & 20mm magazines
37. & 42. 4.7in magazines
38. & 43. feed water tank
39. hoist compartment
40. gyro room
41. engineers' tube store
44. 6in shell room
45. & 46. 6in magazines
47. boiler room
48. dynamos & evaporators
49. aux machinery compartments

50. shaft passage (P&S)
51. gearing room
53. WOs' cabin & uptakes
54. engineers' workshop
55. uptakes
56. fan chamber
57. & 60. stores
58. cooks' lobby
59. marines' mess
61. stokers' drying room
62. 20mm & 40mm MA room
63. engineers' stores
64. victualling issue room
65. sailmakers' shop
66. laundry room
67. laundry

68. ship's galley & flour store
69. WCs & optical workshop
70. cabin
71. Type 79 RDF office
72. feed water gravity tanks
73. & 91. 40mm quads (P&S)
74. 40mm directors
75. radar workshop &
   lieutenants' cabins
76. bath & WC
77. charthouse
78. RC office
79. plot room
80. admiral's bridge
81. Type 285 RDF office
82. DF coil

83. 16in DCT
84. HA director tower & 285 RDF
85. Type 253 RDF aerial
36. Type 243 RDF aerial
87. 6in DCT
88. officers' dormitory
89. VS office
90. CT
91. 40mm quad mount
92. radar power room & 3rd W/T office
93. lower steering room
94. dynamo rooms
95. hydraulic machinery
96. ERAs' mess
97. 'X' 16in turret
98. LP generator room

Type 6 office &
20mm AA positions

ALO position showing
20mm AA singles

6in barrage directors

Type 79 transmitting
office

16in DCT

after CT platform showing
2pdr Mk VI pom-poms

40mm quad
mountings

accentuated by leakage past the rear door of the starboard tube, which was found to have been damaged. Both tubes were loaded, with bow and rear doors closed and drain valves open.

The Middle Deck was flooded to a depth of 2ft between 43–60 bulkheads through the hole caused by the armoured manhole cover blown up from the Lower Deck and through the ventilation supply trunk to the Prison Flat below.

The compartments affected were: Lower Deck: Prisons, Lobby and Music Room; Canvas Room; Awning Room; Provision Rooms; Canteen Store; Flour Stores; Lobby. Platform Deck: Torpedo Tube Rooms; W.T. Compartment; Torpedo Body Room; W.T. Compartment;

Refrigerating Machinery Room; Cold Room and Lobby; E.A. Plant Room. Hold: 'A' Pump Room Drain Tank; Torpedo Tube Drain Tank; Warhead Magazine; Torpedo Gunner's Store; Warhead Magazine; Air Bottle Compartment; No. 3 Central Stores (Forward); No. 3 Central Stores (Aft). Double Bottoms: W.T. Compartments.

DAMAGE CONTROL:

Shoring: Some time elapsed before the forward boundary of the flooded area was established, due to the flooding of the Middle Deck, but it was quickly ascertained that no flooding had occurred forward of 23 bulkhead. At the after

boundary of the flooded area, the Watchkeeper escaped from the Refrigerating Machinery Room and closed the watertight door, but only clipped it on the side nearest the hinge (this door opens into the compartment and is hinged on the fore side). The hole in the Middle Deck was plugged by hammocks shored from the deck over. Shores, closely spaced, were erected between Main and Middle Decks throughout the flooded area, the work being continued incessantly for 48 hours. More than 24 hours after the explosion, when the ship had been lightened sufficiently to partially empty the Lower Deck compartments (43–60) which were open to the sea, the surge of water caused the Middle Deck to bulge upwards

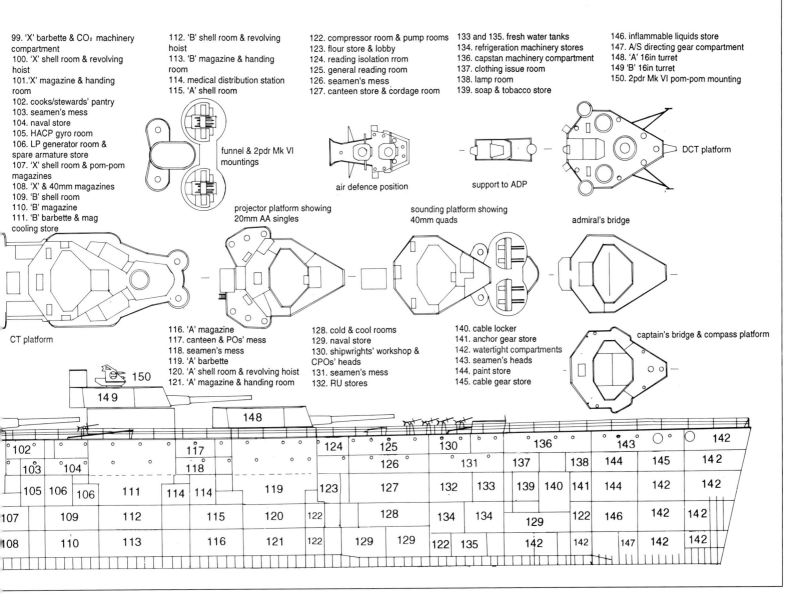

99. 'X' barbette & CO$_2$ machinery compartment
100. 'X' shell room & revolving hoist
101.'X' magazine & handing room
102. cooks/stewards' pantry
103. seamen's mess
104. naval store
105. HACP gyro room
106. LP generator room & spare armature store
107. 'X' shell room & pom-pom magazines
108. 'X' & 40mm magazines
109. 'B' shell room
110. 'B' magazine
111. 'B' barbette & mag cooling store

112. 'B' shell room & revolving hoist
113. 'B' magazine & handing room
114. medical distribution station
115. 'A' shell room

122. compressor room & pump rooms
123. flour store & lobby
124. reading isolation rroom
125. general reading room
126. seamen's mess
127. canteen store & cordage room

133 and 135. fresh water tanks
134. refrigeration machinery stores
136. capstan machinery compartment
137. clothing issue room
138. lamp room
139. soap & tobacco store

146. inflammable liquids store
147. A/S directing gear compartment
148. 'A' 16in turret
149 'B' 16in turret
150. 2pdr Mk VI pom-pom mounting

funnel & 2pdr Mk VI mountings

air defence position

support to ADP

DCT platform

projector platform showing 20mm AA singles

sounding platform showing 40mm quads

admiral's bridge

CT platform

116. 'A' magazine
117. canteen & POs' mess
118. seamen's mess
119. 'A' barbette
120. 'A' shell room & revolving hoist
121. 'A' magazine & handing room

128. cold & cool rooms
129. naval store
130. shipwrights' workshop & CPOs' heads
131. seamen's mess
132. RU stores

140. cable locker
141. anchor gear store
142. watertight compartments
143. seamen's heads
144. paint store
145. cable gear store

captain's bridge & compass platform

about 9in in the vicinity of the hole and further shoring was carried out overhead between Main and Upper Decks. Shores were erected between Main and Middle Decks in way of the bulged plating on the Middle Deck, port side, 60–70 stations. Small leaks were plugged and shored and leaks in the boundary angle were stopped with cement.

Effect on Fighting Efficiency: Torpedo tubes were out of action and of 12 torpedoes carried 10 were destroyed or rendered unfit for service. Speed of ship was reduced on account of the amount of water in the flooded compartments and the risk of undue strain on structure in the

immediate vicinity of compartments open to the sea. Except for the possibility that firing the 16in guns would have disturbed the shoring of the Middle Deck, the fighting equipment was not affected. She was out of action until April 1942.

OPERATION 'BRONTE', BOMBING TRIALS IN NELSON

Nelson showed resilient qualities when used as a target ship for 1,000 and 2,000lb bombs. The trials were carried out in the Firth of Forth near Inchkeith Island from 4 June to 23 September 1948. The trials were divided into stages and the objectives were not only to test her armoured

decks, but to test the efficiency of the armour-piercing bombs used.

One trial showed that although her 6in armour could be pierced by a 2,000lb bomb, it would have to be dropped from more than 4,000 feet to obtain this penetration. *Nelson* was moored fore and aft to buoys laid about position 260° Inchkeith Light 1.14 miles, lying along a line 045°/225°, bows to the north-east.

Six Barracuda III naval aircraft were used, and there were four pilots, i.e., two aircraft were always in reserve. The aircraft were based on the Royal Naval Air Station, Arbroath, and were controlled when over the target by R/T from Inchkeith Island. Bombs were released in diving

Displacement (tons): (1942) *Nelson* 34,955 (light), 40,628 (average action), 42,740 (deep); (1945) *Nelson* 44,054 (deep); *Rodney* 43,100 (deep).
Draught: (1942) 34ft forward, 35ft 4¹/₂in, 34ft 8¹/₄in (mean); (1945) 34ft 7in forward, 35ft 3in aft (*Rodney*).
Armament: Main and secondary as original.
AA guns:
6 x 4.7in
48 x 2pdr
16 x 40mm (*Nelson*)
32 x 20mm (*Nelson*) 13 x 20mm (*Rodney*)
Original saluting, boat and field guns
Original TT
All guns except 20mm were radar-controlled.
Radar: Type 284 for main guns, Type 285 for 4.7in, Type 283 for light AA, AW Type 279 (*Nelson*), Type 281 (*Rodney*), SW Type 271, GW Type 291 (*Rodney*), MF/DF.
Searchlights:
Nelson 2 x 44in, *Rodney* 4 x 44in, 6 x 24in signalling in both.
Aircraft: none, but aircraft crane retained in both.
Complement: 1,631–1,650
Speed: Stated to have been reduced to about 22 knots owing to additional weights added since 1939.

attacks at 55° to the horizontal, diving to the point of release from a height of 4000 feet at 280 knots. Attacks were made either along the middle line of the ship from astern or from the starboard quarter diagonally across the ship towards the port bow. Two cameras to record the path of the bombs prior to striking, striking velocity and angle of strike, were positioned at Pettycur Battery, Kinghorn Ness, on the north shore of the Firth of Forth and on Inchkeith Island.

The original order for Stage IV was: 'Bomb, A.P., 2,000lb, Mk IV, filled inert and exploding charge 23¹/₄lb T.N.T., fitted pistol and detonator delay, dive dropped from 8,000ft.'

The pistol used was No. 65 Mk IX. The stage commenced with detonator delay No. 60 Mk II (0.07 seconds) and was to have continued with detonators No. 56 Mk II (0.05 seconds) or No. 50 Mk II (0.14 seconds) if the delay proved too long or too short respectively.

After 39 bombs had missed from 8,000 feet the dropping height for Stage IV was amended to 6,500 feet to give a reasonable chance of hitting, since only 60 of the specially exploding bombs had been supplied for the whole trial. Hit J, the first in the stage, was scored with the 42nd bomb. The stage was then discontinued as the exploding charge appeared to be too powerful.

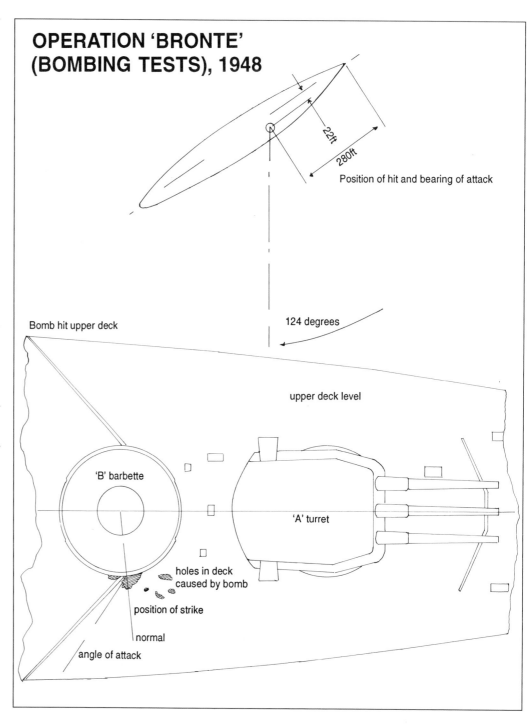

OPERATION 'BRONTE' (BOMBING TESTS), 1948

22ft
280ft
Position of hit and bearing of attack

124 degrees

Bomb hit upper deck

upper deck level

'B' barbette

'A' turret

holes in deck caused by bomb

position of strike

normal

angle of attack

The system of numbering of hits gives the stage no., the serial no. of the drop in that stage and the letter of the hit.

RESULTS:

Hit IV/42/J Date: 15th September, 1948 Time: 1715.
Type of Bomb: 2000lb A.P. explosive, 0.07 seconds delay detonator.
Force and Direction of Surface Wind: North West, 5 knots.
Weather and Visibility: 3/10ths cumulus, extreme visibility.
Conditions of Release:

	Ordered	Actual
Height of Release	6,500 ft	5,900 ft
True Air Speed	285 kts	280 kts
Striking Velocity	807 fps	780 fps
Striking Angle (to vertical)	20°	28°
Time of Flight		11.3 secs
Angle of Attack to ship's head.		Green 124°

PATH OF BOMB:

The bomb struck the starboard side of 'B' Barbette on the armoured ring bulkhead at station 126 about 6ft 6in above the Upper Deck, and exploded on impact. The angle of strike was 70° to the normal to the armoured ring at the point of impact. The marks on the armour indicated that the centre of explosion was very close to the point of impact. Since the centre of the burster charge was situated at about one-fifth the length of the bomb from the base end, it follows that the nose of the bomb had slid down the armour towards the deck, bringing the tail nearer to the armour, when the explosion occurred. There was no evidence either way as to whether the explosion had occurred before or after the tail actually struck the armour.

A large number of fragments was produced by the explosion, varying in size from a few pounds to more than 100 pounds in weight. Some of these fragments were seen to hit the water some distance ahead of the ship (estimated at 300 yards maximum). An Ingersoll-Rand air compressor, standing close to the point of burst, was damaged beyond repair by fragments and blast.

'B' Barbette Armour: Thickness of armour 600lb. The plate was scooped at the point of impact to a depth of $^3/_{16}$in on an area of 6in x 2in. The plate as a whole was dished $^3/_4$in on a 4ft datum and loosened slightly at the butts. There were a few small cracks on the cemented face. There was no apparent damage to the turret roller path.

Upper Deck: There were six main holes in the Upper Deck, the largest of which was directly beneath the explosion and appeared to have been caused mainly by the air blast of the explosion. The deck plating in the area was 30lb S.Q. The main holes were:
1. 4ft wide by 8ft long from about station 124 to 127 just beside the barbette armour.
2. 4ft 2in long by 1ft 8in wide at 120 station at 20ft 6in to starboard of the middle line.
3. 12in long by 6in wide at 119 station, 23ft 9in to starboard of the middle line.
2ft 8in long by 6in wide at 121 station, 25ft to starboard of the middle line.
5. 6in x 3in at 123 station, 24ft to starboard of the middle line.
6. 3ft long by 1ft wide from 127 to 128$^1/_2$ stations, 20ft to starboard of the middle line.

No. 1 hole had a large petal of plating hanging downwards at the forward edge of the hole. All the other holes had little or no petalling and showed signs of brittle fracture. The deck girder, 8in x 6in x 6in x 35lb S.Q. I bar, in way of hole No. 1 was carried away completely from stations 124 to 127. At station 128, this girder was distorted and split where a fragment had struck the upper deck. Hole No. 6 was just inboard of this girder.

Main Deck. This deck was perforated in several places both by bomb fragments and pieces of the Upper Deck carried away by these fragments or by the blast of the explosion. The W.T. door in bulkhead 127 was perforated by a fragment which carried on through the Main Deck abaft 127 station. The principal holes in the Main Deck were held below No. 1 in the Upper Deck. One or both may have been caused by the nose of the bomb which may have been broken by the explosion. The base-plug of the bomb was found on the main deck.

Middle Deck. The deck armour, of 250lb with 30lb S.Q. backing plate, was struck at 122 station, 21ft to starboard of the middle line close to the barbette armour ring, presumably by the nose of the bomb or part of the nose. The armour plate struck was one cut diagonally at the after end to fit the casting supporting 'B' barbette. The plate was 15ft long on the inboard side, 21ft long on the outboard side and 6ft 6in wide. The inboard seam was 14ft to starboard of the middle line. The seams were tongued and grooved and the butts plain faced. The hit occurred on the point of the plate where it was cut diagonally at the after butt. This point was set down, with some removal of metal from the face of the plate, to a maximum of 4$^3/_4$in, the tongues and grooves being opened up in way. There was a scoop in both the adjacent casting and the next plate outboard with no depression in either. Pieces of the nose of the bomb were found scattered on the armour in the Mess space between bulkheads 95 and 127. The fragment which caused hole No. 2 in the Upper Deck passed through the Main Deck, travelled forward through a vent trunk, struck a ladder removing the bottom rungs and was deflected upwards to strike and force open the W.T. door at bulkhead 95. Some distance forward of this door, a jagged fragment of ship's structure was found embedded in the side of a kit locker at station 82. This may have been a piece of the main deck carried away by the fragment described above or it may even have come from the upper deck and been itself the fragment which damaged the ladder and door. The total distance of this fragment from the point of explosion along its path was about 90ft.

Underside of Middle Deck. The backing to the deck armour was smooth bulged to a depth of 5in on a 4ft datum in a way of the impact of the bomb nose. The 9in x 7in x 7in x 53lb S.Q. I bar under the outboard seam of the damaged armour plate had its top flange and upper part of the web split at the point of impact.

DETAILS OF BOMB:

2000lb, A.P., Mk IV. Makers: Thomas Firth & John Brown Ltd.
Bomb No. P. 4110.
Filled HES/RD 1057.
Pistol: 65Mk. IX.
Detonator (delay): 60 Mk II 0.07 seconds delay.
Tube: T.N.T. Exploder, 23$^1/_2$lb and C. E. Pellet – 12 oz 3 drachms.
Tail unit: No. 47 Mk I

The bomb exploded instantaneously, the centre of burst being very close to the point of impact of the nose. It broke up into a large number of fragments varying in size from a few pounds to more than 100 pounds in weight. The nose was found in three pieces on the armour deck and it could not be ascertained whether it had been broken up by the explosion or by impact with the deck. The base-plug was found on the main deck and no explanation could be found as to why it had been projected downwards. No conclusive evidence could be obtained as to whether the delay had been shortened by a blow transversely on the tail of the bomb or whether it had simply not functioned correctly.

Flooding caused: Nil.

Damage to Machinery, etc.: Firemain supply to main and middle decks, 95–127 starboard, fractured on main deck.

Damage to Electrical Leads: Lighting and power leads, both permanent and temporary, were severed on main and middle decks between 95 and 127 starboard. These included the degaussing circuit and telephone and fire control circuits of the ship's permanent system.

In the last trial a 2,000 AP Mk IV bomb hit the deck at 232 station, 22ft 6in to port of middle line just abreast the funnel. It perforated all decks and transverse bulkhead down to the middle deck, where it penetrated and rebounded

whole on top of the deck. Another similar bomb, dropped in the same fashion, also pierced the armour deck, at 219/220 station. The plating was heavily dished over a wide area and some holding-down bolts blew down and pierced the lower deck.

The conclusions drawn from these tests were:
1. All bombs needed to be dropped from at least 5,000 feet to be effective.
2. Dropped from 3,000 to 4,000 feet, in practice the bombs only penetrated 2.95in to 4.75in.
3. It was not easy to hit the ship from these heights and certainly not from 5,000 feet.
4. It was noted that the ship was a stationary target.
5. It had not been an easy task to pierce *Nelson*'s 6in armoured deck, but the fact remained that it had been pierced and this proved once and for all that battleships were very vulnerable to this kind of attack. In fact the tests proved that the days of heavily armoured ships were over.

HISTORY: NELSON

1922 Programme. Laid down by Armstrong Whitworth & Co., Newcastle on Tyne 28 December 1922. Launched 3 September 1925. Began trials April 1927. Completed trials June 1927.
Commissioned at Portsmouth 15 August 1927 to relieve *Revenge* as flag Atlantic Fleet. Carried out further extended trials August to October 1927 and did not hoist flag until 21 October 1927.

ATLANTIC FLEET (FLAG) October 1927 to March 1932.
Collision with SS *West Wales* spring 1931. Slight damage.
Embarked King Amanulah of Afghanistan for exercises off Portland April 1928.
Atlantic Fleet redesignated Home Fleet March 1932.

HOME FLEET March 1932 to July 1941 (fleet flag to December 1939 and from August 1940 to April 1941).
Grounded in Portsmouth harbour January 1934 when leaving for spring cruise. No damage.
Jubilee Review, Spithead 16 July 1935.
Extensive refit Portsmouth 1937 to January 1938.
With *Rodney*, paid official visit to Lisbon February 1938.
Took part in operations against *Scharnhorst* & *Gneisenau* 23–30 November 1939 following sinking of *Rawalpindi* by *Scharnhorst* on 23rd.
Considerably damaged by magnetic mine in Loch Ewe 4 December 1939.
Refitted at Portsmouth January to August 1940.
Temporarily replaced as fleet flag by *Warspite* pending return of *Rodney* from refit January 1940.
Rejoined fleet August 1940.
Norwegian coast operations September 1940.
Took part in operations against *Scheer* following

sinking of *Jervis Bay* 5 November 1940.
Operations against *Scharnhorst* & *Gneisenau* January to March 1941.
Relieved as fleet flag by *King George V* 1 April 1941.
Detached April 1941 to escort Middle East troop convoy via Cape.
Rejoined Home Fleet June 1941.
Transferred to Force H (Gibraltar) July 1941 for Malta convoy; left Clyde with convoy 11 July.

FORCE H (Gibraltar) July to September 1941 (flag from 8 August).
Malta convoy 21–27 July 1941.
Relieved *Renown* as flag 8 August.
Selected (with *Rodney*) in August 1941 for transfer to Eastern Fleet in December 1941 or January 1942 (see *Ramillies*). Later cancelled.
Malta convoy 24–30 September 1941; damaged forward by aerial torpedo 27 September, during this operation. Ship brought 10ft down by head, reducing speed to 15 knots and later to 12 knots. Refitted at Malta and Rosyth September 1941 to April 1942.
Rejoined Home Fleet on completion of refit.

HOME FLEET (2nd BS) April to November 1941.
Transfer to Eastern Fleet again proposed April 1942.
Left Clyde 31 May 1942, with convoy for Freetown, en route to join Eastern Fleet, via Cape, but recalled from Freetown in July for Malta convoy.
Rejoined Home Fleet at Scapa 26 July.
Flag (VA) convoy escort force hoisted at Scapa 27 July. Left Clyde with convoy 4 August.
Malta convoy 10–15 August (flag VA Escort Force).
Rejoined Home Fleet later in August.
Transferred to Force H October 1942 for North Africa invasion.
Left Scapa 30 October and joined at Gibraltar 6 November.

FORCE H (Gibraltar) November 1942 to October 1943 (flag from 15 November 1942 to May 1943 and from June 1943 on).
Took part in North Africa invasion November 1942.
Relieved *Duke of York* as flag 15 November.
Temporarily relieved as flag by *King George V*

May 1943 and came home to work up at Scapa for Sicily invasion.
Rejoined Force H June 1943. Left Scapa 17th. Arrived Gibraltar 23rd.
Took part in invasion Sicily July 1943 and Italy September 1943.
With *Rodney*, bombarded defences at Reggio 31 August, prior to Italian landings. Supported landings at Salerno 9 September.
Italian armistice signed on board at Malta 29 September 1943.
Left Gibraltar to rejoin Home Fleet 31 October.

HOME FLEET (2nd BS) November 1943 to June 1944.
Unit of bombardment force for Normandy invasion June 1944.
Carried out twenty bombardments of batteries, including Houlgate battery, and troop concentrations 11–18 June.
Damaged by mine 18 June.
Left Portsmouth 22 June to refit in the USA for service with Eastern Fleet.
Refit Philadelphia Navy Yard 1944 to January 1945.
Rejoined Home Fleet January 1945 for working-up.

HOME FLEET (2nd BS) January to April 1945.
Left home April 1945 to join East Indies Fleet (ex-Eastern Fleet) via Suez Canal.
Continued work-up in Mediterranean en route and arrived Colombo 9 July, relieving *Queen Elizabeth* on 12 July as flag 3rd BS and fleet flag.

EAST INDIES FLEET July to October 1945 (flag 3rd BS and fleet flag to September 1945).
Surrender of Japanese forces in Singapore area negotiated on board at Penang 2 September 1945.
Present at surrender all Japanese forces in South-East Asia at Singapore 12 September 1945.
Relieved as flag by *Howe* 20 September and left for home 13 October.
Arrived Portsmouth 17 November 1945.
Recommissioned at Portsmouth 24 November to relieve *Rodney* as flag 2nd BS and fleet flag Home Fleet.

HOME FLEET November 1945 to October 1947 (flag 2nd BS and fleet flag to April 1946. Seagoing Training Ship from April 1946. Flag

Home Fleet Training Squadron August to October 1946).

Relieved as fleet flag by *King George V* 9 April 1946 and became Seagoing Training Ship in Home Fleet.

Hoisted flag (RA) Training Battleships Home Fleet 14 August 1946 on formation of special Training Squadron, to comprise *Nelson*, *Anson* and *Howe*.

Relieved as flag by *Anson* October 1946 and became private ship in squadron.

Collision with submarine *Sceptre* at Portland 15 April 1947. Slight damage.

Replaced by *Victorious* and reduced to reserve at Rosyth 20 October 1947.

RESERVE (Rosyth) October 1947 to May 1948.

Paid off to Disposal List, Rosyth 19 May 1948.

Used as bombing target 1948 (see Operation 'Bronte').

Sold to British Iron & Steel Corporation 5 January 1949 and allocated to T. W. Ward & Co. for scrapping.

Arrived Inverkeithing 15 March 1949.

Hull arrived Troon for final demolition December 1949.

HISTORY: RODNEY

1922 Programme. Laid down by Cammell Laird, Birkenhead 28 December 1922. Launched by Princess Mary 17 December 1925.

Began trials August 1927.

Commissioned at Devonport 7 December 1927 for 2nd Battle Squadron, Atlantic Fleet. Because of further extended trials, did not actually join fleet until 28 March 1928.

ATLANTIC FLEET (2nd BS) March 1928 to March 1932 (temporary fleet flag April to May 1930 and July 1931).

Temporarily replaced *Nelson* as fleet flag April to May 1930.

Conveyed British Parliamentary Delegation to Iceland June 1930 for 1000th Anniversary Celebrations of Icelandic Parliament.

Again temporary fleet flag July 1931 while *Nelson* refitting after collision damage.

Atlantic Fleet redesignated Home Fleet March 1932.

HOME FLEET (2nd BS) March 1932 to

September 1941 (Fleet flag January 1934. Flag 2nd BS and 2nd fleet flag January to May 1936. Fleet flag June 1937 to February 1938 and January to August 1940).

Became temporary fleet flag January 1934 after *Nelson* grounded in Portsmouth harbour at commencement of spring cruise. Flag re-transferred during cruise.

Jubilee Review, Spithead 16 July 1935.

Again fleet flag June 1937 to February 1938, replacing *Nelson* for refit.

With *Nelson*, paid official visit to Lisbon February 1938.

Refit Portsmouth September to November 1938.

Took part in operations against *Scharnhorst* and *Gneisenau* 23–29 November 1939 following sinking of *Rawalpindi* by *Scharnhorst* 23 November. Developed serious rudder defects during these and forced to break off search on 29th and return for repairs.

Refitted at Liverpool December 1939 (completed 31st).

Rejoined fleet 1 January 1940 and became fleet flag, relieving *Warspite* which had temporarily replaced *Nelson* after latter mined 4 December.

Norwegian operations April to June 1940.

Hit aft by bomb off Bergen 9 April 1940. No material damage. Fifteen casualties.

Detached to escort homeward-bound Halifax convoys after sinking of *Jervis Bay* by *Scheer* 5 November 1940.

Took part in operations against *Scharnhorst* and *Gneisenau* in North Atlantic January to March 1941. Briefly sighted them 16 March but unable to maintain contact.

Detached 24 May 1941 from escorting SS *Britannic* to take part in operations against *Bismarck*. Joined *King George V* on 26th and assisted in destruction of *Bismarck* on 27th. Third salvo scored first registered hit on the German ship. Sustained only splinter damage to one HA director during the action.

Refit Boston Navy Yard to August 1941.

Selected (with *Nelson*) in August 1941 for transfer to Eastern Fleet in December 1941 or January 1942 (see *Ramillies*). Later cancelled. Worked-up at Bermuda after refit and then joined Force H (Gibraltar) late September for Malta convoy.

FORCE H (Gibraltar) September to November 1941 (flag from 30th September).

Malta convoy 24–30 September.

Replaced *Nelson* as flag Force H 30 September after latter damaged by aerial torpedo on 27th during convoy operation.

Relieved as flag by *Malaya* and rejoined Home Fleet November 1941.

HOME FLEET (2nd BS) November 1941 to November 1942.

Based at Hvalfiord, Iceland November 1941 to February 1942 to meet threat of attack on North Atlantic convoys by enemy heavy ships.

Refit Liverpool February to May 1942.

Transfer to Eastern Fleet again proposed April 1942. Left Clyde 31 May 1942, with convoy for Freetown, en route to join Eastern Fleet, via Cape, but recalled from Freetown in July for Malta convoy.

Rejoined Home Fleet at Scapa 26 July.

Left Clyde 4 August with convoy for Malta.

Malta convoy 10–15 August.

Rejoined Home Fleet later in the month.

Transferred to Force H (Gibraltar) October 1942 for North Africa invasion.

Left Scapa for Gibraltar 23 October.

FORCE H (Gibraltar) October 1942 to October 1943.

Took part in North Africa landings November 1942.

In action with batteries at Oran 8–10 November. Engaged fort Djbel Santon on the 9th until it capitulated.

Came home May 1943 to work-up at Scapa for Sicily invasion.

Rejoined Force H June 1943. Left Scapa 17 June. Arrived Gibraltar 23rd.

Took part in invasion of Sicily July 1943 and Italy September 1943.

With *Nelson*, bombarded defences at Reggio 31 August prior to Italian landings. Supported landings at Salerno 9 September.

Rejoined Home Fleet October 1943.

HOME FLEET October 1943 to November 1945 (2nd BS to September 1944. Fleet flag later).

Unit of bombardment force for Normandy invasion June to September 1944. Attacked by shore batteries, bombs and human torpedoes during this period but not damaged. Bombarded Houlgate and Benerville batteries on D-Day (6 June).

On 30 June, heavily hit concentrations of armoured vehicles seventeen miles behind 'Gold' beach.

Bombarded enemy troop concentrations at extreme range on 2 July.

Bombarded defences at Caen 8 July, prior to assault.

Knocked out shore batteries on Alderney (Channel Islands) 12 August.

Unit of covering force for Russia convoys September to November 1944.

Relieved *Duke of York* as flag Home Fleet September 1944.

Relieved by *Nelson* November 1945 and reduced to reserve at Rosyth.

RESERVE (Rosyth) November 1945 to March 1948.

Reduced to Care & Maintenance status August 1946.

Placed on Disposal List 1948.

Sold to T. W. Ward & Co., March 1948.

Arrived Inverkeithing for scrapping 26 March 1948.

Left: *Rodney* in her warpaint, 1942.

Left: *Nelson* enters Portsmouth after a most impressive war career, 1945. She is seen here after her service with the Pacific Fleet. Note AA additions, camouflage and RDF installations.

Below: *Rodney* pulled into position by the workers of Thomas Ward scrapyard. Shortly after this photograph was taken, all drawings (hull, electrical, gunnery and torpedo) were taken off the ship by Royal Naval officers and destroyed by fire. March 1948.

KING GEORGE V CLASS

DESIGN

As with *Nelson* and *Rodney*, the *King George V* design was not settled without a great deal of deliberation, and was carried through against a background of restrictions and difficulties. The Admiralty had planned for the ships as far back as 1933 although their idea of a suitable ship to enhance the battle fleet was not popular with Britain's allies or indeed among some departments of the Admiralty itself. In all essentials the class was built under the restriction of the 1921 Washington Treaty which was extended by the 1930 and 1935 naval agreements between Britain, USA, France and Russia and severely limited displacements, the entire scope of the design suffering accordingly.

During the great lull in construction from 1925 to 1935 there had been an enormous amount of experimentation regarding the entire infrastructure of British capital ship design, and this was fastidiously examined by the Post-War Questions Committee, which in turn sent its deliberations to their Lordships. It was noted that there had been much activity in the way of foreign development; ships such as the German *Deutschland* (1931) and the French *Dunkerque* (1935) were two of the most formidable to date. Both were considered to be of a battlecruiser type and it was thought that their primary role would be for use against commerce for which both were the ideal type. The USA had modernized its fleet to an unprecedented degree and Japan had also gone some way along this road. The USA had three 16in gunned ships and Japan two; the other ships in both navies were armed with 14in and 12in guns. France now had 13.5in guns in her new ships, Germany 11in and Italy still had 12in but for how long was uncertain.

The conclusion of many years of careful study culminated in a summary delivered to the Board showing just what the Royal Navy would require in any fresh battleship construction:

1. *Disposition of Main Armament*
Not less than four twin turrets, placed as in *Queen Elizabeth* class.
2. *Calibre and Disposition of Secondary Armament*
Twelve 6in guns in battery mountings, capable of 30° elevation.
3. *Anti-Aircraft Armament*

Six guns each side, or two twin mountings each side and one on centreline. Design of ship to be such that 4.7in or 4in can be mounted (decision as to which calibre to be given later) in between deck twins. Four Mk M pom-poms and eight 0.5in multiple machine-guns if possible; a minimum of two pom-poms and four multiple MG if it is necessary to reduce numbers.
4. *Torpedo Armament*
Torpedoes to be carried in above-water tubes, quintuple mountings.
5. *Armour Protection*
(a) If displacement is not reduced, 1928 proposals to be accepted, i.e., aginst 16in shell and 2,000lb bombs; but protection to be given to machinery spaces against 1,000lb 'terminal velocity dive' bomb attack.
(b) If displacement is reduced, standard of protection to be against 14in fire; anti-bomb protection as before.
6. *Under-water Protection*
(a) Anti-Torpedo: Against 1,000 pb. charge in contact with the ship's side. (b) Anti-mine – ('B') Bomb, etc.). Best protection possible; *Nelson*'s standard being a minimum. Close subdivision of compartments.
(c) Near-Miss (by a heavy bomb). Areas outside anti-torpedo protection to be considered.
7. *Speed.*
A maximum of 23 knots. (Endurance required at various speeds is detailed)
8. *Endurance*
14,000 miles at 10 knots.

On this foundation the DNC Department was asked in 1935 to submit suitable sketches. This they did, but because of the large number of designs proposed, all still being restricted to about 35,000 tons, the concept gave the department an almost impossible task. More than twenty designs were forwarded from July 1935 to April 1936 and a design prefixed '14.0' was considered the best possible all-round layout. The DNC said:

'In view of the very great importance of getting the best design of ships possible, a design which must be able to withstand the development of design of the next twenty years, the naval staff have been at great pains to examine '14.0' design in every aspect. The staff memo has the appearance of being written by an *advocatus diaboli* pointing out all the weak spots of an admittedly fine design. But this is all to the good

as it brings out these points which require modification. The raising of the armoured deck is of great importance and definitely should be adopted.' With slight modification of armouring and armament the prefix was changed to become design '14.P' and was approved on 28 May 1936. The design can be best understood by referring to the official Admiralty History of Design, *King George V* class:

'The last capital ships completed for the Royal Navy prior to *King George V* and *Nelson* and *Rodney* which were designed to meet the requirements of the Washington Treaty. At the Geneva Conference in 1927 the British contingent were prepared to accept a reduced standard displacement and smaller calibre of gun for capital ships, but the USA was not prepared to discuss size of capital ships.

'At the London Conference in 1930 the major powers agreed not to exercise the right provided in the Washington Treaty to lay down the keels of capital ships replacement tonnage during 1931–6 inclusive. Thus the earliest date for laying down keels of replacement tonnage became 1.1.1937. The London Treaty of 1936 between the USA, France and Britain was arranged because of the forthcoming expiration of the Washington Treaty (1921) and London Treaty (1930).

'An important clause affecting capital ship design was to the effect that no capital ship should carry a gun over 14in calibre provided however that if any of the parties of the 1921 Washington Treaty should fail to enter into an agreement to conform to this provision not later than 1st April 1937 then maximum calibre shall be 16in. (Japan did not enter into the agreement.)

'*King George V* class were designed to Treaty limitations of 35,000 tons and 14in guns. Great Britain decided to lay down two capital ships at the earliest date permitted by the Treaty, namely 1st January 1937.

Great Britain then became committed to the 14in gun although in the event of Japan refusing to accept this size consideration was given to designing the ships so that the 14in guns could be changed over to 16in guns at a later date. This, however, would have involved an appreciable increase in citadel length and armour weight and delay and it was therefore decided to design the ships with 14in guns. Many sketch designs

Below: *Prince of Wales* fitting out at Cammell Lairds early in 1941.

Original proposal for battlecruiser, 8 August 1935

Equipment	1,200 tons
Machinery	3,350
Armament	6,850
Armour	10,550
Hull	13,050

Total displacement of ship to be 35,000 tons.

Design '14P' Final Legend
Displacement: 35,000 tons.
Length: 700ft(pp), 740ft (w2).
Beam: 103ft.
Draught: 28ft mean.
Freeboard: 22ft 9in.
SHP: 110,000 for 28½–29 knots.
Fuel: 4,000 tons oil.
Armament
10 x 14in (80rpg)
16 x 5.25in (200rpg)
2 pom-poms Mk VI (500rpg)
4 x 0.5in MG

Catapult and aircraft (4 aircraft to be carried).
Armour
Main belt 15in, 15–7in below water.
Turrets 13–9–7in, deck: 6in over magazines, 5in over machinery.
Weights (tons)

General equipment	1,050
Machinery	2,635
Armament	5,880
Armour	12,845
Hull	13,040

Designs

	'15C'	'14H'	'14G'	'14J'	'14K'
	9 x 15in	9 x 14in	12 x 14in	12 x 14in	12 x 14in
	29½ knots	30	27	28	29
	108,000shp	112,000	80,000	90,000	100,000
	14in armour	14in	14in	13in	12½in
	6¼in deck	6¼in	6¼in	6in	6in
	740ft long	750	750	740	750
	35,000 tons	34,545	35,345	35,300	35,200

were prepared before approval. The earliest sketch design included 12 x 14in guns in three quadruple turrets and 20 x 4.5in guns in ten twin turrets. The middle deck was the armoured deck. In later sketches the secondary armament became 16 x 5.25in guns in eight twin turrets and the armoured deck was raised to main deck level, increasing the depth of side armour by about 8 feet. To meet this increase adhering to 35,000 tons it was found necessary to reduce the main armament to ten 14in by making 'B' turret a twin mounting.

'Every effort was made to economize in weight.

'On 28th May 1936 approval was given to design 14.P.

'On 29th July 1936 two ships were ordered (*King George V* and *Prince of Wales*).

'The Board drawings were completed, approved and delivered to the ship builders on 30th September 1936.'

The design as completed was probably the best 35,000-ton limited displacement battleship ever produced. True the main armament was not powerful enough, but the 14in was a good gun, and in all other apsects they were excellent ships; the armour protection was in fact second to none. Lessons embodied in the design had all been learnt during the Great War and augmented by the experiments with *Emperor of India* and *Marlborough* in 1931. They included:
1. Magazines below shell rooms.
2. Main machinery re-arranged and sub-divided to reduce possibility of complete disablement.

King George V: Launch figures, 21 January 1939
Length: 700ft (pp), 700ft 0$^{1}/_{4}$in as measured, 745ft 0$^{1}/_{8}$in (oa).
Beam: 103ft 2$^{9}/_{16}$in.
Depth of keel to upper deck: 51ft 1$^{5}/_{16}$in.
Breakage:
Longitudinally in a distance of 688ft: 1in hog.
Transverse in a distance of 98ft: nil.
Draught: 13ft 2$^{1}/_{8}$in forward, 15ft 10$^{1}/_{4}$in amidships, 18ft 6$^{7}/_{8}$in aft.
Hull: 11,790 tons.
Displacement at launch: 18,120 tons.
Displacement (tons) at launch for others

Prince of Wales:	18,578.
Duke of York:	18,852.

Duke of York: GM and stability, 19 August 1941
Ship in 'A' condition: Draught: 32ft 5$^{1}/_{2}$in, 55 tons water protection, 2,530 tons oil fuel. GM: 7.36ft.
Ship in 'B' condition: Draught: 33ft 3in, 55 tons water protection, 3,270 tons oil fuel. GM: 8.14ft.
Stability.
Maximum in 'A' condition: 34°
'B' condition: 35°
Stability vanishes at:
'A' condition: 67°
'B' condition: 70°
Displacement: 38,126 tons load condition.

Particulars of ships, as completed
Construction
King George V: Vickers; laid down 1.1.1937; launched 21.2.1939; completed 11.12.1940. *Prince of Wales*: Cammell Laird; laid down 1.1.1937; launched 3.5.1939; completed 31.3.1941. *Duke of York*: John Brown; laid down 5.5.1937; launched 28.2.1940; completed 4.11.1941; *Anson*: Swan, Hunter; laid down 22.7.1937; launched 24.2.1940; completed 22.6.1942. *Howe*: Fairfield; laid down 1.6.1937; launched 9.4.1940; completed 29.8.1942.
Displacement (tons):
Duke of York: 37,754 (light), 41,858 (average action), 42,046 (deep); *KGV*: 38,151 (load), 42,245 (deep); *Howe*: 39,138 (load), 42,630 (deep).
Dimensions
Length:

King George V	700ft 0$^{1}/_{4}$in (pp)	745ft 0$^{1}/_{8}$in (oa)
Prince of Wales	700ft 1in,	745ft 1$^{5}/_{8}$in (oa)
Duke of York	699ft 11$^{7}/_{8}$in	745ft 0$^{5}/_{8}$in (oa)
Anson	700ft 0$^{1}/_{4}$in,	745ft 0$^{1}/_{4}$in (oa)
Howe	699ft 11$^{1}/_{2}$in	744ft 11$^{1}/_{2}$in (oa)

Beam:

King George V	103ft 2$^{9}/_{16}$in
Prince of Wales	103ft 2$^{3}/_{16}$in
Duke of York	103ft 1$^{3}/_{4}$in
Anson	103ft 0$^{1}/_{4}$in
Howe	103ft 0$^{3}/_{8}$in

Draught: Ranging from 28ft 6in through to 33ft 7$^{1}/_{2}$in depending on condition.
Armament
10 x 14in 45cal Mk VII (80rpg)
16 x 5.25in 50cal Mk I HA/LA dual-purpose (200rpg)
32–48 2pdr AA
1 x 40mm AA (*Prince of Wales*)
11–15 x 20mm AA (*Anson* and *Howe*)
4 x 3pdr saluting
3 to 4 20-tube AA rocket-projectors (*King George V* and *Prince of Wales*).
Freeboard: (as designed) 30ft 10in forward, 26ft 10in aft.
Armour
Main belt 15–14in
Bulkheads 12–10in
Barbettes 14–13–12–11in
Turrets 13–9–7in
Secondary turrets 1in–1$^{1}/_{2}$–1in
Splinter protection to secondary magazines 1$^{1}/_{2}$in 'D' steel
Underwater protection 1$^{3}/_{4}$–1$^{1}/_{2}$in
Deck: 6in over magazines, 5in over machinery.
Lower deck forward of citadel 5–2$^{1}/_{2}$in, aft of citadel 5–4$^{1}/_{2}$in,
Conning tower (and bridge) 4in sides, 3in face.
Machinery
Parsons single reduction geared turbines driving 4 propellers.
Separate cruising turbines.
Turbines arranged in four compartments.
Boilers: 8 Admiralty 3-drum boilers in 4 compartments.
Designed SHP: 110,000 for 28$^{1}/_{2}$/29 knots
Working pressure: 380/410psi
Steam temperature: 750 degrees.
Length of engine rooms: 'A' and 'B' 43ft 11$^{1}/_{4}$in, 'X' and 'Y' 43ft 11$^{1}/_{4}$in.
Length of boiler rooms: 43ft 11$^{5}/_{8}$in
Fuel: 3,770 tons oil (average).
Radius of action:
King George V, Prince of Wales, Duke of York, 15,600nm at 10 knots; *Anson* 16,700nm at 10 knots; *Howe* 15,400nm at 10 knots.
Weights (tons)

General equipment	1,150
Machinery	2,770
Armament	6,570
Armour	12,460
Hull	13,780

Costs

Hull	£2,578,034
Armour	1,140,000
Machinery	1,116,153
Armament	2,243,162
Stores and equipment	315,785
Stores and equipment	315,785

Total of each ship on average: £7,393,134.
Ship's boats
3 x 25ft motor boats
3 x 45ft motor pickets
1 x 45ft motor launch
2 x 32ft cutters
2 x 27 whalers
2 x 14ft dinghies
1 x 16ft dinghy
1 x 13 6in balsa raft
47 life floats.
Searchlights
6 x 44in: 2 on lower bridge, 2 on platform abaft fore funnel, 2 on platform on second funnel; 2 x 24in signalling on lower bridge.
Upper deck to fore truck 121ft 6in.
Top of fore funnel from upper deck 63ft 9in.
Upper deck to after truck 103ft.
Upper bridge to upper deck 59ft 6$^{1}/_{2}$in.
Complement
King George V and *Prince of Wales*: average 1,400 (1941); *PoW* 110 officers, 1,502 men (December 1941); *Duke of York* as squadron flagship 84 officers, 1,530 men, as fleet flagship 104 officers, 1,578 men.
Total cost of each ship on average: £7,393,134.

3. Side armour substantially lengthened and thickened.
4. Thick armour at top end of side armour and splinter protection covering all magazines.
5. Anti-flash arrangements in all turrets.
6. Ventilation arrangements to handing rooms.
7. Important underwater protection.
8. Close watertight sub-division and pumping facility extensions.
9. Technical improvements, particularly in propulsive machinery and structural application of armour.

Features of the design were:
1. The only British battleships to have 14in guns (apart from the ex-Chilean *Canada* taken over in 1914) and quadruple turrets.
2. First design since 1877 with a dual-purpose HA-LA secondary armament and the first completed without any torpedo armament.
3. The first completed with radar.
4. The first designed to carry aircraft.
5. The first since 1877 completed without a heavily armoured conning tower.

The ships had a flush deck hull and a very slight sheer forward, this having been curtailed to an undesirable extent to meet an Admiralty requirement (in force prior to 1941) that all turrets be able to fire at 3° depression over their entire safety arcs. The sheer forward was inadequate, however, and was aggravated by a reduction of about three feet in the original design freeboard due to the addition of extra weights added during construction. This caused the ships to be wet at high speed and inclined to bury in head seas, the class suffering appreciably from this defect. During the action with *Bismarck*

in May 1941 'A' and 'B' turret rangefinders in *Prince of Wales* were blanked by heavy spray coming in over the low forecastle and, as the main armament radar was not functioning, the fighting efficiency of the guns was seriously impaired.

Such was not the case in *King George V*, however. On her preliminary trials (2 December 1940), Constructor H. S. Pengally said of her general seaworthiness:

'During full power trials the ship was dry except for broken water over the bow which was well cleared by the breakwaters. The fairing at the fore end of the side armour and the streamlined refuse chute were effective in reducing spray. The flying-off space and quarterdeck were dry, the latter even when going astern at 10 knots.

'The movement of the ship was generally easy, periods measured on many occasions being about 7½ seconds' pitch and 14 seconds' roll. The ship was remarkably free of vibration at all speeds and I was informed that the rangefinders could be used without difficulty. The Captain and officers have all expressed themselves as

being pleased with the ship and her performance.'

They were the last British battleships to have the conventional (cruiser) stern, a new square-cut type being adopted in the later *Vanguard*. The tight, almost square bilge offered greater resistance to rolling. The metacentric height was 6.1 feet in the average load and 8.1 feet deep, this being greater than in any previous British armoured ship since *Inflexible* (1874). Electric welding was extensively used in the construction but was limited to certain areas.

ARMAMENT

In 1931 staff requirements called for a main armament mounted in not less than four twin turrets placed as in the *Queen Elizabeth* class. After many tests this method of disposing the armament was strongly advocated. It was thought that if for reasons connected with adequate protection and limited tonnage it was found impossible to mount the armament in this way, the method should follow that as fitted in *Nelson* and *Rodney* (triple turrets). The calibre of

gun as proposed ranged from 14in to 16in and in all forms of disposition. That the 14in was finally adopted came about as a direct result of the 1936 London Naval Conference, which suggested a reduction in maximum permitted gun calibre from 16in to 14in, and the design of the *King George V* class was prepared on this basis. The other powers concerned failed to ratify the agreement, but as the delay of one year required for the preparation of new designs was unacceptable the 14in armament was retained. Designs for 15in guns were available at the time, but the 14in was considered to offer a better-balanced design on a displacement limit of 35,000 tons.

Numerous alternative plans were considered with a view to mounting the maximum number of guns, and both twin, triple and quadruple turrets were discussed. Three quadruples were eventually approved although it later became necessary to reduce this to two quadruple and one twin to offset the weight of extra magazine protection which trials with new projectiles had shown to be desirable. The *Nelson*-class arrangement for the original three quadruple turrets was considered, but rejected because of severe blast

effects when the after turret trained abaft the beam, and because of difficulty in accommodating the longer machinery space required in the fine stern section. The arrangement of two turrets forward and one aft was finally adopted, the second (superfiring) quadruple being later replaced by a twin. They were the only British battleships to have 14in guns (apart from the ex-Chilean *Canada* taken over in 1914) and quadruple turrets. They were also the first to complete with radar control.

Because of the complexity of the quadruple turrets the crews had problems that were noticeable during the action against *Bismarck* in 1941, for example, when main armaments in *Prince of Wales* and *King George V* were at times only 20–50 per cent effective. *Prince of Wales* had one gun in 'A' turret defective throughout, and 'Y' was temporarily out of action through mechanical failure. In *King George V* one turret was inoperative for nearly twenty minutes. These problems were later overcome and at the sinking of *Scharnhorst* in December 1943 *Duke of York* fired 52 broadsides of which 31 straddled and sixteen fell within 200 yards of the target, a remarkable performance even if the efficiency of the radar control is taken into consideration.

The secondary armament for the *King George V* group was extremely problematical although it had been under development since the time of the original proposal in 1928, which called for twelve 5in guns mounted six on each side. The contentious issue was whether to include a gun that could cover both LA and HA fire. The low-angle gun needed to be powerful enough to stop attacking destroyers and yet have sufficient elevation to counter diving aircraft, and there was no such dual-purpose weapon in production at that time. The questions of armament allocation and weight distribution were hotly argued throughout the early 1930s, but on 1 January 1936 it was finally decided to replace the 4.5in gun by the new 5.25in which was about to go into production. At a DNO's meeting on 1 May 1936 the positioning of the 5.25in guns was debated:

Position 'A': Eight guns on each side in two groups. The entire 5.25in battery being fed from common groups of magazines and situated just before the foremost boiler room.

Position 'B': To separate the guns on each side into two groups, the foremost group each side to be fed from magazines positioned forward, and after group from magazines positioned aft.

Disadvantages of Position 'A':

1. The two after mounts required long-distance transportation of ammunition between decks.

2. As all 5.25in magazine and shell rooms came together serious dislocation would result from an underwater hit.

3. Could be put out of action completely by shell or bomb hit.

4. Close-range AA difficult to position away from blast of 5.25in guns.

Disadvantages of Position 'B':

1. Arrangement required two separate funnels and fore funnel would have to be closer to the bridgework.

Advantages of 'B':

1. Magazines widely separated.

2. Less vulnerable to all being knocked out by single blow.

3. Better internal arrangements.

4. Better arcs of fire and no interference to bridge.

Although *Nelson* and *Rodney*'s secondary guns were fitted in turrets, the recommendations of the 1928 committee did not favour a return of this mounting and strongly advocated the battery system of the *Queen Elizabeth* and *Royal Sovereign* classes.

The advantages of the broadside battery as opposed to the turret system were:

1. More reliable due to absence of machinery and probable effect of splinters.

2. Crews fairly well protected.

3. A better chance of a fair proportion of the armament being fit for service after a day's action.

4. Local control of whole battery easy.

5. Upkeep easy and cheap.

6. Cost of mounting twelve guns about one-third that of mounting the same number in turrets.

Disadvantages:

1. Arcs of fire not as good as those of turrets.

2. Rate of fire falls off as personnel become tired.

3. Adequate supply arrangements more difficult to arrange.

4. Difficult to protect from weather unless mounted higher than in *QE* and *RS* classes.

The final recommendation was for twelve guns in a battery of high command.

The backup HA armament was to consist of eight 4.7in twin mountings as had been dis-

cussed in the 1928 prospoals. At a later date, however, weight restrictions imposed on the design forced a reduction in calibre to 4.5in. More discussions led to the favouring of a dual-purpose battery (both LA and HA) and for this the turret system seemed best, although at the same time it was seen as a flaw in the protection because secondary turrets could not be heavily armoured because of displacement restrictions. The final recommendations were for 5.25in guns separated into four groups of four guns (i.e., two twin mountings) situated in the corners of the citadel, the magazines and shell rooms to be divided into groups before and abaft machinery spaces.

Both the 1928 and 1931 Battleship Committees had problems in deciding whether to fit any torpedo armament. The 1928 Board showed a certain dislike for the idea, but three years later favoured the addition. The 1931 proposal was for above-water tubes which would be advantageous for night fighting. Later, however, the whole question of torpedo armament was dropped because of weight problems.

They were the first British battleships to be designed with the dual-purpose (LA/HA) sec-

ondary armament, but in service the 5.25in gun was found to be too heavy for rapid fire, particularly sustained AA fire at close ranges.

Light AA armament was variable in the earlier and later ships of the class, as completed.

The original design had provided for thirty-two 2pdrs in four multiple (8 barrels) mountings, two P&S on the superstructure before and abeam the fore funnel. The first two ships (*KGV* and *PoW*) completed thus (1940–1) plus a single 40mm in breastwork right aft on the quarterdeck in *Prince of Wales* only. *King George V* carried four and *Prince of Wales* three 20-tube rocket projectors, one each on 'B' and 'Y' turrets in both ships. *King George V* also carried an additional rocket launcher on her quarterdeck. *Duke of York*, *Anson* and *Howe* completed with an extra pair of multiple 2pdr mountings, one on 'B' turret and one on 'Y' instead of the rocket launchers. There were also some 20mm AA in *Anson* and *Howe* mounted on the forecastle and quarterdeck in both, and on the forward superstructure as well in *Anson*.

Rocket-projectors in *King George V* and *Prince of Wales* were replaced by multiple 2pdrs (8 barrels) and four 20mm AA added in place of the

rocket projector on the quarterdeck in *King George V*. There was radar control for the secondary armament and the 2pdrs; four directors in *King George V*, *Prince of Wales* and *Duke of York* as completed, but six in the last two of the class.

These ships were the first British battleships to be completed without any form of torpedo armament.

ARMOUR

The original desired scale of protection was that first envisaged during the early 1930s when proposals were made to protect new battleships against 16in shells at ranges between 12,000 and 30,000 yards. In foreign navies, however, there were only five 16in gunned ships (1935, USA three, Japan two) and it was thought highly improbable that any new ship would have to face one of these. Most heavy guns were 14in, however, and it was thought that this size might well become the 'standard' so protection would only need to be effective against this calibre, especially when displacement limitations would play such a big part in construction of any new ships.

A more daunting aspect when considering adequate protection was the ever-increasing danger from aerial bomb attack, the efficiency of which was improving steadily. In 1930 the weight of the high-explosive bomb was limited to 2,000 pounds, but it could not be ruled out that before long more powerful bombs would be available. It had been estimated that the following thicknesses of NC steel could be penetrated by the 1,000lb bomb:

Aircraft speed at end of dive:	Height of release:	NC steel:
320mph	1,200ft	3.43in
400mph	1,200ft	4.20in

Protection would need to be:

Magazines: Against penetration by 14in shells between 12,000 and 30,000 yards.
Against 2,000lb bombs AP dropped from 10,000ft and lower.

Engine and boiler rooms:
1. Against 14in plunging shell fire up to 26,000 yards; the side armour not being penetrable outside 12,000 yards at 70° inclination.
2. Against 2,000lb bombs when dropped from 4,000ft and below.
3. Against 1,000lb bombs of 'terminal velocity dive' type.

Main armament:
Ammunition supply arrangements and gun-houses to be protected from 14in shells between 12,000 and 26,000 yards
Same protection against bombs as for engine rooms and boiler houses.

Secondary armament:
Against splinters and blast of 14in shells or 2,000lb bombs bursting in the vicinity plus weather, blast from own guns and machine-gun fire from attacking aircraft.

Steering gear:
The need for protection against all but direct hits.

It was found practicable to include protection against guns of greater calibre than their own, the scale in fact being second to none compared to any capital ship afloat (1937) or indeed any proposed designs of the time (with the exception of the Japanese *Yamato* class). As built, they were protected against 16in shells between 12,000 and 30,000 yards and against 2,000lb bombs from 10,000ft (side armour and decks). The main armament was proof against 16in shells at ranges between 12,000 and 26,000

yards, the machinery spaces against 16in plunging fire up to 26,000 yards, and the side armour was impenetrable outside 12,000 yards during normal battle conditions.

Extra consideration was given to underwater protection and it was concluded that the following was needed:
Anti-torpedo: To provide against 750lb charge in contact with ship's side.
Anti-mine: To provide at least 5 feet between bottoms of inner and outer hulls.

Anti-torpedo protection was built in and fitted internally for as far forward and aft as possi-

ble on the given weight restrictions, and during construction consideration was given to protection against 1,000lb torpedo charges rather than 750lb after reviewing the scale of protection in *Nelson*.

As with the battleships that had been 'modernized' during the 1930s (*Warspite*, *Renown* etc.), there was no provision for a heavily protected conning tower as had been normal to that date (1933), all control positions being adequately protected beneath the deck, and bullet-proof protection being provided for bridges, etc. In any case officers were reluctant to use a con-

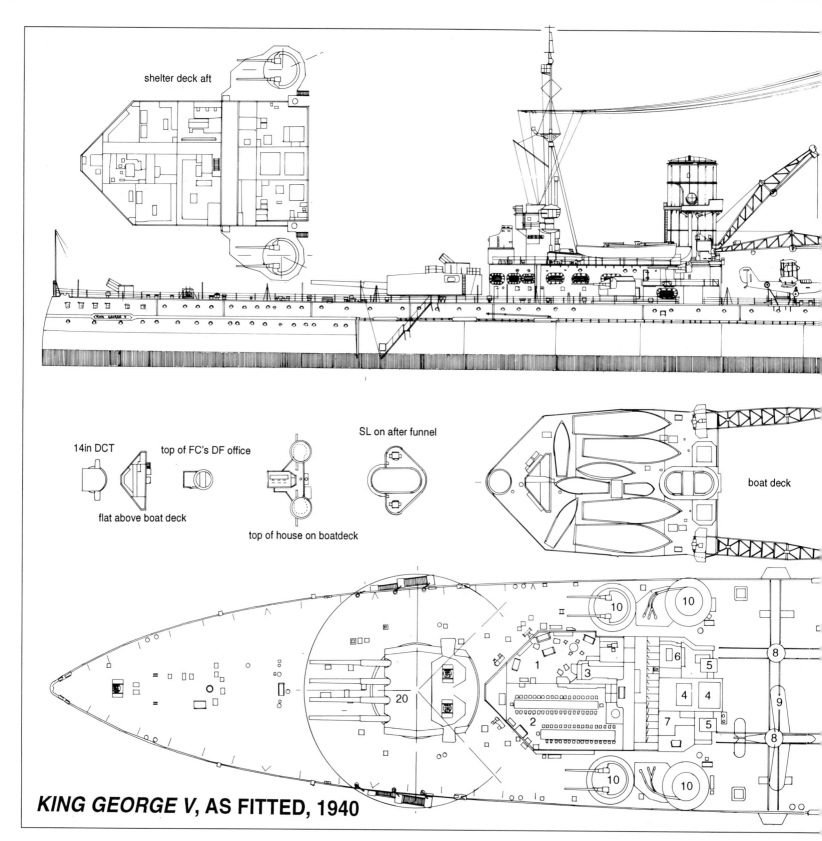

shelter deck aft

14in DCT

flat above boat deck

top of FC's DF office

SL on after funnel

top of house on boatdeck

boat deck

KING GEORGE V, AS FITTED, 1940

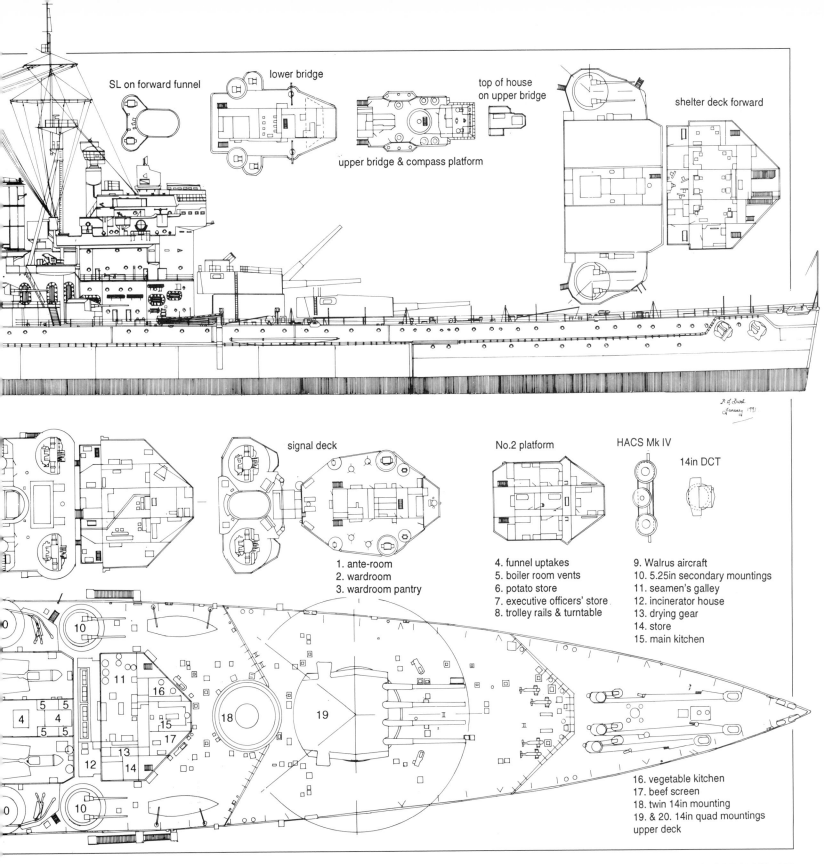

SL on forward funnel

lower bridge

top of house
on upper bridge

shelter deck forward

upper bridge & compass platform

R A Burt
January 1991

signal deck

No.2 platform

HACS Mk IV

14in DCT

1. ante-room
2. wardroom
3. wardroom pantry

4. funnel uptakes
5. boiler room vents
6. potato store
7. executive officers' store
8. trolley rails & turntable

9. Walrus aircraft
10. 5.25in secondary mountings
11. seamen's galley
12. incinerator house
13. drying gear
14. store
15. main kitchen

16. vegetable kitchen
17. beef screen
18. twin 14in mounting
19. & 20. 14in quad mountings
upper deck

ning tower because of the poor view from the position and the fact that a direct hit would probably put the personnel out of action – and this saw the demise of the conning tower within the Royal Navy's designs.

The entire philosophy underlying the protection given to the *King George V* class was a direct result of full-scale tests carried out during the 1930s against structures built on to 'Job 74' which were tested against heavy contact charges. The two most important tests involved 1,000lb TNT charges exploded against a heavy two-ply riveted protective bulkhead of 'D1' material, and showed that a riveted bulkhead resisted explosive charges much better than a welded one. Many experiments were carried out with models and against older ships such as *Emperor of India, Marlborough, Centurion* and the monitor *Roberts*. The drawings show some of the tests.

Conclusions of the *Excellent* tests were highlighted in the report made to the Admiralty:
1. Both systems of defence were heavily defeated and, had either system been incorporated in a ship, sea water would have entered two, possibly three, main compartments behind the holding bulkhead.
2. The principal cause of the extensive damage was brittle failure which was associated with welded joints.
3. Steel ranging in thickness from 1½in to 5/16 was used in the construction of the target and thick metal was the most susceptible to brittle fracture; in fact, examples of ductile breaks in 1½in metal were rare, whereas, in 5/16in steel they were numerous.
4. The evidence of the tests and Job 74 trials indicates that riveted joints in thick protective bulkheads are superior to welded joints for resistance against explosive loading.
5. Valuable information was obtained on the efficiency of various design features of the defence system.
6. The damage obtained was far more extensive and different in type when full-scale trials rather than ¼-scale models were used.
7. The trials emphasize the importance of metallurgical research on structural steels.
8. The trials emphasize the importance, in the buiilding of large warship structures, of the highest quality of workmanship.

As completed, the *King George V* class had an external armoured belt instead of the internal

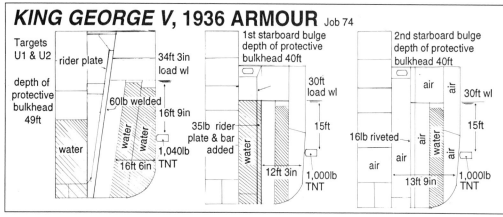

KING GEORGE V, 1936 ARMOUR Job 74

Targets U1 & U2

depth of protective bulkhead 49ft

rider plate

34ft 3in load wl

60lb welded

water

water | water

16ft 9in

1,040lb TNT

16ft 6in

1st starboard bulge depth of protective bulkhead 40ft

35lb rider plate & bar added

water

12ft 3in

30ft load wl

15ft

1,000lb TNT

2nd starboard bulge depth of protective bulkhead 40ft

16lb riveted

air

air

air | water | air

30ft wl

15ft

1,000lb TNT

13ft 9in

arrangement adopted in the *Nelson* class and the armour belt was carried lower beneath the waterline than in any previous battleships, this being demonstrated during firing tests against the German battleship *Baden* (1921), *Superb* (1922), *Monarch* (1924) and *Emperor of India* (1931). Despite this increase in depth of armour, however, *Prince of Wales* was hit beneath the armour belt during the *Bismarck* action in May 1941.

The belt armour was carried one deck higher than in *Nelson* with a maximum increase of 1in over that class. The flat armoured deck, adopted in *Nelson*, was retained but placed one deck higher. Thickness was reduced by ¼in over magazines, but increased 2in over machinery and boiler spaces. The 6in maximum deck thickness was based on the extensive trials since 1922 which all indicated that this thickness was adequate against any bombs then considered likely to be developed. On the other hand, only the Japanese had estimated that a 6in thickness was not enough to keep out really heavy bombs, and during tests carried out from 1934 had concluded that at least 7in to 9in was needed to resist AP bombs dropped from a great height. As in *Nelson*, the external bulge system was not used and a new arrangement of bulkheading was adopted with increased pumping facilities.

The loss of *Prince of Wales*, which capsized after being hit by many torpedoes, showed up a whole series of minor defects, however, one of the most important being the lack of watertight integrity in the ventilating system. The ship settled rapidly before capsizing. The torpedoes caused more damage than they should have done, but it is believed that the ship could have been saved had it not been for a bomb which pierced the catapult deck, burst in the cinema space below and blew out the side of the hull, causing rapid flooding. The cinema space extended right across the ship and the free flooding collected in this and was mainly responsible for her capsizing. With the abandonment of aircraft in battleships after 1942, this hazard was reduced by relocating the cinema and various offices on the catapult deck in the former hangar space and eliminating the free flooding area below. Additional tanks for watertight integrity were also fitted following the loss of *Prince of Wales*.

With a view to increasing waterline protection, arrangements were made, for the first time,

for flooding the fuel tanks outside the anti-torpedo bulkheads as oil was expended so that these would never be empty. Later, however, it was found that this offered no advantage over empty spaces in absorbing shock.

The main armoured belt as completed was 15in abreast the magazines, 14in abreast machinery and boiler spaces with a lower edge of 5½in and 4½in respectively. The total armoured side was 414ft long by 23ft 6in wide and extended to just beyond the outer faces of 'A' and 'Y' barbettes. The upper edge of the belt was at main deck level some 14ft 9in above the waterline (at normal load), the lower edge being approximately 8ft 6in below. The entire side protection of the citadel reached 40ft before and 36ft abaft. Bulkheads were 12in–11in–10in clos-

ing forward and after extremities of belt armour between main and lower decks. The main deck was 6in–5in thick and laid flat over the length of the belt; 6in over magazines and 5in over machinery and boilers (also 5in–2½in and 5in–4½in on lower deck outside citadel). Barbettes were 13in–12in and 12in–11in according to position ('A' and 'B' 3in–12in–11in and 'Y' 13in–12in).Turrets had 13in faces, 9in sides, 7in rears and 6in crowns. Secondary turrets (5.25in) were given only 1½–1in bullet-proof plating. Splinter-proof protection for secondary magazines was 1½ 'D' steel. Anti-torpedo bulkheads were 1¾in running the whole length of the armoured belt and finishing in a 1½in bulkhead. The conning position in the bridge face was given 4in armour plates on the sides, 3in on the

DUKE OF YORK: FEBRUARY 1942

Inboard profile key:
1. admiral's day cabin
2. admiral's dining cabin
3. admiral's pantry
4. midshipmen's study
5. officers' baggage room
6. and 7. passages
8. teleprinter office
9. admiral's lobby
10. capstan machinery compartment
11. WOs' mess
12. steering gear compartment
13. captain's cabin
14. propeller warning room
15. admiral's steward's space
16. canteen manager's space
17. officers' bedding store

18. wardroom store
19. bathroom
20. annexe
21. annexe extension
22 cabin spaces
23. pump space
24. spirits room
25. and 29 fresh water tanks
26. water tanks
27. 'Y' shell room
28. WT compartment
30. 'Y' magazine
31. 'Y' handing room
32. 14in DCT
33. pom-pom RU magazine
34. junction-box space
35. 'Y' 14in quad mounting
36. 2pdr Mk VI pom-pom
37. No.8 RDF office

38. No1 RDF office
39. boat store
40. DF W/T office
41. HACS
42. pom-pom director
43. gunners' instruction gear store
44. electricians' workspace
45. shipwrights' RU store
46. engine room vent
47. spare engine store
48. wardroom officers' WCs
49. wardroom pantry
50. ante-room & wardroom
51. wardroom officers' bathroom
52. passage

53. sub officers' bathroom
54. kit lockers
55. billets
56. church
57. main naval store
58. machine shop
59. medical distribution store
60. central communications office
61. CCOs' annexe
62. electricians' gear store

63. engineers' fitting shop
64. HA/LA calculations office
65. pom-pom magazine
66. 'Y' magazine
67. strongroom
68. 5.25in shell room
69. 5.25in magazine
70. engine rooms
71. boiler rooms

72. boiler & funnel uptakes
73. engine room exhaust
74. catapult machinery space
75. kit lockers
76. SL & emergency conning platform

PROFILE AS FITTED, TRIALS PERIOD NOV 1941-FEB 1942

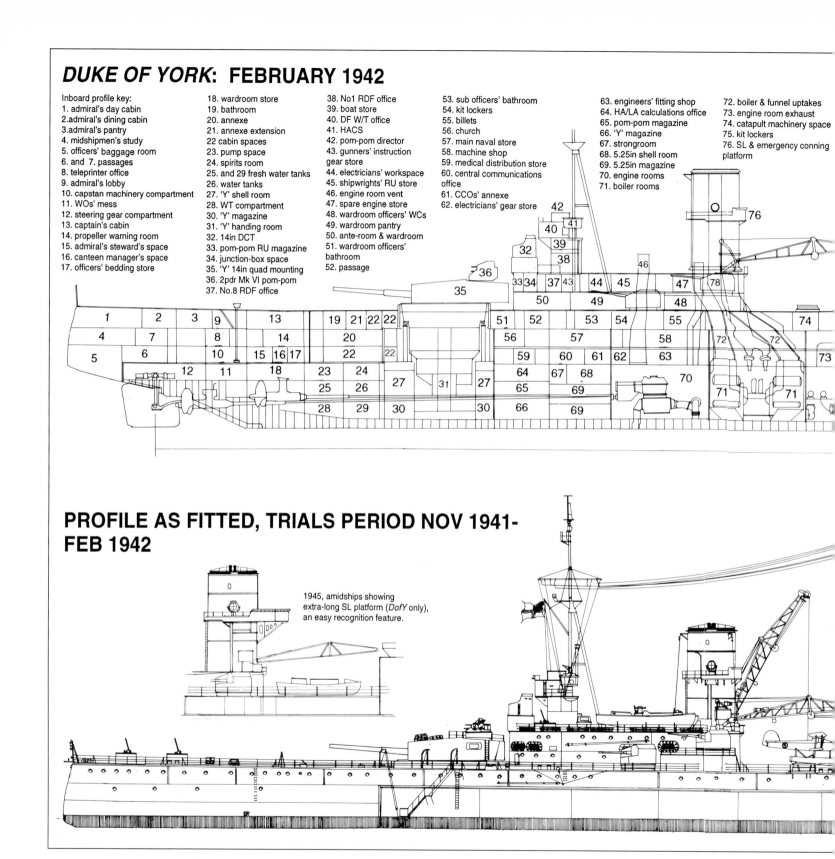

1945, amidships showing extra-long SL platform (*DofY* only), an easy recognition feature.

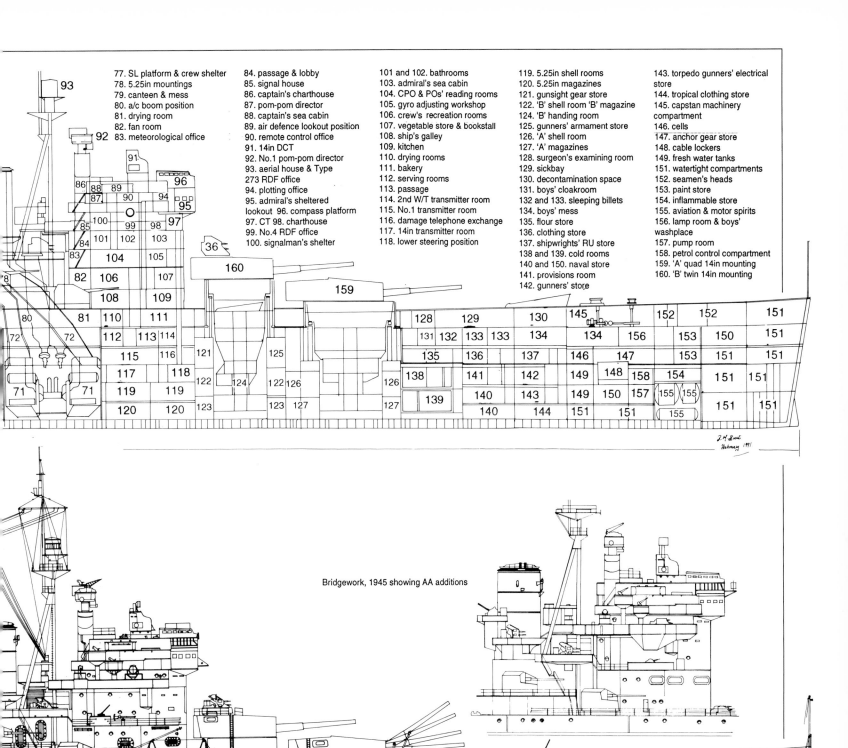

77. SL platform & crew shelter
78. 5.25in mountings
79. canteen & mess
80. a/c boom position
81. drying room
82. fan room
83. meteorological office
84. passage & lobby
85. signal house
86. captain's charthouse
87. pom-pom director
88. captain's sea cabin
89. air defence lookout position
90. remote control office
91. 14in DCT
92. No.1 pom-pom director
93. aerial house & Type 273 RDF office
94. plotting office
95. admiral's sheltered lookout 96. compass platform
97. CT 98. charthouse
99. No.4 RDF office
100. signalman's shelter

101 and 102. bathrooms
103. admiral's sea cabin
104. CPO & POs' reading rooms
105. gyro adjusting workshop
106. crew's recreation rooms
107. vegetable store & bookstall
108. ship's galley
109. kitchen
110. drying rooms
111. bakery
112. serving rooms
113. passage
114. 2nd W/T transmitter room
115. No.1 transmitter room
116. damage telephone exchange
117. 14in transmitter room
118. lower steering position

119. 5.25in shell rooms
120. 5.25in magazines
121. gunsight gear store
122. 'B' shell room 'B' magazine
124. 'B' handing room
125. gunners' armament store
126. 'A' shell room
127. 'A' magazines
128. surgeon's examining room
129. sickbay
130. decontamination space
131. boys' cloakroom
132 and 133. sleeping billets
134. boys' mess
135. flour store
136. clothing store
137. shipwrights' RU store
138 and 139. cold rooms
140 and 150. naval store
141. provisions room
142. gunners' store

143. torpedo gunners' electrical store
144. tropical clothing store
145. capstan machinery compartment
146. cells
147. anchor gear store
148. cable lockers
149. fresh water tanks
151. watertight compartments
152. seamen's heads
153. paint store
154. inflammable store
155. aviation & motor spirits
156. lamp room & boys' washplace
157. pump room
158. petrol control compartment
159. 'A' quad 14in mounting
160. 'B' twin 14in mounting

Bridgework, 1945 showing AA additions

Below: The ill-fated *Prince of Wales* in full fighting shape, August 1941. Note the camouflage – 5 colours – which made her one of the most colourful battleships in the fleet.

front. There was also extra armour in the way of circular bulkheads under the barbettes; 2in splinter-proof screens for main magazines ('D' steel) and a small 4in bulkhead on the after end of the steering compartment. The ships had a double-bottom 4 feet deep.

MACHINERY

In 1928 the Post-War Questions Committee examined the requirements for a superior battleship and its conclusion was: 'A slight superiority in battlefleet speed on either side is of little account.' With this in mind and the fact that it would still be to some advantage to have at least equality with most of the foreign battleships at sea, the terms for the Royal Navy's new ships were laid down. At first the suggested speed was only 21 knots' which was much slower than the *Nelson* and *Queen Elizabeth* classes. In October 1928 the Board considered the following alternatives: 'Either design for 21 knots with the purpose of maintaining that speed throughout the

life of the ship, or design for 23 knots, which would be obtained by forcing the boilers and which would be subject to reduction with age.'

The conclusion reached was that the best policy was to aim for a speed of 23 knots in the standard condition and that a greater forcing of the boilers than had previously been allowed should become common practice. The figures were based on a ship of 35,000 tons and carrying 16in guns. In 1929 when the matter of a smaller battleship was being investigated the question of speed was aired: 'The staff were unable to recommend a policy of increasing speed at the expense of main battleship requirements'. At this meeting the notion of 'a balance' in speed from the tactical point of view was put forward and it was pointed out that if battle fleet speeds increased, so too would the speeds of other new types of vessels which would have to keep up with them. The DNC Department did not like or accept this view and, even at the expense of another 1,000 tons, it was thought necessary to raise the speed of the new battleship to at least

25 knots. The argument about high speeds was based on the supposition that speeds would rise in the future in all types of ships and that high speeds were essential to deal with the attack of 'extraneous weapons'.

It became extremely difficult to work out the propulsive power that could be worked into the new ships. Moreover there were many reports reaching the Admiralty regarding speeds of the modernized Japanese battle fleet, and it was known that the French fleet and reconstructed Italian ships were all showing greater speeds than before. In the light of this it was almost impossible for the Committee and the DNC not to give the new ships a speed of at least 26 knots, and when the final legend was drawn up the speed had risen to 27 knots – which was still considered by many to be too slow.

As built the machinery consisted of Parsons single-geared reduction turbines driving four screws. There were separate cruising turbines and they were arranged in four separate engine rooms in four compartments. Eight Admiralty 3-

CUIRASSÉ

Left: Aerial view of *Duke of York* in 1943, showing additional AA guns mounted on the forecastle near the breakwater.

Preliminary Steam Trials
King George V: Displacement 41,700 tons. 108,290shp = 28.4kts.
Prince of Wales: Displacement 42,650 tons. 111,900shp = 27½kts.
Duke of York: Displacement 42,550 tons. 111,300shp = 28.6kts.
Anson: Displacement 42,600 tons. 111,850shp = 27.62kts.
Howe: Displacement 42,630 tons. 112,105shp = 27½kts.

Duke of York: Trials, 1 November 1941
Ship complete with ammunition plus 35 tons trial ammunition.
Displacement: 42 ,970 tons.
Under way 08.30 hours. Firth of Forth.
Full power trials commenced 12.00 hours.
Sea: slight.
Wind: moderate.
Mean SHP: 28,720.
RPM: 153.
Speed: 20.6 knots.
Mean SHP: 111,200.
RPM: 232.
Speed: 28.6 knots.
Constructor and DNC aboard.

drum boilers in four compartments with a working pressure of 380–410psi. Steam temperature was 750°. Machinery and boilers were arranged alternately to reduce the risk of complete disablement. It was reported that the cruising turbines were seldom used during the war as the fleet speed was set at a knot or two above their capability and so they could not be employed.

BRIDGEWORK

The bridgework of *King George V* was basically a development of that in *Nelson* and *Rodney* but was a more square-shaped construction with a less pointed front. Over the years it was found that although *Nelson* was much better bridgewise than previous classes of battleships with their open tripod fittings, there was still a considerable back draught throughout the bridge and compass platform, especially if the doors were left open.

In an endeavour to alleviate this problem a slightly lower and more square flat-faced superstructure was chosen after many tests of a modified *Nelson*-type structure had been carried out at the National Physical Laboratory from 1934 to 1936. As completed, however, it was found in practice that although less draught was evident

Right: *Anson* in 1942. As completed, *Anson* and *Howe* were extremely difficult to tell apart.

Below right: *King George V* on 4 February 1943.

as compared to *Nelson,* there were still cross-flows of draught up and over the various levels at knee height.

Further tests were carried out from 1940 to 1943 in the interests of future battleship construction, but it seems that the situation was never rectifed – even for *Vanguard* (1944), the last British battleship. Although it had probably the best-designed and constructed forward superstructure fitted in a British ship, *KGV* was never draught-free, just more tolerable than most of the older ships. The problem was that the more closed-in and draught-free a bridge structure was, the less vision the staff had. A more open structure obviously meant strong or severe draughts and the answer had to be a compromise to attain an acceptable level.

Throughout the history of British battleship construction from 1906 to 1944 (*Dreadnought* to *Vanguard*), many tests were undertaken (as seen in previous chapters), all leading to the final conclusion that a sharp-faced or round front was far worse regarding draught and up-winds than a less streamlined, flat-faced type of structure. It was proved that the wind hitting the flat face would disperse around the sides rather than carry on across as it did with rounded off edges or smooth, streamlined fittings.

The open bridgework of the *Queen Elizabeth, Royal Sovereign, Renown* and *Hood* types were at best practicable; at worst they proved downright uncomfortable, but it was claimed that from the point of view of fighting efficiency they were much easier to man and were more favoured by the personnel than the closed-in efforts that became normal in all new battleships and reconstructions throughout the 1930s.

APPEARANCE CHANGES, MODIFICATIONS AND REFITS

The ships were very distinctive, with a long, low flush deck hull with very slight sheer forward. They had very large superstructures that were separated amidships by catapult space. The forward superstructure and bridge tower was especially massive. Large quadruple turret forward and aft with twin turret in superfiring position forward. Secondary turrets port and starboard amidships in two groups. Large, flat-sided strongly ribbed funnels spaced well apart. Searchlight platform on second funnel.

Prominent aircraft crane port and starboard over catapult space amidships. Rocket projectors or light AA guns on 'B' and 'Y' turrets. Very light rig: light tripod masts. Main tripod legs raked forward. Short topmast to each mast, no topgallants. Radar aerial at head of each topmast. Prominent radar aerial screen (lantern type) on foretop in *Anson* and *Howe.*

Individual differences:
King George V:
1. Rocket projectors on 'B' and 'Y' turrets and right aft on quarterdeck (removed 1941–2 and replaced on turrets by multiple 2pdrs).
2. Lantern radar screen on bridge tower between HA directors (relocated on foretop 1941–2).
3. Type 279 radar aerial at each masthead.
4. External degaussing cable (relocated internally later).
5. Square ports right aft.

Others:
1. Multiple 2pdrs on 'B' and 'Y' turrets (*Anson, Duke of York* and *Howe*). Rocket projectors (*Prince of Wales*) replaced by 2pdrs 1941.
2. Lantern screen on bridge tower (*Prince of Wales*), foretop (others). Added in *Duke of York* 1941.
3. Type 279 radar aerials at mastheads (*Howe*). Replaced by Type 281 in 1943.
4. Internal deguassing cables.
5. Round ports right aft.

Prince of Wales:
1. Single 40mm in breastwork right aft (only ship thus).
1941–2
1. Radar control (Type 285) fitted for 5.25in guns in *King George V* and *Prince of Wales,* as others (by June 1941 in *Prince of Wales*). Multiple 2pdr mounting (8 barrels) added on 'B' and 'Y' turrets in *King George V* and *Prince of Wales* (June 1941 in *Prince of Wales*). Rocket projectors removed from both ships. Nine 20mm AA (singles) added in *Duke of York* (May/June 1942): five on forecastle abaft breakwater, four on quarterdeck. Four 20mm (singles) added on quarterdeck in *King George V,* replacing rocket projector.
2. Surface warning radar (Type 271) added in *Duke of York.* Aerial in lantern screen on foretop.
3. Protection to magazines and machinery fur-

ther improved in *King George V* and *Prince of Wales* in 1941 following loss of *Hood.* Other three ships similarly modified while building.
4. Camouflage painted up in *King George V* and *Prince of Wales.*

1943
Howe:
Air warning radar Type 279 replaced by Type 281 (March 1943).

1944–5:
1. Type 284 radar on forward 14in director replaced by Type 274. Type 274 fitted to after director as well in all except *King George V* (Type 285). New Mk 6 directors with Type 275 radar fitted for secondary armament in *Anson* only. Quadruple 40mm AA mounting added port and starboard on after superstructure abeam mainmast. Eight 40mm (singles) added in *Howe* (1945): two port and starboard on lower bridge, two in place of SL on second funnel, two port and starboard on forecastle and quarterdeck. Two 40mm (singles) added port and starboard on superstructure abaft second funnel in *King George V.* Four multiple 2pdr AA (8 barrels) added in all. Two port and starboard on superstructure abaft second funnel and on quarterdeck (not certain that *Howe* and *King George V* had after pair). Four multiple 2pdr AA (4 barrels) added in *Anson* and *Duke of York*: two port and starboard on lower bridge and on upper deck abeam rear of 'B' turret. Some or all 20mm AA removed. *King George V* carried two in place of the SL abaft forefunnel. Additional light AA directors (Type 283 radar) fitted port and starboard on superstructure abeam and abaft second funnel in all, in place of SL abaft forefunnel in *Anson* and *Duke of York* and on centreline abaft mainmast in *Duke of York* and *King George V* (*Anson* and *Howe* completed thus). Type 282 radar control to LAA directors where fitted replaced by Type 283.
2. Surface warning radar Type 271 replaced by Type 277. Air surface warning radar Type 293 added. Aerial at head of foretopmast in place of forward Type 281 aerial. Identification (IFF) radar Type 242 fitted high on foretopmast and at head of maintopmast. HF/DF aerial added right aft on quarterdeck in all. VHF radio communication equipment fitted in *Anson,* aerials on main tripod legs.

Right: An excellent view of *Howe* in 1944, showing her camouflage and extensive radar aerials.

3. Searchlights removed from bridge and abaft forefunnel in *Anson* and *Duke of York* and from bridge and second funnel in *Howe* and from abaft forefunnel in *King George V*.

4. Aircraft and catapult removed (1944), cranes retained for boats. *King George V* reported to have been the last British battleship to fly-off its own aircraft.

5. Superstructure built up between second funnel and mainmast and boat stowage shifted to catapult deck.

6. Heavier foretopmast fitted to carry the additional radar aerials.

7. Pacific camouflage painted up (1945).

Appearance was very cluttered with many light AA guns and numerous radar aerials, etc., but no major changes. Any type of camouflage deleted by later 1945.

Individual differences:

Anson 1. Very large secondary directors (only ship thus). 2. Multiple 2pdr mounting port and starboard on lower bridge and upper deck abeam 'B' turret. 3. Prominent DF aerials on main tripod legs.

Duke of York 1. SL platform on second funnel extended well forward. 2. Multiple 2pdrs as *Anson*.

Howe 1. Forward of SL platform around second funnel enlarged and enclosed. 2. AA guns in place of SL on this platform.

King George V 1. 20mm guns in place of SL abaft forefunnel. 2. Type 279 radar aerial at head of mainmast (Type 281 in others).

1945
1. DF aerial on quarterdeck removed.

1946-8
1. All 2pdrs and 20mm AA (with exception of two 20mm in *King George V* removed; 2pdr mountings retained on turrets and superstructure. 2pdrs removed from *Howe* and *King George V* in early 1946. Quarterdeck 2pdrs removed from *Anson* and *Duke of York* in 1946, others 1947-8. Quadruple 40mm AA retained in all plus four singles in *Anson* (on bridge and second funnel platform) and two in *King George V* (abaft second funnel).

Particulars of ships in 1945
Original length and beam.
Displacement (tons): *King George V* 44,460 tons; *Duke of York* 44,790 tons; *Anson* 45,360 tons; *Howe* 45,400 tons. All deep load.

Draught had risen about 1½ft with an average addition of 1,500 tons per ship since 1941.
Average draught: 35ft 10in to 38ft 3in deep load.
Armament
Original main and secondary. Light AA guns were variable throughout the class. 8 x 16 x 40mm AA. Two quadruples in all plus 8 singles in *Howe* and 2 in *King George V*. 80–96 x 2pdr. 10 x 8 barrels in all plus four quadruples in *Anson* and *Duke of York*. Nil to 4 x 20mm AA. All guns except single 40mm and 20mm were radar controlled.
RDF: Type 274 for main armament. 275 for secondary in *Anson*, 285 in others. Type 283 for light AA. Air warning Type 279 in *King Goerge V* and 281 in others. Surface warning Type 277. Air/surface warning Type 277. IFF Type 242. HF/DF and MF/DF. VHF communication in *Anson*.
Searchlights: 4 x 44in *King George V*; others 2 x 44in; 2 x 24in signalling in all.
Aircraft: All removed including most of the equipment.

2. VHF equipment removed from *Anson* (1946-7).

All laid-up from 1950-1.

BATTLE DAMAGE

Prince of Wales Bomb Damage, 31 August 1940

While fitting-out at Cammell Lairds, *Prince of Wales* was subjected to a low-level bombing attack during which she was struck by a 250lb bomb. The raid took place at about 20.30 and *Prince of Wales*, whilst lying in the fitting-out basin, was hit at 20.40. The bomb actually exploded between the basin wall and the hull of the ship, causing damage to the hull plating. There was flooding to the port longitudinal protective bulkhead and the ship heeled to about 8 degrees. Water rose in the lower deck compartments (184–228) to about 18 inches below the middle deck. The lower deck was flooded through holes which had recently been made for the internal degaussing cable. The ship had to be dry-docked once more and the damage was repaired without any serious delay to her completion.

Armour: as original with some minor modifications to the magazines and machinery areas.
Machinery: as original.
Speed: slight reduction owing to additional weights added during the war. Admiral Vian reported that *King George V* could not manage more than 26 knots by 1945.
Aircraft hangars utilized for officers and cinema space.
Boats stowed on catapult deck.
Rig: Original except for heavier foretop mast.
Appearance: Very cluttered with AA guns, radar aerials, etc., but no major changes.
Individual differences (1945)
Anson: Very large secondary directors (only ship thus). Multiple 2pdr mountings P&S on lower bridge and upper deck abeam 'B' turret. Prominent DF aerials on main tripod legs.
Duke of York: SL platform on second funnel extended well forward. Multiple 2pdrs as in *Anson*.
Howe: Forward section of SL platform around second funnel was enlarged and enclosed. AA guns in place of SL on this platform.
King George V: 20mm guns in place of SL abaft fore funnel. 279 RDF aerial at head of mainmast (281 in others).

Duke of York action against Scharnhorst, 26 December 1943

Although *Duke of York*'s action against the German battlecruiser *Scharnhorst* was an overwhelming success, she received some damage. The battle damage report is given below:
'*Duke of York* sustained no serious structural damage due to enemy action with the exception of one hit from an 11in shell which passed through the port strut of the mainmast and the mainmast itself. The shell did not explode but carried away about two-thirds of the structure of both mast and strut in the track of the shell.
1. Extremely hasty repairs were carried out at Kola Inlet by welding on steel straps and the ship's staff performed well in making staging for and carrying out these repairs in distinctly difficult conditions.
2. The repairs, although of some help, could certainly not be considered effective and, since the ship experienced fairly bad weather on the passage back to Scapa, the fact that the mainmast stood is regarded as a definite tribute to the tripod system of construction.
3. The damage in *Duke of York* to weather deck fittings, particularly mushroom heads and covers to ventilation openings and lengths of ventilation trunking below the upper deck, was severe and

392 KING GEORGE V CLASS

extensive. This damage was mainly due to blast from the 14in broadsides but was accentuated somewhat by the trunking systems filling with heavy quantities of water due to continuous hard driving in bad weather before, during and after the action with *Scharnhorst*.

4. The potential weaknesses of the ventilation system were already well known, as ample experience had been gained in all ships of the *King George V* class. The present action experience, with the ventilation system extensively damaged by blast, strongly emphasized the urgent need for fitting the stronger type steel or metal weather deck ventilation valves instead of the existing

aluminium type. Most of these stronger valves were ordered months ago for all four ships and every opportunity taken to fit the new type of valve to all ventilation openings in the weather deck including those openings not yet fitted with a valve.

5. In addition, the trunking below the weather deck developed numerous gaping cracks through which water poured into the living spaces. As renewal by stronger trunking of the round section is hardly practicable in wartime, it is necessary for the corners of all trunking liable to exposure to gun blast to be reinforced by extensive strapping.

6. Weather deck leakage also developed through bolt fastenings of Oerlikon screens and ammunition lockers and rivet fastenings of breakwaters, skylights and girders under the upper deck. These leaks were numerous and mainly due to the whip of the forecastle deck under blast from forward arcs of fire; the breakwater defects were due to heavy seas. Pillars under the upper deck suffered from blast and dished washers between the heel of the pillar and the main deck appear to assist the tap rivets securing the heels of these pillars. It is clear that the weather deck fittings should be secured in general by welding instead of through fastenings. Many of the fittings caus-

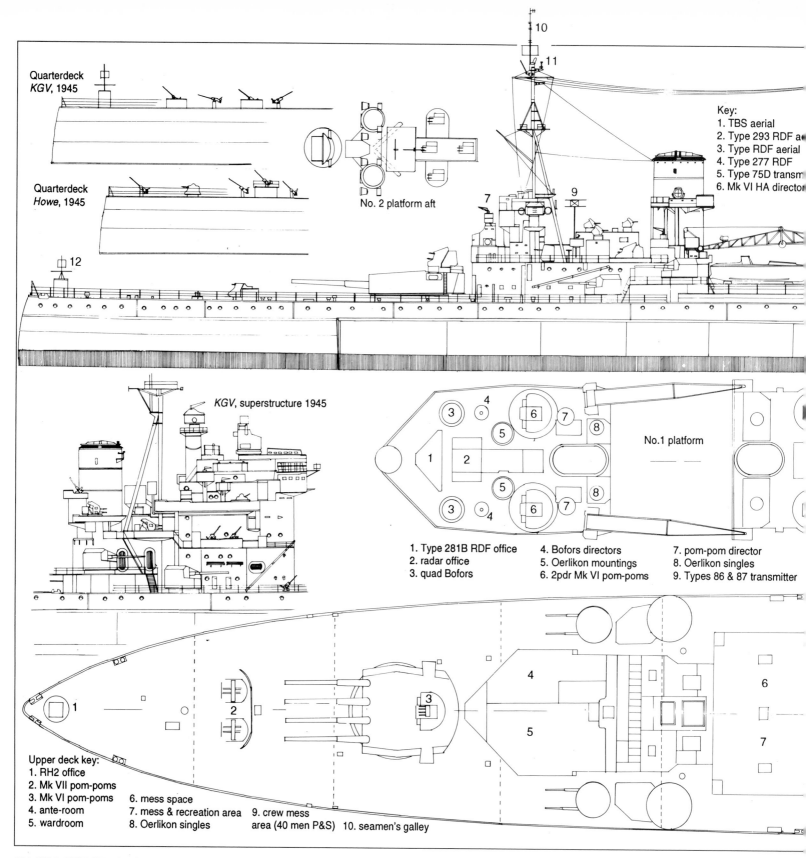

Quarterdeck
KGV, 1945

Quarterdeck
Howe, 1945

12

10

11

No. 2 platform aft

7

9

KGV, superstructure 1945

No.1 platform

4

3

5

6

7

8

1

2

3

5

6

7

8

4

1. Type 281B RDF office
2. radar office
3. quad Bofors
4. Bofors directors
5. Oerlikon mountings
6. 2pdr Mk VI pom-poms
7. pom-pom director
8. Oerlikon singles
9. Types 86 & 87 transmitter

1

2

3

4

5

6

7

Upper deck key:
1. RH2 office
2. Mk VII pom-poms
3. Mk VI pom-poms
4. ante-room
5. wardroom
6. mess space
7. mess & recreation area
8. Oerlikon singles
9. crew mess
area (40 men P&S)
10. seamen's galley

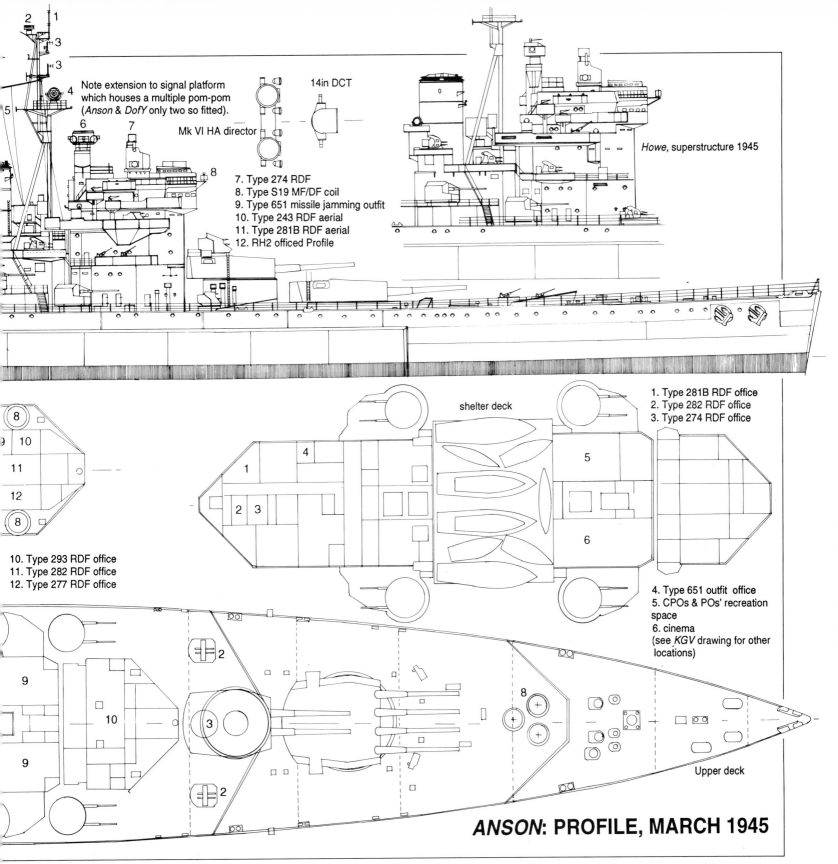

Note extension to signal platform which houses a multiple pom-pom (*Anson* & *DofY* only two so fitted).

14in DCT

Mk VI HA director

7. Type 274 RDF
8. Type S19 MF/DF coil
9. Type 651 missile jamming outfit
10. Type 243 RDF aerial
11. Type 281B RDF aerial
12. RH2 officed Profile

Howe, superstructure 1945

shelter deck

1. Type 281B RDF office
2. Type 282 RDF office
3. Type 274 RDF office

10. Type 293 RDF office
11. Type 282 RDF office
12. Type 277 RDF office

4. Type 651 outfit office
5. CPOs & POs' recreation space
6. cinema
(see *KGV* drawing for other locations)

Upper deck

***ANSON*: PROFILE, MARCH 1945**

ing leakage had been secured by bolting when little time and labour were available for using alternative methods.

7. Severe leakage occurred past "A" barbette on the main deck and weather shields around these barbettes, particulary "A", are a necessity for bad weather.

8. Some leakage occurred into the fire control rooms, 14in magazines, action machinery rooms and power control room through the ventilation system and this might easily have proved serious since some fans went out of action from this cause.

9. Altogether the large amount of water which accumulated below presented a serious and continuous problem which was dealt with later.

10. An interesting case of blast damage occurred in "Y" boiler room where the divisional plates above the eyes of the boiler room fans were split open at middle deck level.

11. As will be seen from the above the damage was confined to subsidiary equipment with effects which, although highly inconvenient and in some cases temporarily serious, did not affect the main structure of the ship. It is satisfactory to note that, in spite of the more or less continuous hard driving to which the ship was subjected in the course of these operations, no structural failure occurred.

12. Radar Type 281, F.V.1, 91 and 251M, W/T Type 75D were put out of action by wiring being severed.

13. Gun armament – No damage was caused by enemy action to the main armament. Five Oerlikon shields and the supports on the forecastle were extensively damaged by weather and blast and had to be scrapped before the homeward passage. P2 and S2 the GRU was blown from its supports, all by blast from "Y" turret. Repairs were made after arrival in harbour the following day.'

HISTORY: KING GEORGE V

The ship would normally have been named after the reigning monarch, King George VI, but was named *King George V* at the special request of the King to commemorate his father.

1936 Programme
Laid down by Vickers-Armstrongs, Newcastle-on-Tyne, 1 January 1937. Launched 21

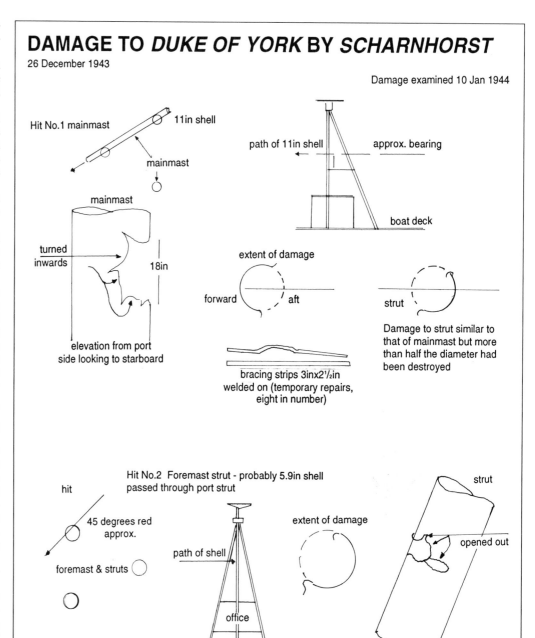

DAMAGE TO *DUKE OF YORK* BY *SCHARNHORST*

26 December 1943

Damage examined 10 Jan 1944

Hit No.1 mainmast   11in shell

path of 11in shell   approx. bearing

mainmast

boat deck

mainmast

turned inwards   18in

extent of damage

forward   aft

strut

Damage to strut similar to that of mainmast but more than half the diameter had been destroyed

elevation from port side looking to starboard

bracing strips 3inx2½in welded on (temporary repairs, eight in number)

Hit No.2 Foremast strut - probably 5.9in shell passed through port strut   strut

hit

45 degrees red approx.   extent of damage

path of shell   opened out

foremast & struts

office

hangar top   elevation looking forward

February 1939.
Commissioned at Newcastle 1 October 1940 for 2nd Battle Squadron, Home Fleet. Joined Fleet at Scapa 2 December 1940.

HOME FLEET
December 1940 to May 1943 (2nd BS to April 1941, fleet flag later).
Conveyed Lord Halifax to the United States as British Ambassador, January 1941. Left Scapa 15 January and arrived at Annapolis on the 24th. Left for home on the 25th, escorting a special convoy, and rejoined Home Fleet at Scapa late February.
Unit of covering force for Lofoten Islands Raid 4 March 1941.
Temporarily attached to the Battlecruiser Squadron, Home Fleet, early March 1941.
Took part March to May 1941 in covering Halifax convoys against possible attack by enemy heavy ships, specifically *Scharnhorst*, *Scheer*, and *Hipper*.
Relieved *Nelson* as fleet flag, Home Fleet 1 April 1941.
Took part in operations against *Bismarck* and *Prinz Eugen* 22–27 May 1941 and with *Rodney* in destruction of *Bismarck* on 27th, experiencing difficulties with main armament during this action.
Took part in search for *Scheer* and *Prinz Eugen* off Norwegian coast 20–23 February 1942.
Flag of covering force for Russia convoys March to May 1942.
From 6 to 10 March a force comprising *King George V* (flag), *Renown* (flag VA), *Duke of York*, *Victorious*, *Berwick* and twelve destroyers provided special cover for an outward and homeward convoy during a sortie by *Tirpitz*.
Contact with *Tirpitz* established off the Lofoten Islands by aircraft from *Victorious* but a torpedo attack by these failed and the German ship was able to return to base without being brought to action. Convoys not attacked.
Rammed and sank *Punjabi*, one of her screening destroyers, in low visibility on 1 May 1942 during Russian convoy operation. Sustained considerable damage to bows and also damaged by explosion of *Punjabi*'s depth charges.
Refitted by Cammell Laird, Birkenhead, May to July 1942, flag behind transferred to *Duke of York* on 6 May.
Rejoined fleet at Scapa and reverted to flag CinC

11 July.
Unit of covering force for Russia convoy January 1943.
Transferred to Force H (Gibraltar) with *Howe*, May 1943 for Sicily invasion.
Left Scapa for Gibraltar 21 May.

FORCE H
(Gibraltar) May to October 1943 (flag May to June).
Temporary flag of Force H May to June, relieving *Nelson* for working-up at Scapa.
Flag reverted to *Nelson* 23 June.
Took part in invasion of Sicily in July and Italy in September.
With *Howe* intended to serve as a reserve for Force H in these operations to carry out diversionary bombardments, assault convoys and replace any other Force H battleships that might be disabled.
On night of 10/11 July both ships carried out bombardment of Marsala and Trapani on west coast of Sicily to simulate another intended landing and pin down enemy troops.
Stationed at Augusta 7 September with *Howe* as reserve force for Salerno landings but detached on the 8th, following the signing of the Italian armistice, as unit of special squadron (under command Vice-Admiral Malta) comprising *Howe* (flag), *King George V*, four cruisers of the 12th CS and the minelayer *Abdiel* sent to Taranto to occupy and hold the port. Force entered Taranto 10 September.
With *Howe* escorted the larger of the surrendered Italian warships from Malta to Alexandria 14–16 September.
Left Alexandria 1 October to rejoin Home Fleet.

HOME FLEET
(2nd BS) October 1943 to February 1944.
Detached December 1943 to bring Prime Minister home from the Cairo Conference.
Withdrawn from Home Fleet February 1944 to refit prior to transfer to Eastern Fleet.
Refit by Cammell Laird, Birkenhead February to July 1944.
Worked-up at Scapa and left for Ceylon 28 October 1944.
Proceeded via Suez Canal and bombarded Lakida Battery on enemy-held island of Milos in the Aegean 15 November 1944 while en route through the Mediterranean.

Left Alexandria 1 December, arrived Trincomalee 15 December and transferred to the Pacific Fleet then being formed there (see *Howe*).

PACIFIC FLEET
2 BS December 1944 to January 1946 (Flag VA 1st BS and 2nd fleet flag February to October 1945).
Left Trincomalee for Pacific Fleet base at Sydney Australia on 19 January 1945 together with *Indomitable* (flag RA carriers), *Illustrious*, *Victorious*, *Indefatigable*, *Argonaut Black Prince*, *Euryalus* and ten destroyers, the force carrying out air attacks on oil refineries at Palembang, Sumatra, on 24 and 29 January while en route.
Arrived Fremantle 4 February where flag Vice-Admiral second in command Pacific Fleet hoisted in *King George V*.
Arrived Sydney 10 February.
At Sydney flag CinC Pacific Fleet transferred ashore from *Howe*, the Vice-Admiral in *King George V* assuming seagoing command.
Fleet left Sydney for operational area 28 February 1945.
Joined US 5th Fleet and commenced operations against the Japanese 26 March 1945, being designated Task Force 57.
Carried out bombardments of Japanese airfields on Formosa and Sakashima Gunto Islands March to May 1945 as part of the Okinawa campaign.
On 4 May with *Howe* and cruisers bombarded airfields on Mikayo Shima in the Sakishima Gunto group of islands.
On 27 May the US 5th Fleet became the 3rd Fleet, following a change in command, and the British Pacific Fleet was renumbered Task Force 37.
On 17 and 29 July *King George V* took part with US fleet ships in bombardments of industrial areas on Japanese coast north of Tokyo, being the only British battleship in the operational area, *Howe* having been withdrawn earlier in July for refit.
Flag of British Force, comprising *King George V*, *Indefatigable*, *Gambia*, *Newfoundland* and ten destroyers, selected on 12 August 1945 to remain with the US Fleet off Japan following news of the impending Japanese surrender, the remainder of the British Pacific Fleet returning to Australia.

Present at the signing of the Japanese surrender aboard USS *Missouri* in Tokyo Bay 2 September 1945.
Relieved as flag 1st BS by *Anson* October 1945 at which time flag VA 1st Carrier Squadron replaced flag VA 1st Battle Squadron as 2nd fleet flag.
Refit Sydney October to December 1945.
Conveyed Duke and Duchess of Gloucester from Sydney to Hobart, Tasmnia, December 1945.
Returned home March 1946. Arrived Portsmouth on the 1st.
Relieved *Nelson* as flag Home Fleet 9 April 1946.

HOME FLEET
April 1946 to September 1949 (flag to December 1946. Training Squadron Portland from May 1948).
Relieved as flag by *Duke of York* December 1946.
Refit Devonport December 1946 to November 1947.
Joined Home Fleet Training Squadron, Portland, May 1948, replacing *Howe*.
Reduced to reserve, Portsmouth, September 1949 until April 1957 (Portsmouth to June 1950. C. Category Clyde later).
Laid up in Clyde in extended reserve (C Category) June 1950.
Placed on Disposal List 30 April 1957.
Sold to Arnott Young, Dalmuir, January 1958.
Arrived Dalmuir for scrapping 20 January 1958.
Hulk arrived Troon for final demolition December 1958.

HISTORY: PRINCE OF WALES

1937 Programme. Laid down by Cammell Laird 1 January 1937.
Launched 3 May 1939.
Commissioned at Birkenhead 18 January 1941 for 2nd Battle Squadron, Home Fleet.
Joined Fleet at Scapa 25 March 1941 in incomplete state with contractors' men still on board. Two turrets not finally handed over to the Admiralty until 27 April 1941.

HOME FLEET (2nd BS) January to September 1941 (flag VA 2nd BS and 2nd Fleet flag from July).
Left Scapa 22 May 1941 with *Hood* and destroyers *Icarus*, *Echo*, *Electra*, *Achates*, *Antelope* and *Anthony* to cover area south-west of Iceland and

Below: *King George V* leaving Sydney with the Duke and Duchess of Gloucester for Tasmania and the UK, January 1946.

support cruisers *Norfolk* and *Suffolk* in Denmark Strait following report of sortie by *Bismarck* and *Prinz Eugen*.
German ships sighted on 24 May and action opened at about 25,000 yards. Scored two hits on *Bismarck*, flooding one boiler room, reducing speed, causing oil leak and putting ship one to two degrees down by head. Received five hits by 15in shells and three by 8in. One 15in hit on compass platform and killed or wounded nearly all bridge personnel although CO unhurt. Broke off action owing to turret failures, serious damage to bridge and four hundred tons of water shipped.
Refitted at Rosyth May to July.
Rejoined Fleet 16 July as flag VA 2nd BS and 2nd fleet flag.
Detached 4 August 1941 to take Prime Minister to and from the Atlantic Charter Conference with the President of the United States, held on board at Placentia Bay, Newfoundland, on 10th.
Rejoined Fleet at Scapa 18 August. Flag temporarily transferred to depot ship at Scapa during this period.
Temporarily attached to Force H (Gibraltar) September 1941 for Malta convoy but continued

to wear flag VA 2nd BS.
Left Clyde with convoy 17 September.
Force H (Gibraltar) September to October 1941.
Malta convoy 24–30 September.
Rejoined Home Fleet early October.
Reached Cape Town on 16 November and Colombo on the 28th where *Repulse* joined and the Force was given the code-name Force 'Z'. Arrived Singapore 2 December.

EASTERN FLEET (Force 'Z' Singapore) November to December 1941.
Force 'Z', comprising *Prince of Wales* (flag) and *Repulse*, with the destroyers *Electra*, *Express*, *Vampire* and *Tenedos*, left Singapore on 8 December 1941 to attack supply lines for a Japanese invasion force which had landed on the east coast of Malaya during the night of 7/8th.
The original plan for the formation of the Eastern Fleet was to concentrate *Nelson*, *Rodney*, *Repulse* and four *R* Class battleships with appropriate number of cruisers and destroyers and for them to proceed in company to Singapore, but it was not thought that such a fleet could arrive at Singapore before the spring of 1942 for the following reasons:

1. The necessity for refitting ships before leaving UK, and equipping them with the most modern RDF available. 2. Light craft could not be made available without reducing the Home Fleet, Mediterranean Fleet and the ships required for the Battle of the Atlantic. No modern aircraft carrier was available at that time because: 1. *Illustrious* and *Formidable* were not ready to leave the UK before February 1942. 2. *Victorious* had to remain at home, being the only operational carrier with the Home Fleet. 3. There were urgent demands for two modern carriers in the eastern Mediterranean and one modern carrier with Force 'H'.

It had been hoped to send *Ark Royal* to the Eastern Fleet when her refit in America was complete in about April 1942.

Revenge arrived at Durban on 28 September, *Repulse* on 3 November and *Royal Sovereign* on 17 December. *Ramillies* left the UK on 8 December and *Resolution* was due to leave on 7 January. The plan to send *Nelson* and *Rodney* proved abortive when *Nelson* was torpedoed and it became necessary to change *Rodney*'s guns. By 21 October the situation in the Far East had deteriorated and it was decided to send *Prince of Wales* instead of *Rodney*. She arrived at Colombo on 28 November and reached Singapore in company with *Repulse* on 2 December. To provide the necessary screen for *Prince of Wales* two Home Fleet destroyers and two Mediterranean Fleet destroyers (both of which could be ill afforded) plus four Australian destroyers (which it had been planned would be added at a later date) were sent along. In addition the US Navy promised eight destroyers to bridge the gap until sufficient destroyers could be made available (four of these arrived at Singapore shortly after Admiral Phillips had left on 8 December).

The reason for sending *Prince of Wales* and *Repulse* to Singapore prior to the concentration of the Eastern Fleet was that it was hoped that they would act as a deterrent to the Japanese threat. If, however, Japan decided to take the plunge it was hoped that these ships might prevent them sending their expeditionary force into the Gulf of Siam. It was realized that it was within the ability of the Japanese to bring down a much superior force, but it was felt that the strong American Fleet at Hawaii would deter them from doing so.

On 1 December the Admiralty suggested that *Prince of Wales* and *Repulse* disappear into the blue, and that the uncertainty of their whereabouts would disconcert the Japanese, but the appearance of Japanese submarines off Saigon meant that to put to sea without adequate back-up forces would be unwise.

In judging the action of the Commander-in-Chief, Eastern Fleet, one must strike a balance between what is known now and what we think he knew when he took his decision to put to sea. He had no definite knowledge that Japanese aircraft carriers were in the Gulf of Siam. War experience had shown that high-speed warships with full freedom of manoeuvre would have a good chance of avoiding torpedo aircraft attack, earlier torpedo attacks on the enemy having borne this out. It must be remembered that it was only the third attack on *Bismarck* that did vital damage. Neither he nor the Admiralty had any reason to suppose that the Japanese torpedo aircraft were in fact of a higher degree of efficiency than the British. The weather was such that detection and attacks by aircraft would be very difficult to execute (a north-eastern monsoon was blowing). The fact that the weather cleared not only on the evening of the 9th but also in the morning of 10 December was seen to be unusual. Admiral Phillips was operating at such a distance from enemy shore-based aircraft in Indo-China that the chance of a torpedo attack from them could with all fairness be considered minimal. He probably reckoned that the destruction of the large Japanese convoy (known to be in the Gulf of Siam on 7 December) might well turn the scale of military operations in the Malay Peninsula decisively in favour of the Allies. It would be idle to say that the Admiralty was not anxious about these ships. They considered that the submarine risk was the most potent and that Admiral Phillips would have to rely on the high speed of his ships to avoid danger. The air threat was appreciated, but with the incomplete information available to the Admiralty at that time it was felt that Admiral Phillips was in the best position to assess the threat.

Admiral Phillips realized the danger of sailing into this area without fighter protection, hence his request for it. The facts that he could not have it and that the weather had cleared were probably the factors that induced him to return to Singapore on the night of the 9th.

LOSS OF PRINCE OF WALES

1. *Prince of Wales*, *Repulse* and four destroyers left Singapore after dark on 8 December. Before sailing the Commander-in-Chief asked for: (a) reconnaissance 100 miles to the north of force at daylight on 9 December; (b) 100 miles mid point Singgora, 10 miles from coast leaving first light on the 19th; (c) fighter protection off Singgora daylight 10 December. After sailing the CinC was informed that it was hoped to provide (a) and (b) but not (c).
2. At 1700 on 9 December the weather cleared and *Prince of Wales* was sighted by Japanese aircraft. Phillips decided to return to Singapore at full speed.
3. At midnight on 9/10 December he was informed that a landing was taking place at Kuantan and he decided to investigate. At about 1000 shadowing aircraft were again observed and at 1115 air attacks on *Prince of Wales* and *Repulse* began.

The attack developed in several waves (see *Repulse*), being carried out by high-level bombers and torpedo-bombers. *Prince of Wales* was hit by six torpedoes and one bomb (no hit in first attack with bombs). In the second attack (torpedo) *Prince of Wales* was hit aft by two torpedoes which crippled her rudder and both port propellers. One shaft was torn off, ripping a large hole in the hull and causing the port turbines to race to destruction. The ship listed 13° out of control and speed reduced to less than 15 knots. She was also incapable of manoeuvring.

The third attack was directed entirely at *Repulse*.

The fourth attack saw *Prince of Wales* being hit by four more torpedoes, forward, midships and aft on the starboard side, and in the final attack one bomb penetrated the catapult deck and blew out the side of the ship. Following this the ship settled rapidly and capsized two hours after the first hit. *Electra*, *Express* and *Vampire* picked up 90 officers and 1,195 ratings. Twenty officers, including the Admiral and Captain, and 307 ratings were lost. On hearing of the disaster the Press had a field day, levelling severe criticism at the government and those responsible within the Admiralty staff. Headlines were displayed everywhere.

1. *Sunday Express* criticized the tradition by which the Admiral and Captain on board *Prince of Wales* went down with their ship.

2. *Daily Herald* (1) alleged delay of CinC Eastern Fleet in asking for fighter support; (2) alleged delay in their arrival when asked for and (3) asked why was there a change of course to the northward after being sighted by Japanese reconnaissance aircraft.

3. *Evening Standard* asked whether there were enough aircraft in Malaya for both military and naval needs.

4. *Daily Express* and *News Chronicle*: Gravity of initial loss of airfields not appreciated; folly of divided responsibility for airfields' defence.

5. *Daily Herald*: Unpreparedness in Far East especially in mechanized equipment.

6. *Daily Mirror*: The higher Command should be sacked for not appreciating the importance of air protection for ships at sea. Also quoted a similar demand made by *Sydney Daily Telegraph*.

7. *Daily Mail* (Sydney Correspondent) Revelation in Australia by the Minister for External Affairs that the Australian Government had suggested an agreement with Russia that either nation would make war on Japan if Japan attacked the other, but that the suggestion had been turned down.

8. *News Chronicle*. Naval losses were due to failure of inter-service co-operation. Navy mainly to blame (no reason given, the article went on to show that the chief omission was proper defence of the aerodrome at Kota Bharu). The same was said by several other papers.

9. Letter from Admiral Bacon to *The Times*: 'Battleships should not be used to repel invasion. It is most disquieting to find the First Lord to be still of the opinion that battleships can be used for inshore operations.'

As can be seen the loss of *Prince of Wales* and *Repulse* caused dismay and misgivings throughout the country, coming, as it did, within a few days of the Prime Minister's announcement of the opportune arrival of these two fine ships at Singapore. To those who were aware of the superiority and strength of the Japanese fleet and its naval air service it was obvious that this small squadron would not be able to operate far from the protection of Singapore and the fighter cover of the RAF. Sir Roger Keyes, writing in the *News Chronicle* on 18 December 1941, summed it up: 'Until all the facts are known it would be fruitless to speculate. But it is quite certain that the Admiralty utterly underrated the strength of the Japanese Naval Air Service and that Sir Tom Phillips, his Squadron and some hundreds of seamen were the victims of the failure of the Admiralty and the Government to provide the fighting Navy with an efficient Naval Air Service under the direct control of the Admiral, and must bear all the responsibility.'

HMS *PRINCE OF WALES* COMPASS PLATFORM NARRATIVE:

This record was taken by Paymaster-Lieutenant W. T. Blunt, RN, who had his action recorder with him, and wrote out a fair copy as soon as possible after being picked up by *Electra*.

1113. Opened fire on eight high-level bombers which attacked *Repulse*. *Repulse* was straddled by bombs and reported some damage and small fire from two near misses.

1141½. Opened fire on nine torpedo-bombers coming in to attack from port side.

1144. Torpedo hit on port side aft of the bridge (exact position not known).

1144½. One aircraft shot down, falling in sea close on the starboard side.

1145. Close miss past the starboard quarter by torpedo passing from forward aft.

1149½. *Repulse* attacked by one aircraft which dropped one torpedo.

1150½. Reported: One aircraft crashed in sea, Green 140. At this stage a heavy list to port had developed.

1157½. Opened fire on six aircraft on the starboard side, thought to be attacking *Repulse*.

1158. Cease fire.

1159. Aircraft seen to have turned away.

1205. Man overboard, port side.

1206½. *Vampire* ordered to pick him up.

1210. Hoisted 'Not under control'.

1213. Out of touch with 'X' engine room. (Noted that bridge was out of touch with Damage Control Headquarters since shortly after hit).

1220. Seven aircraft on starboard bow.

1221½. Opened fire.

1223. Two hits by torpedoes on starboard side, a few seconds apart. One very near the stem, the other in the after part of the ship.

1224½. One hit starboard side under compass platform, by torpedo.

1226½. *Repulse* shot down two aircraft.

1227. *Repulse* observed to be listing to port. ? hit by two torpedoes.

1228. Destroyers ordered to close *Repulse*.

1230. Nine high-level bombers on port bow.

1230. 'X' engine room only working.

1232. *Repulse* sinking.

1233. *Repulse* sunk.

1241. Opened fire on eight high-level bombers on port bow.

1244. Hit by one bomb (reported as being starboard side catapult deck).

1250. Asked Singapore for tugs.

1310 (approx). Order to inflate lifebelts.

1315 (approx). List to port began to increase rapidly.

1320 (approx). Ship sank, capsizing to port.

EXTRACT FROM REPORT OF FLIGHT-LIEUTENANT T. A. VIGORS TO C. IN C., FAR EASTERN FLEET; dated 11 December 1941, from RAAF Station, Sembawang:

'I had the privilege to be the first aircraft to reach the crews of the *Prince of Wales* and the *Repulse* after they had been sunk. I say the privilege for, during the next hour while I flew low over them, I witnessed a show of that indomitable spirit for which the Royal Navy is so famous. I have seen show of spirit in this war over Dunkirk, during the "Battle of Britain", and in the London night raids, but never before have I seen anything comparable with what I saw yesterday. I passed over thousands who had been through an ordeal the greatness of which they alone can understand, for it is impossible to pass one's feelings in disaster to others.

'Even to an eye so inexperienced as mine, it was obvious that the three destroyers were going to take hours to pick up those hundreds of men clinging to bits of wreckage and swimming round in the filthy oily water. Above all this the threat of another bombing and machine-gun attack was imminent. Every one of those men must have realized that. Yet, as I flew round, every man waved and put his thumb up as I flew over him.

'After an hour lack of petrol forced me to leave, but during that hour I had seen many men in dire danger waving, cheering and joking as if they were holiday-makers at Brighton waving at a low-flying aircraft. It shook me, for here was something above human nature. I take off my hat to them, for in them I saw the spirit which wins wars.

Below: *Duke of York* after the war at Portsmouth in 1947.

'I apologise for taking up your valuable time, but I thought you should know of the incredible conduct of your men …'

HISTORY: DUKE OF YORK

1937 Programme.
Laid down by J. Brown & Co., Clydebank, 5 May 1937 as *Anson*.
Renamed *Duke of York* 12 July 1938 in honour of King George V who had served in the Royal Navy as Duke of York.
Launched 26 February 1940.
Began trials June 1941.
Completion for service delayed by improvements to protection following loss of *Hood* .
Completed 4 November 1941.
Hoisted flag VA 2nd BS and 2nd flag Home Fleet at Scapa 6 November 1941, replacing *Prince of Wales*.

HOME FLEET
November 1941 to October 1942 (Flag VA 2nd BS and 2nd fleet flag November to December 1941 and April to May 1942. Fleet flag May to July 1942. Private ship in 2nd BS later).
Flag transferred to *Renown* 9 December 1941 and ship left Scapa for Clyde to embark Prime Minister and party for the United States.
Left Clyde for USA December and arrived at Annapolis on the 22nd.

Below: *Duke of York* in Portsmouth Dockyard, 1949 –
HMS *Victory* in the background.

Prime Minister returned home by air and *Duke of York* worked-up at Bermuda 5–17 January.

Left Bermuda for home on 17 January and rejoined Home Fleet at Scapa on 30th.

Unit of covering force for Russia convoys March to May 1942.

From 6 to 10 March, a force comprising *King George V* (flag), *Duke of York*, *Victorious*, *Berwick*, and twelve destroyers provided special cover to an outward and homeward convoy during sortie by *Tirpitz*.

Contact with *Tirpitz* established off the Lofoten Islands by aircraft from *Victorious*, but a torpedo attack by these failed and the German ship was able to return to base without being brought to action. Convoys not attacked.

Flag VA 2nd BS transferred from *Renown* 3 April 1942.

Temporary fleet flag May to July 1942, replacing *King George V* for refit after ramming *Punjabi* on 1 May.

Flag hoisted at Scapa 6 May.

On 6 June 1942, King George V visited Home Fleet at Scapa and was accommodated on board.

Flag of distant covering force (*Duke of York*, USS *Washington*, *Victorious*, *Nigeria*, *Cumberland* and fourteen destroyers) for Russia convoy (PQ17) from 27 June to 8 July 1942.

Fleet flag reverted to *King George V* at Scapa 8 July on return from this operation and *Duke of York* became private ship.

Unit of covering force for Russia convoy September 1942.

Transferred to Force 'H' (Gibraltar) as flag (VA) October 1942 for North Africa invasion.
Hoisted flag at Scapa 30 October and left same day for Gibraltar.

FORCE 'H'
(Gibraltar) October to November 1942 (flag).
Took part in North Africa landings November 1942.
Force 'H' employed in covering both the initial British task forces and follow-up convoys against

DUKE OF YORK

attack by Italian or Vichy French forces.
Relieved by *Nelson* 15 November and left Gibraltar for home on the 18th.
Rejoined Home Fleet at Scapa on 26th.

HOME FLEET
November 1942 to September 1944 (2nd BS to May 1943. Fleet flag from May 1943).
Refit Rosyth December 1942 to March 1943.
Became flag CinC Home Fleet May 1943 on transfer of *King George V* to Force 'H'. Flag hoisted 8 May.
Flag of covering force for attack on enemy shipping off Norway by aircraft from USS *Ranger* 4 October 1943.
Flag of covering force for Russia convoy November to December 1943.
Sank *Scharnhorst* off North Cape 26 December during this operation, putting up a remarkable shooting performance with thirty-one straddles out of fifty-two broadsides and placing sixteen within 200 yards of the target.
Sustained minor damage to both masts that were hit by shells which failed to explode. This was the last occasion on which battleships were in action with one another. Proceeded right through to Kola Inlet with convoy after the action, being the first Home Fleet capital ship to enter Russian waters during the war.
Returned to Scapa 1 January 1944.
Flag of covering force for Russia convoy March 1944.
Flag of force supporting attacks on *Tirpitz* in Altenfiord by aircraft from *Formidable*, *Indefatigable* and *Furious* on 17 July, 22 and 24 August 1944 and from *Formidable* and *Indefatigable* on 29 August 1944.
Withdrawn from Home Fleet September 1944 to refit for Pacific service.
Refitted for Pacific at Liverpool September 1944 to March 1945.
Worked-up at Scapa and left for Pacific Fleet base at Sydney, Australia on 25 April. Proceeded via Mediterranean with further work-up period at Malta, Suez Canal, Colombo, Fremantle and Albany. Joined fleet at Sydney July 1945.

PACIFIC FLEET
July 1945 to July 1946 (fleet flag to June 1946).
Hoisted flag Admiral Sir Bruce Fraser, CinC Pacific Fleet, at Sydney 31 July 1945.
Arrived too late to take part in offensive opera-

tions against the Japanese, which were terminated on 15 August 1945, and employed mainly on occupation duties.
Had been intended to be unit of second British Task Force (TF 38.5) comprising *Anson*, *Duke of York*, *Colossus*, *Venerable* and *Vengeance* (11th Carrier Squadron), to work with the main body of the British Pacific Fleet (Task Force 37) in the US Third Fleet for the proposed invasion of Kyushu (Operation 'Olympic'). Following end of hostilities conveyed Admiral Fraser to Tokyo Bay for signing of Japanese surrender aboard USS *Missouri* on 2 September 1945.
Relieved *Anson* as base ship at Hong Kong December 1945.
Left Hong Kong for home 6 June 1946.
Flag CinC transferred to Admiral Boyd at Singapore 11 June en route.
Arrived Devonport 11 July 1946 and flag Admiral Fraser struck on the 12th.
Refit Devonport July to November 1946.
Joined Home Fleet November 1946.

HOME FLEET
November 1946 to April 1949 (flag from December 1946).
Relieved *King George V* as fleet flag December 1946.
Flag Home Fleet for Clyde Review 22–23 July 1947.
Refit Portsmouth December 1947 to February 1948.
Flag of division of Home Fleet comprising *Duke of York*, *Cleopatra*, *Diadem*, *Sirius* and six destroyers, visiting West Indies and Bermuda during autumn cruise, September to November 1948.
Relieved as flag by *Implacable* and reduced to reserve at Portsmouth April 1949.

RESERVE
April 1949 to April 1957 (Portsmouth to September 1951. Flag Reserve Fleet from July 1949. Clyde C Category from November 1951).
Refit Portsmouth April to July 1949.
Became flag Reserve Fleet, Portsmouth July 1949.
Relieved by *Dido* 2 September 1951.
Refit Cammell Laird, Birkenhead, September to November 1951.
Reduced to C Category Reserve and laid up in Clyde on completion of this.

Below: Looking over to the *Duke of York* from underneath the long, silent guns of *King George V* anchored in Gairloch shortly before scrapping commenced, 27 September 1957.

Left Birkenhead in tow for Gareloch 6 November 1951.
Placed on Disposal List 30 April 1957.
Sold to Shipbreaking Industries Ltd., Faslane, 18 February 1958.
Arrived Faslane for scrapping.

HISTORY: HOWE

1937 Programme.
Laid down by Fairfield, Govan, 1 June 1937 as *Beatty*.
Renamed *Howe* February 1940 on grounds that the name Beatty commemorated a too recent Admiral.
Launched 9 April 1940.
Commissioned at Govan 1 June 1942 for 2nd Battle Squadron, Home Fleet.
Joined Fleet at Scapa 29 August 1942.

HOME FLEET
(2nd BS) August 1942 to May 1943.
Unit of covering force for Russia convoys December 1942 and February 1943.
Based on Hvalfiord, Iceland, March to April 1943 to cover North Atlantic convoys against possible attack by enemy heavy ships.
Transferred to Force 'H' (Gibraltar) with *King George V*, May 1943, Sicily invasion. Left Scapa for Gibraltar 21 May.

FORCE H
Gibraltar May to October 1943 (2nd flag from September).
Took part in invasion of Sicily in June and Italy in September 1943.
With *King George V*, intended to serve as a reserve for Force 'H' in these operations, to carry out diversionary bombardments, cover assault convoys and replace any other Force 'H' battleships that might be disabled.
On night of 10/11 July, both ships carried out bombardment of Marsala and Trapani on west coast of Sicily to simulate another intended landing and pin down enemy troops.
Stationed at Augusta 7 September, with *King George V*, as reserve force for Salerno landings but detached on the 8th following the signing of the Italian armistice as flag special squadron (under command Vice-Admiral Malta), comprising *Howe*, *King George V* and four cruisers of the 12th CS and the minelayer *Abdiel*, sent to

Taranto to occupy and hold the port. Force entered Taranto 10 September.
Flag RA 2nd in command Force 'H' transferred to *Anson* from *Warspite* at Malta 12 September.
With *King George V* escorted the larger of the surrendered Italian warships from Malta to Alexandria 14–16 September.
Left Alexandria 1 October for home to rejoin Home Fleet.

HOME FLEET
2nd BS October 1943 to January 1944.
Withdrawn from Home Fleet January 1944 for refit prior to transfer to Eastern Fleet.
Refit Devonport January to April 1944.
Worked-up at Scapa and left for Ceylon 1 July 1944 via Mediterranean and Suez Canal.
Joined Eastern Fleet at Trincomalee 3 August 1944.

EASTERN FLEET
1st BS August to December 1944.
On 22 November 1944, formation of a Pacific Fleet to be based on Sydney, Australia commenced with the appointment of Admiral Sir Bruce Fraser as CinC and the Eastern Fleet redesignated East Indies Fleet.
Howe transferred to Pacific Fleet as flag 2 December, Admiral Fraser's flag being hoisted at Trincomalee on that date.
By end of December 1944 following ships allocated to the Pacific Fleet although some had not actually joined: *Howe* (flag), *King George V*, *Formidable*, *Illustrious Indefatigable*, *Indomitable*, *Victorious Swiftsure*, *Ceylon*, *Gambia* (NZ), *Newfoundland*, *Achilles* (NZ), *Argonaut*, *Black Prince* and 22 destroyers.
Pacific Fleet Battle Squadron became the 1st BS and the East Indies Fleet Squadron the 3rd BS.

PACIFIC FLEET
December 1944 to September 1945 (fleet flag to February 1945. 1 BS later).
Arrived Sydney late December 1944 being the first of the Pacific Fleet ships to reach there.
Conveyed Admiral Fraser to New Zealand January 1945 for conference with the New Zealand government.
Fleet finally assembled at Sydney 10–11 February 1945 at which time Admiral Fraser transferred his flag ashore, Vice-Admiral Rawlings assuming seagoing command with his

404 KING GEORGE V CLASS

flag in *King George V* while *Howe* became private ship in 1st BS.

Fleet left Sydney for operational area 28 February 1945.

Joined United States 5th Fleet and commenced operations 26 March 1945, being designated Task Force 57.

Carried out bombardments of Japanese airfields on Formosa and Sakashima Gunto Islands March to May 1945 in support of the American operations against Okinawa.

On 4 May *Howe*, *King George V* and cruisers bombarded airfields on Miyako Shima in the Sakashima Gunto group. *Howe* narrowly missed by Kamikaze aircraft off Sakashima Gunto Islands 9 May. Aircraft heavily hit by AA fire and deflected in course, passing close over quarter-deck and crashing into the sea.

On 27 May 1945 the US 5th Fleet became the 3rd Fleet after command change and the British Pacific Fleet was renumbered Task Force 37.

Howe withdrawn in June for refit.

Refit Durban June to September 1945.

Transferred to East Indies Fleet on completion and relieved *Nelson* as flag late September.

EAST INDIES FLEET

Trincomalee September 1945 to January 1946 (flag).

Returned home January 1946 arriving at Portsmouth on the 9th.

Transferred to Home Fleet February 1946 relieving *Queen Elizabeth*.

HOME FLEET

2nd BS February 1946 to April 1949 (Flag 2nd BS to August 1946. Training Squadron later).

Attached to new Home Fleet Training Squadron, Portland, August 1946 (see *Anson*).

Clyde Review of Home Fleet 22–23 July 1947.

Refit Devonport May 1948 to April 1949.

Transferred to Reserve, Devonport (as Senior Officer) 21 April 1949 on completion of refit.

RESERVE

Devonport April 1949 to May 1957 (SO to July 1950. C Category from February 1950).

Reduced to C Category Reserve February 1950.

Placed on Disposal List Devonport April 1957.

Sold to T. W. Ward & Co., Inverkeithing 2 June 1958.

Arrived Inverkeithing for scrapping 4 June 1958.

HISTORY: ANSON

1937 Programme.

Laid down by Swan Hunter Wigham Richardson, Newcastle-on-Tyne 20 July 1937 as *Jellicoe*.

Renamed *Anson* February 1940, prior to launch, on grounds that name *Jellicoe* commemorated a too recent Admiral.

Launched 24 February 1940.

Commissioned at Newcastle 22 June 1942 as flag (VA 2nd Battle Squadron and 2nd fleet flag, Home Fleet).

HOME FLEET (flag VA 2nd BS and 2nd fleet flag June 1942 to June 1944)

Unit of covering force for following operations September 1942 to April 1944:

Russia convoys September 1942 and January 1943.

Attack on enemy shipping at Bodø, Norway by aircraft from USS *Ranger* 4 October 1943.

Russia convoy November 1943 and March 1944.

Attack on *Tirpitz* in Altenfiord by aircraft from *Furious* and *Victorious* 3 April 1944.

Attack on enemy shipping at Bodø and in the leads to the south of Bodø by aircraft from *Furious* and *Victorious* 26 April 1944.

Withdrawn June 1944 to refit for Pacific service.

Refit Devonport June 1944 to March 1945.

Commissioned at Devonport 7 March 1945 for Pacific Fleet.

Worked-up at Scapa March to April and left for fleet base at Sydney, Australia, with *Duke of York*, 25 April.

Proceeded via Mediterranean, with further work-up periods at Malta, Suez Canal, Colombo, Fremantle and Albany.

Joined fleet at Sydney July 1945.

PACIFIC FLEET

July 1945 to July 1946 (2nd flag RA 1st BS August to October 1945. Flag RA later VA October 1945 to January 1946).

Joined too late to take part in offensive operations against the Japanese, which were terminated on 15 August, and employed mainly on occupation duties.

With *Duke of York*, *Colossus*, *Venerable* and *Vengeance* (11th Carrier Squadron) intended to form a second British Task Force (TF 38.5) to work with the main body of British Pacific Fleet (Task Force 37) in the US Third Fleet for the proposed invasion of Kyushu (Operation 'Olympic').

Following the end of hostilities on 15 August selected as flag (RA) Singapore Occupation Force, comprising *Anson* (flag), *Vengeance* and four destroyers.

Singapore Force later cancelled because of logistic problems and this group added to Hong Kong Force, comprising *Indomitable* (flag RA Harcourt), *Venerable*, *Swiftsure*, *Euryalus*, RCN *Prince Robert* and ten destroyers.

Entire force (less *Vengeance*, detached to Rabaul en route) arrived off Hong Kong on 29 August and on the 30th Rear-Admiral Harcourt transferred his flag to *Swiftsure* and entered the port accompanied by *Euryalus*, *Prince Robert* and the destroyers, the heavy ships remaining outside because of risk of mines.

Rear-Admiral Harcourt appointed Governor-General immediatley afterwards and Rear-Admiral Daniel in *Anson* assumed command of the force.

Anson subsequently served as base ship at Hong Kong until December 1945, landing 400 ratings and 230 marines for garrison and police duties, etc.

Japanese surrender of Hong Kong signed on board, 16 September 1945.

Relieved *King George V* as flag 1st BS in October 1945 and also became Flag Officer Western Pacific Area. At the same time, 2nd fleet flag transferred from 1st BS to 1st Carrier Squadron.

Detached to Tokyo as guardship in November and returned to Hong Kong early December.

Relieved as base ship by *Duke of York* in December and left Hong Kong for Sydney on 26th.

Flag VA transferred to *Belfast* (2nd CS) January 1946.

Refit Sydney January to February 1946.

Conveyed Duke and Duchess of Gloucester from Hobart, Tasmania to Sydney February 1946.

Returned to forward area in March, visiting Yokohama, Kobe and Kure. Later again stationed at Hong Kong.

Flag RA 5th CS temporarily flown from May to June 1946 while *Bermuda* refitting.

Left Hong Kong for home 21 June 1946 for transfer to Home Fleet.

Below: An aerial view of *King George V* returning from the USA with the Prime Minister, Winston Churchill, on board, 1941.

Below: *King George V* in dry dock under preparation to be mothballed, 1951.

Flag VA shifted to *Belfast* in January 1946, rehoisted at Singapore for passage home.
Arrived Portsmouth 29 July 1946.
Refit Portsmouth July to October 1946.
Selected in August for Home Fleet Training Squadron, formed in that month, comprising *Nelson* (flag), *Anson* and *Howe* and based on Portland.
Joined squadron 19 October 1946, relieving *Nelson* as flag.

HOME FLEET
(Flag RA Training Squadron, Portland) October 1946 to November 1949.
Present at Clyde Review of Home Fleet 22–23 July 1947.
Refit Devonport 1947.
Took part in NATO naval exercise summer 1949.
Withdrawn from Training Squadron November 1949 for refit prior to being placed in reserve.

Refit Devonport November 1949 to August 1950.
Reduced to extended reserve (C Category) August 1950 and laid up in Clyde August 1950 to April 1957.
Placed on Disposal List 30 April 1957.
Sold to Shipbreaking Industries Ltd., Faslane, 17 December 1957.
Arrived Faslane for scrapping.

Below: *King George V* arrives at Gairloch to be laid
up, 1951.

CONCLUSION

When hostilities began in 1939 no one could have foreseen the many changes that the Royal Navy would be forced to make as the war progressed. The panic-stricken rush to build big-gunned ships during the 1930s, although not exactly in vain, had in all essentials been a mistake. Even though the Admiralty knew that the German Navy had only seven large surface ships that constituted a threat, it was not obvious to them that the fighting was going to be very different from that of the Great War. In fact the Germans concentrated their efforts on commerce raiding by surface and underwater craft. Nevertheless, at the beginning battleships were still considered to be prime factors, and even more so by 1941 when Japan entered the war.

It would not be fair to say that money spent on battleships would have been better directed towards other types of vessels because nearly all the leading maritime powers still believed that there would still be the classic surface action during any hostilities. So long as any nation had the type within their fleet, the others were obliged to conform.

During the early years of the Second World War, except at Taranto, the aircraft carrier did not fulfil its promise as the weapon of tomorrow, as so often forecast during the 1930s. Most of the existing carriers had no experience of conducting successful airborne to surface attacks – especially at sea. When *Prince of Wales* and *Repulse* were sunk in 1941 it was land-based aircraft that did the job; the aircraft proved their worth, not the carrier.

It is true that the attack on Pearl Harbor showed the value of the carrier in conveying aircraft for an attack on a fleet in harbour – an emulation of Taranto in 1940, and it was then that all the powers became really aware of the carrier's potential. But this did not make the battleship obsolete; it still had an important role to play within the infrastructure of any surface action. It was still a very capable weapon of war, but it was clear that it was vulnerable to air attack and needed support from AA ships and its own protective carriers, in the same way as those ships needed big gun protection.

The role of the battleship from 1942 turned towards protection for other ships and their big guns also played a superb part in bombarding beaches in support of landing troops. There were

limitations of course, as can be seen in this passage of a report made by the Commanding Officer aboard *Warspite* in November 1944 while bombarding land positions:

'There are bound to be limitations as to what the bombardment can and cannot effect and it is thought proper that these should be set out by the Commanding Officer verbally to the Officer planning and/or conducting the operation, or that particular part of it. The Captain of a heavy draft bombarding ship has his hands very full when he must maintain his ship in a strong tideway, within a space of, perhaps, no more than twice the length of his ship. If he is continuously assailed by doubts as to details of the undertaking, it can but reduce the efficiency of the hammering, which the enormous hitting power of a 15in battleship should make possible AND IS KNOWN TO BE PARTICULARLY DISLIKED BY THE GERMANS.'

In many previous publications the comparative worth of British battleships has been much debated. The answer is very simple; they were as good as any built for any other nation within the limitations of displacement and size, and any statements from 1919 to the present suggesting that British battleships were not on a par with those of foreign powers are nonsense.

Let us look at some of the arguments that have been repeated for so long:
1. The *Royal Sovereign* class were too slow and were weakly protected over the decks.
2. *King George V* class (1936) were undergunned and had poor radius of action.
3. British battlecruisers were poorly protected.
4. British underwater defence was poor.

In answer it would have to be said that, yes, of course, the *Royal Sovereign* class were slow by 1939 standards, and short of being given new engines and boiler equipment how could they fail to be anything else – after all they were nearly 25 years old. The deck armour, although poor by 1939 standards, was all that could be applied (see class notes) because of stability problems within their design, but they were still a match for any contemporary foreign battleship, surviving as they did until the Second World War. When the *R*s were sent to the Indian Ocean in 1942, with the likelihood of having to face the Japanese *Kongo*-class battlecruisers, it was seen as a disastrous move, but the British ships would in fact have given a remarkably good account of

Below: The last appearance of *Queen Elizabeth*, off the Isle of Wight (Motherbank) – 'not wanted any more' – autumn 1946.

themselves against ships armed with 14in guns and protected by a relatively thin 9in belt. Had they been caught by the Japanese aircraft carriers it would have been a different story, but then it would have been the same for any modern battleship.

The second generation of British battleships, the *King George V* class, were under-gunned, etc! Maybe, but the Admiralty knew that before continuing construction. But under-gunned against what? They would not have to face US 16in-gunned ships, and it was highly unlikely that they would ever face the Japanese *Nagato* and *Mutsu* (16in). That left the German and Italian ships with their 15in guns. Against these the 14in gun had a lower rating on paper, but in practice at sea the 14in gun proved itself an excellent weapon although lacking the extra punch of the heavier 15in.

The 14in gun made big holes in the German battlecruiser *Scharnhorst* on 26 December 1943, and she had 14in KC belts. The gun wrecked the so-called superior battleship *Bismarck* in 1941, against 12in KC armoured strakes. It seems that the 14in gun acquired its poor reputation early in its life before the minor faults in its mounting had been rectified, and the troublesome quadruple turret in *Prince of Wales* and *King George V* during the *Bismarck* episode lent strength to its critics. But apart from that, when and where did the gun and turret ever fail to perform admirably?

Poor radius. Well, this was true, but because of the restriction to about 35,000 tons, the weight was directed elsewhere instead of being used for large tanks for much-needed fuel supplies. Many British battleships fared badly in this regard when serving in the Pacific, whereas in home waters replenishment was close to hand.

British battlecruisers were poorly protected. Again, one must agree, but they were built for speed. All the battlecruisers that survived to serve in the Second World War were old ships by 1939.

They had been designed to outrun rather than outfight the enemy. Even in modernized ships this poor protection was never rectified. *Hood*'s armoured deck was weak and the Admiralty knew it before she was completed in 1920. *Renown* remained the weakest unit in the battle fleet, but she was certainly no weaker than the Japanese *Kongo*-class ships and there never seem to be any derogatory comments made about them.

Poor underwater protection in British ships? Not excessively, when compared to ships of the same age. The *Royal Sovereign* and *Queen Elizabeth* classes had old systems of underwater protection which could not in all cases cope with severe damage. *Royal Oak* and *Barham* were most effectively sunk by submarine attack; hit by at least three torpedoes in quick succession, they

Below: A close up of *Revenge* on 4 September 1948, now a worn-out relic of the past. Note the additions to the bridgework and the extra deck level at the rear of the funnel.

Bottom: 'Let's go down and see the "old lady"!' was the cry when *Warspite* ran aground in 1947. She cheated the scrapyard but sadly did not escape the scrapper's torch and was cut up where she lay.

could not fail to sink. But would not similar foreign battle ships have sunk in the same circumstances? Of course they would, and it would be foolish to deny it.

Prince of Wales was effectively sunk by torpedoes and bombs, but in view of the damage she received it is not surprising. Her own turbines opened up her bottom aft when she was hit in that area. No other ship, new or old, could have sustained that punishment and lived to tell the tale (with the exceptions perhaps of the giant *Yamato* and *Musashi*). The underwater system of the *King George V* class was as good as anything fitted to any foreign battleship of the 1930s, in fact it outclassed some rivals in that it was a more complete system.

These reflections on British designs may seem very chauvinistic, of course, but that is exactly what they are. They do not seek to denigrate the foreign opposition, nor skate over the fact that there were many faults, but when all the relative factors have been carefully considered, the conclusion is that British battleships stood well the test of time and do not deserve the adverse criticism that has been levelled at them.

BIBLIOGRAPHY

The hundreds of documents consulted during the writing of this book are too numerous to list but below are some of the more important ones.

NATIONAL MARITIME MUSEUM:
Ships Covers:
King George V 1911
Iron Duke Class 1912
Queen Elizabeth Class
Royal Sovereign Class 1913
Renown Class 1915
Glorious and *Courageous* 1916
Furious 1916
Hood 1916
Nelson Class 1925
King George V Class 1936
Foreign Battleships (general)

Manuscripts:
Sir Tennyson d, Eyncourt. DNC.
Sir William May.
Admiral R. E. E. Drax.
Admiral William Tennant.
Admiral Alfred Chatfield.
Admiral Sir Cyprian Bridge.
Admiral Sir B. E. Domville.

PUBLIC RECORDS OFFICE:
ADM papers.
Naval Policy. 1936.
Aircraft versus battleships. 1937.
Firing tests. (Job 74 etc)
Uses for capital ships. 1943.
Bombardment etc. 1943.

De-gaussing experiments.
Shell and bomb damage. 1939/45.
Washington Naval Treaty. 1921.
London Naval Treaty. 1930.
Capital ship policy. 1921.
Bridge construction in capital ships.
Battleships design. 1919, 1921, 1928, 1934.
Battlecruiser design. 1921.
Aircraft in battleships. 1937.
Armour in capital ships.
Endurance in capital ships.
Replacement. 1933/4.
Design *King George V*. 1936.
Reconstruction of *Renown*. 1923.
Reconstruction of *Royal Oak*. 1924.
Reconstruction of *Glorious* and *Courageous*. 1923.
Camouflage in warships.
Radar installations.
Loss of *Prince of Wales*.
Loss of *Royal Oak*.
Loss of *Barham*.
Loss of *Hood*.
Loss of *Glorious*.
Loss of *Courageous*.
Proceedings: *Ramillies, Furious, Revenge, Renown, Queen Elizabeth* and *Warspite*.
Ships Books: *King George V*; *Hood*; *Anson* and *Howe*.
Ships Logs: *Queen Elizabeth*; *Warspite*; *Barham*; *Valiant*; *Royal Sovereign, Revenge, Royal Oak*; *Resolution*; *Repulse*; *Renown*; *Glorious*; *Nelson*; *Rodney, Hood*; *King George V*.
Vulnerability of battleships. 1933.
Models of capital ships. 1940.
Painting of ships. 1939.

Uses for old battleships 1944.
Gas and chemical attacks. 1923.

PUBLISHED BOOKS CONSULTED:
Raven, Alan and John Roberts. *British Battleships of World War Two*. Arms and Armour Press and Naval Institute Press, 1976
Parkes, Dr Oscar. *British Battleships*. Seeley Service, London, 1957.
Roberts, John. *Hood*. Anatomy of the Ship Series. Conway Maritime Press, London 1982.
Transactions of the Institute of Naval Architects. All volumes from 1911 to 1948
Brasseys Naval Annual. 1916 through to 1950
Jane's Fighting Ships for recognition and photograph identification (not for data however).1919 to 1945.

PERIODICALS AND NEWSPAPERS:
The Sphere.
The Illustrated London News.
Navy League.
Mariner's Mirror.
The Times.
The Daily Mail.
The Evening Standard.
The Daily Graphic.
The Daily Telegraph.

Large drawings are based on Admiralty 'As Fitted' plans now held in National Maritime Museum; small drawings on official drawings and photographic evidence; isometric drawings on photographic evidence.
Photographs are from author's collection.

INDEX